FUNDAMENTALS OF PERSONALITY

THE LIPPINCOTT COLLEGE PSYCHOLOGY SERIES

UNDER THE EDITORSHIP OF
DR. CARL P. DUNCAN, NORTHWESTERN UNIVERSITY
AND DR. JULIUS WISHNER, UNIVERSITY OF PENNSYLVANIA

FUNDAMENTALS
OF
PERSONALITY

A FUNCTIONAL
PSYCHOLOGY
OF PERSONALITY

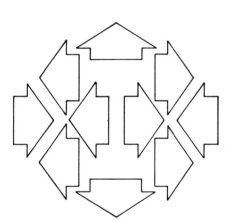

RALPH MASON DREGER

PROFESSOR OF PSYCHOLOGY
JACKSONVILLE UNIVERSITY

PHILADELPHIA AND NEW YORK
J. B. LIPPINCOTT COMPANY

PREFACE

One of the most fascinating subjects in the world, the study of human personality, is also one of the least understood. We thus have what seems like a paradox: that which is closest to us we know the least about. On the one hand, because everyone seems to use the term "personality" freely, it appears as if everyone knows about personality. Yet on the other hand, there is a common belief that human nature is so complex and unpredictable that we could never have scientific knowledge about it.

In actuality, only relatively recently has there come to be a science dealing with personality. Scientists, both psychologists and others, have been testing what we "know" about personality to sift what can or cannot be verified. In addition, they have advanced our knowledge into realms unknown in previous centuries.

The pages of this book deal with the science of personality, sometimes called personology, from the viewpoint of a larger science, that of psychology. Many gaps exist, and many concepts presented will have to be reinterpreted as further knowledge is gained by research. Nevertheless, an attempt has been made to co-ordinate knowledge and theory from various branches of science in order to present a scientific understanding of the fundamentals of per-

sonality. The general plan of the text is to discuss the normal adult personality from several different approaches. Data from all sources are subjected to several cross-classifications, none of which is "true" but all of which contribute to insight into personality. Although these cross-classifications may be regarded in some senses as theories about personality, this text is not one which could be regarded as a book on "theories of personality." All major and most minor theories are represented in these pages; but they are utilized here as lenses through which to view the main subject, the normal adult personality.

In accord with the general plan, Section 1, "Introduction to Personality," places the study of personality in its scientific and psychological frames of reference (Chapter 1), and sets forth definitions of personality, each of which constitutes its originator's theory of personality in miniature (Chapter 2).

Section II, "Personality Functioning in General," seeks to answer the question as to whether we have a subject indeed to study. Is there anything at all that extends across an individual's present, from past to future, which can be considered continuous or across all his functions consistently? (Chapter 3) If there is in whole or part anything like this, is there any organization to it; and if so, what kind of organization is there? (Chapters 4 and 5)

In Section III, "Personality in the Adult Individual: Topographical Structure-Functions," a broad view of personality is taken, based upon, but not by any means limited to, that presented by Sigmund Freud. First, personality data are classified according to four main functions: basic life urges (Chapter 1); general methods of controlling stimulation from within and without the organism (Chapters 7 and 8); the special methods of handling internal and external stimulation arising in connection with society's demands (Chapter 9); and the ways of living in social groupings (Chapter 10). Here personality is regarded as a kind of topographical map on which areas may be marked corresponding to the immediately preceding classification: id, ego, superego, and roles. A cross-classification of the same data, with topographical areas overlapping those just named, recognizes conscious and unconscious functions of the personality (Chapter 11). And still another cross-classification overlapping both of the preceding ones takes account of central and peripheral functions (Chapter 12).

Section IV, "Personality in the Adult Individual: Dynamic: Structure-Functions: Dimensional Traits," views the individual from the well-established position of trait-psychology. What traits are or may be and what traits have been found by those who are looking for them are made the subject of this section (Chapters 13 and 14).

In the final portion of the book, Section V, "Personality in the Adult Individual: Economic Structure-Functions: Distribution and Utilization of Energy," motivational aspects of personality are considered specifically, focussing on those which in the rest of the text are only regarded obliquely. What kinds of movements are there within the personality and between the organism and its environment which contribute to "Why we do what we do"? (Chapter 15) And what directions does the personality take in its course of life? (Chapter 16)

The general plan of the book and the specific outline presented above should be kept in mind in a reading of this text. If the student does not "lose sight of the woods on account of the trees," he should have a far broader and deeper knowledge of personality than at present, he should be more understanding and tolerant in his estimation of his own and others' personalities, and he should have an introduction to a science of personality whereby he is equipped to judge the validity of new data as it comes to him.

Some books appear to be written out of the experience of their authors without much direct help from others. Unlike such texts, this one owes most of its contents directly or indirectly to others. Appropriate acknowledgments are made where they are called for, but the author wishes to express his gratitude for some especially who, wittingly or unwittingly, have made contributions beyond that which can be expressed in formal footnoting:

Dr. Gordon W. Allport, dean of personologists; Dr. David D. Eitzen, teacher and friend; Dr. Otto Fenichel, psychoanalytic systematizer *par excellence*; Dr. Sigmund Freud, creative penetrator of the unknown; Dr. Haim G. Ginott, revealer of the child's mind, friend; Dr. J. P. Guilford, teacher, explorer in creativity; Dr. Arthur R. Orgel, friend and friendly critic of parts of this text.

Dr. Carl P. Duncan and Dr. Julius Wishner, able editors of the Lippincott College Psychology Series, particularly Dr. Wishner for his conscientious reading of the manuscript and his fruitful suggestions; Mrs. Betty Thompson, typist and secretary; the author's family, patient and understanding supporters.

All these and countless others, students, especially in psychology of personality courses; counselees; friends and enemies, all who have helped put flesh and blood on the skeleton which a science of personality would otherwise be.

JACKSONVILLE, FLORIDA   RALPH MASON DREGER, PH.D.
DECEMBER, 1961

CONTENTS

SECTION II. PERSONALITY FUNCTIONING IN GENERAL

SECTION III. PERSONALITY IN THE ADULT INDIVIDUAL: TOPOGRAPHICAL STRUCTURE-FUNCTIONS

SECTION **I**

INTRODUCTION TO PERSONALITY

CHAPTER 1

FRAMES OF REFERENCE: GENERAL

GENERAL SCIENTIFIC CONCEPTS

Certain general scientific principles stand in direct relation to the science of psychology and to the study of personality in particular. These principles serve as "frames of reference," that is, larger vantage-points from which personality psychology may be viewed and by which it may be interpreted. One may consult any modern textbook in scientific logic for detailed discussion of scientific principles. Only those, however, which seem most appropriate to the field of personality are presented here.

Facts

In his Presidential Address to the Royal Astronomical Society several years ago, an outstanding British scientist repeated an essential dictum of science, ". . . the voice of science is now as it has always been: 'Never mind what seems the proper thing to believe; what is the *evidence* for what you say?' " (Dingle, 1954). It seems as if there should be no need to emphasize this simple principle. And yet much of the spirit of the twentieth century has built up pressures to force men of science to tailor their data to "proper" political, religious, and even "scientific" ideologies.

Just the gathering of facts is not science, but without the gathering of facts there is no science. There are many subtleties con-

cerning the meanings of the term "fact" [1] into which we cannot go now (Larrabee, 1945). In the final analysis, "facts" or "data" refer to *observations* reported by scientists. One of the major differences between nonscience of yesterday or today and the science of any day is that armchair speculation predominates in the former and patient gathering of observations characterizes the latter. Although there is room for what may be called fancy in the science of psychology as well as "fact," a science without facts is an anomaly.

Systems and Classifications

It is not facts alone, but classified and systematized facts which constitute the elements of any science. Men have been aware of some of the most obvious facts of psychology for centuries; but it was not until these facts began to take their place

---

[1] The word "fact" is in quotation marks because in recent years it has become increasingly evident that a "fact" rather than being an absolute entity seems to be only an instrument of a certain frame of reference. That this interpretation of "fact" is not entirely acceptable to philosophers of science is revealed in a reading of the various selections in the text by Feigl and Brodbeck (1953). However, the implications of the formulations in the "grammar of science" tend toward the acceptance of the interpretation above. At the very least, a naive view on "facts" is no longer permissible to the student of science.

in a systematic body of data that psychology could claim to be a science. It is not only desirable to have some kind of system to lend meaning to the scientist's observations (Bain, 1861), but it seems almost impossible for a scientist to dispense with a system of some kind even to make his observations. Even though the scientist may not be aware that he has some system or preconceived plan by which he determines what facts he is going to gather, he most likely has such a formal or informal system (Myrdal, 1944). His very choice of where to look for his "facts" and his selection of what variables he intends to study reveal that he has a notion of "what goes with what."

Without classification of a group of facts, just as without the facts themselves, there can be no science (Cunningham, 1924). Placing facts in what seems to be a logical framework brings order out of a heterogeneity of seemingly unrelated data.[1] Most of us have known "walking encyclopedias" whose amazing memories for facts have made them the envy of their comrades. Television shows turn up such prodigies every so often. On the whole, however, these individuals are not scientists, for their vast accumulation of facts is not set in a systematic framework.

There are dangers in any systematizing or classification procedure. It has been said that an idea tends to get itself organized, then the organization tends to kill the idea. Systematic organization of data may kill the growth of scientific ideas by preventing new slants on old facts or excluding new data. A system operating like Procrustes' bed, stretching or lopping off the facts, is not unknown in personality study—or any scientific field. Theoretical systems like psychoanalysis, learning theory, Gestalt psychology and others which are mentioned in the following pages have all resulted at

times in distortion and suppression of facts. In the vast majority of instances such a result has come by honest intent, not deliberate falsification.

In a science of man, as elsewhere, classificatory systems are to be regarded as handy tools, not eternal verities. From early days of scientific psychology (Herbart, 1834) to the present, systems of psychology have arisen, each of which has claimed to be *the* explanation of psychological phenomena. An ironical and amusing comment on this tendency was made some years ago by a prominent psychologist:[2]

The adoption of a closed system and rigid adherence to inflexible rules of observation make for the same sort of satisfaction as that accompanying the performance of any other relatively perfected skill. Swimming, teaching statistical method, or participating in the modern dance all derive from similar motives. They yield the sheer joy of unimpeded activity. This is, of course, the original 'pleasure principle,' doubtless known to the first polar bear sliding down his cake of ice. No, there is no vexing explanatory problem when one has at hand all the explanation he needs at the outset (Geldard, 1939).[3]

No matter what system or explanatory principles we may use, the scientific principle is that to be *used;* it is a servant not the master of the scientist. This caution keeps a system or theory from crystallizing into rocklike rigidity in any science.

Students of psychology will find reference in the literature of psychology to "scientific models" or "theoretical models." Any group of explanatory statements describing relations among observed phenomena can be called a "model." These statements can be in mathematical form ("mathematical models"). For example, Pythagoras' theorem expressed algebraically,

[1] ". . . in spite of the fact that classification and definition have been largely deposed, at least in scientific circles, from their ancient thrones as final arbiters of thought; as instruments of clarification and organization their value has become increasingly recognized as the sheer quantity of knowledge to be handled has mounted apace" (Larrabee, 1945). (Cf. also London, 1949.)

[2] Dr. Frank Geldard, at that time President of the Southern Society for Philosophy and Psychology. One might quarrel with Geldard's main argument that all explanation consists in further description, unless "further description" includes relations among facts (Spence, 1942).
[3] Geldard, F. A., Explanatory principles in psychology. Psychol. Rev., 1939, 46, 411–421. Reprinted by permission.

$a^2 + b^2 = c^2$, is a limited mathematical model setting forth relations between the two shorter sides of a right-angled triangle and its hypotenuse. It sometimes comes as a surprise to many students of science to discover that the seemingly absolute "models" of their high school physics or biology or chemistry are only the best explanations of data *thus far*. The exact formulae of mathematics are really *conditional* statements: "If such-and-such assumptions hold, then these formulae are true." Nothing seems surer or more self-evident than "two-plus-two equals four." Yet this "self-evident truth" appears to mathematicians as part of a man-made system which depends upon certain human assumptions (Wade & Goodner, 1953). Theoretical models, including mathematical ones, are probably only selections from a multitude of explanations for observed phenomena (Altschul & Biser, 1948).[1]

Laws

Whatever theoretical system may be adopted by a scientist, one of the aims of modern science is to formulate laws by which the behavior of the events, persons, or things under observation may be predicted. In some ways modern science differs from ancient science in this respect. Following Galileo, scientists today seek laws which will enable them to predict not only common events, but those which occur "once only" (Lewin, K., 1936a). An-

cient (Aristotelian) science sought to discern the "essens" (essence) of things, *i.e.*, the essential common characteristics belonging to all members of a group of events, persons, or objects. Thus in ancient science, events occurring once only, having no characteristics in common with anything else, cannot be classified scientifically. Therefore, they are "accidens" or accidental deviations to which no attention can be paid.

This distinction between ancient and modern science is highly pertinent to personology. The individual (human) case has proved to be an "accidens," for each personality apparently occurs only once. In fact, the "problem of personality" lies in just this: How can there be anything lawful about phenomena which seem to possess so little of "essens" and so much of "accidens"?

Sometimes it has seemed as if there can be no laws (in the sense which Galileo meant) in the social sciences, to which personality study is more closely allied than it is to the natural sciences. In part, however, the social sciences have succeeded in developing laws (Brown, R., 1954). Scientists even in the most exact of sciences have come to realize in recent years that their "laws" are merely statements which hold with greater or less *probability* for certain relations among phenomena. In this respect, then, laws derived from the scientific study of personality are not essentially different from those in physics.[2]

Assumptions

Reference has already been made to the conditional nature of "self-evident" arithmetic or mathematical principles. For such apparently absolute operations as addition and subtraction, a number of postulates must be made (Wade & Goodner, 1953). It is reasonable to conclude, then, that if in that most exact of disciplines, mathematics, assumptions are necessary, certainly they are required in less exact sciences.

[1] Somewhere in this discussion a statement of the "principle of parsimony" or "Occam's razor" should be made. The author thought he understood the principle until reading a discussion (Newburg, 1954) which muddied the waters for him. His original conception of the principle was that if two or more alternative explanations are available for a given set of facts, the one requiring the fewest assumptions is preferable to science, even though it might not be "truer." Thus the Copernican system won out over the Ptolemaic system of astronomy because it requires fewer positings of "epicycles" and other necessary assumptions. If this is not the "true" understanding of William of Occam's principle, it is one understanding of it. For a fascinating discussion of models in genetics and the use of Occam's razor, cf. Stadler (1954).

[2] Einstein and Infeld in *The Evolution of Modern Physics* (1938) have shown the statistical nature of laws governing atoms.

Even before the scientist sets foot in his laboratory or adjusts his microscope or telescope, or sharpens his pencil to record his observations of whatever sort, he has accepted many assumptions or presuppositions. Two examples from many can be cited here. One of these deals with relations among events, the other with relations among people. In the eighteenth century David Hume initiated a long series of criticisms of the notion of *causality*. We can never again be as naive concerning causality as men were prior to Hume. Nevertheless, some form of causality is assumed in all scientific work.[1] Another assumption made by scientists is that of the honesty of men of science. "We accept all scientific conclusions on the strength of the moral improbability that men of science have entered into a conspiracy to deceive the rest of the world" (McDougall, 1926b). This assumption is a dangerous one which has proven false in some instances. For example, a supposed discovery of the "inheritance of acquired characteristics" in the salamander proved to be the action of India ink which had been used to touch up the original figures (Zirkle, 1954)! And yet, scientists tacitly assume the honesty of their fellows; ordinarily the last thing attacked even in vituperative scientific debate is the integrity of the opponent.

Scientists may disagree as to what assumptions are made in science. Any scientist who claims, however, that he is not making any assumptions has the weight of present-day philosophy of science against him. These presuppositions are not regarded as being "written into the nature of things" (so-called "metaphysical presuppositions"), but are merely working propositions which the scientist is not at the time testing in his investigations (Feigl & Brodbeck, 1953). It would be an endless task for a scientist to try to investigate everything connected with his observations; just from sheer physical limitations he has to assume some things.

Social Frames

The society and culture in which we live provide a framework of presuppositions closely related to the general scientific assumptions mentioned above. These presuppositions are not scientific ones; they must, however, be regarded as a background for science. Although physical and even some social sciences may flourish in cultures other than ours, possibly a science of personality could only appear in a culture such as we have inherited. The emergence of individualism in Greek and Hebrew thought, the forms of law and government stemming from ancient Rome, and Christendom's struggles for democracy have all served as a foundation for an emphasis on the importance of the individual.

Even in those areas of the West where official propaganda decries "the cult of the individual," such influences are strongly felt. Readers of Russian literature from Dostoevsky to Pasternak recognize the importance of the individual to Eastern Europe's common man. The science of Eastern Europe has also been influenced by the heritage of the West. Of personological significance is important research in human conflict (Luria, 1932) carried out in a Russian laboratory. One of Pavlov's associates, Bechterev (1932), wrote an instructive text on personality. However powerful official dogma and pressures are in shaping a culture, a civilization cannot escape its history entirely.

It does not seem to be an accident, however, that personality study has been pursued more vigorously in the democracies which have more closely followed the main line of Western traditions. For the "social climate" of democracy provides many of the presuppositions of a science of personality. Psychologists subscribe more or less implicitly (Myrdal, 1944)[2] or ex-

---

[1] From Planck: "The law of Causality is neither true nor false. It is rather a heuristic principle, an indicator that points the way and, to be sure, in my opinion, the most important indicator (Wegweiser) that we possess." (Quoted in Moore, 1948.)

[2] A thorough reading of Myrdal's (1944) first chapter will give both historical background to

plicitly (American Psychological Association, 1954) to a social philosophy of individual liberty within a framework of laws for the common good.

Likewise, the general Western standards of morality related to the main conflict areas of personality—sexuality and aggression—i.e., main areas for most civilized societies, serve as a frame of reference within which personologists work. Most students of personality seem to agree with Freud in his protests against over-rigid sexual morality and to regard some expression of aggression as normal for most cultures. Yet they do not in their writings advocate the same relatively unlimited sexual freedom or unleashing of aggressive impulses found in some primitive cultures.[1] Statements of basic cultural standards in textbooks on ethics or even somewhat popular listings of the values of our society (Hardee, 1953) reflect the presuppositions within which most personology is carried on.

The very existence of a science of personality seems predicated on the Kantian concept that persons are valuable in themselves, not merely as means to ends. If it were not for the presence of some very potent cross-currents in our culture, one general proposition concerning the worth of persons might be taken as the radix from which more specific cultural assumptions are derived. But the contrary trends serve also as expressed or unstated premises upon which personality study also rests. Not only have other traditions contrary to the assumption of the worth of persons influenced our culture vastly, from the exposure of infants in Sparta to genocide in Nazi Germany, but also the "acids of modernity" (Walter Lippman) have eaten into the structure of our society and culture, so

that some social presuppositions have changed and will presumably change considerably more. Psychological study of ethical principles (Hollingworth, 1949) may in itself contribute to altering the value system which sponsors the study of personality. It is conceivable that further changes may take place of such an order that a different social climate will result in which little impetus is given to a science of personality.

Setting forth the presuppositions of our present culture provides one instance of the general influence of society and culture on the development of any science. In the case of personology the influence of a social frame of reference is especially evident.

GENERAL PSYCHOLOGICAL CONCEPTS

A science of personality rests upon general scientific bases, including scientific presuppositions, and upon the broad, general base of our society and culture. But it also has more specific foundations in general psychology. Stern (1938), who has had a profound influence on American psychology of personality especially through Gordon Allport (1937a, 1937b), maintained that general psychology as traditionally conceived is a part of "personalistics," his term for a science of personality. Whether personology is more inclusive than general psychology or not, and it does not seem so to most psychologists, it is a good-sized branch of psychology today. Taking results from all other branches of psychology, a science of personality utilizes them in understanding the person-as-a-whole as well as his separate functions. In this way the study of personality very closely approaches a general psychology.

Personology is not, however, general psychology. The debate which raged for many years as to whether psychology can study persons as individuals, inasmuch as science is devoted to the general and not the particular case, finds its echoes even now (McNemar, 1954; Prothro & Teska, 1950). But what Allport (1937a) foresaw

---

and clearer perception of "Americanism" than many of the fuzzy discussions offered by chauvinistic propagandists.

[1] The late Wilhelm Reich, who *seemed* in recent years to have advocated greater sexual freedom than is usually considered necessary, is viewed with disfavor by most of his psychoanalytic colleagues. Albert Ellis goes beyond most psychologists at present as well.

has come about: Psychology has learned to a remarkable degree how to deal with intra-individual consistencies (or inconsistencies) as well as inter-individual uniformities. And it has sought laws governing minds-in-particular as well as minds-in-general which is the province of general psychology.

Undergirding the science of personality are the data and principles of a general psychology. Included as a branch of psychology is comparative psychology from which are drawn implications for personology as well as other fields of psychology. Methods and principles developed anywhere in the broad spectrum of psychology are utilized in the study of the individual.

Position of Man Among Animals

In placing man at the top of the evolutionary scale (or scales), the psychologist accepts the results of comparative psychology and comparative biology as to the relative nature of this supremacy. In certain functions man is inferior to other animals; in others he is far superior.

In orientation functions [1] man appears to be inferior to several species of insects (Buhler, 1951) and birds,[2] except as he implements his natural orientation capacities with artificial direction-finders. Complexity of function increases as we ascend the phylogenetic scale (Nissen, 1951), but in terms of behavioral plasticity, less complex creatures may be more "free" than man, thus superior in "freedom." Hearing is one function in which man is surpassed by a number of "lower animals." Chimpanzees,

---

[1] Buhler's (1951) account of research in orientation of ants and bees is informative.

[2] We know only part of the mechanisms by which pigeons home. An "internal clock" appears to define compass directions for pigeons, though other factors may operate even in defining direction (Schmidt-Koenig, 1960). How geographical position is determined is still a problem—to us if not to the pigeon. Orgel and Smith (1954, 1956) who have tested the magnetic theory of homing are engaging in further research to check whether or not the earth's magnetic field gives pigeons guidance.

dogs, white rats, crickets, cats, porpoises, mice, and bats all exceed man in respect to the upper threshold of hearing (Kellogg, 1953). The adult human upper threshold is about 20,000 cycles per second. Bats can respond to nearly 100,000 cycles per second. Other animals have developed an olfactory sense superior to that of man.

In terms of complex learning processes, concept formation, and symbolization, man seems to be preeminent in the field. A scaling of relative intelligence (or "behavioral complexity") of man among the animal kingdom (Figure 1) indicates how much superior man is to the other creatures. The top curve is dotted since we know so little about early forms of man. One criticism of this rough comparison is that greater overlap between man and the lower organisms should be allowed, for many complex functions can be performed by the primates.

Many definitions of personality, including the one employed in this text, by inference, assign personality to members of the animal kingdom below man. The question is asked: How far can we apply studies of animals to human beings? So many rat studies are made in psychology and are used as a basis for interpreting man that the possibilities and limitations of such extrapolation must be recognized. Sometimes such an extension is unwarranted because of the greater complexity of man's behavior. Yet because of many basic similarities a number of conclusions from animal studies are justifiably applied to man (Moss, 1942). Personality study takes account of man's place among the animals and also of the possibilities of research with animals for an understanding of human personality.

Methods of Psychology

General psychology has already introduced the student to methods employed in this field. These methods may be reduced to two fundamental kinds: controlled observation and experimentation. The former may be of the naturalistic variety (Dreger, 1955) in which the observer seeks to stay

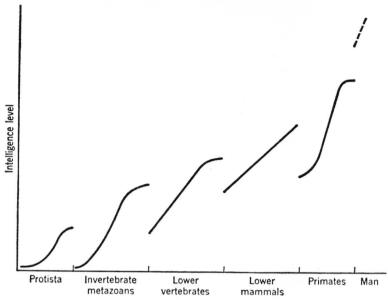

Figure 1. A tentative estimate of comparative intelligence in the animal kingdom. (From S. S. Stevens, *A Handbook of Experimental Psychology*, p. 382)

out of the psychological field of his subject as much as possible; or controlled observation of the clinical variety in which the observer is intentionally a part of the subject's psychological field. Experimentation may include any of the following: (1) open-air laboratory experiments such as those utilized in Kellogg's famous porpoise researches (Kellogg, 1953, 1958), in which animals too large to be placed in a traditional-style laboratory are subjected to experimental handling; (2) the more traditional and exact laboratory investigation; or (3) the less well-controlled tests and measurements of the psychometrician or clinician.

Some texts on personality devote considerable space to the methods of assessing personality. These methods have become so extensive that only a minimum description is provided in this text. The student is referred for more detailed treatment to those texts which discuss personality measurement in full.[1]

[1] For several broad aspects of personality measurement consult Allen (1958), Ferguson (1952), and Harsh and Schrickel (1950). For attempts to

In addition to the techniques of investigation generally employed in psychology and specifically in personology, nonscientific approaches to personality are used; the data thus obtained must be evaluated in the light of scientific understanding. Wisdom was not born with us, nor will it die escape subjectivity in personality assessment see Bass and Berg (1959). Eysenck, Granger, and Brengelmann (1957) present physiological measures concomitant with normal-abnormal psychological dimensions. Cattell (1946, 1957), Eysenck (1952b), and Guilford (1959) are the most complete discussions on factor-analytic methods of measurement. Objective recording of interpersonality functions is described in Bales (1950). Holt (1958), Meehl (1954), and Taft (1959) weigh the relative values of clinical judgments and statistical procedures in personality assessment. Cronbach and Meehl (1955) discuss the validation of tests in terms of construct validity, and Meehl (1945, 1954) the value of objective or structured tests. Methods of multiple judges and multiple tests, with pooling of information, are evaluated by Taft (1959). Cronbach and Gleser (1957) apply decision theory to test development and use, especially "wide band" techniques (interviews and projective tests, for example) which may be less valid but more productive of information than "narrow band" methods (like objective inventories).

with us,[1] nor yet is it confined to science even today.

Those observers who have *felt* with others—poets, dramatists, and artists in particular—have enabled us to see behind the façades of life. There is a reciprocal relation between literary men and psychology. How much, for example, James Joyce reflects psychological (particularly psychoanalytic) understanding and how much psychology reflects James Joyce[2] is difficult to know—even for the writer himself. Possibly scientific psychology influenced Edwin Arlington Robinson in "An Old Story" or perhaps the influence is the other way around:

> Strange that I did not know him then,
>   That friend of mine.
> I did not even show him then
>   One friendly sign;
>
> But cursed him for the ways he had
>   To make me see
> My envy of the praise he had
>   For praising me.
>
> I would have rid the earth of him
>   Once, in my pride.
> I never knew the worth of him
>   Until he died.[3]

Goethe, Shakespeare, Dante, Augustine, Paul, Theophrastes, all without benefit of modern science, have given us insights into ourselves without which we would indeed know less about personality than we do.

An important factor, however, that is often unrecognized by critics of scientific psychology is that these literary "insights" must be tested by science in order to be accepted as scientific. Sometimes a popular speaker cites a passage from literature and parallels it with some scientific finding and concludes that the genius who originated it was scientific. Many of that same author's passages may not have been borne out by research. Those that are accepted

by scientists are accepted not because the "great man" said it, but because patient, plodding investigation has given the inspired structure a foundation.

Principles of Psychology [4]

The search for some sovereign principle to explain all behavior and experience has not been confined to philosophy as one might expect. Psychology, too, has had its share of seeking for such a principle. In the heyday of a crude behaviorism, the "chain reflex" could explain everything (Holt, 1931). Most general psychology texts today do not even mention this master principle which proved inadequate. In the Gestalt tradition, Kurt Lewin, to whom we are indebted for many brilliant ideas, produced the simple equation, $B = f(P,E)$. In essence this equation states, "Behavior is a function of person and environment." Few psychologists would object to this equation. Yet it states in pseudo-mathematical terms the person-environment problem without putting us any closer to an answer. Others besides behaviorists and Gestaltists have tried to explain all behavior by single principles which ultimately break down.[5]

Psychology at present must utilize not *a* principle but a number of fundamental propositions [6] which for want of a better term are called principles here. The follow-

---

[1] Cf. Job 12:2 in the Bible.

[2] *Ulysses* especially.

[3] From "An Old Story" by Edwin Arlington Robinson, published by Charles Scribner's Sons.

[4] Acknowledgments for several valuable criticisms of the Principles are expressed here to the late Dr. Henry W. Nissen of Yerkes Laboratories of Primate Biology. Of course, Dr. Nissen is not responsible for any infelicities of statement of these principles. Only after this chapter was in print was the writer's attention called to a similar attempt to set forth the principles of psychology by W. Edgar Vinacke: The basic postulates of psychology. *Scientific Monthly*, 1948, 67, 110–114. There is a close parallel in the two attempts, remarkable in some ways, but gratifying.

[5] Contrary to much popular and scientific opinion, Freudian psychoanalysis does not seek to explain all behavior by "sex," even broadly conceived. This point is amplified in Chapters 5 and 6.

[6] More modestly than "sovereign principle" advocates, Wheeler (1932) presented eight "laws of behavior" which serve to some extent as inspiration for the attempt at formulating principles set forth in the text. An excellent résumé of these laws is found in Hartmann (1935).

ing set has been elaborated from the works of many psychologists,[1] as either fundamental beliefs concerning behavior or rules of action for a general science of psychology. They divide naturally into three groups of propositions, those dealing with psychology as a science *per se*, those dealing with behavior, and those dealing with the individual. Explanations are appended where it is deemed necessary.

PRINCIPLES RELATING TO PSYCHOLOGY AS A GENERAL SCIENCE

1. *Psychology is primarily a science, and only secondarily an art.*
   a. *The practice of psychology which does not relate itself to the body of scientific psychology and to other sciences is pseudo-science.*
   b. *The art of psychology may go beyond the science for practical purposes, but only in the direction the science is tending.*
2. *Explanation in psychology consists of describing as fully as possible the relations among variables* (Spence, 1942).
   a. *Naming is not explaining.* Unless the name is part of a system of classification which shows relations, to assign an impressive Latin, German, or unfamiliar English word to some phenomenon is only an exercise in magic, the "magic of names."
   b. *The most significant relations among variables are not necessarily the most obvious ones.* Joe's father may be satisfied with relating Joe's behavior to a trait he calls "laziness." The clinical psychologist who knows that in certain activities Joe behaves industriously, activities which he likes

[1] Others have been consulted, but the following books have been employed especially: Brown & Gilhousen, *College Psychology* (1950); Bugelski, 1960; Dockeray and Lane, *Psychology* (1950); Hilgard (1957); Munn, *Psychology, the Fundamentals of Human Adjustment* (1956); Ruch, *Psychology and Life* (1953); and Woodworth, *Experimental Psychology* (1938).

to do, is not satisfied with so superficial an explanation.
   c. *Correlation does not mean causation.* Two highly correlated variables may be related through a third variable or through a set of other variables.
3. *The aim of psychological investigation is to predict and/or control behavior.*
   a. *Pure research that has no practical end in view is legitimate.* Extension of knowledge without regard for applied consequences is a legitimate concern of any science.
   b. *Control of behavior is a valid concern of psychology.* Education, the military, business, and other applied fields are rightly areas of application of psychological principles. As with other sciences, however, applications of psychology are directly or indirectly the results of pure research.

PRINCIPLES RELATING TO BEHAVIOR

1. *The behavior of the organism is the raw data of psychology.*
   a. *Behavior may include introspective data in the form of "verbal report"* (Boring, 1953).
   b. *Social and physical conditions surrounding the organism may provide interpretive data.* Social psychology and sociology blend into each other at this point.
2. *Behavior is determined.*
   a. *Spontaneous behavior, i.e., response without stimulus is unknown to psychology.* Skinner (1953) whose research has had a great influence on learning theory (though he denies being a learning theorist) holds rightly that certain stimuli do not precede the response which they reinforce. He, too, however, eschews spontaneity.
   b. *Behavior may result from the operation of needs.*[2] Both drives and

[2] We do not have to side at this point with either S-R drive-reduction and Freudian motivation theorists or cognitive theorists (Scheerer,

"cognitive needs" (Maslow, 1948a) are involved in human and some higher animal behavior.

c. *Determination or causation of behavior is interpreted in probability terms.* Even laws in physics may be regarded as "probability statements" (Einstein & Infeld, 1938): "If event A occurs, event B will occur within certain limits of probability." [1] Such limits in psychology are usually much wider than those in physics.

3. *The individual behaves as an organism.*
a. *Mind and body are aspects of behavior, not separate entities.*
b. *Whole and part functions are analytically separable.* Vision is not hearing, discrimination of weights is not solving a water-jar problem, learning a poem is not testing a saline solution. The trait of generosity can be discriminated from the trait of honesty.

4. *The behavior of the organism is the resultant of maturational and environmental factors interacting.* Mathematically and physically, a resultant signifies a direction and a distance which are a compromise between the directions and distances of the original forces.
a. *The heredity-environment problem is not an either-or problem, but a question of relative weights.* Contributions of genetic and environmental factors can be statistically determined.
b. *Biological and cultural factors are necessary determinants of behavior.* With the possible exception of reflex

action, behavior is so determined that it would be different if either biological or cultural factors were subtracted.

5. *Behavior at any one time grows out of behavior in the past history of the organism.* Phenomenologists (Combs & Snygg, 1959; May, Angel, & Ellenberger, 1958) maintain that the present perceptions of the individual are the important focus in his adjustments. They would not deny, however, that present perceptual behavior has its roots in past behavior. [2]

6. *Certain aspects of behavior can be measured.* "Whatever exists, exists in some amount" (Thorndike, Bregman, Cobb, & Woodyard, 1927) and its accompanying clause, "and therefore can be measured," might not be accepted by all psychologists. But from Wundt to the present, psychologists have endeavored to assign numbers to psychological events. [3] Although description predominates in psychology, psychologists appear to believe that verbal description is inferior to measurement. [4]

[2] Existentialist psychology (May, 1958) appears to come close to rejection of this position.

[3] An excellent early statement of the need for precise quantitative expressions to summarize data, not merely numbers assigned to such data, is given by Spearman (1904).

[4] Lewin (1935, 1936) has applied nonmetrical mathematics, that is mathematics of relations rather than numbers, to personality study. Most psychologists either because of lack of mathematical sophistication or for more adequate reasons have not accepted Lewin's mathematical-but-not-numerical formulations. Yet it may be that nonmetrical mathematics are genuinely applicable to psychology. If so, this corollary would have to read: *The mathematization of behavior is a desirable goal,* and the general principle would be: *Certain aspects of behavior can be mathematized.* These statements are not only awkward, but unnecessary from the standpoint of most psychologists.

Some psychologists might add to the principles here a statement, "Normal and abnormal behavior are on a continuum." This principle is acceptable for elementary psychology, but not for any advanced statement. In abnormal psychology there is no agreement that differences of degree do not amount to differences of kind. Nor is there agree-

1954). Sociologists and anthropologists have raised objection to need concepts, usually because needs are equated with drives (Kluckhohn, Murray, & Schneider, 1953, ch. 1). Murray (1938) limits the term "need" unnecessarily by the inclusion of one word in his definition: ". . . we may loosely use the term 'need' to refer to an organic potentiality or readiness to respond in a certain way under given conditions." By dropping "organic" we can apply the concept to more than drives. Murray actually does go beyond his own definition.

[1] This, of course, is not a rigorous statement of the meaning of probability.

PRINCIPLES RELATING TO THE INDIVIDUAL

1. *The individual is the locus of psychological functions.*

   a. *Suprapersonal functions exist only because there are individuals.* The inseparability of individual and social functions does not obviate the fact that neither could exist without individuals.

   b. *The individual derives his existence from society and functions only as a social being.* Whatever its ultimate origins, life as we know it now comes from life. Even ". . . hermit souls . . . that dwell apart in a fellowless firmament,"[1] apart from human interaction, could not have come into existence; their perceptions and thoughts are socially derived, however far from society they may withdraw.

2. *The individual is a unit within an interacting society and a series of units within himself.* Whatever the units are called, traits, needs, functions, dimensions, or other, the individual is a dynamic complex of such units within himself and he in turn moves in the complex of society. This much at least has a science of personality contributed to psychology in general.

Personological Point of View

Apart from the general scientific and general psychological orientation which personologists share with other psychologists, there is a special frame of mind which characterizes personologists. For it can hardly be said that all psychologists share one point of view when we go beyond the general principles enunciated above. A study of Fellows of the American Psychological Association (Thorndike, R. L., 1954) found three factors differentiating psychologists from one another. Factor I which is of most interest to us here distinguishes (1) those whose primary interest is in laboratory experimentation from (2) those who are interested in studying the individual.[2] We may recognize that personality study takes its material from both clinic and laboratory. However, most personologists probably are classified among the second group.

Beyond having a strong interest in individuals, an interest characterizing the clinical disciplines in general, the personality psychologist shares the clinician's "nonjudgmental attitude" towards human beings, insofar as his own personality organization makes him able to be nonjudgmental. Essentially, being nonjudgmental refers to the *acceptance* of personality facts, no matter how praiseworthy or how reprehensible

---

[2] A whole chapter could be written on the problem of personality. (Indeed, a first draft of this text included one which had to be excluded for various reasons.) Essentially, the problem is: How can a science be constructed which takes account of the *variety* of individuals and at the same time derives generalities which are applicable to all individuals (Allport, 1937a; Kantor, 1938; Mateer, 1924; Prothro & Teska, 1950). In one way this is the problem of all sciences. But it seems to be expressly a challenge to personology in that focus of concern of the latter *is the individual.* The physicist is not concerned about any particular rock or inclined plane; he draws general laws and ignores the individual event. In psychology the problem has been expressed as a dichotomy between those who claim that personality study should be idiographic and those who press for nomothetic study. Idiographic refers to dealing with particular persons as do literature and biography, nomothetic to dealing with general laws (of perceiving, learning, motivation, etc.). To think that psychology has developed general laws as clearly applicable to the individual as are the laws of physics to individual physical events would be indulging in a fond hope at this time.

It was thought at one time (Freeman, 1934) that differential psychology would supply the answer to the problem of individual-vs-group. But the psychology of individual differences turns out to be instead the psychology of group differences, between sexes, among ethnic and racial groups, etc. Personology, especially in clinical situations, often studies the single case, on the other hand. McNemar (1954) ironically points out, however, that if one takes the time necessary to develop principles for predicting every fragment of behavior for

---

ment that neurosis and psychosis form one dimension with normality (Eysenck, 1952b.)

[1] From Sam Walter Foss, "The House by the Side of the Road."

these may be from a moral or legal standpoint.[1] These facts are accepted as scientific data, not as so many pointers by which to condemn or condone an individual. Many personality psychologists are also clinical psychologists facing persons day after day, some of whose "built-in governors" have failed to control the driving powers of their lives, others whose governors are too tightly adjusted, and still others in whom it seems as if governors were never installed in the first place. Many personologists are also teachers in colleges and universities, dealing regularly with a high-average representation of Western youth. From a scientific standpoint these persons faced by the clinician or the teacher (who may be both) are neither

good, bad, nor indifferent, but are all data for objective study.

The psychologist does not—cannot—sit on his Olympus and in Jovian detachment watch the struggles of men as if they meant nothing to him. As pointed out previously, a scientist cannot escape his cultural heritage. Psychologists hold ideals and have feelings in respect to others. Sam Walter Foss's words are not by any means inapplicable to the psychologist's position:

Let me live in my house by the side of the
    road,
Where the race of men go by—
The men who are good and the men who are
    bad,
As good and as bad as I.
I would not sit in the scorner's seat,
Or hurl the cynic's ban—
Let me live in a house by the side of the road
And be a friend to man.[2]

A psychologist might add a line or two about not being impressed by the good deeds men do any more than he is depressed by their evil deeds.

Many years ago a forerunner of modern personology, John Cooper Lavater, wrote of his profession (physiognomy or physionomy, now considered unscientific):

Oh! if I were but endowed with the spirit of those sublime men who possessed the gift of discerning the inmost recesses of the heart, and of reading the thoughts, how many additional touches should I yet add to the moral character pertaining to the physionomist! He ought to know the world perfectly; and to attain this knowledge, he must associate with men of all ranks and conditions, he must attend them in every possible case and situation, and study them in all circumstances and situations. A retired state will impede his designs; nor should the active scenes of life be copied from one circle; in fact, the physionomist must travel, he must procure details of facts extensive and various, commence an acquaintance with artists, and such of the learned world as have made a serious study of the knowledge of men; he must converse with persons who are

---

a single case, the subject will have ceased to exist, and further that two and a half billion sciences would be required!

One answer to the dilemma is that a single case may be studied scientifically for its own sake, setting up hypotheses and testing them against as objective data as possible under the circumstances (in psychotherapy, for example). Additionally, the single case may be studied for patterns which may be applicable to large groups, possibly all persons. This type of investigation is precisely that in which psychophysics engages; very few psychophysical experiments employ large samples of subjects, yet their generalizations are regarded as applicable to large groups. Personology generally, to be sure, deals with more complex functions of the personality. And yet, with due regard for increased complexity it seems reasonable to suppose that regularities observed under scientific controls in one case may be used in understanding similar regularities in others (Preyer, 1888; Scheerer, 1946; Smith, Bruner, & White, 1956; White, 1952). In studying the single case, we should recognize that even the single case is only investigated scientifically in terms of others' patterns of responses. Unique as each individual's response patterns are, the unique pattern uncompared is hardly scientifically studied at all.

[1] The nonjudgmental attitude of modern science was preceded by religion's "Judge not that ye be not judged." The writer has found, however, few religious persons who can achieve the same degree of freedom from judging that he finds the rule among his psychological and psychiatric colleagues. Those who have had psychological and sociological training, whether religious or not, and who have dealt with human beings of all kinds extensively, seem to be able to free themselves of judgment more than others.

[2] Sam Walter Foss. *Dreams in homespun.* ("The House by the Side of the Road"). New York: Lothrop, Lee and Shepard Co., Inc., 1897. Reprinted by permission.

eminently vicious, as well as with those who are eminently virtuous; with those who are intelligent, and with those who are uninformed, nay with children; he must have a taste for letters and for painting, and indeed for all the other works of art.

The physionomist must possess a soul not to be easily shaken; and yet he must be gentle, innocent, and mild; no rude or boisterous passions must invade the peaceful territories of his heart, all the various avenues and windings of which must be under his own guidance and direction. If he is not generous and noble himself, he cannot discover generosity and greatness in the character of another (Lavater, 1797).

With minor and appropriate changes a personologist recognizes the same needs in modern days. Stern (1935) wrote, "Any condemnatory prejudice or criticism is capable of obscuring a factual view; thus no one who starts with the a priori thesis that human nature is inherently bad is qualified to be a scientific characterologist." Perhaps a personologist should keep the record straight by inserting the words, "or that human nature is inherently good."

Those valuations which the personologist holds, at least consciously, are such that he hopes he can have as undistorted a viewpoint on the facts of personality as possible. It is further his hope that students exposed to his approach to personality may develop similar attitudinal patterns. This hope is qualified, in that a psychologist recognizes that only those who are prepared by previous experiences (and perhaps even by constitutional factors) are prepared to adopt the seemingly paradoxical, scientifically-detached, nonjudgmental "interest in individuals."

SUMMARY

Principles accepted by all scientists underlie a science of personality. First, we may cite the importance of gathering facts or data rather than merely speculating about what the facts may be. The necessity of classifying or systematizing the data in any field and deriving laws of prediction are manifest in scientific endeavor. Science accepts certain general presuppositions or assumptions which are not specifically tested in any one investigation; personology as a science accepts these, too, and additional presuppositions peculiar to Western culture.

Personologists adopt the general frame of reference of psychology, specifically in relation to man's usual but not complete preeminence among the animals, and in relation to experimental and other controlled observation. Personology additionally utilizes literary products for beginning its investigations or filling the scientific gaps.

Rather than seeking a sovereign principle to explain behavior and experience, psychologists now recognize the need for a number of principles. And as psychologists, those who are also personologists strive to maintain an "interest in individuals" which is at the same time objective and nonjudgmental.

QUESTIONS

1. Why is science not a mere gathering of facts?

2. What are some dangers in the use of systems and hypotheses?

3. What are some advantages in the use of systems and hypotheses? Are they or are they not necessary to science?

4. What are scientific laws?

5. Cite assumptions, either from the text or your own experience and observation, upon which scientists depend.

6. How has culture as a broad frame of reference influenced the development of science of personality?

7. What are some of the "social frames" or value premises accepted by personality experts?

8. What is the place of man among the animals?

9. What are the two basic methods of psychology?

10. How does "nonscience" contribute to personology?

11. Discuss the section in this chapter on the principles of psychology.

12. What is the personological point of view?

CHAPTER 2

FRAMES OF REFERENCE: DEFINITIONS OF PERSONALITY

ON PERSONALITY DEFINITIONS IN GENERAL

In a way, defining personality is almost like defining life itself, in more ways than is apparent—as is pointed out later in this chapter. Biologists, however, find it very difficult to arrive at a satisfactory concept of what they mean by "life" (Von Bertalanffy, 1952).[1] Carlson and Johnson (1948), representative physiologists, define biology as "the science of life." But they do not give a specific definition of "life," instead characterize "living things" as having certain peculiar properties: living things metabolize; living things grow; living things reproduce; living things adapt themselves to their environment; and living things are highly organized. Modern science accepts this form of definition, which constitutes an "operational definition" of a sort.[2] The above operations characterize life rather fully, hence to that extent *define* it.

Thus to define personality we could describe the various operations of personality and say, "Now, there you have it—personality." Many years ago Oliver Goldsmith said, "Handsome is that handsome does," and Chaucer wrote, "That he is gentil that doth gentil dedis" (He is gentle that does gentle deeds). Similarly personality might be characterized definitely by its deeds (functions). Perhaps, then we should not define personality, but explain what it does, and then draw together a summary. Indeed, Raymond Cattell (1946) states in one of his personality texts, "The ritual of beginning a dissertation with a precise definition of what is being studied seems to be beloved almost as much by students as by professors. Yet it frequently implies a serious misunderstanding of scientific method. If anything can be fully defined, it is pointless to investigate it." True as these words may be in terms of "fully defined," the student usually likes to know, and is entitled to know, a definition according to which he can delimit the field of study. All definitions are somewhat arbitrary, yet serious attempts at definition are not to be scorned. One's conceptions of personality should become more intensive and extensive as he discovers what men have conceived personality to be. Definitions of personality, like scientific ap-

---

[1] Bertalanffy declares that the definitions of "life" are legion.

[2] The term "operational" has been used in many ways. Its usage stems from, among other sources, P. W. Bridgman's *The Logic of Modern Physics* (1927). But as both Stevens (1951) and Bridgman point out, making *meaningful* operational definitions is a difficult task.

16

proaches, are not comparable to a debater's definition, a mere preliminary to the real thing; they are instead ways of understanding personality. As we study the following definitions in their various classes, we should gain a broader view of personality than we could get without such definitions.

If there were no entity which could be called "personality," no functionally operating *system* of behaviors or responses as B. F. Skinner (1953) seems to imply, then we need not even consider a definition. But we need not then consider having a text on personality at all! Under such circumstances this would not be the first time many texts had been written on a nonexistent "science"—astrology texts illustrate this condition. Yet if there is no such "thing" as personality, it would have to be invented to account for psychological facts. Historically, psychology did not hold to a concept of personality, but gradually, a need for an explanatory concept as a kind of grand "intervening variable" [1] arose; as Lecky (1945) states succinctly:

The personality is a concept of the organism, created by us as a means of assisting our understanding of psychological phenomena. Without the concept of personality, we cannot study psychological topics, for physical systems by definition have no psychology. We have not changed the organism, of course, but we have changed our conception of it and think about it differently.[2]

Consequently, even though we find considerable lack of agreement in definitions of personality, psychologists continue to attempt definitions. The drawback in attempting a definitive statement is demonstrated by the criticism of one of the most acceptable definitions ever proposed. Allport's (1937a) definition, frequently quoted, is: "Personality is the dynamic organization within the individual of those psycho-

physical systems that determine his unique adjustments to his environment."

Roback (1938), writing a review of Allport's book, stated:

The definition seems to be both abstract and redundant. Every psychophysical organism may be said to be dynamic. The organization is naturally within the individual. Where else could it be? And if we are speaking of systems within the individual, they would have to be psychophysical. Furthermore, all adjustments are unique; and every psychophysical system determines adjustments to an environment.

We thus see that in spite of the explanations which follow every term in the definition, nothing remains of it after we take it apart.[3]

Such a peculiar *reductio ad absurdum* reminds the author of the relatively familiar story of the fishmonger who hopefully put out a sign one morning, "Fresh fish for sale today." A friend dropping by called his attention to the redundancy of his sign. "If you have the sign out, of course, you're selling the fish *today*." So the fishmonger erased the last word. The friend continued, "Why do you have '*for sale*' when everyone knows you are *selling*, not giving fish away?" The offending terms were dropped. "But what other kind of fish would you have but *fresh* fish?" persisted the friend. "Why, of course, I wouldn't have any other," indignantly responded the fishmonger. And finally the remaining word was erased and the sign hauled in, "For after all," the friend remarked acidly, "it *is* a *fish* store!"

Despite such treatment of a very good definition less severe criticisms usually are made; and psychologists still essay to define something as elusive as personality.

CLASSES OF DEFINITIONS

In his scholarly historical survey of the term "personality" from its origin in *prosopôn* (Latin, *persona*), the theatrical

---

[1] Intervening variables refer to the processes occurring between the observed stimulus and observed response, or at least processes we *infer* are occurring.

[2] Lecky, P. *Self-consistency, a theory of personality*. New York: Island Press, 1945. Reprinted by permission.

[3] Roback, A. A. Review of G. W. Allport, *Personality, a psychological interpretation. Char. & Pers.*, 1938, *6*, 243–249. Reprinted by permission of Duke University Press.

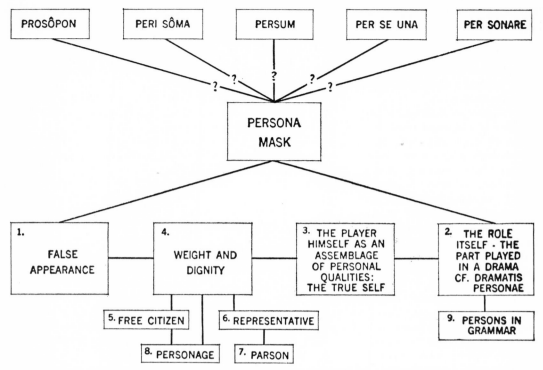

Figure 2. The early derivative meaning of *persona*. (From G. W. Allport, *Personality*, p. 27)

mask used by Greek and later by Roman actors to denote different characters, Allport lists an even 50 definitions. First he divides into four basic meanings those derived from the original usages and found in Cicero's writings:

(a) as one appears to others (but not as one really is);
(b) the part someone (*e.g.*, a philosopher) plays in life;
(c) an assemblage of personal qualities that fit a man for his work;
(d) distinction and dignity (as in style of writing).[1]

Figure 2 which is reprinted from Allport's book presents these derived meanings in relation to the original Latin term. Although Allport himself appears to concen-

[1] Allport, G. W. *Personality: a psychological interpretation.* New York: Holt, 1937. Reprinted by permission.

trate on the third and fourth meanings, others have regarded these as only partial.

Following his groupings of original usages of "personality," Allport brings together subsequent historical definitions into the following groups:

1. *Theological* meanings—*e.g.*, Persons of the Trinity.
2. *Philosophical* meanings—*e.g.*, for Locke a person is "a thinking, intelligent being, that has reason and reflection and can consider self as itself."
3. *Juristic* meanings—a person in law may be an individual or an incorporated group of people.
4. *Sociological* meanings—ranging from "person" in the French language (meaning "no one," a contemptuous designation) to concepts including an integration of traits determining one's role and status.
5. External appearance (*biosocial*) meanings—*e.g.*, the popular "superficial attrac-

tiveness," or the more scientific "social-stimulus value." [1]

6. *Psychological* meanings—in terms of "sum-totals" of traits, integration of attributes, hierarchies of selves, and adjustment. Allport's own definition quoted previously classifies here.

A thorough reading of Allport's second chapter is recommended to get the overtones of what can only be presented here in fundamentals. Note, however, that the *philosophical* meaning relates to what the individual believes is going on within—i.e., to his self; the *sociological* to his ways of maintaining social standing—his role; the *biosocial* (at least partly) to the impression he makes on others—his "It" or "Oomph"; and the *psychological* to his organized internal adjustment qualities—a sum-total of traits.

The above classifications are not the only ones which psychologists have constructed to bring some order out of the welter of ideas as to what personality is. Brand, writing more recently (1954), cites a number of attempts and makes his own classification into: (1) *individual behavior* definitions which seem to parallel Allport's "Psychological"; (2) *general-behavior*, which, emphasizing the chance variations of individuals as only unsystematic deviations from the general average, really "define personality out of existence"; and (3) *functional*, which direct attention to both the individuality and the purposiveness of a person's behavior patterns, or putting these aspects together, to the experiential and the characteristic ways in which an individual selects alternative means to an end.

Further sets of classifications might confuse more than enlighten. However, though the Allport classifications are related to the following,[2] meanings of some terms have changed over the years. Therefore, we

classify definitions of personality under these rubrics:

1. *Characterological*—which has no precise parallel in the other two systems, but has reference to enduring psychological qualities.

2. *Phenomenological*—which may correspond roughly to "philosophical" with its emphasis on internal workings.

3. *Biopsychological*—which corresponds roughly to "psychological" and "individual-behavior."

4. *Sociological*—which takes in what Allport called "biosocial" as well as "sociological," with the contemptuous overtone eliminated.

5. *Biosocial*—which in keeping with its component linguistic parts has come to include both social and individual functions.

Although probably no one likes to think of his definition as being "partial" in the sense of incomplete, some of the definitions quoted below are more inclusive than others, related to more or less inclusive aspects of the individual.

Characterological

The first broad set of concepts yielding definitions of personality center in the word "character." Allport only hints at the definitions involving character, though these derive from his third "basic meaning" in Roman and Greek usage ("an assemblage of personal qualities that fit a man for his work"). Before most psychologists included personality in their texts, Ogden (in his 1916 *Introduction to General Psychology*) devoted three chapters to "personality" and one to "character." His definition of character comes fairly close to some meanings of personality: "In a general way, . . . it is possible to say that character is the expression of individuality, which is in turn founded in the ultimate determinations of organic life as modified by the intellectual developments of reason, appreciation, morality and religion." In 1922 Myerson in essence equated character and personality. Such usage indicates a confusion in meanings, a confusion possibly explained etymologically. Commenting on

---

[1] Based on Mark A. May's definition of personality quoted in *ibid*. Reprinted by permission.

[2] It is only fair to say that Allport might not agree with either the rough reduction of his classes or the alleged correspondence between his classes and the writer's.

the vagueness of terminology in the study
of personality, McDougall (1932a) pointed
out that part of the difficulty arose in that
the German term *"Charakter"* is virtually
equivalent to the English "personality,"
whereas "character" in English refers to the
portion of the personality having to do with
an achieved system of enduring properties.[1]

Phenomenological

When we investigate behavior, not from
the standpoint of observable behavior, but
from the point of view of the behaving individual, we are using a phenomenological
approach (May, et al., 1958; Snygg &
Combs, 1949; Combs & Snygg, 1959). The
question asked in phenomenology is not
"What is the objective situation?" but
"What does the situation mean to the individual?" This approach has to do with the
self, with the internal workings which have
to be inferred by the observer, by what
the individual conceives he "really is."
There have been a number of psychologists
who have identified self or self-consciousness and personality. In Ogden's text mentioned above, personality meant *self*-con-
sciousness in the sense of "awareness of
self" (not that of an awkward embarrassment). Among famous psychologists of a
generation ago who held this concept was
W. B. Pillsbury (1911) who in 1911 and
again in 1920 wrote a chapter on "the self,"
but none on personality as such.[2]

Though giving no definition of personality *per se*, a text in phenomenological
psychology (Combs & Snygg, 1959) defines the "phenomenal self" as inclusive of
the physical self, and perceptions of the self
as good, honest, guilty, and so forth, and
by identification persons and objects outside of the physical self. It includes all the
aspects of the perceptual field which may
be referred to as "I" or "me."

Both the less and the more conscious

aspects of experience are comprehended
in the phenomenal self according to Snygg
and Combs who state elsewhere that the
latter is the self of which the individual is
aware; the less conscious is included, but
definitely not an "unconscious." From
Snygg and Combs' discussion it seems as
if they deny any unconscious functions in
the individual; if they do deny such, they
appear to go contrary to much evidence
(Miller, 1942).

While approaching the notion of personality "from the inside" as it were, these
authors are compelled to include functions
outside the organism in the "self." This inclusion of something "outside the skin,"
then, does not come only from sociologi-
cally oriented sources, as might be supposed.

Biopsychological

In Allport's (1937a) own classification
his well-known definition is subsumed under "psychological." In the more general
classification we use here, it is classed under
"biopsychological." It is given here again
to put it in its appropriate setting: "Personality is the dynamic organization within
the individual of those psychophysical systems that determine his unique adjustments
to his environment." Allport elaborates on
each section of his definition, emphasizing
the self-regulating activity of the organization, the biological *and* psychological nature of personality, the fact that personality
does something, the variations among individuals, and the broadly adjustive—not
merely biologically adaptive—nature of
personality functioning. It should be noted
that this classical definition confines its
meaning to "within the individual," as do
other biopsychological definitions.

Allied to Allport's definition are such as
Humm's (1942): "Personality may be defined as the entire fabric of an individual's
attributes. While it is possible to analyze
it in various ways, the minimum consideration would be to say that it includes disposition or temperament, intelligence, skill,
aptitude, interests, and physical make-up."
Note that "physical make-up" is included

---

[1] McDougall used "sentiments" for these enduring properties.
[2] In the *Handbook of General Psychology*, however, published with L. A. Pennington (Pillsbury
& Pennington, 1942), a chapter on personality appears.

here, as presumably referring to both physique and physiological functioning.

One of the most prolific researchers and writers in the field of personality is H. J. Eysenck, a British clinician. A demonstration of the possibility of going ahead in research without a fixed definition, just as biologists have done, is found in Eysenck, for at times he accepts one definition, at times another. In *The Structure of Human Personality* (1953) he accepts Allport's formulation. Earlier in *The Dimensions of Personality* (1947) he recognized Roback's definition [1] as "perhaps nearest to a general consensus of psychological thought": Personality is "The integrated organization of all the cognitive, affective, conative, and physical characteristics of an individual as it manifests itself in focal distinctness to others" (Warren, 1934). Eysenck in *The Dimensions of Personality* constructs a further definition:

. . . personality is the sum-total of the actual or potential behaviour-patterns of the organism, as determined by heredity and environment; it originates and develops through the functional interaction of the four main sectors into which these behaviour-patterns are organized: the cognitive sector (intelligence), the conative sector (character), the affective sector (temperament) and the somatic sector (constitution) (1947).[2]

Presumably this statement is more acceptable to Eysenck than Roback's.

While Roback indicates that the social aspects of personality cannot be ignored, as practically all of the definitions thus far do ignore them, it does not appear that even Roback goes much beyond others, in that the actual roles in society played by the individual do not seem to enter his definition unless they are implied by the phrase "as it manifests itself in focal distinctness to others." Perhaps Roback meant to include these roles, but the remainder of the

[1] Eysenck attributes this definition to Warren— but Roback (1950) was quick to point out that the attribution was incorrect.

[2] Eysenck, H. J., Dimensions of personality. London: Routledge & Kegan Paul, 1947. Reprinted by permission.

text in which he works out the implications of his definitions comes closer to incorporating sociological emphases.

Sociological

A strictly sociological definition is found in Frederick Thrasher's, *The Gang* (1927), where he equates personality with "the role which the individual plays in his group." Since the biological and psychological aspects seem to be almost neglected by Thrasher, his is too one-sided a definition. Close to Thrasher's are concepts which, taking their departure from one meaning of "role," that of the "unit of socialization," assert personality to be the internalization of roles (Lindzey, 1954, Vol. I, Ch. 6). And, of course, the "social-stimulus value" type of definition in general is classified here.

A problem of fundamental importance in this connection is the distinction to be made between a person's "social stimulus value" and his roles. As we shall find later, the term "role" has nearly as many meanings as has personality. But the objection raised by Mowrer and Kluckhohn (Hunt, 1944) to including "social stimulus value" as part of the personality because one *has* such value rather than *is* such value can hardly apply to the sociological concept of role. A family doctor's role exists in part *within* the doctor's organism, as his internal knowledge and feelings are represented and he incorporates his role in himself; but it could hardly exist without others, i.e., it is *interpersonal*. Both intrapersonal and interpersonal aspects of the role are *his*, however, one as much a part of this (complex) role function as the other.

One would not wish to class the carefully thought out definitions thus far presented as being only "part definitions." As we gather different kinds of definitions together, it appears that the elephant *is* different things to different men. Yet those conceptions of personality which include "within the individual" aspects only are not sufficient, for there are other aspects of the individual which are of greater importance in his ongoing way of life than some internal functions. A person's role as father is usually more important than his characteristic way of solving arithmetic problems or whether he is more interested in athletics than in intellectual things or whether or not he is a slight introvert. The common sense notion that personality *is* one's way of affecting others should act as a corrective here.[1]

On the other side of the ledger, definitions of the "social-stimulus" and role varieties sometimes leave out the internal organization which in part moves the individual to produce impressions or carry out his roles. Reference to the principle of psychology, "The individual is the locus of psychological functions," helps us to realize that discussions which center personality in its effect upon others make of personality a kind of mirror phenomenon. If your personality is only a reflection in others' eyes, as it were, *you* become a kind of ghost, a mirrored image. The principle cited is neglected, leaving us with no real locus of psychological functioning, almost it seems a reflection without a mirror, or to use a familiar figure from Lewis Carroll's *Alice*, a grin without a Cheshire cat. Both from the original "persona" meanings, indicating the character manifested in public and the inner structure of the "actor," as well as from the actual historical usages of "personality," it would seem well to define our terms in a larger way.

Biosocial

Definitions of the type classified here are termed "biosocial," because they take both biological and social functions into account. Such a definition is implied in the following statement from Gardner Murphy (1947), "A personality is a structured organism-

environment field, each aspect of which stands in dynamic relation to each other aspect. There is organization within the organism and organization within the environment, but it is the cross organization of the two that is investigated in personality research."[2]

A definition which, with its related discussion, has exercised greater influence with succeeding years is that of Andras Angyal (1941): "We use the term personality to denote the total organism when, as in man, the latter includes the social self and other factors which bind the individual into superindividual relationships." Angyal amplifies his meaning in another place in his remarkable text, *Foundations for a Science of Personality:*

The integration of the individual into the social group, the assimilation of its culture, of its written and unwritten codes, are just as essential for the personality development and personality organization as any of the physiological functions. Thus it appears that personality is a larger unit than a mere individual organism, because it also includes those factors through which it functions as a participant in the superindividual units of society and culture.[3]

Inasmuch as the writer has a definition to offer which strongly relates to these biosocial definitions, we hasten to the next section where that definition is set forth.[4]

---

[1] Allport declaims strongly against psychologists who neglect common sense of a high order when they step into their laboratories and forget the usage of traits in describing personality. But he himself neglects common sense of equal order when he holds personality entirely "within the individual." It seems that the man-on-the-street's notion of personality, seasoned as it is with experience, does not deserve the rebuff Allport gives it.

[2] Murphy is one of a number who have extended the concept of personality beyond the skin.

[3] Angyal, Andras. *Foundations for a science of personality.* New York: The Commonwealth Fund, 1941. Reprinted by permission of Harvard University Press.

[4] A miscellaneous group of definitions could be included, difficult to classify, but important in giving us an understanding of scientific concepts of personality. A few of these are:

"I am using the term 'personality,' by the way, in the inclusive sense of referring to the individual's organization of predispositions to behavior" (Newcomb, 1950).

Character (signifying personality) is "*l'ensemble des dispositions congenitales cui forme le squelette mental d' un homme*" (LeSenne, 1945).

Personality is "a complete realization of the fulness of our being" (Jung, 1939).

Raymond Wheeler's suggestive concept brings

AN INCLUSIVE DEFINITION

As the student learns the definition below—not a very difficult task!—it is well for him to keep in mind that definitions though helpful are arbitrary to some extent and that a definition can become a paralyzing thing in respect to the concept or entity it is supposed to symbolize. The definition given here is a point of reference, not a final statement of what personality is. It will be bettered, perhaps by someone reading these words; we know from the history of science that no final statements are really final.

PERSONALITY CONSISTS OF THE ORGANIZED FUNCTIONS OF THE INDIVIDUAL.

So simple, one may say, why, it has nothing to it! Quite to the contrary, the major objection should be to the fact that it seems to have *everything* in it: Personality consists of the organized functions of the individual. *All* functions. Some one may ask, does this include my growing of fingernails (toenails too?) and the passage of neural impulses along a nerve cell, and my being a student in school and the secretary of the Junior class? The answer is "Yes" in each case. One need not then, as we shall see, go over to the other extreme and reject the definition, now not for its simplicity but for its complexity.

Perhaps the key term in the above defini-

tion is "function."[1] Although there are relations of the mathematical meaning of "function" to the term we are using here, we do not mean anything like $y = f(x)$ (*i.e.*, y is equal to the f-function of x so that whenever a value is assigned to x, at least one other value of y is determined). We do mean by function *characteristic action* of the individual, usually normal, but sometimes special, even once-only. The use of the term implies a dynamic conception of personality. Is a man "honest"? What is meant is that he is behaving,[2] thinking, feeling, striving honestly. Honesty is not static, but a specific, dynamic manner of living. Is a man just or cruel or sensitive or masculine or obsessive? The same meaning holds true, in that he is behaving, thinking, feeling, striving in these ways. Like Heraclitus' stream, into which no man can step twice, personality and its individual components are dynamic—not only is the stream never the same again, but the man is not quite the same man and his traits are never quite the same. It is well to add on the other hand that viewing personality as a set of functions does not imply that personality has no permanency. A function as a dynamic process is a changing one, but may be changing as the physical organism changes, whose functions themselves may be considered as elements of personality; the physical organism replaces its substance but retains its structure.

It seems appropriate in discussing this "dynamic totality" to make a distinction between "organized" and "integrated." No authority has maintained that personalities are any more than *more or less integrated;* it is not that *all* parts work as *one* for the

---

together Gestalt contributions which, as we know, emphasize "wholeness" in and of all functions. ". . . personality is not the sum total of so many traits of character, not an integration of habits. Rather, it is a field property of the individual's total behavior" (Wheeler, 1932).

"Personality is not a technical, psychological term, but it may serve for convenience to include a number of varieties of mental traits which are not intellectual and yet which depend, in some measure at least upon the individual's native or inherited make-up" (Freeman, 1936).

Cattell gives what he calls a denotative definition in his *Personality*. "Personality is that which permits a prediction of what a person will do in a given situation" (Cattell, 1950).

"Personality, then, is the basis for psychological unity, coherence, and identity" (Kantor, 1938).

[1] Although there are semantic differences between the terms "function," "operation," and "process," they are used nearly synonymously in the text primarily for variety's sake.

[2] Behavior and behaving are not restricted here to muscle movement, but include what some psychologists would call conduct. In the first meaning behavior signifies "response," in the second it signifies any activity of the individual observable by others directly or indirectly, from bloodflow to presiding over a board of directors' meeting.

furtherance of some common activity, except under most exceptional circumstances. Even Lecky asserts that prior to recognizing that certain ideas are inconsistent with the individual's conception of himself they are maintained in the mind. The meat of what is meant by "organized" is instead in the state of being "organic," that is, parts of a living whole, of an organism when speaking of the biological functions, of the personality when speaking of functions which go beyond the organism. When we conceive of the organized functions of the individual thus, we do not need to defend the thesis that all the parts work together in an *integrated* fashion. Part functions, organized within themselves, may be operating at variance with one another, as in the conflict between an adolescent's conscience (which may be organized but not integrated) and his role as a member of a group seeking greater license. Even within the physiological organism there are sometimes malfunctions, processes which run counter to the health of the whole organism.

In one way, however, without pressing the concept of organization to the extent of meaning integration, we can conceive of an "organization of the whole personality." When cancer cells suddenly proliferate, their organized activity may be unwelcome to the total physiological organism, and yet *they are still part of the organism*. On the psychological plane when the person becomes a "dissociated personality," *even this dissociation takes place in the same individual*. In the self-functions, for example, as Murphy points out, a conflict is a demonstration of an organization of one kind: ". . . the fact that there is conflict is evidence of wholeness of a sort, for instead of functioning at two levels and developing two completely independent spheres of activity, the individual's picture of the self forbids even the temporary mutilation of the image" (Murphy, 1947). This concept is in keeping with Lecky's self-consistency idea as well. For other than self-functions, the same kind of argument might hold.

Pursuant to the ideas already expressed, the term "consists of" has been employed to link the subject and the predicate of our definition. In ordinary usage the term does not signify any necessary consistency among the elements enumerated in the predicate, but instead that something is composed of something else. In this case the composition is a set of functions which may be more or less consistent with one another, but at the very least are all related to the individual.

Emphasis in our definition is rightly placed on the *individual*, for the individual is the locus of all the functions to which we have referred; "mankind" or a "group mind," for example, are metaphysical terms to a large extent (Allport, 1954). One does not by any means deny the *reality* of the functions to which reference is made in what other sociologists called the "group mind"; all we need to recognize is that such functions would disappear were there no individuals. Nevertheless, it must also be recognized that these interpersonal functions are necessarily included in personality, *given* so many biological individuals.

A short digression is called for at this point. Some reflection on the definition given here reveals that it does not seem to differentiate between "life" and "personality." As previously stated, biologists find great difficulty in defining "life." A highly reputed biological authority, Von Bertalanffy (1952),[1] does venture to set up an admittedly limited definition of the living organism, a definition which may serve our purpose: "A living organism is a hierarchical order of open systems which maintains itself in the exchange of components by virtue of its system conditions." These "open systems" are the biological systems, integumentary, musculoskeletal, respiratory, circulatory, etc.; and the maintenance, exchange, and "system conditions" are normal functions of the organism. Life so defined is the prime requisite of personality, but personality includes in addition to the life functions: (1) those phenome-

---

[1] Von Bertalanffy (1952) was apparently the first to use the *organismic conception*.

nological characteristics which have been mentioned previously, the individual's interpretation of the self and the environment, his hopes and dreams, his feelings of shame and joy (more than visceral reactions), his self-consciousness, and so on, (2) those functions which commonly are classified as psychological beyond the phenomenological, judgment, reasoning, learning, and so forth, and (3) the social functions, of making impressions on other individuals, acting with or against them, and maintaining certain roles. Furthermore, should further research substantiate claims of Oriental and some Western scholars that there are supra-sensible functions of the individual, these would have to be differentiated from life.

Life is too narrow a term in some ways to be equated with personality; in others it is too broad. Living does not distinguish one individual from another, while personality is that which distinguishes one from another; functions are *characteristic* actions.

A striking example which may help to differentiate life and personality at least in one respect is the instance of a man who loses his arm by a clean cut near the shoulder. For a very brief time the arm remains *alive,* as long as the exchange of the components mentioned by Bertalanffy continues. Since the physical functions of the arm, however, are no longer part of the individual's functioning, these *physical* functions are not any longer incorporated as part of the organized functions of the individual. Yet the internalized *body image* still includes the arm, so that the functions of that portion of the body image are still (*psychological*) functions of the personality (Schilder, 1950).[1]

Thus, life functions may be included in personality, and are included in fact under most circumstances for our purposes; but according to the conception here, life and personality are not synonymous, except for metaphorical usages such as in the religious statement, "I am come that they might have life, and that they might have it more abundantly" (John 10:10).

Just as there is no way of separating certain life functions from personality functions, so there is no way of separating certain functions of a number of individuals one from another. "National policy" is a function of a number of individuals, but not of any one of them specifically. When we get beyond the individual to functions which he shares indistinguishably with others, then we can no longer consider that we are studying personality functions. The line between those functions which yet pertain to the individual (like role, status, group membership) and those supra-individual functions which do not pertain is not clearly marked at all. It seems safe, however, to keep the definition as we have it, even though we are not always certain as to what can be referred to the individual: "Personality consists of the organized functions of the *individual.*"

"PERSONALITY CORRELATES"

In the light of *various* definitions of personality and especially of the one just given, it seems that the use of a phrase like "personality correlates of visual functions" or "personality correlates of such-and-such attitudes" is rather anomalous. Even though the writer employed a fairly inclusive definition in carrying out his doctoral research, his dissertation was inconsistently entitled

---

[1] In this connection we may inquire whether physique is a part of personality. Our physiques certainly are factors distinguishing us from one another. In one way it may be agreed that the physique is only the sub-stratum for various functions of the individual, the *sine qua non* of personality without actually being part of the personality. We react positively or negatively to our physiques as do others; we play roles on the basis of them, as in the case of a football player or

circus midget. Usually, however, we would not consider physique itself as being a function. Today, especially in the study of body mechanics, the physique is viewed dynamically, so we may even be able to include physique as a function or set of functions, and thus an integral portion of personality. However, the writer is not prepared at present to subsume physique under personality, but only to consider physique and personality related.

"Personality Correlates of Religious Attitudes as Determined by Projective Techniques." Indeed, such titles, like the speeches of Hamlet's actor, can be said "trippingly on the tongue." But even if personality refers only to "those psychophysical systems which make for unique adjustments to environment," a person's religious attitudes are as much a part of his personality as any other of these systems. The psychological journals are replete with such studies of "personality correlates," performed by scholars who just as solemnly define personality in terms similar to the *sum-total* of all the organism's adjustment systems.

Is there any justification for this paradoxical procedure? To save his own and other psychologists' faces, the writer finds some justification in the usage, in that there are some more central and proximal portions of the personality which might be more important, as relatively enduring portions of the personality, than, say a passing attitude. In keeping with much authoritative research in the field of personality we may speak of "personality" as referring to emotional-motivational aspects (which may be called "temperamental-social functions"), and speak of the intellectual and physiological functions as "correlates." Why these latter functions should be excluded from personality is difficult to see, inasmuch as any of the more inclusive definitions of personality given above logically includes them. Despite chagrin over catching himself in an inconsistency, however, the writer is glad that neither his research nor that of others must wait until a perfect consistency is achieved.

Personality in Lower Organisms

Not only the definition of personality given above but many other definitions as well leave room for personality in animals and possibly even in plants. Although ordinarily personality research is limited to human beings, there seems to be no reason to deny personality in animals. Almost any dog fancier insists that his Rover has personality and offers details about the way in which Rover's personality is expressed.

Work on chimpanzees (Hayes, et al., 1950, 1952, 1953a, b; Kellogg & Kellogg, 1933) and other animals does not allow us to deny mentation or emotions or social functions to animals. In fact, with the *possible* exception of self-processes and introspection we admit all other functions of personality in animals; and even some of the self-processes, such as self-concepts, levels of aspiration, and the like, can be inferred for animals as well as man—at least, for the higher animals. Murphy (1947) speaks of such lowly creatures as chickadees (representing other similar organisms) as "primitive individual personalities." It seems, though, that it would be neither interesting nor profitable to carry such a study very far down the phylogenetic scale.

Plants, including trees, present a different problem. Inasmuch as they are without nervous systems, the fact that both social and individual functions can be found—one of our distinguished sociologists delivered a lecture on "The Sociology of a Garden" [1]—does not seem to warrant extending personality to individual plants. Great trees, of course, possess "character" in more than a metaphorical sense. Lapsed-time photography shows us the striving, seeking, even problem-solving nature of some very lowly plants. If someone cares to attribute personality to plants, there should be no objection, as if we had to defend the dignity of man by refusing lower organisms a term so highly valued among men; but neither does there seem to be much advantage in the practice.

Summary

Difficult as it has been found to define personality, a review of definitions and kinds of definitions yields considerable understanding of personality itself. Although different classes of definitions may be determined, those which appear to satisfy modern concepts are:

[1] Dr. Raymond F. Bellamy.

1. *Characterological*—referring to qualities which represent more or less enduring psychological properties of an individual.

2. *Phenomenological*—referring primarily to self-concepts, all that may be identified as "me."

3. *Biopsychological*—including concepts of psychophysical adjustment systems, which consist at least of intelligence, character, temperament, and constitution.

4. *Sociological*—referring to role functions.

5. *Biosocial*—inclusive of intrapersonal and interpersonal functions. The definition employed by this text is related to other biosocial definitions: Personality consists of the organized functions of the individual. As thus defined, personality may be differentiated from life in that it refers to the individual, and in that it includes functions not properly subsumed under life, psychological and social functions at least. Also, as defined, personality encompasses those functions sometimes considered only correlative, attitudes, intellect, and physiological processes, for example. Personality need not be denied to creatures other than man, but this text concerns itself with human personality.

QUESTIONS

1. What do definitions of personality provide for us besides a delimitation of subject matter?

2. Distinguish among the various classes of personality definitions given in the text: characterological, phenomenological, biopsychological, sociological, and biosocial.

3. Give verbatim the definition of personality employed in the text.

4. What is meant by "function" as the unit of personality? what by the term "individual"?

5. Distinguish between: "organization" and "integration" in personality; "life" and "personality"; role functions rightly included in personality and social functions of groups of individuals.

6. What are "personality correlates"?

7. Discuss the possibility of personality in lower organisms.

SECTION II

PERSONALITY FUNCTIONING IN GENERAL

CHAPTER 3

CONTINUITY AND CONSISTENCY OF FUNCTIONS

The expression "unity of personality" [1] is not employed in this book in part because it begs the question involved in the very study of personality. If one assumes that there is a unity, actually a complete integration, then research on what relatedness there is to personality functions, cross-sectionally or longitudinally, is purely academic. If on the other hand, one assumes with most personologists that many part-functions may overlap and may be interrelated, but that also they may be relatively uncorrelated and even inconsistent with one another, then an inquiry into the degree of relatedness is in order. In reality, how much consistency there is across present functions and how much continuity there is across a period of time occasion most of the research in personality today. To the uninitiated any question about whether we are "the same person" from time to time smacks of the inane if not of the insane. Yet the assumption of continuity of personality has been challenged—with reason. So, too, personology has found no *a priori* reason for assuming that all part-functions of personality are directly correlated at any one time.

In this chapter the results of research into longitudinal continuity and cross-sectional consistency are presented. Examples of the kinds of investigations employed in the several areas of personality research are described briefly in order to show how

[1] Cf. Allport, *Personality* (1937a), Chapter XIII.

personologists have arrived at the present stage of understanding. It will be seen that a scientific viewpoint today steers between the Scylla of a "fuzzy totalism" (as Stern termed it) and the Charybdis of a complete specificity which allows no consistency or relatedness to the personality at all. [2]

LONGITUDINAL CONTINUITY

A continuity from one stage of development to another seems to hold on the physiological level of functioning, even

[2] Scheerer (1946) states a position that is not out of harmony with that held here: "Following William Stern's suggestions, however, we should expect that the whole person will manifest his individual characteristics, not to the same degree, but to different degrees in different activities. For example, he would express himself with varied uniqueness, in handwriting, in projective test or problem solving situations. With this qualification, not only the thought processes should bear the stamp of the person's organizational matrix, but perceptions, feelings, and motor-acts as well. On second thought, these apparently different processes may actually be one unitary performance in which no true separation exists, but, instead, one definite pattern, in which emoting, thinking, and perceiving articulate in a configurated dynamic relation to each other. If all this be true, then the terms, perception, emotion, and thinking, in their separate applications, would be only conventional abstractions which the psychologist is forced to make, in order to maintain the control of otherwise boundlessly merging and numerically overwhelming variables. . . ." Reprinted by permission.

though new functions appear and old ones disappear (Gesell, *et al.*, 1938, 1939, 1943, 1947). New materials replace old in cells of heart and lungs, in veins and all functioning cells, yet the same functions continue from first appearance until final degeneration. At a higher level of organization there is, to be sure, the appearance and disappearance of certain functions which are called for in the development of the organism, sometimes for reasons not understood. Instances of these ephemeral functions are the "grasping reflex" and "Babinski reflex" of the infant. In the former the child has a grasp strong enough to support his entire weight by one hand; and in the latter his toes fan out when parts of the soles of his feet are stroked with a fine-pointed object. These reflexes appear in the first half-year of life and then are gone, except in persons manifesting pathological conditions. Yet despite these exceptions to a general rule, when children are followed longitudinally, their characteristic manner of functioning physiologically is evident. Most children seem to follow an over-all pattern of development of such functions, allowing for the establishment of developmental norms like those found in good infant tests. Each child, however, appears to possess an individual pattern of his own, his own manner of unfolding the over-all pattern; and what is important here, his characteristic expression of the physiological functions can be recognized from one stage to the next. There is no insistence here that the functions under consideration are exactly similar from one period to the next. All that can reasonably be asserted is that they are recognizable as belonging to the same individual when observed over a period of time.

What has been said for children concerning the relative continuity of physiological functioning is even more applicable to the adult. His personal physician can often identify the characteristic manner in which his organ systems operate. Indeed, what for one person would be a dangerously high rate of basal metabolism in another is the usual thing; and what for one is a normal pattern of brain waves for another is an evidence of abnormality.

Thus, while many processes bring about a change in the organism, there is a continuity to the organism physiologically. There is also a continuity of psychological functioning which appears to keep the same individual's functions of yesterday *in some sort of relation* to his functions of today. We need not maintain that, for example, the "self" of yesterday is exactly the same "self" as that operating in the individual today, any more than we need deny that there may be "selves" contemporaneous to one another in the same individual. All that is claimed, on the basis of much evidence (*e.g.*, Tuddenham, 1959), is that there is some measure of continuity of psychological functions, including self-functions, across a period of time.

Inasmuch as the self-concept is so important in modern psychology, and especially since in personality psychology the concept of self-consistency has been stressed (Lecky, 1945), an experiment which tends to raise questions about the continuity of the self is cited here (Bach, 1952). Following up his patients in group therapy, the investigator makes a practice of presenting to each person 300 cards on which are typed statements representing memories of childhood which a number of persons, including the subject, uttered in the beginning of group therapy. Statements are taken from several sessions, individual and group, but all from the first four to six weeks of psychotherapy. In the small experiment reported, twelve persons were given the 300 statements, including from six to 45 of their own, after periods ranging from three months to three years and ten months. Each subject sorted the statements into three groups, his own memory statements, those not his own but true of his past life, and those not applying to him at all. The first group is of special interest to us. On the average, individuals claimed as their own only 52 per cent of the memories they had actually uttered in the first weeks of therapy. Further, the percentages recalled correctly ranged from only 10 per cent in one case to 82 per cent in another. The interpretation which the therapist put on the rejection of so many memory statements is that the memory is among other things an *instrumental agency* reinforcing the person's *present* self, not a static repository of a stable past.

One could protest against these results by saying that possibly people carry former self-concepts in their unconscious memories, or that the sample is too small to draw conclusions, or that these individuals were not well-integrated anyway, else they would not be in therapy. Nevertheless, research that the writer and his colleagues have done with several hundred university students, supposedly normal individuals, tends to support the previous conclusion. This research, done in relation to changes of specific attitudes and practices in the first three months of the Freshman year, revealed much change in some fairly fundamental self-attitudes *without the individual's being aware at times that these had changed.* One epitomized this lack of awareness as she looked over the first form she had filled out (after completing the second one), "Did *I* say that!"

The recovery of memories under hypnosis or narcoanalysis suggests, however, that memory functions are more stable than either of the preceding experiments would lead us to conclude. And as far as is known, these memories are regarded by subjects as belonging to themselves, at least under the narcotic or in hypnosis. "Memories" may sometimes be implanted by suggestion; consequently we cannot always be sure that what one "remembers" is what actually took place in the past. To the extent that "memories" are false they cannot be regarded as evidence of continuity. Enough genuine recovery of memories, of self as distinct from others, has been effected in states of hypnosis and narcosis, to suggest strongly that a fairly strong relation obtains between "yesterday's personality" and "today's personality." Such evidence for the continuity of the self cannot be disregarded and must certainly be set along side of the

data concerning changes in self-concepts.

An acceptable interpretation of longitudinal continuity of functions, including self-functions, appears to lie between the almost indignant position of most psychologically naive persons, that, of course, they are exactly the same persons they were ten years ago, and a system of psychology which appears to deny any real relation among past and present functions. Most major systems of interpretation of personality have assumed some continuity across time to psychological as well as physiological functions. Even in Lewin's system of dynamic psychology in which there is a strong emphasis on the *present* life-space in the individual's existence the past is regarded as somehow continuous with the present. Some have been led to believe that Lewin virtually neglected past experience in the history of the organism. But a careful reading of his pertinent writings (K. Lewin, 1935, 1946) shows that the "life-space" includes *both* past and present (as well as projections of thought and feeling into the future). Even in Lewin's system, then, some interrelatedness of past and present functioning is maintained. (Cf. Figure 13, p. 85.)

CROSS-SECTIONAL CONSISTENCY

General Consistency and Integration of Functions

Integration of Functions. Clinical psychologists tend to assume that there is a general consistency to personality within any brief period of time. They do not usually doubt that by getting enough information about an individual they can find a general over-all consistency, even to the place of a high degree of predictability. This assumption of clinicians must not be dismissed merely because it is not based entirely or even to a great extent on experimental evidence. Nor should the assumptions be ignored of other workers outside the field of psychology who maintain consistencies of the personality. The detective, for example, by patient study of a person's varied movements may be able to predict with considerable accuracy the subsequent movements of a criminal. He, like the clinician, is trying to take "all the facts" about a person into account. The family doctor is another who may make wise forecasts of physiological and psychological behavior of some of his patients whom he has come to know "inside and out."

On the whole, however, the evidence which does not depend on lucky guesses and "clinical intuition" does not uphold a general consistency of personality. It may well be that our instruments for measuring are crude, and that as they become more refined and capable of handling more variables with greater accuracy, more subtle consistencies will be manifest. For centuries in natural science certain physical phenomena, namely gravitation and electricity, seemed inconsistent with each other. If modern physical theory holds true, however, these phenomena are lawfully related (Einstein & Infeld, 1938). Perhaps the various functions of personality which now seem inconsistent with one another will some day be drawn together in a comprehensive theory. It seems safe to predict that any such unifying theory would have to be a "field theory" parallel to modern physical "field theory"; for all of the interpersonal functions of personality and probably most if not all of the intrapersonal ones are diadic rather than monadic (related to others rather than existing within the individual apart from other persons) (Sears, 1951). It is doubtful, however, even with a unifying theory based on far more adequate measures of personality than we have now that all functions will be discovered to be directly correlated with one another in even the most highly integrated individual.

At present our data do permit us to say that some individuals are more consistent from one function to another, are far more integrated than others. In the experiment cited above the patients ranged from 10 to 82 per cent in the correctness of identifying memories. While we may not say that the latter individuals are thoroughly consistent, they are at least more consistent in some areas than are others. (We say, "You can always count on John.") However, such statements do not mean that any individual is perfectly consistent, or integrated, or even that in the most highly consistent individual there will not be broad areas which are relatively uncorrelated with most other functions of his personality.

Consistency and "Congruence." A useful concept to help order the actual observable phenomena is Allport's doctrine of "congruence," though this concept needs expansion if it is to take account of the individual differences we know to exist among human beings. According to Allport's analysis, individual items of behavior may be at considerable variance with one another. As the psychologist probes beneath these external forms of behavior, however, as he must if he does not view the organism as a stimulus-response mechanism (Skard, 1937), he discovers that there are often reconciling elements in the personality which make the contradictory behaviors understandable and "congruent." In the accompanying diagram (Figure 3) a graphic demonstration is made of congruence in the case of D, a teacher. His manifest behavior is indeed contradictory. His individual acts are sometimes orderly, but ofttimes disordered, sometimes meticulous, sometimes careless. (These acts are depicted as small black and white squares.) But analysis of the behaviors leads to recognition that in respect to his personal possessions D is careful and neat, indicating a trait of neatness in this regard. His slovenliness in respect to others' possessions is the other of the opposing traits. These two seemingly diametrically opposed traits are seen, however, as the resultant of a single cardinal trait of self-centeredness. Thus, the discordant behaviors and traits are congruent in that they can be traced to the *radix* or root in a single basic trait.

A similar case is that of a young girl who went to a psychologist after getting into trouble with the school authorities. She was one of the neatest, most orderly young women the psychologist had ever counseled. Her general deportment was exemplary. And yet, she was apprehended for

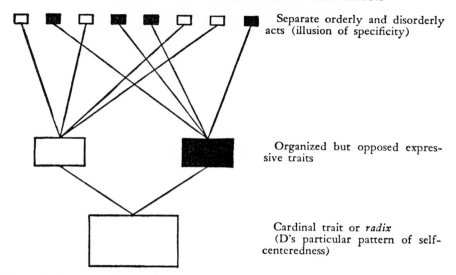

Separate orderly and disorderly acts (illusion of specificity)

Organized but opposed expressive traits

Cardinal trait or *radix* (D's particular pattern of self-centeredness)

Figure 3. An illustration of congruence. (From G. W. Allport, *Personality*, p. 358)

having in her possession many books from the library—not charged out. In the course of her counseling treatment she revealed that her kleptomania had been expressed in other ways. An interview with the parents revealed that she had been a "model girl" in most of her childhood activities. Her mother therefore was at a loss to explain what seemed like most uncharacteristic behavior when the girl entered the menarche; so neat and tidy in every other way, she took her soiled pants and hid them among newspapers or magazines where her mother would run onto them a month or more later.

The psychologist could have accepted these as merely discordant bits of behavior: the neatness, cleanliness, and usually moral behavior, as opposed to the isolated uncleanness and socially unacceptable behavior. Of course, he was not satisfied and probed deeper. He found that an exceedingly strict toilet training—the mother was proud of having trained the child by ten months—symbolized an equally strict upbringing, an anxious mother accomplishing what she set out to accomplish, the production of a "good" daughter, clean, obedient, and pure, but also accomplishing more than she intended, the production of a daughter

who inwardly rebelled and outwardly engaged in compulsive forms of "contradictory" behavior whose meaning was just as puzzling to her as to her mother. The behaviors turned out to be "congruent" in the light of the deeper analysis.

"Yet the conception of congruence must not be carried too far," Allport (1937) writes. "To say that whatever occurs in a personal life is *ipso facto* consistent with everything else is going to a pointless extreme." Not only must the conception not be carried to an extreme, it must also be recognized that it cannot be applied with equal force to all persons. We know from many studies that individuals differ widely in ability to generalize, both on the conscious and unconscious levels of thought. Therefore, some persons are capable of operating more "congruently" or consistently than others. Other things being equal, there is probably a curvilinear relation between intelligence and ability to be consistent or congruent: The very simple of intellect and the highly intelligent are most likely more capable in these respects than the middle levels. Of course, other factors of culture and emotion distort a simple curvilinear relation.

Another extension to the concept of congruence which is implied in Allport's original discussion, but not made explicit, is the degree of consistency between role functions and inner experiences. "The Colorado River has a wonderful power," a preacher once said. "People who all their lives until coming to Southern California have been pillars of their churches back in Iowa or Kansas suddenly on arriving in California lose their religion and never darken the doors of a church." The speaker's psychological insight did not extend to a comprehension of what is the most probable explanation, that the person's needs for recognition and status were met in his midwestern community where the church held a high position. They were not met in the materialistic culture of Southern California where the church competes for position, not always successfully, with seven-day markets, Hollywood, beaches, mountain resorts, and race tracks. Thousands, of course, do not "lose their religion" at the Colorado River. Their roles in different subcultures are thus relatively consistent. In the first case, however, seemingly contradictory roles and inner experience may not be as inconsistent with each other as they at first seem to be. In California the inner needs for status may very well have been met by *different* roles (in a lodge, club, or community organization), but not *dissimilar* roles.

Differentiation and Integration. The "doctrine" of congruence (and also Lecky's self-consistency) is admittedly an attempt of a highly abstract nature to fit facts together which might otherwise be disparate. There are other less abstract principles which can assist us in interpreting our data. One of these principles stemming from biology is the twin process of differentiation and integration in the development of organisms.[1] In the course of development from single cell to adult individual a process of *differentiation* of structure and accompanying functions occurs in multicelled creatures by which the original cell becomes a group of organs, each organ performing its separate function and each part of an organ functioning in its peculiar way. Yet at the same time the group of organs becomes a system of organs functioning interdependently in a more *integrated* way. We should not expect biological functions to be either completely consistent (correlated), or yet completely discordant with one another in the total organismic functioning. If we take one function of the integumentary system (which is primarily the skin), that of growing fingernails, we shall presumably find some, but not great, correlation with fluctuations in blood flow, a function of the cardiovascular system. Perhaps if our measurements were fine enough, however, even these widely separated functions of specialized organs would be found to correlate more highly. Demonstrable correlations can be found between the operation of adrenalin in the blood and of the sympathetic nervous system; indeed, adrenalin is called "a sympathicomimetic substance" because it mimics the sympathetic system.[2]

In respect to more complex psychological functions, Lewin (1946) has spoken of the "differentiation of the various dimensions of the life space." Not only are there successively greater differentiations, Lewin maintains, within the *present* life space of the developing person, but the older individual in contrast to the younger differentiates within his life space along the psychological *time dimension*. He separates both near past from far past and near future from far future. And along the reality-

[1] The most lucid discussion of this process the writer has found is in Morgan, *Child Psychology* (1942), which is admittedly a tertiary source for knowledge of embryology and especially organogenesis. Gardiner, *The Principles of General Biology* (1952) gives an account of the process, as would presumably any good biology text. Murphy (1947) attributes to Herbert Spencer the concepts of differentiation and integration, then gives credit to Heinz Werner for documenting the concepts. The writer first became acquainted with these ideas in Morgan where Paul Weiss is given credit for the elaboration in experimental work on animals.

[2] The adrenal medulla which secretes adrenalin is under direct control of the nervous system, so there is an initial relation here as well (Carlson & Johnson, 1948).

irreality dimension he makes more accurate differentiations between truth and lying, and between perception and imagination. Further, the degree of differentiation of life space, like that of physiological functions, proceeds at different speeds for different individuals and at different rates within the same individual from stage to stage. While psychological differentiation is going on, integration is proceeding likewise as part of the "twin process." An infant responds as a whole perceptual-motor being; he "looks" with his hands, literally "takes in" an object via his mouth. An adult, on the other hand, thinks of or perceives an object with little or no observable perceptual-motor behavior except the remnants of former psychomotor activity registered by action currents in the muscles. But the adult's *coordination* of hand and eye, of perceptual and motor apparatuses is certainly superior to that of the infant.

In other words, differentiation and integration serve to *lower* some correlations and *raise* others. We should expect from the operation of the process, then, to find some functions more consistently linked together at some stages of development and less consistently at other stages, and vice-versa with other functions. So with even a "highly integrated" individual we should find some functions with low correlations among themselves; in fact, the more highly integrated the individual, since integration and differentiation are two sides of a coin, the lower would be the correlation expected among some spheres of activity. It is probably no accident that the persons who seem capable of acting most consistently (on a mature intellectual level) also seem to be capable of making the finest discriminations in judgment.

To carry the differentiation-integration process into social and cultural functions of the individual may be extending it too greatly and may not add much in the way of explanation for the consistencies and inconsistencies of the individual. It is true that the role functions of the person become more highly differentiated as he gets older. At first his role is "just baby," but contrary to Shakespeare he soon "plays many parts," all at one time, not seriatim. His roles differentiate into sibling, play partner, boy or girl, nursery school child, and so on in a bewildering profusion. Just as there is a differentiating process, there seems to be a comparable mechanism which could be called role integration. This process may be related to some type of self-consistency, whereby the organism strives to keep a coherent self in the midst of conflicting external demands, and hence endeavors to keep its role functions consistent. The fact of role differentiation does aid us in finding a superficial explanation for lack of correlation among functions; unless something like self-consistency or congruence is present, however, role integration does not help very much in showing why some individuals play generally consistent roles, or refuse to play some that are inconsistent with these. They respond to approximately the same external demands which stimulate others but with different role-behaviors from others'.

Levels of Personality. One other "explanation" of apparent consistencies and inconsistencies within the personality is the concept of "levels of personality," or sometimes we may say "layers of personality" to correspond with biological facts.[1] As the biological organism develops in layers of cells, especially as the three germ layers (ectoderm, mesoderm, and endoderm) develop, and out of these develop further complex structures, so we can judge from depth analysis (free association, dream analysis, hypnosis, narcoanalysis) that the psychological and social functions of the

[1] Chapter 12 gives a more extended discussion of central and peripheral functions of which the discussion here is a special case. A further discussion of "levels of the mind" is found in contributions to David and Von Bracken's *Perspectives in Personality Theory* (1957) by Lersch and Gilbert. The latter suggest on the basis of European stratification theory that overlapping strata are found integrated in personality: vegetative (associated with the "old brain"), orectic (conative and affective), cognitive-volitional, and super-conscious intentions. Thus far the last-named is only regarded as potentially present, inasmuch as "there is no evidence against its existence."

organism may figuratively develop layer upon layer. In the deepest layers are those experiences which perhaps are forever buried from coming to conscious awareness, but they are still operative, are still functions of the individual. These, even for the individual himself, can only be inferred from their effects. In relatively more outward layers are those functions which may, under various conditions, come to awareness, but ordinarily are hidden even from the awareness of the individual possessing them. In even more outward layers are functions which are "known" to the person, but which he keeps from others as best he can. Then finally are those layers open to others, layers including psychomotor and psychosocial functions.

Along this line, two social psychologists suggest the relatively simple formulation of three levels; because of the context the statement of these levels is phrased in social psychological terms:

Level I, the level of public communication, the overt, interpersonal behavior of the subject as rated by professional observers, or by his peers in the group; Level II, the level of conscious description, what the subject reports about the interpersonal activity of himself and others, in conversation, on questionnaires, on check lists; and Level III, the interpersonal themes expressed in dreams, fantasies and projective tests (Leary & Coffey, 1955).[1]

Whoever has done any research in personality (or whoever has been observant) recognizes the usefulness of the level concept in whatever way it is expressed. And as the authors of the above statement point out, psychological or psychiatric diagnoses appear sometimes to be inconsistent because the observer slips unwittingly from one level to another in his personality description.

A logical deduction from the "levels" concept might well be that the "deeper" one goes, the more consistency there is to

be found. After all, are not the deeper layers more basic and thus more "real"? This deduction is sometimes implied in the belief that if the unconscious (deeper level) functions can be uncovered, we are getting down to the "real person." Why the unconscious processes should be regarded as more real than conscious problem-solving or taking the role of a tool-maker is difficult to see. In actuality, according to both theory and empirical observation, there is to be expected less consistency on the deeper levels rather than more. The levels concept derives in part from psychoanalysis (Fenichel, 1945); and the latter postulates greater inconsistency in deep layers than in superficial ones.

In one place Freud wrote:

The strangest characteristic of the unconscious (repressed) process, to which no investigator can become accustomed without the exercise of great self-discipline, is due to their entire disregard of reality-testing; they equate reality of thought with external actuality, and wishes with their fulfillment . . .[2]

And somewhat later he stated that these processes are not only slightly related to external reality but are also timeless, *i.e.,* bear no relation to time, so that facts of long ago lie side by side with facts of today even though both sets of facts are entirely contradictory to each other. An example of the latter would be both believing and disbelieving that a dead loved one still lives. Such contradictions seem so manifestly absurd to the average "normal" person that he dismisses the contention that there are such "crazy ideas" except in mentally ill persons. It is only necessary, however, to cite the processes occurring in dreams to show that normal persons hold these "crazy ideas," too. In dreams, absurdities are the rule, dead people live, "impossible" situations occur unsurprisingly, people and things are transformed from one state to another as

[1] Leary, T., & Coffey, H. S. Interpersonal diagnosis: some problems of methodology and validation. *J. abnorm. soc. Psychol.*, 1955, *50*, 114. Reprinted by permission.

[2] From the new edition: *The standard edition of the complete psychological works of Sigmund Freud*, edited by James Strachey, Vol. 12, p. 225. Reprinted by permission of the publisher, The Hogarth Press of London, England.

easily as in any fairy tale, and the individual sees himself doing things he "would never do in actuality." These apparently universal phenomena suggest that such contradictions within deeper parts of the individual cannot lightly be dismissed as Freudian balderdash.

In general, we may expect more consistency on the outer levels of personality. In the daily contacts we make, in our usual roles, we must act more "logically" and must find "reasonable" meanings for our activities. And yet, some of the most glaring inconsistencies may be found in overt behaviors, that is, on the outermost levels of personality. In some parts of the country the most outspoken advocates of "State's rights" vote regularly against "home rule" for local municipalities. Apparently the evident contradiction between their behaviors in the two situations escapes them entirely.

As contradictions exist within any layer, so between layers there may be inconsistencies. If there are portions of a person's being operating without regard for reality, sometimes an individual may behave rationally and think irrationally. Or he may take roles which do not jibe with his self-concepts. In some cases the individual recognizes the inconsistency and takes various defensive or alteration measures. In other cases, acting consciously but under the influence of unconscious motives, he reasons in devious ways—rationalizes—to explain his strange behavior.

If the above reasoning is in accord with facts—and even though its biological analogy may not be acceptable, the evidence of different "layers" is extensive—then many of the inconsistencies of personality, factors lowering coefficients of correlation sometimes to the vanishing point, are recognizable as differences *between* layers or contradictions *within* the same layers.

There are other explanations of the consistencies and lack of consistency of the personality, but the ones presented here are probably inclusive in one form or another of the major endeavors to cope with the issue.

Specific Consistency and Interrelatedness

Thus far we have been speaking in general terms concerning the extent to which various functions of the individual go together. In this section we present more specific evidence as to that "going together." The aim here is not to support doctrines of "specificity" or "generality" of personality traits, but to indicate by experimental evidence the degrees of consistency found among a number of representative functions. Of necessity the materials presented here encroach upon later chapters, but a more inclusive viewpoint is taken here. Only a limited number of the multitudes of experiments can be reported, of course.

One caution is noted in regard to experiments outlined here and others which may be read in the psychological literature. In the main, correlation coefficients are intended to express the degree of relationship between or among various part-functions. It is well to emphasize at this point that a coefficient of a certain size does not indicate a percentage of relationship. When a Pearson product-moment r is squared, it signifies the proportion of variance of one set of *measurements* associated with the variance of another set. Note that the association is between sets of measurements; and that these measurements are subject to all the errors to which measurements are liable. Therefore, coefficients may or may not be representative of the actual degree of association or lack of actual association between or among functions. If a coefficient is high or if it is low, it may be so by chance. Nevertheless, if we can be fairly certain our measurements are valid, a correlation coefficient is far superior to unaided judgment.

Psychophysiological Functions. The autonomic nervous system and other physiological activity has been investigated as measures of personality in several ways. Experiments with infants and adults (Wenger & Irwin, 1936) indicated that electrical skin resistance (psychogalvanic skin reflex, mediated by the autonomic nervous system) decreases with much muscular tension and increases with relaxation. Small fluctuations in resistance occur at low resistance levels (much muscle tension) and large fluctuations at high levels. But when measures are standardized to have equal means and standard deviations, relatively the same degree and pattern of variability may be found from individual to individual, regardless of the actual level of resistance. Children at the Fels Research Institute (Wenger, 1943), ages six to twelve, were rated on a five-point scale of muscular tension (with a fair degree of agreement among raters). These ratings and a number of objective measures of physiological functions and one anatomical index, together with the child's age, were intercorrelated. Intercorrelations were low generally, except where a direct or inverse relation would be expected (*e.g.*, diastolic blood pressure and pulse pressure). Sufficient relation was found, however, among the measures to extract two factors by factor analysis: (1) An autonomic factor, and (2) a muscular factor which correlated positively with the muscle tension ratings. The same or very similar muscle tension factor was produced in another investigation (Duffy, 1946) in which sixteen different measures of muscle tension were taken under stress conditions. The conclusion in the last experiment is that the presence of a general factor of the nature measured suggests that individuals are characteristically high, low, or intermediate in muscle tension.

Related experiments involving stress (Lacey, 1943; Lacey, Bateman, & Van Lehn, 1953; Lacey & Van Lehn, 1952) have disclosed that there is individual patterning of cardiovascular variables, although some variables are more discriminative among individuals than others. Further, general autonomic reactivity is not so characteristic of an individual as is a pattern of being relatively hyporeactive in one function and hyperreactive in another. Contrary to theories in psychosomatic medicine (Alexander, 1948), to the effect that every emotion has its characteristic physiological

syndrome, these latter results are more in keeping with a personalistic emphasis: Autonomic nervous system reactivity shows a variety of individual patterns depending on the genetic and experiential factors brought by the person to a specific stress situation. Some individuals tend to respond with a given pattern virtually always, regardless of the stress, others may do so most of the time, and still others exhibit what appears to be a random choice of reactivity patterns.

Supporting the relations found in other work are correlation coefficients ranging from .28 to .49 among skin temperature, skin resistance, and pulse rate (Baker, 1954). Measures were taken at rest and under stress conditions, so that evidently in either rest or stress some association is present among these functions, but not a striking relation in any case.

Generally, then, there is some measure of correlation among psychophysiological functions, but the degree of correlation differs from individual to individual. Insofar as high correlation signifies consistency in the personality, it may be deduced that there is moderate to fair consistency among these functions. The same principles seem to hold among psychomotor functions.

Psychomotor Functions. Expressive Movements. A classic set of experiments relating to physically measurable functions of the organism is that of Allport and Vernon (1933). These researchers, relating their work to physiognomy and graphology, and to previous experimental work, put twenty-five men through a series of tests eliciting their "expressive movements." The authors define these latter as "*individual differences in the manner of performing adaptive acts, considered as dependent less upon external and temporary conditions than upon enduring qualities of personality.*" These movements, recorded several times, consisted of various aspects, over thirty in all, of reading and counting; walking and strolling; estimation of known sizes, distances, angles, and weights; arranging cubes; strength of grip; tapping; compression of a stylus with fingers; drawing geometrical figures; handwriting; muscular tension; and self-ratings of expressive characteristics. These measures were correlated by means of Spearman's ρ, which is a correlation coefficient approximating Pearson's r.

Allport and Vernon discovered that their subjects were consistent in the repetition of their tasks (both within the same experimental session, and across about eleven weeks) to the extent of a ρ of $+.68$ on the average; this figure is not as high as repeat-reliabilities expected in intelligence tests, but for the type of test employed, with a median of only about 30 seconds in length, it seems that the authors' conclusion is justified that, "Specific performances are to a rather high degree constant." That is, in a species of longitudinal investigation, individuals prove relatively consistent.

Further results of this well-known group of experiments lead us to believe that in respect to cross-sectional study of expressive movements "the left hand knows what the right hand is doing." But it does not always know completely by any means. For example, nothing like a "general speed factor" showed up in the investigations. That is, most of the subjects were not either generally speedy or generally slow on all tasks, tending instead to be slow on some and fast on others. Nor was there a "general motility factor" or anything like a man's being "consistently variable" about his own mean on all tasks.[1] And yet, in some fields a consistency was found; for instance, a kind of an "areal factor" appeared, relating such variables among others as area of total writing, over-estimation of angles, and length of walking stride. (Strangely, the length of strolling stride did not correlate highly with length of walking stride.)

Athletic Skills. Are the conclusions drawn in regard to the Allport and Vernon experiments borne out by other research? In the other psychomotor functions, have other investigators found the same limited consistency? From an overview of the literature it appears that the emphasis on "limited" would be greater in more recent research.

One instance of this emphasis is in an area in which many nonscientists would consider themselves authorities, that of athletic ability. It is often stated, "If a man is good in one sport, he'll be good in almost any." But correlational research does not bear out this dictum. In gross athletic skills the "all-round athlete" is the exception rather than the rule.[2] And when modern methods of mathematical analysis are applied to the skills underlying various sports and active games, specificity rather than generality turns out to be prevalent. Most evidence points in this direction.

An experiment (Hempel & Fleishman, 1955) in one series of investigations of psychomotor functions illustrates the trend of recent research. Four hundred basic trainee airmen were administered forty-six carefully standardized tests of motor skills. The correlations among the tests were subjected to factor analysis. Only about thirteen or fourteen of the seventeen factors revealed have real meaning from either a psychological or physiological viewpoint. The experimenters group the factors into what seem like meaningful areas somewhat independent of one another:

a. Strength of limbs and trunk.
b. Flexibility of legs and trunk (ability of muscles to endure and recover from strain and distortion).
c. Balance, static or equilibrium, and dynamic or performance.
d. Gross body coordination.
e. Energy mobilization—ability to mobilize quickly and effectively a maximum of energy or force.
f. Manual dexterity—ability to make skillful, coordinated arm-hand movements.
g. Finger dexterity.
h. Arm-hand steadiness—precise, steady, arm-hand movements of the kind that minimize speed and strength.

[1] This finding appears to be in contradiction to Herrington's (1942) results, but the latter's findings concerning variability are limited strictly to physiological functions.

[2] In Helson's text (1951, ch. 4) Bayley gives a brief understandable discussion of work in this area with children and adolescents.

i. Aiming—movements requiring precise, visual alignment and motor control (eye-hand coordination).

j. Nonverbal reasoning factor.

What is the significance of these results in terms of personality? Although various interpretations can be given, we can say that prediction from one athletic ability to another is not as good as common opinion seems to hold. A person may be strong but not flexible, have general, over-all body coordination, but not finger dexterity, have high arm-hand steadiness but not good aiming ability. At the psychomotor level, and as we see later at other levels as well, various kinds of functions tend to be more specific than commonsense opinion recognizes.

Perceptual-Motor Behavior. The relations holding between perceptual and motor functions are logically the next area to which our attention should be drawn. In this case, the (nonscientific) man-on-the-street postulates a dissociation between perception and motor behavior to which the scientist cannot subscribe.

In the text *Mind: Perception and Thought*, which brought together much pre-World War II research in psychology and psychiatry, Schilder (1942b) illustrates the thesis that "Primitive perception . . . contains motion." While it is difficult to define "primitive perception," it may be identified as the basis of all highly developed, complicated perceptions. The reader may wish to try one of Schilder's experiments according to the following directions:

Hold your arms straight out in front of you so they are parallel to each other. Now raise one arm to about 45 degrees above the horizontal. Hold your arms in position for 25 seconds. Then close your eyes and lower the upper arm to the same position as the lower one, *i.e.*, parallel to it. Open your eyes then and look at your arms. Stop and do these things before reading any farther in order not to spoil the experiment.

Now, if you are approximately normal in muscle tone, your mobile arm came to rest about an inch higher than your resting arm. The kinesthetic perception of your arms in space has been altered by the movements in which you have engaged.[1]

Besides demonstrating the relation between movement and kinesthesis, Schilder likewise cites experiments in time perception where body rhythm and activity are important, though apparently not all-determining. Other kinds of perception also seem to be related to movement. Movement and visual perception have been shown to be involved with each other. In one representative experiment (Krus, 1953) subjects who had engaged in a pushing exercise saw significantly fewer moving objects in still pictures flashed on a screen than did subjects who had not exercised.

The intrinsic relation between perception and movement should not be surprising. After all, the organism's sensory and motor neurons are bound up in one nervous system. Indeed, it is sometimes surprising to discover how little related may be functions which are mediated by the same nervous system.

Psychomotor and Higher-Order Functions. When psychomotor behavior is correlated with other "psychological" functions, does the pattern of limited consistency still obtain? Roughly speaking, here again it does; but now we are in research territory where more variables and more complex ones are found.

In another pioneer experiment following Allport and Vernon's, Eisenberg (1937a) endeavored to relate expressive movements to dominance-feeling as measured by a "Social Personality Inventory." Eisenberg took men and women who scored at the extremes of the Inventory to represent those persons who are most dominant and least dominant in their concepts of themselves. Expressive movement tests similar to those employed by Allport and Vernon were supplemented by several unusual tests, like holding a hand dynamometer at half the individual's maximum grip for as long as possible. It was found that dominant-feeling men write and draw more rapidly

[1] Schilder, P. *Mind: perception and thought in their constructive aspects.* New York: Columbia Univer. Press, 1942. Reprinted by permission.

than nondominant-feeling men, cover more space on a page, exert more pressure on a pencil, and are less distracted under distraction conditions. Fewer reliable differences exist between women in expressive movements as related to their dominance-feelings. Eisenberg concluded that there is a "syndrome" of dominance and nondominance expressive behavior paralleling the comparable self-concepts. At any rate, some consistency is shown by the experiment between an individual's psychomotor and more complex psychological functions.

Of special interest to students of psychology is the relationship between handwriting and other functions of personality. Every so often amateur graphologists tell their audiences that they can "read your personality from your handwriting." How adequate are the claims of either amateur or professional graphologists? The only study to which most reference has been made in American psychological discussions [1] is not sound enough to warrant draw-

ing the negative conclusions usually drawn. Murphy (1947) calls attention to the values of graphology, but leaves unanswered the most important question: How valid are the judgments?

Several graphological experiments can be represented by one of Eysenck's (1947) and another (Pascal & Suttell, 1947) drawing opposite conclusions. Fifty hospital patients were given the task of copying a "personality questionnaire," [2] and also of answering the questionnaire for themselves. The hand-written copies were given to a female graphologist who was asked after studying them to answer the questionnaire as the individual would have answered it. She was then to match the handwriting with a personality sketch written by the patient's psychiatrist. By chance the graphologist should have agreed with the questionnaire 50 per cent of the time; in actuality the number of agreements was about

[1] Ever since 1919 many American psychologists have cited an experiment done under the direction of the late Clark Hull at the University of Wisconsin as proof of the failures of graphological study of personality (Hull & Montgomery, 1919). Seventeen students of a medical fraternity copied some lines from a magazine. Each of these students then rated the others in six character (personality) traits. "Graphic signs" for these traits, as manifested by various rather minute measurements of the handwriting, were correlated with the traits, and found to be unrelated to these latter. Roback (1934) and Allport and Vernon (1933) maintain (a) that the manner of obtaining personality ratings is invalid, and (b) that the microscopic, atomistic type of measuring handwriting does not follow any method employed by outstanding graphologists. It seems that both Roback and Allport and Vernon in their second objection missed the point of the experiment which was plainly to test the *specific signs alleged by graphologists* to be associated with certain "character traits" (with references to graphologists' writings in which the claims were made). The writer agrees that the experiment does not invalidate graphologists' general methods, but it did not set out to do so. Nevertheless, the experiment was not highly adequate methodologically in part because of the first objection raised above.

The work of a Britisher, Robert Saudek (1929), leaves one puzzled. One of the founders of the

Journal of Personality, Saudek was evidently highly regarded by McDougall. If the reports Saudek made of his graphological accomplishments are true, personologists are leaving one of the most potent instruments of personality examination out of their test batteries. In one case Saudek predicted which two out of about 70 bank employes would embezzle funds! Strangely, although this unusual graphologist left a record of his methods of handwriting analysis, no serious attempt has been made to replicate his work.

Werner Wolff (1948) made a number of experiments in graphology. Again, one is puzzled by the failure of personologists either to refute or support his work. Somewhat of a beloved "enfant terrible," Wolff seemed to skirt the fringes of academic, even clinically-oriented psychology. As in the case of Saudek, Wolff's ideas should be put to the test and accepted or rejected, not merely ignored because of their not being couched in familiar terms.

German graphology, represented primarily by Klages in *Handschrift und Charakter*, has not appealed to most American psychologists, possibly because it is more or less tied up with a more philosophical German psychology than Americans like.

[2] If the definition of personality employed in this text is used, "personality questionnaires" measure only part-functions of the personality. These are, to be sure, usually exceedingly important functions, self-attitudes, affective reactions, and so forth. But the questionnaires should be called "temperament inventories" as Guilford terms them.

62 per cent, a statistically significant rise above chance. Where the graphologist felt especially sure of her judgment, the number correct was about 68 per cent. For practicality, matchings with psychiatrists' "personality sketches" were made in 10 groups of five patients each. By chance here, then, one out of five matchings would have been correct; actually 2.4 matchings were correct on the average, again a very significant result over chance.

Eysenck warns rightly, that the coincidence of the graphologist's judgment and personality traits expressed in questionnaires and sketches does not prove actual correspondence between traits and handwriting signs. Nevertheless, there is a presumption that the signs and questionnaires are related to the actual psychological behavior of the individual.

Another study of a somewhat simpler nature (Pascal & Suttell, 1947) gave a graphologist the gross (and presumably less difficult) task of distinguishing between psychotics and normal controls. Psychotics wrote passages; then from typed copies normals wrote exactly the same passages, each abnormal subject having a matched normal control. There was one fairly accurate portrayal of a subject from his handwriting. On the whole, however, no better than chance differentiation occurred between normals and controls.

Consistency within the personality is neither proved nor disproved by the success or failure of a graphologist, of course. The handwriting expert may be inexpert. The question concerning the validity of handwriting analysis still awaits definitive answers. The question of how closely handwriting is related to the rest of the personality consequently must also wait.

Relating of even as complex a psychomotor function as driving skill to others illustrates the same principle that correlation of simpler skills to higher functions reveals. In one investigation (Parker, 1953) those truckers in a concern who had preventable accidents were distinguished from those who had nonpreventable accidents. (The former are not called "accident prone" be-

cause the term is a misleading one.) The only physiologically related variable differentiating the upper and lower halves of the "nonpreventable" group was visual acuity. But a number of variables from psychological tests differentiated the two halves of the "preventable" group. The fact that a number of such variables did not prove significant in predicting the separations into upper and lower halves underscores the thesis of this section: The individual has some consistencies among his functions, but it is not by any means nearly complete consistency.

Claims of relations between simpler and more complex functions, that perception of the vertical on which individuals differ widely (Witkin, Lewis, Hertzman, Machover, Meissner, & Wapner, 1954) is related to neuroticism and extraversion, seem not to be borne out by subsequent research (Taft & Coventry, 1958). It would be convenient if we could diagnose people as normals or neurotic on the basis of their ability to judge the verticality of a rod without an adequate frame of reference, or place them on some (possible) continuum of introversion-extraversion in the same way. But correlations between the perceptual-motor behavior and temperament patterns do not at present allow us to be so quick and easy in diagnosis.

Borderline Functions. Somewhere in the shadowy territory surrounding psychomotor functions lies the so-called "autokinetic phenomenon." If a subject is enclosed in a darkened room with only a tiny point of light in front of him, in a short while the light seems to move. It may "move" different estimated distances under certain circumstances. Sherif (1935) seems to have been the first to do any experimental work with this phenomenon although others had noted it many years before. And still others have worked on it since. A relatively recent experiment (Young & Gaier, 1953) employing the autokinetic phenomenon is reported here to represent studies of the relations among various personality functions which include this "psychomotor" (?) function. Despite the relatively small numbers involved in the experiment, it is more satisfying methodologically than many more extensive experiments.

The researchers first tested twenty high school boys in an experimental group and twenty in a control group (these and other subjects matched for intelligence). To the former group the suggestion was made after each had reported how far the light had "moved" that the estimate was incorrect, but that most subjects missed the correct distance by from three to nine inches. The control group received no suggestion. Forty-eight hours afterward both groups were tested again. A *t*-test revealed that the two groups differed in "suggestibility," as measured by amount of change between first and second presentations, at the one per cent level of confidence. The experimental group also took the "Bernreuter Personality Inventory" and the "Minnesota Multiphasic Personality Inventory." A group of indices was taken from the tests to represent Introversion-Extraversion, Ascendance-Submission, Self-sufficiency, and Hysteria. These various measures were correlated with one another and with "suggestibility" on the autokinetic phenomenon. A multiple correlation coefficient and a multiple regression equation were then calculated. The multiple correlation coefficient shows the relation between one variable and a number of others. A multiple regression equation enables the experimenter to predict from a group of variables what an individual's most probable score will be on another variable. In this case prediction was from the various indices derived from the inventories to "suggestibility."

At this place most experiments stop. But this one continued. Another group of twenty individuals was divided into two sub-groups, in the first of which were individuals predicted by the regression equation to be more "suggestible" than those in the other sub-group. Then both groups were exposed to the darkened room with its tiny point of light. They were asked to report how far the light "moved" under the same conditions that prevailed for the ex-

perimental group in the first part of the experiment, that is, being told their first estimates were "incorrect," and being retested 48 hours later. In accordance with the prediction, the two sub-groups differed in their estimates at the 5 per cent level of confidence on the second testing.

The authors conclude that individuals do differ as to "suggestibility," and that prediction as to "suggestibility" can be made from selected "personality traits." They are careful to warn that they are not predicting to other situations of suggestibility and that their experiment does not prove the existence of a generalized trait of suggestibility. From this experiment, however, we may draw the conclusion that some individuals manifest a relation between the "borderline" function called the autokinetic phenomenon and some more complex functions of personality.

There seem to be other "borderline functions," like the false estimates of comparisons of lines under "prestige suggestion" and possibly some hypnotic phenomena. The one instance here is sufficient for representing others in terms of possible consistency among functions in individuals.

Psychosocial Functions. In our pursuit of consistency among personality functions, considerably more than passing mention must be made to one of the outstanding psychological research projects of the first half of the twentieth century. This project involved one of the major areas of personality, that of character. The Character Education Inquiry, directed by Professors Hugh Hartshorne and Mark A. May, under the auspices of Columbia University and the Institute of Social and Religious Research, entailed five years of research during the mid-nineteen-twenties. It required the use of a number of thousands of school pupils, principally from grades five through eight, the administration of many, many thousands of tests, and (for the time) refined statistical handling of the masses of data. Results were published in journal articles and in three volumes, *Studies in Deceit* (Hartshorne & May, 1928), *Studies in Service and Self-Control* (Hartshorne,

May, & Maller, 1929), and *Studies in the Organization of Character* (Hartshorne, May, & Shuttleworth, 1930).

Children were observed for moral conduct on the playground, given opportunities to play fair or to cheat in classroom situations where they thought they could not be detected, checked as to their home conduct, and asked to express their attitudes toward moral and religious standards. One test, for example, required the child to decide whether he would perform tasks for the benefit of hospitalized children or not. Another called for doing a task for the child's own profit and another for the benefit of his school class; which task he did more eagerly was a test of his service motives. Still other tests of character in the child included one in which an arithmetic test was given, the papers collected and duplicated, then returned to the child for scoring with an opportunity provided to change his original answers. In one test children could grade their own papers at home. Stealing or not stealing a small sum of money, under circumstances in which the child was supposed to think there was no possibility of his being checked, served as still another test in the Inquiry. These are only a few examples of a host of ingenious devices designed to measure character objectively.

Hartshorne and May's preliminary conclusions from their original studies in deceit, service, and self-control were that:

. . . deception, helpfulness, cooperation, persistence and inhibition were groups of specific habits rather than general traits. We found that, when situations involving the possibility of deception were almost identical, the behavior of individuals did not greatly vary from occasion to occasion. But when the situations permitting dishonesty were altered, as when one moves from a classroom to a party or an athletic contest or has the opportunity to steal money rather than to copy the answers of a test from an answer sheet, then there was considerable alteration in the practice of deception. As the situations became less and less alike there was found greater and greater diversity of behavior, so that one could not predict from

what a person did in one situation what he would do in a different situation.

Similarly in the case of service and self-control, the unselfishness, persistence, or inhibition that characterized a child's behavior was closely tied up with the situation calling it forth and could not be made the basis of generalization about what would happen under other circumstances (Hartshorne, *et al.*, 1930).[1]

In the light of their preliminary conclusions Hartshorne and May set themselves to discover if there is an "empirical organization" of those specific tendencies which they felt they had discovered in the early portions of their research. Concerning themselves with the problem we have been taking up, "the inner consistency or self-integration of the individual," as well as of his closely allied social functions, the experimenters tested 850 children grades five to eight in three different communities selected to represent differences in privilege. Various measures were made and intercorrelated; these comprehended selected aspects of conduct, the relation of knowledge to conduct, a comparison of the standards of conduct of groups (communities, schools, grades), reputation with teachers and classmates, the relation of foresight to character, the character of the "child as a whole," and his social functioning in home, club, and school.

Correlation coefficients in most instances in the tests cited are relatively low, some not significantly different from zero, a few ranging as high as .49.[2] The correlations average for 23 tests +.30. Two major exceptions to the general low level are found: When scores of children in particular groups are correlated (rather than the scores of all individual children), correlations run high. In "moral knowledge and opinion" tests, for instance, r's range from

---

[1] Hartshorne, H., May, M. A., & Shuttleworth, F. F. *Studies in the organization of character;* studies in the nature of character by the Character Education Inquiry. Vol. III. New York: Macmillan, 1930. Reprinted by permission.

[2] When "corrected for attenuation" by the methods detailed in *Studies in Deceit* (Hartshorne, May, & Shuttleworth, 1930).

.40 to .60, in "conduct" tests from .44 to .58, and in a group of "reputation" tests from .51 to .72. Second, for 100 children "portraits" or "character sketches" were made up from all areas of testing. These sketches were sorted into eleven different groups, representing a normal curve going from "low character" to "high character," by sixty-three "judges." The resultant average rankings of the children were correlated with sub-test scores and other factors like school marks and age. The correlations are high here, too, in many instances.[1]

On the basis of the low average correlation among all tests for individuals, however, Hartshorne and May, following their final experiments, concluded that, "the general principle of specificity is fulfilled. In proportion as situations are alike, conduct is uncorrelated" (Hartshorne, et al., 1930). The authors also concluded that if there is any consistency of character it resides in the prosocial individuals (honest, service-oriented) rather than in the antisocial.

For impact upon the scientific world (and religious education) few research projects can compare with the Character Education Inquiry. Debate over its conclusions has not entirely quieted down after 30 years. The most well-known criticisms are Allport's (1937a), but others are not far behind (Cattell, 1950; Eysenck, 1953–56; Roback, 1934; Stagner, 1948). Only a myopic critic could fail to give credit for the monumental labors of the CEI. Eysenck refers to the books, reporting the results, as a landmark which has not been surpassed, and pays tribute to the authors' scientific integrity which sets forth all the data, thus enabling others to draw conclusions of their own which may differ from the original conclusions.

Actually, re-examination of the data does force different conclusions. Children, it can be seen, often behaved consistently, not in terms of what adults prescribed as "moral behavior," but in terms of their own codes.[2] This consistency is recognized in part in the first major exception noted above to the generally low correlations. But also it is found in the low correlations themselves—they are low, but all positive, indicating that complete specificity of behavior did not exist (Maller, 1934). Further, the second major exception mentioned above, that concerning the "character sketches," suggests that the closer one gets to judging in terms of the "whole personality," the greater is the degree of consistency. Other similar conclusions can be drawn from a new look at the data.

As Eysenck (1953c) states, summing up modern attitudes to the issues raised by the CEI,

. . . we will do well to bear in mind that although Hartshorne and May have failed to show that human conduct is completely specific, they have shown conclusively that it is far less general than we tend to imagine, and far more strongly determined by the specific situation in which it occurs than used to be thought at one time. There is truth in the contentions of the adherent of the theory of specificity, as well as in those of the adherent of the theory of generality; the problem ceases to be a theoretical one, and becomes instead quantitative and empirical.[3]

The CEI is but one representative of a number of investigations which purport to prove inconsistencies of personality factors, studies predicated on a theory of personality as a bundle of specific habits. Today even the most ardent advocates of specificity recognize some consistency to personalities. The path of investigation researchers have followed in recent years has been to proceed with gathering evidence as to *how* consistent personalities are, devising meth-

---

[1] These correlation coefficients are spuriously high because the records of individual tests are included as part of the basis for the character sketch.

[2] Hartshorne and May checked whether children were functioning in relation to adult standards by correlating scores on moral knowledge and cooperation (in school social service activities, easily known to adults). The resulting r is .17. Even when children *know* what adults expect, they are not under compulsion to *act* that way.

[3] Eysenck, H. J. *The structure of human personality.* New York: Wiley, 1953. Reprinted by permission.

ods which allow us to find consistencies where they may be present.

SUMMARY

Although the average individual thinks of himself as the "same person" from year to year, research evidence points to greater lack of continuity than is commonly recognized. A general consistency or integration of personality at any one time does not appear to be borne out either, though wide differences are found among individuals. In some cases where inconsistencies appear, however, they may be found to be "congruent" by tracing them to their sources within the personality. Correlations among functions may be both raised and lowered in the course of differentiation and integration of both physiological and psychological processes, as separate functions become at once more independent and more interdependent. Sometimes, too, an understanding of inconsistencies is gained in terms of the different layers of the personality, laid down biologically and chronologically, and between which at times communication is not adequate.

An investigation of each of the roughly defined areas of the personality ranging from psychomotor functions through psychosocial functions reveals a general principle: We must be cautious in claiming too much continuity or consistency across all the functions of the individual. It appears to be going too far to say with Stern that when a person is *sick*, the *whole* person is sick; such a statement is a metaphysical assumption, not a testable hypothesis. One only needs to say that when a person is ill more functions are affected than the local organ. As Francis Parkman, historian of *The Oregon Trail*, dragged his pain-wracked body from bed to write a few lines before dropping back exhausted, his intellectual processes were probably affected to some extent, but his "whole person" was not as sick as some parts of it, for his intellect was performing brilliantly. It is enough to say with Goldstein (Purdy, 1937) that a man with a brain injury is not just a brain-injured individual, but an *altered man;* it is not necessary to say he is a *completely* altered man, or that every function of his personality has been changed. It is poetic to speak of the universe as so closely bound together that one can "pluck a flower and trouble a star," but the poet goes beyond his facts. So, too, the personologist may be so carried away with his idea of the unity of the personality that he claims greater interrelationship than can be proved.

QUESTIONS

1. In what ways are physiological and psychological functions continuous across a period of time?

2. How does "congruence" help to explain behavior? How should the doctrine be limited and how expanded?

3. Relate the biological concepts of differentiation and integration to personology.

4. How do concepts of "levels of personality" aid in understanding personality? Are deeper layers more or less consistent than surface levels?

5. Cite specific instances of consistencies and interrelatedness as set forth in the experimental literature. Describe briefly at least the work of Allport and Vernon, Fleishman and Hempel, and Hartshorne and May. Relate these studies to the general problem of personality consistency.

CHAPTER 4

OVER-ALL DYNAMIC STRUCTURE—I

PERSONALITY STRUCTURE

Various theories of personality imply that there is a structure to personality. At the outset it is well for us to recognize, however, that there is no general agreement among personologists as to *what* structure there is to personality, or even *whether* there is an over-all structure. While we cannot here take up whole theories of personality, those parts of certain theories dealing with structure or lack of it are presented in order to gain an understanding of how structure of personality is conceived by serious theorists.

There are several distinct meanings to the term "structure": (1) We could mean a series of elements lying contiguous with one another, but having no inherent pattern or cohesiveness. A physical parallel to this type of structure is a pile of stones. It may have a chance arrangement or may even have been constructed by someone, two of the elements required by a dictionary definition of "structure." Some theories of personality offer a personality "structure" analogous to a pile of stones. (2) Another meaning of structure is that of a relatively patterned group of factors, rather loosely related but having some sort of functional unity. A building represents a physical parallel to this conception. Parts of the building are not organically connected with one another, but may be removed, altered,

or added to without substantially destroying the "structure" or its function. The building may change but is still a structure in this sense. Again, some personality theories appear to follow a building analogue in respect to personality structure. (3) A third meaning of structure holds that the parts are *organically* related to one another. The biological organism is the representative parallel. Parts of the organism may, it is true, be destroyed, altered, or removed, but insofar as they are essential their changes affect the structure and function of the organism. As with other meanings, some theories of personality structure may be subsumed under "organismic" concepts. (4) The term "structure" may also be applied to a grouping of elements which are related in both organic and superorganic ways. In sociology there is what is known as "family structure" with units having organic structure, but consisting of more than these. An electrical field likewise may have relations which are beyond the organized structures within the field and have superorganic structure because of these relations. While our actual division of systems of personality structure differs somewhat from these categories on account of the realities of the systems, general concepts of structure will be seen over and over in the following discussion on views of personality structure.

Whatever actual structure personalities

possess, whether more like a pile of stones or an organism, the principle holds here that there may be an infinite number of scientific models for explaining or "structuring" natural phenomena. If one is expecting to find *the* expression of personality structure which correlates perfectly with some "actual structure" of personality, he is most likely pursuing a will-o'-the-wisp. Psychological models of personality, like physical models (theories) of the universe, are apparently doomed always to be only approximations. There are, however, some conceptions which appear to take more of the observable data into account and make more sense of such data than others; these should be accorded higher rank as being better approximations to the elusive "real personality structure." From each of the systems recorded here, though, we can gain some knowledge of the structure of human personality, for each has been advanced on the basis of some empirical investigations.

How Personality Structure May Be Conceived

Although structure concepts may be classified in various ways, any one theorist's position may not fit into a neat classification of such concepts. Like personality itself— indeed, no doubt as a resultant of the overlapping of personality functions—structure concepts overlap one another and spill over from one precisely-verbalized category into another. Some of the authorities mentioned in the following paragraphs may find their concepts in a category not to their liking; in each case, however, there is an explanation where one seems called for.

Personality as a Group of Elements

Faculties. Prescientific psychology sought elements in the personality just as it sought larger units. Democritus of ancient Macedonia held to a materialistic philosophy which suggested atoms as elements of the soul as well as of "material" bodies (Weber, 1925). Reid and Stewart of Scot-

land in the late eighteenth and early nineteenth centuries sought indivisible, independent elements as the structure of the soul or mind. Reid, for example, proposed specifically that there are twenty-four "active powers of the mind" such as imagination, hunger, self-esteem, and pity, and several "intellectual powers" like memory, judgment, and perception. Reid's fellow Scotsman, Stewart, building on the former's foundations, popularized what came to be known as "faculty psychology." In personological language, faculties would be regarded as the elements of personality.

In France the anatomist, Franz Joseph Gall, who with G. Spurzheim is credited with the establishment of phrenology, took Reid's and Stewart's lists of faculties and purportedly localized some of these in the brain. One major difference between other faculty psychologists of the last century and Gall is that he was endeavoring to establish attributes which *differentiate* individuals from one another, rather than attributes of mind-in-general. Hence his phrenology, despite its indefensible correlations of faculties and skull protrusions, was closer to modern personology than most of the faculty psychology of then and later. At least, Gall's psychology is closer, for it may be that his phrenology and psychology can be separated (H. D. Spoerl, 1936). Allport maintains that Gall was a century ahead of his time in recognizing the need to *distinguish among men*, not merely to gather data on abstract faculties belonging to no man in particular.

Whether or not faculty psychology has been maligned indiscriminately as Allport implies, psychologists at least since Wundt and James have discredited the psychology of faculties together with the belief, shared by Gall and others of his day, that various combinations of faculties will produce the man.

Sensational Elements. With Wilhelm Wundt, the father of experimental psychology, came other elements.[1] These ele-

[1] Foreshadowed most likely by the highly empirical *sensationism* of Condillac and other Frenchmen.

ments were the psychological parallels of chemical elements, capable of being resolved by analysis and synthesized by compounding. The "mental chemistry" of Wundt was not a mechanical compounding but a *creative synthesis,* wherein new properties are found in the combination of elements different from the properties of any constituent element. Thus for Wundt, the man is not merely a sum-total of elements (as faculty psychology implies); man's experience is an organic process (Boring, 1950). From a personality standpoint Wundt's elements, combined or separate, are attributes of universal types of minds, having very little to do with the individual. They could just as well be the interchangeable parts of block-boring machines governed by automation.

Associationist psychology, especially that propounded by the famous Mills (father and son), held ideas very similar to Wundt's about the structure of the mind. Ideas and sensations were regarded as elements to be fused or compounded.[1]

[1] Very close to, sometimes almost indistinguishable from, faculty psychology and Wundt's elementistic psychology, was James Mill's *associationism.* For Mill sensations comprised one of the primary states of consciousness, and ideas as copies of sensations a second class. Sensations and/or ideas in Mill's view united in the organism by associating themselves together, by compounding themselves; but this associating within occurs only because external objects which produce the sensations and ideas are associated. Although Mill did not employ the terms we employ today, for Mill personality would consist of a series of successive or synchronous sensations or ideas. With synchronous sensations or ideas a new principle is introduced, that of fusion, rather than simple association. Fusion produces complex elements; an example of a complex idea is that of brick and mortar (objects which produce sensation) and position and quality (ideas) which altogether make up the complex idea of wall. Boring indicates the final absurdity of this type of reasoning; if the logic is pursued we find that the idea of Everything is a compound of individual ideas of *every thing!* (Boring, 1950). While there may not be in any actual personality as closely knit an integration of the elements of personality as some critics of elementaristic psychology claim, the components of personality do not seem to be as fragmented as Mill supposed.

Once again, in respect to the Mills' compounded or associated sensations and ideas, and Wundt's elements, and most "faculties," the personologist has to shake his head over these disembodied factors which only incidentally have a local habitation and a personal name. The individual, the person, only serves as a *vehicle* for these general elements and their various "laws" of combining or compounding. To even the most element-minded personality psychologist today, the individual, uncorrelated as some of his functions may be, is still the locus of elements. It is in the person that these elements combine, if they do, or are dissociated, if not combined; the person gives substance to these elements and to their peculiar combinations or constellations.

One aspect of the "element" concepts thus far presented is the doctrine of dualism held by most faculty and elementistic psychologists, usually in the form of a psychophysical parallelism or interactionism. Mind and body were conceived as separate entities, usually considered as being independent in their operations but parallel, or else "exerting an influence on each other." This doctrine as we have seen in Chapter 1 is not held by modern psychology. It is not entertained in the following position either.

Identical Elements. We come to the most modern of the group-of-elements concepts of personality structure based on the extreme behaviorism with which, rightly or wrongly, the name of John B. Watson is associated. In the discussion on consistency of functions, especially in the review of Hartshorne and May's research (Chapter 3), the essential features of the identical

John Stuart Mill, James Mill's even more illustrious son, carried his father's association concept of intellectual processes to a more logical conclusion than did his father. Like Wundt, the younger Mill held to a mental chemistry rather than a fusion of sensations and ideas. If we translate this concept into personological terms, it seems to signify that the elements of personality are not isolated or fused building-block factors, but instead complex factors more like chemical compounds. In addition, there may still be "simple" ideas and sensations which serve as elements of personality.

elements type of stimulus-response personality structure were made evident: Personality is a bundle of specific habits, dependent on particular stimuli and particular responses. Generalized traits cannot be the elements of personality at all, for the person will respond in the same way from time to time only insofar as situations he confronts contain identical or nearly identical elements. This doctrine of specific habits as the elements of personality does not maintain complete specificity, only that traits of personality are not so general in their operation as suggested in other systems of psychology. Since others have presented extended critiques of this doctrine (G. W. Allport, 1937a), no further treatment of the subject is necessary here.[1]

---

[1] Goodenough (1945) makes a colorful case for specificity, basing much of her argument on Hartshorne and May:

"Not long ago it was rather generally supposed that such characteristics as honesty, cooperativeness, seclusiveness, perseverance, and so on were rather stable qualities of the individual; that, for example, an honest person is honest in nearly all situations, that a resourceful person will show his resourcefulness under almost any circumstances, that a persistent person can be depended upon to stick to almost any kind of task, and that an optimist goes about whistling in all weathers. But recent investigation does not bear out this idea. It is true that both grown people and children show a good deal of consistency in their conduct from one time to another, if the situation remains about the same. Because we do often observe persons repeatedly under similar conditions we become impressed with this consistency and assume that they will behave in just the same way under all circumstances. The teacher who sees Jimmie and Johnnie only in the classroom and finds that Jimmie seizes every opportunity to copy his lessons from his neighbor while Johnnie's eyes never wander from his own paper no matter how many chances for cheating are given him concludes, not unnaturally, that Jimmie is a wretched little cheat and Johnnie is the soul of honesty. If questioned about their 'personality traits,' she will almost surely rate Johnnie high and Jimmie low on all aspects of honesty and trustworthiness. But she fails to take account of the fact that Johnnie has little need to cheat, for he is at the head of his class anyway and doesn't have to worry about promotion. Moreover it would be silly for him to copy from his neighbor when the chances are that his own answer is the right one. The situation for Jimmie is very different.

Whether or not personality "actually" consists of groups of elements not much related to one another, the theories which maintain specificity of elements are of little use to a science of personality. Either they have no reference to any *individuals*, as in the case of faculty psychology (except insofar as faculties vary in strength from person to person), or they allow no genuine possibility of structure to personality, as in the case of specific habits as alone the constituents of personality. Perhaps there is no "actual structure" to personality, as the "group of elements" doctrines imply. Both

He is on the verge of failure, and his father has promised him a "good licking" if he doesn't bring home a better report card next time. The two boys differ in classroom conduct, to be sure, for Jimmie cheats and Johnnie doesn't. And there is a real difference in 'personality' besides, for Jimmie feels the need to cheat and Johnnie doesn't. But are we safe in assuming that Johnnie is consistently honest and Jimmie dishonest?

"Let us follow them out to the playground. Now Jimmie, who is shaky on the multiplication table, who mixes up all the dates in his history lesson, and who spells sugar with an h is a 'cracker-jack' when it comes to marbles, but Johnnie is all thumbs. If an opportunity for cheating comes will it be Jimmie or Johnnie who yields to the temptation?" (Reprinted by permission from Goodenough, Florence L. *Developmental psychology, an introduction to the study of human behavior*. (2nd ed.) New York: Appleton-Century, 1945.

Goodenough's final question invites a reply from a Mutt and Jeff story. Jeff describes a friend of his with an effeminate name and effeminate ways whose whole early career consisted of a gentle life of refusing to fight vulgarly when other boys fought, of refraining from rowdyism and boisterousness, and generally of being a "sissy." Jeff asked in fervor, "Do you think that when Uncle Sam issued the call for volunteers to serve our country he waited to be drafted?" Rising to the gallantry of the occasion, Mutt cried out, "No!" To which Jeff responded, "You bet your sweet life he did!"

Note that Goodenough implicitly takes account of a greater degree of structure than she recognizes explicitly. Some kind of *self*-defense is operating when "Johnnie has little *need* to cheat" and Jimmie fears his father's licking. It appears that both boys are acting more in keeping with a self-structure that operates more generally than could be supposed if they exhibited merely identical behavior in two similar situations or different behavior in dissimilar situations.

common observation and present scientific study disclose that in most individuals some *specific items* of behavior tend to go with other specific items, and further, that even some of these *groups* of behavioral items tend to go with others. We are forced, in other words, to turn to more generalized concepts of personality structure.

Personality as a System of Traits

There are two general concepts of personality structure which come under the heading of personality as a system of traits, namely those concerned with independent and interdependent traits. Employing for the present a dictionary definition of "trait" as "a distinguishing quality of character, mind, etc.," and adding the proviso that the quality is usually long-lasting, we examine these two trait concepts briefly. We will discover that they share much common ground.

Independent Traits. As interpreted in some ways, some systems of factor analysis give us illustrations of independent traits operating as a system in personality. Such a conception seems almost like a paradox. But listen to the dean of American factorists, the late L. L. Thurstone:

In factorial investigations of mentality we proceed on the assumption that mind is structured somehow, that mind is not a patternless mosaic of an infinite number of elements without functional groupings. The extreme, opposite view would be to hold that mind has no structure at all. *In the interpretation of mind we assume that mental phenomena can be identified in terms of distinguishable functions, which do not all participate equally in everything that mind does.* It is these functional unities that we are looking for with the aid of factorial methods. It is our scientific faith that such distinguishable mental functions can be identified and that they will be verified in different types of experimental study. Our work in the factorial study of the human mind rests on the assumption that mind represents a dynamical system which can eventually be understood in terms of a finite number of parameters [1] (Thurstone, 1947).

[1] Thurstone, L. L. Multiple-factor analysis. Chicago: The Univer. of Chicago Press, 1947. Re-

Extending the concept beyond "mental abilities," some factor analysts have held to a system of personality-in-general consisting of these "independent" factors. These are "traits" in the sense of representing distinguishable qualities or unitary functions of the organism as revealed mathematically, such as fine muscle coordination, gross muscle coordination, numerical ability, radicalism, and esthetic understanding. These traits are independent in the correlational sense, that is, they do not go together when tests of the various abilities or characteristics are given to a large number of persons. Not only are they independent, but they are common, in that a trait such as any of those named may be recognized by common characteristic features from one person to another. Individuals differ in both the kinds of organization of their trait systems and in possession of differing degrees or quantities of each factor.

General and Specific Factors.[2] The roots of factor analytic conceptions of personality structure reach back a long way (at least insofar as the science of personality goes). In 1904 Charles Edward Spearman reported a general factor, "g," and specific factors, denoted by "s," in the area of intelligence (Spearman, 1904, 1927).[3] The neutral letter, "g," refers to the common intellectual function (or functions) which in Spearman's view underlies all intellectual activity, a kind of "general intelligence"

printed by permission. Thurstone uses the term "parameter" in the following sense: "*A parameter is one of the measurements that are used for describing or defining an object or event.*" He means, however, not the *original measurements*, but *derived* measurements like the "verbal comprehension factor" which he considers a functional unity. Any person may have a "factor score" in "verbal comprehension factor," such scores from many persons representing the measurements which constitute the parameter, or factor. For other meanings of "parameter" see Mode (1951), Sisam (1949), and Yule & Kendall (1949).

[2] The appendix offers a simplified explanation of factor analysis.

[3] Some authorities would not say "discovered." They would insist that the very method of factor analysis employed requires the conclusions to which Spearman came.

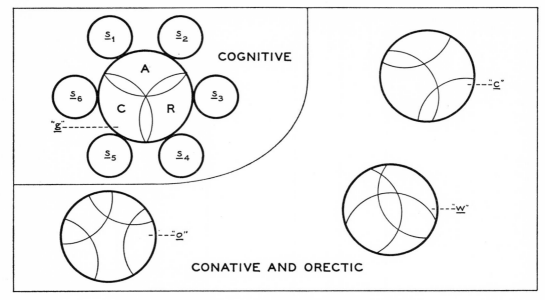

Figure 4. Spearman's conception of personality structure.

running through all intellection.[1] "s" is a specific factor in any ability and peculiar to it alone; there may be any number of "s's" depending on the number of abilities possessed by an individual. Beyond these factors, however, Spearman accepted two other "cognitive factors" which certainly border on the noncognitive or orectic (referring to appetites or desires). These are *perseveration*, which is denoted by some as "p" (or its opposite number "c," which is freedom from perseveration), and general *oscillation*, sometimes designated as "o." The former refers to the kind of disposition rigidity which is manifested by a persistence in perceptual or motor behavior, a "general mental inertia or lag." The latter factor has to do with lapses of attention, fluctuations or oscillations in consciousness of stimuli. A final noncognitive or orectic factor accepted by Spearman is character or *will*, "w."

Figure *4* portrays very roughly the structure of personality implied by Spearman's

analysis of "g." There are three processes involved in cognition, according to Spearman: (1) the apprehension of one's own experience, (2) the eduction of relations, and (3) the eduction of correlates. In regard to (1) it is stated ". . . that a person has more or less power to observe what goes on in his own mind. He not only feels, but also knows what he feels; he not only strives, but knows that he strives; he not only knows, but knows that he knows" (Spearman, 1927). While we might quibble over how much the person knows, Spearman's proviso "more or less power" allows room for unconscious "knowledge." (2) The second process is that of bringing to mind the relations between two or more items of mental content when one has the items in mind; and (3) the third process is that of bringing to mind an item of mental content when one only has in mind another correlated item and the relations between the two. Each of these abilities like the first is possessed in greater or less degree by individuals. While these processes are exhaustive of all *new* cognition (that which is not purely reproductive), they are over-lapping.

[1] At first Spearman was cautious in saying that "g" is only found when scores on ability tests are correlated in a certain way. But later he stated unequivocally that "g" is universal.

Although these intellectual functions are independent of the conative and orectic, interdependence within the cognitive sphere is found in the fact that "*g*" is present in all of the processes. And to a much lesser degree specific abilities, "*s's*" sometimes overlap, making for some interdependence. These overlappings make for a few "group factors." In the diagram (Figure *4*) this interdependence is only suggested for "*c*," "*o*," and "*w*," with their (presumably discoverable) fundamental processes shown as overlapping within their respective spheres.

In interpreting the diagram of Spearman's implied concept of structure of personality, it should be noted that each of the spheres and all parts of them vary from individual to individual, so that one person has more of A (apprehension of his experience) than another, or more of "*g*" than another, and different "*s's*" than another or different amounts of the same "*s.*"

First- and Second-Order Factors. Other factorists have changed and improved Spearman's factor system both mathematically and methodologically. One who has probably made more contribution to psychological theory of personality structure than any other from a factor analytic standpoint was L. L. Thurstone, whose *opus magnum, Multiple Factor Analysis,* was published in 1947. Thurstone (1938) discovered in the intellectual field the "primary mental abilities," factors obtained by correlating with one another a large number of tests on a group of college students. When it was pointed out that there was also correlation among the (oblique, rotated) [1] primary *factors,* Thurstone added to his system what he called "second-order factors." These latter are obtained by performing a factor analysis on a correlational matrix derived from "primary factors" in

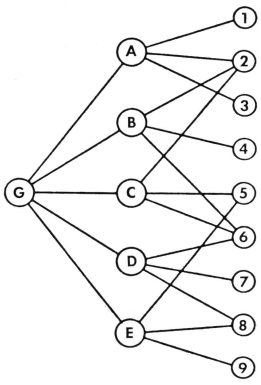

Figure 5. A second-order factor derived from correlated first-order factors. (From L. L. Thurstone, *Multiple-factor Analysis,* p. 417)

somewhat the same fashion as are original "first-order factors" which are obtained from a correlation matrix derived from tests on individuals.

Thurstone illustrated various types of second-order factors, but the illustration most apropos to our subject (shown in Figure 5) demonstrates the interdependence within a group of traits or factors revealed by a factor analysis of tests of abilities. A, B, C, D, and E are traits of intellect corresponding to verbal comprehension, fluency, spatial visualization, and so forth. If there is any correlation to speak of among these factors (traits), at least one second-order factor, G, is found, in this case a general second-order factor accounting for all the correlations among the first-order factors.

Viewing the Thurstone conception of

---

[1] "Rotated" refers to the mathematical treatment of the axes which changes the reference frame of the tests, considered as vectors in multidimensional space. "Oblique" refers to the axes as not being perpendicular to one another; cartesian coordinates are perpendicular to one another. (Cf. Appendix.)

first-and-second order factors from the standpoint of personality structure, and supposing that personality factors other than intellectual ones may also have such second-order derivatives, we may conceive of personality as a number of groups of factors, each with interdependencies within the group. How much interdependence there is among the various *groups* of traits is not answerable yet. The work of Guilford, who has done a huge amount of work in the Thurstone tradition, tends to indicate that among temperamental functions there are some second-order factors, though in recent years, Guilford has found more and more separate factors among interests and abilities (Guilford, Christensen, Bond, & Sutton, 1954; Guilford & Merrifield, 1960). Thus there may or there may not be second-order factors in various areas of personality. If there are, the picture of personality structure is one of interdependent traits within groups of factors, the groups being relatively independent from one another.[1]

[1] Generally, personologists accept the results of factor analysis. Nevertheless, strong arguments can be made against the conception of personality structure as a system of independent factors; the most important are the following:

(1) Can people be assumed to have the same factors even though differing in degree? As Loevinger (Helson, 1951, ch. 12) stated, "Why should all minds be organized in the same fashion? May people differ not only in amounts, not only in mental profiles, but in the whole pattern of mental organization?" Years before, Allport raised the same objection.

(2) The second objection is: Are factors real? Do they in fact correspond to real qualities of personality? Are these "traits" discovered by mathematical analysis only artifacts of the method used to "discover" them? Can they be arrived at by other methods than factor analysis? If they are real, they should be discoverable by other means.

(3) The last objection is a technical one having to do with the basic assumption (or equation) of factor analysis, but also in a deeper sense with the very concept of personality structure: Is an individual's (standard) score on a certain test a resultant of *adding* his scores on all factors (or traits) together? In terms of personality structure one may ask whether the factors are independent and merely add to one another within the personality or whether they are interdependent. This

Interdependent Traits: Unique, Focalized Dispositions. Several attempts have been made to conceive of personality as a system of interdependent traits. Representative of these is the system associated

phrasing of the question simplifies it too greatly. Mathematically, the objection should ask: Does a linear equation represent the function which in turn represents the factors or parameters, or would some higher-order function be better?

These objections are weighty ones. In part, the first may be answered by saying that factors or traits here may not characterize any single personality. All personalities may differ even in basic organization. But if there are not some common features which may be roughly represented by factors, then our whole *scientific* search for structure is fruitless (and indeed search for a science of personality). It may be granted that each personality has its unique organization, differences in heredity and environment and their interactions being what they are; yet if there are no relatively common structural patterns, there is hardly a science. McNemar's (1954) trenchant criticism of having innumerable sciences of psychology is applicable here. Factor traits may not be adequate to the description of personality; yet the objection that there are unique organizations of personalities is not to be laid against factor analysis alone. Any endeavor to get at common elements can be similarly criticized. However, we have only answered this objection indirectly; it may still hold for *all* efforts to discover personality structure. Indeed, it may apply to all scientific endeavor.

In answer to the second objection concerning the reality of factors, factorists maintain that if factors show up in different studies, even though they have no "psychological meaning," they must have a reality beyond the factor analysis process itself. This answer is weak, however, in that the principle of many possible scientific models has been forgotten in pressing this argument. Perhaps all factor studies are exercises in autism. On the other hand, in line with general scientific practice it may well be that factor-traits are not "real" ones, but they may serve as rough approximations until better ones are brought to light. Further, the additional argument, that such traits must be arrived at by several methods not only by factor analysis if they are to represent anything real in personality, appears to be fairly well answered by the marshalling of evidence by Cattell (1950) and Eysenck (1953c) to the effect that other studies than factor studies *have* found similar traits. We may never know what the "real personality structure" is; but that factor analysis does not represent the "real" structure is not a fault of factor analysis alone.

We can hardly enter into argument over the last objection concerning the additivity of factor with the name of Allport [1] more than any other, which emphasizes both the *individual nature* of traits and their *interdependence*. In order to understand Allport's position his definition of trait must be introduced: ". . . *a generalized and focalized neuropsychic system (peculiar to the individual), with the capacity to render many stimuli functionally equivalent, and to initiate and guide consistent (equivalent) forms of adaptive and expressive behavior*" (1937a). While this definition of trait is limited in terms of our text's definition of personality, it is in harmony with Allport's famous personality definition [2] quoted in Chapter 2.

---

scores. Nevertheless, the technical question is exceedingly important, for a system stands or falls on its assumptions, and the assumption of the basic equation of factor analysis may be utterly false. Cattell maintains we have little reason thus far to deny the usefulness of the assumption. Others make use of factor analysis as if the assumption holds. For the present all we can say is that while the equation stating the relation among the factors may not be "true" it is useful. Until better means are devised, the factor solutions of personality structure can serve as scientific models.

[1] Allport's latest text on personality, *Pattern and Growth in Personality* (1961), a revision of the famous 1937 text, arrived too late to be examined for this text. A cursory examination suggests that Allport's basic position is not essentially changed. He changes the term "trait" to "personal disposition," apparently to distinguish his concept from that of factor analysts and other "common trait" advocates. (Cf. Chapter 13 in this text.)

[2] There is room for considering roles of the individual as "traits" even more than some of the "neuropsychic" functions. The college student may during his career have traits of an intra-personal nature, such as a consistent inner system of rebellion against campus regulations, which may render many stimuli equivalent and guide his behavior into deviant channels. Even here his role on the campus may not be separable from the neuropsychic disposition. But possibly much longer-lasting and determinative of his behavior is the role he plays as son of a family. This role cannot be separated from the neuropsychic disposition, but it is primarily interpersonal. With the exception that it is not primarily neuropsychic such a role function fulfills the other characteristics of a trait as defined by Allport. That Allport does not discount social factors in psychology is evidenced by his work since 1937. Both his research and theorizing in social psychology have

One of the main points here from a structural standpoint is that the trait is "peculiar to the individual." [3] Allport declares:

Strictly speaking, no two persons ever have precisely the same trait. Though each of two men may be *aggressive* (*or esthetic*), the style and range of the aggression (or estheticism) in each case is noticeably different. What else could be expected in view of the unique hereditary endowment, the different developmental history, and the never-repeated external influences that determine each personality? The end product of unique determination can never be anything but unique" (1937a).[4]

Thus each of the focalized units, or traits, which enter into structure of personality is unique to the individual even though it shares common features with similar units in other persons. Additionally, in Allport's system, these unique traits are overlapping. No trait is probably isolated from others completely. Reflexes and "logic tight compartments" are not *entirely* separate from the remainder of the organism's activities.

A single act may, and usually does, result from the mobilization of available energy through *many* channels. Consider the task of writing a letter; it requires the convergence of mental sets, habits, motives of the moment, skills, stylistic traits, as well as the deepest of personal convictions and values. Such adaptive behavior always demands the effective convergence of many determining influences, traits among others. Generalizing the illustration, it may safely be said that no single performance is ever a univocal product of any one single trait (1937a).[5]

The boundaries between and among traits, in this view of personality structure are permeable to a greater or lesser degree;

been highly influential. In Lindzey's *Handbook of Social Psychology* (1954), among the hundreds of authors referred to, Allport has more references than Lewin, who is second.

[3] Allport does not deny the use of the term "trait" to common dispositions as measurable aspects of personality common to mature people in a given culture.

[4] Allport, G. W. *Personality: a psychological interpretation.* New York: Holt, 1937. Reprinted by permission.

[5] *Ibid.* Reprinted by permission.

thus in this system traits are *interdependent* rather than *independent*. The overlapping of traits, however, does not make for an amorphous condition, but instead there are distinguishable traits which appear more or less stable in their operation. These are *focalized*, an important quality in this system.

The trait, then, is identifiable, not by clean-cut contours or boundaries, but rather by a nuclear quality, by its *focus*. This focus is essentially the *telic* significance of the trait, that is to say, its meaning to the individual as a mode of survival and mastery. The loquacious disposition of the talkative man is, for him, a *modus vivendi*. So too are all the other focalized (and interdependent) systems of his personality; his esthetic interests, his thriftiness, his timidity, his neatness, his affectionate attachments, and his political conservatism—they are all *modi vivendi*. In this same sense attitudes as well as traits are focalized dispositions (G. W. Allport, 1937a).[1]

An integral part of the dynamic structure is the operation of the "functional autonomy of motives." Objecting to genetic theories of personality which trace a person's behavior to a limited number of "presumably innate" needs or drives, Allport maintains that there are many motives (dynamic traits) which may at one time have been directly derivative from innate drives or needs, but which in the course of development of the individual have become autonomous, ". . . self-sustaining, *contemporary* systems, growing out of antecedent systems, but functionally independent of them" (1937a).

Workmanship is a good example of functional autonomy. A good workman feels compelled to do clean-cut jobs even though his security, or the praise of others, no longer depend upon high standards. In fact, in a day of jerry-building his workmanlike standards may be to his economic disadvantage. Even so he cannot do a slipshod job. Workmanship is not an instinct, but so firm is the hold it may acquire on a man that it is little wonder Veblen mistook it for one (1937a).[2]

[1] *Ibid*. Reprinted by permission.
[2] *Ibid*. Reprinted by permission.

There are a number of objections to Allport's concept of functional autonomy. (These are discussed more fully in Chapter 15.) But at this point our interest is in reviewing the structure of personality as conceived by the outstanding exponent of the interdependent trait position. That most if not all traits are not independent of one another does not in Allport's scheme of personality obviate the possibility that some traits can be "functionally autonomous" of others in the complex structure of personality.

Whatever "functional autonomy" traits may have for Allport, the structure of personality is a system of unique, overlapping, focalized dispositions or traits, many of which are presumed to be practically independent of the basic drives or needs which are the roots of the (living) structure. Emphasis again should be laid on the unique nature of these traits, that no two are alike in any individuals.

Personality as a Hierarchical System

While the two general concepts of personality structure thus far considered, personality as a group of elements and as a system of traits, imply at times a hierarchical structure, they are not strictly theories which self-consciously set up a hierarchy of higher and lower, outer and inner, or of more or less vital functions. Allport's interdependent traits concept and Murphy's need system (considered later) could be subsumed here. But there are more representative conceptions of personality structure actively employing hierarchical arrangements to serve as conceptual models of personality.

Concentric or Superimposed Layers. A simple teaching device the author has used for a number of years to help students conceive at least portions of the structure of personality is directly related to the "levels of personality" given as an explanation for consistency and inconsistency in Chapter 3. The device is pictured in Figure 6 (a). It is intended as an analogue of biological development with a primary emphasis on control functions of the individual. As

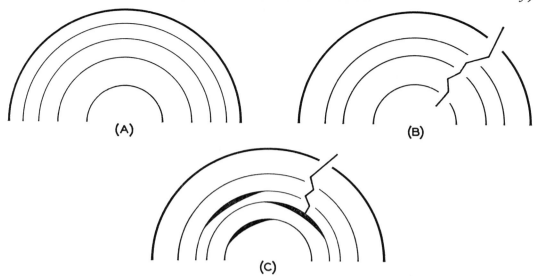

Figure 6. Concentric layers of personality.

the biological organism develops layer on layer of cells, so the personality is conceived as developing layer on layer of control functions. The core of energies with which the individual begins life is rapidly overlaid with controls, perceptual, motor, ideational, and role functions, which are forced on him or accepted by him willingly. Each successive layer of controls exerts a dominant effect on those beneath (hence the use of "hierarchy" to denote this schematization).

Since this is not the place to take up personality development in detail, it is not necessary to trace how layers are built up. An attempt at understanding of many of the phenomena of personality can be made, however, by considering that there may be weaknesses in some layers of controls. A severe trauma, like loss of one's mother in infancy or early childhood, may so disturb the development of the layers which normally grow at that time that a permanent weakness may be found at one spot in these control layers. Layers above may be weakened in consequence, that is, those controls which depend on previously developed controls may suffer in turn from inadequate development in the latter. An example might be the "psychopath" (here meaning

one whose conscience has many lacunae not found in most persons of his society), whose early traumatic experiences disturb lower layers of (self-) controls that normally develop in our culture; as a consequence these disturbed controls prevent later (primarily superego) controls from developing (Lindner, 1944).

Sometimes the weakness in various layers may remain there, so that crisis situations bring about a "break-through" as layer after layer gives way at its weak point or points. Such a condition is represented by Figure 6 (b) where what is known as "regression" has occurred. The upper levels of controls are penetrated and the individual acts in the uncontrolled fashion of a tiny child. There is no need to argue, as authorities do, whether regression is an actual return to childhood ways of behaving or is merely an altered way of responding (Cameron, 1939). In either case there is lack of control, and one may consider the behavior as resulting from a break-through of levels. Sometimes weaknesses may be found only in the upper levels, so that a break-through to lower levels stops with some of the outer layers, possibly with less ego-involved role functions or some higher ideational functions. An actor may forget his lines and lose the controls he has developed in his role as an actor; he may retain most of his intellectual, perceptual, and motor controls intact. Or it may be that he does lose, say, some of his perceptual controls and paranoid-fashion sees others making fun of him when they really are not. Such a condition is diagrammed in Figure 6 (c) where a breakthrough has occurred, but only in the upper layers.

Of course, instead of having weakness in certain layers of control when traumata occur, compensatorily the person may develop greater strengths in these layers, as a tree may develop a specially tough, thick layer where some injury has occurred during the course of a year. This situation is shown in Figure 6 (c) where extra-thick layers have developed. The reader may be able to conceive of many more situations which can be diagrammed as the ones named already have been.[1]

By using the "layers of personality" (or levels) as a *developmental*, structural concept, we may add to our understanding of consistencies and inconsistencies mentioned in Chapter 3. Those levels representing greater maturity of control are sometimes manifest in the behavior of the individual; but sometimes lower levels are exposed, so that behavior today may be contradictory to that of yesterday because it stems from a less mature level of control, one which the person may usually seem to have outgrown. Concentric or superimposed layers concepts of personality structure may also help us to understand both some of the order that actually is present as well as some of the apparent contradictions and disorder which are evident from common observation and scientific study of personality. They constitute only one kind of suggested structure, however, so we move on to others.

Typological Structure. Not all type theories of personality structure have been viewed as hierarchical. In fact, some of

them have not been much concerned with the *structure of personality;* rather they have been concerned with *classifying persons* into broader or narrower categories. From the viewpoint of personology, merely being able to pigeonhole an individual among those who are cycloid or schizoid (Kretschmer) or introvert or extravert (Jung) or tetanoid or Basedow (Jaensch) illuminates very little of what the actual personality is and especially of the way in which part-functions of the personality relate one to another to make one such-and-such a type.[2] Granted that some persons may for convenience be classified according to "type," we have to ask how the *varying combinations* of internal and external elements operate to produce the type; in other words if a person may be typed, what is the structure of his personality that makes him that way?

The clearest exposition of the structure of personality from a typological viewpoint is given by Eysenck (1947, 1953c). Look at Figure 7 in which a representative picture of the hierarchy of personality is given. It does represent a hierarchical arrangement in personality, for each level is subordinate to the one above until the highest is reached. The specific response level refers to the observable items of behavior of any person. These are the raw data from which the other "levels" are inferred. Various specific responses are noted to go together to form what we call "habits," the next higher level in the hierarchy. Habits in turn group themselves together to suggest the existence of traits. Since Eysenck is demonstrating the type of an introvertive personality, the traits are chosen here from among those that char-

---

[1] A more elaborate schema based upon a system devised by the author for setting up "levels of maturity" is found in Dreger (1952).

[2] If we try to classify many people, they seem to fall between types; the recognition of this fact is evident in common parlance in a negative way when someone is described, "He's a type!" or "She's just the type!" Further, when we consider all the types offered by so many scientific as well as popular authors, the cross-classifications in which an individual is caught remind one of the description the blind men made of the elephant. The utility of type theories is discussed by Stagner (1948).

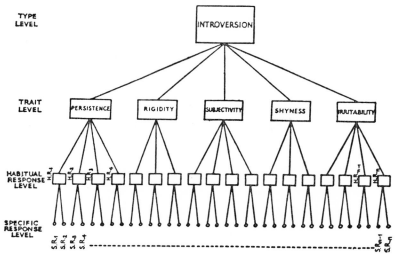

Figure 7. Diagrammatic representation of hierarchical organization of personality. (From H. J. Eysenck, *The Structure of Human Personality*, p. 13)

acterize introversion. Finally, the fourth level, in this case "introversion," is inferred because the individual has a predominance of traits regarded as introvertive.

Note several things in this diagram. Identification of individual traits at the trait level is not intended to be exhaustive—there could very well be other traits included to represent introversion. Further, there would have to be a similar diagram to depict the extravert, with correspondingly different specific responses, habits, and traits. And last, the choice of introversion as a type is not happenstance in Eysenck's system; he accepts with modification Jung's introvert-extravert dichotomy as representing observable types. This dichotomy is not accepted in an absolute sense; *i.e.*, the types are represented in most individuals by degrees rather than in a clearcut fashion.

Eysenck's system is bound up with his factor analysis methods. Each of the levels corresponds either to testable data or to correlational results which tie together observable events. The lowest level consists of responses which may occur only once and are of necessity characteristic of the individual. The habitual response level roughly coincides with the consistency an individual shows from one situation to a similar situation, measurable in terms of reliability coefficients. Traits are inferred from inter-correlations of habitual responses. At the top is the person's type as determined by correlations among traits. It is notable in Eysenck's system that it is inductive in large part, that is, the connections among responses and in turn among traits are not deductions from a type system, but are recognitions of empirically determined habitual linkings.

One of the implications [1] of the concept of structure indicated by Eysenck is of main interest to us here. The higher one goes in the hierarchy the less predictable are specific responses. Knowledge of habitual responses gives better basis for prediction than knowledge of traits and knowledge of traits than knowledge of type. If then there is poorer prediction the higher one goes, why go through the labors of factor analysis to find higher levels? Eysenck's answer is that if the scheme sup-

[1] Another implication is that factors are not absolute but relative to tests and behavior measured. This implication is an objection to the system only if we consider that a scientific model has to take in everything and is *absolutely* true, two conditions not met by any model.

plies us with a fairly accurate picture of personality organization, the problem of prediction is a secondary one which may be solved by more appropriate methods.

Several observations are called for by the proposed theoretical structure and Eysenck's representations concerning it.[1] Negatively considered, the structure may not apply to a number of personalities. Both from factor analytic and psychological viewpoints the bringing together of traits into types may not be justified. The factor argument cannot be discussed at this point. But psychologically the number of persons who can be "typed" appears limited. Recognition of this limitation is made in psychology texts where Jung's introversion-extraversion theory is pictured (very inadequately) as a normal curve with introversion and extraversion at the extremes and what has been termed ambiversion occupying most of the curve (or area under the curve, more precisely). It is usually not recognized that such a picture tends to destroy the type-theory, for if most individuals are "ambiverts," they merely possess *varying degrees* of both introvert and extravert *traits* and cannot be classed as types.

A further psychological difficulty makes itself felt as one examines the systems of most typologists. In this case we shall limit ourselves to Jung, inasmuch as Eysenck's system of personality structure is so closely bound in with Jung's typology; but some of our remarks apply to other typologies. Jung has cross-classifications of sensation, intuition, feeling, and thinking types, any of which may be extraverted or introverted, and which in turn are divided into rational and esthetic (Jung, 1926). The complexities of let us say, a "Dionysian,[2] esthetic, sensation extravert" can hardly be represented by a simple typological scheme. Then taking account of the complexities and cross-classifications of the system Jung describes, Eysenck cheerfully adds other complexities in the form of multidimensional analyses and hundreds of correlation coefficients. It would seem as if the simplicity of Figure 7 hides many complications. When one considers all the cross-classifications and conditions inherent in any carefully constructed typology, he may be inclined to agree with one critic (Stagner, 1948) that the type may serve as a reference point for orienting the psychologist toward any individual, but that some psychologists may find it of no help in understanding the origin of personality structure or in planning therapy for an individual.

After saying these things, we do well to see that Eysenck *has* made a contribution to the understanding of personality structure in his recognition of levels of generality *in interpreting personality*. If there is no actual hierarchy of generality in the structure of personality, we are forced to construct one to help order the data of personality. While astronomers recognize that constellations are artificial clusterings of stars from the observer's viewpoint, they use these artificial clusterings to order some of their data. Observed correlations among items of behavior and among groupings of these items may not represent intrinsic structure of personality, although the continued finding of similar clusters again and again from one sample of persons to others does lead one to suspect that

---

[1] The general objection that the writer has to systems which include only "within the individual" or "within the organism" functions holds here. There is no need of laboring this objection too often. A semantic difficulty arises in Eysenck's use of factor terms, at least as the writer understands these terms. When Eysenck uses "group factor" he evidently means "common factor" as employed by others, and "general factor" for "group factor." The difference can be represented as below in a Thurstone-Eysenck comparison:

Eysenck	Thurstone
Error	Error
Specific	Specific
Group	Common
General	Group

In Eysenck's personality structure schema error variance corresponds to the specific response level, specific factors to the habitual response level, group factors to the trait level, and general factors, conceived as responses divested of error, specific, and group factor variance, to the type level.

[2] Nietsche's term.

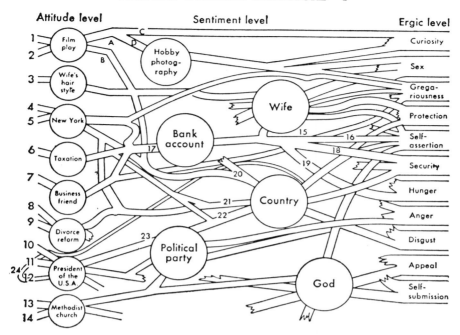

Figure 8. Fragment of dynamic lattice, showing attitude subsidiation, sentiment structure, and ergic goals. (From R. B. Cattell, *Personality*, p. 158)

there may be some intrinsic relations involved. Whether there are or not, the concepts of personality derived from these correlations serve as useful schemata.

Dynamic Subsidiation. One of the most comprehensive systems of personality organization, taking in research data and broad suggestions from clinic, laboratory, field work, speculative and scientific psychological theory, and everyday thinking, is Cattell's "dynamic lattice" of personality. Figure 8 is the pictorial representation of this system. Cattell has been influenced, especially in his recent work (1957a), by typological theories. The concept of "dynamic subsidiation," however, is hierarchical without being typological.

In this hierarchy the ergic level is "lowest," the sentiment level next, and attitude level at the "top." But as is evident from even this portion of the "dynamic lattice" of personality, no simple relations hold.

To understand the significance of the diagram it is necessary to know something of the derivation of Cattell's terms and of his

psychology in general. Cattell has taken as a framework for personality the "purposive" or "hormic" psychology of McDougall (1923, 1932b) and the kindred "psychodynamic" purposiveness of Freud. It is perhaps better to say that McDougall and Freud contributed much to Cattell's system, for the latter is not a copy of either original, but a distinct and fruitful contribution in its own right. Both McDougall and Freud regard behavior and higher-level attitudes as purposive in the sense that they serve the basic urges of the organism. Both of these keen students of personality were aware that "higher" attitudes and the manifest behavior from which they could be inferred are determined by forces other than basic urges. But each traced these manifest items to their lowest common denominator, instincts in the case of McDougall and sexual or aggressive drives in the case of Freud. Purposiveness, then, signifies that the individual's behavior serves purposes of which he may be partly or entirely unaware.

Besides purposiveness in the organism's

functioning, a further portion of McDougall's system of psychology having direct bearing on Cattell's dynamic lattice is the concept of "sentiments." For McDougall a sentiment was "an enduring conative attitude toward an object set up by the experience of the individual" (1923b). As Eysenck (1953c) remarks, the term has gone out of fashion, but could be revived to convey the generalized meaning of a large area of tendencies directed toward a major object in the individual's environment. The term has dropped out of even personological vocabulary possibly because some psychologists have loosely equated it with "attitude" (Murray, 1938) or "trait" (G. W. Allport, 1937a). In psychoanalytic work Freud's term "cathexis" has been employed, meaning the "evoking power of an object" (which does not reside in the object at all, but in the individual). It may also be that in the scramble of psychologists to throw out McDougall's "instinct psychology," several worthwhile babies were emptied out with the admittedly murky bath water.

At any rate there appears to be need for a term to identify those relatively enduring conative (striving) tendencies of an individual directed toward what he feels are very important objects in his life. Although there is no absolute dividing line between attitudes and sentiments, a good case can be made for the less-enduring qualities of *some* attitudes as compared to the continued power of others which can be distinguished by being called sentiments. Father may at times become worked up over some passing political figure and express a strong attitude toward him. At other times we see a tear stealing down his cheek and ask him, "What's the matter, Dad?" He responds, "I was just thinking about Mother." Yet we know that Mother has been gone for fifteen years. Certainly these are comparable "direction tendencies" in some ways; but the passing political figure and the beloved wife are hardly in the same category in the affective life of the one who regards them. "Sentiment" seems to be as good a term as any to refer to the class of attitudes of the more enduring na-

ture. It is in line with this thinking that Cattell (1950) makes his distinctions: ". . . attitudes are connected with minor, relatively superficial interests, whereas sentiments are stronger and deeper attitudes."

Introducing a new term for an old class of functions, Cattell offers the word "erg" for a whole group of determiners of behavior. Derived from the Greek *ergon* (meaning "work"), "erg" is the chief constituent in "energy." It comes closest in meaning to McDougall's "propensity" which he employed in later years to replace the much-derided "instinct." "Erg" refers to a constitutional, unitary pattern of reactivity found both by unaided observation and by measurements and correlation techniques. Cattell refers to an "erg" as one of the class of traits called "source traits" which according to Cattell can be either environmentally molded or innately determined (cf. Chapter 13); "ergs" are source traits of the innate variety.

Thus we find the principal concept in subsidiation is that some functions subserve the purposes of other functions which in turn may subserve still others. A motive-behind-a-motive type of sequence occurs, *subsidiation* in the sense that subsidiary streams contribute to larger streams and they to still larger ones. If, Cattell states, you should ask Horatius, a hero in Macaulay's *Lays of Ancient Rome*, why he did battle with so formidable a foe as Lars Porsena, Horatius would probably first reply he wanted to keep the Tuscan (or more generally Etruscan) soldiers out of Rome. Why? Because he was a Roman with patriotic sentiments. Why was Rome important? Because Horatius wanted to have a place of security and opportunity for his children. Why did he love his children? Here Horatius would consider your question a foolish one. In like manner one can trace other behavior-attitude-sentiment-drive sequences to their biological origin, each intermediate goal subserving the next in line. Figure 8, representing these sequences, shows a *dynamic* lattice, a diagram of forces, each subpart generating activity in other parts. Cattell admits Freudian concepts of id, ego, and superego as well as a self-sentiment into his structure of personality as major functional aspects. It is not clear how these fit into the dynamic lattice, but we need not ask a diagram to represent everything.

Calling attention to the dynamic nature of the forces or functions which may be directly visualized from Figure 8, but apparently having other unrepresented portions of personality in mind as well, Cattell shows how cultivating one's business friend, seeking tax reduction, and avoiding expensive visits to New York, all of which are on the attitude level, converge on the sentiment toward the individual's bank account. The bank account in turn subsidiates to another sentiment, wife, and to "ergs" like self-assertion, security, and hunger.

It may be noticed that the diagram representing Cattell's concept of personality structure is only a fragment of the entire lattice. Other "ergs" named by Cattell, though the list is not exhaustive in its scope, are: to seek air; to avoid physical pain, heat, and cold; to seek water; to seek food; to urinate and defecate. Sentiments also are more numerous than depicted, and attitudes even more so. Far from being a simple subsidiation sequence, the personality is a vast complex of such sequences which intermingle with one another.

Any dynamic trait whatever is therefore like a busy crossroads, or at least a corridor, to something else. Its importance and strength depend upon the number of further satisfactions to which it can contribute. This is the essential point that is brought out by representing the personality trait structure by a *dynamic lattice*. . . . Reluctant though the student or the lover of mathematical simplicity may be to face such a complex mode of representation, the fact remains that this is how human dynamic traits are structured, and we shall get ahead most quickly by admitting it. To the clinician, who may spend a year tracing the dynamic entanglements of a neurotic patient, the truth of the lattice concept will be immediately evident, though he may object that the present diagram is an especially simplified one, since it contains practically none of the instances in which a

subsidiation chain doubles back upon or recrosses itself (R. B. Cattell, 1950).[1]

Already, no doubt, even before reading about Cattell's concepts, the student has realized the high complexity of human personality structure. Cattell only underscores what research and intuitive psychologists such as great dramatists and poets have revealed. Simple formulations of personality may evolve in the future, but at present any such formulations are simplicistic. The easy generalizations about people made in common parlance run counter to science.

Organismic Structure. In a sense most psychologists subscribe to an organismic view of man as represented in Behavior Principle 3 in Chapter 1. Yet, in respect to systems, the term "organismic" is usually reserved in psychology for theories of personality structure influenced by or parallel to Gestalt theory. Probably the most consistent advocate of the organismic approach to personality is Andras Angyal whose *Foundations for a Science of Personality* (1941) has gradually been making itself felt among psychologists. Angyal designates his approach both "holistic" and "organismic." The former term is spelled unfortunately, following Smuts' spelling in *Holism and Evolution* (1926). Its meaning is that of "Gestalt" or "totality" rather than "holiness," and is better spelled "wholism" as in Howell's *Hunger for Wholiness* (1940). While recognizing the emptiness of much "holism," and the negative nature of some Gestalt theories which are merely opposed to any kind of *analysis*, Angyal maintains essentially with Gestaltists that an examination of parts in isolation from their function in the whole does not even give the correct picture of the parts, to say nothing of the whole.

Turning directly to Angyal's concept of personality structure, we find a highly dynamic system of systems as the over-all pattern.

---

[1] Cattell, R. B. *Personality, a systematic theoretical and factual study.* New York: McGraw-Hill, 1950. Reprinted by permission.

Personality can be regarded as a hierarchy of systems. In the larger personality organization the significant positions are occupied by constituents which themselves are also systems; the constituents of the secondary system may also be systems; and so on. Thus personality may be considered a hierarchy with the total personality organization at the top; below it follow the subsystems of first order, second order, third order, and so on (Angyal, 1941).[1]

Subsystems of the hierarchy may be broadly classified as those with a broad range of variation, and those systems that are (relatively) rigid. Exemplifying the first order are sensory-neuromuscular functions which occupy the outer regions of the organism. These are highly variable functions, with very little automatization; they are associated with considerable conscious awareness and conscious direction of activity, and they meet an external environment which is only slightly homeostatic. The second group of subsystems includes the visceral functions which occupy the internal regions and which in contrast to the sensori-motor systems face a highly homeostatic environment, become automatized readily, have small variability, and yield little to consciousness either in awareness or control. In between the two groups are the Janus-like functions such as the excretory functions, which are midway between the plastic and rigid systems. It is obvious that there is high survival value in having some systems capable of great variation to meet the almost infinite variability of the external world and other systems which function automatically without many energy-consuming adjustments.

The relations of subsystems to other subsystems of the same order or of different order and to the whole are determined partly by the rigidity or plasticity of the part-systems. A rigid system is localized in its activity, while plastic systems spread their effects to other systems both above them (superordinate) and below them (subordinate) in the hierarchy. Although Angyal does not illustrate these relations, we may suppose, for instance, that the ordinary functioning of the small intestine does not spread its effects to the student's understanding of these paragraphs. On the other hand "that certain person" may have happened by a short time ago; in consequence, a number of the student's sensory-neuromuscular functions, responding to this portion of the variable environment, spread their effects to a whole series of subordinate and superordinate functions, including the understanding of these words!

Changes in one system affect other systems in a distant region of the personality through intermediary systems. Angyal helps interpret some of the correlational results (or lack of correlation) among functions of the personality by pointing out the effect of intermediary systems which may alter direct connections:

. . . we may state that such attempts as, for instance, tying up *directly* some physicochemical changes with some complex form of behavior are very deceiving. If one neglects the intermediary steps one may bring into relationship members so distant that the connection between them remains entirely incomprehensible. The connections between the influence of a given drug on cell metabolism and some of its distant effects, for instance, a friendly, communicative attitude, cannot be understood if one disregards the various stages in the spread of influence through the intermediary systems. Correlations between processes in distant parts have, of course, a definite value from a theorectical as well as from a practical point of view. The establishment of such correlations should, however, be only a beginning. The next step is the tracing of the passage of change through the intermediary systems (Angyal, 1941).[2]

Changes in one system, however, may spread relatively locally within the system, in a limited way to other systems, or they may affect the whole personality. It is at this point that Angyal differs most widely from those who might be called "idealistic

[1] Angyal, Andras. *Foundations for a science of personality*. New York: The Commonwealth Fund, 1941. Reprinted by permission of Harvard University Press.

[2] *Ibid*. Reprinted by permission.

Gestaltists" who would hold that nothing can happen in any subsystem of a system of systems without affecting all subsystems, just as no part of a system can be disturbed without affecting all system parts. For Angyal, however, both within any one system and among systems changes may occur which do not affect the whole of the system or the entire organization of systems.

Dynamics *between* systems of different orders and *within* any system differ. Those between systems might be called relational or connectional; those within systems must be considered as "system action." There are no elements acting in isolation in a system. Even stimulus-response processes are not isolated elements but follow a pattern of: part $_1 \rightarrow$ whole (system) $\rightarrow$ part $_2$; this pattern represents the difference between S-R, stimulus-response, and S-O-R, stimulus-organism-response. Furthermore, within a system a part function may play either a variable or a relatively fixed role, unlike systems themselves which usually are definitely plastic or rigid.

In Angyal's concept of structure, "part" (as referred to part-function) has a special meaning. It does not mean "fragment." Walking, for example, could be arbitrarily *fragmented* into one-fourth steps or into portions like lifting of the leg, advancing it a bit, and putting it down; these are not *parts*, but fragments. But a fully completed step which enters into the total process of locomotion is a "part," because it is relatively complete in itself and it contributes directly to the completion of the whole function. "Directly" has a significance here also; a part has meaning only as an *immediate* part of an *immediate* whole. In a parallel way a letter is part of a word, but not directly of a sentence (unless it is a single-letter word), a word is part of a sentence but not directly of a paragraph, a sentence is a part of a paragraph but not of the chapter, and so on. To extend these concepts to personality functions we may say that a single act may be part of a habit but not directly a part of a trait; and a habit may be directly part of a trait, but not of a temperament.

One important element in Angyal's system is that any part-function may subserve several or many systems. Various physiological organs may be utilized for several functions, as is the urethra in the male, for example. And activities like earning money may answer any number of needs. "As a rule we try to kill two birds —or many—with one stone" (Angyal, 1941). At one time a part-function may subserve one major system, at another time another. As we can readily see, this conception of "structure" where parts may interchange their functioning makes for a dynamic personality—Angyal's representation is a picture of a *fluid* personality. In actuality, however, any system of personality structure has to take account of this cross-functioning, of part-functions subserving many major functions.

It is recognized that this discussion of Angyal's concepts has been fairly abstract. (Actually, Angyal's entire book tends to be even more abstract.) A summary of the concepts is in order to view the structure Angyal presents: We may start at the top with the personality as a whole, then come down to first-order subsystems as parts of the whole, then to second-order subsystems which are parts of the first-order subsystems, then third-order, and so on. Cutting across these orders of systems is a cross-hierarchy of rigid, semirigid, and plastic systems extending from the internal to the external regions. Even though, however, there are "rigid" systems, the personality structure is dynamic; that is, there is "system action" within even rigid systems, and there are forces affecting systems from other systems. Personality structure is not a mere heaping of parts on parts and systems on systems in a kind of static pyramidal arrangement; it is instead an "organismic hierarchical structure."

One criticism applies peculiarly to Angyal's system but holds as well for some other hierarchical systems. We recall from definitions of personality (Chapter 2) that Angyal uses the term personality "to denote the total organism when, as in man, the latter includes the social self and other factors which bind the individual into super-individual relationships" (1941). It is difficult, however, to fit these social factors into Angyal's hierarchy. Where does a man's role as union member or choir singer or husband enter into the hierarchy? Angyal does not make this matter explicit. Others who define personality in a manner that excludes interpersonal functions make no pretense of providing for such functions even by implication; Angyal definitely should include social functions in his hierarchy, but apparently finds it hard to do so.

Another criticism of Angyal's system is that it has not yielded fruit in research studies to the degree that some other systems have. Possible reasons for this lack of productive testing of its positions are the abstractions of Angyal's writing and the noncommercial publishing of his book—it is virtually unknown to many psychologists even many years after its publication. More important, much like psychoanalysis, Angyal's position is not stated so as to make his propositions easily testable. This criticism holds equally for some other Gestalt formulations.

Although a number of other questions and criticisms could be made of Angyal's system, it has appealed to some personologists because it takes a systematic account of many facets of personality. (Further description of Angyal's outlook on personality is found in Chapter 15.)

SUMMARY

Although some do not agree that personality has structure, most theorists have constructed "models" of the personality. Among the concepts of personality as a loose group of elements, faculty psychology regarded the mind as a group of independent "powers"; middle and late nineteenth century psychology as a compound of mental or sensational elements; and psychology in the first quarter or more of the twentieth century as a bundle of specific habits, the "identical elements" concept.

Regarding personality as a system of traits, factor analysis has looked upon the mind and other portions of personality in terms of distinguishable, mathematically-defined functions, both independent from one another and found commonly in all (in degrees). As Thurstone modified the original Spearman method of factor analysis, it became evident that the "independent" factors (first-order) can participate in larger wholes (second-order factors). Objections raised against the factor model of personality turn out to be objections against any scientific model. Allport's model looks upon personality as a system of interdependent traits, each one focalized and possessing telic significance, and each maturely-developed trait being "functionally autonomous" of its origin in drives or tissue needs.

Personality has been conceived as a hierarchical system, first and most simply as a set of concentric layers developing as the organism develops, with strengths and weaknesses in various layers. Type theories of personality, usually only classificatory, have been fashioned into a hierarchical system by Eysenck, spreading from the specific response level to the highest or type level. Similarly, Cattell has shown in "dynamic subsidiation" how parts of the personality are subordinate to others, and these to others, though they may change places in the hierarchy. Angyal represents organismic hierarchy concepts, maintaining a general (dynamic) system of systems, part-systems contributing to the operation of larger part-systems until the whole system consists of all part-systems.

There are still other ways of looking at the structure of the personality. In Chapter 5, however, it will become evident that even though different theories have unique features, all serious attempts to formulate structure bear some relation to one another. Some common elements are found even in seemingly diverse concepts.

QUESTIONS

1. Discuss the meanings of "structure" in general. What kinds of personality "structure" are there?

2. Discuss the implications for personality study of faculty psychology.

3. What value and what general criticism can be given in relation to Wundt's and the Mills' concepts of mental structure?

4. Describe and criticize the identical elements concept of personality structure.

5. Give the fundamentals of Spearman's and Thurstone's concepts of the personality.

6. What are the strengths and weaknesses of Allport's view of personality structure? Discuss "functional autonomy."

7. How can personality be conceived in terms of a hierarchy? Present several concepts which employ the hierarchical schema; include at least Cattell and Angyal in this discussion. What are the common elements in all of the concepts of hierarchy as presented in this chapter?

CHAPTER 5

OVER-ALL
DYNAMIC
STRUCTURE–II

In this chapter several additional views of personality structure are discussed. Although all of them are self-consciously "dynamic" systems, it is evident from the preceding chapter that those taken up now can lay no exclusive claim to such a designation. The structure of personality may be conceived in various ways. But as the student reads the succeeding pages the likenesses among various theories should become apparent as well as their dissimilarities.

PERSONALITY AS A CONFIGURATION OF TRENDS: THE "RORSCHACH PERSONALITY"

Almost any educated American knows a little about the Rorschach Ink Blot Test.[1] Possibly this is one case where a little knowledge is a dangerous thing. For experts are not agreed on major problems concerning the Rorschach.[2]

From a psychometric standpoint the test or technique is certainly not very satisfactory. Many clinicians, however, are not concerned about the statistics derived from or employed on the Rorschach, but insist that it gives a "personality configuration" or the patterned structure of per-

Eysenck, 1947; Ferguson, 1952) express concerning the Rorschach is pithily summarized by Eysenck (1947) who counts himself among "more cautious psychologists":

"Opinion regarding the value of the Rorschach test in its orthodox form is sharply divided. To many Rorschach experts, this test seems to fulfill in the realm of psychology the functions which in physics fall to the cyclotron, the Wilson cloud chamber, the thermionic valve, and the spectroscope all in one; in other words, the test is used for a great variety of disparate measurements which make it seem likely that if any of the fields is accurately covered by the test, none of the others can very well be so covered. To many more cautious psychologists, the test appears as one whose reliability is known to be low, whose validity has never been established with regard to most of the claims made in its favour, and whose subjective nature does not attract the scientific worker." (Reprinted by permission from Eysenck, H. J. *Dimensions of personality*. London: Routledge and Kegan Paul, 1947.)

Cattell (1946), no less caustically, states: "It remains a mixture of ill-defined intentions, analogous to a patent medicine, devoid of clear-cut theoretical bases which would permit refinement through research."

A review of the literature of validation problems of the Rorschach is out of place in a text like this. Suffice it to say that even a symphathetic

---

[1] It is difficult to know how to categorize the concept of personality as set forth in the Rorschach Test. Rorschach "trends" are not usually thought of as "traits," but are distinguishing qualities similar to factors in factor analysis—which are regarded as traits.

[2] It is with considerable hesitancy on the part of the writer that the personality structure as purportedly revealed by the Rorschach Ink Blot Test is included. There is a strong question concerning just what the Rorschach measures, if indeed it is a measuring instrument at all. The scepticism which factor analysis authorities (Cattell, 1950;

sonality.[1] It is with the latter consideration in view that the Rorschach personality structure is presented. If the pattern is helpful in understanding actual personalities, it may be admissible in our text on personality even though the Rorschach may not be a measure of the pattern.

Probably the first essential item of interpretation of a Rorschach protocol is the assumed principle that all the trends of personality are related to one another, so that different "scores" on the Rorschach cannot be considered apart from their interrelations. Consequently, though there are differentiated functions in the resultant personality structure, fundamental in that structure is the mutual interaction of all the part-functions in a *unitas multiplex,* similar to Stern's conception (1938).

Next in importance for the structure of personality is the balance of *introversion* and *extratensive* trends shown by the individual. Whether the former or latter prevails determines the "experience type" of the person. Extratensive means the quality of being *responsive* to the environment, both human and animal, animate and inanimate. Some people are passively responsive and others actively, even creatively so; therefore, the kind of extratensiveness makes for qualitative differences in personality structure. Introversion, somewhat unlike Jung's concept, refers to the internal resources available to the individual rather than to his being withdrawn from the world. A person may even enjoy society as an introversive individual, but he is not too dependent on others inasmuch as he has good inner resources. From the standpoint of structure we may find various individuals with "balance" of introversive-extratensive trends; in this case "good balance" is not mere balance, but rather a richness of both trends. Nevertheless, numerical balance between these trends is expected to a considerable degree (an expectation not borne out by research).[2]

Besides introversive and extratensive trends, another major function of personality is the kind of control the individual exerts over himself and his environment.

---

reviewer finds many difficulties in the way of validating the technique. Considering the Rorschach as a "method of observation" (B. Klopfer, Ainsworth, W. Klopfer, & Holt, 1954) rather than a "test" of personality seems inadequate. Even the most objective test is a method of observation. The same questions of validity apply to both methods.

On the whole experimental testing of Rorschach hypotheses has been eminently unsatisfactory. Individual signs and "global judgments" derived from the test have shown little relation to objectively determined functions of personality, except in a few isolated instances (*e.g.,* King, 1958). Nevertheless, many clinicians continue to use the test because it *seems* to reveal data about personalities which other instruments fail to uncover. Extensive standardization similar to that of the Stanford-Binet and Wechsler Intelligence Scale for Children is called for. A good start, and only such, has been made in work like that of Ames and her collaborators (Ames, Learned, Metraux, & Walker, 1952).

[1] Sometimes the cart goes before the horse, as the personality structure is derived from the test and not the test from the structure. As long as the user of the Rorschach recognizes that the device only sets up a model of the personality structure and does not reveal the "real" structure, no harm is done, of course.

[2] To maintain a proportion between fantasy life and emotional reactions to the outer world, the proportion between the human movement and color responses is examined at this point. Although the theoretical position is that an even balance is best, practical considerations would allow a slight imbalance one way or the other (Mons, 1949). In one study (Dreger, 1952) this slight imbalance became a great one. In a group of persons virtually all of whom were clinically normal—that is, they were not at the time receiving clinical help, and only two or three had ever received such help—the introversive trends outweighed the extratensive almost six to one. This result seems strange in terms of "balanced structure" in Rorschach theory. The subjects were of higher than average intelligence, so according to theory would be expected to have "scores" indicating a rich inner life (introversion), but also a rich responsiveness to external stimuli. It may be that the personality structures of these subjects as "revealed" by the Rorschach were in reality awry, for according to Rorschach theory there should have been more "balanced personalities." Either there is much greater introversiveness in the average personality, or the meaning of what the Rorschach reveals is different from what interpreters have thought (or as some might say, there is nothing to the Rorschach!).

There is either a relaxed, mature, nonanxious type of control or a rigid, anxious, almost consciously gritting-the-teeth type. In most instances there is a combination of both kinds which makes for more or less secure handling of one's impulses and of perceptual-motor contacts with the external world. The structure of any one personality is characterized, according to Rorschach theory, by the relative quantity and quality of different kinds of control and the interactions among them.

Still another function which makes up the dynamic structure of the personality is the intellectual approach a person makes to problems. This approach is revealed in the perceptual approach to the ink blots. Does the individual approach the blots as "wholes" or does he see details first? The inference is that he approaches problems (or life in general) by "wholes" or by piecemeal analysis. Again, does he have a positive approach or is he negativistic—does he tend to see "figure" where other people see "ground?" [1]

Related to the preceding functions directly is one last major set of functions entering into the total structure of personality, the manner of conforming or not conforming to usual ways of perceiving and of thinking. On the Rorschach blots there are actually meaningless portions which are perceived in similar ways by most of the members of any one society. How close the individual comes to viewing these blot portions as others in his society perceive them is in Rorschach theory a measure of the personality's conforming to social standards (at least in thought and feeling).

A lucid explanation of the personality structure from a Rorschach viewpoint is given in the little book, *Principles and Practice of the Rorschach Personality Test*

[1] No doubt this aspect of personality functioning is an important one, but the same study cited in note 2, p. 71, revealed discrepancies between empirical results and the introversive-extratensive theory also gives evidence that the accepted proportions of "scores" relating to "mental approach" had little validity for the group under test, who in turn were representative of much larger groups.

(Mons, 1949). Like others this text suggests the use of a "psychogram" (Figure 9) to represent personality structure. Not all of the elements for which the Rorschach is "scored" are on the psychogram, for we should need several more dimensions than the two a textbook page affords to include them all.

The meanings of the letters need not concern us except that they each refer to a quality "scored" on the test. Each functional element in this picture of the personality is dependent for its interpretation upon its relative position (and quality). To the Rorschach interpreter the psychogram pictured here is a symbolic representation that the individual whose responses have been "scored" thus is (among other things) relatively well-balanced in terms of introversive-extratensive trends; that he has sufficiently strong hostile-aggressive impulses and primitive (in an adult probably mainly sexual) drives to occasion some anxiety, but that he also has fantasy outlets and mature controls over his impulses as well as enough "will power"; that he is sensitive to the world about him, being artistically inclined in all likelihood; that under most circumstances he will not give way under external pressures; that he has a measure of insight into himself and a fair degree of empathy for others. To the student it may seem like magic that a picture of personality can thus be derived from a diagram—and not only to the student but to many seasoned psychologists as well. And yet, regardless of how adequate or inadequate the Rorschach psychogram is in assessing any personality, it must be confessed that the concept of personality structure represented by the psychogram is a consistent and compelling one.

Taking the various functions of the personality suggested by Rorschach analysis, we may possibly gain considerable understanding of personality structure. Of course, the question remains: Does the Rorschach reveal this structure by its assessment methods? This question we can only ask in a textbook such as this. It may be that if the student goes on in his study

The Rorschach Test

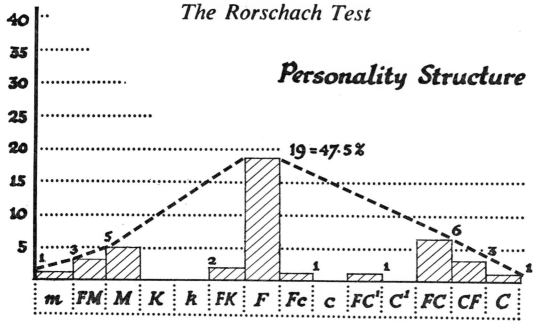

Figure 9. Rorschach representation of personality structure. (From W. Mons, *Principles and Practice of the Rorschach Personality Test*, p. 92)

of psychology to the point where he can do research in personality, he may be instrumental in helping to answer the question.

PERSONALITY AS A NEED-TENSION SYSTEM

A number of conceptions of personality structure as a need-tension system could be instanced at this point. Adler's conception of personality as a set of dynamic patterns built upon the basic feeling of inferiority and the compensatory striving for superiority could be cited.[1] Striving from "below" (feminine) to "above" (masculine) is in Adler's (1912, 1920, 1927) system the basic need, a tension being constantly felt as long as the person is below. Likewise McDougall's instinct system could be dis-

cussed here, although it seems more like a "hierarchical system." Even Jung's complex yet logically (and psychologically) worked out schema of psychic structure with its dynamic representations of types and subtypes could be placed among need-tension systems because of its emphasis on the striving nature of man, on his basic urge (libido, life-energy) which constantly moves him. The conceptions which are examined below, however, have been selected as being fairly representative of structure concepts based on the principle of unfulfilled needs'-creating-tension-arousing-action.

Biophysical

"Within-the-skin" need-tension systems may be classified as biophysical, a term which could apply to some other conceptions discussed already. From a structural standpoint, however, these other formulations have been taken up elsewhere because their major characteristics do not lend themselves to need-tension structural

[1] Adler seemed to have refrained for the most part from setting up anything so apparently rigid as a personality structure. The only place that the writer has found a suggestion of the "personality structure" as such is in *The Neurotic Constitution* (1912, p. 73), where the neurotic "abstract psyche" is pictured.

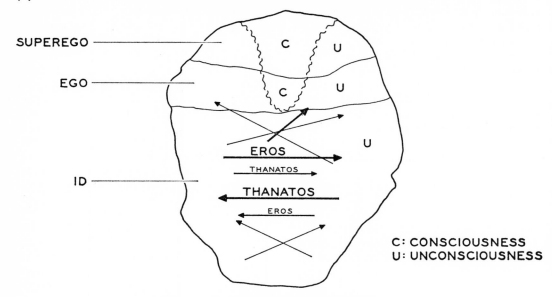

SUPEREGO

EGO

ID

EROS

THANATOS

THANATOS

EROS

C: CONSCIOUSNESS
U: UNCONSCIOUSNESS

Figure 10. Freudian personality structure.

conceptions. The systems of Freud and of Murray represent biophysical theories of personality structure.

Id, Ego, Superego; Eros, Thanatos. It is impossible to do justice to psychoanalytic concepts in the few paragraphs we have allotted to them. Certainly the importance of these views is not proportional to the small amount of discusion offered here. Rightly or wrongly it has been assumed that the average student is more familiar with Freudian concepts of personality structure than with others. Less space is thus devoted to the former.

A pictorial and over-simplified representation of Freudian theory (Figure 10) may be based on Freud's own simple diagram (Freud, 1927) and on the expressed concepts of Freud and of others who have discussed these matters in direct relation to Freud (Fenichel, 1945). The main systems in the structure as we know are id, ego, and superego. Id is a driving chaos of forces seeking release without regard to time, place or circumstance (operating according to the "pleasure principle"). Ego develops out of id in response to demands from without and within for controls of incoming stimuli and of motor expression (op-

erating according to the "reality principle"). Superego develops out of ego as the representative of society's demands related to "expected" behavior (primarily parental "introjects").[1] Within the structure various life urges operate in ways that lead to life or death in varying degrees (arrows aimed at different degrees from horizontal). The "life-instinct," Eros (sexual drives), and the "death instinct," Thanatos (movement of organic back to inorganic), operate sometimes in fused ways or sometimes in opposed fashion to each other. At times Eros and Thanatos work together (as indicated by small arrows going in the same direction as the counter-force), but generally in opposite directions. Not all psychoanalysts accept the "death instinct" (Fenichel, 1945), but since this concept was one of Freud's major adaptations in his basic system, it is included to represent Freudian psychoanalysis.

The structure of personality according to this system is a need-tension structure: The organism is moved by its needs to

[1] "Introjects" refer to those things "taken in" figuratively to become part of the personality, just as objects (food) are taken in literally to become part of the organism.

function at any one time according to its strivings for discharge or dynamic control, to move toward life or death. But there are in this process forces and counter forces creating tension. In connection with this concept of personality structure, it is to be understood that it is both general and individual; all persons possess or develop the major functions, but endowment and development are individual. Thus, for instance, the contents of the superego depend on the culture in which the individual resides and on what models he has for his parental "introjects."

Need-Press System. Accepting Freud's general divisions of the personality into its three components, ego, id, and superego, Murray (1938) sets forth a concept of personality structure which elaborates on these fundamental components.[1] The conception is known widely among psychologists in its "need-press" aspects through the Thematic Apperception Test, which is probably familiar to the student as one of the popular tests in psychological and psychiatric diagnosis.

It is difficult to diagram the structure of personality here. We will have to imagine something like Freud's conception of structure with interrelated subdivisions called "needs." A need, according to Murray is a construct (a convenient fiction) standing for a force in the brain region. This force, of unknown physicochemical nature, organizes perception, apperception, intellection, conation and action. And it organizes them so as to change an unsatisfying situation "in a certain direction," in most cases leading the organism to search for, avoid, attend and respond to certain stimulus situations called "press" (defined below).

There are primary or viscerogenic and secondary or psychogenic needs. Representative of viscerogenic needs are: "n Inspiration" (oxygen) from the group of needs designated as "lacks"; "n Sex" is included among "distentions"; and "n Nox-

avoidance" among "harms." The letter n in each case stands for "need." The last term "n Noxavoidance," ". . . refers to the tendency to avoid or rid oneself of noxious stimuli: to look or draw away from repulsive objects, to cough, spit or vomit up irritating or nauseating substances" (Murray, 1938). Psychogenic needs can be represented by "n Acquisition," one of the needs directed toward inanimate objects; "n Superiority" which is self-explanatory; "n Inviolacy," referring to desires and attempts to preserve self-respect and one's good name; and "n Affiliation," need to form friendships, to join groups, to love. Primary in Murray's scheme is the conception that needs are dynamic factors, virtually forces within the organism. Murray thus employs the term "energy" in connection with needs in a two-fold manner, first to mean general energy associated with being "energetic," and secondly to parallel McDougall's drives or fundamental urges of life. In the latter sense needs are *tensions* built up in the organism. They are stronger or weaker in their intensities, but never completely absent, else not only would the entire structure of personality disappear, but life itself would be gone.[2]

Meeting or thwarting the *needs* of the individual are *press*, for example: "p Nurturance," those objects both human and nonhuman which give protection, sympathy, and nourishment; "p Dominance," those objects which offer domination and overriding of the individual's will or desires; and "p Affiliation," objects serving the individual in a friendly, loving, or companionable way. Murray writes: "We have selected the term *press* (*plural press*) to designate a directional tendency in an object or situation," (Murray, 1938). Physical objects or social situations are classified

---

[1] In Kluckhohn, Murray, and Schneider, *Personality in Nature, Society and Culture* (1953), a conception of personality closer to the writer's functional concept is proposed.

[2] Homeostasis, the physiological balance of forces within the organism, is not freedom from tension, but a dynamic balance of tensions. See W. B. Cannon, *The Wisdom of the Body* (1932). Physiologists do not necessarily accept Cannon's doctrine of homeostasis, but apparently accept a "level of tension" rather than a lack of tension as characteristic of life (Heilbrunn, 1952).

from the individual's standpoint, not according to responses *per se* which they invoke in the organism, but according to whether they are perceived to benefit or harm the individual.

Needs may subserve one another in the general structure of personality, thus making Murray's theory an hierarchical one as well as a need-tension theory. Also needs unite with press or "pre-actions" (any actions determining future behavior) or with outcomes of events (o) to form what Murray calls "themas" (from which the name of the Thematic Apperception Test is derived). These themas are structures of events comprising *molar* [1] aspects of behavior (large units of behavior). Simple themas can be exemplified by the following (adapted from Murray, 1938).

p Rejection——→n Rejection: the person is rejected (snubbed) by a human object and responds in kind.

o Failure——→n Achievement: the person makes renewed, counteractive attempts to succeed after failure.

Insofar as themas are comprised in part of objects they are not strictly speaking portions of the structure of personality. But there are "thematic tendencies" which are the structured aspects within the personality that meet press, pre-actions, or outcomes. Murray states, for example, regarding the unconscious portion of the personality, "In our experience, the unconscious . . . of a person may be formulated best as an assemblage or federation of thematic tendencies." (Murray, 1938).

Summing up the structure of personality as abstracted from Murray's writing, we can say that besides possessing the over-all Freudian type structure, id, ego and, superego, the personality contains sub-elements known as needs which interact with press, preactions, and outcomes to form larger dynamic structural wholes known as themas (or thematic tendencies).

[1] *Molar* refers to the gross, general characteristics of behavior in contrast to *molecular* facts provided by physiology and physics. These terms are usually attributed to Tolman in his *Purposive Behavior in Animals and Men* (1951).

Two comments must be made concerning Murray's concepts. In the first place needs are confusingly sometimes called by the name of the state of the organism and sometimes by that of the object which satisfies the state of tension. Two examples are: "n Sentience," which is the inclination to seek sensuous gratification (not necessarily sensual gratification), particularly taste and tactile sensations, and "n Water," which is the object of seeking (though not the aim of seeking). This confusion may be only a semantic difficulty and Murray may mean by such terms as "n Water" the inner state he defines; sometimes, however, one gets the impression the confusion is in concepts, not words. The other comment is not a negative criticism; it stems from our present understanding of personality. Virtually all of the structure of personality in Murray's system is within the individual, except as it seems to reach out for objects. Interpersonal functions do not seem to be recognized as portions of the personality, even though needs for interpersonal relations are recognized. Perhaps these latter needs could be extended to include roles, but the possibility of such an extension is not made clear.

Biosocial

Related in some ways to Angyal's concepts, biosocial formulations take account of "outside-the-skin" functions of personality. As one surveys the story of personality study of the past twenty-odd years against the background of previous study, there seems to be little doubt that the trend is toward greater inclusiveness in respect to what personality is. Social psychology, in spite of rather chaotic conditions in many of its areas, has been forcing personologists to take account of functions hardly to be considered as residing inside the biological organism, yet just as distinguishing of the individual as the feelings he has about himself. Anthropology and sociology have likewise forced psychology to consider larger wholes than it had previously taken notice of. To the major biosocial personologist's system of structure we now devote attention.[1]

Gardner Murphy in his masterly volume, *Personality, a Biosocial Approach to Origins and Structure* (1947), sets forth many different meanings for "organization" and "structure" of personality. Very catholic in his acceptance of different suggestions from widely scattered sources, Murphy presents his need-tension system clearly, weaving the sources into a more or less consistent, and highly instructive view of personality structure.

Basic to Murphy's concept are the three stages through which every individual passes on the way to maturity: Stage 1, in which there is undifferentiated mass activity; Stage 2, in which differentiated parts function more or less autonomously; and Stage 3, in which action is integrated, inasmuch as parts are interdependent. With these stages in slightly different form we have already become acquainted in Chapter 4, though Murphy's formulation of the processes is his own.

Before considering these stages from a structural standpoint, Murphy discusses the possible ways in which traits (or more generally, in our terms, functions) can be related in the personality. Some traits may grow directly out of others, such as compensation out of feelings of inferiority. Two or more traits may also converge on another one, as the desire to be a hero may stem from both narcissism and father identification. Furthermore, traits may arise from conflict, as for example in the Oedipal situation impulses of love toward one parent and fear toward the other lead to possibly long-lasting feelings of frustration, since the individual is pulled one way and pushed the other. In any concept of organization like this, there is the dynamic quality of balance among traits, "a chronic suspense," as Murphy calls it, as in the balancing of extratensive and introversive trends in a Rorschach view of personality. And related to balance is the mutual influence

traits have on one another, limiting the range of variability of one another; when too much success or too much failure distorts the self-picture, the organism moves homeostatically to reduce the one and raise the other to the place where the individual can "be himself again." In addition to these general ways in which traits can be related (in personality organization), "reversible reactions" may occur in the personality similar to reversible chemical reactions; for instance, unsuccessful attempts to rebel against parental domination may alternate with moves toward compliance, an uneasy balance with neither tendency able to get the ascendancy. Sometimes, of course, no kind of balance is possible, so a new equilibrium must be set up; inability to resist disease may, for example, lead to adaptation of host and disease parasite at a reduced health level.

Like many others, Murphy thinks of traits as interdependent inasmuch as they are aspects of a larger field (Gestalt). A parent's courage and patience in caring for a sick child are distinguishable as traits but interdependent. More complex instances of trait interdependence may be found in which local traits are aspects of the whole personality system, as the ". . . courage of the sick child's mother is an aspect of her entire personality that is focused upon one supremely important goal." (Murphy, 1947). One must not take too literally the "entire personality . . . focused," for Murphy indicates, in a succeeding suggestion concerning trait interrelations, that the entire system is not homogeneous, but instead, that there are dominant focusings of energy *among* other less dominant focusings. Murphy does not use the illustration, but his example of the sick child's mother could be expanded to show that a portion of the mother's personality is focused on having to take *some* care of her own bodily needs (she does, after all, eat and drink), or of those of other family members, while *most* of her personality is focused on the supremely important goal of the occasion.

After the various relations among personality traits are presented, in Murphy's

---

[1] Norman Cameron (1947) also classifies as an outstanding biosocial psychologist.

words, "We come at last to structure as a specification of an architectural whole . . ." (1947). Only when mature interdependence of traits is present, as when differentiated functions have arisen from undifferentiated ones and these in turn have become integrated, can architectural wholeness be spoken of. The *degree* of interdependence and of organization (actually, integration) differs for different members of a group and even for the same person from time to time. The "architectural whole" is a dynamic one, "with areas of relative stability, but with a capacity for internal reorganization as well as free adaptation to new situations" (1947).

Murphy does not follow the Gestaltist's claim that all functions of the personality are literally interdependent. He adheres to the same principle to which we have been led inductively (in Chapter 5), that there is insufficient evidence to show that consistency of personality is complete. The fact of conflict is too potent to be dismissed; some parts do seem to be autonomous from others. (Yet Murphy is the one who makes the interesting suggestion cited previously that the very existence of conflict is evidence for wholeness of a sort, in that complete dissociation of the self into two [or more] *completely* independent spheres of activity does not take place). Instead of complete interdependence then, among all the elements of structure, there are "degrees of organizedness" and some groups may be relatively autonomous from others.

Despite his use of the term "trait" throughout his discussion, for Murphy "traits" are needs or tensions rather than semistatic elements and are the fundamental units of the structure.

From the present point of view the *ultimate elements in personality structure are the needs or tensions, and they are interrelated by means of the functional connections between regions which permit the spread of these tensions.* The result is a *tension system* whose lawful structure is expressed in terms of the relative strengths of tensions and the relative rigidity of barriers to their diffusions. Our hypothesis therefore claims that *the organism's tension system is organized,* in the sense that each event is limited and controlled by the relations between elements, as in homeostasis. There is organization at every moment in time, in the form of a "static" system. There is also temporal or dynamic organization, each tension or group of tensions initiating changes which eventually bring the organism to a new balance, or restore it to the first. (Murphy, 1947).[1]

There is an additional element in Murphy's conception of personality structure which carries it well beyond Murray's need-tension system. This element is the "structured organism-environment field" which constitutes the personality. Personality can be investigated from three levels of complexity: (1) that of its being an event or object as in statistical enumeration; (2) that of its having internal structure, as most concepts of personality would hold; and finally, (3) that of its being supra-organismic. It is this last level which places Murphy beyond Murray, and indeed beyond many personologists. Citing biological facts of reciprocity between organism and environment, Murphy declares it is difficult to conceive of personality as lying entirely within the skin. Personality can be viewed as a field in which boundaries are vague and continually changing, with the organism as a node in the field. As *social* structures, personalities studied in their interrelations constitute a society. And even beyond being a related portion of the social structure, man is also a portion of the *cosmos*, so his "field" is the universe. Murphy parallels a pantheistic conception of the universe in his concept of personality:

Personality is social, but it is more. It is a drop of the cosmos, and its surface tensions bespeak only a fragile and indefinite barrier that marks a region of relative structuring, relative, that is, because of the confluence of the self and the nonself. As the musician melts into and identifies with his beloved instrument, the Hopi Indian on the rim melts into his Grand Canyon (Murphy, 1947).[2]

[1] Murphy, G. *Personality: a biosocial approach to origins and structure.* New York: Harper & Bros., 1947. Reprinted by permission.
[2] *Ibid.* Reprinted by permission.

For its most adequate expression personality structure is schematized as three-dimensional in Murphy's view. We find, however, the field concept of personality conceptualized in Figure 11 which depicts the personality as an organism-environment field. Letters represent needs which are interrelated one with another. These needs are not, as they appear to be in Murray's system, all within the organism, but in part lie "outside the skin." [1] Murphy states, "All the functional relations within the shaded area, and between the shaded and unshaded areas, constitute personality. The shaded area is the organism" (Murphy, 1947).

In Murphy's concepts of personality structure we find a number of fruitful concepts to help order personality data. Whether the "structure" is superior to others or not—and we recall that any scientific model may be utilized which takes account of what we know—, it is well-reasoned and brings many of the complexities of personality within its scope.

Topological

Among the brilliant scientists Germany has contributed to America, Kurt Lewin was one of the most influential. Whether he was a "great man" or not,[2] his original ways of thinking and his inspiration to extended research in psychology are evident in the record. Lewin's "topological psychology," which he later called "hodological" (from *topos*, a place, and *hodos*, a way) may not be familiar to the student. But studies in aggressive and regressive behavior performed

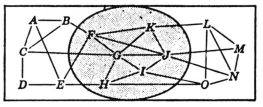

Figure 11. Murphy's biosocial concept of personality structure. (From G. Murphy, *Personality*, p. 8)

by Lewin and his students in elaboration of his system have their place in many beginning psychology texts. One experiment may be recalled in which children were exposed first to toys of ordinary attractiveness, then to very delectable toys, and then were shut away from the more attractive toys by a wire partition. In this situation most children "regressed" by measurable age-units in the quality of their play, while a few became more constructive or "older" in their play behavior. This experiment on frustration and regression was one of Lewin's (Barker, Dembo, & Lewin, 1941). Also may be recalled the experiment on "autocratic," "democratic," and "laissez-faire" social climates in which boys were placed in different social climates to determine what type of behavior resulted from each "climate." Again, this study was performed under Lewin's direction (1934). Lewin's influence on social psychology, particularly experimental social psychology, has been and still is extensive.[3]

We cannot take up Lewin's entire system of psychology,[4] even though his concept of personality structure is embedded in it. Several principles of Lewin's general psychological system must be understood, however, to make his personality concepts clear. As stated in a memorial volume of Lewin's basic papers (1951), the construct

---

[1] The writer came to the view of personality as *inter*personal as well as *intra*personal independently of his study of Murphy. He gladly gives priority to Murphy and others in this recognition. It was a source of real gratification to discover that so eminent an authority as Murphy had arrived at the same conclusions concerning the scope of personality as had the author. It seems that one can hardly be aware of the cross-currents of research and theoretical discussion without coming to similar conclusions; but this view may be a narrow one, for not many writers in personality are as explicit as Murphy is.

[2] Boring (1950) is doubtful.

[3] Lewin (1951; Lindzey, 1954) is one psychologist whose influence seems to grow with the years after his passing.

[4] Leeper (1943) has given a digest and critique of Lewin's system which helps to understand it, though the student who goes much farther along the road of psychology will probably want to read Lewin directly (1935, 1936a, 1936b, 1946).

most fundamental to Lewin's psychology is that of "field."

In treating individual psychology, the field with which the scientist must deal is the "life space" of the individual. This life space consists of the personal and the psychological environment as it exists for him. In dealing with group psychology or sociology, a similar formulation is proposed. One may speak of the field in which a group or institution exists with precisely the same meaning as one speaks of the individual life space in individual psychology (Lewin, 1951).[1]

Taking its cue from electro-magnetism, field theory in psychology uses a general definition of field: "A totality of coexisting facts which are conceived of as mutually interdependent is called a *field*" (Lewin, 1946). There can be no change in the *environment* or in the *person* without effecting a change in the complementary component of the field, just as a change in the electric current running through a wire or in the lines of force surrounding the wire effects a change in the alternate component.[2]

[1] Lewin, K. *Field theory in social sciences, selected theoretical papers*. Edited by Dorwin Cartwright. Published for the Research Center for Group Dynamics, University of Michigan. New York: Harper & Bros., 1951. Reprinted by permission.

[2] Most present-day psychologists would probably agree with this concept of field. Also, the designation of this field as "life space" has come to be fairly well-accepted. It is at the point of considering behavior as a change in the state of the field in a *short* unit of time, however, that many psychologists especially of psychoanalytic persuasion have found fault with Lewin's system. To some psychologists the insistence that only contemporaneous processes can be considered in the change of states of a field means that there is no consideration of past events or of future plans in Lewin's system. For personologists this insistence (if Lewin actually so insisted) would seem to undercut any kind of longitudinal continuity to personality. For learning theorists the possibility of learning seems to be thrown out. Even Leeper (1943) seems to misunderstand Lewin's position in respect to the "principle of contemporaneity" in his otherwise sympathetic and discerning discussion of Lewin's position. Some of the criticisms of Lewin remind the writer of Dampier's epigram concerning religion and rationalism: ". . . religion always mistakes what it says for what it means. And rationalism, so to

It is difficult to get the concept that the life space does not coincide with the physical person and environment. For example, parts of the body of a schizophrenic may become estranged from him—they are no longer a portion of *him*. (There may be self-mutilations, sometimes literally fulfilling the biblical injunction, "And if thy right hand offend thee, cut it off, and cast it from thee.") On the other hand, a person's children or even his clothing may be so much a part of him that he is not "all there" when separated from them. Thus even the "person" may be more or less than the physical person. Likewise the "environment" is not to be understood as corresponding directly with the physical world

speak, runs after it pointing out that what it says is untrue" (Rall, 1940).

In this connection Lewin makes a distinction between "historical" (Aristotelian) causation and "systematic" causation ("systematic" referring to changes internal to a system like Angyal's "system action"). One can imagine the horror of "historically minded" psychologists on reading Lewin's bold statements:

"Though we are justified in setting up 'historical' questions and looking for causal sequences, yet we must be careful to avoid historical or half-historical answers to 'systematic' questions of causation. It was typical of the Aristotelian way of thinking not to distinguish between historical and systematic questions. The result was that one took past or future events as causes of present events. In opposition to this assumption we shall here strongly defend the thesis that neither past nor future psychological facts but only the present situation can influence present events. This thesis is a direct consequence of the principle that only what exists concretely can have effects. Since neither the past nor the future exists at the present moment it cannot have effects at the present. In representing the life space therefore we take into account only what is contemporary" (Lewin, 1936a. Reprinted by permission from Lewin, K. *Principles of topological psychology*. Translated by F. Heider and Grace M. Heider. New York: McGraw-Hill Book Co. Inc., 1936. Copyright, 1936.)

So psychologists and psychiatrists and especially social workers who take life histories are Aristotelian (old-fashioned) as opposed to Lewinians who are scientific! And yet, it appears to be a misreading of Lewin's position and a misunderstanding of behavior to maintain Lewin is *wrong* in his "principle of contemporaneity." At any one moment of time I cannot be moved by my *actual* past but only by my *psychological* past which is about the person. A natural mistake must not be made here in thinking that the environmental portions of the life space need to enter *awareness*. Experiments in hypnosis would seem to indicate that portions of the environment of which we are unaware may influence us psychologically (Hunt, 1944, Chapter 15). Sherif and Cantril as social psychologists in summarizing research up to 1947 demonstrate the experimental formation of attitudes under social influences of which many subjects are not cognizant (Sherif & Cantril, 1947). Both person and environment which constitute the life space in Lewin's system, therefore, are partly but not by any means entirely coincident with the physical person and environment. In either case, too, there are portions of the field which may be out of the individual's immediate awareness.

One aspect of Lewin's model of the life

present with me now. It is not what *actually* happened to us as children that moves us to action (behavior) now, but *our present conscious or unconscious interpretation of our childhood* combined with whatever present circumstances exist in our environments. Bartlett's (1932) famous experiments on remembering and forgetting and considerations such as are advanced in phenomenological analysis (Snygg & Combs, 1949) tend to bear out Lewin's contentions in regard to past events. And in addition, we are moved not by the actual future but by our *present* plans of the future.

Lewin did not assert, however, that historical causation is nonexistent. Even in the quotation above it was stated, in a dependent clause to be sure, but still stated: "... we are justified in setting up 'historical' questions and looking for causal sequences. ...."

Lewin's position is given relatively clearly in another place:

"One could argue that psychological facts are intrinsically of a historical nature. As a matter of fact the structure of the person and the psychological characteristics of the environment at each moment and in each point are in a decisive way dependent upon the previous history, as experimental investigations show impressively. ... However, this influence of the previous history is to be thought of as indirect in dynamic psychology. From the point of view of systemic causation, past events cannot influence present events. Past events can only have a position in the historical causal chains whose interweavings create the present situation" (Lewin, 1936a). (Reprinted by permission.)

space deserves a few words, and that is the nature of the boundary between the life space and the "foreign hull" of facts which are not governed by psychological laws (*i.e.*, in respect to any one individual). Lewin insists—in keeping with much that we know of personality—that the life space is "dynamically not closed," that is, every point in the life space can be a boundary point with those physical and social facts which do not at present influence the person psychologically. In other words, every region within the person and within the environment is open to potential influences which are not now affecting the psychical functioning of the individual. The dog lurking in a shadowy fence corner is in the immediate *physical* environment of the unwary traveler even before making his canine self known, but he suddenly enters the life space of the traveler as he springs out—and brave is the man into whose inner-most portions of life space the influence of the charging dog does not penetrate, even though the traveler knows that normally the dog is only capable physically of penetrating the outer portions of his person.

In representing the personality in its life space the emphasis in Lewin is on *system* rather than on *history*, *i.e.*, Lewin emphasizes the interplay of forces at the present time. ("Present" here may be momentary [microscopic unit] or a fairly extended period of time [macroscopic unit].) These contemporaneous considerations of the life space are in rather sharp contrast with the usual theories of personality structure which implicitly assume historical causation.

With the concept of the field in mind, we may put the person into his life space, thereby depicting the personality structure. Essentially, but in an exceedingly simplified fashion the person himself is represented in Figure 12 as if drawn on an elastic sheet so that no matter how one stretches the sheet, changing the shapes and sizes of (a) or (b) and their constituent parts, the fundamental relations of the parts to one another still hold.

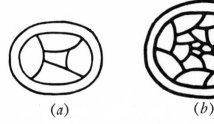

Figure 12. Lewin's topological concept of personality structure. (From K. Lewin, *A Dynamic Theory of Personality*, p. 208)

As is evident, (a) stands for a child and (b) for an adult. In each case there is a "boundary region" between the person and the world, called either the motoric or the motor-perceptual region, the portion of the life-space wherein contacts are made through receptors and effectors with the remainder of the life space, the environment. Within the boundary regions are other regions or systems (comparable to Angyal's systems).

In the case of the child as compared to the adult, two outstanding facts are to be noted by use of the diagrams. First, the boundary lines between system and system are lighter, indicating greater permeability of the boundaries in the child. He appears to behave more as a whole than does the adult, that is, regions or systems are more readily accessible; as for instance the child is more "transparent" in manifesting his thoughts and feelings than is the adult.[1] Second, the child's personality[2] is considerably less differentiated, has fewer regions, than the adult's. Devious as are the ways of children, it is freely admitted that their lives are *relatively* undifferentiated or less complex.

[1] One reason both Lewinians and Freudians speak of "regression" is that behavior seems to be more "transparent" in this sense when the individual reacts to stress conditions. The schizophrenic like the child asks, "Why do you ask me? You know what I'm thinking anyway."

[2] One hesitates to use the term "personality," for nowhere does Lewin define the term. But presumably in a text like the *Dynamic Theory of Personality* Lewin was speaking of personality when he spoke of "persons."

A question arising from biosocial considerations should be asked here: Does Lewin include among his systems or regions of the person the social or interpersonal functions of personality? Sometimes it seems as if he does and other times not. In discussing differentiation he asserts, "The fact that various life-spheres (profession, family, friendships with definite persons, and so on) as well as different needs are much more differentiated in the adult than in the one-year-old child scarcely demands extensive demonstration" (Lewin, 1935). On the other hand, the very use of the term "motoric" for the boundary region seems to imply a "within-the-skin" conception of personality. A cautious presumption is made here to the effect that the general tenor of Lewin's dynamic, field system seems to imply that the person (or personality) cannot be considered as limited to internal processes.

As we look at Figure 12, we are not to imagine it as representing a static entity. It is a living diagram of personality structure—in fact, Lewin sometimes speaks of regions as "cells" which in biology are living entities.

We have to read into the diagrams something not symbolized here, that is, that each region is in a state of lesser or greater tension. It is this property of the field that makes Lewin's system a need-tension system. Tension has reference to the state of any one system relative to the state of surrounding systems (regions). The states of the organism, especially its needs and quasi-needs, determine to a large extent what responses an organism makes to certain stimuli. As a dynamic element of the organism, a need corresponds to a "system in tension," and satisfaction of a need to "release of tension." Intention (or "will") corresponds to "setting up a tension," just as a need such as a state of hunger is a setting up of tension.

Out of these concepts of a need-tension system grew a series of important laboratory experiments like that of Zeigarnik (1927) on the resumption of completed and incompleted tasks (the "Zeigarnik effect"). These researches though dealing with isolated phenomena never lost sight of the place of any one tension system in the total of tension systems of the organism—and of the field, of the life space. We are led directly from the changes of state within the person to tension systems and changes of state in the life space as a whole, for the person cannot be conceived of in a vacuum. Lewin's later research or that inspired by him tended in the direction of discerning larger fields, first from individuals to small groups of children, and then to larger groups of persons in the military and industry.

There is much more to Lewin's diagram than meets the eye. One should not be misled, however, into thinking that Lewin *intended* to cram all the complexities of personality into the relatively simple diagrams of Figure 12. In other diagrams not shown here Lewin indicates, in addition to divisions into motor-perceptual and inner-personal regions, sub-regions in the motoric region. These sub-regions are, first, those differentiated ways by which the needs or other states of the inner-personal region serve as "paths of influence" to the environment. For example, speech and gestures and smiling may be considered as dynamic regions or processes within the motoric region. Second, there are differentiated ways by which the inner-personal region is affected by the external world, different perceptual systems, eye, ear, skin receptors, and so forth, functioning in their special capacities.

Both within the motor-perceptual region and within the inner-personal region distinctions may also be made between major central and peripheral regions. Such a distinction is a familiar one in perception where we differentiate between "figure" and "ground" or what is central and peripheral in attention. In motor expression, each of us has probably at some time sat writing a paper with the radio on, tapping out rhythms with his foot, a peripheral activity (we hope) to his more central activity of writing. Experiments by Lewin's students have particularly con-

cerned themselves with inner-personal distinctions between central and peripheral. A person reacts differently to influences which reach his peripheral regions only and to those which also touch his central areas. If someone questions us about our lack of faithfulness in attending some school organization which to us is of peripheral interest, we are not anywhere nearly so inclined to react emotionally as if someone should question our loyalty to our country, which is presumably more central. What *is* peripheral and what central may, of course, differ greatly from one individual to another.

Not only are central and peripheral different from person to person, but conditions may alter boundaries within the same individual. In what Lewin calls "an easy situation" the person may very well allow access of the world to a number of inner-personal, but not central, regions. When the traveler discusses with a stranger many of his personal feelings, there are yet some things he will not (or if unaware of them, cannot) discuss. In other circumstances, however, the person has perhaps been aroused by something he considers damaging to himself. Then, even those regions which he normally would express freely and to which he would allow free access are closed off.[1] In still another case affective tension may reduce internal boundaries so that the inner state of the person is "primitive," as in a high rage. And still another situation might find a relative dissolution of boundaries between inner-personal and motoric regions, as in a state of extreme panic or rage the person behaves from mostly uncontrolled impulses arising in the inner core of his being, and strikes

[1] Not very many teachers were directly accused in the heyday of McCarthyism of being communists. But the fearful way in which teachers refrained from expressing their normal judgments on social affairs indicated that the boundaries had changed so that some of the normal peripheral regions became central. Some of the regions have been allowed to become peripheral again, but in the period of extreme international tension probably not all the former peripheral regions will ever become so again.

out in "blind rage" or engages in senseless flight. What is central in the inner-personal region has become peripheral even in the motoric region.

Before closing the discussion on Lewin's concept of personality structure, one of Lewin's most important contributions in later years to the understanding of personality must be mentioned, namely his distinction between levels of reality and irreality. He considered this distinction one of adding another dimension to his representation of life space.

A daydream, a vague hope, has in general less reality than an action; an action sometimes has more reality than speech; a perception more than an image; a faraway "ideal goal" is less real than a "real goal" that determines one's immediate action. . . . Action itself can be of very different degrees of reality. Processes which concern strong needs of the person and in which he has to surmount strong physical or social barriers have usually a high degree of reality (Lewin, 1936a).[1]

These levels of reality and irreality are diagrammed topologically by planes lying one above another as represented in Figure 13; here each plane coincides with regions of the life space at a certain level of reality-irreality.

Although Lewin conceived of many planes of reality-irreality, Figure 13 which is one of his best known diagrams, depicting only two planes to represent reality-irreality levels, is reproduced here. It pulls together a number of the concepts discussed previously as well as the dimensions I and R at two different developmental stages, the complexity of the real and irreal life spaces, the distance between real and irreal, and the extensions into psychological past and future differ. This diagram represents children, but presumably the adult's life space exceeds the child's in complexity just as the older child's exceeds the younger one's. We should not consider psychological past and future as coinciding with actual past and future. All of the psychological past, present,

and future are present now according to Lewin's formulations.

Locomotion is possible within any one plane of reality and between different planes. From a psychological standpoint what is real or irreal may not correspond to objective reality or unreality, any more than person and environment need to coincide with "objective" factors. The adult's irreal levels correspond to some of the child's real levels. The child's or primitive man's magic system may be more real for him than are scientific systems. These magic systems for him may be more rigid and less permeable than objectively real systems. Planes of irreality are, however, not only usually more fluid but also less differentiated. In his everyday life the individual may make careful distinctions between the possible ways to different goals, may figure out obstacles, give credence to certain facts and not to others, and so forth; in his fantasy life, however, the impossible is achieved, barriers are melted magically, hero status comes without effort or with "really" impossible effort.

Personality structure, then, for Lewin may be summarized as a need-tension system, consisting of regions designated as motor-perceptual, inner-personal, boundary, and psychological environment—denoted altogether as the life space—in which movements may occur within and among regions and whose levels extend from reality to irreality and from psychological past to psychological future.

With Lewin's system as with all the others discussed in this text there are critical questions one can ask. There is one major criticism especially which has been made of Lewin's work, and that is his use of mathematical models in a way which leaves some authorities unsatisfied (London, 1944). Lewin's mathematical representations, either in the nonquantitative topology or in the equations which indicate quantitative relations, sometimes seem to have a quality of "irreality" to them. It may be a misinterpretation of the system, but it appears as if Lewin *could* fill in the quantities of his quantitative equations, yet

[1] Reprinted by permission from *Principles of topological psychology* by K. Lewin. Copyright 1936. McGraw-Hill Book Co., Inc.

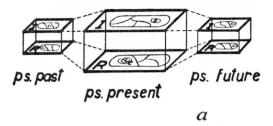

ps. past

ps. present

ps. future

a

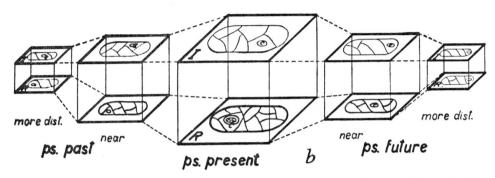

more dist.

near

ps. past

ps. present

b

near

ps. future

more dist.

Figure 13. Lewin's concept of the life space at two developmental stages. (From L. Carmichael, *Manual of Child Psychology*, p. 798)

never quite does it—about as satisfying as a picture of a banquet. Topological and hodological diagrams seem to fit personality characteristics, but likewise make one think that here must be relation equations which can be applied exactly to such characteristics—but the promise does not appear to be fulfilled.

As with several of the other concepts of structure, however, the capacity of Lewin's system to order the data already at hand and to provide a framework for future research is high. While there are "bugs in the machinery," many of which have been pointed out by a friendly critic of Lewin (Leeper, 1943), the personality structure as conceived by Lewin is relatively consistent with itself and with the experimental data—indeed, it grew out of much experimentation. Although the presentation of Lewin's or any other system of structure is not *primarily* intended to give one further insight into himself and others —one does not become a psychologist by reading a textbook—nevertheless, a person should have a better understanding of

his own experience by an overview of Lewin's system.

PERSONALITY AS A DYNAMIC, MULTIDIMENSIONAL, TOPOGRAPHICAL SYSTEM

It should be evident by this time that simple formulations of personality structure are hardly admissible today in a science of personality. The naïve way in which the man-on-the-street expresses his view of personality, such as, "Well, one has to take personality factors into account, *too*," overlooks all the multplicity of interrelation within even the narrow framework of what the man-on-the-street conceives personality to be; and it fails almost entirely to consider the extensiveness of personality factors beyond so restricted a view of personality. Each of the structures considered thus far discovers to us some different set of functions which must be accounted for, some more complex relations (or system actions), some new architectural (structural) features.

No one system has been able to take account of all we know. It is to be doubted if any one system will ever do so, for in accord with the history of science any system which has been able to account for most of the data gathered up to a specified time has had to yield to new facts, which may have been gathered even as a result of the implications of that system.

It is not only in facing new social exigencies (which brought forth Lowell's well-known challenge in his day) but in the conduct of science as well that:

> "New occasions teach new duties;
> Time makes ancient good uncouth;
> They must upward still, and onward
> Who would keep abreast of Truth."
> (Lowell, *The Present Crisis*)

In the new science of personology, however, we may well expect that no one system of structure proposed yet would be able to take even the facts known thus far into its purview. As in physics in its early stages, multitudes of so-called "facts" in personality study, gathered from time immemorial, are no doubt "fancies," but we do not yet know that they are and so we try to incorporate them into a system. At this stage in the history of personology, hundreds of articles appear yearly reporting research done in laboratory, clinic, and field. The best any theorist can do is to construct his personality model so as not too greatly to abuse the data sampled or the directions in which the data seem to point.

In offering the following concept of personality structure titled "a dynamic, multidimensional, topographical system," the writer recognizes the strengths and limitations of such models. A major strength of this model is that it seems to take account of many of the data of personality at hand. A major weakness is that its diagrammatic representation (Figure 14) may be taken too literally, although it is only intended to "give an idea of" the possible connections among the major and minor functions of personality. Like the other conceptions presented, the concept of personality represented here is intended to express as close an approximation to "actual personality structure" as the writer can devise at present; the topographical diagram is only an aid in understanding the concept, which ought not be made "to get down on all fours."

Therefore, if the student will consult the diagrams, Figure 14, he may find help in understanding the concept of personality structure presented in this volume. But he should remember that the diagrams are only used here for didactic purposes. After digesting the previous pages, the student may still think that the diagrams are over-complex; however, it is possible that they are not complex enough to represent the vast mazes of personality.

Figure 14(a) portrays the traditional Freudian schema of personality plus the role functions which, in the model followed in this text, are held to be integral portions of the personality as are id, ego, and superego. By definition, these four major functions are nonoverlapping. We may say that an ego function has become differentiated from the id when a control function develops, as for example when the organism achieves control over the sphincter muscles of the rectum. A superego function arises from the ego as specialized controls develop in response to the demands of society. An example is the internalization of the parental prohibition against uninhibited masturbatory activity; no longer does the child refrain from such activity because of fear of real or remembered parental voices (an ego reaction), but because the voice of the parent has become his own, his own conscience. The distinction between roles and the other major functions represented in Figure 14(a) is not as clear-cut as in the other cases. However, insofar as the personality is of the external world as well as of the individual, roles may be distinguished from the other major functions. They are the interobject and interpersonal portions of the personality. A family role function, such as being little brother to big sister, is distinct from the learning process (an ego function) by which the child achieves his sibling status and from the feeling of oughtness (a super-

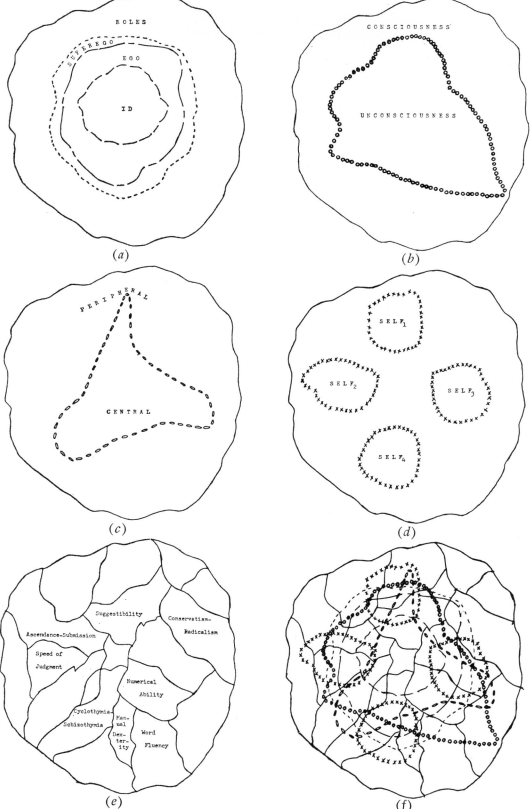

Figure 14. Diagrammatic representation of personality structure as a dynamic, multi-dimensional, topographical system.

ego function) the little boy may have in respect to obeying big sister.

Farthest from the external world is the id, next is the ego, closer is the superego; and roles are of the external world as well as of the individual. This representation is fairly accurate in terms of how much the external actually contributes to each function. Because many superego and role functions are acquired relatively late and are not so deeply entrenched as other portions of the personality, they may be very easily shed. And yet, roles like that of child to mother or superego reactions like repugnance to killing may persist after trauma has impaired the ego function of judgment.

Overlapping all of these functions except id are the two major part-functions of consciousness and unconsciousness, as seen in Figure 14(b) and 14(f). There is no room here for argument as to whether there is an Unconscious, a boiling, cavernous foul depth of Repressed Evil, as opposed to the innocent surface of consciousness. (Cf. Chapter 11 for consciousness and unconsciousness.) All that is necessary here is to conceive that some of our functions are in our awareness and others not. Id forces are virtually by definition unconscious. Most of our memory functions (which belong to the ego) are unconscious. Superego, as well as id and ego may be unconscious.

Also overlapping all other functions except id are those which we may call central and peripheral, which are represented alone and with other functions in Figure 14(c) and (f) respectively. Lewin's concepts are adopted here in making a distinction between those portions of the personality which are open to others and those which are not. It is important to recognize that central and peripheral are *not* synonymous with conscious and unconscious.

The self (or selves) is found in various places in the diagrams, Figure 14(d) and (f). Further explanation will be made concerning the lack of continuity of the self-regions. Only the fact is noted here. Likewise, it should be observed that self-regions overlap *all* other areas, including id.

Figure 14(e) and (f) endeavor to take account of the dimensional nature of personality as conceived in modern trait psychology. Representative traits, from various areas and, in connection with temperament traits, on one level of abstraction (surface traits—cf. Chapter 14), are named in Figure 14(e). These diagrams suggest how the cross-categorization of personality data in terms of dimensions may overlap functions, like central and peripheral, consciousness and unconsciousness, and so forth, which also legitimately classify personality. A trait like *Cyclothymia-Schizothymia* reaches into the depths of the personality (the id, unconscious, central), has conscious and peripheral aspects, expresses part of the self (selves), has some share in ego functioning, possibly in the superego as well, and has a place in several roles one individual may play. Trait names are used here which suggest polar qualities (*Ascendance-Submission, Conservatism-Radicalism, Cyclothymia-Schizothymia*), degrees of ability (*Word Fluency, Numerical Ability*), and other functions which can be measured. The polar traits are deliberately used as examples to imply that one's traits may be one thing viewed from outside and another viewed from inside.

More extended discussion of the actual concepts of personality structure underlying Figure 14 is called for. First of all to be noted in the schema under consideration is that it is a nonmathematical model of personality structure. Unlike Lewin the writer does not think the science of personality is ready for *over-all* mathematization. There are some specific functions, for example, some self-concepts, some roles, some attitudes, ego and superego strengths, as well as many other part-functions, which have been and will continue to be measured. But it seems like pseudo-mathematics at this time to endeavor to have an over-all mathematical model to represent personality structure. Yet some notions are borrowed from Lewin's topology: The roughness of regions and boundaries and the connectedness or lack of connectedness within and among regions as described in topology are not denied but incorporated in the system and in the diagrams. In the conceptual schema represented here these characteristics of regions are kept in mind as showing that some functions can be related to other functions but may be relatively unrelated to still others even though they are in the same personality.

Second, the fundamental unit of the personality is denominated a *function*. These are organized portions of the personality and usually discernible from one another, sometimes by logical analysis, sometimes by more or less refined empirical techniques like factor analysis. Sometimes they are not distinguishable when the individual is behaving in certain ways, as in emotional states. The minor elements within the major ones may be roughly equated with needs, at least if needs include tension systems beyond the biophysical organism, the role functions especially. Needs regarded as tension systems impart the dynamic aspect to personality in the "dynamic, multidimensional, topographical system."

Traits could be regarded as the fundamental units of personality, as some personologists have considered them. However, as usually used, traits are not general enough to cover all the aspects of personality which must be taken into account. It is difficult within the ordinary or scientific meaning of trait to include a gross construct like the ego, very real states like consciousness, and the role of mother. It is also difficult in considering the structure of personality not to make hierarchies of traits which result in super-traits or types (as suggested below), so that some more general term has to be used to encompass the lower and the higher levels. And going the other way, we find that one has to have some term to include the habit level of personality, that level made up of (let us say) functions which are not general enough to be classified as traits and yet are definitely organized and continuing activities of the organism which tend to distinguish it from other organisms. A more neutral and general term, like function, is required to cover both those activities of the individual which are more general and

those less general than traits. Nevertheless, if anyone wishes to regard functions as traits, his concept is not in keeping with the treatment of personality here. (Cf. Section IV where traits are treated as functions.)

Just as functions may be coincident with traits, so too functions may combine to form gross functions called types. Cerebrotonic or extravert types may result from such dynamic combinations. At this point, however, we must insist upon mathematical delineation of types rather than armchair classifications such as found in Kretschmer's system (1951). Unless correlation coefficients resting upon a large number of variables and a large sample of subjects reveal gross patterns of functions, the speculative typologist tends to overlook the contradictory evidence against the existence of his types. Cattell (1946), Eysenck (1953c), and Guilford (1959) have proposed typologies based on factor analysis which support the notion that combinations of functions may issue in types.

Neither traits nor types are considered here as the fundamental elements in personality partly because in most discussions of these elements they are viewed as within-the-skin units, while we are committed to a view of personality which includes the role functions. At times also both types and traits have been treated as if they were static entities fixed and certain for all the life of the individual, whereas the scheme here is a dynamic one. To be sure, the lack of rigidity which might be implied by use of the term *function* does not signify that there are no permanencies in some portions of the personality structure. A penurious individual may play his role from toilet training (Abraham, 1927) to the tomb, and a happy-go-lucky person may likewise play his role from childhood to old age.

Of either type or trait we sometimes say, "He has a certain trait," or "He is of a certain type." What we ultimately mean is, "He is functioning honestly, and this function of honesty is a long-lasting one; it seems to be part of the dynamic structure of his personality." Or again, "He is functioning in an ascendant manner, and has been for a long time, so that this function seems to be a *very* long-lasting one."

It is the different combinations of functions, some of which may be peculiar to an individual, but many of which are common (somewhat similar in all persons), which make for the practically infinite variety of traits for which Allport so convincingly argued as characterizing personality. When these functions are organized in a certain way, including some functions and excluding others, certain traits or even certain types appear in the personality organization of the individual. These combinations, of course, cannot be shown in our diagrams, for they are individual for the individual. But the structure of personality cannot be considered complete unless these combinations can be taken into account. This is the "multidimensional" aspect of personality structure to which some of the ablest personologists have devoted themselves.

There is an acceptance in the dynamic, multidimensional topographical system of the hierarchical principle, first in that there are higher-order and lower-order functions, and second in that the functions are conceived, layer or level fashion, arising in part out of one another, as ego out of id, and superego out of ego. Conscious and unconscious and central and peripheral are hierarchical to an extent. And yet, this system is hardly to be considered a hierarchical one in the usual sense, for there are too many overlappings of most functions to constitute a true hierarchy in which each part has its fixed place subordinate or superordinate to other parts. In a dynamic system, minor functions may become major, a whole set of peripheral functions may become central, or conscious ones unconscious, or ego functions may slip back into id (as in sleep), so that the "hierarchy" of functions changes constantly. Hierarchy is still preserved after a fashion, however, in the general distinctions among major functions.

When we regard the major functions as cross-categories, the overlapping nature of consciousness and unconsciousness with the ego and superego is an aspect to be considered seriously. Identification of ego with consciousness is not an uncommon error. To be sure, one may define ego as the conscious portion of the personality, as Jung has done. But if he stays close to the tradition established by Freud, ego must include unconscious functions as well. As suggested above, both ego and superego may be partly unconscious.

It is probably difficult for the average individual to imagine an unconscious conscience, but evidence seems to support the idea. Edmund Bergler (1948), a psychoanalytic psychologist, speaks of "the criminal who bargains for the electric chair." Bergler summarizes his and others' clinical research thus:

The cynic, "the man who knows the price of everything and the value of nothing," to quote Oscar Wilde, who should have known, tells us that inner conscience is just a fable that everybody agrees on. He uses for his argument criminals with or without acknowledged social position, whose "hardboiled" actions can hardly be described as being influenced or restricted by conscience. And still, interestingly enough, the majority of outstanding criminals of the political or simple murder variety, end in the electric chair, on gallows, or before firing squads. In other words, the cynic does not look far enough; he focuses his attention on the *initial* action, not taking into account the fact that these actions are possible only with the *unconscious* condition that *final* detection and punishment must be reckoned with. Every criminal bargains *unconsciously* for the electric chair. Of course, he is not aware that he does so, with the result that the cynic (nobody is more easily fooled than the cynic!) comes to false conclusions, believing the criminal's rationalization (Bergler, 1948).

We need not be uncautious and say that "Every criminal bargains for the electric chair." All we need to say for our purposes here is that *some* criminals do, *unconsciously*. And, of course, criminals are not the only ones in whom an unconscious superego may be found (Alexander, 1943).

A logical question to ask at this point is

[1] Reprinted by permission of the author.

whether or not role functions can be unconscious. The answer is that they can be. Here is a naïve soul who fills the role of simpleton in his community. As far as the citizens of his town are concerned, who define personality as the way one impresses others, his personality *is* that of simpleton; but he may never be aware of it, thinking that his words and actions are taken seriously. Pagliacci may play the role of cuckold and be completely unaware for a time of this function which he has unwittingly taken over. Modern social research underscores again and again the fact that the social roles we play, as upper or lower or middle class, as Americans or Britons or Frenchmen, or Mexican, or white, are partly unconscious. It may be noted, for instance, how many persons identify unconsciously with the role of "the fortunates" as they speak about how they must be sure to help "the poor unfortunates."

What has been unconscious can, under certain conditions become conscious. Pagliacci "wakes up" and discerns the role he has been playing. A student wakes up to the class and caste role he has been playing and says with Eugene V. Debs (1948), ". . . years ago I recognized my kinship with all living beings, and I made up my mind that I was not one bit better than the meanest on earth. I said then, and I say now, that while there is a lower class, I am in it, while there is a criminal element I am of it, and while there is a soul in prison, I am not free." [1] The lad with a speech disorder discovers that what has been below his threshold of awareness, his hostility to his parents, is a root of his difficulty.

On the other hand, functions that are conscious may become unconscious. The typist may become confused if she tries to reverse the process of her learning and make conscious the individual acts of typing which she has carefully filed among her automatic acts, acts of which she is normally unaware but of which she was painfully conscious as a typing novitiate. Amnesia may result from psychic conflict or physical trauma; the very name one owns, one *is*, may be forgotten.

Not only are there the cross-classifications of conscious and unconscious functions which overlap other part functions, but there are central and peripheral functions of personality [2] which do not entirely coincide with biophysical versus social functions. Some roles, it can be readily seen, are more central than many seemingly more private functions. A man's love for his child, deep-rooted (central) as it may be, may be evident to others; it may be peripheral in the sense of being open to others. So, too, a number of role functions may be exceedingly private even though we may be conscious of them. Several examples of the latter are: a boy from a respectable family who keeps his gang membership hidden; subordinate secretaries to the late President Franklin D. Roosevelt whose personal secretary asked that his assistants have "a passion for anonymity"; and a member of the Communist underground in America. All these roles are social functions, but may be privately played. However, in general it would seem with most of us role functions are more peripheral than superego, ego, and id functions.

In the last major item of the topography of personality as represented by Figure 14, the student may be surprised by the isolation of the areas labeled "self." [3] While we can adopt the Lewinian notion that there

---

[1] From Statement to the Court in *Writings and Speeches* of Eugene V. Debs (1948), p. 437. When the writer recalled the statement from memory before verifying the quotation, a significant omission occurred; the clause concerning the "criminal element" was omitted and a clause, "as long as there is a class deprived," substituted. "Remembering" that one may be of "a class deprived" does seem different from identifying with "a criminal element."

[2] The writer had, like many another, come to the distinction before studying Lewin. But Lewin should be given credit for his clear discussions on central and peripheral systems.

[3] It might seem strange that social psychologists have been most insistent on studying the self. It is not so strange that a seemingly interpersonal set of functions should be subject-matter for social psychology when one realizes that any analysis of self sooner or later leads to role functions somewhere along the line (Symonds, 1951).

can be communication between distant regions through intermediate regions, the diagrams endeavor to set forth what we know of the facts of selfhood. One's self-concepts appear to be different when one is awake than when he is dreaming. His self-concepts may differ even from reality-thinking to day-dreaming. They may be different from one role to another. To say that any one of these is not the "real self" is to invite the question, "How do you know which is your 'real self'?" It may be that there are a large number of *more or less* consistent functions which are operating in *more or less* united fashion and are identified as the "real self." There are probably other selves, however, which gather together still different functions (or perhaps overlapping ones). One of the other selves may be more "real" in the sense that it is more central than the larger, more peripheral self which we have identified as the real one.

If there are different selves, what happens to Lecky's principle of "self-consistency" which we have accepted as a valid principle? We can only at present engage in speculation on this point, for the empirical data seem to indicate selves rather than a self. It may be that the personality is devoted to a self-consistency for *one* of the major selves or for the self that is *felt* to be the basic pattern. Or there is the possibility that various selves may really be only outcroppings of a basic self to which all things must become oriented. Perhaps psychologists who hold to a unified self rather than a number of selves in the individual would insist on a three-dimensional topographical model with possibly underlying connecting strata from one manifest self to another, much as Allport's principle of congruence would seek for connections among apparently disparate forms of behavior. In actuality there may be strata connecting self-concepts with one another; but only empirical research implementing such a concept can determine whether self-concepts *are* all connected.

Implicit in the diagrams of Figure 14 is

the possibility of conflict. The very complexity of personality structure suggested by the admittedly over-simplified drawings indicates that conflicts are almost inevitable among the various functions. Even recognizing a unity of a sort in the fact that conflicts do take place within the personality, we are made aware by the model that at the boundaries of id and ego, ego and superego, superego and role, and among the overlappings of these with selves, consciousness and unconsciousness, central and peripheral functions, any set of functions may come into conflict with any other. Then, by the nature of specific functions, further potentialities for clashing may be seen. Id and ego, for example, are regarded as operating according to different principles; many times the resultant affect, behavior, or thought processes may be harmonious, but often desire may outrun judgment or drive the capacity to control it. Superego functions may be opposed now to the expression of impulse or to the consideration of sober reality. And again, superego may allow open expression of fierce impulses, as in a lynching. Roles may clash one with another. One self may abominate another. And so on.

As we study the diagrams, and endeavor to conceptualize the vastly complicated realities of personality which they adumbrate, we are forced to recognize the conflictful nature of personality and to marvel at the measure of harmony that does exist among the many interacting parts.

SUMMARY

(For completeness, the summary of Chapter 4 should be read first.)

Assuming personality trends to be related one to another, Rorschach concepts of personality regard the balance of introversive and extratensive, the kind of control an individual exerts over internal and external stimuli, his mental approach, and his conformity or lack of conformity to common modes of perception as the important elements of structure.

Among concepts viewing personality as a need-press system, Freud's theories see three major dynamic elements, id, ego and superego; and general life and death trends operate in opposing fashion throughout the structure. Akin to Freud's system, Murray's regards the basic elements of personality structure as needs, which meet press in the environment. Murphy's biosocial system also views needs as basic units of personality structure, interdependent and interpersonal, both within and outside the organism. Applying topology to personality study, Lewin recognizes each element of personality and personality as a whole to be operating in a "field." In the life space, present, past, and future, exist an inner-personal region and a motor-perceptual region, levels of reality and irreality, and all in a state of tension. Boundaries exist between need elements, but these are more or less permeable and elastic.

A dynamic, multidimensional, topographical system of personality structure is Dreger's model.[1] The neutral (but dynamic) term "functions" identifies the basic elements. Personality is conceived as a system of hierarchical functions, the highest of which are id, ego, superego, roles, consciousness and unconsciousness, central and peripheral, and self or selves. Consciousness and unconsciousness and central and peripheral functions overlap dynamically, as do self-concepts overlap all other "areas" in the topography. The remainder of this book is taken up with detailing the major

and some minor functions which have been described thus far in broad outline.[2]

QUESTIONS

1. What major functions of personality is the Rorschach intended to reveal?
2. Describe briefly personality structure as conceived by Freud.

[2] Our text would be extended indefinitely if we included all the concepts of personality structure that have been advanced. The concepts presented may not, in some authorities' eyes, be the most important. All the writer will claim is that they are representative. Some of the most important omitted here are:

Jung's psychoanalytic view is expressed especially in *The Integration of Personality* (1939), but is also scattered throughout his writings. One of the major differences between his structure and that expressed here is that the ego consists of *conscious* control factors. Since, however, Jung recognizes unconscious functioning, any quarrel over naming these would be logomachy.

McDougall sets up in both the *Energies of Men* (1932) and the *Outline of Psychology* (1928) a rough structure of five "classes" of personality: disposition, temperament, temper, intellect, and character (though these may not exhaust all of personality).

Stern (1935) was one of the first to call attention to the note sounded in the text, that a listing of traits is only the beginning of personality study. Stern speaks of the "enduring potentialities" which are "dispositions," like character, intelligence, temperament, and memory. Specifically, character is the totality of personality viewed from the definite standpoint of "the predisposition to acts of will." Traits of character, then, may be stratified and be possessed of lesser or greater *embeddedness*, some deeper and more central, others more superficial and peripheral, some stable, some more labile: ". . . what is crucial to the *notion* of character is not so much definite features in definite degrees of intensity, but the manner in which the qualities just indicated are incorporated in the unity of the structure, or more properly speaking, the manner in which they assume their relative weight and rank order by virtue of this unification." Traits may be inventoried for personality or character delineation from (a) a descriptive view as to their intrinsic nature, (b) an inter-individual comparability, on scales or as types, and (c) a personal accent, or place in the total character scheme (profferred by Stern).

Roback in *Personality in Theory and Practice* (1950) holds that the units of personality are traits, thousands of them. A hierarchical structure

[1] The topographical representation of structure is related to but not the same as the topological. The topographic diagram pretends to no mathematization whatsoever. In fact, the diagram actually is not necessary to the concepts expressed in the text, whereas the topological diagrams are virtually the essence of the Lewinian system. Topography as used in this book follows psychoanalytic usage, merely designating that there are recognizable structures within the general structure of personality. Topology and topography differ also in that the latter expressly represents the personality as inclusive of its role functions, while the former seems to include roles at times and not at others, although as indicated in the discussion on Lewin's system the tendency is there.

3. What place do needs, press, and themas have in personality according to Murray?

4. Discuss Murphy's "structured organism-environment field." How do Murphy's concepts of balance and interdependence compare with the Rorschach's?

5. Consider the place of the individual's history in Lewin's conceptual system. What is the "life space"? Inner-personal and motor-perceptual? Tension and release of tension? Central and peripheral? Child and adult personalities? Reality and irreality?

6. Discuss personality as "a dynamic, multidimensional, topographical system."

is present, first of traits, then attitudes, then disposition, and finally mood (humor in the ancient Hippocratic scheme). One aspect of "levels of personality" which Roback maintains as significant is that some areas are more importantly personality than others, for example "personality" as measured by "personality tests" than that measured by "intelligence tests."

Haggard and Fry in their text *The Anatomy of Personality* (1936) set up five "elements of personality," physique, impulse or driving force, intelligence, temperament, and ego. Presumably they mean "self" by the last. Their inclusion of physique and "driving force" as part of personality was in opposition to narrower concepts of personality of the day.

Fenichel, by far the most systematic and inclusive of psychoanalytic authorities, in *The Psychoanalytic Theory of Neurosis* (1945) sets up the structure of personality in a formal Freudian way, id, ego, superego, but also brings together throughout the book the "layers of personality" developed at various developmental stages of these dynamic structure-functions.

PERSONALITY IN THE ADULT INDIVIDUAL: TOPOGRAPHICAL STRUCTURE-FUNCTIONS

Thus far we have seen the various approaches which scientific psychology makes to the study of personality. A number of representative definitions of personality have been examined. Likewise we have considered just how far the evidence allows us to go in regarding personality as continuous and consistent. Differing views of the structure of personality have led us to recognize that different authorities, endeavoring to order the known or presumed known data, may hold widely divergent views of the manner in which personality is structured.

Within all the theories of structure, except that which regards personality as a group of independent elements, one common theme is found: The various sub-functions of the personality are organized into larger units, and these in turn into major structure-functions. Each theorist says or assumes, "There must be *some* structure to personality which includes the grouping of smaller units into larger ones." Beyond this common theme it is sometimes difficult to find similarities among the different concepts of structure. And yet, a rough approximation may now be made of the congruities among all the divergent views. There is some agreement as to the gross outlines of the major functions and to a lesser degree in respect to part-functions. The following sections present those major functions of personality on which there seems to be a considerable agreement, not necessarily in name but in fact.[1]

In the organization of personality it has usually been held that some sort of hierarchical arrangement of functions prevails. As we have seen, however, different authorities regard different functions as "top man on the totem pole." For our purposes the three general cross-classifications of functions which have been discussed briefly in Chapter 5, namely, topographical, dimensional, and economic, serve as the highest-order functions. Within these higher-order functions those of lower-order are operative, again in a series of cross-classifications.

Some authorities have endeavored to identify certain functions with anatomical divisions of the organism, for example, consciousness with the cerebral cortex and unconsciousness with subcortical structures. Although there may be such parallels between personality functions and anatomy, our focus would not be on these possibilities for their own sake. The interest here is in the functioning individual, many of whose most important psychological and social functions can scarcely have an anatomic locale and cannot be identified even with physiological functions.

In the seven chapters which follow, the first of the major cross-classifications of personality will be taken up, topographical structure-functions. These are regarded as "topographical" in the sense employed in psychoanalysis, identifiable *functional* areas of the personality. On the whole, as on a map, these areas are nonoverlapping func-

tions in any one cross-classification. From the diagram of the "dynamic, multidimensional system" of personality structure, however, it is evident that there is considerable overlapping among the cross-classifications. Three such cross-classifications are recognized: (1) id, ego, superego, and role functions; (2) consciousness and unconsciousness; and (3) central and peripheral functions. These gross functions may at some times be composed of one set of sub-functions and at another time of slightly or greatly different sub-functions, but altogether they subserve the personality in approximately the same capacity year in and year out.

Although psychoanalysis has enriched our understanding of the topography of personality, the discussion in the next chapters departs significantly in places from standard psychoanalysis. One major example of the difference is in the formulations regarding the id in Chapter 6. Freud's conception of the id as a mental or psychological representation of physical processes distinct from psychic processes seems to suffer from a dualism of body and mind which psychology eschews.[2] His view ap-

---

[1] One omission will be found by some, especially by psychoanalytic psychologists. No function called the "psyche" has been included among the major functions of personality. This is a deliberate omission. "Psyche" conveys to modern psychologists too much of an atmosphere of a mind-body dichotomy. The term may be used roughly to refer to all "mental functions," and from time to time for convenience the derivative "psychic" is employed in this text. But no suggestion is made here, as the usage of "psyche" as a separate function implies, that psychic and somatic can be separated.

[2] The near reification of portions of the psychic apparatus of which Freud has been accused may not have been Freud's intent. But by separating body and mind so sharply from each other, Freud creates the impression that id, ego, and superego are little engineers in the organism. Faithfully paraphrasing Freud, in their review of Freudian concepts Hall and Lindzey (1954, ch. 4) describe id operations thus: "The psychic process employed by the id is called the *primary process* (Freud, 1900). This process consists of discharging tension as soon as any tension reaches the id. The first and most primitive operation of the primary process is to expend energy immediately in motor activity. Examples of this are the emptying of the bladder's contents when the pressure on the sphincter reaches a certain level, or the mass activity of a baby when it has colic." The phrases "employed by the id" and "reaches the id" are terms to apply to the superintendent of an organization. When neural impulses reach the brain, does the id as a mental phenomenon (thing?) direct the release of physical energy? Are not these processes, rather, *organismic* processes with the physical energy release and mental representation but two *aspects* of the *same* function? The consciousness of, say, emptying the bladder's content is another

pears to suffer also because it omits some very important functions of personality properly classified as id. With almost any modern understanding of the personality, those somatic components which Freud felt are only *represented* by the id are not only considered bases of personality but are actually individualized patterns of energy-distribution or production which differentiate one person from another. Thus these somatic components constitute personality functions in their own right.

To set the stage for succeeding chapters we may point out another difference between Freud's theory and the present discussion. In the view presented here, *all* control functions of the personality are included in the ego, not merely those classified (artificially, it seems) as psychological. Another major distinction is found in regard to the superego. Folkways and mores are considered here as superego functions, whereas psychoanalysis has generally limited superego to conscience and ego ideal functions. And lastly, among the ma-

jor differences is the entirely new addition to topography of the role functions. Students of psychoanalysis have not been accustomed to include roles among Freud's divisions of the psyche (Freud's term for the personality). While Freud did not by any means neglect the roles which the individual plays [1] in any society, roles for Freud were not endopsychic (within the psyche), hence they are not in his view part of the personality. Freud changed his concept of personality structure in his later years to a model paralleling to some extent the one set forth here (H. Hartmann, 1951),[2] but not to include role-functions *per se*. When we come to these latter functions, we depend on Freud only for intensive study of some of the more intimate roles.

---

accompanying aspect which is strictly—even according to Freud—an ego function distinguishable by subjective analysis from the actual releasing of energy.

[1] Freud recognizes male and female roles beyond anatomical distinctions; family roles in the "family romance"; the transference role of the therapist. He speaks of leaders who . . . "impress others as being 'personalities'; it is on them that their fellow-men are specially likely to lean; they readily assume the role of leader, give a fresh stimulus to cultural development or break down existing conditions" (Freud, 1950, ch. 23).

[2] Historically and in actuality the influence has been the other way around.

CHAPTER **6**

TOPOGRAPHICAL STRUCTURE-FUNCTIONS ID: BASIC LIFE URGES

First among the major topographical functions of the personality are those which can be grouped under the shorthand term *id*.[1] We may cautiously define id as the life urges of the individual. These may be regarded as a dynamic source of energies [2] for other functions. Source is used in this connection as it is used in reference to a river's waters, with full recognition that the id is a *transmitting* agency rather than an absolutely *originating* agency.[3] The term id is employed for the whole set of functions which provide physical and psy-

[1] The translation of the German term *das Es*, "the it" literally, was complicated in part by employing Latin *id* for German *Es*. Freud's title is *Das Ich und das Es*, "The I and the it."

[2] What is meant by "mental energy" and how it coincides or overlaps with or is distinct from physical energy is a problem too difficult to handle here. Psychoanalysts have posited the term "mental energy" in the same way physicists have posited physical energy. The latter can be measured in various ways, but the former cannot as yet be measured in comparable ways. Cattell (1950) takes up the problem from the psychologists' point of view and concludes that our instruments are not adequate yet. Whether this reason is sufficient or whether others are more important, such as the possibility that mental energy is of a different kind, is a moot question (Fenichel, 1945). Psychical energy is posited here as it is in psychoanalysis. There is only justification for such an assumption if it seems necessary to account for behavioral data which could not be explained without it. There should be another assumption to account for the data—but the writer has found none yet.

[3] It is not the purpose of an eclectic approach to personality to engage in doctrinaire debates about the meaning and qualities of the id. Leavitt (1953), a modern psychoanalytic writer, asserts with some reason that the id is an organized structure, while Fenichel (1945) in opposition, following Freud very closely, describes it as a "dynamic, driving chaos of forces, which strive for discharge and nothing else." (And yet when comparing the ego to the ectoderm and the id to the endoderm, Fenichel speaks of *organization* as proceeding from surface to depth, meaning from ego to id.) All we are interested in doing now is to establish the fact that there is a set of functions which constitute the basic energies of the individual. Whether we call these functions, drives or instincts or needs or ergs (Raymond Cattell's term, it may be recalled), makes little difference here (though in general psychology and especially in emotion, motivation, and learning theory this issue is very important).

Freud spoke of the id as operating according to the "primary process," that is according to blind discharge principles, as opposed to the "secondary process" which is the ego's way of functioning, regarding time, place, and circumstance (Freud, 1949a).

98

chical energy for the personality's other activities.

It is essential to keep in mind in the following discussion that the term id is employed here primarily to group together a set of functions. In psychoanalytic literature the id has often been reified, so that it has seemed to be a little (mad) man inside the individual. Even in his latest formulations of psychoanalytic theory, Freud (1949a) continued to speak of the id in a manner inviting the criticism that the id is an homunculus rather than a unifying construct serving to show relations among observable phenomena. The id has no more —or less—reality than has the mind which has been re-admitted to psychology (after an extreme behavioristic exile) as a descriptive term for functions of judging, thinking, and so forth.

Metabolism, Tissue-Needs, and Drives

Metabolism is the most general of the id functions; it is the life process which consists of all the chemical and mechanical activities of the organism related to utilization of food and production of energy. This general process is sometimes subdivided into anabolism and catabolism, the building up and breaking down processes, or the storing and production of energy. However, the distinction between the two is not very clearcut at times.

In the over-all complicated process of metabolism individual patterns have been discovered; for example, one man "metabolizes" faster than another, his BMR (basal metabolic rate) being higher than another person's. Authorities working at the Mayo Clinic (Heilbrunn, 1952) determined the basal metabolism (as measured by rate of oxygen consumption, one method of determination used widely) of each of 639 males and 828 females from six to 70 years of age. While the rates declined markedly from early to late years, with the rate for men higher than women on the average, it appears that despite a general lowering as one ages a person's basal metabolic rate remains characteristic for him. The probabil-

ity is that if he is below the mean or above the mean at one time, he will remain in that position from childhood to old age.

Metabolism thus fulfills the definition of personality functions employed for our investigation of personality. It is organized as the basic energy-providing function of the individual. In addition, it is unique to the individual (Williams, 1959).

Included in metabolic activities are nutrition, respiration, secretion, excretion, and growth. Let us take just one of the subfunctions and see what place it may have in the entire personality. The digestive functions are roughly mediated by the digestive system, but are certainly not limited to it. Food hunger and satiation can be considered as the psychological components of the digestive functions, and these are not limited to one organ system. In personology we go beyond the assertion that there are digestive functions which provide energy to the recognition of individual patterns of energy-production in nutrition. On the one hand, ". . . the hunger mechanism appears to be inherited and is not essentially modified by the experience of the individual" (Carlson, 1948).

On the other hand, modern use of the self-demand schedule (Gesell & Ilg, 1943) has come about as a result of recognition of the individual "organic times" in hunger rhythms (Aldrich, Sung, & Knop, 1945) as well as other life rhythms. The rigid schedules demanded in years gone by proved to be a passing pediatric fad. That further fads have developed in conjunction with self-demand schedules themselves is evident from the pediatric literature (Wolfenstein, 1953). At first it was supposed that if the natural rhythm of the individual child should determine the times of gratification, a routine could be established and psychological and psychological needs could be met more easily (Weinfield, 1950). Then, it was found that mothers and nurses could not tell the difference between hunger and other cries of the infant, so that feeding "on demand" led to vomiting and diarrhea, especially with bottle-fed babies (Lapin, 1954). Some mothers have been shown to be ready for self-demand schedules, others not. Indeed, some seem to use the schedules as compulsively as other mothers used to use the four-hour routine. The connection between infant-paced feeding and psychosocial adjustment is not established, indeed may be questioned in the light of some work (Newton, 1951) in which children who were the products of the most and the least rigid feeding schedules tended to be better adjusted in kindergarten than the middle group. The effects of letting the infant determine everything may be to upset the household and especially "orderly and executive" type mothers (Lapin, 1954). "Demand feeding within reason" is being called for now, advice that takes account of the individual characteristics of hunger rhythms and yet recognizes the legitimacy of social demands, a balancing of id and social requirements. The general pattern of digestive functions, admittedly similar from person to person, is expressed in different ways.

The evidence for "biochemical individuality" (Williams, 1953, 1959) suggests that metabolism and related processes are not only different from person to person, but that their patterns tend to be characteristic for any individual. That is, individual patterns are impressed upon the complex processes which are much the same in gross outline (Duffy, 1946; Lacey, 1950; Lacey, Bateman, & Van Lehn, 1953; Lacey & Van Lehn, 1952; Wenger, 1943; Wenger, & Irwin, 1946).

One of the most significant investigations is that of Herrington (1942). His subjects were eleven male medical students, ages 19 to 24. For 90 days (45 observations *in toto*) Herrington measured them on four physiological functions, metabolic rate (two different measures), systolic blood pressure, respiration rate, and pulse rate. Each of these, as might be expected, showed a different mean for the 45 measures for each subject. In addition, variability as indicated by the standard deviation proved to be characteristic for each subject, although there was no correlation between means and standard deviations. The investi-gator drew a preliminary conclusion that the variability of itself constitutes a measure of some type of "general factor of intra-organic control."

Herrington went further, however, and predicted that a combination of standard deviations on the four physiological measures would predict a psychological variable, general activity. To gain a measure of the latter, three raters familiar with the subjects rated each subject after a 90-day period of observation in respect to physical vigor manifested in work and play, excitability of speech and pressure for verbal expression, and energy and enthusiasm in meeting class requirements. The composite ratings correlated .51 with the combination physiological variability measure, a substantial correlation. Mean measures of physiological functions correlated even higher with the activity ratings. And when Herrington paired systolic blood pressure variability with mean pulse rate, the multiple correlation coefficient was .91, a truly astounding result.

Even if Herrington's findings should not be duplicated exactly in replications of his experiment—and regression to the mean is the usual result of such replications—, findings anywhere nearly approximating his would justify his conclusion that pressure of activity, conceived in a psychosomatic sense, is an important aspect of personality. The underlying autonomic nervous system activity apparently makes itself felt throughout the personality strongly enough to determine an organized pattern which Herrington called *Pressure of Activity*, a factor on which individuals differ greatly.

Besides the functions which may be more strictly classed as metabolic, other common but partly individualized life-processes or tissue-needs serve as id functions. These are less "sources" of energy than are metabolism; they are drives or urges which seek discharge in an imperative manner. Sleeping and the avoidance of pain or noxious stimuli are found in this group of functions. It would only be laboring the obvious to point out that there are individual patterns of sleep. Napoleon's dictum, "Six hours for a man, seven for women and children, and eight for a fool," has the virtue of an epigram and the vice of ignorance. Even in Napoleon's day people had individual sleep needs which could hardly have failed of recognition by astute students of human nature. (Cf. Chapter 11 for further discussion of sleep.)

As for avoidance of pain, the sensitivity to pain stimuli is characteristic for any individual. In whatever manner also that we seek release from pain, our responses may be categorized roughly into aggressive or withdrawal behavior, but we recognize the individual nature of such behavior in specific cases. To what extent pain is a "learnable drive" is still a moot question (Stevens, 1951, Ch. 13). Yet little doubt exists that, added to the constitutional differences in pain responses among individuals, are some differences which come from experience. Much research is called for in the field of pain in relation to personality especially. Anecdotal material galore tells of the differences in pain responses from tribe to tribe and class to class,[1] but such uncontrolled observations must be checked by scientific means. On the basis of present research we may conclude (the obvious) that pain does act as a drive, but that it acts differentially in many cases. Even more research than that which has been done on pain avoidance is required in determining general and individual patterns of with-

drawal from noxious stimuli unrelated to pain.

Emphasized strongly in research in the middle 1950's, especially following Harlow, Nissen, and their associates in this country (Harlow, 1951, 1953; Harlow, Harlow, & Meyer, 1950; Nissen, 1951, 1954; White, 1959) and Berlyne in Great Britain, is the exploratory drive. Most of the research on this urge which has been called a drive has been done on animals. The manifestations of this push-from-within are a tendency to move about sniffing, pawing, digging, pinching, poking, or otherwise exploring or manipulating the environment in the apparent absence of any other drive state which might, according to some learning theories, be postulated for activity. Harlow's descriptions of monkeys which keep looking through a window curiously each time the experimenter lifts the shutter to look in, until at last after many, many hours the experimenter stops the activity from sheer exhaustion, are humorous to the point of hilarity.

Whether, however, the exploratory motive is a drive comparable to hunger and thirst or not is a question (Leuba, 1958). Even in animals the tendency verges on perception and cognition. In human beings it seems better denominated as a more or less complex attention process (Dember & Earl, 1957) or perceptual curiosity (Berlyne, 1957). One authority (White, 1959) maintains that because experimental psychology and psychoanalytic ego psychology have discovered this urge to explore, move about, and manipulate, the whole concept of motivation needs overhauling. But this motive was known long ago (Warden, Jenkins, & Warner, 1936). At any rate, whatever unconscious components this drive, need, or urge may have, and however it will finally be classed, it does partake of some of the characteristics of a life urge, possibly a vital one. Genetic differences in exploratory behavior have been discovered among several strains of rats (Carr & Williams, 1957); but differences among individuals, especially as related to their other functions, have yet to be demonstrated.

[1] A (white) woman who worked for the writer's mother at one time delivered a child about eight o'clock in the morning. "By noon," she said, "I was so hungry I got up and cooked myself a beefsteak." Fads in the amount of pain, and consequent length of the period of debility, are manifest within the same social class. Popular articles today emphasize that childbirth can be fun. Classes of expectant mothers are prepared for delivery by being told that it need not be painful. How much *sensitivity* to pain is altered by these instructions or changing customs and how much relaxation of tense muscles merely prevents painful tearing of the flesh is a question. The same question could be asked of hypnotic delivery, although there seems to be evidence in the literature on hypnosis that the gross quantity of pain is reduced under hypnosis, *e.g.*, in dental practice (Anonymous, 1957a, 1957b).

AGGRESSION AND SEXUALITY

Aggression and sexuality are two functions which seem to be in a special class by themselves. Sexual functions, complicated as they may become very early in life, yet seem to be more closely allied to tissue needs than is aggression. Whether they are on the same level of fundamentality, however, a unique place has to be made for them in the study of personality, for they differ in many ways from other urges. Eating, like sex and aggression, has been subjected to many prohibitions and regulations, but eating must continue or the organism perishes. And other life processes must be consummated or death results. In their turn, however, neither sex nor aggression, urgent as their demands may be, is a vital process, even though they may be tissue-generated (Fenichel, 1945). Howbeit, sex and aggression are urgent at times and apparently (at least for sex) sources of energy for more derived functions of the personality. Individual patterning of these two functions is more apparent than that of the digestive functions. Especially is individuality evident when learned behavior is present; but sex and aggression may be individual even prior to learning.

As has been remarked previously (in Chapter 5), Freud in his later years came to think that there are two basic forces in living materials, a Life and a Death Instinct. These may be roughly equated with anabolism, converting inorganic substances into living matter, and catabolism, changing organic matter to inorganic. But the Life and Death urges may also be equated with sex and aggression, and were so equated by Freud. This dualistic conception is accepted by some influential psychoanalysts (Bergler, 1948, 1949; Menninger, 1938) and rejected by others just as eminent (Fenichel, 1945; Reich, 1949; Szasz, 1952). Among other evidence cited contradicting the existence of a Death Instinct and supporting only a Life Instinct (Szasz, 1952) is that stemming from Alexis Carrell's "immortal chicken heart." In Carrell's experiments a portion of a heart muscle from an un-hatched chicken embryo, cultured *in vitro*, continued to live for many years. When food was available and metabolic products could be eliminated directly to the outside world, apparently tissues could go on living, dividing and multiplying, for all practical purposes forever. This same principle appears to hold with certain unicellular organisms. Aging and death may not be primary forces, but frustrations of the primary force which might be termed the Life Instinct, grossly sex or libido.

Whatever the fate of Freud's later theories, there is little doubt of the existence of urges known as sex and aggression which we may regard as sub-functions of the id. These urges directly or indirectly provide energies affecting the major attributes of the personality if not its entirety; that they exist in some form makes life and thus personality as a whole possible.

TENSION AND WISH-FULFILLMENT

Freud limited the id to the psychic content of the life urges. For him the id contained solely wishes striving for fulfillment. A tension exists; the organism strives to reduce the tension. The unconscious mental representative of this striving for reduction of tension is specifically an id function. Going beyond Freud, however, we may add that the physiological drive and its mental representation are indistinguishable psychophysiologically or organismically, even though they may be logically distinguishable. Hence both are considered to be id at this point.

In its "psychological aspects" Freud at first maintained that the id operates according to the "pleasure principle" or seeking to be rid of all excitation and thus all tension. Freud's insistence that the individual seeks for complete freedom from tension has been criticized (G. W. Allport, 1937; Schilder, 1942) and rightly so. For we appear to possess an automatic control process which prevents our seeking a dead level of tensionless immobility. By 1924 Freud (S. Freud, 1925, Chapter 22) had come to realize that sometimes the organism instead of seeking reduction of tension at all times seeks increase of tension sometimes. At any rate, as Fenichel (1945) theorizes, the principle seems to be a homeostatic one, seeking a certain level of tension, rather than abolition of tension. Energy-exchanges of a physiological nature do not usually result in reducing muscle tonus completely or unhealthy flabbiness results. Now, however, in support of Freud's early position it is well to point out that the automatic process which prevents complete loss of tension is an ego function by definition rather than an id function. Id seems automatically to develop controls (ego), but the seeking of discharge of tension is strictly speaking id. Consequently, the way Freud (1932) expressed the matter in one place sums up the situation: ". . . where id was, there ego shall be."

One of the higher functions of discharge or tension-releasing consists of the wish-fulfilling tendencies of the id.[1] These are sometimes called hallucinating, which in reality is a form of striving for discharge of tension uniting both id and ego functioning. If direct discharge of an impulse, hunger, sex, or other urge, is prevented, then an hallucination of a forbidden or inhibited act will be substituted. Tension from hunger could not be discharged directly by the young men serving as "semi-starvation guinea pigs," so their dreams and thoughts

were forced into concocting food images (Keys, 1950). Sexual tension generates "wet dreams" on the part of the male without direct opportunity for discharge. After the Judge, in Whittier's "Maud Muller," had "closed his heart" toward marrying the peasant maiden who would have demeaned his proud family, he saw Maud Muller's hazel eyes looking out from the fire on his hearth. And hallucinatory wish-fulfillment was hers, too:

Sometimes her narrow kitchen walls
Stretched away into stately halls;

The weary wheel to a spinnet turned,
The tallow candle an astral burned;

And for him who sat by the chimney lug,
Dozing and grumbling o'er pipe and mug,

A manly form at her side she saw,
And joy was duty and love was law.

It should be evident that both id and ego are operating, in the drive, in the wish and the channeling of the wish, in this poignant tale of "what might have been."

POSITIVE ID FORCES

Historically, the study of id has been primarily in the service of psychopathology. "It is grimly unfortunate," one psychologist has written vividly, "that in a period when rationality, insight, and creative social invention are in such urgent demand, science is prepared to throw light mainly on man's irrationality and helplessness." The concept of the id as a "driving chaos of forces" which operates only according to the "pleasure principle" (disregarding considerations of appropriateness, time, and objectivity) as opposed to the "reality principle" would not seem to leave much room for positive, creative forces. It is true that the net impact of Freudianism has been a heavy emphasis on the irrational and negative. Yet even in the concept of libido there is abundant room for regarding the id as positive. It is this latter aspect which has been emphasized in this chapter for the most part.

[1] In conjunction with both wishes and hallucinations psychoanalysis has employed a term unfamiliar to most students, *cathexis*. The essential meaning is the "drawing power" that an object, including a living object or even an idea, has for an individual. Murray speaks of the "evoking power" of an object. Lewin's parallel term is "valence," an analogy with chemical attractions or repulsions (the latter is anticathexis in psychoanalytic terms). In actuality, any definition which speaks about the "pull" or attraction or repulsion or valence of an object is only a figure of speech, for the cathexis is within the individual; it is an impulse of the individual, an id function, directed toward or against an object by the ego. The term *countercathexis* is used when energies are directed by the ego against the id, a concrete example being that of the hypermoralist who has exceedingly strong impulses to do immoral deeds but has built up correspondingly strong defenses against his impulses.

Recognition of the positive id forces does not mean denial of that which might be called negative. All the aggressive, lustful, cannibalistic, magical, superstitious, megalomaniac—all the "evil" impulses which issue in man's inhumanity to man (including himself) are not denied. They are only set in their appropriate context here. If the individual has "evil" impulses, he also has "good" ones. We can do no better than repeat the words of some authorities who have profited greatly from Freud but who present a corrective view:

In due time it became apparent to other analysts, if not to Freud, that the concept of id could not be limited to unacceptable dispositions. In infancy, for example, when the ego system is non-existent or at best very rudimentary, the mind is a hive of involuntary spontaneities, emotions, and needs, many of which are not only acceptable to the child and its mother during these early years, but continue to be acceptable and, what is more, culturally encouraged throughout life. It would not be proper to say that respiration, ingestion of food, defecation, expression of affection, endeavors to master the environment, and so forth, had their source in the ego. Also, as Jung, Rivers, and others have pointed out, the id is evidently the breeding ground of love and worship, as well as of the novel imaginations which are eventually applauded, instituted, and cherished by society. For these and other reasons, it seems best to think of the id as consisting of all the basic energies, emotions, and needs (value-vectors) of the personality, some of which are acceptable when expressed in a culturally approved form, towards a culturally approved object, in a culturally approved place, at a culturally approved time (Kluckhohn, Murray & Schneider, 1953).[1]

RECIPROCITIES OF ID AND OTHER FUNCTIONS

It has been indicated that the id and the ego operate conjointly in wish-fulfillment. This particular instance indicates how id

may function in reciprocity with other functions of the personality. Topographically the id can be regarded as a separate gross function. Dynamically, however, id does not operate in isolation. It is first the supplier of energy for all other personality functions. These in turn "dispense" energy as secondary sources (H. Hartmann, 1948)[2] which are continually replenished from the id.

Second, there is a reciprocating process in terms of a giving back to the id, as it were, those sub-functions which have developed out of the id. During every period of sleep some functions of the individual over which he has gained control (ego or superego) become id functions again. Motility, for instance, over which almost complete mastery has been acquired, is no longer "under ego control," but instead we are at the mercy in many ways of accidental external or internal stimuli (viscerogenic, for example). This loss of ego control is dramatically demonstrated to nearly anyone who has engaged in unaccustomed strenuous physical activity during the day. Sometime in the night he is sharply awakened by a violent twitching of his leg or arm as a result of imbalance in the body chemistry. Perceptual controls which are also well-established become inoperative. And especially ideation rarely admitted to adult consciousness becomes the rule rather than the exception, as the impossible becomes possible in dreams. Superego controls over aggressive and sexual inclinations may be relaxed. But when awaking comes, functions which were allowed to slip into the id during sleep become "controlled" again in the normal adult.

Not only in sleep is there reciprocity, but under stress conditions some functions which are under ego or superego control may give way and be uncontrolled. The taxi driver who admitted rape slayings of his sister-in-law and her little daughter expressed the matter unusually but probably not untruthfully: "Inwardly I feel that I

[1] Kluckhohn, C., Murray, H. A., & Schneider, D. M. (Eds.) *Personality in nature, society, and culture.* (2nd ed.) New York: Knopf, 1953. Reprinted by permission.

[2] Hartmann (1948) from whom the notion is taken does not include roles as a fourth system as we do here among the secondary sources.

want to be the best Christian in the world and outwardly I'm a damn maniac," he told the police. "I can't control the outward part and I don't know why." (The Tallahassee Democrat, 1955.) Working in the opposite direction, functions which are not ordinarily under ego or superego control may become "controlled" in excitement. Even in nonstress conditions some id functions may be temporarily controlled and thus for the time being become ego rather than id functions strictly. How accurate the stories are of Indian holy men who are reputed to be able to slash their wrists and control the flow of blood from the incision is a matter yet to be settled—why they would want to slash themselves in the first place is a puzzle to most Westerners. (The need for research beyond the bounds of Christendom is evident at this point.) The writer has been able to demonstrate control of blood circulation to graduate psychologists by forcing blood into his head and neck "at will," though at the cost of considerable expenditure of energy. Sad to say, the control does not operate in reverse; when blushing occurs, nothing seems to force the blood down except cessation of the emotion-provoking situation.[1] Certain id functions may, it seems, come "under control" in either stress or nonstress conditions.

Id Strength

In some ways every experiment reported in the preceding pages of this chapter presents a measurement of id strength. Specifically, however, there have been measures of the relative strength of drives in animals (Moss, 1924; Tsai, 1925; Warden, Jenkins, & Warner, 1936). Theories of learning have assumed relative strength of drives (Hull, 1943, 1952; Hull, Hovland, & Ross, 1940).

For a start at measuring id strength in terms of drives we could use the simple formula (from Hull in Stolurow, 1953),

$$D = D' \times \epsilon,$$

where D is the primary motivation, D' is the drive condition (like hunger) which is an increasing function of the length of time of deprivation, and ϵ is an exhaustion component (in the hunger state, inanition). D is not referrable to a specific drive, but is a general level of drive of the organism with all of its interacting needs (Hilgard, 1956). Such a formula may be satisfactory for hunger, thirst, air deprivation, and sleep. For the reaction to pain, the exploratory motive, and the sex drive, it seems that it either needs considerable revision or replacement. However, it can serve as an approximation to measurement of strength of some drive modalities. Possibly other more general formulae can be derived which will encompass both physiological drive conditions and other components of the id. Perhaps this is too large an order, and we may have to be content with more specific function measurement, as may be the case also in respect to ego, superego, and role functions.

These specific function measurements, some of which have been mentioned in this chapter, include basal metabolic rates, heart rates, and so forth, all of which have been measured with great accuracy in contrast to most psychological functions. Many studies have been done on the effects of anoxia, but the writer knows only one similar study in which air deprivation was measured as an invoker of air hunger drive. Sleep, pain, the exploratory motive, aggression, and sexuality (and the maternal motive) have been subjected to more or less exact measurement. Tension in the form of anxiety has been measured indirectly by verbal questionnaires (e.g., Taylor, 1953) and projective measures (e.g., Murray, 1938). More direct psychophysiological methods have also been employed. Hallucinatory wish-fulfillment tendencies have only been very indirectly measured by such techniques as level of aspiration tests in which some subjects set altogether unrealistic goals for themselves (Diggory, 1949; Lewin, 1944).

[1] Erythrophobia (literally, fear of blood, or in psychoanalytic usage, reddening from displaced fears) has deeper roots than we normally think, at least in some cases (Dreger, 1949).

SUMMARY

The first of three major cross-classifications of the dynamic structure-functions of the personality is topographical. Basic in the topography of personality are id functions, basic life urges arising in metabolism and tissue-needs. These functions include aggression and sexuality among other urges. Discharge of tension through wish-fulfillment constitutes a substitute activity for direct expression of impulses of the id. There are positive, creative forces in the id, as well as the negative ones recognized by classical psychoanalysis. Id and other functions reciprocate as id supplies energies for all other functions and gives up or takes back various sub-functions. Measurement of specific id functions is more advanced than that of id strength in general.

QUESTIONS

1. How does the text differ from Freud in its presentation of the topography of personality?

2. What basic id functions are there and in what way are they included as personality functions?

3. Discuss the positive aspects of id.

4. How does id reciprocate with other major functions?

CHAPTER 7

TOPOGRAPHICAL STRUCTURE-FUNCTIONS: EGO—I

Because we have been dealing with the living personality, with its interweaving and overlapping of functions, in discussing id, considerations about the *ego* were necessarily introduced. In both our discussion of Freud's conceptions of personality structure (Chapter 5) and in the chapter on the id we have assumed that the term "ego" was relatively clear in meaning. Now we must be more precise regarding this major part-function of the personality.

EGO AND SELF: EGO DEFINED

In common speech "ego" is often equated with "self." "And was my ego deflated," confesses Mr. Smith, meaning he as a self has been humiliated, and especially that portion of his self which is "inflatable" or "deflatable" by external circumstances. The man on the street is not alone in equating ego and self, however, for scientific authorities have done the same thing. Sherif and Cantril in *The Psychology of Ego-Involvements* (1947) reject the term "self," but proceed to use "ego" as approximating "self"; and many others from William James to Gordon Allport and Gardner Murphy have used the latter in a similar fashion.

In one way, the meaning we place upon a term like ego is an arbitrary one, just as in the case of a definition of personality itself. But our meaning is not entirely arbitrary. If we decide, in a kind of operational way, that we mean certain identifiable personality functions, then we have a common ground to proceed in further discussion. Here we define ego to mean "the control functions of the personality," and distinguish it from the self by referring the latter term to those functions which the individual identifies as "I" or "me." (Cf. "Self formation and preservation" in Chapter 8.) Self is, therefore, both more and less than ego, as can be seen from Figure 14 (p. 87), for self includes portions of id and superego and role as well as ego functions. And ego in turn includes more than self among its functions. Whenever some form of control develops within the personality, this is *by definition* an ego function. Symonds comes close to our conception of ego in *Dynamic Psychology* (1949) when he says the term ego is "used to refer to that phase of personality which determines adjustments to the outside world in the interest of satisfying inner needs." If in "adjustments to the outside world" Symonds subsumes those controls over inner impulses or drives and over ideation and imagination, controls which, of course, eventually determine adjustment to external factors, his concept is in accord with the definition above.

As we have given warning at the beginning of the chapter on the id, a similar warning is issued at the start of the two chapters on the ego: For convenience the construct ego is employed to refer to control functions. Such use does not imply that the ego has any reality beyond the existence of these functions. Any reading of the text which reifies the ego is putting more into the meaning than modern personology intends. The same stricture holds for the discussion on the superego (Chapter 9).

EGO PSYCHOLOGY

A few remarks must be made at this place which ordinarily would be relegated to a footnote. These concern Freud's contribution to "ego psychology." It has been the fashion recently to deride Freud for his having been interested in the id and its devious ways and having neglected the ego. As with so many of Freud's contributions, however, his writings in this field have been misunderstood. It is true that in recent years "ego psychology" has developed remarkably; but it is not true that there was virtually no "ego psychology" in the early years of psychoanalysis. No less an authority on psychoanalysis than Anna Freud, Sigmund Freud's most distinguished child and herself a highly original contributor to psychological understanding, protested against the prevalent notion that psychoanalysis was interested only in the id in early years, and wrote in 1936:

From the beginning analysis, as a therapeutic method, was concerned with the ego and its aberrations: the investigation of the id and of its mode of operation was always only a means to an end. And the end was invariably the same: the correction of these abnormalities and the restoration of the ego to its integrity (Anna Freud, 1937).

Although Freud did not *seem* to be occupied with ego problems until his *Group Psychology and the Analysis of the Ego* in 1922, and especially *The Ego and the Id*, published in 1927, problems of control functions were in his thinking from very early in his psychoanalytic career. In 1894 Freud published his paper on "the defence neuropsychoses" in which he described his patients' having thoughts that were unbearable and their being unsuccessful in making these thoughts inoperative even though pushed out of consciousness. Aside from the fact that Freud used the term "ego" repeatedly in the article, his concern was with what the ego did with these unacceptable thoughts, or in our terms what control measures were exerted in respect to them. It was one of Freud's great contributions to psychopathology that he recognized the symptoms of neurosis and psychosis as expressions of abortive control measures of the personality rather than as inexplicable foreign intrusions. Throughout his career Freud was concerned with ego functions. In addressing the College of Physicians in Vienna in 1904 he spoke of "will power" and then struck a theme which he was to repeat in different form in one of his last publications; speaking of the effect of impulses when conscious or unconscious he said in 1904, "It is only by the application of highest mental energies, which are bound up with consciousness, that we can command all our impulses." (Freud, 1950) Other pioneer psychoanalysts like Karl Abraham (1927), though not exponents of what is now called "ego psychology," wrote on character-formation and were concerned both theoretically and in their psychoanalytic practice with the development of controls.

EGO: CONSCIOUS AND UNCONSCIOUS

It is well to recall, since mention has been made of consciousness, that in the Freudian theory of the structure of personality, ego and consciousness are not at all equated though they are overlapping. Control functions are present in the individual of which he is not aware, most of the time at any rate. Although there may not be, as suggested previously, much if any modification of the hunger rhythms by experience, the very fact that there *are* rhythms and not disintegrations is a manifestation of the organism's control over its own processes. Chemical and physical regulators make for a kind of homeostasis (Cannon, 1932) [1] or at least a balancing of forces by means of internal operations supplemented by materials from the external world. These controls are then unconscious ego functions, developed in part long before the individual becomes aware of himself or of the rest of the world. The point should be emphasized that in the view expressed here, the ego and consciousness cannot be equated, for many of the controls developed over physiological functions are unconscious ones. Furthermore, many of the controls developed in the forms of intellection (mental functioning in general) are unconscious. If one is asked as an American what is the first stanza of "America," or as a resident of the British Empire what is the first stanza of "God Save the King," until he is reminded, he is unconscious of these words. Memory functions, as has been stated previously, are not *dead* storehouses, but dynamic, living ones; they are ego functions, primarily unconscious in their operation.

Although we are not discussing personality development as such, control functions which develop early may very well be the "most unconscious." *In utero* some controls develop; these are over *physiological* processes primarily.[2] If, however, we define

psychology with Munn (1956) as "the science of *behavior*," these controls develop over *psychological* processes as well; for the neonate is not a congeries of disorganized functions, but already a complex *organism*. Even some of the higher control functions such as learning may develop before birth, functions which we usually refer to postpartum existence (Spelt, 1948); we are not yet in a position to be sure of this possibility.

Both psychological and physiological processes which are control functions constitute ego. Consequently, ego, as defined, cannot be conscious only, for some of these processes operate outside of the awareness of the individual. Ego is thus both conscious and unconscious.

MAJOR SUBFUNCTIONS OF THE EGO

Having distinguished ego from self and consciousness, and having subsumed control functions under ego, we take up now the specific functions which have been considered traditionally in psychoanalysis as parts of the ego. Both general and child psychology provide sources for material in these pages. But the organization of materials and some of the terminology come principally from psychoanalysis, inasmuch as the latter has approached these functions from a personological point of view. This overview of ego functions does not supplant a general psychology text which offers much of the same information, but in greater detail, on attending and perceiving, psychomotor behavior, emotions, learning and thinking, and the like. General psychology does not view these functions from the personalistic standpoint; here we do.

Fenichel (1945) sets forth four major functions which are specific to the ego: (1)

---

[1] It is recognized that not all biologists accept the concept of homeostasis.

[2] Most authorities have not included in the ego physiological controls of the nature instanced in the text. But if there is to be a comprehensive view of personality, *any* controls which are developed must be included, for these along with all other individualized functions help to make up personalities. The fact that basic physiological functions are *more or less* similar from individual to individual and that the controls developed over them are *more or less* uniform does not make these drives or their controls any less significant for personality. It is the similarities of these functions in part which make possible *some* categorization of personalities, *some* temperamental *types* or *traits* which serve as a basis for a science of personality. Because such ego functions are not "psychological" they might be overlooked; but

from the time of Galen at least (200 A.D.) the study of temperaments has been considered a province of psychology, and the temperament one possesses (phlegmatic, sanguine, choleric, melancholic) is probably rooted in the general level of drives and the kinds of controls developed over these drives.

perception, (2) motility control, (3) "binding" tension, and (4) judgment. To these may be added a function suggested by Symonds (1951) which includes elements psychoanalysis has emphasized in so-called "character analysis." This is: (5) synthesizing. To the first three of these the remainder of Chapter 7 is devoted. Judgment and synthesizing functions are taken up in Chapter 8.

Perception

How, one may ask, is perception a control process? Is not perception something that *happens* to us? Yes, in part, but in part we make it happen, too. First, we must realize that perception is of internal as well as of external data. We perceive our muscle motions, the changes of leg and arm positions; we perceive our stomach's distress signals and sometimes other internal operations. Perception is oriented both toward the organism and the environment (as well as toward the symbiotic relations of organism and environment). Then it is to be noted that perception is considered a control function in that it is developed as a *means of coping with* the data from within and without which present themselves to be perceived.

Perception as Motivated Behavior. Perception is motivated behavior (Nissen, 1951) in part, in the sense that it serves the purposes of the organism or personality in general. When we have maintained that perception is a form of control, we do not mean, of course, that the individual has complete control over stimuli arising from without or within.[1] But both clinical and experimental psychology (Blake & Ramsey, 1951; Fenichel, 1945; Witkin, *et al.*, 1954) tend to coalesce in holding that what the individual perceives is directly related to what the organism needs at the time.

Woodworth, one of the "grand old men" of psychology, wrote,[2]

. . . perception is always driven by a direct, inherent motive which might be called the will to perceive. Whatever ulterior motives may be present from time to time, this direct perceptual motive is always present in any use of the senses. It is impossible to look without trying to see or to listen without trying to hear. To see, to hear—to see clearly, to hear distinctly—to make out what it is one is seeing or hearing—moment by moment, such concrete immediate motives dominate the life of relation with the environment. . . . (Woodworth, 1947).[3]

Woodworth makes almost too strong a case, however. To deny at this point the overwhelming part external and internal "objective" factors play in the perceptual process would be to flout common sense and experimental evidence. We might not agree *what* tree we are observing, but given sufficient illumination and appropriate *distance*, most of us would agree that we perceive a tree. (The semantic problem as to why we agree it is a *tree* need not concern us here; we shall agree that when we say "tree" we mean approximately what our neighbor means when he says "tree." When a pure tone is heard by two laboratory subjects stimulated by sound waves from a tuning fork, they may not agree to call it "F" or "C," but they can reach a measure of agreement as to the relative place the tone has on the scale. Perception is not authochthonous in most instances, but is determined in some part by objective factors, even in the most ambiguous of projective methods.[4]

Perception as Related to Psychophysical Structure and Experience. Perceptions, determined in part by factors not under the

---

[1] Whether this is a native, *i.e.*, genetically determined, form of control or not has no bearing on the argument. All that admission of "native" controls would mean is that some ego functions are hereditarily determined; the position that ego functions develop does not mean they are *entirely* learned phenomena.

[2] The writer is indebted for this reference to Martin Scheerer in Lindzey, *Handbook of Social Psychology* (1954).

[3] Woodworth, R. S. Reinforcement of perception. Amer. J. Psychol., 1947, *60*, 119–124. Reprinted by permission.

[4] Even Stern's (1937) "cloud pictures," possibly the most ambiguous stimuli ever offered in a projective technique, still have certain definite forms, which are perceived differently, but could be described as objective measures.

individual's control, are nevertheless control functions developed by the organism in accord with its own nature. Take one of the familiar Gestalt visual processes like closure. Does one perceive a triangle in the accompanying diagram (Figure 15) only because the three separate lines are objectively arranged in a certain way? Probably not, but instead the organism seems to organize the lines into a triangle perception, a form of control over the stimuli. In unpublished research (Dreger, 1960b) the author found that even when subjects recognized the incompleteness of sets of lines (tending towards a triangle and a rectangle respectively), they *thought* immediately of the forms which the lines suggested. Here the principle that cognitive inference enters into the perceptual process (Vernon, 1957) is relevant. But most subjects *perceived* a triangle or a rectangle. These forms of control which the individual exercises over incoming stimuli are not, as once thought, unchanging from age level to age level, but develop throughout childhood and adolescence (Solley & Murphy, 1960).

Even when the determination of much of our perception by objective data and by our general psychophysical nature is recognized, the individual way in which we perceive the "same" situation tends to carry the lesson that perception develops in large part in relation to individual personality organization. Any general psychology class which has studied how we observe becomes aware of the individual nature of perception. Students may observe and report on some adaptation of the scene in which a professor is interrupted in his lecture by an assistant who annoys the professor until a shooting occurs (Ruch, 1953) or on a showing of a film like *Fidelity of Report* (1946) in which a double hold-up takes place. It is vividly demonstrated to the student how little he is *prepared* to observe all the activities in the situation. The same stimuli are perceived in different ways; many things totally or partially overlooked by some are easily taken in by others.

We are prepared by our previous experience to single out (to "pay attention to")

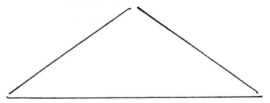

Figure 15. Diagram representing Gestalt principle of closure.

particular aspects of a situation. And our perceptual experience in turn is a series of *selections* from our environment, without or within, related to the needs we have. Individuals, further, are units in whole classes and cultures, and deviate not only from others in their own group, but with those others, deviate in their perceptions of objects, of persons, and of relations from other groups. Group and cultural differences in needs are determinative in part of perceptual differences.[1]

"Object Relationships"; Self and Role Awareness. Within the perceptual functions, sub-functions can be distinguished which everyone develops individually. The first of these is developing and maintaining "object relationships." Here the operation of id functions must be assumed. As id urges are constantly seeking discharge, so these energies come to be channeled in more or less appropriate ways toward objects which can satisfy the urges or reduce the tensions (or increase them under some circumstances). In the course of personality development certain objects, like milk, or a symbol with which at first it is always as-

[1] These assertions need considerable bolstering. Ever since Muensterberg's *On the Witness Stand,* published in 1908, if not before that, psychologists have been experimenting with individual differences in perception. The classical experiments by Sherif (1935) on social influences on perception, of Bruner and Goodman (1947) on social class differences in perception, of McGinnies' (1949) "perceptual defense" have all been subjected to critical analysis, especially on the grounds that it is not perception which is influenced by these other variables but the report of what is perceived. It seems, however, that enough additional evidence has accumulated, much of which is set forth in Chapter 11, to enable us to make the statements in the text safely.

sociated, the breast or bottle, serve to reduce tensions; presumably awareness of the
object develops only as the object relieves
tension.

It is the psychoanalytic contention that
the basis of love and hate in our human object relationships is found in the fact that
apparently the only reason the object exists for the infant is to ease his tensions, and
thus the object exists to be gotten rid of,
as it were. Ambivalence toward the same
object, both hate and love of children toward siblings or parents, of parents toward
children, and so on, has its origin in the
primitive dual attitude toward the same
object. Research has not yet shown
whether this contention is adequate or not;
its promulgation has come principally from
the analysis of adult neurotics or psychotics. It may tentatively be accepted until it is shored up by better evidence than
has been presented, or has been shown to be
inadequate. In any case, it may be that the
explanation holds for some individuals and
not for others. The joint operation of id
and ego is, thus, found in developing and
maintaining object relationships, the control functions serving to direct id energies
positively or negatively toward objects.

The second sub-function of perception
in its role as part of the total personality
functioning is very closely allied to the
maintenance of object relationship, and that
is the awareness of one's self or selves [1] as
distinct from the not-self. Perceptions may
be roughly divided into those which are
"internalized" and those which are not.
That is, some perceptions, transformed
into memories, become "a part of one"
while others are merely experienced without becoming or being part of one. Those
portions of the internal or external environment which become internalized are
part of the self; possibly they constitute
the self. As long ago as the philosopher

Protagoras, the Sophists maintained that
the only object with which one should occupy himself is the self, for it is the only
really accessible object. Differing widely
from the Sophists in his essential view of
man as an ethical being, Socrates nevertheless appropriated the motto inscribed on
the temple at Delphi, *Know thyself*. Socrates thought that man could know himself
absolutely (or that some men could thus
know themselves), even though absolute
knowledge of the external world is denied
to him. Alas for absolute knowledge of
any kind! Long before modern clinical investigation demonstrated how little we
often know even of ourselves, Immanuel
Kant in the eighteenth century of our era
had fairly well shown the inaccessibility of
the self to direct knowledge.[2]

Part of the knowledge of self, if not the
very beginning of the conceived self, is
awareness of one's body. Psychoanalysis
and academic psychology (Fisher, 1958;
Schilder, 1950) have brought out the importance of the experience we have with
our bodies, experience, however, which
may not be any more reliable a reproduction of the facts pertaining to one's body
than experience with the rest of the world.
Actually, William James, some time before
Freud made his impact on our thinking, described "the Material Me," including the
body and its sensory excitations and clothing, much of which we perceive to be part
of ourselves. Carlyle's *Sartor Resartus* ("the
tailor retailored") sets forth the notion that
man has indeed become too much identified with his clothes which ought not, Carlyle maintains, to be considered as part of

[1] Isham (1955) identifies ego with the linguistic
usage of "I" and the self with "me." Such usage
may be satisfactory for distinguishing ego and self
but does not take account of ego as a vast system
of control functions such as we envision ego to
be here.

[2] There are so many metaphysical aspects of
Kant's philosophy of the self that we should bog
down attempting to discuss them. It is sufficient
to say that in *The Critique of Pure Reason* Kant
maintained that the self is a phenomenon just as
is the external world—and phenomena can never
be known directly. According to Weber and
Perry in *History of Philosophy* (1925), though
Kant never advocated the identify of the self and
not-self, his close identification of self and world
led to the idealism of Fichte, Hegel, and Schelling
with their expressed identification of the inner
and outer.

oneself. Whatever "ought" to be, James' analysis and Carlyle's coincide.

Knowledge of the self is partly the perception of one's thoughts. Although Hume in the eighteenth century claimed that the self consists only of perceptions "of heat or cold, light or shade, love or hatred, pain or pleasure" (Hume, 1896), his list of self processes must be extended to include thoughts of more general nature, that is, concepts and generalizations. We can, as James stated, think of *ourselves* as thinkers; and we can also think about the thoughts we have.

A third sub-function of perception relates very closely to those of maintaining object relationships and of perceiving the self, indeed overlaps with them; this is the perception of one's roles. Sometimes, these may be perceptions of one's "social self," or as James insisted "social selves," of which we have as many as there are groups of people about whose opinion we care. The term "role" is larger than "social self," as we shall see later, for the latter is found in conjunction only with those roles with which one may personally identify himself, or in which one may become "ego-involved," to use a phrase from Sherif and Cantril. There may be some roles the person consciously enacts with which he identifies virtually not at all (Gouldner, 1957), an extreme example being that of the spy who adopts roles which are not "his" in the country upon which he is practicing espionage; he rejects them as part of "himself." There may be other roles of which the person is partially or completely unaware; in whole or in part then he "does not have control over them," for he perceives them either only dimly or not at all.

Motility

Mastery of the motor apparatus can hardly be distinctly separated from perception in some aspects. Indeed, the tiny child's perception is largely perceptual-motor behavior. Gesell and Ilg (1943) write:

He spends many moments looking at his hands, fingering his hands, mouthing his hands.

These sensory experiences—visual, tactile, wet, dry, still, moving, stop-go, oral, palmar, touching and being touched, provide him with a medley of data. By gradual degrees he comes to realize that he has a hand which feels when it contacts (active touch), which feels when it is contacted (passive touch), which feels when it moves (sense of motion, or kinesthetic sense mediated by sensory end organs in muscles, joints, and tendons). His ceaseless manipulation, therefore, acquaints him not only with the physical universe and the physical presence of other persons, but with the physical presence of himself.[1]

Gesell and Ilg's research on infants and children leads them to conclusions in this regard (though definitely not in some other ways!) similar to those which psychoanalysts have reached by clinical investigation. Probably the connection between perceptual and motor behavior, based upon the unity of the nervous system and perhaps the related conductivity properties of all protoplasm, is never outgrown.[2] However, as intermediary thought processes intervene in a highly complex fashion between initial perceptions and final motor behavior in the adult, we can for practical purposes distinguish perception and motility.

Psychologists have been interested, along with other scientists, in the effects of the *lack* of such control in varying degrees among persons who have never achieved mastery of portions of their physical apparatus or have lost such control having once gained it, as in various paralysis states. Authorities differ on these effects (Larson, 1958; Mussen & Newman, 1958; Panton, 1958; Potter & Fiedler, 1958; Saxer, 1959; Simmel, 1958), although the general consensus is that there are strong effects. There is assuredly enough evidence even from a common sense standpoint to enable us to recognize reverberations throughout much

[1] Gesell, A., & Ilg, Frances L. *Infant and child in the culture of today.* New York: Harper & Bros., 1943. Reprinted by permission.

[2] Research on motor accompaniments to thinking, especially of the "thinking toward" type (Hull, 1933; Jacobson, 1932) tends to support this statement.

of one's personality under the influence of failure to develop motor control or to lose it, when once one has developed it. One who has experienced these lacks or losses himself, or has had an opportunity to study them intimately, is aware of the way in which a person's outlook on life is altered when he does not have what he deems to be normal control of his musculature.

Distortions of feelings, of body image representations, of levels of aspiration, of attitudes toward self and others, and many other effects of inability to have complete control over one's own motor behavior are not confined to individuals with gross differences from the norm. Indeed, Alfred Adler's psychological system is built upon the alleged fact that the normal child possesses "organ inferiorities" which handicap him in his start in life. Among these inferiorities is the relative lack of control of his muscles, so that compared to adults he is clumsy and inept. Far from being able to overcome his resultant inferiority feelings as he develops more mature controls, his life is devoted to strivings prompted by these feelings. Actually, Adler, who like Freud and Jung extended his clinical findings to nonclinical personalities, maintained in his later years that the basis of a child's educability is his need to overcome not only these inferiorities, but also primarily the feelings associated with them (Adler, 1927).

In some situations, as depicted in the structure of personality diagram, Figure 6 (p. 59), break-throughs may occur when motor controls have long been established. One of the writer's counselees during most of his life has probably had better gross motor coordination than the average individual. As a child he competed in athletic contests with fair success. As a youth he played tennis, not excellently, but well. Over forty now, he is still active physically, capable of carrying out motor tasks from which many of his age have long since retired. But when the great crisis of his life came—the results of which drove him to counseling—he was dismayed by a strange failure of his muscle controls, particularly

quivering of muscles over which he could recall no similar loss of control previously. For a full year or more following his crisis, these conditions continued with diminishing intensity. Whether as a result of counseling or of his learning to live with them—or both—he did come to view his muscle symptoms with a rather humorous detachment, a kind of "estrangement" similar to the schizophrenic's decrease in cathexis for a particular body organ. At first, however, the loss of control was very disturbing. Follow-up of this man's case reveals that he has not had recurrence of his symptoms for a number of years. Apparently he has regained control; but he insists, "It was not by any conscious effort; they (the symptoms) just gradually went away."

Ego controls in respect to motor behavior are not limited to the voluntary musculature. One of the reasons for maintaining that ego functions are partly unconscious is that the operation of some muscle systems is relatively automatic, continuing whether we are in a sleeping or waking state. When once the neonate's respiratory system has been set in motion, the muscles continue their operation without conscious direction. The writer has not tried the experiment; but it seems reasonable to suppose that, as some say (Carlson & Johnson, 1948), committing suicide by holding one's breath (closing the glottis) is just about impossible; for, the reasoning goes, as soon as one has become unconscious, his muscles relax and respiration begins again.[1] Or in another area of control, sphincter muscles over which some voluntary control has been established are also governed by other than conscious portions of the brain.

Motility and its corresponding ego controls cannot be limited to the musculature alone. Glands as well as muscles serve as re-

[1] Probably because of the continual stimulation of vagus fibers and especially the operation of carbon dioxide on the respiratory center in the medulla oblongata. "When CO_2 reaches a great enough concentration, the most determined effort of the 'will' cannot nullify its effect on the center. One could not commit suicide by voluntarily holding the breath" (Carlson & Johnson, 1948).

sponse mechanisms. In the relation of motility control to higher functions, the complex of responses of a glandular-muscular nature should not be overlooked as a set of personality functions.

While the *average* functioning of motor controls is of primary interest to the physiologist, to the personologist the individual patternings of motor controls is of greater interest. Especially does personality psychology ask "What place does a certain form of control have in the total functioning of the individual?" The respiratory cycle and especially the inspiration-expiration ratio have been used to measure emotional reactions of individuals (Herrington, 1942). Characteristic patterns of respiration may disclose a person's anxiety or freedom from anxiety (Postman, 1949). Individual patterns of control over sphincters are found even in adults. In Milton Mayer's *They Thought They Were Free* (1955) one of the ten Nazis who supplied information was an enuretic until he was 22 years of age, establishing it would seem some sort of record for inability among nonhospitalized persons to gain control over the bladder's sphincter muscles. It is not necessarily such extreme cases in which we are interested, although students find abnormal psychology among the most fascinating parts of their study of psychology. Normal individuals under *normal* conditions provide enough characteristic ways of controlling their motor apparatuses to make such personality patterns of great interest. Normal individuals under *stress* conditions yield further scientific data. A. R. Luria (1932), the Russian psychologist, invented a recording technique for measuring muscle tremors in natural and artificial conflict situations which revealed that there are relations between feeling of stress and motor expression in normal persons. The individual places his hand on a "tremorgraph" which records tiny movements of which the person himself may be unaware. Inducing stress to the degree permitted in the laboratory increases the amount of tremor, with characteristic patterns for different individuals.

We include, then, mastery of motility among important ego functions. Such mastery cannot be entirely separated from perceptual conrol. It is closely related also to various self processes and emotions, as a basis for developing a body image, attitudes, and so on. Finally, both conscious and unconscious voluntary and involuntary motor controls are included.

"Binding" Tension

Inasmuch as there is constant demand on the part of the id functions for discharge or exchange of energy, unless there is some holding of tension in check there could be a constant process of tension-release-tension-release. We know, however, that "binding" of tension occurs in the normal adult, such that discharge takes place under circumstances acceptable to both the individual and society. Under normal conditions in any society when, for example, an adult is hungry, he waits until there are acceptable times and places; he does not eliminate waste products just anywhere or anytime; he holds off, sublimates, or substitutes for his aggressive impulses; he deals with his sexual tendencies appropriately. To be sure, even for the normal person control measures may break down or be less than perfect, as when a man's "risibilities" have been touched and he breaks out into uncontrollable laughter.

Very wide differences are found from society to society regarding acceptable times and circumstances for relieving tension (Benedict, 1934). Every society, however has some regulations governing these expressions. Likewise, within any one society there are wide differences among individuals both as to their ability to control and the kinds of controls they exert. Whether Rorschach theory is adequate or not for organizing the data of personality, the suggestion made by Rorschach and his followers concerning the types of control we employ is fruitful. In varying degrees people seem to utilize either the relaxed, easy type of control or the more or less conscious, rigid kind in dealing with their tensions, or more precisely seem to use both. The balance between these types of control determines differences among individuals in respect to ability to "bind" tension. But the kind of tension involved also determines our behavior.

Physiological and Psychological Tension. When we think of tension (apart from muscle tension with which we have dealt previously, pp. 114–5), we may only have reference to physiologically-based "tissue needs," like hunger, thirst, and pain. With even these we deal according to the social structure in which we find ourselves and the particular type of personality structure we have developed. There are tensions of a fairly normal nature in any society which may have physiological components but which are primarily psychological in content. For these tensions, principally psychological controls are necessary. A young man envisions a career in business or a profession and has a "burning desire" both to make his name known and to bring help to those whom he will serve. In this case "binding" tension overlaps with the judging and synthesizing functions of the ego (Chapter 8), but is logically separable from them. Ordinarily the young man refuses to allow tension to release itself in hallucinating the fulfillment of his dream. Instead, he holds himself to the task of preparation, waiting for auspicious times to seek discharge of his tension. When these bindings become habitual, we can consider them major elements of character.[1]

Anxiety: Defenses Against Anxiety. Inordinate tension may be beyond the capacity of the individual to control by ordinary methods. This inordinate tension is called anxiety. Either the fear that overwhelming tension will flood the being, or the very tension itself which has been built up may be termed anxiety. Different kinds of anxiety have been revealed by experimental methods (Dreger & Aiken, 1957; O'Connor, Lorr, & Stafford, 1956; Taylor, 1953). Possibly the overwhelming excitation of the infant in his helpless state is the direct prototype of anxiety states in later life (Fenichel, 1945). As ego controls develop, anxiety is "tamed," serving now to prevent the individual's being overwhelmed by excitation. If, however, the rising tide of excitation is too great, then ego controls of an ordinary nature fail, the "tamed" anxiety no longer serves merely a warning function, but becomes instead panic.

It is against this panic that defense has to be erected. The so-called "defense mechanisms" are among the devices employed for this purpose. It is usually not made clear in elementary discussions that these are in reality "defenses against anxiety," not strange, inexplicable devices which can only be described and not understood. Various classifications and cross-classifications of the defenses against anxiety can be made (Fenichel, 1945; Anna Freud, 1937; Reich, 1949), but for our purposes two major classes can be distinguished, those which may be classified as successful and ordinary, and others which may be regarded as unsuccessful and pathogenic, the "defense mechanisms" of classical psychoanalysis. The distinction in this case is no more absolute than in most classifications of personality phenomena. Sometimes a defense device is "successful," at other times "unsuccessful." It is the use to which the device is put by the individual that usually determines what it is. Nevertheless, that some devices are successful in "binding" anxiety and others are unsuccessful is a useful distinction, even though a particular device shifts from one category to another depending on the use to which it is put.

Before carrying out our classification of

[1] Fenichel (1945) as a psychoanalytic systematist considers character as an ego function only. Symonds (1951) as a psychologist appears to agree with Fenichel. It should be recognized first that we are making arbitrary divisions of various control functions when we speak of ego and superego. In psychoanalytic theory superego arises as part of ego. This concept is in keeping with our understanding of psychological development. We learn to adjust to (develop controls for) what we conceive of as reality; the general adjustmental or control functions may be called ego. Part of the "reality" to which we have to adapt positively or negatively is a moral or custom-laden part; functions which develop in connection with these aspects of reality may be called superego.

specific mechanisms, a difference in point of view, or possibly only of emphasis, needs to be recorded, a difference between the classical psychoanalytic view and the more interactionist type of outlook represented in modern psychology. Psychoanalysis has seemed to ignore the situation often and concentrated on the intrapsychic nature of the defenses, especially on the individual's anxiety level which generates the need for defense. However, differences in the level of anxiety may interact with the situation in which a defensive device is used.

In one study (Doris & Sarason, 1955) subjects were classified into high and low anxiety groups on the basis of a special questionnaire. A pre-arranged success-failure sequence of tasks induced failure feelings and projection of blame in the high anxiety subjects when the series of tasks was presented to experimental and control groups in one way. Presented to a similar set of groups in reverse order, the series did not elicit significant differences. And yet, the blame (self-blame) scores for the second set of experimental and control subjects actually averaged higher than in the first case. For some presently inexplicable reason, the projection mechanism worked equally successfully (or equally unsuccessfully) in both high and low anxiety groups under the second conditions. The main point to be noted is that the low anxiety group in one situation did not feel impelled to employ the projection mechanism, but in the other situation they did. Situation and level of anxiety may thus interact.

Successful and Ordinary Defenses. In the first category of defenses are those which accomplish their purpose of controlling the drives or impulses without at the same time blocking their discharge. Among these defenses are those called *sublimation,* which is actually not one defense mechanism among others as is implied in most discussions. In actuality, most of the common "defense mechanisms" can be employed in a sublimatory fashion. Sublimation can be defined as the turning of one's instinctive energies from expression unsatisfactory to the individual and possibly to his society to ex-

pression which is satisfactory both to society and to the individual (*i.e.,* meets his needs).

Probably the two most cited examples of sublimation are those of the unmarried teacher who dearly loves children and turns to teaching so that she can "mother" many children and of the surgeon whose aggressive tendencies to cut and tear are turned into a useful and satisfying vocation. These examples represent two different kinds of successful defenses, the latter a true sublimation and the former not. In the case of the surgeon the drive is satisfied by his actually being able to engage in the natural activity required by the drive, whereas in the case of the teacher a large part of the natural activity required by the drive is inhibited. A large component of "mothering" children begins with the satisfaction of sexual impulses in intercourse with a loved husband whose children a woman bears as a consequence. Another large component is the bearing and nursing of the child to be "mothered." These components are missing in teaching.

And yet the sublimation employed by the unmarried teacher, though not strictly similar to that of the surgeon, may bring more satisfaction to herself and her charges than actual physical mothering may bring to another woman. Mere satisfaction of the physical urges necessary to motherhood or even carrying out many of the "psychological" tasks associated with actual mothering is no guarantee of happiness or ability to serve.

In connection with the surgeon's sublimation it should be recognized that merely being able to cut and tear or to do anything else aggressive without social purpose seems to satisfy neither the individual nor society *in the long run.* The surgeon's sublimation is a world apart from either the temporary destructive behavior of the one who has to "let off steam or I'll bust" or the continuing criminal destructiveness which, compulsively motivated, makes the criminal hated and feared by himself and others.

Besides the devices which are considered in a more or less precise fashion to be sublimatory, there are others which may be called "ordinary defenses" which accomplish their aim in whole or in part as defenses against anxiety, defenses which cannot be classified as "defense mechanisms" in the classical sense. Some of these operate on an entirely unconscious level, others are partly conscious, and still others are mostly or possibly entirely conscious. Although they are included here among "successful" defenses, as dynamic functions they may change character from time to time in the same individual, becoming unsuccessful if the balance of internal and/or external forces is upset.

There are among "ordinary defenses" those which operate only indirectly against the expression of impulses which could generate anxiety. Their immediate reference is the external world. Indirectly they serve to keep the individual from feeling the panic which arises from within should his anxiety get out of hand.

1. *Forgetting, procrastination, lateness.* When these behaviors are directed against persons or things distasteful to the individual, they constitute defense phenomena. The child who dawdles on the way to school, the person who is habitually late for certain social events but not others, the Hamlet who puts off the day of revenge, all may represent the operation of defense.

2. *Disparaging others, arguing, negativism, lying.* These all have in common an element of hostility with more of an "edge" to it than is found in the immediately preceding group of behaviors. When a person makes belittling remarks about another or engages in the other forms of more or less hostile behavior represented here, astute observers recognize that these are directed against others for the sake of hiding shortcomings in the person himself.

3. *Pseudo-sexuality, glamor, "manliness."* On a pathological level Don Juan seems to be hyper-sexual, but "the apparent plus conceals a real minus" (Fenichel, 1945). On the nonpathological level, if the individual is not convinced that manliness or womanliness is his or her essential nature, he must defend against his real feelings which are

too painful to admit. The defense operates as a parading before others, so that they will say, "What a man!" or "What a woman!" [1]

4. *Clowning.* The defensive nature of clowning has been recognized in the implied pathos of the bidding, "Laugh, clown, laugh!" Figaro says in *The Barber of Seville*, "I hasten to laugh at everything, for fear of being obliged to weep." Besides the pathetic aspect of clowning is another with different motivation, that of allowing hostile expression indirectly. Clowning of this kind can allow the original instinct to be expressed in a manner partially acceptable to the individual and society, for was it not "all in fun?" [2]

5. *Pseudo-hostility.* To prevent the expression of positive feelings, the individual expresses hostile feelings. Somewhere the heroine of a play declaims tearfully, "I hate him! I hate him! I hate him! I love him!" Although the hatred may be genuine and intense, the more basic feeling is not sufficiently defended against and comes through.

6. *Perceptual-blocking.* Related to more pathological hysterical defenses, like hysterical blindness, deafness, and anesthesias, this defense is seen most clearly in "cultural blindness" to which sociologists and anthropologists have called our attention. It would be painful, it would be inconvenient and upsetting, for members of a dominant group to recognize superior group characteristics in a subordinate group of persons. The "heathen Chinee" with his wiles and his treachery could not be honest like the white man—ever!

---

[1] This simple reconstruction of the dynamics of pseudo-sexuality is not based on experimental evidence. It comes from the writer's clinical experience and observation of many individuals without clinical investigation. It is, however, an extrapolation to "normal" persons from carefully observed clinical materials.

[2] Tarachow's (1951) fascinating discussion on circuses and clowns presents documented arguments as to the exhibitionistic, and genital and anal anxiety-producing character of at least professional clowning. There may very well be attemps even in "normal" clowning to reassure oneself of his masculinity by such exhibitionism.

Some of the "ordinary defenses" operate directly against impulses, rather than as in the previous group indirectly, in order to prevent being overwhelmed by anxiety.

1. *Distraction devices.* Study, work, games, shows, drinking, whistling, talking, reading, and a host of other behaviors may be used to fend off unpleasant affects.[1] "Partial regression" (Berg, 1953) may take place in the recurrence of obsessive tunes or of ideas and may represent deep-lying conflicts (Freud, 1950) or current stress situations. One may employ various devices to fend off the pangs of conscience; in this case in the colorful expression of psychoanalysis the superego imbued with the fierce energy of the id is seeking expression, but the individual seeks to silence the "voice of conscience" by distractions.

2. *Day-dreaming.* Strong erotic components may be found in day-dreaming, so much so that the fantasy outlet of sexuality is obvious. Fantasy release of aggressive feelings, of omnipotence feelings lingering from childhood, and of aspirations for recognition and status may occur in daydreams. To express these various impulses directly would occasion too great anxiety, so the latter is warded off by the "denial in fantasy" of reality (Fenichel, 1945).

3. *Inferiority-feelings, compensation, and counteraction.* Contrary to common educated opinion, inferiority-feelings do not constitute an inferiority complex which is by definition unconscious. Surprisingly in some cases, inferiority-feelings may be a defense against more basic omnipotence feelings. On the other hand, compensation consists of carrying out activities which serve to "make up for" real or imagined deficiencies; too great anxiety results if the individual has to face his feelings of inferiority. Counteraction may be represented by the young lady who on receiving a coveted offer stated, "I'm thrilled, but humble."

She could not allow herself to be overwhelmed by joy and counteracted the joyful impulses by humility.

4. *Doubt.* When doubts cannot be dislodged by normally effective, rational methods, the suspicion is that they are employed defensively. Although the dynamics of doubt are probably very complex (Abraham, 1927; Freud, 1950), doubting may express ambivalence not toward the object or idea about which it is expressed, but toward seemingly remote impulses. At the very least, a doubter, a sceptic, need not act, hence his doubting is a defense against expressing his impulses one way or another.

5. *Passivity, avoidance, withdrawal.* Avoidance and passivity may represent attempts to get away from others, but may likewise represent a desire to keep from disclosing oneself to oneself. Walking alone is a fairly literal attempt to "get away from it all"; in the course of such activity the walker may be able to overcome his own feelings which made it necessary to get away in the first place. A "poker face" is one means of avoiding others' prying into one's emotions, and at the same time directly serves as an attempt to fool oneself into thinking he has no emotions. Seemingly meaningless rituals of everyday, like "How do you do?" or "How are you?" and "Oh, I'm fine," (when the one responding may be in misery) make sense in part as defenses against revealing to oneself as well as to others how one really does feel.

6. *Distortion, condensation, perceptual invention.* Schilder (1942) and Bartlett (1932) have demonstrated by introspective and objective methods the distorting and condensing activities of memory. According to Bartlett, memory is "functional" in the sense of altering incidents to suit the needs of the individual. In ordinary reproductions of materials perceived well enough to give an "impression," various changes occur to justify the impression; details may even be manufactured and others distorted to allow a reasonable setting for the impression. Changes and inventions in reproduced materials come about as a conventionalization process wherein unconventional and

---

[1] The "extremely busy" person who is so obviously escaping something as he or she goes from one activity to another desperately is close to being pathological. We are trying here to keep to relatively normal defense activities which usually succeed. Such a defense does not succeed.

unfamiliar incidents or objects are rationalized by being reduced to the more familiar and acceptable. Unable to tolerate the memory of a humiliating incident, a person gradually changes the incident to a less disturbing one.

Sublimation and the other successful and ordinary defenses are probably employed by the average person to a far greater extent than are the "unsuccessful and pathogenic" ones. The latter have been subjected to more clinical and experimental investigation. Consequently, a whole area of research is open in respect to ordinary defenses. But by the same token not a great deal of verified evidence can be adduced in their behalf. Most of the preceding section has come from the thoughtful observations of psychologists and others without benefit of either laboratory or clinical controls.

Unsuccessful and Pathogenic Defenses.[1] Anna Freud (1937) delineated nine of these defenses in her father's writings: regression, repression, reaction formation, isolation, undoing, projection, introjection, turning against one's self, and reversal. Others have added to the list until 16 or 17 fairly distinct defense mechanisms have been described. Any of these may be utilized by normal individuals, just as the most abnormal deviate in our society may employ the "successful" defenses. Inasmuch, however, as pathogenic defenses are by definition ones which do not achieve the purpose of satisfying both drive and society, and the classical defense mechanisms generally are not capable of doing so, the latter are more usually pathogenic.

Among the unsuccessful defenses is a spe-

cial class which Anna Freud called "permanent defense phenomena." These constitute an admission that success in certain directions is impossible. They are not defenses of a high energy-expending kind as are the other defenses. Such defenses become part of the permanent character structure of the personality, which now is limited and bounded but no longer required to expend great quantities of energy in "binding" tension.

Depth analysis of even balanced individuals would most likely reveal trends which if allowed to come to fruition would issue in the most pathological of defense functions. The average individual engages in defensive operations in order to "bind" tension, usually by means of successful defenses, but often also by the use of pathogenic ones. Indeed, students of psychology studying classical mechanisms of defense are more often impelled to say "Why, I show signs of all these!" than in their study of any other area of abnormal psychology.

SUMMARY

Topographically distinct from id in even the partly developed organism, the ego can be identified with neither self nor consciousness. It consists essentially of all the control functions of the personality. Its major sub-functions are (1) perception, (2) motility, (3) "binding" tension, (4) judgment, and (5) synthesizing. The first three are taken up in this chapter. Perception operates in part according to the organism's needs, shutting out and letting in as called for. Developing and maintaining "object relationships," and mediating awareness of self and roles are major sub-functions of perception. Not entirely distinguishable from perception, motility involves development of control over the motor apparatus; loss of such control or failure to develop it affects much of the entire personality. Motor patterns are found to be characteristic for individuals.

"Binding" tension is part of the tension-release cycle, but manifests itself in widely different patterns from society to society

---

[1] It is difficult to give credit for all the work done on these. Some basic references are: Abraham, *Selected Papers of Karl Abraham* (1927); Fenichel, *The Psychoanalytic Theory of Neurosis* (1945); Anna Freud, *The Ego and the Mechanisms of Defence* (1937); S. Freud, *Collected Papers* II, starting with "The Defence Neuropsychoses" (1924); Sears, *Survey of Objective Studies of Psychoanalytic Concepts* (1943) and "Experimental Analysis of Psychoanalytic Phenomena," in Hunt, *Personality and the Behavior Disorders* (1944); Symonds, *The Dynamics of Human Adjustment* (1946) and *Dynamic Psychology* (1949).

and individual to individual. Physiological and psychological tensions of an inordinate nature, anxiety in its various forms, is met by manifold defenses. A classification of defenses into successful and unsuccessful recognizes that some activities enable impulses to be expressed satisfactorily to the individual and society and some do not; countercathexis is employed in unsuccessful defenses, and conscious "self-control" in both types. Defenses sometimes are employed against "good impulses" as well as "bad." Successful and ordinary defenses include sublimations and those operating indirectly against impulses (*i.e.,* forgetting, negativism, pseudo-sexuality, clowning, pseudo-hostility, and perceptual-blocking), and those operating directly against impulses (*i.e.,* distraction devices, day-dreaming, inferiority-feelings, doubt, passivity, and distortion). Unsuccessful, pathogenic defenses are the common "defense mechanisms" and permanent defense phenomena which perform as part of the character structure.

QUESTIONS

1. What is meant by "ego"? Relate ego to self and to consciousness.

2. In what ways can perception be regarded as a control function? Discuss perception in relation to needs, awareness of self and others, and motor control.

3. Consider motility as a personality function.

4. How does tension "binding" differ from society to society and individual to individual?

5. Distinguish between successful and unsuccessful defenses against anxiety. Cite defenses which operate directly against impulses and others which operate indirectly. What are the pathogenic defenses?

CHAPTER 8

TOPOGRAPHICAL STRUCTURE-FUNCTIONS: EGO—II

In Chapter 7 three major ego functions were delineated: perception, motility, and "binding" tension. Attention was directed to the defenses against anxiety, especially to the ordinary defenses. Pathogenic and permanent defense phenomena were only mentioned in order to complete the picture. Returning now to the normal ego functions, we take up the two major sub-functions which remain, judging and synthesizing. In the last portion of the chapter, the concept of ego strength which has been made the subject of research and theorizing for some years is discussed.

ADDITIONAL MAJOR SUBFUNCTIONS OF THE EGO

Judgment

Reasoning and "reality testing" have been considered primary functions of the ego from at least the middle years of psychoanalysis.[1] Judgment (distinguishing truth

from fiction, rationally weighing alternatives, etc.) has been considered a function of "mind" for generations in psychology, having been designated as "thinking" or "reasoning" and sometimes "problem-solving." In personology we are not concerned with specific modes of thinking and reasoning; these are the concern of general psychology. Our interest is primarily in the dynamic structural position of judgment in the ego and in the "total personality." Additionally, from a personological viewpoint, several main aspects of judging, not ordinarily discussed in general psychology, may be distinguished.

Reality Testing. As the id operates according to an "unreality principle" (or "pleasure principle," according to Freud), that is, without regard to appropriate times or places for discharge of tensions, so the ego operates according to the "reality principle,"[2] that is, with due regard to considerations of appropriateness. It must be emphasized that these are "considerations of appropriateness," not what would necessarily be objectively appropriate. Here we have to take account of what has been said of the ego function of perception, part of which may be summarized by saying that percep-

---

[1] "We shall place reality-testing among the major *institutions* of *the ego,* alongside the *censorships* which we have come to recognize between the psychical systems . . ." From *The Standard Edition of The Complete Psychological Works of Sigmund Freud,* Vol. 14, p. 232. If we replace "institutions" by "functions" and "censorships" by defenses, we can see two major aspects covered in the text.

[2] Lewin's levels of reality and irreality are certainly applicable here. (Cf. Chapter 5.)

tual reality for the person may not correspond at times very closely to objective reality (Combs & Snygg, 1959; Solley & Murphy, 1960; Tuddenham, 1958a, 1958b; Tuddenham, MacBride & Zehn, 1958). One of the ego's functions is to try to bring perceptual reality and objective reality as close together as possible, to "test reality," first by reasoning and secondarily by verifying the results of reasoning by a comparison process.[1] In one way the whole of the scientific enterprise can be regarded as the operation of judgment in reality testing. Likewise, the process of development in the individual from infancy to old age is one of testing reality, "bumping one's nose against the hard facts of existence."

Both stimuli from inside the organism and environmental stimuli need to be subjected to the judging process. When is it appropriate for hunger impulses to be allowed satisfaction? In private or in public? Anywhere there is food, responds the American immediately, public or private makes no difference. (But considerations of class—"John, don't stop there, what if some of our friends should see us eating there!" —and of caste—"How can you *think* of eating with *them!*"—enter into American judgments of appropriateness.) For the Balinese, however, public or private expression of hunger impulses constitutes a question of shame (Mead & Macgregor, 1951). When is it appropriate for bladder tension to be relieved? In public or in private? Why, in private, of course, responds the American. But the Frenchman may reply that public or private has much less to do with expression of such impulses than other more important considerations. Testing of reality

involves weighing the strength of impulses against the time, place, and circumstances in which discharge may occur.

Thinking, Speaking and Impulse Control. Thinking is the heart of the judgment process; in fact, it is sometimes very difficult to make more than academic distinctions between thinking and judging, except that the latter seems to be inclusive of a decision process leading to action. Thinking helps to handle reality. Prior to the development of speech, thinking may be considered purely a means of reacting to whatever the individual perceives as real (Goodenough, 1945). The older behaviorist position (Watson's) maintained that thinking is implicit speech, but observations of animals (Fields, 1942; Kellogg, 1948) and of children not yet capable of speech (Gesell, 1943) fairly well dispel such a notion. And as Fenichel observes, there is a wordless state in all thought, something that goes beyond the capacity for verbalization. As a means of controlling reality, thinking may involve words, but need not always employ them.

When, however, speech and thought are conjoined in the individual, an enormous increase results in his ability to control himself and things external to him. There is first the *action* power of words. As the child gains control of an object, after a fashion, by learning its name, so most likely in the adult there is a residue of action-control in the words he uses to name objects. One can have more privileges of acting toward those whom one can name, especially by their first names; the very name is a form of control.[2]

Very closely associated with action power of words is the *magic* power of words. Although research on childhood language development has been very extensive, direct research on magic in children's use of words is very limited. Freud made the statement, "Words and magic were in the beginning one and the same thing . . ."

---

[1] Several processes are telescoped here. Hall and Lindzey (1954, ch. 4) make the distinction between "secondary process" and "reality testing" by saying that the former is mental-problem solving while the latter is the behavorial means of verifying the solution reached by reasoning. Such a distinction takes care of two important processes, testing appropriate discharge avenues in thought and comparing the actual discharge with the "objective facts." It is doubtful that Freud (1925, 1955) made the same distinction between reality testing and the secondary process.

[2] It may be pure happenstance that in slang usage a name is a "handle." Depth analysis, however, has taught us to be suspicious of such "happenstances."

(Freud, 1949). Piaget's work on children's language and thought processes (1926, 1930, 1952), one of the few attempts to put the widely accepted notion of children's use of word-magic to the test, appears to substantiate Freud's contention.

The use of words in a magical way is more evident among primitive individuals. A story well-known to Bible students is that of the "blessing of Jacob," recorded in the Book of Genesis. Under false pretenses Jacob persuaded his aging and nearly blind father, Isaac, to bestow the patriarch's blessing on him rather than on the rightful heir, Esau. Scarcely had Jacob left Isaac's presence before Esau came in with food prepared for his father to receive the old man's blessing.

"His father Isaac said to him, 'Who are you.' He answered, 'I am your son, your first-born, Esau.' Then Isaac trembled violently, and said 'Who was it then that hunted game and brought it to me, and I ate it all before you came, and I have blessed him?—yes, and he shall be blessed.' When Esau heard the words of his father, he cried out with an exceedingly great and bitter cry, and said to his father, 'Bless me, even me also, O my father!' But he said, 'Your brother came with guile, and he has taken away your blessing.' (Gen. 27:32–35, RSV).[1]

There is probably more than a hint of magical usage in many other expressions of the power of a word or the Word in the Bible. Frazer (1940) refers to the Sulka of New Britain who speak of their enemies as "Rotten tree-trunks" and believe that by so doing their enemies legs will become ponderous and clumsy. A thief, according to a Gaffre superstition cited by Frazer, may be reformed by shouting his name over a kettle of boiling water, clapping the lid on the kettle, and letting the name steep in the water for several days; the thief need not be aware of this procedure to be reformed.

[1] Reprinted by permission from *The Holy Bible*, Revised Standard Version published by Thomas Nelson & Sons, New York. Copyright 1946 and 1952 the National Council of the Churches of Christ in the United States of America.

However, there is a *real* power of words presumably growing out of their action power and magic power. This is the power resident in the interaction of the hearer and the perceived utterances of the speaker. A whole science of communication (Brillouin, 1956) has grown up in recent years concerned with how much information can be transmitted from agent to recipient. Telephonics engineers have been especially interested in "information theory," but psychologists and speech experts have taken part because of the human variables involved. Social scientists, including psychologists, have been attacking the problem of how we get our ideas across to one another. Whatever other means we use, and there are many, much of our communication is by words. And as the ultimate purpose of the communication seems to be to bring about action, words as a form of communication serve also as a form of control.

Both words and the "wordless states" of thought in the reasoning processes are used not only to control external objects directly or indirectly, but to control drives or impulses as well. One of the writer's counselees, a very moral individual, after living a number of years in a cloistered environment, found himself among those whose language regularly included terms not classed as the King's English. This counselee developed a mild compulsion in respect to the forbidden terms; he was in some fear that he might say them inadvertently, especially in company which would be shocked by some of the more obscene terms. He developed a substitution type of defense. Every time an unacceptable word tried to force its way into his consciousness, he formed similar more acceptable words which he said to himself, "darn" for "damn," and so on. The acceptable words after a fashion served to control the impulse toward profanity and obscenity. (This defense appeared to work well for some time, but would be classed as an unsuccessful defense because of the high amount of countercathexis necessary to maintain it.)

The judgmental process relating to the

control of id functions, beyond serving defensively, is associated with the second major ego function, mastery of motility. By "taming the wild impulses" the ego can direct them into purposeful action. Over and above reality testing for appropriateness of discharge is the process of directing id energies into the positive activities which make individual and social life possible. The highest pursuits of civilization must depend upon the purposeful utilization of the deepest-lying energies of individual personalities.

Besides control over physiological tension functions, judgment is exercised over what has been called "hallucinatory wish fulfillment." Piaget (1929) cites an example of a boy's thinking he could change the accuracy of his father's rifle shooting by changing the angle of his father's cigar which he was holding. This is one instance probably of both a worded and wordless magical thinking of this type. As the individual develops, controls are exerted over these wild imaginings which are transformed into useful imaginations or symbols (Fenichel, 1945).

Thus judgment is exercised through thought and speech as one of the means of gaining and maintaining mastery over id and environment.

Curbing Frustration. One special office of the judgment function of the ego is to meet and solve deprivation and frustration problems. Some authorities (Maslow & Mittelmann, 1951) distinguish deprivation from frustration; the former is a failure to meet needs of the individual which do not necessarily threaten him as a person, while frustration is privation which does so threaten him. Another authority (Hunt, 1944) has a somewhat parallel distinction in describing primary and secondary frustration. The former is really privation or deprivation, the latter is failure to meet a need because of the intervention of a "third party" or obstacle. An example of the first is hunger; the second is represented by being kept from eating by an unexpected visitor. Whether deprivation or frustration is involved, there has to be a judging

process by which either the emergency is foreseen and circumvented, or once having been encountered, it is controlled because means of handling it have been devised. That the process is not always successful is evident in some cases where the means of prevention or solution are at hand but the level of intelligence is not sufficiently high to achieve a solution; or it may be that neurotic difficulties prevent use of the intellectual capacities that are present. It is also evident that failure may result when the obstacles in the way of satisfaction of the need are too great, as in a famine.

"The Will." It may not be evident to the student of psychology that the concept of "will" or "will power," so common in everyday thinking, is virtually absent from the psychologist's thinking. William James (1892) devoted a whole chapter in his briefer course in psychology to "The Will." Today general psychology texts scarcely mention the term. When "will" or "will power" is mentioned at all, it is most likely either in a slighting fashion or in an endeavor to redefine the concept in line with our present knowledge of motivation. "Will is not," one text states, "a 'power,' but a term that represents the organization of habits and interests that make one motive dominant" (Dockeray & Lane, 1950).

In recent years the idea of "decision-making" has sneaked into psychology through a statistical back door (Diamond, 1957). Therefore, we are forced to devote some attention to "the will" which used to occupy a major position in psychology. We have made mention of "conation"[1] previously (in connection with Spearman, Chapter 4), but conation appears to be a composite of a number of functions, among which are several ego functions.

Whatever other conative functions there are, however, or whether conation includes "the will," willing, deciding, or choosing is certainly a function of the personality. The fact that psychologists cannot find a special energy called "will power," does not

[1] Conation is not exactly what is meant by "the will" either.

thereby eliminate one of the activities in which we engage continually. Judgment enters into the process of deciding, but it would appear to be only one element in decision-making, and perhaps not the most important. Theories of decision-making (Cronbach & Gleser, 1957) tend to assume that we are rational when we make our choices among alternative courses of action. But when we analyze *why* we make certain decisions rather than others there seem to be so many nonrational factors that the assumption appears untenable. By definition judgment as an ego function is rational. Consequently, wish-fulfilling tendencies which show up especially in clinical research as major components in our making choices of alternatives must be taken into account, as well as the rational judgment elements. Actually, in terms of modern psychology, what we are discussing is motivation, or in personological terms psychodynamics. The best we can say, then, is that "the will" probably refers to the conscious concomitants of motivation. Judgment, therefore, as both a conscious and unconscious function may include "the will" in the form of willing or choosing, but not even judgment comprises the whole of decision-making.

In summary, it can be said that judgment is first a process of "testing reality ahead of time," that is, the reality perceived by the individual. Both words and wordless states enter into thinking or judgment and the control of impulse and fantasy. Meeting frustration and making decisions may be subsumed under judgment, although decision-making is a function of many personality processes.

Synthesizing

The final and in many ways the crowning function [1] of the ego is its synthesizing one,

the task of bringing together the materials of life and endeavoring to achieve some kind of harmony with them. Employing the term "synthesizing" in its adjectival form, "synthetic," as occasionally is done in the following pages, does not imply that the functions to which reference is made are in any way "substitute" or "ersatz." The latter meaning of "synthetic" arose in Germany during World War II to designate substances, usually of an inferior nature, like the much-maligned "ersatz coffee," which were chemically constructed (synthesized) rather than produced from "natural" sources. Only the organic union or integration of elements implied by chemical synthesis is related to "synthetic" in the personological sense, not the "ersatz" aspect.

Submental Synthetic Functions. Whatever synthesizing factors there are in the structure of living matter at the molecular, atomic, and subatomic levels have to be assumed in personology. It may ultimately be that the individual capacities which each of us has for "holding things together" depend upon differences among our microscopic reciprocities and interdependencies, especially electrochemical processes (Overton, 1958). These may very well have considerable influence in those functions of the nervous system which make for individuality and relative strengths of synthesizing abilities, of memory functions, perceptual functions, and so forth. Regulatory forces within the cell, the structural unit of life, must make for some of our over-all personality differences in synthetic ability.

Whether the suggestion that intracellular differences in organizational (synthesizing) activity form a basis for higher synthesizing activities is accepted or not, however, we can see that there are synthetic functions of over-all organismic activity which may be defined as ego functions. Maintenance of body temperature, of pH concentration, of oxygen and carbon dioxide balance, of sugar content, and the bal-

[1] "A well-integrated ego implies that a person has a good ego-control instead of being impulsive, that he is able to concentrate his energies on tasks before him instead of scattering his efforts in aimless or destructive behavior; that he is able to harmonize his wishes and needs with those of individuals with whom he associates instead of being selfish and ego-centric; that he is able to pursue his objectives to a satisfactory termination; that he is not too easily disorganized and is able to tolerate frustration" (Symonds, 1951. Reprinted by permission).

ancing of other substances or processes seem to consist of a series of interrelated synthesizing functions. In the vertebrates, including man, the circulatory system and the nervous system serve as integrative agencies; the nervous system has a task beyond that of the former, for it has more direct connections with the external world, and thus takes part in a more complex type of synthetic function, that of harmonizing the internal activities of the organism with the external environment of the individual.[1] Homeostasis (Cannon, 1932) appears to appeal more to psychologists as a principle of regulation than it does to physiologists and biologists. Nevertheless, some principles, if not a principle, of harmonization and organization of various portions of the organism seem to be operative (Hartmann, 1948; Róheim, 1947).

Psychological Synthetic Functions. For the present we are more concerned in personality study with the broader synthetic functions of the ego, those we usually style "mental." Although we cannot neglect those physiological synthesizing activities which enter into broader psychological functioning, it is ordinarily the mental functions that differ sufficiently to enable us to separate individuals from one another. At any rate, we can distinguish one person from another more easily if we know about his higher ego functions than if we have only cell metabolism or temperature regulation on which to judge, even though we may recognize individual patterns of physiological processes.

As we take up specific synthesizing functions of the ego in this broader sense, it is well to recognize that there are *failures* of synthesis as well as *successes*. The discussion in Chapter 3 on interrelatedness and consistency of functions demonstrates the success and/or failure of individuals in their synthesizing of factors within and without. It is not entirely a matter of ego functioning, for regardless of success in organizing internal factors into a coherent whole, there are also roles which the individual plays which may appear inconsistent.

There are at least four major synthesizing subfunctions which can be classed together as the "synthetic function of the ego." These are: (a) remembering, (b) self formation and preservation, (c) character formation and preservation, and (d) reconciliation. The last has sometimes been taken as the sole content of synthesis (Symonds, 1951), but the others are organizing and integrating functions as well.

Remembering. The more usual designation of this function is "memory"; but in several places research has demonstrated the *dynamic* nature of storing and utilizing memories (*e.g.*, Bartlett, 1932), a factor not conveyed by the more static term "memory." One writer (Symonds, 1951) considers the memory function so important a part of the ego's tasks that he designates at least the *building* of memories as a major function of the ego, along with what we have called, following psychoanalytic usage, judgment, synthesizing, and "binding" tension. But it should be apparent that remembering, both unconscious and conscious, makes psychological (and physiological) synthesizing possible.

Insofar as any one individual is concerned, remembering begins before he is *conceived*. Such a paradoxical statement is clarified when we think that much of our total functioning as individuals is built into the structure of our organisms by heredity, the ways in which our nervous systems operate, our blood flows, our digestive organs transform food into organism, and our eliminative organs transform organism into environment, and the determination of "higher" processes of perception and possibly thought.[2] It does not seem necessary in

---

[1] Angyal (1941) insists that this is a "biological total process," that "life is a process which takes place between individual and environment."

[2] *E.g.*, the Gestalt "laws of perception" and possibly logical "laws" such as that of contradiction or of identity. While the "laws of thought" may not be part of external reality, as an idealistic philosophy maintains (Robinson, 1930), they may be part of the internal, inherited structure of the mind. It seems more reasonable to believe that our minds are not so much a *tabula rasa* when we are born as a *tabula groeve* (Middle Dutch for

this connection to adopt Jung's (1939) position that there are innate ideas and symbols (archetypes). But neither is it necessary to reject Jung's position merely because some psychologists and philosophers are frightened by the thought of innate ideas. All we need emphasize here is that *some* of our remembering is racial, genetically representative of the experience of the species.

Beyond these "memories" that are more or less common to all individuals, specific memories are formed which serve to integrate the individual to a lesser or greater degree. For legitimate purposes of analysis, it may be necessary to separate learning and remembering; but as we contemplate the personality of any one individual, these functions are not so distinct as they might appear. We can see that in the personality these functions are dynamically related. A *person* learns in order to remember.[1] If we go on [2] and ask why a person needs to remember, a good answer might include many more factors, but it would include at least this: Because there is need to tie together what has occurred at one time with whatever else has occurred, is occurring, or will occur at another time. The storing and using of memories is one means of synthesizing various parts of experience in time.

Self Formation and Preservation. Sometimes "ego" and "self" have been used interchangeably. In the view of personality offered here, they are considered not to be synonymous, though they are sometimes overlapping. Reference to the diagram of personality (Figure 14, p. 87) reveals the self (selves) to be both within and without

the ego, just as it (they) can be said to overlap id, superego, and role functions. Self and personality have sometimes been used synonymously, but such a usage is not acceptable, inasmuch as personality includes self. What then is the self? For purposes of keeping distinct the various portions of the personality, even though some may overlap, the self can be defined as those functions of the personality which have an "I" or "me" or "mine" quality. Like other functions which cannot be directly observed, the self must remain a construct, inferred to order or explain observable behavior. The self appears to be an object of value to the individual (Hilgard, 1949). It may be viewed from without as "personally involved attitudes" (Sherif & Cantril, 1947), or from within as the "phenomenal self" (Combs & Snygg, 1959), that portion of the individual which is subjective, the "personal viewer." [3]

Despite the fact that the self (used loosely to gather various selves into one term) is not only an ego function, it can generally be conceived of as a product of ego operations. Begun originally as an interaction between what others, especially mother or mother-surrogate, think I am and whatever there is present within my personality (including roles) which would modify the perception of what others think of me, the self is partly formed as a perceptual process (Mead, 1934). In addition, it is a perceptual-motor process. Not only does the individual perceive others, he perceives those portions of

---

groove or rut). Kant's analysis of the proleptic determination of perception and thought is not out of keeping with much of modern research.

[1] So broad a statement needs qualification. "Latent learning" experiments seem to indicate that there is no specific need, such as drive-reduction, which is met by much that we learn incidentally. There is still much argument on this point. But if we can allow such incidental learning, then the statement in the text could be translated, "Learning is of no economic value to the person unless it is remembered."

[2] We could go on indefinitely, of course, asking "why" until we traced motivational patterns to basic drives and social necessities.

[3] Symonds (1951) identifies the ego as the objective self and the *self* as the subjective self. Although his terminology is rather confusing, we can fathom his meaning, that the ego is the objectively observable portion of the personality which has such-and-such functions and the self is what is subjectively observable. In Moustakas' (1956) edited text on the self, there are so many contrasting concepts of the self that the array is bewildering. One factor which appears to be common to all writers in Moustakas' compilation is that self is taken almost uncritically to be one. Lecky alone of the writers seems deliberately to set forth his concept of the personality (self) as a completely consistent, unified structure (an organization of values felt to be consistent with one another).

the world which are different from others, that is, the physical portion of himself. By gaining control over this physical portion, he learns it is part of himself. The quotation from Gesell and Ilg cited in Chapter 7 in connection with motility serves also to convey how these concepts of the physical self develop, and it bears repeating:

He (the infant) spends many moments looking at his hands, fingering his hands, mouthing his hands. These sensory experiences,—visual, tactile wet, dry, still, moving, stop-go, oral, palmar, touching and being touched, provide him with a medley of data. By gradual degrees he comes to realize that he has a hand which feels when it contacts (active touch), which feels when it is contacted (passive touch), which feels when it moves (sense of motion, or kinesthetic sense mediated by sensory end organs in muscles, joints and tendons). His ceaseless manipulation, therefore, acquaints him not only with the physical universe and the physical presence of other persons, but with the physical presence of himself. (Gesell & Ilg, 1943).[1]

Throughout this self-development the judging-synthesizing process is in operation as well as perceptual-motor processes.

Not only self-formation but also self-preservation may be classified as an ego function (Hartmann, 1948). "Just as the id is directed exclusively to obtaining pleasure, so the ego is governed by considerations of safety. The ego has set itself the task of self-preservation, which the id appears to neglect" (Freud, 1949a). While the concept of self-preservation in all of nature goes beyond preservation of the *self* as it is understood here and elsewhere,[2] the operations which are usually subsumed under self-preservation include protection of that which is identified as I or me or mine in the specifically human sense.

Formation and preservation of the self also include building and maintaining self-esteem [3] (functions in which the superego

has a part as well). How the individual comes to value his self and develop thus a self-esteem is a complex process, apparently beginning with valuation by the original supplier of nourishment and with the feeling of being loved (Fenichel, 1945). Self-esteem is closely tied to the body at the beginning and possibly all the way through life (Symonds, 1951). Later experiences of success and failure may contribute to the valuation of the self, but the original feelings of self-esteem, developed in relation to one's parents, especially mother, *seem* to have more to do with how the person (ego, here) values himself than do his success experiences. The "seem" is emphasized here because there is strong debate especially between modern phenomenologists like Snygg and Combs and psychoanalytically inclined authorities as to the origin and continuance of self-esteem. The writer's clinical experience tends to bear out the contentions of the analysts; but presumably others (*e.g.*, Phillips, 1956) with different orientations find their ideas confirmed by their clinical practice, too. However, experimental evidence bearing on the regulation of self-esteem is presented in Chapter 9.

At the heart of client-centered therapy, which leans toward the position that therapeutic experience can change essential self-concepts without reorganization of the ego, is the change that is supposed to come in the counselee's self-acceptance. One hypothesis which the chief apostle of client-centered therapy, Carl Rogers, has maintained is, "In the course of therapy an experimental and effective type of learning about self takes place in the client" (Rogers, 1955). But Rogers grants that such an hypothesis might be difficult to prove at present. Whether the growth of self-esteem stems from the provision of early "narcis-

---

[1] Gesell, A., & Ilg, Frances L. *Infant and child in the culture of today.* New York: Harper & Bros., 1943. Reprinted by permission.

[2] That is, an amoeba can engage in self-preservation, but hardly in preservation of the self.

[3] Jack Block (1950) and Jeanne Block (1950) divide the ego into two parts, (a) ego need, the

need for self-esteem, and (b) ego control or ego structure, "the individual's characteristic means of handling or mediating both his internal need tensions and the demands imposed upon him by the external world." The writer considers establishing and maintaining self-esteem part of the control functions shared by the ego and its derivative, the superego.

sistic supplies" (food coupled with affection), and self-esteem thus always related to our earliest experiences, or whether there can be radical alterations in self-esteem in later life, it is partly an ego function to form and preserve such self-esteem; regulation of self-esteem *per se* may be a function which properly can be said to be specialized under superego functions (Chapter 9).

Formation and preservation of the self is probably a continual and never entirely successful process. To find out what parts of the world are *mine* and then to maintain these as mine is a complex process of synthesizing factors which are sometimes seemingly and sometimes actually disparate. What is mine? This body which keeps continually changing its substance? These impulses to do good or bad? Are these ideas mine which appear so good to me, so creative and sparkling, or are these others mine which keep intruding themselves as unbidden guests? Is this lodge or club or church in which *I* take an active part *mine*, even if *I* do not own it as *mine?* The pronoun "I" is one of the most common in usage in our language [1] (I guess so, I think, I believe, I hope, I'm sure, I did, I will, etc.). But who am *I?* The one who today drudges through the routine of daily tasks or the one who lives excitingly above the routine? The one who says, "Yes, sir." "No, sir," "Not yet, sir," or the one who dominates his family in Napoleonic fashion? Is it the one who at the beginning of therapy states, "I have absolutely no grudges against anyone," and from every indicator which we can observe he really believes he has none, or is it the one who as he reveals him*self* to him*self* comes to a realization that he has strong grudges against many persons—which self is "I" in this case? As was suggested in the discussion on the structure of personality, there may be unconscious links between these diametrically opposed self-attitudes, links which may make them appear less contradictory. Nevertheless, the struggle on

the part of the reasonable ego to bring together apparently unrelated factors each of which claims to be "the self" is not easy. So difficult is it in some cases that "depersonalization" occurs—whole portions of the self are disowned, including at times even portions of the body.

Character Formation and Preservation. The differentiation of "character" and "personality" cannot always be made distinctly. The German term *Charakter* means approximately what personality has meant to many English and American authorities. In a large sense of the term, character is a moral concept. It refers to the ways in which the individual *habitually* adjusts to the demands of the id and of the external world, and to the demands of the representatives of the external world, the superego and roles. Character, then, can be classed primarily as a psychological function of the ego, although these habitual modes of response are manifest in superego and roles as well as in strictly ego functions.

We could make the traditional distinction between *character* and *reputation;* but present-day socio-psychological analysis has tended to make obscure the lines between the two. Character, the popular saying goes, is what you are; reputation is what people think you are. In actual character formation, however, we become in part what people think we are. And yet, upon further analysis we find that there is an aspect of character which differentiates it from reputation in that a man may have an habitual *inner* mode of response which belies to some extent his *outer* modes (including his roles). Sometimes the difference is known to the individual, as in the legendary, and probably apocryphal, story of Galileo's remark after his recantation before the Inquisition. It is said that after he abjured his belief in the earth's moving about the sun he arose from his knees muttering, "Nevertheless, it does move." Although the story may be false, it is not untrue to a scientist's habitual mode of *thinking* in spite of his external behavior to the contrary, a situation that most likely occurs many times under totalitarian regimes.

[1] Though it is notable that some languages subordinate the "I" to a place only as part of the verb. Does this usage reflect a lack of self-distinction in some cultures?

Sometimes also it may be that what the person thinks his habitual modes of response are may not truly be his; he may believe, in other words, his own reaction formations which are the opposite of his more basic reactions.

It was stated above that in a broad sense character is a moral concept. We may lay emphasis upon the beliefs and values determining the habitual conduct of the individual (Urban, 1930) in respect to his society. In this respect then, superego functions are certainly present in character; and there are ego reactions to the superego. What the person habitually believes in matters of ethical import is a superego question. How he habitually obeys his superego dictates is a matter of character going beyond superego functioning itself. In our ways of adjusting to inner and outer demands there may be both "good" and "bad" [1] character displayed, as well as acquiescence or rebellion. Further, there may be "strong" or "weak" characters which may represent strong or weak egos. There may be various combinations of good and bad character traits, of acquiescent and rebellious ones, of strong and weak ones, and so on. The synthesizing abilities of the ego are not ordinarily, if ever, sufficiently strong to make for complete consistency of the various traits of character either within or among themselves or to make an individual a completely "good" or completely "bad" character.

In addition to the foregoing we may emphasize the usual considerations of "moral," that character has a moral aspect. By this is meant that character consists of the habitual adjustments an individual makes to the world at large, including man but more than man. The ways in which one regularly accepts or rejects the universe, cooperates with or endeavors to run counter to it, not only to the personal but the impersonal portions of the universe, constitute large portions of his character.[2]

The habitual modes of response called character are not entirely the result of the ego's synthetic efforts, but stem partly from the materials on which the ego's broader operations are performed. Whatever patterns of temperament enter into character, whether generally slow or easygoing or mercurial or melancholic, must in part be determined by genetic factors. Perhaps steadiness of character is as much metabolic as social. What the social and possibly the physical environment provide, however, also determines character. A wealth of research tends to confirm the concept that the human environment determines one's habitual modes of response to a considerable extent. Controlled research may or may not verify common views that the mountain or the desert, the country or the city, apart from their human aspects, "enter into the soul of man."

Reconciliation. Looked at in one way each of the subfunctions of the synthesizing activities of the ego is a form of reconciling. Specifically isolated here, though, are the harmonizings that must occur, or at least be attempted, among *conflicted* areas of the personality and between areas of the personality and external world conditions.[3] Although various areas of the personality need harmonizing with the external world and with one another, conflict is not the necessary outcome of this need. It is only

---

[1] As defined by the person's society.

[2] A scientist may be more "religious" in his reactions to the universe than many self-acknowledged religious persons, if one takes faith as a major mark of religion. The scientist trusts the operations of nature in a way which some "religious" people may not, for one of his assumptions is the "uniformity of nature." This assumption, or any other, need not be metaphysical (Pap, 1953), but may very well be arrived at inductively. The scientist does not wearily endeavor in every observation or experiment to prove that the results of his operations today will be the same tomorrow; he assumes that they will be. Some religious people on the other hand are apparently convinced of the capriciousness of the universe in that they have to cajole the powers that be either not to change or to change for some special purposes.

[3] Symonds' (1951) instructive section on synthetic functions of the ego concerns itself only with conflicted areas, "warring functions"; but other major synthetic functions do not necessarily exist to resolve *conflicts,* even though *differences* must be harmonized.

when there is competition among incompatible responses that there is conflict (Miller, in Hunt, 1944, Chapter 14). There may be a choice between wanting to engage in skin diving and fear of going into the depths of the water, but there is little conflict unless the desire and the fear are somewhere nearly equal. If they are not nearly enough equal to produce a "stable equilibrium," one response wins out, the response prompted by fear or by desire. When, however, these responses compete with each other on close to equal footing, there is conflict.[1]

In the first place, conflict may be between the entire or most of the personality and the world. "The time is out of joint; O cursed spite, That ever I was born to set it right!" was Hamlet's plaint. Yet it is not alone in fiction that one becomes convinced that the *man* may be against his times. The so-called "weeping prophet" of the Bible, Jeremiah, finally felt that everyone was against him, even the Lord who gave him the message that brought him into disrepute. "O Lord, thou has deceived me, and I was deceived, thou art stronger than I, and thou hast prevailed. I have become a laughing-stock all the day; everyone mocks me." (Jer. 20:7) Another case is that of the individual who is at odds with society, so that he "is in conflict with the law."

Solution to such conflicts as these, in which a personality is out of line with his society are sometimes beyond the capacity of the individual ego. In Jeremiah's case the prophet tried to cease his prophesying, but could not because of his inner compulsion. "If I say, 'I will not mention him, or speak any more in his name,' there is in my heart as it were a burning fire shut up in my bones, and I am weary with holding it in, and I cannot." (Jer. 20:9) He was going to withdraw, but his defense did not work: reconciliation as such was impossible. In Jeremiah's case as in that of many another prophet, not the man but the society must

be altered to solve the conflict. In the case of the criminal, where laws that have been found necessary to hold *any* society together are at stake, it may be that the primary conflict is not between the man and society but within the man, intrapsychic, so that his overt illegal behavior is an attempted solution of his internal conflict. The resolution of the conflict, ostensibly an overtone, must take place within. The man only uses society as a means to an end. Punishment is a means of relieving his guilt. (To be sure, not all criminal behavior is to be interpreted in this way.[2]) Here as in the case of the prophet, the solution of the overt or covert conflict may be beyond the ego's synthetic capacity.

Taking conflicts of a less extensive nature, we can sometimes see how the wishes of the id or learned (ego) drives are often at variance with the demands of the external world to a conflictful extent. Whereas in the "man against world" situation the intrapsychic nature of conflict is not manifest, here it is evident, for as long as the world's demands are not internalized to some extent, these may be experienced as *deprivation* or *frustration* but not necessarily as conflict. The difference among deprivation, frustration and conflict may be seen in animal experimentation. Sometimes an animal for various purposes is deprived of food; it is neither in conflict nor frustration (primarily), but is simply hungry. At other times a male animal may be frustrated by being excited in the presence of estrous females, then being removed before intromission can occur (Kagan, 1955); conflict is not present, but frustration is. On the other hand, conflict in laboratory animals has been induced on the model of Pavlov's "neurotic dog" who had to learn to discriminate between a circle of light and an ellipse. As the ellipse was reduced to the proportions of a circle, starting with semi-axes of ratio 2:1 and progressing until the ratio was 9:8, the animal could still differentiate to an extent between circle and el-

---

[1] Several types of approach-avoidance and approach-approach conflicts have been delineated by Miller (in Hunt, 1944) and by Miller and Dollard (1941; 1950). Lewin's analysis (1935, 1946) in terms of valences differs primarily in terminology.

[2] See Thorpe and Katz, *The Psychology of Abnormal Behavior* (1948), for a summary of theories of criminality.

lipse even at 9:8, but his behavior became pathological (Pavlov, 1927). In this case the dog was in conflict, not being able to choose between competing responses. The external world in the form of the experimenter, tones, rewards and other paraphernalia presented demands which called for responses of an incompatible nature, since the dog had internalized (learned) the demands of the environment. If we may use the term with dogs, the ego mechanism failed in its endeavor to provide a solution to the conflict. But, of course, all conflicts do not eventuate in breakdown; reconciliation can occur in many cases.

Drives and superego demands must be harmonized also, or at least attempts at harmonization must be made. The engaged person's superego introjections may include parents with strong disapproval of premarital intercourse; but often his proximity to the loved one arouses intense sexual urges so that strong conflicts are set up which must be met in one way or another by ego synthetic (reconciling) functions. Sometimes too, conflict occurs between superego demands and those of the external world. Young people whose consciences tell them it is wrong to engage in drinking or "partying" find themselves in conflict over the demands of two taskmasters. It is up to the rational, reality-facing functions of the personality to endeavor to harmonize demands like these. Perhaps such conflicts as those described are in terms of the self and the world. In this case it is often a matter of conflict between a concept of self and a role one must play or thinks he is expected to play. "With this (self) I identify, with that (role) I don't, yet I am expected to act as if I am like the role which is called for. I just can't imagine myself in that position." How to bring the conflict to a successful resolution is the ego's task.

Conflict of self with self has often been dramatized in world literature and in recent years in the scientific literature. Fenichel cites the example of a physician who in his analysis revealed that he had a feeling of wonder that a (grown-up) druggist should accept a prescription from him (a child) as an order to be filled; probably this conflict was between selves, between his still present child-self and his grown-up self. A woman psychologist (Calkins, 1915), whose researches involved the self from an introspective standpoint quotes a poem in which the poetess complains of having a self that likes to be polite, another that is mannish, another that loves solitude of an adventurous type, another that loves the solitude of the nunnery, a mother self, an ideal self, and a nonparticipant self (Calkins, 1907). That such a division among ourselves is not merely poetic fiction is attested by the contrast between our waking and sleeping "selves." This division is to be inferred also from the way in which the self (used as a collective noun) develops from often contradictory social perceptions (Sherif & Cantril, 1947; Snygg & Combs, 1949). The ego must struggle to bring these selves into harmony with one another.[1]

Within the ego itself may be inconsistencies which call for harmonization. Perceptions may be contradictory in whole or in part with one another. In certain parts of the world there are natural "optical illusions." A car rolls backward up grade, or what seems like up grade. People lean at an angle to the seeming horizontal, an angle which to actual horizontal is an impossible one. Amusement parks capitalize on the perceptual habits we have developed by constructing "crazy houses" which offer the same illusions. Psychology has constructed such illusions, especially under the impetus of Gestalt experimentation. These inharmonious perceptions arising from ego functioning call for reconciliation. One of the commonest questions in this connection is "Why is it? Why do we perceive in this way when we know it is false?"[2] Some kind of synthesis of such perceptions which

[1] The use of the term ego in this manner implies no reification; we are dealing with functions of the individual not homunculi.

[2] Both the perceptual habits and the inquiring mind may be learned in part and may differ from culture to culture. But there appears to be an inquiry of some sort about contradictions in many if not most cultures. Moses' turning aside to investigate a bush that appeared to be burning but

appear contradictory to normal ones is called for.

Related to illusory perceptions are differences between present perceptions and memories. Once more we emphasize that memory is not a static entity in the personality but a dynamic function. Therefore, even if the external situation stays relatively the same, a new perception may differ from the memory of the same object. What can be done to bring the memory and present perceptions together? The person may have changed in many other functions even if the object and the memory have remained relatively the same. How often have individuals returned to childhood scenes and found them disappointingly small. That great big barn is hardly much larger than a fair-sized house. That huge tree which took the courage of Daniel to climb seems of ordinary size now. The lane which long ago seemed endless is in actuality only a few car lengths. Present perception and memory do not jibe, but the reasoning ego declares, "You were only a small youngster then. Everything seemed much larger to you as a child than it does to you as an adult." And the explanation is usually satisfying (consciously at any rate, although the lingering disappointed feeling may indicate that unconsciously the same acceptance has not been accorded the rational explanation).

In a related manner it has been suggested (Symonds, 1951) that one of the ego's tasks is to reconcile "the painful past and the hopeful future." By this is meant that a tendency to avoid scenes and activities which represent past failures has to be overcome by a discrimination process of subjecting past situations to analysis in order to determine what led to failure so that future activities may be more successful. As such a discrimination process, this function seems to involve only judgment which would not of necessity be reconciliation. But taking the psychological past, present, and future as does Lewin (Chapter 5) we

can see how vast a reconciling task there is for the ego. Psychologically, we live not only in the past (remembering) and present (perceiving) but also in the future (hoping, expecting, fearing). Consequently, just as perception and memories must be harmonized, so an attempt to bring the psychological future into line with the past and present is a necessary endeavor on the part of the ego.

Joint id- and ego-derived conflicts call for reconciling by the synthesizing capacities of the ego. How difficult a reconciling task this is can be judged from the way sometimes "our imaginations run away with us."

Does the following monologue reflect *only* a counselee's fantasy? It seems not. "And people will look at me and say, 'There goes B——. He's the one who did that marvelous piece of work.' And the other guy'll answer, 'You don't have to tell me what he did. Who doesn't know about it?' And one of the things that'll please me most is that old fat George will have to eat crow. The son of a b—— has kept me from getting anywhere—you know the story, I told it to you before. Old man J——'ll call him in and tell him off, 'What's the matter with you? This whole damned organization is in disgrace now because we haven't given him any real recognition. And *you're* the guy'——no, the 'one,' old man J—— wouldn't use such undignified language—you're the one that's responsible.' I wouldn't want George fired, he's got too nice a wife and kids, but I'd like to see him sent back to the sticks. I'll get big offers, and when G—— C——— Company has signed me on, I'll go in to old man J—— and tell him if he wants to hold on to good men he's going to have to change some of the policies around here."

Under normal circumstances there is an effective, if imperfect adjustment of hard realities with fanciful imaginations which is more or less satisfactory. Sometimes, however, the process fails and the individual turns to the never-never world. At this point the ego has broken down in its function of adequate reconciliation.

A final reconciling task is adjustment of role with role. It may be that the roles are

---

not consumed comes from a primitive people's experience (Exo. 3), "ego-involved" [1] ones, so that the reconciliation is of self with self as discussed previously, as well as role with role—in some instances it is almost impossible to make the distinction between self and role. The case may be that one role is ego-involved, another not. Or neither role may be deeply ego-involved, for the person may play his roles "for duty's sake" or because convention requires it, but may never identify with them so much as to say within, "This is my role." Sometimes, then, the ego-reconciliation process may be on a fairly superficial level. "Neither the organization nor its members means very much to me," a friend said, "but I got to thinking that it didn't look right for me to be a member and not accept some responsibility, so I took the office when they offered it to me. I did the job well—several said better than they'd seen it done before—but I never really got into it—myself." Reconciling such roles with others of a similar nature does not require alterations within the ego or self to speak of.

When, however, the individual has accepted as "mine" various roles, the conflict over contradictory aspects of these roles may reach to the depths of the personality. A counselee was referred by the courts for engaging in pederasty under a suspended sentence on the condition of taking treatment. Some of the important roles he was playing were being husband to a social-climbing wife, father to two teen-age sons, a salesman in a medium-sized concern, and paid director of a large church choir; one additional role of whose extent he was only partly conscious was being son to a still very domineering mother. To reconcile the role of homosexual and seducer of boys with these other roles was, as can well be imagined, a tremendously difficult, even impossible, task.[2] What was very distressing to the counselee was the high invest-

ment he had in each of the roles, high ego-involvement, or high cathexis in psychoanalytic terms. Under "normal" circumstances the roles may not have so much element of conflict in them as in the roles of this individual.

Reconciliation thus must be undertaken by the ego when incompatible responses are called for. The personality as a whole may be in conflict with the world; or id and superego demands must be harmonized within or between themselves. Self may clash with self, perceived past with perceived present and future or even present perception with present perception; and combining other conflicts, role may conflict with role. Among the synthesizing functions of the ego, reconciliation is not least in importance and is perhaps the most difficult.

Considering the synthesizing functions of the ego all together, an outstanding psychologist spoke along similar lines as our discussion, cautioning that the synthetic function [3] is a process, not a completed activity in any case:

The healthy self, however, will achieve an integrative organization. Note that I say integrative and not integrated. It is the integrative personality which can handle the complexity of relationships with other persons in a culture like ours, a culture which makes plural demands. An integrated personality soon leads to its own isolation or destruction if it is not also integrative. Lest this seem to be an idle play on words, let me point out that the paranoid psychotic with highly systematized delusions is among the best integrated of personalities. He is integrated but not integrative (Hilgard in Brand, 1954).[4]

These, then are the main functions of the ego: (1) perception, (2) mastery of motility, (3) binding tension, (4) judgment, and (5) synthesizing. These are all "control functions" which together consti-

---

[1] Really "self-involved" as the term is used in this text. "Is it mine?" is the question. In psychoanalysis the expression is "cathected."

[2] In ancient Greece the man's ego would have had an immeasurably easier time of it. Cf. Fisher, *The Beginnings of Christianity* (1916).

[3] Hilgard in Brand (1954) does not call it the synthetic function but means the same thing.

[4] From *Human motives and the concept of self* by E. R. Hilgard in Brand, H. *The study of personality.* New York: Wiley, 1954. Reprinted by permission of *Amer. Psychologist.*

tute the ego. An attempt has been made to be exhaustive in the listing, but there is no guarantee that something perhaps very important has not been omitted. (No pretense at thoroughness of coverage of individual functions is made; each of them deserves a book by itself.) Overlapping as these functions may be, they can be delineated sharply enough to be recognized as separate functions within the ego.

Ego Strength

A number of authorities have used the concept of "ego strength." Roughly, the term refers to the degree to which the ego succeeds in performing its respective functions. In one Rorschach text (Klopfer, Ainsworth, Klopfer, & Holt, 1954), it is suggested that the main ego strength components are reality-testing, emotional integration, self-realization, and mastery of reality situations. These components are given coordinate scores on the Rorschach to indicate whether an individual is high or low in ego strength. It is to be expected that an individual may show different degrees of strength and weakness in different areas. Not only in Rorschach theory, however, is ego strength an important concept.

Qualitative criteria of ego strength, which might in the long run be quantified, are detailed in one influential text (Kluckhohn, Murray, and Schneider, 1953). These criteria cover the general areas of perception and apperception, intellection, and conation, areas which overlap the major sub-functions outlined in these chapters on the ego; more emphasis is placed on conation in the other treatment than we have given. Conation seems to be a function of the entire personality more than it is of the ego; accordingly, it is given fuller treatment in Chapter 16 which takes up styles of life and directional trends.

Quantitative criteria of ego strength are found in various scales, some of which explicitly speak of ego strength. Most of the so-called "personality inventories" and "behavior schedules" endeavor to assess some aspects of the omnibus quality of ego

strength.[1] Part of the problem in psychiatric and psychological screening of military personnel is to assess ego strength in a gross way. Objective scales may be used in such screening, especially by the psychologist.

A pioneering attempt to measure what we would now call ego strength resulted in the discovery of a factor called "w" which was derived by Spearman's factor method (Webb, 1915). This factor, on which different scores may be obtained indicating more or less strength, represents persistence of motives, depending upon consistency of action resulting from deliberate volition or will. (Cf. Chapter 14 for further elaboration of this factor.) Eysenck (1947) believes that his *Neuroticism* factor corresponds to the negative of "w." Cattell's *Ego Strength-vs-Proneness to Neuroticism* (Cattell, 1957) also seems to parallel "w" but is more inclusive than the latter which is principally conative. On Cattell's factor one measures as stronger or weaker in being emotionally stable, free of neurotic symptoms, not hypochondriacal, realistic about life, unworried, steadfast and self-controlled, calm and patient, persevering and thorough, and loyal and dependable.

One very important research project (Peck, 1958) by two teams of social scientists discovered a factor which comes close to Cattell's and is likewise labeled *Ego Strength*. Characterizing this factor are the elements of emotional maturity, locus of concern (from egocentric to altruistic), internal consistency (roughly, personality integration), rationality of behavior, accuracy of self-perception, accuracy in assigning responsibility (to self or others), accuracy of social observation, functioning intelligence (largely, test-IQ), insight into others' motives, autonomy (inner-directed), relations with same-sex peers (positive), and positive feelings toward mother. The major problem of most attempts to measure ego strength (or any aspect of personality) by questionnaire or inventory methods is circumvented in this research;

[1] Cattell (1957) has quantified the concept by factor analysis.

the problem is to find how closely related the artificial measure is to actual ego strength manifest in "real life." Because the investigation reported here was a longitudinal study of children from ages 10 to 18, and a great deal of the assessment of their behavior came from "real life" situations, it is impressive that mathematical treatment of the data resulted in so coherent a factor and one which matches so clearly the clinically-derived concepts of the ego and ego strength.

Possibly the most extensively investigated scale of ego strength is Barron's Es which was developed from Minnesota Multiphasic Personality Inventory items. In research (Barron, 1953a) on patients who before psychotherapy had received several tests, including the MMPI, it was found that the latter predicted the outcome of therapy with a fair degree of accuracy. When, however, 68 specific items were selected on the basis of their ability to forecast improvement, the scale, called the Ego-Strength Scale (Es), in several cross-validations with both clinical and nonclinical samples showed differences between normal and clinical subjects and a moderate degree of correlation with Improvement-Unimprovement in therapy (Barron, 1953b). Because of the kinds of items which constitute the Es and its correlation with other measures, its author suggested that the test is an "estimate of adaptibility and personal resourcefulness," of "effective personal functioning," and represents a "capacity for personality integration," all of which could well be considered descriptive of strength in ego functioning, especially of synthesizing.

A number of studies (Barron & Leary, 1955; Cartwright, 1956; Quay, 1955; Taft, 1957; Wirt, 1955) offer support to the Es as a discriminator between patients who improve and those who do not and between clinical and nonclinical groups. Of great interest to students of personality is the finding in one re-examination of a study which did not at first seem to differentiate between patients who had therapy and those who had not had it (Barron &

Leary, 1955). The re-appraisal of the first study (Cartwright, 1956) revealed that *individuals* differ in relation to the effects of therapy or of remaining on a waiting list. Distinctions between normals and patients holds up in another, the Australian, culture (Taft, 1957).

Reasoning that if the Es is an indicator of ego strength, it should be able to differentiate between diagnosed patient groups with presumably different degrees of ego strength in terms of psychosis and psychoneurosis, investigators (Tamkin, 1957; Tamkin & Klett, 1957) administered the Es to several such groups, but found no significant differences. Although to a small degree these negative studies support the interpretation of Barron's scale, their general pattern suggests that the Es is not as overall a measure of ego strength as originally assumed. The question is, therefore: to what extent does the scale cover the areas of ego functioning?

Some of the postulated elements of ego strength have been found in a factor-analytic comparison of the Rorschach and Es (Williams & Lawrence, 1954). One of the factors discovered in this study shows, along with high loadings (correlations with the factor) for Es, a wide range in the use of different categories of Rorschach responses, an ability to perceive the blots as organized wholes, and a capacity to be open to stimuli from outside oneself—all capacities related to ego functioning discussed in this chapter.

One aspect of ego strength which we might suppose should be measured by any scale, the ability to "bind" tension, appears to be assessed by the Es (Grosz & Levitt, 1959). Twelve normal subjects were administered the Es under waking, ordinary hypnotic conditions, and in an hypnotic anxiety state. Under the anxiety instructions—which were intense—the scores on the scale decreased significantly, presumably because the subjects could not handle the tension as well as in their normal states.

A breakdown of the Es items by factor analysis (Crumpton, Cantor, & Batiste, 1960) uncovers some of the reason for the discrepancies in validational studies. The generality of the test, as suggested above, is upon inspection of the results, found to be considerably less than complete; but it is still sufficient to cover a number of areas one might expect in a gross measure of ego strength. Of fourteen factors extracted, six seem reasonably interpretable. One refers to freedom from phobic and schizoid symptoms. A second represents a kind of resistance to being "pushed around." Freedom from guilt and obsessive anxieties is apparently the essence of one factor, as is freedom from neurasthenic symptoms that of another. Still another factor indicates degrees of adequacy in interpersonal relations. The last fairly clear factors seems to measure heterosexual attitudes. Because the majority of factors appear to be measures of freedom from symptoms rather than of positive qualities, the investigators declare that the scale seems to be misnamed, that it ought to be "ego weakness" rather than "ego strength." They feel that a scale of ego strength ought to measure positive qualities, one that should be able to differentiate with greater definiteness between the well-adjusted and ill-adjusted subjects in their analysis.

We can agree with the conclusions of the last paragraph, but recognize that the criticism of the Es is not to be limited to that scale only. As an attempt to assess ego strength it seems to be as good as anything we have. The Es, its parent, the MMPI, and many other instruments in the personologist's armamentarium are derived from abnormal personalities. They are couched in terms of psychopathological symptomatology. Therefore, strength is represented by the absence of the latter. On the physical level, to be sure, it is probably easier to define illness than wellness (even the awkward term signifies something, for good health is not merely the absence of ill health). That the Es does measure some positive aspects of "effective personal functioning" is so much to the good.

When a construct has been hypothesized, such as ego in this case, and scales have been devised to measure its relative strength in the individual, psychologists wish to test under controlled conditions various predictions made on the basis of theory as to what an individual with a certain degree of the quality will do.[1] A good illustration of such a test of one major aspect of ego strength is a series of experiments on what the experimenters call "ego control" (defined as the individual's characteristic mode of handling his need tensions). In this series (Block, J., 1950; Block, J., & Block, J. L. H., 1951; Block, J. L. H., & Block, J., 1952; Block, J. L. H., & Morton, 1955), one of the experiments (Block, J. L. H., & Morton, 1955) carried out interesting variations of the famous study of frustration and regression by Barker, Dembo, and Lewin (1941). A group of children were divided into those who were called Under-controllers and Over-controllers on the basis of two tests of "ego control" (and a ranking by observers). In one test children were allowed by means of a crank to raise pieces of candy one at a time in a little cart which emptied into a large glass vessel. The child was told the game would be over when he stopped to eat any candy, but that he could have as many pieces of candy as he put in the jar. The conflict situation of wanting to eat candy and of wanting more candy to eat was presumed to test the child's capacity to "bind" tension, his "ego control." Scoring this test consisted merely in counting the number of pieces of candy put in the jar before the child ate any candy.

The other test of "ego control" in this series involved Lewin's theory of permeability of boundaries within the personality. Predicting that Over-controlling youngsters would show less decrement in constructiveness of play and less overt, verbal or physical, desire to get beyond the frustrating barrier, and Under-controllers more of each behavior (and intermediate controllers in between), the experimenters placed the children in the Lewinian frustrating situation. For 30 minutes each day

[1] What is called the "predictive validity" of a test (Technical, 1954), although other elements of validation may be found here.

the children played with ordinary toys with a wire mesh barrier visible, but no toys beyond it. After three days they were again brought into the room, this time behind the barrier where now very attractive and desirable toys awaited them. Just as they became highly involved with these toys they were led to the other side of the barrier where only the ordinary toys were found. Quantitative measures were then taken of the amount of time spent at the barrier expressing desire to get at the delectable toys and of the constructiveness of the play with the more prosaic toys during the frustration period. (The children were allowed to return to the desirable toys for a period following the experiment.) Both predictions concerning constructiveness of play and barrier behavior during frustration were modestly supported. Overcontrollers tended to show less decrement in play and less time in direct expression of frustration at the barrier. For our purposes the most important aspect of this experiment is not the result *per se*, however, so much as it is that quantification of "ego control" (as one measure of "ego strength") determined in one life situation enabled prediction to another life situation where presumably "ego control" would operate to bring about measurable differences among individuals.

Summary

The fourth main sub-function of ego, judgment, subsumes reality testing and, in part, thinking and speaking; thought and speech assist as means of control over impulses and wishes. Deprivation and frustration problems are met by judgmental controls. Decision-making or "the will"

(conscious concomitants of motivation) is also in part a judgment function.

Last of the identified major sub-functions of ego is synthesizing, which begins in biological, homeostatic mechanisms, but includes psychological functions as well. These latter are: remembering, both genetic and learned; self-formation and preservation, including building and maintaining self-esteem; character formation and preservation, forming in conjunction with other functions the person's habitual modes of adjusting to inner and outer demands; and reconciliation of conflicted areas: of personality and world relations, of id and superego, of self and self, of ego function and ego function, of past and future, of id and ego, and of role and role.

Criteria of "ego strength" include aspects of all control functions. One need, to quantify measures of ego strength, has been met in part by some researchers.

Questions

1. In the judgment process what is meant by "appropriateness" in respect to reality testing?

2. How do speech and thought serve as control functions?

3. Illustrate the judgment process in curbing frustration.

4. What place does judgment have in decision-making? Discuss "the will" and "will power."

5. As a synthetic function (synthesizing function) how does memory operate?

6. How are the self and character formed and preserved?

7. In what types of conflicts is reconciliation needed?

8. What is meant by "ego strength"?

CHAPTER 9

TOPOGRAPHICAL STRUCTURE-FUNCTIONS: SUPEREGO

The Freudian "trinity," as is well known, has one other major element in its constituency besides id and ego, that is, the superego. In the view of personality maintained here there is still another, a fourth, major element of personality topographically considered, the role functions. Now, however, we take up the third major distinguishable function, the superego. Once more it is well to recall that there are no sharp distinctions which can be made between these major part-functions of the personality. They overlap one another in their operations and shade so imperceptibly into one another, that of a particular subfunction it may at times be said it is a joint operation of several major functions or at other times that we cannot be sure where to categorize it. Since all of the categories and classifications which can be employed are to an extent arbitrary anyway—nature, including human nature, not being neatly divided up into obsessive-compulsive-classes— we should expect some fuzziness at the (functional) boundaries we have set up.

REGULATION ACCORDING TO SOCIETY'S DEMANDS

What is the superego? [1] It is, broadly speaking, that set of control functions of

[1] Most of the following is based on Freud (1923, 1924, 1925, 1949a, 1950) and Fenichel (1945) with

the individual which regulate his behavior (including thought and affects) in accord with what the individual believes are the ethical and conventional demands of society. But someone may say that the ego is supposed to include all the control functions of the individual. Now does he say that there is another set of control functions relating to certain of society's demands? No, not another set, but a special set *within the ego.* Freud called the superego "a step within the ego" and "a precipitate in the ego." In the origin of the superego discussed below it can be seen what Freud meant by these terms. It is only necessary here to recognize that the superego is not, any more than id or ego, a separate "entity" in the personality, but only a recognizably distinct set of functions. These functions are distinguished by their "oughtness," and by the guilt which arises if any of the prohibitions or standards are violated. Often, the superego is conceived of as divided into two major portions, the conscience and the ego ideal.[2] These have been interpreted respectively to mean the self-

incidental reference to Alexander (1948) and to Hall and Lindzey (1954, ch. 4).

[2] Kluckhohn, *et al.* (1953) speak as if the ego ideal and superego are separate from each other; but they seem to mean conscience when they speak of superego, so that together conscience and ego ideal would—if integrated—constitute what others have conceived of as superego.

judging portion which metes out punishment when the rules are broken and second, that part which sets the rules. There are reasons why the two aspects should not be separated (Fenichel, 1945; Freud, 1927). Here the distinction is observed, but the two aspects are subsumed under several functions related to the self and character.

There is another distinction within the superego which has not commonly been made, yet it is one that needs emphasis. It is the difference which can roughly be made between elements of the superego which have reference to actual moral commands and those which refer to conventions, customs, and traditions not imbued with primary moral denotation. These latter "folkways" of a people may be internalized by the individual even if, for society as a whole, they are not classified with demands possessing the character of "mores" or morals. Sometimes an individual is much more distressed by his violation of a social custom, such as a breach of table manners, than he is by what he considers to be a "moral problem." Freud recognized the class of extra-moral characteristics which can enter the superego in his posthumously published *Outline of Psychoanalysis:* ". . . what is operating is not only the personal qualities of these parents but also everything that produced a determining effect upon them themselves, the tastes and standards of the social class in which they live and the characteristics and traditions of the race from which they spring." (Freud, 1949).

Not enough has been made of this distinction in research on the superego. The fact is that a person can engage in just as strict self-judgment for his violations of relatively amoral customs as for violating those of acknowledged moral character (Dreger, 1960c). Such a fact should give rise to serious questions as to what the society as a whole *really* values—which is a social psychological question—and then as to what happens in the individual to enable him first to detect what society actually values most and second to internalize such values—which is a personological question.

The writer is keenly aware of such questions in regard to the predominant social issue of the American South where he resides. For many southern whites, violation of the social custom forbidding eating with Negroes appears to generate more distress than flagrant flouting of widely accepted ethical standards, such as "Do unto others as you would that they should do to you"— when these standards have reference to the other race. The confusion of ethical and customary issues and the resultant superego anomalies according to which more guilt and pain are felt in respect to the latter than the former can be found indirectly demonstrated in such works as Dollard's *Caste and Class in a Southern Town* (1937) and Myrdal's comprehensive summary in *An American Dilemma* (1944). Considerably more research needs to be done on the personological significance of well-known sociological data concerning rigid adherence to amoral and even antimoral social expectancies.

RELATIONS TO EGO, ID, AND ROLES

Ego functions derive their energy from the id as the transmitting source of energy. So, too, as a portion of the control functions, superego receives its energy from the drives we have classified in the id. But superego functions are peculiar in that they serve to regulate release of the very impulses (instincts) which give them life in ways that may go directly contrary to those impulses. Psychoanalysis expresses the situation by stating that the superego is that portion of the id which has been changed into counter-instinctual energy. This portion of the control functions is that which determines which impulses are and which are not acceptable. In this case, acceptable means what the individual believes to be acceptable to society. Functions which are classified primarily as ego functions, those of perception and judgment especially, thus enter into superego operations in performing the latter's counter-instinctual tasks.

There can be harmonious relations

among the functions of id, ego, and super-ego, as the demands of the id may be handled in a directly satisfying or sublimated fashion in such a way that the external world's demands as mediated by the super-ego are also met.[1] An instance of this harmony can be seen in a happy marital relation where the striving id, the judging ego, and socially-oriented superego are "satisfied" by the married person's sexual behavior.

On the other hand, conflicts can occur between the superego and each of the other sets of functions, as the id seeks outlet in ways that violate society's demands embodied in the superego, or the rational considerations of ego are confronted with irrational prohibitions or standards which are internalized in the superego. A common instance of the former type of conflict is found in the individual whose aggressive drives seek expression directly against an offending person, but brought up in a middle class American culture he has internalized the parental admonition, "Good boys don't fight." A common example of the second type of conflict is that in which a woman has so thoroughly internalized the strictures against releasing sexual tensions that under circumstances where all the reasonable portion of her nature says that it is legitimate and rational to give herself up to her sexual urges, she cannot. It is *as if* the ego were saying, "You are married to a man you dearly love. You have the sanction of the church and the state, of parents and friends, of custom and convention. You are free to engage in and enjoy sex activities." But *seemingly* a harsh superego says, "O, no you don't! You cannot engage in or enjoy sex. Sex is bad. It is wrong." Whether such an imaginary dialogue occurs or not,[2] reliable surveys of sexual behavior (Kinsey, Pomeroy, Martin, & Gebhard, 1953; Terman & Miles, 1936) reveal a high incidence of frigidity among women;[3] and psychoanalytic studies (Benedek, 1952; Deutsch, 1944) indicate that a good many of the frigidities are psychogenic in origin, representing in general a conflict between the drives of the woman and her interpretation of society's prohibitions.

Intimately related as it is to ego and id functions, the superego is also bound up with many role functions.[4] The superego is involved indirectly in determining some role functions, as the (judging) ego decides that certain roles will not be played, or that certain ones will be played, else guilt feelings will result. Whenever there is conflict over what role the individual should play, there is also operation of the superego. The conflicts of aggressive and sexual drives with conscience demands mentioned above, may be interpreted in orthodox Freudian terms as intrapsychic, or they may (not contradictorily) be interpreted in modern social psychological terms as role conflicts: "Shall I play the role of a

---

[1] It is neither in keeping with Freudian thought nor with a logical analysis of the functions of ego and superego to say that "In every sense, the superego stands in opposition to the ego" (Lindzey, 1954, ch. 4). Freud spoke in connection with this point that an investigation of normal, stable states is not profitable for learning about the psychic structure, for in such states besides a relative balance of the ego and id, ". . . the superego is not distinguished from the ego because they work harmoniously" (Freud, 1949). And Fenichel, in speaking of neurotic conflict states, used the simple formulary that at times the conflict is ego and superego vs. id, and at others id and superego vs. ego. Further, from a logical standpoint it would be a completely neurotic world if in every individual the reasonable, judging, reality-considering portions of the personality were always at odds with the demands of conscience. We are neurotic enough without that!

[2] In many cases the person does actually verbalize at least to himself some of his conflicts.

[3] Kinsey (Kinsey, Pomeroy, Martin & Gebhard, 1953) reports on previous studies: The average from all studies is about one-third of all married women.

[4] Here we depart from at least Freudian expression if not meaning. It may be argued that orthodox psychoanalysis has not taken the social field functions of the personality into account; but under various forms of expression it seems that Freud recognized these, even though he never formally incorporated them into his concepts of psychic structure. He did say concerning the ego ideal (superego), "In addition to its individual side this ideal has a social side; it is also the common ideal of a family, a class, or a nation." From *The Standard Edition of the Complete Psychological Works of Sigmund Freud*, Vol. 14, p. 101.

fighter or pacifist?" "Shall I play the role of wife or of (infantile) daughter to my parents?" and so on.

UNCONSCIOUS OPERATION OF SUPEREGO

Among the ancients, Aristotle allowed only a possibility of the "moral virtue's" being unconscious.[1] A less systematic but more penetrating analysis is that of Jesus, "Out of the *heart* are the issues of life."[2] Kant protested against "psychologizing" the sense of obligation, by which he meant that conscience cannot be reduced to the results of forgotten associations with early pleasurable or unpleasurable consequences. He was not thereby denying that some of the roots of the present content of conscience are forgotten. On the whole, however, Kant and most ethical thinkers from the Greeks until nearly the current era have regarded conscience as almost entirely conscious (Sidgwick, 1931).

It remained for contemporary thought to recognize that a great portion of the conscience may be unconscious. However, some counselors may not find anything unconscious (Phillips, 1956), but others (*e.g.,* Bergler, 1948) are convinced that the individual is driven to certain forms of behavior by an unconscious superego.[3] Postulation of a portion of the superego beyond the boundaries of consciousness does make plausible some otherwise inexplicable phenomena. There are acts in which we engage about which we say, "I feel good about that (or bad)," but we honestly add, "I don't know why." Somewhere in our development associations of a superego nature have been made and we have forgotten the connections. The particular operation seems to be unconsciously determined, whether repression or some other type of forgetting has taken place. (Cf. Chapter 11.) In defining the self (selves), as discussed in the later portion of this chapter, behavior which seems to be unconsciously determined has been experimentally demonstrated. Wolff's work (1933, 1935, 1943) on expressive movements (Chapter 3) has been followed up in more recent years by comparisons between schizophrenics and normals in the ability to evaluate themselves from their expressive products (Epstein, 1955). In this experiment, samples of the expressive behavior of four persons including his own, obtained surreptitiously, were presented to each subject. These samples were voice recordings played backwards, handwriting presented upside down and in mirror image, voice recordings played forwards, handwriting rightside up and in mirror image, first names presented tachistoscopically, and figure drawings. Subjects rated the samples for liking for the persons who produced the samples and for degree of similarity to their own behavior products. Only three out of the 60 subjects identified their own voices or handwriting. And yet, for the group as a whole there is a strong positive relation between liking and similarity ratings, *i.e.,* the greater similarity to his own behavior the subject rated the expressive behavior the more liking he expressed for the producer (who in the extreme was himself!). Unconscious self-evaluation appears to have been operating, because so few subjects recognized their own work.

Inconsistencies and lacunae in respect to moral standards also appear explicable in terms of an unconscious portion to the superego. Often the question is asked, "Will

---

[1] In the *Nicomachean Ethics* Aristotle does say that "sleep is an inactivity of the soul as regards its goodness or badness, except in so far as certain impulses affect it slightly and make the dreams of good men better than those of ordinary people." Such a view allows for some unconscious activity of the "moral virtue." Modern research on dreams enlarges Aristotle's "slight effect" to "immeasurable effect" and adds a host of question marks to his reference to the dreams of "good men."

[2] Insights of ethical philosophers could be brought into our discussion here and elsewhere. A fruitful area of research would be one relating the insights of psychoanalysis, academic psychology, anthropology, and ethical philosophy. Much of the discussion in psychoanalytic writings proceeds as if no one before Freud had ever given thought to the phenomena represented by the term "superego."

[3] Of course, the unconscious part of the superego is inferred, just as any other hypothetical construct is.

a person go against his moral standards under hypnosis?" Popular articles reiterate the theme that no one will do anything contrary to his conscience in the hypnotic state. Experimental results (Rowland, 1939; Wells, 1941) indicate that at the very least a subject will commit acts which under ordinary circumstances he will not do. One may very well ask, however, who knows what a person's conscience is or what his moral standards really are? It does not take a clinician or experimental evidence to determine that not all a person believes deeply is manifest to others; the individual himself knows some areas of lack or distortion in his conscience which others do not know. But pertinent to our theme here is the suggestion that not even the individual himself is aware of his entire superego functioning. Strange lapses in moral or customary behavior find one kind of explanation in the postulated existence of superego functions which are unconscious. Not all of the strange forms of behavior associated with custom and conscience can be thus explained, to be sure. Other types of explanation must be invoked, including the development of superego functions.

DEVELOPMENT OF SUPEREGO

Superego and Ordinary Learning

Although we deal primarily with the adult personality in this book, we cannot understand the operations of the adult superego without an elementary knowledge of its origins.[1] Whatever the basis of the actual sense of obligation of which Kant spoke (Sprague, 1958), that is, the bare possibility of having a feeling of oughtness, just about all authorities agree that the contents of conscience toward which the

sense of obligation is directed are acquired by experience (Kluckhohn, *et al.*, 1953; Hall & Lindzey, 1954; Mackenzie, 1925; McDougall, 1908; Urban, 1930; White, 1948).

Whether the processes by which the superego develops are maturational or learned,[2] there appear to be two puzzling differences between ordinary learning and superego functioning. These may be differences of degree and not differences of kind. If the degree is great enough, however, it may substantially amount to a difference of kind. The first distinction lies in the *demanding* character of superego commands and prohibitions, together with the *guilt* aroused if these are flouted. There is, of course, a compelling aspect to the multiplication tables which may be used to represent ordinary learned materials. But somehow, these tables do not seem to possess the same type of demanding or guilt-evoking capacity that "Thou shalt not" possesses. Or even with lesser superego content, the convention in Western culture, for instance, that men must wear trousers rather than a dress, we can reasonably suppose that violation of this custom would produce greater intensity of feeling than would citing the incorrect answer to "9 × 7." At least, this inference may be made on the basis of research on superego functions (Dreger, 1960c) in which "Finding yourself in a public place without your trousers or dress" ranks very much higher in imagined guilt production that "repeating the multiplication tables with a number of errors."

Superego demands involving either morals or custom seem to possess a special intensity or drive character that does not inhere in learning of other kinds. There is guilt or embarrassment which may rise to an intense degree in conjunction with the superego.[3] It was the guilt factor among others that impelled psychoanalysis to

---

[1] Henry Sidgwick points out in his *History of Ethics* (1931) that as long as the moral sense is only regarded as a way of knowing what is good for us, no one is interested in its origin. But when it comes to be considered as a conscience, operating without reference to whether its rules are for our good, the claims of conscience are disputed and an appeal to its origin has to be made; the question is then asked, "Is it part of man's original nature?"

[2] Maturation and learning are not, to be sure, contrasting but complementary processes.

[3] Because of the extreme severity of some guilt reactions, some authorities have spoken of the "sadism of the superego."

posit the superego as part of the psychic structure (Freud, 1922, 1949, 1950). The intensity may be the resultant of the same factors operating in partial reinforcement experiments, for which no satisfactory explanation has yet been advanced (Bugelski, 1956). The inconsistent and aperiodic reinforcement which moral and customary standards receive certainly appears to be closer to the partial reinforcement paradigm than to one hundred per cent reinforcement. It is usually the case that partially reinforced responses are extinguished more slowly than fully reinforced ones. So, too, superego responses have a persistent character, difficult to extinguish. The guilt aspect may be some function of the persistent nature of the responses.

The other major difference that seems to hold between superego "learning" and other kinds of learning is that so much of the irrational exists in the former as compared with the latter that a qualitative distinction must be made. Usually parents or parent-surrogates in our culture at least serve as the core of that which is "learned" in the superego. No matter what the actual models are like, however, the individual's superego may contain so distorted a "picture" of these parents that it seems autistic rather than realistic. In addition, the irrational character of guilt responses often manifests itself to even the casual observer at times. A Nazi bully in a high position who could order thousands to death and show tender compassion toward a bird in his home evoked comment all over the world. The Inquisition with its excesses of cruelty all "done in good conscience" was paralleled by the Counter-Inquisition with similar phenomena. Abraham Lincoln shook his head sadly over the ones who could live as the result of the work of others. Those who suffer the agony of the damned because they know they have committed "the unpardonable sin" have lesser counterparts among those who suffer bitter pangs of regret over a gauche remark they have made or a social ineptitude they have perpetrated.

These two characteristics of superego experiences, their demanding and irrational guilt aspects, which contrast them to other types of learned experiences require some special considerations which do not enter into the learning of other kinds of responses. The learning theorists, Dollard & Miller (1950), have analyzed extensively how anxiety and fears may be produced. Their work may be utilized here to give a "learning theory" approach to superego development. Applying their analysis to the learning of superego responses, we might say that in the early years, during which time all authorities agree conscience functions are developing, there are many experiences which are unverbalized, hence they are not under the verbal control which we gain over verbalizable materials. Consequently, superego models are perceived imperfectly because the child lacks experience in interpreting the sensory data presented to him and cannot verbalize resulting distortions which might be corrected to some extent if he could speak about them to himself and others.

As the child grows capable of verbalizing, he expresses his percepts and thoughts, but meeting with sharp rebuff for unacceptable behaviors, including words, he "stops talking" so that his thoughts again become unverbalized, especially if there is extreme severity involved in the rebuffing process. The fear associated with the forbidden acts and thoughts will be disproportionate to their rational importance. Directed especially towards aggression and sex but also towards a host of other matters, some of these forbidden behaviors objectively amount to relatively nothing at all (inasmuch as the parents' superegos are irrational too). There is a further generalization of originally irrational fears to other matters which may have no logical, but only happenstance, connection with the original thoughts and acts. Therefore, on the basis of the initial distortions, the subsequent "repressions" from undue fears over certain behavior and from the generalizations of these fears, the partially irrational and peculiar form of anxiety which we call guilt comes to be formed in the individual. This analysis is admittedly sketchy; many portions will have to be filled in, and the general outline made far more rigorous than it is here.[1] Nevertheless, it seems to be in keeping with the facts of development known today, although there may be inherent factors not accounted for in learning theory.

Oedipus Complex, Introjection, and Identification

Whether the processes involved in development of the superego as a human function are all learned processes or not is still a moot question (Sanford, 1955) which depends for answer in part on whether identification and/or introjection are functions classifiable under learning or something else. These two mechanisms, identification and introjection, have only been mentioned thus far in these pages. They are very confusingly represented in the literature, sometimes as the same process and sometimes as different (Brand, 1954; Fenichel, 1945; Lindzey, 1954; Sanford, 1955). Fenichel, who summarizes psychoanalytic concepts of identification and introjection, reveals why the confusion has arisen: introjection is regarded as a primitive form of identification, so that the earlier (introjection) carries over into the later (identification). For our purposes, including possibilities of interpersonal research, the two mechanisms are regarded as relatively distinct from each other, and both of them distinct from love or object relationships to which they may contribute.[2]

Introjection, identification, and love may be assumed to lie on a developmental continuum from primitive (infantile) to mature interpersonal relations. The model for the mechanism of introjection is the infant's literally incorporating his environment ("Everything is grist for his mill"). Psychologically, introjection signifies taking in, in a more or less global fashion, the characteristics of another person. One may say, "taking in the other person" in two senses, first a relatively undifferentiated mimic or imitation without regard for the other's finely discriminating or distinguishing characteristics, a kind of "swallowing whole hog" some other person, mother or father or another; and second, an inconsiderate use of the other as if he were, to use the slang expression, being "taken in." There may be aspects of introjection which are unlearned, although a reasonable analysis suggests that introjection is an entirely learned process (White, 1948).

How close the process of introjection is to that known as imprinting is difficult to tell. Imprinting refers to fixation upon an object by the neonate or very young creature (Beach & Jaynes, 1954; Jaynes, 1956, 1957). Human infants have been observed to make the same type of response animals make (Gray, 1958). In the course of imprinting, a parent or parent-surrogate (including an inanimate object) is taken as an object to be followed with blind loyalty, with certain attending and vocalizing responses. This process has to occur at certain very early, critical periods, or it does not occur at all. Imprinting seems to resemble introjection in several ways: It seems to be irrational, like introjection, in that the object to be imprinted does not have to be of the same species or even animate, the response is intense out of proportion to the action of the stimulus object, and rewards and punishments of the usual variety are not required. Further, there may be a parallel in that fear responses tend to succeed imprint responses as the creature gets beyond the critical period; with introjection it has been pointed out that incorporation of another generates fears of retaliation. Introjection may differ from imprinting in being apparently a less immediate type of response, although this point is not clear. Also, imprinting seems to require some type of motion on the part of the object to be imprinted, a condition which may not be necessary for introjection.

Farther along the continuum toward ma-

[1] One matter not made clear in such an analysis is the force of the ego ideal or positive aspect of the superego. How does guilt arise from not living up to a positive ideal?

[2] Sanford (1955) points out a number of differences between introjection and identification.

ture interpersonal relations lies identification, which refers to the process of consciously and/or unconsciously imitating another for power, prestige, beauty, or other desirable characteristics. A greater degree of differentiation exists in identification than in introjection, that is, a finer discrimination among characteristics of the object of identification. Also, there is a greater consideration for the other person, regarded as an end in himself and not merely a means to an end. Such consideration merges into the portion of the continuum occupied by love or object relationship, which is at the opposite end to that containing introjection. In love there are elements of incorporation and identification, but the loved object is regarded with real concern, the loved one's welfare tending to mean as much as one's own.

With the foregoing distinctions in mind, we may better understand the psychoanalytic theory of superego development which underlies much of present-day learning theory applied to the superego (Dollard & Miller, 1950).[1] Clinical observations which suggest the order of development of the superego are not as adequate as more controlled research, but for the time being they are the most comprehensive and systematic we have. [Piaget's work (1932) is classed here with clinical observation.]

Classical psychoanalysis from which we draw material assumes the Oedipus complex, an assumption which is certainly not gratuitous, but which is unproved. By being unproved in this case we mean that a sufficiently large sample of clinically normal individuals has not been examined as intensively as clinical cases have been to show that what seems to be a very widespread phenomenon among neurotics and psychotics is also characteristic of normal individuals. For the purposes of exposition of Freudian concepts of superego development, we shall assume the generality of some form of the Oedipus situation, possi-

bly the "nuclear complex" proposed by the anthropologist Malinowski (1927).

In the early years, according to orthodox Freudian doctrine, there is no superego proper.[2] By introjection the child takes the mother's (or mother-surrogate's) moral prohibitions and ideals into himself to become a portion of his early ego.[3] This introjection comes from both a fear of loss of favor or affection and fear of punishment. If the parents, especially the mother, can be introjected, they cannot hurt the child, but neither can they be lost. As a means of defense against punishment and loss of love, the introjection has two main characteristics. It is very close, first, to a direct satisfaction of aggressive, sadistic impulses, as well as to plain hunger instincts, for actual incorporation (i.e., eating) to which introjection is very closely allied causes the object toward which it is directed to disappear. Hence the "forerunners of the superego," or internalized parental ideals and prohibitions, are tinged or possibly saturated with sadism. Secondly the introjection defense may fail fairly easily, for introjection actually does not get rid of the feared (and loved) parents; furthermore, the internalized parents may be projected into the world again. Because, too, the process by which the parents' prohibitions are internalized is so close to an instinctual one, the portion of the ego which can be called preconscience is pos-

[1] Freud's first enunciated theory of repression in hysteria was the forerunner of Dollard and Miller's "unverbalized" type.

[2] Melanie Klein (Lorand, 1944) who accepts much of Freudian doctrine pushes the Oedipus complex into the oral-sadistic state of development; the superego as directly connected with the Oedipus complex also is pushed back into the same stage (Lorand, 1944). Ernest Jones (Thompson, Mazer, & Witenberg, 1955, ch. 5) goes along with Klein in this respect. Klein's view does coincide more with learning theory than does the usual Freudian view in some ways, especially in regard to the fantastic aspects of the superego and the greater continuity between early and later stages of the superego.

[3] Psychoanalysts make much of the auditory nature of the superego, for prohibitions and commands are received auditorially and in psychotic processes parental voices may be "heard" again. But there must be much more to the processes of "taking in" parents, because deaf people appear to develop superegos.

sessed of drive properties, including both intensity and irrationality. These properties carry over into the later superego, and enter into the explanation of the strange ways in which the latter sometimes operates.

When the time comes for the Oedipus complex to be resolved, that is for the Oedipal objects, mother and/or father, to be given up as love objects, a decisive change in relation to the parents occurs. After having developed object relationships (love) in respect to parents the child now regresses to an identification with and even introjection of the parent, as if the child unconsciously were saying, "If I can't have my father as a lover, I'll get rid of him by taking him in (eating him)." The same process holds for the mother, except that what is called "identification with the aggressor" takes precedence, in that the child usually seems to introject more fully the parent who frustrates the child's oedipal feelings more completely. In our culture this aggressor is usually the father, although identification with the mother also takes place; if the mother is the greater frustrator, identification with her may be stronger.[1] The new and markedly different post-oedipal introjections of the parents unite with the earlier introjects, taking in the irrational and instinctual character of the latter, and become "parents within," [2] now never to be evaded completely.

ACCRETIONS TO THE SUPEREGO

Later additions may be made to the superego from peer groups, as Piaget has sug-

[1] This seems to be one of the weak places in psychoanalytic theory. Why should identification be with a parent who is not the original oedipal object? Brodbeck (1954) has given an experimental answer to this problem. His work may be crude in some ways, but is a worthy attempt to supplement or correct psychoanalytic theory by controlled research. In effect, Brodbeck states that the Oedipal attachments only reinforce the identification process preceding them, and then later experiences contribute possibly as much as or more than Oedipal experiences.

[2] In Allport's terms the conscience could now be considered to be "functionally autonomous."

gested (1932), although the actual influence of the peer group may not be as great in changing the dynamic structure of the superego as it is in molding the overt behavior of the child (Burt, 1925; Healy & Bronner, 1926, 1936). A study (Kutash, 1943) of "psychopathic defective criminals," individuals who were supposedly without conscience and were actually incarcerated for antisocial behavior, revealed that on the Thematic Apperception Test the fourth most frequent category of inner feelings which these "hardened criminals" utilized was that of conflicts and guilt feelings. [This finding is in keeping with Bergler's (1948) notion that criminals "bargain for the electric chair," striving to escape tyrannical superegos by seeking punishment.] Supposedly, these criminals, whatever their early experiences, had conformed to the criminal subculture, taking on antisocial behavior and seared consciences. Yet the very existence of guilt suggests operation of superegos not entirely or perhaps even basically altered from earlier times. Nevertheless, it does seem as if the normal superego develops from contact with peers; so too the pre-criminal superegos were probably changed to some extent through peer influence.

Besides peer groups, teachers form a class who may contribute to the formation of the superego. Nursery school, kindergarten, and primary teachers are often amused by a child's calling them "mother," for confusion seems to exist in some children's minds between teacher and mother—though the actual verbalization should not be taken by itself to establish the fact of confusion, for "mother" may be a generic term, or the child may forget that mother actually is not present, despite the fact that he knows the difference between teacher and mother. But from what we know of the transference relation where confusion occurs even in adults between therapist and parent (Rioch, 1955), we can be reasonably certain that such confusions can occur in a child—and sometimes at the very same time as Oedipal conflicts and resolutions are occurring. Even later, however, the authority of parents may be usurped by teachers. Parents may be amused or annoyed by Johnny's coming home from school and announcing, "I'm going to brush my teeth every day from now on." And he does! Why has he adopted this minor (but important) addition to his superego-instigated behavior? Because Miss Jones said to. And Johnny's parents who have been trying to get him to do exactly the same thing for some years are baffled as to why all their efforts seem to have failed and one simple remark from Johnny's teacher effects what looks like a miracle. The psychodynamics of even so simple a situation as this one may be very complex. The least we can say is that probably the parents enter into Johnny's decision through his original superego development far more than they think they do, inasmuch as teacher is misperceived to be a parent. Such additions to the superego as teachers may provide, however, would appear to be genuine additions to dynamic structure and not merely temporary superficial changes.

Kluckhohn, Murray and Schneider (1953) suggest further that the developing superego absorbs within itself the conflicting standards provided by literature. One may well add the conflicting standards provided by radio, television, movies, and comics as well. Here again, how far into the inner core of the superego these additions penetrate, so that the actual *basic* functionings of the superego are affected, it is difficult to tell. Studies of the influence of movies, comics, and radio have for the most part been on a mass basis which does not get at what is happening within individuals (Bakwin, 1953; Cantril, 1935; Charters, 1933; H. S. Lewin, 1953; Spiegelman, 1953). A few studies have been on the comparatively new medium of television, but, these, too, seem to be mass studies. Only as deeper analyses are made of normal individuals to find out what is really happening in their secret beings can we be more certain that the inner workings of conscience are strongly affected by later accretions which appear to affect the overt behavior of individuals to considerable extent.[1] Television may pose new problems in respect to the formation of conscience in that children of oedipal age view many programs with conflicting standards. On the basis of psychoanalytic theory, however, none of the extra-familial educational agencies except peer groups and teachers can have as much influence as the family for *none of them can give or withhold love*. Research of the future could well devote itself to testing this part of psychoanalytic theory—in such an exceedingly important area of personality development—by separating educational agencies into those with which object relationships may be established and those with which only passing identifications seem possible.

Psychoanalytic theory of superego development like learning theory is one kind of explanation for the observable facts of child and adult adherence to moral and traditional ways. We cannot forget that it is only one kind of explanation. Thus far it seems to be the most complete and satisfactory to clinicians, although academic psychologists tend to look askance at it. As long as and as far as it provides what appear to be near-adequate relations among the complex variables involved, it will serve science. Beyond these considerations it needs no defense as part of a system. However, support from experimental sources is welcome to the personologist. For example, a study (Jourard, 1957) of identification with parents relating it to the ego-ideal, disclosed a positive relation between these variables, a finding which tends to support the theory of superego development outlined by psychoanalysis. Further research which is reported below, relating self-esteem to a variety of other factors, also lends credence to clinically-derived hypotheses.

[1] Though how much comics, for example, have to do with even overt behavior is questioned by Coggan (1955) who has shown that the choices of comics by institutionalized delinquent boys almost exactly parallel the choices of nondelinquent boys!

Major Subfunctions of the Superego

We need not, to be sure, accept any one theory of superego development in order to study the set of correlative functions which make up what is known as the super-ego. Clinical and to some extent experimental analyses provide a broad outline of the sub-functions logically grouped together as major components of the super-ego. A comparison of the gross sub-functions detailed here with Cattell's (1957) and Peck's (1958) lists of trait elements, factorially derived, defining the superego reveals a close parallel. Few texts in academic psychology have made it their sole province [1] to examine the total area of ethical-customary behavior. We are forced, therefore, to rely upon clinical sources primarily for the general organization and much of the content of the following discussion.

On the basis of the available studies, five interlocking and contingent functions can be discerned within the superego: (1) representation of society, (2) generation of guilt, (3) regulation of self-esteem, (4) regulation of instinctual gratification, and (5) definition of self, character, and roles.

Representation of Society

If society could count only on a fear of external reward and punishment to assure conformity of its members to its demands, there would have to be a policeman with every individual; and the logical question in such a case arises, "Who then polices the policeman?" [2] In order to regulate its members according to its needs (or supposed needs) any society, at least according to logical analysis, must have either the unlearned automatic behavior of some sub-human societies, behavior that might be termed instinctive, or the learned behavior

which higher forms of social organization depend upon. These latter responses, determined in part by something drawn from without but now acting from within the individual, must serve as an internal warning system that operates even in the absence of *external* reinforcement, a partly learned "automatic pilot" keeping the individual on course.[3] Whether the superego has elements of both instinctive and learned behaviors, society does come to be *represented within the person;* we can call this representation process by the name of supergo.

Society's demands may be rational or irrational, or in the limited circumstances of any one society demands may be rational which would not be so in another large framework. The potlatch ceremonies [4] among the West Coast Canadian Kwakiutl Indians (Boas, 1897) may have their roots in rational behavior, but from a long-term standpoint they are economically ridiculous and wasteful. Yet the very name of the individual is tied up with these ceremonies, and he must keep on with the custom, irrational as it is in terms of a larger framework. Other forms of behavior may be dictated irrationally. Sexual behaviors are as rigorously regulated by some societies as are any kinds of behavior; and as irrational regulations as any are found among societal demands concerning sexuality. Kinsey and his associates (1948, 1953), late comers in the field, point out what Freud and many others had made evident for years concerning the irrational character of many sexual prohibitions and ideals. Yet many of these latter are passed on from generation to generation, becom-

---

[1] One of the few serious attempts is that of Hollingworth, *Psychology and Ethics* (1949).

[2] A difficulty with some congressional committees' approach to the matter of loyalty to the country seems to be the assumption that loyalty can only be guaranteed by external means. Totalitarian regimes at times seem to make the same mistake.

[3] An addition to the Biblical statement, "The wicked flee when no man pursueth," has been made by some anonymous wit, "but they flee faster when some man pursues." There is a kernel of truth in the witticism, for probably few of our superego internalized prohibitions and standards are completely automatic.

[4] Giving away or destruction of blankets or coppers in an endless exchange ceremony in which nothing is produced. To be sure, some of our own Stock Exchange procedures may have similar lack of rationality.

ing internalized in a hopeless confounding with rational, justifiable regulations. Inasmuch as society's demands may be irrational, the superego which represents these demands may be also, and conflicts arise between the ego and the superego, between the rational, judging portions of the personality and those elements of the internalized demands which are contrary to reason. (The structural conflict of ego-vs-id with superego "siding" with one or the other can be represented as id + superego-vs-ego at this point.) In the extensive investigation of adolescents in Prairie City (Peck, 1958), case studies revealed that some children tend to have rigid, arbitrary superegos while others tend to have superegos which operate more rationally.

Even when the demands of society are reasonable, the superego will not always represent society accurately. The parents and other superego models are not themselves perfect representations of their society. They, too, internalized the environment *as they perceived it.* So their misunderstandings of even a rational set of demands may be passed on to their children or superego heirs. In turn, even should the parents represent fairly the moral and customary standards of society, the child with his limited perceptive capacity and inner distortional mechanisms may misinterpret the parental *imagos* (images for imitation) and develop a superego which may be far from representing the society. Lastly, since the child may rebel against the parental (and other) standards, reaction formations may be incorporated which not only distort the original standards, but actually produce what Nietsche offered as a way of life, the "transvaluation of values," a complete reversal of the values society expects to inculcate in the child.

It is small wonder that psychoanalysts speak of "vicissitudes of the superego," considering all the possibilities for distortion and misdirection to which the superego is subject. And yet, after all is said, there remains the fact that unless a society can count on the inner ally which an individual develops, there can hardly be a so-

ciety any more permanent than the tenure of the King of the Golden Wood, [1] who lived only as long as he could prevent his successor from assassinating him.

Generation of Guilt

Anxiety or general tension over fear of pain becomes specialized into guilt in the superego. [2] Remorse for deeds or thoughts has been a topic for dramatists and story tellers for many ages. It does not seem to be a peculiarly human institution, for animal fanciers have insisted that their charges possess guilt feelings over doing something "they know is wrong." The dog with his head bowed down and tail between his legs indicates that possibly he feels guilt. [3] It

[1] Sir James Frazer (1940) began his long study, leading to twelve volumes of *The Golden Bough,* as an effort to discover why the ancient king or priest of the grove beside the lake of Nemi in Italy maintained his rule only by keeping constant vigil. He had won his priesthood by killing his predecessor. He ruled until his successor killed him. Hence his strained and grim outlook and the insecurity of his term of office.

[2] Shame and disgust are two emotional responses sharing many of the characteristics of guilt. These may be analyzed in somewhat the same fashion that guilt generation is analyzed in the text. Fenichel (1945) applies his paradigm of motivation for neurotic defenses to anxiety, guilt, disgust, and shame, and finds the same dynamic elements: (a) Trauma. In each case some experience or experiences have been painful, as in disgust, "This is inedible and should be spit out." (b) Danger. The ego uses the emotions of guilt, shame, disgust, or in general, anxiety, to warn against expression of certain drives or repetition of certain experiences. (c) Panic. Going beyond the normal, anxiety in some of its forms becomes overwhelming.

[3] Mowrer and Kluckhohn (1944) maintain that rats who learned a D-maze did not develop guilt in a "socialization" experiment which Mowrer and Whiting performed. In this experiment rats were allowed to choose the longer or shorter way from one end of a maze shaped like a D to the other, either along the straight side or around the curved side, to a feed box at the lower corner of the D. When they had established the easier way as a habit, they were divided into three groups, one of which was shocked in the straight alley, one of which was prevented from using the shorter alley by a plate of glass, and the last of which was not given any food at the end of the shorter alley. All groups learned to take the longer alley, with the first group learning fastest

may be, however, that animals, even dogs, do not possess a real superego which goes with them regardless of the presence of the owner (counterpart of the parent?). Has a dog ever been observed through a one-way vision screen apart from human companionship to do some act which "it knows is wrong," then manifest "hang dog" behavior which owners report as the evidence that the dog is feeling guilty? As far as the writer knows, no such experiment has been performed. Yet science cannot reject summarily animal observers' contentions concerning guilt in animals. Human beings on the other hand testify over and over again, not only by their direct verbalizations, but by their indirect ones as in projective tests, that they have feelings of remorse over their deeds or thoughts. Whether gods and goddesses, who as external authorities are believed to judge men for sin, are projections of parents or not (Freud, 1952), from a psychological standpoint the grief men have felt over their sins [1] has been a part

of them as truly as their knowledge of the multiplication tables and even more independent of outside bolstering or interference.

Of itself this function of guilt generation may not seem to serve much of a useful purpose in the personality. To see patients in depressive subjection, moaning and wringing their hands over real or fancied sins, does not encourage belief in the "survival value" of guilt. The writer's mental hygiene professor in college stated almost unequivocally that "guilt is a bad thing," and that it would be better if there were no guilt feelings. Such value judgments may not be called for in science; whether they are or not, however, guilt is a very real factor in many personalities in Western Christendom, possessing in many cases the intensity of a drive, even to overcoming of self-preservation in some instances. But as we consider the regulation of instinctual gratification below, it will be apparent that there is a value in the economy of the personality to feelings of guilt, for without having experienced guilt, the function of warning in the regulation of drive-expression would be greatly weakened.

Guilt appears to be composed of at least two emotional reactions (Stein, 1958). An anxiety-type reaction seems to have external referents; an outside agency may be feared. Also, an internal referent may be present, with self-directed anger as the reaction. Accordingly, a person may respond to one type of infraction of the rules with one kind of reaction, and to another type with the other kind. Perhaps animals are only capable of guilt reactions with an external referent, but human beings of both kinds. Yet for some, one type of reaction may predominate, possibly making for the major differences between inner-directed and other-directed persons (Riesman, 1950).

Differences of a similar nature appear in

and the last one slowest. The shock group, corresponding to children punished for disapproved behavior, did not develop any "guilt," for as soon as the rats were no longer subjected to shock they went back to the straight path. The other two groups of rats were not thought to represent conscience development in children; but it would be better to consider that they do represent some kind of conscience development. Superego development is not only the result of punishment, but of barrier and no-reward situations as well. In the shocked group, however, there seemed to be no residue of "guilt" which would prevent the rats using the short path any more than with the other non-punished rats. Mowrer's analysis may confuse the warning function of conscience or regulation of instinct gratification with the actual guilt or remorse functions; it may also serve to illustrate the difficulty of assigning human feelings to animals.

[1] "With woe and grief, full of sighs, is his soul;
Tears doth he weep, laments doth he pour forth."
(Penitential Psalm, Babylonian, c. 2000 B.C.)

"For I know my transgressions,
and my sin is ever before me."
(Psa. 51:3)

". . . we acknowledge and bewail our manifold sins and wickedness, which we from time to time most grievously have committed, by thought, word, and deed, against thy Divine Majesty, provoking most justly thy wrath and indignation against us. We do earnestly repent, and are heartily sorry for these our misdoings; the remembrance of them is grievous unto us" (From *The Book of Common Prayer*).

the responses of adolescents in our society, as suggested in the Prairie City investigation (Peck, 1958). Korean prisoners-of-war (Segal, 1957) reacted grossly in the same way, with the Resistors apparently answering to themselves more than to the external world of their captors, and the Participators capitulating to the external authorities. In between were the Middle Men who tried to blend in with the scenery without either actively resisting or actively cooperating. These latter may have blended the two types of guilt reactions.

That superego reactions of the nature under consideration are interpersonally determined, despite their seemingly exclusive intrapsychic quality is demonstrated in both the Prairie City studies and psychological and psychiatric data on Korean POW's. In the former the *Superego Strength* factor, although apparently unrelated to the family *Democracy-Autocracy*, correlates relatively highly (.50) with *Consistency in Family Life*. And *Willing Social Conformity*, which may be regarded as a superego factor, correlates .53 with *Consistency in Family Life* and likewise .60 with *Mutual Trust and Approval* (in the family). Thus, whatever guilt aspects there are to these superego factors is, as theory would predict, associated with family interactions. In the Korean War (Schein, 1957; Segal, 1957), the Chinese captors used social pressures to bring about guilt feelings in prisoners, as noncooperating prisoners used it on collaborators (although evidently not so much as in previous wars). Even more striking were the manipulations of social pressure of the Chinese in relation to their own citizens in the Revolutionary Colleges set up in the early years of the Communist regime (Lufton, 1957). Students were brought to an intense degree of guilt over their deviationist sins by group pressures exceedingly strong even for a group-oriented society like the Chinese. Some of the know-how gained in the Revolutionary Colleges was apparently applied in respect to American prisoners in Korea. We may conclude that whatever components of guilt-generation come from

the original family situation may be reinforced by social interactions at any one stage of existence.

Individual differences in reactivity to present social situations, however, may not only be assumed but experimentally demonstrated. One study (Diggory, 1949) on level of aspiration with a task impossible of solution engendered realistic and unrealistic attitudes by the instructions. Measures taken before and after the failure period showed that although the realistic and unrealistic groups differed in their induced attitudes toward the task, both groups differed from pre- to post-failure in variability. In other words, the variance for the realistic group was less than that of the unrealistic group in the post-failure measures, but both groups' variance was significantly different from their pre-failure variance. This increased variability in both sets of subjects indicates that there is differential reactivity to the failure situation not only in conjunction with the failure itself, which depended upon the immediate social situation, but in relation to the different persons.

Regulation of Self-Esteem

What a person thinks of himself depends in part on what others think of him. Prestige and status are reflected in the feelings of self-esteem (Kluckhohn *et al.*, 1953). But also part of what the person thinks of himself is not so much presently interpersonal as an intrapersonal deposit from past experience with others. The extreme of a lack of self-esteem or an excessive self-esteem is found in the manic and depressive psychoses, sometimes alternating in the same individual. The attitudes of doctors and nurses and aides no doubt fluctuate from time to time in respect to the patient, but the manic or depressive response is out of all proportion to the present social stimulus provided by the patient's environment. There is an *internal* regulator of self-esteem which may operate conjointly with external stimuli, but is sometimes relatively independent of them. In even normal folk there is still a relative independence of external factors in this respect. The admonition, "Come on, buck up, old fellow, you've got nothing to be blue about," ignores the internal determiners of mood. It may be difficult to demonstrate the relation between self-esteem and mood. If one is "moody" or "blue," he may be feeling badly about something in the environment, a rejection by a lover, a failure, refusal by the boss to grant a raise, a loss of some prized object, or something similar. In such cases analysis has usually been able to show among other things that, even for losses which could hardly be traced to the individual's own direct action, his response is, "I'm no good." In some cases, of course, there *may be* sadness without this self-debasement, but ever since Freud's "Mourning and Melancholia" (S. Freud, 1925) clinicians have accepted the connections between external losses and loss of self-esteem. Where the individual actually says, "I'm no good," matters of self-esteem would almost seem certainly to be involved, though not always in the direction which the individual has expressed—strange as it seems, his pronouncement may mean, "I am far better than you think I am."

There are probably physiological determiners of self-esteem, as reflected in moods, just as there are present social determiners. Psychoanalysts especially (Benedek, 1952; Deutsch, 1944) have demonstrated the correlation between "blue" feelings and menstrual cycles in women. Perhaps there are biological cycles which are present in both men and women which profoundly affect their moods and thus their self-esteem, although the sexual periodicity of women seems to have no counterpart in men (Kinsey *et al.*, 1948).

When we eliminate social and biological determinants—recognizing, of course, the interaction of the factors involved—we find there is still a large psychological component regulating self-esteem. It is this internal regulatory process which is the superego function. Self-esteem seems to be regulated in part by the closeness to a feeling of power which the individual has. In psychoanalysis this feeling of power is called "omnipotence." The infant is supposed to possess an original feeling of omnipotence because he is not yet separated from the all-powerful world. When later he is brought close to the original omnipotence feelings, he gains self-esteem, or when he loses such feelings he loses self-esteem. The way in which the child is brought close to omnipotence feeling is by the provision of "narcissistic supplies" of food and affection, which are offered together at first by parents; later affection alone is given (though many persons turn to food or have eating difficulties when affection is withheld). As the superego takes over in place of parents in middle childhood, the superego provides or withholds "narcissistic supplies" in the same way the parents have done previously. In this way, in cooperation with whatever biological and social factors are operating, the superego acts as a regulator of self-esteem.

The only part of the psychoanalytic description of the regulatory process which does not seem to be in accord with objectively verifiable data is the early "omnipotence feeling" of the child. Most child psychology texts refrain from discussing anything except observations of behavior and direct implications from behavior, such as inference of hunger under certain behavioral indices. As far as the writer knows, implications of "omnipotence feelings" are all made from clinical research on adults, especially adult psychotics; and while many of the extrapolations from adult psychotics to childhood have been verified by direct observation of children, inferences about omnipotence have not and possibly cannot be so verified. At any rate, the rest of the theory could stand fairly well without the assumption of omnipotence feelings, and does fairly well fit the observable data.[1]

Regulation of self-esteem in terms of

---

[1] Other explanations could be offered, but with some rearrangements and different terminology the explanation proposed could fit in with others. A biosocial interpretation of depression given by Norman Cameron in *The Psychology of the Behavior Disorders* (1947) is not fundamentally opposed to the text discussion.

self-evaluation and its relation to other variables has been the subject of a fair amount of research. One measure of self-esteem is the "stability of the self-concept" index (Brownfain, 1952; McGehee, 1957). The latter is operationally defined as the discrepancy between a subject's rating of himself giving himself the benefit of every reasonable doubt to make a positive picture and a self-rating denying himself the benefit of every reasonable doubt to produce a negative picture. On the whole, those with a minimum of discrepancy between their positive and negative self-ratings (high stability of self-concept) tend to be high in self-esteem as measured by other techniques, to be well-adjusted psychologically, adequate in interpersonal relations (sociometrically determined), and to view themselves more realistically (at least, in consonance with the way others view them). Surprisingly, those with a high negative self-concept tend to express greater acceptance of themselves than those with high positive self-concepts and to show less discrepancy between ratings of their perceived and ideal selves (Cowen, 1954).

As in the last-mentioned study, ratings of the perceived self and ideal self, with the discrepancy score taken as a measure of self-esteem, have served as the basis for several investigations of the correlates of self-esteem. That there are no simple relations among self-esteem and the other variables has become evident in the course of this research. Taking a cue from client-centered personality theory, one investigator (Zimmer, 1954) tried to find a direct association between ideal-self–perceived-self ratings and conflict areas of the personality, but could find no such relations. The same theoretical impetus instigated investigation of discrepancies between ideal and perceived self in relation to psychological adjustment (Block & Thomas, 1955; Chodorkoff, 1954). Rather than a straight-line relation holding between these variables, a curvilinear association appears: Those with very low and those with very high discrepancies between perceived and ideal selves tend to be well-adjusted, while those me-dium in discrepancy tend to be low in their adjustments. Taking another dimension, academic achievement, with perceived-ideal self-concept discrepancy, another experimenter (Chickering, 1958) found that the lower the discrepancy, the higher the academic achievement, or in other words, the higher the expressed self-esteem, the higher the achievement in school.

Using various measures of self-esteem in terms of scores on self-acceptance tests, some investigators have found its relations to acceptance of others; here, too, these relations are not simple. A fairly clear positive association is found between a person's expressed self-acceptance and his expressed acceptance of others; and also his own self-acceptance is directly related to his beliefs of how others accept him (McIntyre, 1952; Omwake, 1954; Scher, 1955). But *actual* acceptance by others, as determined by sociometric ratings, may not be related to one's feelings of being accepted by others or to one's own expressed self-acceptance. Some who think much more highly of themselves than they do of others may feel accepted, but in reality are not so well liked by others. Those on the other hand whose acceptances of themselves and others are closely related tend to feel more accepted and in reality are more accepted by others than are those with greater discrepancies between their own self-acceptance scores and their other-acceptance scores (Fey, 1955; McIntyre, 1952).

Extending these more personal acceptance concepts to the larger society, associations between self-esteem and esteem of others are found in research on Xenophilia and Xenophobia (marked preference for and marked rejection of an outgroup, respectively). Those who score higher on self-dislike items tend to show preferences for foreign individuals and institutions (Brodbeck & Perlmutter, 1954). However, the study also shows that Xenophilia is probably the resultant, in some cases anyway, of endeavors not to identify with the parent or other socializers. It seems to be a form of resistance against these agents which are superego imagos, a rejection of those close by in favor of acceptance of those afar. Thus, the finding is not out of harmony with other results of a more personal nature which generally support the theory that self-esteem and other-esteem go hand-in-hand.

Measurable disturbances in the personality are associated with disturbances in the perception of and acceptance of oneself and others. For example, conflict over sex makes some women more accurate in their perception of their own sexuality but less accurate in rating others (Harlow, 1956). Subjective self-evaluations show an inverse relation to anxiety as rated by both oneself and clinicians; the greater the anxiety, the lower the self-evaluation (Scheide, 1955). (An inventory of anxiety did not reveal these relations, but presumably direct observation by clinicians and the subject's own report would be more accurate in assessing anxiety than a paper-and-pencil test.) Being a patient in a mental hospital is associated with excessively lowered or raised self-acceptance and acceptance of others. Some type of compensatory elevation or depression may occur in psychoneurotics and psychotics. In one application of self-acceptance measures (Corrie, 1958), psychoneurotic patients scored higher than normals, who in turn scored higher than psychotics. In another study (Zuckerman, Baer, & Monashkin, 1956), the same kind of relation held, with schizophrenics scoring lower than normals. But in the investigation reported earlier on unconscious self-evaluation (Epstein, 1955), schizophrenics over-valued themselves compared with normals. The explanation for the discrepancy between the findings of these last studies is most likely found in methods employed and the depth reached. In the first, ratings were of the pencil-and-paper variety, *i.e.*, conscious evaluation. In the other, it may be recalled that subjects were required to rate liking for the producer of certain expressive products, not knowing that they were really rating themselves, to all intents an unconscious self-evaluation. When, however, these same schizophrenic subjects made conscious self-judgments, they averaged the same as normals, only tending to use the extremes of the scale more than did normals. Thus, consciously they either over-valued or under-valued themselves. That conscious and unconscious ratings of self-esteem should differ should not be entirely a surprise. Nor should it be surprising that schizophrenics do over- or under-value themselves, considering the differences in disturbance, with some openly and secretly rejectant of self, others with open and secret omnipotence feelings, and others with various combinations of open and secret, partially open or secret acceptance and rejection of self.

Relations with other variables can be shown in connection with self-esteem (Hampton, 1955; Lehner, 1956; Lepine & Chodorkoff, 1955; McElvaney, 1958). Enough has been presented, however, from the studies in self-esteem to indicate some of the associated factors which may enter into the regulation of self-esteem.

Regulation of Instinctual Gratification

As suggested previously, guilt (or other similar, sometimes indistinguishable affects like shame) may be used as a warning signal, as well as a response to disapproved behavior. Actually, of course, it seems more accurate to say that there is a warning function of the conscience which serves to forestall guilt feelings. It is as if the superego were saying, "If you give way to your impulses now, you will suffer dreadful remorse later. So don't do it." Extension of the warning system to that portion of the external world which might call forth dangerous impulses is in keeping with the associative processes of learning. "Don't let yourself get into an argument; you know what happens!" or "Don't go to the burlesque show, there's too much danger for you."

But the regulation of drive expression is not negative only. What and where drives *can* be expressed is just as important as the suppression (or repression) of drives under inappropriate circumstances. The expression may not be in ways that society ordinarily expects but according to the *individual's* principles of allowing expression. In a radio dramatization of a "true detective story" a woman very much dominated by her mother, the mother herself, and a policeman confronted the husband as part of the wife's move to get a mother-instigated divorce. The husband was in an upstairs apartment as the trio approached the building. On becoming aware of their presence and their purpose he called out the window to watch out, and in great anger tossed out of the window one piece of furniture after another, including a large mirror. Of course, appropriate sound effects accompanied the orgy of destruction. The climax came as a final horrified wail rose from the wife, "Oh, no. Not the refrigerator!" (An apartment refrigerator would not be too heavy an object for a man operating under the influence of adrenalin and the sympathetic nervous system in aroused states.) When the police finally entered the apartment, the husband cried out, "Why didn't I do this before? I feel so good!"

Such a release of impulses is not uncommon in mob behavior (Brown, 1954), though whether there is the same "good" feeling in mobs is another matter. If as F. H. Allport (1924) states, "The individual in the crowd behaves just as he would alone, *only more so*," then we should expect that there is at least a temporary marked increase in self-esteem ("I feel so good!"), as the superego is circumvented or actually *allows* under the peculiar circumstances of mob behavior the expression of ordinarily forbidden impulses.

Normally the allowance of expression of instinctual urges is in keeping with the usually accepted standards of a society. Among the Balinese, eating must not be indulged in public except under certain conditions, but naturally the "instinct" of eating is allowed under "appropriate circumstances" (Mead & Macgregor, 1951). Aggressive impulses are usually restrained from direct expression in "polite society," but given fairly free reign at a football or baseball game. In Western culture, sexuality has been, and still is, under more restraints than in many cultures, but there is relatively free expression under certain carefully prescribed conditions. If the "education of the superego" has been in fair conformity to these allowances, there is freedom from internal warning signals when the judging portions of the ego give reason to believe social custom is not violated.

It is in this warning function, or lack of it, that idiosyncratic superego formation appears most evident. Several of the writer's counselees have been much distressed over picayunish matters and little distressed over what society might consider graver issues. One man could tell lies "indirectly" as he expressed it, but was painfully compulsive about not telling direct lies, "even little white lies." He was an expert at making the best appearance in most situations, and if the audience believed his rationalization, he was not distressed that the truth was stretched. Lack of distress here would be failure of guilt, but his lack extended also to the *planning* stages of his deception in that if he could convince himself that no "direct lie" would be involved he felt no qualms of warning conscience. Presumably a similar lack obtained in financial tycoons of yesteryear who looted and stole with apparent equanimity (Flynn, 1932). Investigations of political and business chicanery in recent years seems to reveal parallel superego lacunae. It is more difficult to judge in these latter cases, because clinical analysis is usually not part of the investigations. At least, the allowance of expression of certain impulses differs from person to person even within the same society more than the actual customs of such a society might seem to permit.

Definition of Self, Character, and Roles

Perhaps this function should be split into what would appear to be three logical subfunctions. And yet, the very close relation of self and roles has been fairly well demonstrated, though also their independence can be demonstrated to an extent (Sarbin, 1954). There is a similar close relation between self and character and character and roles. Each of these is distinct, but there is sufficiently close interaction among them to include them in an admittedly complex function of the superego. "Definition" here has a dynamic meaning, not merely an intellectual exercise of setting up certain characteristics. Instead, it signifies a delimiting and accepting or rejecting, as fitting or not fitting, those self, character, or role behaviors and affects and intellections in which the individual is constantly engaged or which he is contemplating. Some function of the personality maintains a watchdog attitude toward these potential or actual constituents of self, character, or role. It seems appropriate to classify this function under the general heading of superego.

Many aspects of self-defining in the dynamic sense have been given attention from a scientific standpoint since William James (1920). Self-valuation,[1] self-acceptance, distinguishing between self and nonself, and even distinguishing among acceptable and unacceptable portions of one's self (or selves) are incorporated in the process of defining self. Does the person consider that such and such properties of his personality actually belong to him? Or of all the possible "selves" thus accepted, how many are accepted consciously and how many only unconsciously?

By definition only those aspects of the personality which have an "I," "me," or "mine" quality are the self (or selves more accurately). But the young woman who was so wrought up in the final portion of a Rorschach examination by the examiner's question, "Some people see sex symbols in these cards, do you?" that she became almost violent must have had some self processes which she was denying. Out of more than sixty persons in the experiment

(Dreger, 1952) who were placed in the same kind of experimental situation only the one reacted thus violently. The examiner was taken completely by surprise, for rapport was excellent up to almost the last; the young woman had thrown herself into the production of TAT stories and Rorschach responses with evident enjoyment, and neither stories nor Rorschach spontaneous responses seemed to be overly anxiety-laden. The unexpectedly explosive discharge of affect was very similar to the reaction of a person whose pain nerve endings have been suddenly stimulated. The most economical inference then seems to be that something very painful psychologically had been touched upon. The extreme denial of sexual matters would imply that these painful matters involved sex. Since sex is a part of everyone, it appears reasonable that the subject was denying part of her *self*, because if the part were not ego-involved such violent reaction would not be called for.

Not only socially unacceptable portions of the self can be "defined out" of the conscious self, but sometimes characteristics which are entirely acceptable to society. One young man, a counselee of the writer, denied any feeling of love for his mother, not vehemently, but calmly and matter-of-factly, indicating that if reaction formation were operating it was very mild. He believed for some reason that it was unmanly to have love for his mother (regardless of oedipal components). Later he came to accept on a conscious level a love which was there before as part of himself but denied.

Definition of character, in the sense we are using the term definition, is fairly close to definition of self; a reciprocal relation holds between character and superego. What is acceptable as material for the building of character (or developing habitual modes of adjustment) and which traits are acceptable to be formed out of these materials must be judged. But also a portion of the total character structure is the manner in which the individual forms judgments of good and evil, of customs and

---

[1] Symonds (1951) takes up self-valuation as if self-valuation and values of the self mean the same things. What values the self possesses, however, seem logically to be different from the individual's valuation of himself.

ethical standards, as well as the manner in which he reacts to both traditional and ethical stimuli. Therefore, even the very formation and continuance of the superego as a gross set of personality functions defines character in part. And whether the individual rebels against his superego or complies with it tends to be a characteristic mode of his internal adjustment, forming thus a portion of his character (Fenichel, 1945).

What roles the individual plays are likewise determined in part by his sense of oughtness. Of course, roles are linked to his self concepts as he identifies certain roles as *his;* they are linked, too, to his character, for his habitual modes of adjustment are very often found in certain roles he is playing. When we view roles, character, and self separately for the sake of analysis, however, it can be seen that what the individual judges is *right* for him to be, in respect to various social groupings, determines in part what he *is* in these groups. Being a boy or a girl means playing a sex role, even though there are sex differences which are more fundamental than roles (Mead, 1949). These roles are impressed upon a child early.[1] He comes to believe early that it is right for him to engage in role behaviors appropriate to his sex and wrong for him to engage in behavior which the culture has made clear is appropriate only to the opposite sex. Presumably roles may be superego objects, for the same kind of pain comes from violating one's role expectancies as from committing some act which the individual defines as sin. Thus for a man to wear dresses in our culture would be to violate his conscience; only a transvestite does such things. Accordingly, not only social approval or disapproval, but superego approval or disapproval "defines" his sex role for him. Playing the role of a middle class mother in America, Negro or white, calls for certain kinds of child-rearing practices differing from lower class mothering (Davis, 1953). By implication,

[1] The age at which sex roles are learned differs from social class to social class in America (Rabban, 1950).

if our analysis is correct concerning the necessity for internalization of social customs in order for them to be truly effective, the mother's role is partly "defined" by her superego.

Temporary as well as more permanent roles are superego-regulated to some extent as well. "*Should* I take the office or should I not?" "Can I take the position they've offered me and still look myself in the eye?" In the Korean War some young men capitulated to the North Korean–Chinese tormentors and took on themselves the role of what others called "turncoat." For those young men who did and for the great majority who did not assume such a role the decision was mediated in part, we can almost be sure, by superego factors: "What *should* I *do?*" (Schein, 1957; Segal, 1956, 1957).

Sometimes discussion of the superego has dwelt on its sordid and negative aspects; we know enough about the superego to recognize why clinicians especially have emphasized the harsh, unreasoning character of much of the superego's functioning. But not only debased and ignoble activities can be traced to the superego; definition by the superego of roles to be enacted includes the noblest of behaviors as well. Whether Lincoln ever said about slavery, "If I ever get a chance to hit that thing, I shall hit it hard," there seems to have been ethical compulsion as well as political expediency in his determination to play the role of the Great Emancipator.

In the mid nineteen-thirties, the Nazi government put the tremendous pressure of its resources, its secret police, torture, ridicule, and denunciation, against that section of the Christian church known as the Confessional Church, a group of Christians who opposed the religious dominance of the Nazis and much of their social legislation, especially that concerned with oppression of Jewish persons. The chief spokesman for the Confessional Church was Martin Niemoller, pastor of a large church in a suburb of Berlin. Four days before his arrest on trumped-up charges, Niemoller (1942) said among other things to his congregation:

We have as little thought and as little hope as the Apostles had of escaping from the clutches of the powers-that-be by our own efforts; and we have certainly as little intention as they had of obeying the human command to keep silent regarding what the Lord our God orders us to say; for, as long as the world shall last, one must obey God rather than men! [1]

Recognizing the complex psychodynamics and sociodynamics of such a dramatic situation, in which a popular minister opposed a governing regime, in this case not merely a party in power but a totalitarian government, we can yet conclude that there were probably strong superego elements defining the role that Niemoller assumed. Additional evidence to this effect comes from the fact that concentration camp experiences, including solitary confinement, did not alter the role of opposer which Niemoller had taken on.

SUPEREGO STRENGTH

Some attempts have been made to measure superego strength, just as ego strength has been reduced to quantitative measures. The intensive investigation (Peck, 1958), to which reference has been made several times before, of Prairie City adolescents intercorrelated 29 temperament variables and factor-analyzed the resulting correlation matrix.[2] Of the six factors derived from the matrix three relate to the functions discussed in this chapter: *Superego Strength* (presence of an effectively behavior-guiding conscience), *Willing Social Conformity* (overt conformity to the moral code; emotional stability—largely overt conformity to expected, "controlled" behavior; range of moral horizon—the range of people and groups toward whom the subject is overtly moral; overt acceptance of mother's expectations; absence of overt hostility; and positive relations with opposite-sex peers), and *Hostility-Guilt Complex* (guilt about inner impulses; inner feelings of hostility toward mother; lack of overt acceptance of father's expectations; and lack of inner liking for opposite-sex peers). Each of these factors can be given a factor score so that individuals can be measured as to superego strength in each of these areas.

A multiple approach to superego strength (Friedenberg & Havighurst, 1948) employed a 110-item questionnaire with coverage in 11 (logically-ordered) categories: honesty, loyalty, responsibility, miscellaneous taboos, kindliness, cleanliness, moral courage, religion, self-control, ego ideal, and authority. Five validity items were added. Administered to junior high school subjects in two different ways— "How bad is it to do such-and-such?" and "How would you feel to do it?"—the test had satisfactory reliabilities, but its validity as a measure of superego is not so satisfactory.

One hundred and sixty Australian-born subjects at the University of Sydney rated the seriousness of offenses and improprieties (Sutcliffe & Haberman, 1956). By the method of paired comparisons, about 20

---

[1] Niemöller, M. *The Gestapo defied*. London: The Religious Book Club, 1942. Reprinted by permission of William Hodge & Co., Ltd.

[2] The procedure could be questioned. Usually, as required for computing tetrachoric correlations, a sample of subjects should be at least 200 to have a correlation matrix reliable enough to factor. Only 34 subjects were used in this study. One method of reducing error in the original scores was the use of multiple judges. If Pearson r's were computed, as one might expect with as small a number as 34, another component of error would be reduced. The report does not indicate which type of coefficient was used. Extenuating conditions, of course, have to be recognized in this study: One cannot expect as intensive investigation of 200 as was made of 34; furthermore, there were only 120 altogether from which to choose. And as a general consideration practicality has to be regarded in any experiment (Fisher, 1951).

However, statistical conclusions must be limited to the adequacy of the method regardless of insurmountable limitations. If the factor results were far out of line with what theory predicts, greater question would of necessity be raised. But because the sample is so small, one needs to view with caution even results compatible with theory. Perhaps both the theory and the factor results are biased in some way. This same type of criticism can be made of the early factor-type study of Allport and Vernon (1933) discussed in Chapter 3.

items were ranked (a sizable task, for comparing 20 items one with another requires 190 judgments). Sample items are, "A student proctor observes a fellow student cheating in an examination," "An army sergeant observes a corporal victimizing one of the men," "A citizen observes a murder," "A senior shop assistant overhears a junior being rude to a customer." Instructions were to identify with the role of the first person in each case. Scale values obtained by the above procedure are:

Murder	3.30	Slander	1.05
Rape	3.14	Burglary	.85
Kidnapping	2.33	Abuse of	
Sacrilege	1.98	position	.77
Swindling	1.79	Profanity	.73
Adultery	1.64	Cheating	.65
Assault	1.63	Drunkenness	.57
Blackmail	1.61	Prejudice	.35
Negligent		Gambling	.21
driving	1.50	Bigotry	.01
Breach of		Rudeness	.00[1]
confidence	1.06		

(In the method of paired comparisons, rudeness would be assigned a value of .00; it might have a true degree of seriousness.)

Using a somewhat different method, the author (Dreger, 1960a) has obtained preliminary results with the G-E Scale. On the latter, subjects rank ten items whose real life counterparts are presumed capable of arousing guilt or embarrassment. Instructions include the notations, "If I should be in this situation, how bad would I feel?" and the admonition to judge according to the *intensity* of the imagined reactions, not bothering to distinguish guilt from embarrassment. After the subject has ranked the items, he is told to mark each as G, E, or GE for guilt, embarrassment, or both. The rankings in the next column with the usually overwhelming majority of G or E identifications, were obtained from a sample of mostly mature undergraduate night students.

The coefficient of concordance (which ranges only from .00 to 1.00) is .64 for the subjects of the research, representing a

[1] Reprinted by permission of J. P. Sutcliffe and *Amer. Psychologist.*

Item	Average Rank	Guilt or Embarrassment
Killing someone in a planned murder ("premeditated murder")	1.5	G
A married person, engaging in sexual intercourse with another than your spouse	2.6	G(?)
Stealing an automobile	3.6	G
Finding yourself in a public place without your trousers or dress	4.0	E
Telling a lie (not a "white lie")	5.8	G(?)
Using God's name in a curse	6.2	G(?)
Breaking your hostess' best China platter	6.8	E
Going into a theater without paying (and not getting caught)	7.4	G
Missing a step going upstairs and falling forward ("falling upstairs") in the presence of those before whom you wish to appear dignified	7.9	E
Repeating the multiplication tables with a number of errors	8.8	E

fairly high degree of similarity among the individual rankings. There is a fairly broad spread for several of the items, however, particularly for the item relating to using God's name. One fairly clear conclusion comes from the above rankings, fortifying a contention made earlier in this chapter. Some individuals, at least in imagination, rank some experiences which only occasion them embarrassment as more intense than some over which they experience guilt. These represent the two sets of reactions to which we paid attention earlier, custom and conscience reactions.

In attempts to measure superego strength, those which Hartshorne and May and their associates employed in the Character Education Inquiry (Chapter 3) should not be overlooked. Their whole endeavor amounted to a search for estimating superego strength. Studies carried out under the auspices of the Character Research Project (Ligon, 1956) also have measured superego factors extensively. These latter studies are reported in a somewhat confusing manner, inasmuch as matters of methodology are continually being discussed with substantive material, so that one is sometimes not sure whether the discussion deals with what should be discovered or what has been. And yet, the attempts should be given due credit.

SUMMARY

Third in the main dynamic structure-functions, the superego develops as a differential portion of the ego and serves as the representative of society in respect to the ethical and conventional demands of society. The intimate relation of superego to id and ego is paralleled by its close association with roles. Both conscious and unconscious in operation, the superego's developmental history determines its differences from ordinary learned functions; beginning before verbalization gives rational controls and partaking of primitive perceptual-defensive processes of introjection, the superego may later gain rational accretions but has an irrational core.

Major sub-functions of the superego are: representation of society's demands, rational and irrational; the generation of guilt; regulation of self-esteem; regulation of instinctual gratification, allowance or forbidding present or contemplated release of impulses; and the definition of self, character, and roles, determining what is "appropriate" for inclusion in these closely allied functions.

Scales for measuring superego strength have been developed which either yield factor scores or rankings of the relative seriousness or imagined intensity of offenses.

QUESTIONS

1. What two major distinctions can be made within the superego? Relate the findings on the G-E Scale to one distinction.

2. How does the superego work with and/or against id, ego, and roles?

3. How much can we know of what a man's basic moral standards are?

4. Distinguish between superego and ordinary learning.

5. Trace in outline form the development of the superego according to learning theorists and psychoanalysts.

6. In the later development of superego how do personal agents and the TV, radio, and comics differ in their contributions?

7. Discuss the superego in its relation to: representation of society's demands, the generation of guilt, the regulation of self-esteem, the regulation of instincts, and the definition of self, character, and roles.

CHAPTER **10**

TOPOGRAPHICAL STRUCTURE-FUNCTIONS: ROLES

In the three preceding chapters three major structure-functions of the personality, as viewed from the topographical standpoint, have been detailed. These functions, the id, ego, and superego, have been recognized by many authorities as "areas" in any personality, even though they are individual in expression. There is another area in the topography of personality which has not traditionally been regarded as parallel to the other three, yet which logically complements them.

Without actually including the role functions in the structure of personality, many personologists have implicitly recognized their importance. Lewin's concepts of personality structure take account of differing roles a person plays. Cattell's sentiments and possibly attitudes in the "dynamic lattice" of personality imply a role undertaken voluntarily or involuntarily in each case, such as "husband" in respect to "wife" or "citizen" in respect to "country." Angyal's interpersonal concepts demand role functions in the personality. But even the identical elements view of personality structure suggests by inference that the scholar in the classroom plays a different role on the baseball field. In recent years, however, not only by implication, but directly, personology has come to include roles as distinct

functions of the personality. It is increasingly difficult to ignore the work of social psychology and sociology in discussing personality. To bring the findings of these latter disciplines, as well as those of anthropology and social psychiatry into the service of personology, we shall turn now to a discussion of roles in the social structure.

ROLES IN THE SOCIAL STRUCTURE

One of the original meanings of the term "persona," is that personality may mean the role or part one plays. Thus far, as in the case of several terms we have employed, the assumption has been made that the meaning of the term "role" is clear and definite. In actuality it is not, not even when it is used in scientific work (Bates, 1956).

Several terms must be clarified in order to understand what is meant by "role." [1] A

[1] Gullahorn (1956), p. 299: " 'Role' is used here to mean the way in which a person carries into action the configuration of rights and obligations of a status or structured position he occupies with a group." Neiman and Hughes (1951) trace the concept of role from James with his idea of self or selves, Baldwin with his "dialogue of the self and the other," Dewey who emphasized the importance of language in the development of the self, Cooley with his "looking glass self," and Mead who spoke first of a social role, "taking the

"position" in social psychology is considered to be a set of expected behaviors which may be designated by a single term relative to a certain social structure.[1] Such positions as mother, chef, doctor, husband, military policeman, millwright, paymaster, and so forth have more or less definite be-

role of the other," and the "generalized other." (The student may wish to seek these for himself in Baldwin, 1911; Cooley, 1902; Dewey, 1891; James, 1892; and Mead, 1934.) Neiman and Hughes group definitions of role into three classes which regard the concept in terms of: (1) Dynamics of personality development: role as the basic factor in the socialization process, or a cultural pattern; (2) society as a whole: role as a social norm, or a synonym for behavior; or (3) specific groups: a status-role continuity, or participation in specific groups. The common elements in all concepts, they find, are: (1) An individual's definition of a specific situation or the individual's acceptance of a group's definition of a specific situation; (2) the assumption of symbolic interaction; therefore, only man is a role-playing animal; and (3) human behavior cannot be explained by traits or other "atomized concepts," but must be viewed in a framework of organized and integrated patterns of behavior. On the whole, these common elements coincide with our text position. Methods of investigation, Neiman and Hughes conclude, have proceeded from the armchair to experiment and have carried across areas like the family, child development, cultural norms, social status, deviant social behavior, occupational groups, pathological behavior, and small group dynamics. Disappointingly, after an excellent review, Neiman and Hughes decide that even though role has become an integral part of sociological vocabulary the utility of the concept is questionable, because the concept is vague and has generated so few hypotheses. Their very review seems to contradict their conclusion as does the extensive research since 1951.

Sometimes the term "status" is used indistinguishably from that of "position." Bates redefines position, role, and status in such a way as consistently to apply these terms to groups rather than individuals. His reformulation may appear somewhat radical at first, but his consistency does help to clear up some of the confusion mentioned in the text. In the discussion in the text there is not much distinction made between rather temporary positions and more permanent ones. A rationale for this lack of distinction can be provided, in that any position, no matter how brief its temporal extent, can be defined just as more permanent positions are.

[1] Although many persons hold the title "Doctor" today, the medical profession has so established itself in public opinion that when we say

haviors associated with them, expected of anyone who fills these positions in our society. Positions are not directly referred to any one person, for they exist as concepts regardless of who fills them. It is only as persons take on the roles which serve to show they qualify for positions that we are interested in the latter in personology. "Roles" then, are those relatively consistent patterns of behavior in which individuals engage while occupying certain positions.

Obviously, role and position are closely allied; indeed, a good case exists (Sarbin, 1954) for saying that a position is an organized system of "role expectations," the *actions* and *qualities* which persons enacting the role anticipate of themselves or which others anticipate for them. These role expectations are embodied in "role behaviors." By definition of terms in social psychology we cannot study roles directly by studying a single individual, for a role is a range of behaviors expected of all persons who occupy a certain position; thus all we can study in personology are "role behaviors" which Newcomb defines as ". . . a molar unit which can be identified, by those familiar with the role system, as behavior on the part of a person in his capacity as occupant of some specified position—as husband or wife, for example, or as employee or employer." (Brand, 1954.) "Roles" and the "role behaviors" are used interchangeably here, but the reference in terms of the individual personality is to role behaviors. Study of roles and positions *per se* is a sociological enterprise (Hare, Borgatta, & Bales, 1955; Linton, 1956; Merton, 1957).

ROLE FUNCTION CHARACTERISTICS

It is possible now to continue the discussion on role functions of the personality where we left off in the section describing generally the "dynamic, multidimensional, topographical system" of personality organization (Chapter 5). There it was main-

"the doctor" ordinarily only the medical man is thought of, just as in times past the "parson" was the "person" in the community—etymologically "parson" equals person.

tained that role functions can sometimes be considered just as permanent and necessary parts of personality as any other seemingly "more personal" functions. It is not necessary to belabor the point that personality includes role functions. A person enacts a role in much the same way he metabolizes, performing a general function individually. We shall assume (as common sense has assumed) that roles are parts of the personality, and apply as much of role theory as is useful in understanding personality. Inasmuch as role theory is still only in its infancy, observations here cannot be considered even as exhaustive as the discussion in previous chapters on the topography of personality. Neither can the principles set forth below be organized to the extent materials concerning ego, id, and superego have been. Statements offered here must be viewed as more tentatively held than are most psychological "laws" in general.

1. *Roles are interpersonal functions of the personality*.[1] Since roles are defined in terms of position in a social structure, there could most likely be no roles for any one individual without a society in which to enact his roles.[2] Even when role behavior does not represent the polarity of so-called "reciprocal roles"—mother-child, employer-employee, chief-tribesman, etc.—"others" are necessarily involved in any role one plays. "Others" need not always be human beings, for the possibility of an abstract position such as a castaway on a humanity-

forsaken island exists with only animals as one's companions. In respect to these non-human companions Robinson Crusoe can play the role of master or hunter. (In reality, one of Crusoe's originals, Alexander Selkirk, played the role of voluntary exile and later of rescuee, only in respect to human companions.) Likewise, the status of master in relation to horse or dog in human-animal society leads to the role which a man may play in respect to his particular horse or dog. Usually, however, roles are limited to interpersonal relations. "Reciprocal roles" obviously requiring objects which are loved, feared, cared for, avoided, and so on, shade into what may be termed "non-reciprocal roles" where not such sharply limited classes of individuals are objects or foils, such as the role of a "sport," as one who devotes himself to gay and carefree pleasures, or of a "normal person" in the sense that Cameron (1947) means when he says, "In real-life situations, role-taking means earnestly behaving as, and therefore actually being, a particular social person in relation to other persons."

2. *Role functions may have both inner and outer referents*. The "outer referents" are, of course, others. Others see us in our various roles and from many standpoints consider that they know us as personalities because they know that we perform certain social functions. These are the "social selves" of which William James (1892) wrote:

Properly speaking, *a man has as many social selves as there are individuals who recognize him* and carry an image of him in their mind. To wound any one of these his images is to wound him. But as the individuals who carry the images fall naturally into classes, we may practically say that he has as many different social selves as there are distinct *groups* of persons about whose opinion he cares.[3]

In actuality, these social selves go beyond those about whose opinion we care, for many of our roles are determined by people we do not know or for whom we do

---

[1] The term and concept of "interpersonal" owes much of its vogue to Harry Stack Sullivan's "interpersonal theory of personality" which is expressed briefly in *Culture and Personality* (Sargent & Smith, 1949) and more fully in Sullivan's works (1953). Leary and Coffey (1955) trace their interpersonal concepts to Sullivan.

[2] To employ the phrase "enact a role" or "play a role" means nothing derogatory to the individual. Shakespeare's "All the world's a stage" may have ironic overtones in its implications; but social psychology's borrowing of the stage terms is only a convenience to indicate that a man has to serve a number of social functions. The distinction in social psychological literature between "playing" and "enacting" roles is not maintained in this text. (Cf. Sarbin & Jones, 1955.)

[3] James, W. *Psychology, briefer course.* New York: Holt, 1892 & 1920. Reprinted by permission.

not care. James detailed two such "social selves," one in the mind of the person with whom an individual is in love, and the other the fame, or honor, or dishonor, which a person holds. The latter may very well be in terms of persons about whom we have no concern or a negative concern. In connection with the social self of honor James' illustrations can also serve as (unintended) illustrations of the way a person plays his role in qualifying for a certain position:

The particular social self of a man called his honor is usually the result of one of those splittings of which we have spoken. It is his image in the eyes of his own 'set,' which exalts or condemns him as he conforms or not to certain requirements that may not be made of one in another walk of life. Thus a layman may abandon a city infected with cholera; but a priest or a doctor would think such an act incompatible with his honor. A soldier's honor requires him to fight or to die under circumstances where another man can apologize or run away with no stain upon his social self. A judge, a statesman, are in like manner debarred by the honor of their cloth from entering into pecuniary relations perfectly honorable to persons in private life (James, 1892).[1]

It is no accident that the term "self" has been employed in conjunction with role functions, for the self[2] and role have been held by social psychologists to be reflections of each other (Cooley, 1933). Ontogenetically, self and role arise together (Young, 1952). Even in adult life it is difficult to distinguish between self and role. What I perceive as *my self* is so intimately linked up with the parts I have to play in any social setting that often they seem like two sides to a coin or mirror-images of each other. We might say that the self is the internal referent, as others are the external referent of role functions, except that the formula is too simple. Self and role are assuredly overlapping functions, but they are not merely the same portion of the personality as it is viewed from within (the self) or from without (roles).[3]

On the one hand, while the roots of the schizoid process of fantasy role-taking, for example, may be found in the original interaction of roles and self in the child, many of the fantasy roles are not ordinarily observable *as roles* to the observer. Maslow and Mittelmann (1951) present a case of the individual who lay perfectly still because the world is in a gigantic battle between Good and Evil and the balance of power lay with the immobile individual. If the latter as much as moved a finger, the balance would be disturbed and the vast forces of Evil would overwhelm the world. Such a fantastic self-role, if we may term it such to discriminate it from externally visible roles, cannot be observed—all that can be observed is the role of an immobilized catatonic. Even when the patient informs the observers of the tremendously important role he is playing in the fate of mankind, the "role" is not evident to others directly; it seems to be part of the self which is not referable to role functions as ordinarily defined.

On the other hand, as indicated in the discussion on personality structure, some roles are played without the individual's being aware of them; thus if they are not either consciously or unconsciously accepted as part of the self, these roles have no internal referent as do most roles. Sarbin (1954) maintains that a role cannot be played unless the role expectations have been learned. But many a person, especially on entering a new society where he does not know the roles, has engaged in role behaviors which fulfill the role expectations of a certain position and yet he is not aware for some time, and may never become aware—in fact, may never even per-

---

[1] *Ibid*. Reprinted by permission.
[2] It should be remembered that "self" is shorthand for "selves."

[3] G. H. Mead's (1934) distinction between the "I" and the "me" gets at the distinction between the roles a person plays which are the outer representation of self and the portion of the personality not strictly role-connected. Garfinkle (1958) finds similar differences between the "generalized self concept" as measured by an adjective check list and the "role self concept" as measured by a student behavior check list.

ceive *unconsciously* that he has been playing a role of a certain kind. As far as others are concerned, he *is* that kind of person; insofar as roles constitute interpersonal functions of personality, his personality is partly composed of that role. Others react to him as if he were the kind of person represented by the role; and he may react to their reactions as if he were that kind of person, even misinterpreting their actions and thinking *they* are reacting to the role *he* thinks he is playing.

One southern gentleman had progressed in his thinking concerning race relations to the place where in a discussion with other Southerners he declared that he would allow a certain famous Negro singer to stay in his home. To himself and to others with less liberal notions he was playing the role of a liberal—even a radical! But to the observer who considered the Negro singer by far the greater person the seemingly liberal attitude revealed a role of patronizer which was somewhat like that of a person who says, "Why, yes, I would allow the President to visit my home." This gentleman was—as far as could be ascertained from both the particular incident and many other observed behaviors—completely unaware that he was playing the role of patronizer. To the observer such was his role; and to a considerable extent, therefore, such was his personality.

We may conclude that roles have both inner (self) and outer (others) referents, but that the role is not entirely inclusive of the self any more than that the self is entirely inclusive of roles. A number of roles are accepted by the self, others rejected, as the person says to himself, "That is *my* role or that is not mine," even though some roles which he may neither consciously nor unconsciously accept are really his as viewed from outside.

3. *Roles may be either conscious or unconscious,*[1] *or partly conscious and partly*

unconscious. The discussion under the preceding point leads directly to the recognition that roles are sometimes entirely unconscious (Freedman, Leary, Ossorio, & Coffey, 1951). That roles may be partly accessible to one's conscious awareness and partly inaccessible is attested in common experience where an individual may play the role of "automobile driver" and perform his role behavior so automatically that he cannot recall the part he has played in many of its particulars. Another example comes from the writer's early life. In high school he had a two-mile walk to and from his after-school work. To beguile the time, he took along a book and read as he walked. Although the role of pedestrian in relation to many cars and street-crossings was apparently played successfully, true to the stereotype of the profession in which he eventually landed, he was "absent-minded" about most of the role behaviors of the pedestrian, though probably not all of them.

A friend had a slight speech difficulty of which he was unaware until he had been in graduate school over a year. A speech teacher called his attention to it, but even then he could not recognize it until a record of his reading a passage of literature was played back to him and for the first time in his life he heard himself as others

the multiform ambiguity of this archaic terminology by making our distinctions in terms of the adequacy with which a patient identifies, recognizes and formulates the significant factors in his behavior. Instead of the hypothetical split into a conscious and an unconscious, we shall emphasize *varying degrees in the accessibility* of a person's behavior to his own analysis, through his self-reactions, and in his *relative accessibility* to the motivational analysis of others." Referring his concept to Cameron's discussion of motivation, Sarbin indicates that there are some role behaviors which are not accessible to the conscious awareness of the individual. He cites the case of the customer in a supermarket who may perform all the acts necessary to the role of customer without being able to recall her actions; she may even be engaged at the time of playing the role in playing other, nonpublic roles; also the case is cited of the hysterical amnesia victim who may not recall his roles prior to the amnesia. In this text we are under no constraint to steer clear of the terms "conscious" and "unconscious," so we can identify these roles as more or less unconscious.

[1] Sarbin (1954) prefers to avoid "conscious" and "unconscious" and employs the terms "accessible" and "inaccessible" instead. Likewise Cameron (1947) in rejecting "conscious Psyche" and "unconscious," writes: "We shall seek to avoid

had heard him. The knowledge of his difficulty had apparently not been repressed—in other words that he actually "knew" but could not admit it—for when the matter was brought before him he did not deny or resist the facts but cooperated willingly in speech therapy to overcome the disorder. That others had reacted to him in the role of one with a speech difficulty seemed attested by the fact that his wife was amazed that he did not know of the condition; she had noted it and "accepted" it without comment.

How much repression is involved in unconscious roles is a matter for intensive investigation of the individual. The amnesic probably has employed considerable repression in becoming unconscious of roles played in the past. Present roles may be repressed, too, if we can trust depth psychology for somewhere nearly an adequate analysis of our ways of behaving. Caryl Chessman, author of *Cell 2455 Death Row* (1954) gives considerable sociological and psychological data which serve as partial explanations for his psychopathic criminal behavior. To a psychologist with psychoanalytic orientation, however, the book *seems* to testify to an unresolved Oedipal complex of which the author is unaware. He was, apparently, playing a role in respect to his mother which as far as can be determined was unconscious. Of course, prior to his execution no searching analysis of Chessman's personality was attempted, despite his many examinings, so the inference of an "unresolved oedipus" remains in a speculative stage. Other similar characters, however, have been analyzed intensively and have been found with unconscious roles of the nature possibly found in Chessman (Bergler, 1948, 1949; Lorand, 1944). Repression need not be involved in roles which are wholly or partly unconscious. Only in some cases is it necessary to posit that the role *has* to be hidden from the individual.

4. *Roles are determined in part by the perception of the individual.* As would be expected from the fact that self and roles arise as an interactive social process, what the person perceives to be his role is very important in the formation of the self-role functions. Excluded from these perception-determined roles are those of which the individual is unconscious *and* which are his without even "unconscious perception" (as is the case of the individual entering a new society, as mentioned in #2 above). Where, however, an individual assumes a role by processes of which he is unaware, but it is *his*, accepted as part of himself, unconsciously or consciously, perception is definitely involved. We are not concerned here with "role perception" in general, which is properly the province of social psychology, but with the perceptions of the individual which relate to his own roles. To be sure, these perceptions of the individual's own role-playing and potential role-playing, and his own role expectations, are built up in part on the basis of his perceptions of others. What I am in myself and in the very closely related roles I play seems to depend much upon what I perceive others expect of me. Not alone the verbalized expectations, but the nonverbal, symbolic, and motor behavioral reactions of others are cues to be perceived for guiding me into the roles expected of me.

It is not, however, necessary for an individual to have high perceptual accuracy in respect to others in order to function efficiently in his role behavior, only sufficient accuracy to engage in the category of behaviors called for by the role (Steiner, 1955). But accuracy in perception of oneself tends to facilitate role-taking (Couch, 1957). When others become familiar with the way an individual perceives his own roles, as opposed to the way others perceive them, *they* achieve greater accuracy in predicting what his social attitudes and interests are (Payne, 1957).

Perceptual accuracy does not depend solely upon the person himself when he is called upon to enact a certain role. The role itself may be vaguely defined by the culture. Experimental manipulation of the clarity of definition of roles, that is, from clear to ambiguous, demonstrates the effect of ambiguity in the role itself (Smith,

1957). Lowered group productivity and lowered satisfaction with the situation resulted from lack of clarity in the definition of the role to be played. Even if there were no distortion in the individual's own perceptual processes—a condition difficult to envisage—there could be inadequate role behavior because the social norms defining the role are unclear.

In geographical areas where social stratifications are well marked, social scientists can detect fairly easily how a person's perceptions of the behavior in which he is expected to engage determine the role he plays. He may not, for example, be able to describe all the perceptions which enter into the determination of his role as an inferior or superior. But he has perceived what is necessary to enact his role. After spending a number of years as a close observer of the caste system of India, one authority declared that he had never seen an Indian mistake the caste of another Indian, at least in respect to the necessary superior or inferior behavior in which he was obligated to engage. The Western observer could not in many instances tell what differentiae were utilized by Indians to determine the caste of others. Presumably the expert's experience was limited and/or the mistakes made in caste identification were unnoticed, but there is probably considerable truth to the contention that the caste Indian can judge fairly accurately to whom he should act in a superior manner and to whom in an inferior (unless he is a member of the subcastes of the Brahmans and has no superiors!). A host of signs he perceives in himself and in others lets him know what role to play, signs like clothing, gait, emblems, facial expressions, gestures, perhaps even odors. He probably does not know all the cues he employs to determine his role, a condition not uncommon in the role enactments of any individual.

What has been called the "as if" dimension of role enactment is of importance here.[1] The behavior of the individual may be considered (from a role standpoint) as

an attempt to act *as if* the person were occupying a certain position. A revealing slang expression recognizes this "as if" quality of role-taking when, for instance, a modern mother states, "Now I'm making like a mother," signifying at least partly that she fails to fulfill all the role expectations of being a mother. The person perceives what the role is supposed to be and behaves in the manner he thinks is "like" the expectations. Of course, his perception may be inaccurate—indeed, is subject to the inaccuracies for which perception at times is notorious. And his execution of the role may be faulty as well. He may play it as he sees it and as he can in the "as if" fashion.

There is one peculiar aspect of perception in role-playing which needs considerable research especially in conjunction with research on the self. This is the special perception which we call "self-consciousness." It may refer to the embarrassed awareness of one's role in a situation which generates anxiety, or it may refer to being aware of the role one is playing without such embarrassment. In either case there seems to be the element of observation of one's self in a social situation, as if one part of one's self is viewing what another part is doing. It is only a suggestion which needs further research from a phenomenological and possibly hypnotic experimental approach that the major self system which is consciously identified as the "I" reacts to different roles the individual is playing. But the other roles (and selves) are likewise recognized as "mine" in many cases. And in many cases they are disowned, even as the person recognizes he is playing the role. The relations involved in "self-consciousness" need considerable exploration.

We may conclude that perception does enter into the formation and continuance of the individual's role functions. Not at all incidentally, we may also observe in this connection that perception as a control function (ego) is manifested clearly in the determination of roles. Although other determinants beyond an individual's control enter the process of role-formation—after

[1] Vaihinger's lead in *The Philosophy of As If* (1911) is followed by Sarbin.

all, roles are *interpersonal* functions—what we perceive the position to be according to which we fashion our role behavior partly determines the role.

5. *Roles are primarily learned behavior.* In the early development of self-role theory in sociology and social psychology (Cooley, 1933) it was maintained, following McDougall (1908), that the self (and its accompanying roles) has an instinctive basis.[1] That an instinctive (i.e., hereditary) basis for self and roles is present in many instances can well be accepted today. For some persons of a solid, phlegmatic temperament it would be unthinkable, perhaps even impossible, to play a role of gay, light-hearted, frolicsome playboy. In any case granting the general principle that heredity and environment interact, the acquisition of self and roles is primarily a learning process. Even the meaning to the individual of his physical body, a meaning which plays an important part in our roles and our selves, is a socially derived set of symbols. As has been pointed out by sociologists (Mead, 1934; Young, 1952), the young child does not have a sense of his physical self first and then of his social self; the process is reversed. He *learns* his social-self roles in which his physical body takes its place as that body is perceived first by others then reactively by the individual.

When we go beyond the elementary physiologically-related roles, it is evident from what is now world-wide research that roles are primarily learned. Take an outstanding example in American culture. There is little doubt that American Negroes on the whole perform in an inferior fashion to American whites in most areas of accomplishment demanded by Western culture (Dreger & Miller, 1960; Shuey, 1958). The wide overlap of distributions such as those of intelligence scales cannot conceal the fact that on the average whites outperform Negroes, sometimes significantly, on many, if not most tasks. But over a good many years social scientists have been forced to the conclusion that the Negro is inferior on the average because *he has been taught to be inferior* (Karon, 1958). The expression "forced" is used advisedly; Myrdal (1944) shows that in connection with psychic differences of whites and Negroes, the first scientists observing race differences accepted them as primarily genetically determined, but realized later through force of evidence the cultural nature of many such differences.

Evidence has gathered over the years to support the contention that the *average* inferior role played by any major segment of mankind is a learned one. A Negro learns to play his role just as the caste Indian learns to play his from the thousands of cues and reinforcements provided by his culture (Miller & Dollard, 1941). And the man of the "superior" group learns *his* role in respect to the "inferior" group; he is amazed, hurt, and angered when the role which he perceives to be his naturally is challenged as not by nature his. Because of the close ties of self and role, a challenge of his role is a challenge of *him*. Even the person cast in the inferior role may be uncomfortable if the role is challenged.[2]

---

[1] Cooley, Angell, and Carr's (1933) volume *Introductory Sociology*, does not show familiarity with either the work of K. M. Bridges (1931) on the ontogenesis of emotional behavior, work published two years previously, or that of Sherman (1933), published first in 1927 and 1928. Nevertheless, their general thesis that emotional reactions which have instinctive (or better, hereditary) components enter into formation of the social "looking glass" self would not be quibbled with today. Furthermore, a modern representative social psychologist, Young (1952), does not deny the place of perception of one's body, especially kinesthetic impressions, in self-role development. And body senses are presumably mainly unlearned, though there is room for learning even in these senses (Hunter, 1929).

[2] A value-judgment is not out of order in this place. The fact that certain minorities cannot play roles for which they are fitted is not alone a matter of lack of self-fulfillment for the ones who are so deprived. Since many people are denied opportunity to develop the talents they possess, the country is denied an immense reservoir of potential engineers, physicists, chemists, physicians, academic personnel, and so forth. The country that affords itself the luxury of not developing *all* its human resources in these times may find itself dropping behind those countries which do not afford themselves such luxuries.

Virtually all the roles of which one can think appear to be primarily learned. Being a city man or a farmer is commonly recognized as a learned pattern of behavior. But even the role of "baby" which would seem to be a matter of just being born a baby has many elements which are learned. Sex roles (Rabban, 1950) and ethnic roles (Radke, Trager, & Davis, 1949) are learned and relatively early at that. These and other roles are learned not only because of the face-to-face experiences the child has, but also because the child matures in his ability to conceptualize and employ language in his conceptualization processes (Strauss, 1956). Not only must each role itself be more clearly conceived, but the compatibility and incompatibility of roles, their interrelations, the manners in which they can be simultaneous and successive and complementary, and a host of other complicated data about roles must be learned.

6. *There are degrees of "ego-involvement" in role-taking.* Although this is not the place to view personality dimensionally (as we do in Chapters 13 and 14), we cannot help thinking dimensionally in respect to roles. "Ego-involvement" or "self investment" or "cathexis" in regard to a role signifies that the individual "puts more of himself into" some roles than he does into others. Sarbin (1954) has called this the "organismic dimension," or "intensity dimension," the intensity being gauged by the number of organ systems involved. He distinguishes seven different levels, ranging from those roles where self and role are readily differentiated, when few organic systems are involved, for which little effort and little affect are needed to maintain the role, or in other words where there is little "ego-involvement," to those roles at the other end of the scale where role and self are undifferentiated, the entire organism is involved, and much effort is necessary. A close examination of Sarbin's "levels" reveals more dimensions than one in the organismic dimension; [1] Sarbin has attempted

to reduce exceedingly complex qualitative data to the semblance of quantitative measurement, an attempt that is in line with one of the principles of psychology.

Whatever levels or numbers of dimensions are represented in the degrees of ego-involvement in our roles, each of us recognizes that some of his roles are more important to him than others. But the degree to which we give ourselves to a role is not easily measurable. One may spend many hours enacting a certain role which yet he has cathected little. The amazement of the "top Communist leaders" over the testimony of Herbert Philbrick ("I was a Communist for the FBI") at the trial which sent them to prison for engaging in conspiracy to overthrow the government by violence, indicated that even they, so skillful at taking roles and acting them "as if" they really believed in their roles, were unprepared to find someone who could play a role as expertly as Philbrick did and yet merely be "playing" it.

It is not uncommon for a psychologist to find a person actively engaging in a role for which he cares little or which he even rejects. One counselee was a middle-aged man who was married, had a family, and took a prominent place in his local church. But he played his role as a father and husband only from a sense of duty which was rapidly weakening; and his part in church work, apparently at one time sincere, now was a front. On the side he was having an affair with one of the choir members. The conflict that brought him to the counselor was his desire to maintain his home for its respectability and business advantages while at the same time he really wanted to play the role of clandestine lover. He was more ego-involved in the latter role than

[1] For example, in relation to effort, some of the "casual" roles require more effort than some of the less casual ones, as in the case of being a pedestrian in a hilly town compared to sitting at the deathbed of a loved one enacting the role of a person who knows the loved one is about to depart but can do nothing to prevent the loss. Probably the number of organ systems involved in these cases does not manifest the intensity of the "ego-involvement." Most of the variables dealt with in psychology are complex; this one "organismic dimension" is more so than many others.

in that of householder, and wanted the counselor to help him "have his cake and eat it, too," keep his household and his mistress at the same time. (Of course, the counselor could not—in this case would not—assist him in this task.)

More innocently a person may enact a role from other than desire to enact it, even fulfilling the role expectations well, but not feeling as if it is part of him. He may take an office in a club, head up a charity drive, become a student at a school, act like a bar-fly, engage in any of a multitude of roles, and "not let his whole weight down." It seems that Sherif and Cantril (1947) are correct in stating that investigation of man should begin by placing him situationally in his reference and membership groups,[1] and then take account of his (other) personality characteristics. But for personology the recognition has to be kept in mind even as we place a person situationally that there are many degrees of ego-involvement even in membership groups.

7. *Among other things role functions may be in varying degrees:*

a. *Permanent or temporary.* Role functions like being a three-year-old are only maintained for a short time (though to the three-year-old such a role constitutes one fourth of his life). Playing a feminine role, although there are many sub-roles as the girl grows older, is a rather permanent one. Its temporary or permanent nature does not guarantee either the degree of ego-involvement or the importance of a role to the personality. Enacting the role of hold-up victim may be very temporary but also very traumatic. Being a cousin to another individual may be a long-time role which one plays, but not necessarily a deeply ego-involved one.

It is difficult to conceive of roles which are not part of the personality. Perhaps fleeting roles like "being a passenger on a plane" for a brief period of time just once in one's lifetime might be so considered. And yet, the person considers himself to be

such a passenger and acts according to what he interprets his role to be; others view him temporarily as such a passenger. If this role is so temporary that it has little influence on the rest of his life, we may consider it a relatively unimportant portion of the individual's personality. Or there may be roles of which the individual is totally unaware which might be excluded on the basis that they are not considered by the individual, even unconsciously, to be *his*. But if others observe the behavior going with the role, they react to him as if he is such a person.

Temporary roles which leave little impression on the remainder of the personality's functioning may be disregarded in our study of personality. After all, our major interest is not in fleeting functions but in more permanent ones. It is well to be aware, however, that some seemingly temporary roles may be lasting. The example of the once-in-a-lifetime airplane passenger may signify as important an event to the individual as "my operation."

b. *Reciprocal or nonreciprocal.* Husbands and wives, children and parents, employers and employees, students and teachers, masters and servants, storekeepers and customers, all play reciprocal roles in relation to one another. The role in each case could not exist without the alternate person's role. Other roles have fewer reciprocating features, but they demand other objects, usually persons, as a background for enacting them. To perform their specific role behavior, an athlete, a bureaucrat, a "skinflint," a wise man, and a neurotic, all require others, but not in so reciprocal a fashion. Still others may appear to be reciprocal, but are not so in essence. When a farmer is compared with a city dweller, there are contrasting behaviors which distinguish him from the latter, but if we consider an entirely agrarian society we can see that learning the behaviors expected of a farmer does not need to involve learning to react to city dwellers.

c. *Central or peripheral.* This characteristic is closely allied to ego-involvement, but differs in that a role may be central or

[1] Reference groups are those to which the individual relates himself in some way; membership groups are those which are especially *his*.

private and not be strongly cathected, or may be peripheral and maintain high ego-involvement. A fantasy role or a somnambulistic role is central in many ways for it may be played primarily in private; with the latter the individual engages in overt behavior expected of a somnambulist. On the other hand Achilles' dragging Hector's body behind a chariot before the walls of Troy was the act of a haughty avenger, a role played as publicly as he could play it, a peripheral role, but one that meant a great deal to the childish, egocentric Greek "hero." Generally we can suppose that the roles which are more central are also more ego-involved; but this relation is even more suppositious than most which are discussed in this chapter.

d. *Manifest or latent.* One may fill a position in a given society with role behavior that is regarded as relevant to that setting (the manifest role). At the same time he may have any number of roles which are irrelevant to that setting (the latent roles). That these latent roles are important even in carrying out the manifest role is evident from common observation. A student who is also a husband or a wife, a Cabinet member who is sincerely devoted to public welfare but who is also a director of large companies, an industrial worker from a minority ethnic group, an adolescent in the home whose peers demand of him behavior contrary to his home standards—none of these, it would appear, can escape the influence of his latent roles even though he may enact the manifest role with relatively adequate role behavior.

The investigator who suggested the designations for manifest and latent roles (Gouldner, 1957) studied first the so-called "experts" in a company who are not usually given top management positions, probably primarily because their ego-involvements are not as great within the company as they are without. These are technical or professional individuals with a high commitment to their specialized role skills, engineers or scientists for example whose orientation is towards outer reference groups. They are not "company men."

They may engage in all the consensually recognized behavior within the company relevant to their position in the company. Yet their latent roles are exceedingly important even as they take their manifest roles seriously. Parallel to the company situation is the campus where Cosmopolitans and Locals (Cosmos and Locals) were compared. Cosmos are the faculty members corresponding to the company "experts." Locals are more like "company men." At "Cooperative College" it was found that, compared to Locals, Cosmos indicate they need more time for research, that if the college provided no time for research the job would be less satisfying; they said that the college itself has few people who share their professional interests, that they know fewer members of the faculty, that their intellectual stimulation comes from outside the college mainly, that the American Association of University Professors (the union, as it were, for colleges) is integral to the campus and is not an outside organization, that Communist hunts do affect life on the campus, and that salaries are relatively low. In addition, Cosmos had more Ph.D.'s in their ranks and more publications to their credit than did Locals.

Latent roles in the company or on the campus are important background factors in the enactment of the manifest role. *Mutatis mutandis*, the enactment at an annual convention of the manifest role of professional organization man (not Organization Man!) is conditioned by the latent role of being an employee of X Company or professor at Y University. Other latent and manifest roles are recognizable in respect to other positions.

e. *Voluntary or involuntary.* That there can be portions of a man's personality which are unpleasing to him and rejected by his ego is not any new piece of knowledge. Nor is it something new for us to realize that the individual may enact roles involuntarily. Prisoners of war engage in expected role behavior which is usually distasteful to them, just as prisoners of any kind may ordinarily play roles they do not choose. But here a caveat must be entered, inasmuch as the terms "voluntary" or "choose" may apply only to conscious choices, and in actuality what the individual "wants" unconsciously is often what he gets (Bergler, 1948). A role may be consciously voluntary and unconsciously involuntary; or the individual may unconsciously choose a role which consciously he rejects. Contrasting examples may be cited. In Voodoo and in other primitive activities in which there may be a "taking-the-role-of-a-moribund-person" how much the expected role of a dying person is unconsciously a desired role it would be difficult to say. Cases may be cited (Frazer, 1940) of "hexing" where the individual believed a spell had been cast on him or he had violated a deadly taboo and died from expecting to die. One case (Alexander, 1943) in which an individual died without apparent organic cause was considered by the specialist who worked with him to result from an inverted "death wish." Possibly, to be sure, among cases of "hexing" there must be those who have survived the curse placed upon them and did not play the role expected, that of a moribund person. But where the "hexed" person has died, a reasonable hypothesis—which yet seems almost impossible to test—is that inner voluntary factors united with the external cultural expectations to enable the individual to play such a seemingly involuntary role.

f. *Fantasy or reality*. Roles may generally be considered interpersonal functions; but some roles are played in so central a fashion that the expected behavior is entirely phenomenological. In a sense even fantasy roles are interpersonal in that they are ordinarily imagined behavior in a social situation; however, one can imagine himself alone in space or in a deserted spot. Reality roles are those which are played overtly, but which may have strong fantasy components in the way the person perceives and conceives of himself as playing his role. Thomas Hardy brings out a mixture of fantasy and reality roles in one of his "Satires of Circumstance":

IN CHURCH

"And now to God the Father," he ends,
And his voice thrills up to the topmost tiles:
Each listener chokes as he bows and bends,
And emotion pervades the crowded aisles,
Then the preacher glides to the vestry-door,
And shuts it, and thinks he is seen no more.
The door swings softly ajar meanwhile,
And a pupil of his in the Bible class,
Who adores him as one without gloss or guile,
Sees her idol stand with a satisfied smile
And reenact at the vestry-glass
Each pulpit gesture in deft dumb-show
That had moved the congregation so.[1]

8. *Conflicts in role behaviors can usually be referred to internal conflicts*. This proposition is in line with the orthodox psychoanalytic contention that neurotic conflicts are basically ego-vs-id and with the social psychological concept that conflict is within the individual who occupies a certain position containing inconsistent roles (Bates, 1956). In the case of neurotic conflicts which are the extremes, to be sure, there are role aspects to consider as the individual is confronted with expressing (primarily) his aggressive or sexual drives in an unacceptable fashion. Translated into role terms, if a person is confronted with playing the role of an aggressive individual, the role behavior may violate his role of a kindly, even-tempered person which he ordinarily perceives himself to be. The neurotic aspect may appear if his arm should become paralyzed, or in other words if he plays the role of a person unable to strike aggressively. Other than neurotic conflicts exist, of course. Sherif and Cantril (1947) cite cases of strong conflict over roles a girl should play in a taxi-dance hall. These role conflicts have their internal reference in the individual's quandary, "Am I this kind of a person (self) or that kind?" Role conflicts of the kind faced by an automobile driver wondering whether he should play the part of a generous lift-giver or that of a somewhat more hard-hearted (but probably safer) lift-refuser are not neurotic

[1] Reprinted by permission from *Satires of circumstance: lyrics and reveries with miscellaneous poems*. London: Macmillan, 1914.

ones or as serious as the taxi-dancers'. In any case the conflict is an internal one with superego often siding with the generous impulses of the id against the more "practical" ego.

Where, however, the individual does not consider either consciously or unconsciously that his roles are in conflict, even though others see them so, there is a role conflict which has no direct reference within the person. A high school girl said of a minister in her town that she had seen him first when he was in overalls and could never afterwards see him truly as a minister. As far as his personality was concerned, for her there was a conflict of roles; for him there was probably no internal conflict between wearing overalls, the role badge of physical labor, and his ordinary ministerial role.

The interplay of reactions to external and internal referents in conflict situations has been investigated under somewhat artificial, yet not entirely unrealistic conditions. What would you do if you were proctoring an examination and saw someone cheating? What degree of punishment should be inflicted? What if the person should turn out to be your roommate and friend? How would you expect the school authorities to react? How would you expect your friends to react if they should know about the cheating and your observation of it? Such questions were posed to a social science class (Stouffer, 1949). Students responded with a wide range of reactions which enabled the investigator to distinguish roughly three types of role expectations: Some considered that both authorities and students would react alike, others that they would react entirely differently, and still others that students and authorities would have different, but somewhat overlapping reactions. But for either potential audience, students or authorities, the kinds of actions the subject himself would take would be different depending upon whether the cheating would become public knowledge or not. The conflict could be regarded as internal, but its character and resolution are conditioned by reference to either internal or external referents (Sutcliffe & Haberman, 1956).

9. *Sub-roles may be found within major roles.* A person may become a special officer within an organization; he may also be a boy, a youth, or an adult within the general role of being masculine. India's division of its four major castes into seemingly innumerable sub-castes furnishes a good illustration of how sub-roles are found within major roles. The individual is first a Brahman, a Kshatriya, a Vaisya, or a Sudra, then he plays the part expected of one of his sub-caste. A difference has to be noted between the above example of being in the masculine role and that of castes in that the latter are not successive roles.

10. *An individual's roles may be considered as primary, secondary, and tertiary.* With little doubt roles can be considered from dozens of angles and classified by many systems. But if we make a list of the role behaviors of a society under any classification system we end up with a list of positions [1] in the society rather than with

[1] A list of many of the important positions of our society and some others indicates what role possibilities there are:

Adopted	Counselee	"Go-between"
Aggressor	Counselor	(of various
American	Cousin	kinds)
(etc.)	Delinquent	Gormand
Athlete	Director	Gourmet
Audience	Dominant	Grouch
Aunt	Driver	Hero
Authority	Dupe	Honest man
figure	Easterner	(Brutus is an
Blind, deaf, etc.	(etc.)	honorable
Boy	Economic	man)
Bureaucrat	status	Hostile critic
Child	Employee	Housewife
Chronological	Encourager	Human or
age (infant,	Enemy	created
child, ado-	Entrepreneur	Humorist
lescent,	Executive	Hunter
adult)	Experimenter	Hunted
Church mem-	Failure	Husband
ber	Farmer	Hypnotized
City man	Father	subject
Citizen	Feminine boy	Inferior
Civilian	Follower	Initiator
Class status;	Fool	Innovator
caste	Friend	Inventor
Club member	Gang member	Irreligious
Consumer	(etc.)	Jilted
Coordinator	Girl	Leader

individuals playing roles, a sociological rather than a personological result. For our purposes we can look at the individual and see that he fulfills several roles which seem most fundamental (primary), some which are important but not so fundamental (secondary), and others which trail off to very little importance (tertiary). An infinite series of gradations could be made, of course. By "important" here is meant "of relative significance for existence of the individual and maintenance of the basic human institution, the family." Let us take a male individual and follow him through his primary, secondary, and tertiary roles.

He may fulfill his primary role of *being human* which may be defined in different ways from culture to culture. Is it human to eat "long pig"? In our culture, no; in a cannibalistic culture, yes. As the person plays his (primary) human role, however defined, he may also play the primary reciprocal role of *being a child*. There are probably greater differences from culture to culture in the role expectations of childhood than in being human. Again, at the same time as he enacts his human and child roles, the individual takes on the role of *being a boy*. The conception that being a boy or girl is naturally a result of possessing certain primary or secondary sex characteristics has found little support in present-day social psychological research. Our individual has to learn much, if not most, of his primary role of being a boy. He also starts at birth and carries on with some changes another primary lifelong role, that of *being a consumer*. Thus, a man may have successive or concurrent primary roles such as being human, being a child, being a boy, and being a consumer.

Secondary roles which the person may enact are those of *membership in his racial or ethnic group*, of *being a sibling*, of *being hard-of-hearing*, or of *having the name of Jack Spratt*.[1] He has to learn what constitutes normal behavior in his society so that he can play the role of *a normal person*. As he grows to manhood, he is prepared for his secondary role of *husband* in positive or negative ways and in more or less organized fashion. He may likewise receive training and experience in a role expected of most male members of our culture, that of *producer*. He may grow into manhood in a depression era when he cannot enact his producer role, or he may be one who follows the "theory of the leisure class" (Veblen, 1934) as far as this important secondary role is concerned. Note that these various roles are very important from many standpoints, but that they are not as important as those instanced in the previous paragraph in maintaining existence and the family. For example, to maintain his very existence a man must be a consumer; he does not need to be a producer, for others may produce for him all his life.

Tertiary roles open to the person are so numerous that almost any can be selected. He may as a child, for instance, be a "*spoiled child*," or he may be a *submissive one* (not that these are diametrically opposed). He may become ill for a while and play the role of a *sick individual*. If he becomes a "*sickly child*," the role of being ill would probably assume secondary rather than ter-

Lover	"Partyer"	Success
Masculine girl	Patriot	Superior
Master (to dogs also)	Pedestrian	Teacher
	Performer	Technologist
Military person	Playboy	Traitor
	Producer	Tribesman
Minister	Race (or ethnic position)	Trustee
Mother		Twentieth-century man
"Natural child"	Religious	
	Scholar	Uncle
Neurotic	Seeing-hearing	Villain
Nonathletic	Self-employed	Virginian (etc.)
Normal	Servant	Vocational status (professor, e.g.)
Officer (position on team)	Sibling	
	"Skinflint"	
	Spoiled Child	Well person
One's name	"Sport"	Wife
Opinion-giver	Student	Wise man
Orienter	Subject	World citizen
Parisian (etc.)	Submissive	
Parishioner	person	

[1] The psychology of names should be much more extensively investigated. Geneological studies scarcely touch on what a person's name means to him or to his comrades. Many children, for example, go through a stage of hating their names—why? What connection has one's name with his self? Many research projects could be set up to answer the question, "What's in a name?"

tiary importance. In this day of mass experimentation he may be a *subject of an experiment*, enacting a role which requires special behavior peculiar to our civilization. He may become a gang [1] or *club member*, to a child a relatively temporary role (Dreger, 1955). Even though he may have learned many of the role expectations of being a boy, he may also be a feminine-type boy, a "*sissy*," a role which may generate much scorn from his peers and much discomfort within him. As he grows older, he may either "naturally" or reactively become an *athlete*, a role considered masculine even for some types of women's athletics. He may become a *lover*, even a "*jilted lover*" in his teens or later, roles for which there are often strictly prescribed behaviors.[2] If the individual becomes a *father* after assuming the marriage state, he takes on a primary role in our culture. (In some cultures father's role does not seem to be a primary one [Mead, 1953]. Sometimes in our own culture father's role is belittled as in the comic strip, "Bringing Up Father." It is nevertheless a primary one.)

[1] For childhood "the gang" does not have the serious overtones it has for youth; cf. Thrasher, *The Gang* (1927).

[2] Seventeenth century England had poetic prescriptions for both roles, probably even more than have other eras. Sir John Suckling presents the *lover's* role by indirection:
"Why so pale and wan, fond lover?
  Prithee, why so pale?
Will, when looking well can't move her,
  Looking ill prevail?
  Prithee, why so pale?
Why so dull and mute, young sinner?
  Prithee, why so mute?
Will, when speaking well can't win her,
  Saying nothing do't?
  Prithee, why so mute?"
                    ("Song")
And the *jilted lover's* role is portrayed by Thomas Carew:
"No tears, Celia, now shall win
  My resolved heart to return;
I have search'd thy soul within,
  And find nought but pride and scorn:
I have learn'd thy arts, and now
Can disdain as much as thou.
  Some power in my revenge convey
  That love to her I cast away."
                    (Disdain Returned)

The complexities and interrelations of primary, secondary, and tertiary roles can indeed be confusing. Our male individual whose career we have been following may continue his primary consumer role while he enacts a secondary or even tertiary role while maintaining certain social and economic status.[3] His specific *vocational role* may be secondary or tertiary. In India where a man is born to his vocation and cannot change his occupation, except under the corrosion of what Walter Lippman called "the acids of modernity," vocation is a secondary role. But in many if not most complex societies today a man may change from one occupation to another, sometimes requiring different skills, so that we might regard his vocational role as high among tertiary roles. As for social status *per se*, our individual may be able in a fluid society to change his status fairly readily, so that any status role becomes tertiary rather than secondary. But the role expectations of his class may have been learned too well to allow change, or the role expectations of another class may be impossible for him to fulfill. He cannot become one of the "400" merely by gaining more money. He cannot be entered in the "Social Register" by wanting to be in it (Baltzell, 1953). Therefore, his class or caste may be of the more enduring secondary ranking rather than of tertiary significance in relation to maintaining himself and his family.

A person's geographic role as Westerner, Southerner, Easterner, or Northerner may be secondary or tertiary. At the time of the Civil War *Northerner* and *Southerner* were distinctly secondary in rank. Some of that importance still seems to attach to being a Southerner even today. A *Westerner* and *Easterner* are playing tertiary roles at this time, but in the days of the Old West there may have been greater significance adhering to these roles. In many places the identification of an individual's

[3] Social scientists recently have begun to frown on the use of the term "socio-economic status" as too simplex a term for a complex of variables. It has merit as shorthand if we understand some of its complexities.

geographic role by his speech, manner of dressing, expression of ideas, and even his walk has been held not difficult at all. For example, the attendant at the trial of Jesus declared, "Certainly you are also one of them, for your accent betrays you" (Mt. 26:73b, RSV.) In any individual's case, of course, we have to be careful in making such identifications, for his role learning may have been incomplete or he has rejected his role consciously or unconsciously or both.

The man we have in mind may be a *driver* at one time, a *pedestrian* at another—and many complications enter into his learning and playing these tertiary roles. He may be an *honest man* (in general, and with due recognition of the lack of integration of personality), an *uncle*, a *patient*, a *twentieth century man*, a *friend*, a *humorist*, an *entrepreneur*, or any of the roles he may fill in a tertiary fashion, though most of these may at some times become secondary to him.

It is evident that while most primary roles are distinctly primary, the secondary and tertiary roles may more easily exchange places in the life of any individual. An examination of which roles are secondary and which tertiary may give us a great deal of information about the individual's total personality. It would be naïve, however, in view of all else that we know about roles to assume that a mere tally of the length of time a person spends in enacting one role or the amount of his expressed interest in it give a *direct* index of whether it is secondary or tertiary.

11. *Changes in roles constitute personality changes.* This principle is emphasized partly as a reminder that we are dealing with personality functions when we speak of role functions. To be consistent it is not permissible for us to say, "He has a different job, but it's the same old Charley." The very fact that Charley's role is different makes Charley different. There is little satisfactory evidence that role-playing of the kind used in leadership training and group problem-solving (Klein, 1956) in which someone takes on for a brief period another

person's imagined role leads to permanent changes in the personality structure (Mann, 1956). It may indeed be effective in accomplishing short-term goals, but it seems to lack motivating power for the long run. However, when real life conditions are investigated, changes in roles sometimes appear to effect changes which persist.

We need not go over the same ground covered previously (Chapter 3) on the consistency of personality, except to recall that changes of state or status may result in far-reaching changes of many different behaviors, though some persons seem more consistent from one place (or one role) to another. Changes in what seem to be only position may be in reality extensive changes in the personality.

In a longitudinal investigation (Lieberman, 1956) of factory workers in a medium-sized company, attitudes toward the company and the union were measured in September and October of 1951. Between the initial testing and December 1952, the experimental period, out of the 145 stewards and 151 foremen in the company two experimental groups were selected: (1) 23 workers who were promoted to foremen, and (2) 35 workers who were selected as (union) stewards. Two control groups were set up: (1) 46 workers who were not promoted to foremen during the experimental period, and (2) 35 workers who were not selected as stewards during the same period. These E and C groups were matched on various demographic, attitudinal, and motivational variables, as determined prior to the experimental period. In a retesting in December, 1952, the attitudes of those who had been advanced to foremen had changed to be more favorable to management than their controls, and the attitudes of those who had been selected stewards changed to be relatively more favorable to the union. A related finding was that the attitudes of the experimental group foremen had changed more in favor of management than the attitudes of the corresponding stewards did toward the union. Experimental foremen became more anti-union than were their controls, but experimental stewards did not become relatively more anti-management than did their controls.

Following the experimental period, a recession and other factors brought about changes of position: Eight out of 23 foremen became workers again, 12 still remained foremen, and three left the company voluntarily. Fourteen experimental stewards became just workers again, and 15 left the company voluntarily or were laid off. In June, 1954, the residues of the E and C groups were tested again. Foremen returning to workers' roles returned to their 1951 levels of attitudes, again holding the management and union attitudes they held previously. Foremen remaining such remained management-oriented in their attitudes. Results for stewards were not clearcut. For the foremen, however, it seems reasonable to conclude that the changes in position which they underwent, more distinct than in the case of stewards, brought about changes in the orientation of attitudes. Role changes meant personality changes, in this case in terms of attitudes.

Reinforcement for this principle is seen in another study of adjustment in old age (Phillips, 1957). When the variables of psychological adjustment, being treated differentially by others, and self-concepts (related to "How old I feel") were associated to objective role conditions of being employed or retired, married or widowed, and being between 60–69 or 70+ in age, significant correlations were found for the most part. That is, if one is in the role of a retiree, or a widow or widower, or over 70, he is inclined to be more maladjusted, to consider himself old, and to receive differential treatment. Thus, differences in internal psychological states and in reciprocal role-enactments change with certain other role changes. For those who are either undergoing such changes or are closely observing them, this report merely emphasizes the obvious.

In Chessman's (1954) story mentioned before he describes how he deliberately set himself not to let the state win, and part of not letting the state win was to keep from being imbued with the spirit of fear of Death Row. He said, "I had made up my mind the Row wouldn't change me, wouldn't touch me." But he added, "It finally did." Not that it broke him, but changed him:

. . . you can't spend more than five years in such a place as Death Row and not change, radically. In time the place gets inside you, it eats its way in; it writhes around in your innards. And once it does you'll never be the same again.

Do you doubt this? Do you think you could spend close to two thousand days, more than sixty months, well over five years, on the Row, fighting defiantly for survival, existing all the while in the very shadow of the gas chamber, and not change? That you could watch approximately half a hundred men walk by your cell and believe that, in some insidious way, it doesn't eat at your mind? That you could observe many of the doomed driven either insane or to the borderline of insanity by the stark fear of impending death, and not feel the slugging impact upon your own personality? That you could see men hounded to suicide or attempted suicide by fear and depression and stay wholly impervious to the sickening tug of environment upon your own mental processes? . . . That you could observe the baffled minds and tortured emotions of others of this condemned fraternity laid naked and raw by the mocking imminence of death, and not experience an inner upheaval, an indwelling turbulence? (Chessman, 1954).[1]

Agreeing (unknowingly, to be sure) with Chessman's thesis of the over-all effect of being forced to play a different role, one authority (Newcomb, 1950) cites several studies of the far-reaching effects of role changes, for example, of concentration camp experiences, as prisoners adapted to their roles, changing widely from their usual selves (Bettelheim, 1943), and of British prisoners of war whose "personality disturbances" were not temporary and "self correcting" (Curle, 1947). Of importance to us also is the critique (Newcomb, 1950) of a significant study done by Gordon Allport and his associates (1941) on refugees

[1] Chessman, Caryl. *Cell 2455 death row.* Englewood Cliffs: Prentice-Hall, 1954. Reprinted by permission.

from Nazi terror. Interviewing 90 refugees who had fled Germany after severe deprivation or persecution, these investigators found relatively few "personality changes" in their subjects because of the harrowing experiences. It is pointed out from the very evidence presented, however, that there were probably more temporary changes in personality than the investigators saw. Even if there were no "cataclysmic" personality changes, the critic concludes:

First, these refugees were so strongly addicted to their existing roles and existing self-perceptions that they fled their country rather than abandon them. And secondly, those who managed to escape, and to take up again something like their old roles, did not change radically in personality. We do not know how much personality change was suffered by other individuals whose roles were more permanently altered (Newcomb, 1950).

The only criticism of this critique is that too much distinction is made between "personality" and "role." A change in role is a change in personality. What is meant, it seems, is either that changes in *self* occurred with changes of *role* or that changes in role brought about changes of feeling states.

Sherif and Cantril (1947) give a number of examples of the seemingly drastic reformation of the self and role in adolescence when changing body shape and size reflect themselves in changed perceptions of the self and consequent role functions. But this is a circular process, for as the young person changes in his roles his body-image concepts likewise become different. Changing status in regard to the opposite sex makes for changes in the youth's self concepts, as he or she struggles to become masculine or feminine in the manner approved by society. And changing status in regard to adults makes for feelings of insecurity and inadequacy.

What Sherif and Cantril do not point out is that a change toward more positive self attitudes occurs as well in many if not most young people who gain security and adequacy feelings as a result of being treated sometimes like adults. In general, though,

conflicts between the role of child in which the adult sometimes casts the adolescent, denying him the full privileges of adulthood, and the role of adult, sometimes accorded the adolescent as he *is* given adult privileges, offer some of the best illustrations of the principle that role changes constitute personality changes. The unpublished research (Dreger, 1954) cited previously (Chapter 3), in which first semester Freshmen gave dating attitudes before and after the first three months of university life, revealed the wide changes in self-attitudes, over and above changes in attitude toward institutions and the opposite sex. Residence on a university campus, that is, enacting the role of college student, probably effected the changes. If Riesman is right about the changes in individuals across several centuries from "tradition-directed" to "inner-directed" to "other-directed," then even more widespread changes occur in the entire personality when external historical conditions alter the roles one plays: ". . . the other-directed person tends to become merely his succession of roles and encounters, and hence to doubt who he is or where he is going" (Riesman, 1950).

12. *The individual's roles are usually involved in systems of roles.* In approaching role functions from the standpoint of the individual, it may seem that we are disregarding the strongly interactional nature of role enactments. Viewed personologically and especially topographically, roles may appear like ectoplasmic haloes which the individual carries about with him and whose outer edges may from time to time merge with similar haloes about others. A more accurate picture is that roles form living matrices (Steiner, 1955) or role systems which are comprised of the sets of interrelated behaviors and categories of persons who are expected to behave in specified ways. Accordingly, in most cases the role any one person plays is a dynamic and integral portion of an entire role system in which there are many participants.

One of the clearest examples of this part a person's specified role plays in the role system is seen in clinical practice but should be observable in everyday life. In psychiatric treatment at one hospital, therapists realized that facilitation or failure of treatment occurred not alone in respect to the personality structure (apart from roles), to the individual's own roles, and to his own social norms, but likewise in respect to the roles that others played about the patient. In this study (Rapoport & Rosow, 1957) it was pointed out that a son and husband can react to reciprocal role-playing of mother-in-law and daughter-in-law as well as to the mother and wife with whom he is engaging in reciprocal role-playing. The individual is a different individual because of his reactions to the interactions of others. Role relations between two or more persons acting reciprocally may be improved or disturbed by role relations between or among others in a system of roles (Strauss, 1956).

Some experimental evidence can be adduced to show the relation of the individual's roles to others' roles. In a level of aspiration experiment (Howard & Berkowitz, 1958), subjects were given the task of a (simulated) air defense warning center coordinator. Their performances were judged by three supposed peers, who in reality gave judgments according to a prearranged plan: They gave either moderate (so-called modal) judgments or very high or very low judgments, either with or without other "judges" present. Subsequently, the "judges" were rated sociometrically by the subjects who also estimated their own performance level. The judge who in any one case deviated from his fellow judges was perceived in error, regardless of his giving favorable or unfavorable judgments of the subject's performance. He was also rated lower sociometrically. These judgments on the "judges" interacted with the subject's level of aspiration, as measured by his estimate of his performance level. But our main concern here is in the fact that the reactions of the subjects came from the judges' relative roles as deviant or conforming, not only in terms of their perception of their own roles as successes or failures.

Similar results to those above were obtained in a manufactured situation in which subjects listened to supposed prisoners-of-war who explained why they had capitulated to their Korean captors. The assumed role which the "prisoners" played in respect to their American military administrators affected the judgments the subjects made of the culpability of the former (Jones & deCharms, 1958). Roles which others in the family play in respect to one another were mentioned above. One experimental study (Connor, Greene, & Walters, 1958) gives oblique support to the not unreasonable conclusion of the clinical workers (Rapoport & Rosow, 1957). Husbands and wives agreed more on what "good" parent and child roles should be than did fathers and children; and mothers and children agreed more than did fathers and children.

Satisfaction with one's own role in a system of roles may depend upon the perceived harmony or discrepancy between the role-expectancies the first individual sets up for others' roles in the system and the actual role behaviors of those individuals who fill those roles (Bidwell, 1957). The secretary may expect her boss to be treated in a certain way by the "big boss." If the latter does not play his role as the secretary expects him to, in relation to her boss, she may become dissatisfied with her own role in the system of roles within the company. It may not be necessary for us to be reminded that our reactions to others' interactions, upon which our own satisfaction may be based, are not determined by the actual interactions so much as by our perceptions of those interactions. Children often react to a perceived favoritism displayed by their parents towards another sibling, only to find later that the other sib perceived that it was the first brother or sister who was the favorite! Each has reacted to a perceived favoring parent-favored child role interaction which may not have been an actuality in either case.

ROLE AND TRAIT

What relation is there between roles and traits? We have seen that roles and the self are very closely related. So, too, are roles and traits.[1] Since we have not taken up traits in an extended way, as we do in Chapters 13 and 14, there is no need of extensive comparison here. Using Allport's definition of trait (p. 57) we may recognize traits as internal, relatively long-lasting functions which correspond to certain roles played by the individual. These traits can only be inferred from behavior, from role behavior to a great extent. A person may not always play a role consistent with his trait (Hovell, 1955), but unless he plays the role or engages in some behavior that gives us a hint of his trait, from a scientific standpoint we cannot claim he possesses the trait.

How closely identified the internal and external, the trait and the role, are may be judged from examining the list of trait-elements which represent the extremes of the Source Trait A. *Cyclothymia vs. Schizothymia*, identified by Raymond Cattell (Cattell, 1946, 1950, 1957).

A+ *Positively Loaded*	A— *Negatively Loaded*
Easygoing	vs. Obstructive, cantankerous
Adaptable (in habits)	vs. Inflexible, "rigid"
Warmhearted	vs. Cool, indifferent
Frank, placid	vs. Close-mouthed, secretive, anxious
Emotionally expressive	vs. Reserved
Trustful, credulous	vs. Suspicious, "canny"
Impulsively generous	vs. Close, cautious
Cooperative, self-effacing	vs. Hostile, egotistical
Subject to personal emotional appeals	vs. Impersonal
Humorous	vs. Dry, impassive [2]

Unless, to take one instance, the individual expresses the role of being an easy-going

[1] Stern (1938) recognized different emphases in the personality according to a man's different roles. Allport (1937) speaks of a person's *socius* distinct from his person, though he comes close to the view of this text in stating, "Every person is also a *socius*."

[2] Cattell, R. B. *The sixteen personality factor questionnaire*. Institute for Personality & Ability Testing, Champaign, Ill., 1957. Reprinted by permission.

person in some way, we cannot gather that he possesses this element of the trait *Cyclothymia vs. Schizothymia*. He has to *tell* us by means of a questionnaire, where he gives samples of what he thinks or does or feels, or he has to manifest such behavior in an observable situation. He may be fooled as to whether he has this trait-element or not, or we may be fooled. But unless the person manifests some kind of behavior, primarily playing a role, we are only guessing as to the existence of his trait.

An even clearer illustration of the relation of role to trait is obtained in a study (Dreger & Sweetland, 1960) of college students' characterization of their fathers as they remembered their fathers from childhood. A rating scale embodying the characterization was factor-analyzed, with seven factors representing traits of fatherhood coming out of the analysis. Five of these are: *Secular Non-Punitiveness, Church-Going Religiosity, Ecclesiastical Righteousness, Puritanism*, and *Loving-kindness*. The other two are what may be called ideal fatherhood traits; *Ideal American Fatherhood*, which is a compound of being just, loving, controlled, lots of fun, clean, mild, one who demanded high standards, and industrious; and *Ideal Religious (nonecclesiastical) Fatherhood*, which is compounded of being very religious, clean, lots of fun, industrious, sober, being one who demanded high standards, loving, kind to others in the family, and kind to mother.

The authors regard the traits as double-distilled, in that childhood perceptions may have been inaccurate and memories may have subsequently been distorted. And yet, enough reality shines through to suggest that fathers really possessed the traits ascribed to them by their children, that is, in fair measure. Here, then, are traits of fathers, traits whose outward expressions are the roles in which their children saw them. As far as the children are concerned, these roles constitute father. However distorted the picture the children may have, the fatherhood traits underlie the roles in which the children perceived their fathers.

The answer to our question seems to be,

then, that roles and traits are generally related as outer to inner. Virtually every one of the trait-elements in the Source Trait and fatherhood traits above is socially-directed, and every one is a description of a relation between the person and an object, human or otherwise. There may be traits which are not statements of relations; if so, they constitute exceptions to our answer. But if these traits can be fitted together in some kind of profile or equation, prediction may be made to the kinds of roles the individual will enact. Perhaps oversimplifying, we may say that from one set of role behaviors we infer traits, the existence of which enables us to predict other role behaviors.

It is appropriate in conjunction with the answer to the question concerning relation of traits and roles to remark that the insight of past generations of philosophers and religious leaders in respect to the social nature of man seems confirmed by social psychological research into man's place in society. Although probably more restricted originally in meaning than it may be taken, St. Paul's statement bears pondering, "No man lives to himself, and no man dies to himself" (Rom. 14:7). Lord Tennyson's "I am a part of all that I have met" carries the same theme. A positive response to Cain's question, "Am I my brother's keeper?" signifies a similar recognition of the interpersonal nature of personality. No man lives to himself, for his roles are part of his living, and his roles are not within-the-skin. He is part of all that he has met, for his very being consists of others in part. The ethical conclusion that he is his brother's keeper follows to an extent from the realization that his brother is, insofar as he is co-creator of a man's roles, a portion of his personality.

Role Strength

Almost any of the experimental studies cited in this chapter and most of those involving measurement cited anywhere in this book can be regarded as attempts to measure role strength. For scarcely any aspect of personality does not have its interpersonal implications. Specifically, however,

strength of role conflict has been assessed in one study (Gullahorn, 1956). Subjects, members of a union in one company, were required to imagine roles as officers in a company club and union chief steward, together with varying pressures from the company, the union, or their constituents. One conclusion reached is that as pressures increase, making for greater role conflict, an increasing tendency to unrealistic viewing of the dilemma is found. In another area, prediction of role changes, from constituent to officer or vice versa in a large number of school organizations, has been made (Olmsted, 1957) by means of measuring the strength of psychological involvement and sociometric status and length of time in the group. Degrees of ego-involvement in roles have been suggested in the theoretical discussion to which reference was made previously (Sarbin, 1954).

More general methods of assessments of role strength in terms of interpersonality are delineated in the system of interpersonal diagnosis (Freedman, Leary, Ossorio, & Coffey, 1951; Leary & Coffey, 1955). This system was developed at the Kaiser Foundation and the University of California. It has grown principally out of Sullivan's (1949, 1953) interpersonal psychiatry and Murray's (1938, 1949) need-press system. In the resulting diagnostic scheme the individual is scored in eight major areas of role-taking: Autocratic, Hyper-Normal (compulsive responsibility and empathy behavior), Over-Agreeableness, Docility, Self-Effacement, Distrustful, Aggressive, and Exploitive behavior.

Summary

Roles constitute the major sub-function of personality, topographically considered, in which personality is recognized as interpersonal. A role is the range of behavior expected of all persons occupying a certain position. Technically, only the role behaviors of persons are the concern of personology. Roles are played in reference to others and to one's own selves, both roles and selves being at times conscious, at times unconscious. Perceptual functions determine roles in part in that the position sometimes has to be perceived in order to know how to fill it. Although other aspects are present, learning constitutes the major process in developing role-enactment. "Ego-involvement" is present in varying degrees in different roles. Polar qualities characterize roles, though these are not usually dichotomous; they are permanent or temporary, reciprocal or nonreciprocal, central or peripheral, manifest or latent, voluntary or involuntary, and fantasy or reality.

Conflicts in role behaviors can usually be referred to internal conflicts. Sub-roles are subsumed under major or more general roles. An individual's roles may be considered as primary, such as being a child, secondary, such as being a husband, or tertiary, such as being a club member. Role changes constitute personality changes. The individual's roles are rarely enacted apart from the roles of others, especially their interacting roles, in role systems. The very listing of "personality characteristics" forces a realization of the role aspect of virtually any trait. Role strength is measured in specific and general ways, both indirectly and directly.

QUESTIONS

1. Distinguish role, position, role behaviors, and role expectations from one another.

2. Summarize and give a critical judgment of each of the positive statements concerning roles.

3. What relation is there between roles and traits?

CHAPTER 11

TOPOGRAPHICAL STRUCTURE-FUNCTIONS: CONSCIOUSNESS AND UNCONSCIOUSNESS

STRUCTURE OF CONSCIOUSNESS AND UNCONSCIOUSNESS

Chapters 6 through 10 have considered in some detail the topography of the personality according to a psychoanalytically-based schema. To the major structure-functions of id, ego, and superego which are recognized by orthodox psychoanalysis we have added the role functions which operate in conjunction with id, ego, and superego in a hierarchical fashion. This scheme is not a simple one when the overlappings and mutualities of functioning are regarded, but it is relatively simple in that such a model of personality enables us to classify much of the data at hand and relate many variables of personality in a more or less parsimonious way. Our personalities, however, are more complex than can be represented thus. Accordingly, still viewing personality topographically we must consider other cross-classifications of the phenomena already known. Chapters 11 and 12 are concerned with major functions interlaced in the topography of personality—consciousness and unconsciousness in this

chapter, and central and peripheral in the following chapter.

In a topographical view of the personality, consciousness [1] and unconsciousness are logical "areas" to isolate for consideration. All functions, from the basic ego functions through even tenuous roles, can be regarded at any one time as being divided into two dynamic components, those which are more or less conscious and those which are more or less unconscious. So much we have recognized from the discussion in Chapter 5 on the over-all dynamic structure of personality.

It is only when the attempt is made to say exactly what functions are covered by the expressions "consciousness" and "unconsciousness," that there is difficulty and probably more floundering than in any other aspect of personology. William James, who called consciousness "the Fundamental Fact," wrote at the end of the last century in respect to "personal conscious-

[1] The discussion is limited to finite personality in human beings. The theological and metaphysical questions of consciousness and unconsciousness as cosmic qualities must be laid aside here.

ness," "Its meaning we know so long as no one asks us to define it, but to give an accurate account of it is the most difficult of philosophic tasks" (James, 1920.) Yet even Freud, who seemed to be interested primarily in unconscious functions through most of his long career, testified to the importance of consciousness. After making a just estimate of the enormous influence psychoanalysis had had in uncovering unconscious processes he wrote in 1938 (only a year before his death), "But none of this implies that the quality of being conscious has lost its importance for us. It remains the one light which illuminates our path and leads us through the darkness of mental life" (Freud, 1938). A generation ago, despite James and Freud, some psychologists were ready to discard consciousness, yielding only to the recognition that it might be an "epiphenomenon," a kind of impotent shadow accompanying behavior. Although there appears to have been no determined effort to reinstate consciousness, it has been allowed to return in the form of awareness or whatever is supraliminal.

In connection with unconsciousness much greater disagreement exists among psychologists. Freud wrote confidently at the beginning of the century, "The unconscious is the true psychical reality" (Freud, 1900). But some (e.g., Phillips, 1956) deny flatly that there is any unconsciousness. Such a denial is usually meant only to refer to repressed unconsciousness, indicating that the authors of the denial have not thought through the different kinds of unconsciousness.

The man on the street [1] may regard psychologists as crazy for debating about what seems like a perfectly obvious reality: one is either conscious or unconscious. The complexities of the problems, however, have occasioned extensive discussions (Abramson, 1951a, 1951b, 1952, 1954, 1955) by some of the best minds in various profes-

sions without bringing any satisfactory resolutions. At this point, however, we shall assume that consciousness and unconsciousness exist as (very complex) dynamic major functions of the personality. Our assumption may be incorrect. But many of the data of behavior seem to make sense only on the basis of such an assumption.

As has been repeatedly stated in connection with the previous topographical divisions of personality, there is no intent in these pages to reify consciousness and un-- consciousness. They are constructs, convenient designations of groups of functions roughly divided by certain criteria which are made explicit in the subsequent discussion.

Various theories of consciousness and unconsciousness are drawn upon for the materials presented here. One especially (Collier, 1955, 1956) which concentrates upon the dynamic nature of consciousness appears to coincide with the orientation of this text. Consciousness, according to this theory, is a regulatory field. What becomes more conscious is more available to realistic action. The less conscious any affect or idea, down to the regions of unconsciousness, the less capable it is of entering into the regulatory process. A clinical objection to this deceptively simple theory is that often a counselee may say, "Well, now I know about my hostile feelings toward my child (or sexual feelings toward my mother, etc.). But what can I do about them?" The answer, in accord with the theory, is that some of the ideas and affects, it is true, have now come into the regulatory field of consciousness; but not all the connections have yet entered consciousness. The theory of consciousness as a regulatory field has not been undergirded by research but has merit as an explanatory device for the data already at hand.

Multiplex Forms of Consciousness and Unconsciousness

Let us assume with common sense that there are over-all functions of the personality which we may call consciousness and unconsciousness and ask what forms they

[1] Who is the foil for so much writing in texts that we tend to forget he is not the other person. He is each of us in respect to any discipline in which we are not at home, just as any one of us is in a minority of some kind.

may take. Consciousness and unconsciousness, we may say from the start, can hardly be considered unitary functions of personality. Probably most of the functions that have been named in this book are complex rather than unitary. But in this case there is question whether we should even use the same terms to apply to so many different phenomena.

Consider the following imaginary but not unrealistic incident: Before us is a young man who has just received a spinal anesthetic. A truck struck his car and he was jammed into a corner in such a way that his lower extremities are badly injured; he was not aware (*conscious*) of his plight, however, for his head struck the dash and he became *unconscious*. It was a relatively light and undamaging blow, so that he recovered *consciousness* fairly soon. He is now *unconscious* in one sense, for he is unaware (*unconscious*) of sensory stimulation in the lower portion of his body, but he is also *conscious* in that he can perceive with any of the sense organs in the upper part of his body. He is concentrating with great interest on what the surgeon is doing, very much alive to (*conscious of*) the actions of the surgeon and his associate, but he is so intent on what is being done that he pays no attention to (*is unconscious of*) the internes watching from the benches in the amphitheater. To the young man there are such dramatic elements in this operation on his extremities that he forgets (*is unconscious of*) himself. And yet suddenly a depressing realization dawns on him (*he becomes conscious*) that a deep ambition he had scarcely allowed himself to entertain (had suppressed, had been *unconscious* of desires), on account of the long, tedious, and expensive training necessary to become a surgeon, was desired not only because he wanted to serve mankind, but also because he wanted to cut and hurt people, a desire he had repressed (*was unconscious of*) until this time. Now while he continues to stare, he no longer sees (perceives, or *is conscious of*) what is transpiring in front of and around him, though anyone watching him would say that he is, as psychologists used to say, sentient (*conscious*). A close observer might report that he was "in a brown study" (*slightly unconscious* of his surroundings) and perhaps pass a hand in front of his face. But the unperceiving young man is very much aware of (*conscious of*) his

phenomenological condition, as a torrent of thoughts and feelings generated by memories of events long forgotten floods his mind. No sooner does one memory come than it seems to drag after it another and another out of the well of forgotten (*unconscious*) things. He scarcely knows (*is conscious*) that the rest of the operation is occurring, that he is transferred to a cart, and returned to his room. During the day he receives a sedative, for his surgeon has anticipated some pain, so that he lies half awake and half asleep (*half conscious*) a good part of the day. A troubled sleep comes to him (*he becomes unconscious*) at night during which he dreams (*becomes conscious*) of doctors in armor operating with lances.[1]

What kind of terms are these which refer to such contradictories that a man can be both conscious and unconscious at the same time and can have several different kinds of consciousness and unconsciousness simultaneously or successively? There is, to be sure, some thread which seems to hold together seemingly diverse functions, as we shall see in a moment. But the diversity makes us realize that the simple concepts of consciousness and unconsciousness held by the "man on the street" are unsatisfactory. It may be that single terms will have to be abandoned to describe and define so much diversity. And yet, there likewise is great complexity among the subfunctions of the ego, a major function, whose general validity we recognize. Although at this stage

[1] Adapted by permission from Miller, J. G., *Unconsciousness.* New York, Wiley, 1943, pp. 302–312. Miller lists sixteen ways in which the term "unconsciousness" has been employed, each of which seems to imply a corresponding kind of consciousness. Further suggestions come from a group of experts representing a number of disciplines ranging from physiology to anthropology who met for a number of conferences sponsored by the Josiah Macy, Jr. Foundation, on "Problems of Consciousness"; though they did not reach definitive conclusions about the subject, they contributed considerable light (Abramson, 1951a, 1951b, 1952, 1954, 1955.) In addition, both Freudian and Jungian psychologists have been investigating various aspects of consciousness and unconsciousness for many years. And joined to the multitude of introspective studies of early experimental psychology are numerous experiments of recent years.

of our understanding it is not evident that consciousness and unconsciousness can be divided into component sub-functions in the same manner that id or ego can be, some systematist may yet classify sub-functions of consciousness and unconsciousness in as logical a way. In the meantime we shall assume that the verbal identities found in the use of the terms consciousness and unconsciousness as applied to diverse phenomena represent some real identities among these phenomena.

Some beginning of understanding the multiplicity of introspective and objectively observable data can be made when we regard the different frames of reference from which one can view consciousness (and by implication, unconsciousness). From a *physiological* frame of reference we find, for instance, that there are degrees of sleep and wakefulness according to the diurnal cycle, paralleling variations in body temperature (Kleitman, 1950). Or from a *psychophysical* frame of reference it has been suggested that one individual may be insensible to pain to which another individual registers distress (Stevens, 1951, Chapter 13), as common experience would testify. Or a person may at one time be aware of pain which he fails to sense at another time. From a *psychological* frame of reference an individual may be able to recall material which he either has repressed or that he has been unwilling to tell (Wolberg, 1952).

From a *sociological* viewpoint, Mead in what is considered by social scientists a classic series of lectures (Mead, 1934) stressed how much of our selves and roles is taken over from others without our being aware that we are doing so. Anthropologists emphasize the vast differences in behaviors and attitudes that obtain in one culture as compared to another, practices which are so unconsciously absorbed that the person "knows" that they are natural or inborn, whereas the person in the other culture with directly opposed behavior or attitudes "knows" that his practices are natural.

To take just one example from hundreds,

Inkeles, writing as a sociologist but basing his observation on many cross-cultural studies, states:

It appears that romantic love is a behavior pattern of which very large numbers of Americans are not only capable, but which they manifest with a high degree of regularity. This manifestation of personality, when combined with the appropriate social pressures, insures the continued operation of our courtship and marriage patterns. At the same time, it must be recognized that romantic love is relatively unusual in the known cultures of the world and to the participants in a great many cultures, is essentially incomprehensible. This certainly need not be considered a matter of accident, since in societies where the family structure demands extensive restrictions on the choice of marriage partners, and in many instances precisely prescribes those partners, the appearance of romantic love patterns as we know them would be exceedingly disruptive to the existing system (Kluckhohm, 1953, Chapter 37).[1]

Romantic love is "natural" behavior—to some societies—but would upset the social structures in others. It is unconsciously assumed in our culture that romantic love is fundamental to marriage and the establishment of a home; other cultures make no such assumption. We have for the most part been unaware of many similar cultural assumptions. From a sociological frame of reference the perception and absorption process at least appears to be one of which the individual is only partly aware.

We can be fairly certain that viewed objectively consciousness and unconsciousness are not unitary functions of personality; as is evident, a multiplicity of forms of consciousness or unconsciousness exists. However, rather than substitute other names for the different kinds of functions which appear to be represented in such diverse ways, different frames of reference may enable us to categorize various subfunctions on a logical basis. Of course, there are other

[1] Kluckhohn, C., Murray, H. A. & Schneider, D. M. (Eds.) *Personality in nature, society, and culture.* (2nd ed.) New York: Knopf, 1953. Reprinted by permission.

ways than this one method to accomplish the same purpose.

Consciousness

According to Miller (1942) who has been a major systematizer in the fields under consideration, most observers agree that the characteristic of *subjective awareness* is common to all kinds of consciousness. If so, it is difficult to know what is meant by subjective awareness. Jennings (1906), the noted biologist, claimed that animals right down to the amoeba are capable of becoming conscious. Further, it is commonly accepted even by experts that infants become conscious. In neither case can we be sure that the quality of subjective awareness is present, that is, if the latter term means what it seems to mean: being responsive to stimuli and *knowing* that one is responsive. Introspection in adult human beings does indeed reveal this characteristic as common to diverse kinds of consciousness. But to extrapolate introspective conclusions to preverbal infants and animals may be unjustified. Nevertheless, inasmuch as we are concerned with the adult human individual, subjective awareness may be taken as the element which makes for a phenomonological unity among differing states of consciousness.[1]

Sometimes rather than merely considering consciousness and subjective awareness as related, some have equated them. But whatever possibilities an amoeba may have for consciousness, its consciousness may reasonably be inferred to be so different from the adult human being's that subjective awareness could scarcely be regarded as synomymous with its consciousness. To a lesser degree the same can be said of the neonate or infant human being.

Consciousness and self-awareness cannot be regarded as identical either. By self-

[1] We do not now have to fight through the semantical issue which Freud (Freud, 1955; Miller, 1942) had to meet, that is, the contention that all that is mental is conscious and anything not conscious cannot be called mental. We assume on the basis of practically overwhelming evidence that there are some unconscious psychological processes.

awareness is usually meant awareness of oneself as a responder to one's responses. One philosopher states, "To be conscious means to respond cognitively to a stimulus which is itself a response" (Krikorian, 1938). Unless, however, consciousness is more than this response to a response, a person would not be said to be conscious when he "forgets himself." At such a time the individual becomes so engrossed in his own or another's activities that he is not cognizant of his own responses or aware of his awareness. Yet retrospecting on such periods the individual declares that of all times in his experience he was most conscious then—of certain matters. Consciousness appears to be more than subjective awareness or self-awareness, even though both may be considered elements of consciousness at times.

Perception and consciousness are closely related, but are probably not synonymous. The evidence for unconscious perception is equivocal (Goldiamond, 1958; Howes, 1954), as we shall see later. If, however, there is such a phenomenon as unconscious perception, as claimed by a number of psychologists, perception and consciousness could not be equated. Further, various thinking processes (Bartlett, 1958; McKellar, 1957; Wertheimer, 1959) require considerable conscious manipulation of symbols only remotely connected with the stimuli prompting the thought process. Related as they are, consciousness and perception appear to be distinct functions.

One other identification has been made which in the light of available evidence cannot be maintained. That is, it is sometimes thought that voluntary acts are conscious and involuntary ones are unconscious. Although many studies of decision-making have been made in recent years, work in volition as such has not been extensive since the early years of this century. Our knowledge can be cautiously summarized for the area of volitional-nonvolitional activity primarily in physiological terms: Some muscles of the body (in general, the striped muscles) are under "voluntary control" in the sense that we desire to move them and they move (whatever causal re-lations, if any, are involved). Other muscles (in general, the smooth ones) operate "au-tomatically," in the sense that ordinarily no matter what we desire they move or do not move. Being conscious cannot be equated with voluntary acts in this regard, for sometimes movements of the voluntary musculature occur without volition, as in spasms and tics of which the individual may very well be conscious but over which he has no control. On the other hand, fol-lowing Ach and the "imageless thought" school, psychologists have recognized "de-termining tendencies" or sets for action, some of which are unconscious. Accord-ingly, there appears to be unconscious voli-tion. If by definition an action is voluntary when the individual desires or wills it, then the fact that some actions are unconsciously desired or willed (an unconscious "set" is established for them) negates the equating of voluntariness and consciousness.

The only positive results we can gather from the foregoing paragraphs is that sub-jective awareness seems to be an essential component in the human adult's conscious-ness. Beyond that conclusion we can only affirm that consciousness is more than—but not identical with—subjective awareness, self-awareness, perception, and volition. Topographically, consciousness may be viewed as a more or less distinct area from unconsciousness, with one subregion of sub-jective awareness overlapping with other subregions of self-awareness and so on, and possibly other regions unknown or undesig-nated.

Unconsciousness

It would be a welcome simplification if it would be possible to say that consciousness is one (complex) function and unconscious-ness is its polar opposite.[1] There seems to be a phenomenological unity to adult con-sciousness as represented by subjective

awareness; the personality "region" of un-consciousness, on the other hand, is not merely characterized by lack of awareness, but is a set of sub-regions, whose unity as one grand function may seriously be ques-tioned.

Contributing as he so often did to our in-sights into personality, Freud (1955) gave one fundamental distinction in respect to unconscious processes which has been of as-sistance in ordering personality data. He spoke of both "the unconscious" and "the preconscious."[2] In the former are repressed materials, those affects and thoughts which are unacceptable to the ego. The latter con-tains all the materials which are readily accessible to consciousness, but are not at present "in mind." Debate has continued from Freud until now regarding "the un-conscious," whether it exists and if it does what it consists of; as far as "the precon-scious" is concerned, although the term may not be acceptable, the facts to which it points are not questioned.

Another fundamental lead regarding un-consciousness comes from physiological and

---

[1] A rather involved statement of a Jungian posi-tion concerning polarity of consciousness and un-consciousness may be found in Bash, *Conscious-ness and the Unconscious in Depth and Gestalt Psychology* (1949).

[2] Sometimes "foreconscious" has been used in Freudian literature but seems to have given way to "the preconscious." Others have introduced such terms as "subconscious," almost entirely as a synonym for "the unconscious" but out of re-pute now presumably because of its direct con-notations of above-and-below. Morton Prince's "co-conscious" has similarly lost out in psy-chology; it was used originally to apply to "mul-tiple personalities," but sometimes referred to un-conscious and sometimes conscious processes. Jung (1928) divides "the unconscious" into per-sonal and collective, the latter containing the in-herited images, especially "archetypes" or master images of "mother," "father," "the sea," and other universal images. Oriental thought has proposed a "superconscious" which is beyond both conscious-ness and unconsciousness, but is an integral part of the mind. In Indian thought *samadhi* is the highest form of religious experience, which when experienced and comprehended goes beyond con-sciousness, unconsciousness, and even supercon-sciousness; the experiencer reaches a state where the functioning of the mind is independent of the nervous system (Akhilananda, 1946). A West-erner might irreverently declare, "As far as I can see, the man has voted himself out of existence." To which an Easterner might reply, "Yes, voted him*self* out of existence."

psychophysiological research, especially on sleep and wakefulness (Kleitman, 1939, 1951; Monnier, 1952). From this research we learn about some functions which carry on automatically whether we are aware of them or not, though when we are aware of them their functioning *may* be somewhat different.

From the leads offered by Freud and others, it is possible to establish logical subregions within the major part-function of personality designated as unconsciousness. These subregions, of course, are *dynamic* ones, and are not to be conceived either as representing areas of the brain or as fixed entities. Moreover, they, like the other functions of personality, are not independent but interdependent. They are detailed here to give some kind of structure by which personality materials classified as unconscious may be set in order.

Automatic Functions. These are the functions which rarely if ever come to the conscious awareness of an individual, yet each of them in itself and in conjunction with other functions forms part of the over-all personality. We probably never become conscious of the flow of blood in our veins and arteries. We cut ourselves and the blood flows, or our hearts and the veins in our necks may thump, but in neither case are we directly conscious of blood flowing in the circulatory system. The passage of a nerve impulse along a neuron is a function which with many other nerve impulses may issue in consciousness (Culbertson, 1950). Some functions, like sleep, are virtually by definition unconscious ones, even though there may be conscious activities during sleep in the form of dreams. Other functions arise to consciousness at times; a person's heart action is usually on an unconscious level, but in certain instances his heart's pounding may be highly noticeable to him. Generally, however, the physiological functions operate below the threshold of awareness in respect to any sense modality with which they may be associated.

There may be psychological functions of a nonrepressed variety which never become conscious, such as Jung's "collective unconscious," which is said only to manifest itself symbolically, never directly. Most psychologists do not side with Jung in asserting a collective unconscious, which may be regarded as a series of basic reaction patterns deposited in the individual by inheritance, patterns which include some actual (unconscious) thoughts.[1] Although psychologists tend to reject the concept of these unconscious patterns when they are referrable to the higher psychological functions, Jungians have presented scholarly surveys of the myths of mankind as well as of their own clinical materials (Neumann, 1954) which as evidence for a collective unconscious, cannot be lightly brushed aside. Here we leave the door open and do not assert that Jungian interpretations are false, especially merely because they may sound fantastic to the average "hardboiled" Westerner. In these pages we have had occasion

[1] Neumann (1949), as interpreter of Jung, writes: "The instincts of the collective unconscious form the substrate of this assimilative system. They are repositories of ancestral experience, of all the experience which man, as a species, has had of the world. Their 'field' is Nature, the external world of objects, including the human collective and man himself as an assimilative-reactive, psychophysical unit. That is to say, there is in the collective psyche of man, as in all animals, but modified according to species, a layer built up of man's specifically human, instinctive reactions to his *natural* environment. A further layer contains group instincts, namely experiences of the specifically *human* environment, of the collective, race, tribe, group, etc. This layer covers herd instincts, specific group reactions which distinguish a particular race or people from others, and all differentiated relationships to the nonego. A final layer is formed by instinctive reactions to the psychophysical organism and its modifications. For example, hunger, hormone constellations, etc., are answered by instinctive reactions. All these layers intercommunicate. Their common factor is that the reactions are purely instinctive, the psychophysical unit reacting as a whole by means of meaningful acts which are not the outcome of individual experience, but of ancestral experience, and which are performed without the participation of consciousness." (Reprinted by permission from Neumann, E. The origins and history of consciousness. (Trans. by R. F. C. Hull.) New York: Bollingen Series XLII [Pantheon Books, 1954].)

to call attention to the fantastic nature of much that comes out in a clinician's everyday work. Suffice it to say now, however, that there may be genuinely psychological (nonrepressed) functions which never become conscious and so may be classed under "automatic functions."

The Preconscious. Everything which is not presently in the consciousness of the individual but which is readily accessible to awareness can be considered preconscious.[1] In actuality, these are many of the functions with which general psychology normally deals, learning and memory and thought functions, for example. Only an nth part of these functions can be conscious at any one time; and yet the mechanisms of repression and its companion defenses are not operative in keeping them unconscious. Many materials are functions (in the mathematical sense) of learning and retention; unless they have been learned in some way and retained somewhere during an interval when they are not in the person's consciousness, they are nowhere as far as the individual is concerned.[2] In order to determine what memories are functioning in the individual's preconscious, laboratory methods can be utilized, or clinical probing can get at unrepressed memories more or less readily accessible to consciousness.

What are some of the characteristics of preconsciousness as viewed from a person-ological standpoint? How is it that the "average performance" reported in psychology texts in relation to thinking, learning, and memory does not seem to characterize the actual performance of the concrete person? We can take refuge in statistical abstractions by saying that we can always expect "experimental error," that is, deviations from a mean. But in the study of personality it is just these deviations in which we are interested. A brief glance at the individual's manner of functioning preconsciously is in order.

In the first place, materials which present themselves as possible candidates for the preconscious may never really register at all. One illustration of this factor is the not uncommon manner of introducing one person to another. "I'd like you to meet Mr. B-d-d-l," the introducer mumbles. "Oh, how d'y do, Mr. —— uh," the introducee responds, and has to move on to another person. Afterwards the introducee tries to recall the name and berates himself for being so forgetful; in reality, he did not get the name when he was first introduced. Or the material, depending in part on the motivational state of the person, may fail to impress him. For years, laboratory studies have taken account of motivation in learning and retention. Impression may be greater under reward or punishment than under neutral conditions. But there seem to be other factors which must be taken into account in retention of casual experiences, such as the differential retention of experiences which seem to be about equally neutral or have about equal reinforcement. A person may travel through numerous towns, villages, and cities in an automobile; when he returns to some of them, it is as if he had never been there before, even though he knows full well that he has been. He can recall, however, turns and buildings and streets of other towns which are no more memorable than those in the places not remembered. Of course, exact investigation may be able to extablish the actual inequality of the objects concerned as well as states of the individual which make him receive impressions differentially.

---

[1] Some authorities have stated that psychoanalysis claims nothing is ever forgotten; if this claim were true, it would amount to an untestable proposition, like asserting that "the elephant never forgets." How could such an absurd proposition ever be proved? However, as far as the writer can determine, no such extravagant claim was ever made by Freud himself. In *The Psychopathology of Everyday Life* Freud (1904) asserts the possibility of restoring every original memory. But a careful study reveals that he is referring to repressed memories rather than to all memories. He did say, "In the unconscious nothing can be brought to an end, nothing is past or forgotten" (Freud, 1900). But this statement applies to those memories which have been "purposefully" pushed out of consciousness into what Freud called "the unconscious." Nevertheless, even the statement Freud did make is an untestable hypothesis.

[2] Cf. Woodworth's definition of memory in *Experimental Psychology*, first edition (1938).

Faint or partial impressions may make a difference in one man's storing materials in preconsciousness as compared with another; differential motivational states make such a difference. And the whole complex of intellectual functions serves to individualize materials which go into and remain stored in the dynamic "memory banks" of the preconscious. The over-all intellectual level, the average of intelligences called an Intelligence Quotient, determines individualized observation, retention, and utilization in thinking processes. Likewise, the wide disparities within an individual in his intelligences (cf. Chapter 15) differentiate among the kinds of materials stored and the manner in which they operate.

Furthermore, as suggested in Chapter 9, whatever may be the learning process in stamping in impressions or failing to give correct impressions, psychologists have been aware for many years of the distorting and condensing factors of the memory functions which we classify as preconscious (Bartlett, 1932; Carmichael, Hogan, & Walter, 1932). Many years ago, Freud (1914) spoke of distortion and condensation in respect to the functions denominated "the unconscious." And Koffka exclaimed of the "trace-systems" left in unconsciousness of which some had spoken as if they were in a static storehouse, "A miraculous storehouse indeed!" (Koffka, 1927.) But only relatively recently have distortions of preconscious materials been seriously studied by laboratory psychologists. The main interest of clinicians in these respects has been with repression; but they could very well pay attention to the aberrations of ordinary, unrepressed memories. Experimentalists are beginning to consider in their turn the psychodynamic factors of changes in ordinary memory traces, for dynamic factors which were at one time relegated to "abnormal" persons are now recognized to be operative in normal persons, too.

In this discussion of the preconscious, no more than a surface observation can be attempted. Actually we are dealing with those functions, viewed individually—per-sonologically—which psychology considered as some of its main content until a decade or two ago. Even philosophy (Feibleman, 1955) may present a case for the existence of a "rational unconscious" which includes functions classed as preconscious here, e.g., beliefs of an individual which conform to a culture's expectations, a good deal of problem solving, and a number of assumptions about the nature of things. The vast storage houses of memory and what used to be called "unconscious cerebration" constitute the preconscious when we consider the individual as the locus of these functions.

"The Unconscious." To set off one "psychic region" from others and call it "the unconscious" as if it were a literal section of the personality bounded by rigid barriers, guarded by a censor with Cerberus-like qualities, possessed of characteristics entirely unlike any other functions of the personality, would be entirely misleading. Already the similarities between the "ordinary" functions and unconsciousness should be evident. There seems to be a set of functions, however, which are different from other unconsciousness; for convenience the Freudian designation is applied to them. It is best to emphasize that "there seems to be a set." For there is question yet whether "the unconscious" is any different from other unconsciousness. It was Freud himself who after many years in psychoanalytic work pointed out:

Forgetting impressions, scenes, or experiences nearly always reduces itself to shutting them off. When the patient talks about these "forgotten" things, he seldom fails to add: "As a matter of fact I've always known it; only I've never thought of it." He often expresses disappointment at the fact that not enough things come into his head that he can call "forgotten"—that he has never thought of since they happened.[1]

Freud did go on to show differences which he thought he had found between

[1] From *The Standard Edition of the Complete Psychological Works of Sigmund Freud*, Vol. 12, P. 148. Reprinted by permission of the Hogarth Press, Ltd.

ordinary forgetting and repressive forgetting, the results of which constitute "the
unconscious." Presumably because some
events are so painful, they are repressed
from consciousness and cannot be recalled
by the normal processes employed for
bringing materials from the preconscious.
(Painful in this case may mean shameful,
humiliating, horrible, or even, strangely,
joyful where too great joy might overwhelm the individual with omnipotence
feelings.)

It is here that the issue lies, however. Is
there repression? Is there anything like "the
unconscious"? Clinicians on the whole are
convinced that unconscious processes include some which are definitely shut out
of consciousness, inaccessible to the individual in a way preconscious materials are
not. Experimentalists appear to be inclined
to disfavor such a set of functions as "the
unconscious."

Debate has sometimes been acrimonious
over this issue, a situation suggesting that
emotional factors (perhaps of a repressed
nature!) as well as logical factors are involved. When we endeavor to find the core
of the issue, it seems to reside in one major
question: Are not materials which are said
to be repressed into "the unconscious" only
those which are *not reported* rather than
those which are, like automatic actions, un-
available to awareness? It is not possible to
marshal all the evidence for and against the
existence of a peculiar class of unconscious
functions. Only a sample from the clinic
and the laboratory can be given.

"Failure to Report." A striking illustration of the possibility of having "differential readiness to report," (Bitterman &
Kniffin, 1953) instead of repression into
"the unconscious," comes from a verbatim
record of a therapeutic interview with a
patient under the influence of LSD-25,[1]
a drug that has sometimes startling effects
without danger to the patient; in this case
it was used as a means of relaxing the individual. The patient was a 40-year-old
married woman with psychosomatic and

adjustive difficulties. In psychoanalysis—
four years' treatment—she had been able
to resolve a number of her difficulties, but
her sexual troubles still were partly un-
solved. The analyst and she decided to try
an LSD-25 interview. The following ex-
cerpt (Abramson, 1955b) comes from close
to the middle of the interview; the inter-
jected italicized comment is the therapist's:

Pt. As I say, I never had any opportunity
of discussing sex with anybody, or feeling that
there was anyone I could turn to and ask
questions and get an answer.

Dr. How much difficulty are you finding
now, talking about it?
(*The beneficial effect of LSD-25 is now especially portrayed. Although in a sense, the
patient is a special case in a psychoanalytic
situation, I have seen the same type of production of material during brief therapy with
LSD-25.*)

Pt. Today, I don't feel any difficulty in talking about it. In fact when we had the break,
and I started thinking that this was a big question to begin with, a big problem to begin
with, and unless I come out of, well, unless
something comes out of this today, that to not
have the answers, or to not know where to go
from here, as to my sexual relations, and my
sexual force, actually, it's my feelings about it
that, well, that I've had four years now, and
after four years I certainly must be at a point
where I am able to do something about this
too.

Dr. Well, you just pointed out that that was
one of the most difficult things for you to talk
about. You also pointed out to me that instead
of talking about things you went to analysis
for, you talked about your mother, that that
was easy. The things that really troubled you,
that really were on your mind, you very carefully avoided, because they would disturb you.
Isn't that right?

Pt. Yes, that's right.

Dr. So would you say you've had four years
of avoiding problems rather than four years of
facing things?

Pt. In part. There are times when I deliberately, or rather forced myself into discussing the parts that I found very distressful
at the time, and yet I was able to do it. I think
probably what bothers me more right now is
the fact that after four years I still found it,
and up until today, I guess you could say, so

[1] Diethylamide of lysergic acid.

straining to come in and talk about it. And then I had a time where I really eagerly discussed. I think there have been times when I probably have spoken more or less freely, but not easily. It's always been such a strain to say everything that's been on my mind.[1]

For four years this woman had undergone intensive psychotherapy, and had failed to report what she knew was present. "Failure to report," then, may be the case, rather than repression into "the unconscious," even in many clinical cases which have been adduced to support the existence of "the unconscious." Clinical evidence, sometimes the best available, is usually uncontrolled (in the experimental sense), so that it has been made to support contradictory notions. Therefore, in recent years experimentalists have been testing among other clinical hypotheses that of repression and "the unconscious." Our attention can be turned to three such attempts.

Unconscious Conditioning. If in fact repression of something that has been held in conscious awareness takes place, it must be that the individual knows something without being aware of it. Can it be demonstrated experimentally that a person does know but does not know that he knows? From experiments extending back at least to the beginning of this century, psychologists have been able to to show that behavior can be learned without the individual's awareness that it is being learned (Adams, 1957).

Two interesting experiments serve to il-

lustrate these studies from relatively recent years. In one ingenious attempt (Greenspoon, 1955) to discover whether certain stimuli could increase the probability of occurrence of certain responses, even though the subject would not be aware of the connection between stimuli and responses, the experimenter used simple positive and negative syllables, "mmm-hmm" and "huh-uh" to reinforce the occurrence of plural or nonplural words in free word production. A demonstrated lack of differentiation on nonplural words between control and experimental subjects can legitimately be laid aside, although it must not be entirely forgotten. For the plural words, however, there was significant conditioning of experimental subjects; the relative frequency of plural words increased markedly, although the subjects could not verbalize the purpose of the experiment, did not know that the relative frequency of plural words had changed, and could not guess what the purpose of the "mmm-hmm" or "huh-uh" was.

The other representative experiment (Leventhal, 1959) employed somewhat the same procedure. The reinforcing stimuli were "good" for subjects in one group who used "I" or "We" in conjunction with 80 prepared neutral verbs, "not so good" for subjects in another group who used "He" or "They" with the verbs, "good" for subjects in another group for use of "I" or "We" and "not so good" for use of "He" or "They." A control group received no reinforcement at all. All subjects were restricted to the four pronouns. Normal, neurotic, and schizophrenic subjects were included in the experiment. Most experimental subjects learned to respond more frequently with "I" or "We" (with certain exceptions), but they could not say that they had learned, and they did not know what the experiment was all about. However, the normals responded to reward ("good"), to punishment ("not so good"), and to both ("good" for the correct responses, "not so good" for the incorrect). Neurotics responded under reward and reward-punishment reinforcement, but

---

[1] Abramson, H. A. Lysergic acid diethylamide (LSD-25): III. As an adjunct to psychotherapy with elimination of fear of homosexuality. *J. Psychol.*, 1955, 39. Reprinted by permission. Apparently the criticism which is sometimes laid at the door of clinical, especially psychoanalytic work, that the therapist expects the individual to talk about sex and therefore he or she does, hardly applies here. It is probably true that counselees, who are aware of the part which clinicians believe sex, in its broad connotations, has in adjustment problems, talk about sex sooner than if they did not know a clinician's penchant. Yet if the sexual area, narrowly conceived, is not actually the major problem, the counselee soon veers off to what is really troubling him, unless it is too difficult for him to talk about.

not to punishment alone. And schizophrenics responded to punishment and reward-punishment, but not to reward only conditions.

These and other experiments on "behavior without awareness" answer the question concerning an individual's knowing without being aware that he knows in the affirmative. They, therefore, lay the groundwork for acceptance of the possibility of repression insofar as that process means some materials may be out of consciousness but still have a direct influence on behavior. These experiments do not prove repression in the sense of an air-tight case of inference from laboratory to real life conditions. More real-to-life experiments are called for.

A series of experiments endeavoring to get at more realistic life conditions, initiated by Diven (1937), have sought to show that unconscious conditioning of anxiety reactions can occur. The pattern of these studies has varied from experiment to experiment, but they have employed either the galvanic skin reflex or heart-rate acceleration as an index of presumed anxiety reactions, together with some form of word association test. Conditioning presumably has taken place in such a way as to suggest that, without subjects' being aware of the "critical" words which the experimenter paired with an electric shock, the GSR or heart-rate acceleration varies with presentation of "critical" or neutral words. Diven's original experiment, from which he drew the conclusion that "unconscious conditioning" and "reactivation of a repressed complex" were demonstrated in miniature, has been rightly criticized on methodological and experimental grounds (Cannicott & Umberger, 1950; Haggard, 1943; Lacey & Smith, 1954).

Better controlled experiments than either Diven's or some of his critics' tend to support some of Diven's conclusions (Bindra & Cameron, 1953; Eriksen & Kuethe, 1956; Lacey & Smith, 1954; Lazarus & McCleary, 1951). The evidence is still not univocal (Eriksen, 1960). An ingenious statistical interpretation (Howes, 1954) of apparent unconscious conditioning which depends on the GSR associated with shock on certain exposed syllables makes it seem that no matter how experiments of this nature turn out they cannot prove such conditioning. The reasoning is too subtle to repeat in short compass here, but revolves around the theoretical probabilities of verbal reports. Experimental results would have to be directly contradictory to the statistical theory in order to show that unconscious conditioning occurs. But the experiment (Lazarus & McCleary, 1951) which seems most adequately to demonstrate the process (discrimination without awareness or subception) fits the statistical theory almost perfectly!

Existence of the set of functions known as "the unconscious" is not, however, demonstrated or refuted of necessity by laboratory demonstrations of the kind employed so far. Experiments may not sufficiently approximate life. In all of the experiments except one (Bindra & Cameron, 1953) the individual was aware of concrete factors in the experimental situation, words and shocks, but not of the precise connections between them. Possibly, as suggested by Diven and others, a person's "anxiety" level was raised during conditioning and lowered during extinction. At least, psychogalvanometer needle deflections and EKG tracings were altered. Whether these conditions parallel real-life situations from which "the unconscious" has been deduced is a question. A person may be aware of a punitive father (or some threatening authority figure) and also of a teacher, but not being aware of the connection he has formed between them, he has anxiety in the presence of the teacher. In the experiments either when extinction trials take place or when the subject has been informed of the connection between the conditioned and unconditioned stimuli, "therapy" occurs, or in other words "anxiety" is lowered. But in the real-life situation, especially in neurotic real life, continued exposure to the teacher without fulfillment of threat does not result in extinction of anxiety; neither does merely being intellectually informed of the connection between father and teacher release the anxiety.

Even if the experiments, refined and repeated with far better experimental controls than those previously employed should demonstrate unconscious conditioning well beyond probability limits accepted now, they may not support "the unconscious" unless they can take account of differences between previous laboratory conditions and real life. Only one experiment (Bindra & Cameron, 1953) of those cited above took account of one of the fundamentals of personality research, that individuals differ in their psychodynamics—what one person represses another might not. On the other hand, although there is considerable danger in using the argument, merely because some laboratory studies do not find unconscious conditioning or because certain statistical considerations make laboratory demonstrations of the kind employed in most instances seem unlikely ever to prove such a process, there is no proof that the process does not exist. The null hypothesis is not proved; as Fisher points out in his experimental design text (1951), only a single instance can disprove the null hypothesis, but no amount of experimentation can prove it.

"Perceptual Defense." Another series of experiments begun by McGinnies (1949) purport to show that repression occurs in respect to words which are unacceptable in our culture. Tachistoscopic presentation of neutral and supposedly emotionally toned words reveals that the threshold of recognition seems to be lower for the former than for the latter. Following the first experiment others (Bitterman & Kniffin, 1953; Blum, 1952; Chodorkoff, 1954, 1955; Howes & Solomon, 1950; McGinnies & Sherman, 1952; Postman, 1953; Postman, Bronson, & Gropper, 1953) seek in one way or another to determine whether the lowered "threshold" merely signifies either "differential readiness to report" or the relative frequency with which neutral and emotionally toned words are found in our language. If the first alternative is the case, just as in the clinical example above, subjects of experi-

ments may find it harder to report words that are related to sexuality. If it is a case of relative frequency, the subjects have apparently not responded differentially to neutral and emotionally toned words as defined by the experimenter because of inhibition but because the chances are greater that they would recognize words having greater currency in the language. In neither case is there room for repression of the variety called "perceptual defense."

When group differences as such are ignored, and the reactions of individuals considered, in line with what might be expected from personality studies, there appear to be differences among individuals in relation to so-called "perceptual defense." One experiment (Chodorkoff, 1954), for example, first determined personally relevant threatening terms and terms which individual subjects regarded as neutral. Individuals were then compared in respect to their psychological adjustment and their own threatening or neutral words. The hypothesis that the better the adjustment of the person the less "perceptual defense" operates was borne out at a highly satisfactory level of significance. Another experiment employed the Blacky Test [1] which purportedly measures psychosexual development. Areas of conflict and "repression" (defined operationally) were discovered for a group of graduate students, then four of the 11 Blacky pictures were shown tachistoscopically to them. The subjects, assuming all 11 pictures were shown instead of only four, named all of them. Special experimental and control conditions were employed in such a way as to demonstrate that those subjects who had both conflict and "repression" in respect to a certain picture failed significantly to name that pic-

[1] There may be questions raised about the Blacky Test (Ellis, 1953; Seward, 1950) as well as evidence for its validity (Blum & Hunt, 1952); but the experiment cited here is not wholly dependent upon the assumptions of the test. The students had been trained in the theory and interpretation of the Blacky Test, so that whether the test actually measures the psychosexual dimensions claimed by Blum (1949), for these students the Blacky pictures symbolized these dimensions.

ture in contrast to naming neutral or conflict-only pictures. It is difficult, even considering objections which may be raised against the method employed, to interpret the results of this experiment in any other way that as the operation of a form of "perceptual defense."

Unconscious Motivation. Clinical demonstrations of apparent repression are not as convincing to the psychologist as they are to the layman. Yet they cannot be ignored. From the author's case file comes the example of a young man who was given a post-hypnotic suggestion that he would forget the instructions but would perform a simple task when the counselor placed his hand on the telephone. Following the hypnotic session, the counselor asked the young man if he could recall the instructions given to him. He responded, "I can remember you told me to do something, but I don't remember what it was." In a short while the counselor placed his hand casually on the telephone without any comment. Immediately, the counselee said, "Oh, now, I remember what it was I supposed to do." Then he related—without doing it—what the task was to be.

A more convincing demonstration is semi-clinical. In the film, "Unconscious Motivation," produced by the University of Oregon, the two subjects were not clinical counselees. But real life clinical conditions were reproduced more faithfully than in most laboratory experiments. The subjects, Claire and Don, were given an hypnotic "complex," guilt over supposedly having, as children, taken two pennies from a red purse found in a park on their way to school, and subsequently lying to their parents about their actions. Signs of anxiety, including verbal reports of guilt and need to confess some vague thing, appeared in the two subjects, although in accord with the post-hypnotic suggestion they could not recall with what the feelings were connected. In the post-hypnotic discussion between them Claire and Don offered rationalizations of their symptoms. But at a pre-arranged signal, again by post-hypnotic suggestion, they dreamed of their experi-

ence symbolically. With an analysis of their dreams, discussion of their responses to the TAT, Rorschach, and a word association test, and continued conversation which proved to be a kind of free association, the subjects came to insight concerning the planted experience. What appeared to be real relief manifested itself as the buried reasons for their symptoms came to light.

In this demonstration what seems to be unconscious motivation is operative. It appears that overt behavior has been partially determined by materials which have been forcibly kept below the level of awareness. The film may be dismissed as an exercise in histrionic ability. To anyone, however, who has used hypnosis and reproduced some of the same phenomena, the demonstration has the marks of verisimilitude. Work in experimental hypnosis (e.g., early experiments: Erickson, 1938; Farber & Fisher, 1943; and later experiments, e.g.: Grosz & Levitt, 1959) tends to corroborate the conclusions from clinical demonstrations. Neither, however, is sufficient proof to force sceptics to accept the existence of repressive unconsciousness.

To a clinician working daily with patients who speak freely about even sexual and aggressive matters and yet who seem unable to recognize other patent aspects of themselves it seems like gilding the lily to provide experimental proof of what the clinician "knows." Yet the conditions of the clinic are not as carefully controlled as during an adequate experiment; so despite Freud's demurrer that such proof is not needed, psychologists do feel the need of experimental confirmation of what they choose to consider hypotheses derived from the clinic. The existence of "the unconscious" has not been proved by laboratory studies; and even practice in a clinic has not led a number of clinical psychologists to assume repressed unconscious functioning. Those who believe that the only way that certain phenomena can be explained is to postulate "the unconscious" will no doubt continue to believe that there is such a personality area, holding that experimental conditions cannot reproduce situations which engender repression in life. Those who feel that they can explain all their observations without recourse to what is admittedly an inference will be satisfied with the experimental evidence, or lack of it.

If there is such a set of repressed functions, the assumption is that there is some type of censoring function between these and the preconscious or conscious functions. Even such an assumption, however, does not require absolute barriers. Horney (1937) used a term which many clinicians recognize without difficulty. A piece of presumably repressed material will seem to be kept out of awareness most of the time; but from time to time it may "register" in consciousness. The counselee may say, "Yes, that popped into my head the other day. But I forgot about it." The same kind of registering may take place in hypnosis or under the influence of chemotherapeutic agents.

CONTINUITY AND LACK OF CONTINUITY IN CONSCIOUSNESS AND UNCONSCIOUSNESS

Consciousness and unconsciousness reveal both continuities and discontinuities in their structure. Kleitman's monumental research on sleep (1939) substantiates what common observation has revealed, that there are degrees of being asleep and being awake. Individual differences in sleep-wake cycles are marked (Kleitman, Mullin, Cooperman, & Titelbaum, 1937), as one may be a "morning person" who is more wide awake and efficient in the morning than another person who wakes up more gradually and does better toward evening. As measured by body temperature both kinds of changes in sleepiness and wakefulness are along continua. But when we turn to electroencephalographic (EEG) recordings of sleeping and waking states, there appear to be (relative) breaks in the continuities. In the state of wakefulness an individual may produce from the parieto-occipital lobe of the brain large "alpha rhythm" waves which average about ten

per second when in a relaxed, inattentive state. As soon as a visual attentive state supervenes, however, the alpha pattern is broken up or blocked, and faster, small-amplitude waves are substituted (Monnier, 1952; Stevens, 1951, Chapter 4). The subjective experience one has corresponding to the sudden change in cortical electrical activity bears out the step-character of consciousness in this respect. It is true that there may be increasing or decreasing degrees of wakefulness paralleling increasing or decreasing desynchronization of electrical brain rhythms. And also there are apparently continuous differences from deep to light sleep (Monnier, 1952). And yet, some distinct differences between sleep and waking, manifested by the EEG (Kleitmann, 1939, 1957),[1] are also subjectively judged to be qualitatively different. We do feel that the drowsiness which is not sleep and which may not seem to rest us at all is qualitatively distinct from real sleep.

Other conscious-unconscious phenomena parallel to some extent the person's behavior and experience in sleeping and waking states. There is a continuity among the states of waking consciousness, from a condition close to unconsciousness to an exceedingly heightened awareness; similar gradations are found in the clarity of dreams. Yet (for the adult at any rate because children may not make such distinctions) there are qualities that are distinct about most dreams which seem to place them on a different plane from waking consciousness. In hypnotic states there are degrees in the "depth" of the hypnosis, but also there are qualitative differences among deep and light hypnotic states and unhypnotized states (Wolberg, 1952).

---

[1] As a subject in a colleague's experiment the writer was in a relaxed, reverie-like state in a relatively non-stimulating cubicle, with four electrodes on his scalp attached to an EEG machine. The record suddenly showed the slow, deep rhythms which characterize sleep; from time to time the experimenter who wanted a relaxed but not sleeping subject would have to call to waken the writer. Here the *sudden* appearance of different waves is emphasized.

Even if we consider the Gestalt meaning of consciousness and unconsciousness which refers to being with or without insight, there may be unconscious degrees of approaching the solution to a problem (Hilgard, 1956). And there is no guarantee that when an individual has arrived at an "insight" he has learned all there is to know about the situation, for there may be degrees of understanding either before or after the insight or both. Learning theorists are divided on what happens in so-called insightful learning. Gestaltists maintain there is a sudden change as all the parts of a situation are recognized as belonging to a whole. Association theorists on the other hand suggest an implicit trial-and-error process prior to the actual "insight," thus emphasizing the gradual or continuous nature of learning. But even extreme associationists in learning theory cannot claim there is no disjunction in many cases between the before and after periods. Whatever unconscious trial-and-error is involved, in some instances at one time we are unaware of a solution and then suddenly we are aware; "all at once the pieces fit together," we say, or "it came to me in a flash." Continuities and discontinuities, then, characterize consciousness and unconsciousness of various kinds.

OVERLAPPING OPERATIONS OF CONSCIOUSNESS AND UNCONSCIOUSNESS

Some theoretical distinctions have been made between consciousness and unconsciousness at times, to the effect that the former is logical and rational in its operations and the latter illogical and irrational. But logical and illogical behavior can be either conscious or unconscious. Both daydreams and night dreams are conscious after a fashion (Kleitman, 1957) and are often irrational in content. Even thoughts which are not part of day or night dreams may contain elements of the irrational (Kris, 1950). On the other hand, theorems of mathematics, logical principles, and rational aspirations may be found in the preconscious. And some elements of "the unconscious" are not irrational. In fact, a case may be made for the logicality of the two most famous, and to many the most irrational, complexes of psychoanalytic theory, the oedipus and castration complexes. As *complexes* these are unconscious by definition. Yet given the premises a boy child may hold in respect to father and mother, the development of oedipal desires and castration fears is a logical consequence. Mother is the first love object. The boy's sexuality develops to the point where he desires mother sexually. Why should he not love her with all that he is? But father is in the way. He might not only dislike having his wife taken by another "man," but is big and strong enough to harm that rival. Harm may take the form of depriving the boy of the one thing that makes him a "man" and that is associated with his sexuality. The environment may even reinforce such reactions by providing sleeping arrangements wherein parents are observed in intercourse or make threats to mutilate the genital organ (Pullias, 1937).[1] A system of logic only requires that one proposition be the necessary consequence of the other (Cohen & Nagel, 1934). The oedipus and castration complexes follow logically from the boy's premises (if we can assume he has these). Many unconscious operations are logical in the above sense, outlandish as they appear to ordinary, waking logic.

Overlapping of consciousness and unconsciousness in logical and illogical thought processes is only one area of overlap. Another is found in the motivation of behavior. (Cf. Section V.) Depth psychologies have tended to concentrate on the unconscious determinants of behavior, sometimes almost to the virtual exclusion of conscious factors. Strangely, Freud himself (1949a) regarded consciousness as the one incontrovertible fact. But "ego psychology" arose in psychoanalysis partly to correct a seeming overemphasis on unconscious processes which Freud's work implies. A

[1] Castration in psychoanalytic usage is referrable to the penis rather than to the testicles as in animal gelding.

reasonable synthesis of views is that behavior may be brought about by both conscious and unconscious determinants. A simple illustration—but not *too* simple—is getting a drink. Cellular depletion and blood chemistry changes are not recognizable directly by the individual himself (apart from secondary knowledge derived from instrument analysis). But dryness of the throat is felt consciously. So conscious and unconscious factors thus enter into the motivation of thirst-reduction behavior. To maintain, as we do, that some behavior is motivated from the repressed unconscious does not preclude the conclusion that such behavior is also the result of conscious factors. Sometimes, to be sure, overlapping operations of consciousness and unconsciousness generate conflict, as in the obsessional's firmly turning off the gas to satisfy his conscious demand for safety, then "accidentally" turning it on to satisfy his unconscious demand for punishment. Sometimes, on the other hand, behavior can be described as wholehearted, as consciousness and unconsciousness cooperate.

Overlapping conscious and unconscious operations can be found in self-evaluation and self-judgment. The studies referred to in Chapter 9, especially the two dealing with expressive behavior (Epstein, 1955; Wolff, 1933) serve to illustrate the joint action.

One of the most universal of mental phenomena is symbolization. Freud (1900) accumulated considerable evidence bearing on the use of certain objects to represent sex organs. It is virtually certain that the "sacred pillars" of Semitic culture were consciously regarded as symbols of fertility (Graham & May, 1936). Whether similar symbolism holds unconsciously or not is a question not yet experimentally answered, even though many clinicians maintain that it does. That modern American children may not regard the objects as sexual which psychoanalysis claims do represent sex has been demonstrated (Levy, 1954). Children were asked to name elongated objects, or round, containing objects with male or female names; they did not name them in ac-

cord with the obvious Freudian interpretation. Neither did they respond in the expected direction in a transfer study. To one group of children pictures of the objects were shown tachistoscopically with what would be names appropriate to their presumed sexual significance. To another group pictures of the objects with presumptively inappropriate names were shown. The experimenter hypothesized that if the children unconsciously associated sex with the objects, positive transfer should take place with the group having the appropriate names and negative transfer should take place with the other group when they were tested for retention. The hypothesis was not confirmed. We cannot be sure, then, with such evidence that sexual symbolism is held both consciously and unconsciously and must look further.

A widespread practice which cannot be so easily explained without assuming both conscious and unconscious factors, some of which may involve sex, is the cornerstone laying ceremony. Comparatively innocent in our culture, openly symbolic of the hope of successful completion of the edifice and its successful use, cornerstone laying has bloody antecedents. At the corners of buildings and city walls in many cultures living or dead persons have been buried (Frazer, 1940). Why human sacrifice for the dedication of a building or a wall? It is no answer to say that some cultures have demanded human sacrifice for almost any venture, for that kind of an answer only pushes the question into the general area of motivation of rites and ceremonies; and we may be forced to ask, why human sacrifice at all? Some factors which go beyond the obvious must be operative in the cornerstone ceremony or similar acts. Sexual interpretations (Schnier, 1947) may or may not be adequate. But if we deny sexual symbolism, we must still explain the ghastly history of cornerstone laying; the excess of practices, not required by the innocuous conscious symbolism of our present ceremonies, calls for some rationale. The symbolism may very well be both conscious and unconscious.

One cannot dismiss lightly the mass of evidence gathered by Jung and his followers (*e.g.*, Neumann, 1954) on the well-nigh universal usage of some symbols, not necessarily the Freudian ones. Among others is the noteworthy Uroborus, the serpent encircling (anything) and holding its tail in its mouth, a consciously recognized symbol of the beginning of all which contains the end in itself. Found in modern untutored children's drawings, in the dreams and free associations of neurotics, and in the art productions of cultures far removed from our own in time and space, the Uroborus seems to have unconscious as well as conscious significance.

Other evidence could be adduced for the overlapping of conscious and unconscious functioning. To one who may not accept any unconscious functions at all, even to mention overlap is foolish. To those who recognize preconscious functioning, behavior is explainable in part as a result of presently conscious factors and those others which are not repressed but are not immediately in consciousness. To one who also assumes "the unconscious," few things seem more obvious than the combined operation of conscious and unconscious, sometimes repressed, factors in the production of behavior.

Summary

Analysis of the personality topographically reveals a major cross-classification of consciousness and unconsciousness. Forms of both are multiplex, though introspection appears to reveal a unity to consciousness (phenomenologically) that does not hold for unconsciousness.

The latter can be subdivided into (1) automatic functions, especially the vital processes, (2) the preconscious, all the dynamic materials not in consciousness at present but relatively accessible to awareness, and (3) "the unconscious," or repressed functions, possibly hypothetical in that controlled research has failed to demonstrate conclusively that unconscious conditioning, "perceptual defense," and unconscious motivation actually exist. Continuity and lack of continuity are found in consciousness and unconsciousness. Topographically distinct as they may be, consciousness and unconsciousness overlap in their operations, both, for example, performing in rational and irrational thinking. In a number of personality functions both share jointly, as in motivation, *e.g.*, conscious and unconscious factors are present, in self-judgment aspects of both can be found, and in the characteristically (though not exclusively) human process of symbolization word and objects derive meaning from conscious and unconscious sources.

Questions

1. Describe various forms of consciousness and unconsciousness.

2. Distinguish among automatic functions, the preconscious, and "the unconscious."

3. What experimental proof has been adduced for the existence of "the unconscious"?

4. How does logical mental functioning overlap both conscious and unconscious?

5. Discuss conscious and unconscious aspects of motivation, self-judgment, and symbolization.

CHAPTER 12

TOPOGRAPHICAL STRUCTURE-FUNCTIONS: CENTRAL AND PERIPHERAL

Of the three broad cross-classifications included in the topography of personality two have already been considered. The first is that in which the personality is viewed in terms of id, ego, superego, and role functions. The second roughly divides personality into conscious and unconscious functions. In this chapter the third overlapping division, consisting of central and peripheral functions, is taken up.

Scientific psychology could not at first conceive of anything which is mental as also unconscious. Even today some psychologists doubt that anything like "the unconscious" exists, although they freely admit preconscious functioning. But neither scientific nor lay opinion has ever really been divided on the subject of the existence of what are called here central and peripheral functions. These have sometimes been called private and public functions.

FORMS OF CENTRAL AND PERIPHERAL FUNCTIONS; ACCESSIBILITY TO OTHERS

The terms central and peripheral may occasion some confusion because of differing usage in different contexts. Physiology and physiological psychology refer to the central and peripheral portions of the nervous system. The terms have also been referred to vision; for example, visual acuity is greater in the central line of vision and less at the periphery (Chapanis, 1949). Relatedly, cones are more numerous centrally and rods more numerous peripherally. Sometimes one hears the terms applied to the so-called span of apprehension (Woodworth, 1938): That which is in "the center of attention," or clear, is central; other less clear stimuli are peripheral.

In assessment of others, "forming impressions of personality," (Asch, 1946; Mensh & Wishner, 1947; Wishner, 1960), the terms central and peripheral have been used to designate trait names and by implication the traits themselves. Those trait names which, when embedded in a group of trait names, decisively influence the interpretation of the latter are denominated central. Those which have little or no influence of this nature are peripheral. Although the extension of the influence notion to the traits themselves may not be justified, at the very least the differential influence of certain trait names on others is important to psychology. Rating of others may not be as subject to the "halo effect" as has been held the case for long in psychology, for some terms interact with others and some others do not (Mensh & Wishner, 1947).

These various other meanings of central and peripheral are entirely legitimate. However, the terms are employed here in the way Kurt Lewin used them (Leeper, 1943; Lewin, 1935, 1936a, 1936b, 1946, 1951) to designate on the one hand those layers of personality which are open to others (peripheral) and on the other those layers closed to other persons (central). Without Lewin's repeated insistence on this distinction, we might not so clearly recognize that personality functions can be classified according to their centrality or peripherality as well as according to their conscious or unconscious aspects (Sanford, 1956). The implied dualism of the personality in either of these classifications may be softened somewhat if we accept the analysis of Skinner (1953) of private (central) and public (peripheral) events which, he points out, are subject to the same laws.

In some ways, it seems that the battle between those who believe that there is a repressed unconscious and those who do not could be resolved easily if psychologists could agree that functions classed as conscious or unconscious are really only peripheral or central. Then the degree of accessibility to any functions would be reduced to a matter of differential readiness to report. Many thousands of pages of the psychological literature (including the previous chapter in this text) would be rendered unnecessary—what a boon to students! The heavy guns of sarcasm or irony's lighter caliber weapons would have to be turned elsewhere if the combatants still wished to fight. Unfortunately, the issue cannot be settled so handily. But there would be a great deal less argument if many of those who hold out strongly for or against a repressed unconscious would recognize that often their debate concerns central and peripheral functions rather than conscious and unconscious ones.

Central (or private) functions consist of those functions which the individual will

not or cannot reveal to others by voluntary behavior, including voluntary verbalization. Peripheral (or public) functions consist of those which one is willing and/ or able to reveal to others. As pointed out in Chapter 5 in the discussion on personality structure, central regions of the personality are not coterminous with unconsciousness. There are unconscious functions which are public in that others may easily observe them. On the other hand there are functions which the individual is unwilling to reveal which are not unconscious. Further, just as central and peripheral cannot be equated with unconscious and conscious, neither can they be identified with the id, ego, and superego on the one side of a boundary line and role functions on the other. For though roles are on the whole more easily observed than functions of the traditional "psychic structure" of psychoanalysis, there are many portions of the ego and superego which are openly revealed by the individual, sometimes through his roles, and there are also roles which the individual may take great pains to conceal.

To state as we have that the individual will not or cannot reveal the central portions of his personality is not to say that these portions will not or cannot be revealed under circumstances differing from those of any chosen present moment. Freud's or anyone else's "psychopathology of everyday life" allows unwittingly some private matters to slip into public view. Excesses of alcohol may loosen a tongue which ordinarily would not speak of certain matters, even though known to the person. Projective methods and clinical interviews probe for, and find, materials which an individual either may desire to cover or is unaware he is harboring.

From the foregoing it should be obvious that the boundary line between central and peripheral is not a fixed one any more than any of the boundaries we have previously viewed in this topographic survey of personality. What is central at one time may be peripheral at another and what is peripheral may become central. In forming impressions of personality (Asch, 1946), predictable changes may occur in relation to central and peripheral trait names, *i.e.*, as mentioned before, those trait names having great or little influence upon rating a personality from a group of trait names. If the terms in a list of trait names can be found independently to correlate with specific other trait names, the former have been shown to have a strong effect upon the latter in determining the impression one gets of another's personality from a list of traits. If little or no correlation exists, little or no effect is seen from one trait name to another. Consequently, a trait name will be influential (central) in one context and not influential (peripheral) in another, depending on the degree of correlation it has with the terms in the two lists (Wishner, 1960). As suggested previously, the extension of experiments on trait names to imply similar relations among the traits themselves embedded in the living personality may not be justified. But if there is justification for the extension, the principle that what is central may become peripheral and vice versa, depending on the context, is supported by both experimental and theoretical rationale. At the least, we could reason that by analogy with the experiments the principle holds.

A more complicated expansion of the principle may be something that is observable in everyday life and especially in the clinic: What is private in respect to one person may be public to another, either because of the willingness of the individual to reveal more of himself to some persons than to others or because of the differential perspicacity of the observers. A case of the former is the tease who leads on some naïve person in the group, making the victim think that the tease is a certain type of person, all the while letting the rest of the group know by his doubletalk what he really is thinking. A case of differential perspicacity is seen when a psychiatric patient is presented in clinic to a group of students and professional persons. The patient may successfully conceal from the students what he desires to, but the greater training and experience of the professionals allows them to catch cues of the patient's inner world unrecognized by the students and unwittingly revealed by the patient.

It may be difficult to regard personality functions as central at one time and peripheral at another. In a dynamic system, it must be understood, interactions and transformations are constantly taking place. The circulatory system is a recognizably distinct portion of the physiological organism. Yet constantly it interchanges materials with other parts of the organism. So, too, many functional subregions of the personality may be open or closed to others at different times as interchanges occur. These changes depend upon the individual's ability or willingness at any one time to reveal or conceal certain portions of himself, and upon the observer's ability to read the personality of the other; both of these capacities change from time to time. This interaction between the observer and the observed demonstrates the interpersonal nature of personality, in that what is central or peripheral is determined in part by what others are as well as what the individual is.

Private and Public Domains as Characterized in Literature

It is strange in some ways that problems of the private and public regions of the personality *per se* have not been scientifically investigated to a greater extent, inasmuch as literature and drama have been concerned for centuries with what folk are willing to reveal of themselves. Many examples from literature could be provided [1] to demonstrate the recognition of an outward and an inward world. This is not the place to illustrate these worlds extensively. Only two selections of verse are cited here to display the poet's grasp of central versus peripheral aspects of personality. Neither

[1] Eugene O'Neill's plays with their asides in which the characters tell what they are really thinking differently from their outward behavior; Kahlil Gibran's mother and daughter dialogue in *The Madman;* Shakespeare's Edmund in *King Lear.* These are only some of the better known examples.

one is great poetry; the selections are chosen to typify two kinds of "unwillingness." The first comes from the satirical pen of Sir W. S. Gilbert of the famous Gilbert and Sullivan team. Bunthorne, a character in *Patience or Bunthorne's Bride*, is supposed by literary critics to represent Oscar Wilde at the height of a craze for estheticism, a movement affecting great admiration for works of art of a rather sophisticated nature.[1]

Bunthorne:
Am I alone,
  And unobserved? I am!
Then let me own
  I'm an esthetic sham!
This air severe
  Is but a mere
    Veneer!
This cynic smile
  Is but a wile
    of guile!
This costume chaste
  Is but good taste
    Misplaced!
Let me confess
A languid love for lilies does *not* blight me!
Lank limbs and haggard cheeks do *not* delight
    me!
  I do not care for dirty greens
    By any means.
  I do not long for all one sees
    That's Japanese.
  I am *not* fond of uttering platitudes
    In stained-glass attitudes.

The second literary example carries no connotation of deceitful concealment of the inner world; instead there is a note of pathos or regret that others cannot know what is hidden.

There are those who deem they know me
    well,
  And smile as I tell them "no!"
Who think they may clearly and carelessly tell
Each living drop in my heart's deep well,
And lightly enter its inmost cell;
  But little (how little) they know.
They do not know and they cannot see
  That strong-hinged, low-arched door,
Though I am passing in and out,
From gloom within to light without,

[1] A great over-simplification of estheticism.

Or from gloom without to light within;
  None can ever an entrance win,
    None! for evermore.

                    (Author unknown)

These two illustrations from literature suffice to represent the recognition that poets and dramatists have had of the central and peripheral regions. Many writers have been ingenious in both their descriptions and explanations of the division between private and public functions of the personality. We could revel in literary instances of central and peripheral personality functioning, but the harder and less spectacular task is set for us to discover what psychology as a science has done in trying to order the data which are found so abundantly in both literature and real life situations.

PRIVATE AND PUBLIC DOMAINS AS REVEALED BY SCIENCE

In one way the whole historical controversy between introspectionism and behaviorism was a battle to make either the private or the public world dominant in scientific psychology. And the present movement of phenomenology, which is resisted primarily by neobehaviorists by use of "the silent treatment" rather than by active opposition,[2] when viewed from one angle, is an endeavor to re-establish in psychology the validity of the personal world.[3] Probably there always will be new movements and controversies which will arise to grapple with or to endeavor to settle the problem of inner and outer, private and public, central and peripheral, for the problem is one of the thorniest if not the thorniest in all psychology. Especially in personology is the problem acute, for we

[2] What is more devasting to a man's position than being ignored?
[3] This purpose of phenomenology may be oblique. What phenomenology does try to establish is the givenness of the individual's experience, that the ground of psychology is the experiencing individual, that reality is not found primarily in the "objective" world but in the very experiencing of the world (May, Angell, & Ellenberger, 1958; Sonnemann, 1954).

are dealing here with an individual who is the locus of these private and public functions.[1] At this place our concern is not with the general problem with which psychology as a whole must cope but instead with a more circumscribed problem, that of determining how personology classifies and interprets the private and public functions of the personality. Briefly three representative attempts to clarify these matters are presented, one from William Stern, one from Kurt Lewin, and one from the field of testing, including projective psychology. The warning must be repeated that there has not been adequate scientific treatment of the subject under consideration.

Personal Dimensions

Not offering any specific experimental or clinical evidence for his position, yet bringing a lifetime of experimentation and disciplined observation to his writing, Stern (1938) set up what he called "personal dimensions," especially the "inward-outward dimension."[2] The dimensionality of the concept is not important to us here; in fact, Stern suggests no exact quantification of these dimensions even though such quantification might be attempted. What is important now is that Stern identifies first among several other characteristics a relative polarity of inwardness and outwardness:

The *polarity* of the inward-outward dimension involves the assumption that person and world confront each other in basic opposition. . . . The things and processes of my world, other people who are alien to me, together

[1] What is private, that which the individual feels that he can observe within himself, and what is public, that which others can observe, may require different theoretical models, one phenomenological and one behavioristic. The writer is inclined to think that such a dualistic concept is not the answer to the problem. But thus far "brain models" of a mechanical or electrical nature seem too much like *Hamlet* with Hamlet left out: The experiencing individual, as phenomenologists insist, is just not present in these models, "feedback" to the contrary notwithstanding.

[2] Stern's meanings have been extended slightly, but not beyond the implications of Stern's writings.

with their life-patterns and experiences, are 'outside,' whereas my heart and my lungs, my thoughts and feelings are 'inside.' (Stern, 1938)

The second major characteristic of the "inward-outward dimension" is what is called the "personal present" which refers to the state of the individual when person and object are not in opposition, as is the babe prior to distinguishing himself from the external world or the lover in respect to his beloved. There is, in other words, according to Stern's formulation, not only a (potential) polarity between inward and outward, but a (potential) fusing of inward and outward in the "personal present." There is little if any polarity for the infant, because he has virtually nothing he can conceal. His physiological functions are not impossibly inaccessible to others; his "psychological" functions consist primarily of perceptual-motor behavior, easily observable; and his social functions are open to all. The lover on the other hand, has passed from the "personal present" of the child through a state of polarity to the "personal present" of the adult-in-love in which his private world is shared by another and nothing that he *can* reveal is held back. In the lover some polarity still obtains, for there are those parts he cannot reveal which are thus still in "opposition" to his beloved in the sense of being unshared. The recognition that there are unshared portions often comes in married life, as unconscious factors reveal themselves indirectly to the beloved, sometimes to the latter's joy, but usually sorrow, for the parts unknown are often ones unacceptable to the individual himself.

Stern has elaborated on the inward-outward dimension in such a manner that it is possible to represent it topographically (Figure 16). Stern has his own diagram which is more literally dimensional than that in Figure 16, but the latter is a more familiar delineation in the present context. Both quantitative and qualitative gradations or categories are represented extending from the *personal present* inward into the person and outward through the world.

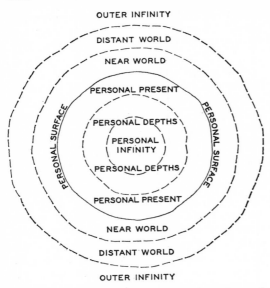

Figure 16. Topographical representation of Stern's "Inward-outward dimension."

"Inwardness" leads through the *personal surface*, close to the personal present, to the *personal depths* representing the "most real" portions of the personality, and finally to the *personal infinity* of the personal depths, the completely indeterminate (unknowable?) portions of the personality. "Outwardness" leads through *near* to *distant* regions of the world to the completely indefinite *outer infinity*, presumably unrelated to the individual. Near and far here refer to both time and space, for a day can be distant as well as a star. But time and space are both psychological and physical. As Stern suggests, the casual traveling seatmate may be "distant," and yesterday may seem "distant" under special circumstances, while on the contrary the friend I am to visit who is physically far away may be "near," and a day long ago may seem "like only yesterday."

This systematization of data of observation and experience coincides with a phenomenological analysis, inasmuch as the person-world continuum (or dichotomy) seems to hold from the individual's own viewpoint. Some aspects of one's *person* appear to him to be farther from the world than others; likewise some aspects of the *world* appear farther from the individual than others.

Nevertheless, Stern's representation is not entirely satisfying as an ordering of all the available data, on several related accounts. First, the diagram and its underlying concept suffers too much from a "within-the-skin" view of personality. Too strict a dichotomy obtains in Stern's view between person and world. Second, a simple continuum (or even dichotomy, since we are practically ignoring quantitative aspects) cannot account for the dynamic nature of inner and outer worlds. As indicated, portions of the personality are open to some portions of the world and closed to others at the same time; in Stern's terms they are both "depth" and "surface" at the same time. Or something hidden today may be revealed tomorrow, or "surface" may again become "depth," in either case wittingly or unwittingly, willingly or unwillingly.

A third source of dissatisfaction with Stern's concept is that it seems to be limited to the individual's outlook, even though it supposedly includes the world. The world is "near" or "far" from the individual depending on its relevance to his "personal present." Psychology in general and personology in particular are not committed to the position that the individual's outlook alone[1] is of importance; indeed, in the extreme behavioristic period the individual's outlook was almost anathema. Although Stern shows in his general position a regard for objective considerations, the interpersonal aspects of the personality and the objectively determinable "psychological distance" of inner and outer "objects" are not given sufficient consideration. A fourth objection is closely allied to the last one. Roles may be central and thoughts may be peripheral, so that a simple distinction between the person and the world cannot very well be maintained.

The dissatisfactions voiced here are not

[1] Even phenomenology (Sonnemann, 1954) does not disregard the "objectivist" ways of treating data in other sciences than psychology.

objections to Stern's position in the usual sense. Stern did not accept the inclusive definition of personality utilized by the present text and others; his position concerning inward and outward is consistent with his view of personality (for the most part). Furthermore, no one should be held responsible for incorporating data or ideas in his system which have not yet been unearthed. Stern was able to systematize many of the materials he had at hand, and due recognition should be given of the value of his attempt as a serious scientific achievement.

Inner-Personal: Central or Peripheral

A second approach to the facts of central and peripheral functions of the personality is that of Kurt Lewin. Reference should be made to Chapter 5 and especially to Figure 12 for the discussion on Lewin's concepts of the structure of personality. Only a few words need be said here as a reminder of Lewin's attempt to take account of public and private functions. Lewin, we may recall, conceived of the personality as composed of regions, the motor-perceptual region surrounding an inner-personal region. The inner-personal region can, according to Lewin, be divided into central and peripheral parts, with the dividing line between them shifting as circumstances are changed for the individual. Illustration of Lewin's concepts is found in his comparison of German and American structures of personality (Lewin, 1936).[1] There are several layers of "resistance to communication" within each personality. But for the German, the boundary dividing his central from his peripheral zones is coincident with lines of resistance away from the center while for the American those lines are farther inside the personality. An American may strike up acquaintances with strangers and discuss relatively personal matters with them. His Rotary Club manner may be manifest in hail-fellow, well-met behavior regardless of his so-

cial position. He is easy of access. Nevertheless, there are portions of his personality he does conceal; he cannot "be read like an open book." About some matters he will not or cannot be open. On the other hand, the German, Lewin asserted, is much more unapproachable, revealing less of himself to others, and having greater reserve.

Lewin recognizes individual differences from person to person, and differences within the same individual from one time to another. Further, however, if we may take Lewin's analysis as representing at least a rough approximation to reality, we must add to inter- and intra-individual differences those cultural differences which make for "types" in personalities in respect to centrality and peripherality. That is, it seems reasonable to suppose that some cultures engender a more "open" type of personality and others a more "closed" type, with each culture generating individual variations upon its own general and peripheral functions. In fact, it was Lewin who introduced the terms, if not the concepts, of central and peripheral. As both a general schematization and as a framework for research Lewin's formulations in this field as in so many areas are fruitful.

Test-Revealed Personality Functioning

As has been indicated in several places, the emphasis in this text is on the individual and not on theories of or methods of measuring personality. It was appropriate, however, in our discussion of the structure of personality to speak of theories of personality which in reality are attempts to set up (assumed) structures which make the most sense out of the data. It is likewise appropriate here, in connection with the discussion of central and peripheral functions, to pay attention to methods which are presumed to assess these functions. For texts which deal with personality testing in detail, the reader is referred to Note 11, Chapter 1. It is obvious from the extent of the material found in texts devoted exclusively to, or even in large part to methods of assessment that too much has accumulated to include here without exclusion of

[1] Types are assumed only very roughly by Lewin.

the object of our primary focus, the personality itself. Yet at this point some discussion of tests and their characteristics is relevant. For here we are on neutral ground where a behaviorism which no longer needs to deny central events and a phenomenology which does not deny reality to peripheral events have no reason to battle. All either needs to do is ask: What can be revealed by temperament or "personality" tests?

Objectively-Revealed Functioning. Since the First World War and the Woodworth Personal Data Sheet the "personality inventory" has been used to get at what the individual believes about himself. As the sum of testing experience grew it became evident that the individual might believe certain things about himself which did not harmonize with what other data revealed. That an individual could claim to be popular and well-adjusted, and not be either, was not so surprising as that an individual could be popular and apparently well-adjusted and look upon himself as inferior and at odds with himself. Also it was recognized that individuals not only could honestly be at odds with objective data but that testwise persons could "fool" the test (Kelly, Miles, & Terman, 1936). And finally, the individual might have ideas about himself which coincided with the ordinarily observable objective data, but not with the more penetrating observation that was beginning to appear in the clinics.[1] In other words by the use of "personality tests," followed by the scientific urge to discuss their validity, realization was impressed on psychology that there are different "worlds," the world about which the individual can and will be open, the world he knows within himself but will not reveal, and the world about which he is not even aware.

[1] Where previous generations had depended on gifted men, dramatists, poets, and "born psychologists," for such penetrating observation, now the clinic adopted new ways of getting at less observable functioning of the personality. After Freud, the techniques of penetrating observation were *teachable*, a prime requisite of any science.

In more recent years personologists have refined "personality inventories"—more properly called "temperament inventories" or "surveys" as Guilford denotes his tests—to try to overcome the defenses an individual employs, voluntarily or involuntarily, against revealing his central processes. Factor analysis has yielded tests which are carefully standardized and statistically treated to discern the basic traits of the individual. Many of the test items are so constructed that a person answering cannot tell what should be the "correct" answer, so that unwittingly he gives responses revealing his more private attitudes. And because there are patterns of test items, sometimes with items apparently logically unrelated going together to make up a factor, an individual who tries to be "consistent" (or to "fool" the test) may reveal just as much about his inner ways as a person who does not try to be sophisticated on the test. Although some test authorities might not agree, a strong case can be made for the contention that even the content of the test items is unimportant. A series of abstract geometrical designs has been shown in several studies to distinguish significantly between clinical and normal groups (Berg, 1959). Books on "How to Beat Personality Tests" will have to become considerably more sophisticated to enable their clients to conceal their inner workings from such methods of assessment.

Those tests which may depend in part upon the content of their test items may be standardized and scored in such a way as to render them relatively valid for differentiating among groups of persons. The Minnesota Multiphasic Personality Inventory appears to be in this class (Hathaway & McKinley, 1951; Hathaway & Meehl, 1951; Meehl, 1945; Meehl & Dahlstrom, 1960). From the viewpoint of ascertaining central and peripheral functions, considerations concerning the MMPI have been raised (Meehl & Dahlstrom, 1960) which apply to any temperament inventory standardized on relatively distinct groups. In the course of research seeking empirical rules for evaluating the MMPI, it was discovered that a number of persons classified by psychiatric diagnosis as nonpsychotic responded in the same way that known psychotics respond. The investigators, although duly cognizant of the patent errors of psychiatric diagnoses and of the inadequacies of test construction and administration, nevertheless ask a pertinent question, "What are we to think about this patient?" Free of overt (peripheral) psychotic symptoms, he has yet responded to 550 verbal stimuli in a way that is statistically similar to that of persons whose clinical pictures show that they are undoubtedly psychotic. Phenomenologically, this patient presents a "schizophrenic way of responding." Such an individual differs from the patient whose clinical and test results coalesce. His private world as revealed by the test appears to be peculiarly different from his public world as determined by ward behavior, mental status examination, etc.

Other ingenious methods of assessment have been devised which try to bridge the gap between the private and public functioning of an individual. Work at the University of California Institute of Personality Assessment and Research has employed several instruments which depart from ordinary "pencil-and-paper tests" (MacKinnon, 1951). Among these is the Gough "Adjective Check List," a simple list of alphabetically arranged adjectives which an individual checks as descriptive of himself and which others check in respect to him. The Barron "Art Scale" developed at IPAR differentiates individuals not only in art taste but in temperament patterns; and what are called perceptual-cognitive tests likewise shows temperament patterns.

An instrument similar to Gough's employed in one research (Van Zelst & Kerr, 1954) illustrates how these newer devices tend to reveal both central and peripheral domains of personality. Five hundred and fourteen technical and scientific individuals were presented a list of 56 trait names abstracted from Cattell's factor-analytic study for self-rating. By guaranteeing anonymity to the self-raters the experimenters believed they had eliminated some of

their subjects' refusal to reveal their inner qualities. The criterion measure against which the trait-checking was compared was productivity in (scientific) literary output. When the effect of age was removed by statistical means, the correlations between productivity and self-rated traits were significant in 37 out of the 56 correlations. The highest correlation was .61. It is interesting to observe that the most productive scientists tended to score highest in "originality" on their self-rated list and showed very little of being "contented" and "conventional." The authors of the report declare that the self-assessment revealed more of the individual than do regular pencil-and-paper tests or clinical assessments. Whether their contention is true or not, the method does appear to make possible the expression of more of an individual's private world than under usual test conditions.

The scorn some psychologists exhibit for "paper-and-pencil" tests is not entirely justified (Meehl, 1945). Still less is the belated recognition on the part of the public of inadequacies which psychological tests possess. What self-appointed protectors of the public point out in the way of errors or the possibilities to fake on the tests, psychologists have known for years (Hathaway, 1959; Kelly, Miles, & Terman, 1936).

In the application of tests to individuals rather than to groups, the psychologist is the main instrument and the test he employs is secondary. The ability of the clinician to judge the individual with or without tests is consequently an exceedingly important variable. Unfortunately, clinicians of various sorts have not performed very well in experimental situations involving judgment of individuals (Kelly & Fiske, 1950; Meehl, 1954; Taft, 1955). There is, however, fairly good evidence, substantiating a commonly held opinion, that some persons are better judges of others than are other persons (Taft, 1955). It is interesting to find, for example, that judges drawn from the physical sciences prove superior to those from the social sciences, contrary to expectation (Taft, 1956). This same principle seems to hold in relation to clinical psychologists who are not all equal, despite their similarity of training (Holt, 1958; Hunt, 1959). As a result, the efficient use of a test or battery of tests applied to an individual depends on how adequate the clinician is.

In the hands of a good clinician, then, one who understands the values and limitations of tests and possesses judging ability, the temperament inventories should be able to discern not only those areas which a person can or will reveal ordinarily but also probe those areas of particular sensitivity in an individual's private world which might escape detection. Surely, the person may at times "fool" the test. But from the remainder of a test or from other personality indicators, such as case study, physical examination, other temperament tests, and so on, there may be areas revealed in one's personality which he is incapable of manifesting directly or is attempting to hide. The very fact that he feels consciously or unconsciously the need to keep these areas private rather than make them public is a clue to what the individual is. Especially is this revelation important if the person has ostensibly come to a counselor for help—why does he need to conceal from the one he expects to help him the very information which might be useful in assisting him? Not only, however, is information elicited when comparison is made with other indicators coming directly from the individual. If the tests are well standardized, the differences which an individual exhibits from the standardizing groups may show up unusual omissions or over-emphases. If there is, say, an utter denial of any hostility, where the standard group has admitted to some hostility, the test interpreter is warned that probably the individual is concealing willfully some important data (which are private and possibly unconscious). If there are over-emphases, the clinician wonders why the person has to be so obvious in revealing what the standard group has failed to reveal so fully.

A further use of inventories of the so-called "nonprojective" or "objective" variety in personality research on central and peripheral functions follows immediately on the individual usage just elaborated. There are advantages when studying either individuals or groups in knowing what most persons in any cultural grouping are willing or able to admit about themselves. Granted that the test may not tell the "basic nature" of these persons or what motivates them, it is a great gain in our endeavor to gather knowledge about personalities to know what the individuals of a specified group know, or think they know, or are willing to let others know about themselves. The peripheral and the conscious are just as much in need of investigation as the private and the unconscious. And "personality inventories" have given us considerable information at this level. When these data are put together with the results of other ways of investigating personality, we have a means of checking and cross-checking from one type of investigation to another.

Projectively-Revealed Functioning. Much of the information about both private and peripheral portions of personality has come from projective methods of investigation to which we turn now. The fact that a method of investigation is called projective does not set it too far apart from the methods we have been considering, for the so-called objective instruments are employed projectively when they fulfill the purposes of revealing that which the person may desire to conceal or be unable to reveal about himself. The projective methods [1] have not usually been considered means of investigating central and peripheral portions of the personality, except insofar as central and peripheral are identical with conscious and unconscious, and especially when central coincides with "the unconscious." It is time

[1] Projective methods can be almost any kind of technique used for deriving information about an individual that he may not divulge directly. Anything from doodling, gestures, and casual conversation to intelligence tests, to finger-painting and non-standardized techniques like the Rorschach and Insight Test may serve the purpose.

to recognize, however, that these methods reveal, insofar as they possess validity at all, central portions of the personality which are not by any means unconscious as well as some that are, and often "reveal" that which is public as well. Indeed, if there were not many instances when projective tests offer information of a public nature, which can be verified by objective observation, and of a private but conscious nature, it would be exceedingly difficult if not impossible to check the validity of such techniques (Purcell, 1958).

Private or Public Conscious Factors. At this point a procedure used by some clinicians demonstrates both an approach by which the validity of projective tests may be partially established and also the fact that private but conscious areas of the personality are uncovered by projective methods of personality assessment. Either as examiner or therapist the psychologist sometimes is required or finds it expedient to interpret the results of tests to the examinee.[1] With the test summaries before him a psychologist could blurt out, "You have an I.Q. of 128, you show a strong Oedipal fixation, you have a minimum of ego strength, you are homosexual, etc., etc." Instead, the skilled clinician may present in terms suited to the counselee's level of intelligence, of ego strength, of understanding and enlightenment certain of the test results as tentative hypotheses of interpretation of the counselee's difficulties, tentative because the tests may be wrong or the counselee may not be ready to accept an accurate statement of his situation.

When confronted with a certain test interpretation, the counselee in turn may respond, "Well, sure, it didn't take a test for you to learn *that* about me, did it?" Or he may say, "I guess you're right. I've never told anyone about that before," and then he may tell more about the attitudes or feelings which the test has sampled and of which he has been aware, but which for any number of reasons he would not mention to others. At times an individual denies he has whatever is suggested by the tests, then later when he has come to trust his counselor he remarks, "You recall what you said about that matter? I knew you were right, but I couldn't bring myself to admit it." Of course, he may not be remembering correctly; he may think now that he was conscious of the matter then, but in actuality his "memory" is of something he has learned about himself since the testing. There is still another possibility, often actualized, of the person's denying and continuing to deny with either calmness or vehemence that the hypothesis advanced applies to him. Then only by weighing other evidence, including other test results and expressive movements of the individual, which serve as projective methods in themselves, can the psychologist conclude temporarily either that the test may be incorrect, that the assigned interpretation to some test indicator may be fallacious, or that the individual may have certain portions of his personality which are private *and* unconscious.

The main point to be derived from the foregoing meager outline of a truly complex procedure is that projective tests provide information about conscious but hidden portions (and sometimes even open portions) of the personality as well as about unconscious portions. By means of checking against the observable or public portions of the personality—public perhaps only in the sense of being revealed by special techniques like the psychogalvanometer—the psychologist may verify for the private and unconscious portions some of the results of his testing. He may also find that the private but conscious portions revealed on the test can be verified as well. Incidentally, although the investigation of the

[1] Some clinicians frown on the practice while others testify to the helpfulness of interpreting tests to the counselee. In a field as little understood as that of psychotherapeutics to say, "This or that procedure is a *bad* one," is to overstep the bounds of our knowledge. Even clinicians who do interpret tests as suggested in the text do not follow the custom of interpreting to every counselee; an individual may have to be chosen with care for interpreting. In one way or another, of course, every clinician who uses tests does interpret the results, directly or indirectly.

same individual cannot logically be used *both* to disclose his inner functions *and* to validate the technique employed, unless there are sufficient correspondences of the test with directly verifiable personality functions, the test becomes—or should become—suspect.[1] If projective methods could only reveal unconscious factors, the problem of validating such techniques would be almost insurmountable.

Private or Public Unconscious Factors. Nothing said in the preceding paragraphs should be construed as a denial of projective revelations of unconscious functioning.[2] The latter is the area for which projective methods are presumed to be preeminently suited as instruments of investigation, and it is not the purpose of this text to deny their efficacy or usefulness in searching out unconsciousness. Already it has been granted that there are functions which are unconscious. Various texts (Abt & Bellak, 1950; Anderson & Anderson, 1951; Bell, 1948) discuss in detail the uncovery of unconscious processes by projective methods. At this place in our study of personality our emphasis is on the private or public nature of the unconscious processes revealed by projective techniques. It does not take special projective instruments to demonstrate that the person himself may be unaware of some very public activities in which he is engaging, namely, some of his "expressive movements." On the other

hand certain attitudes held unconsciously may be amenable to investigation, if at all, only by projective methods. These unconscious functions have been discussed previously (Chapter 11), so that they need no elaboration at this point.

Consistent and Inconsistent Trends. Results of projective and objective tests on an individual may reveal contradictory trends. We are prepared for some inconsistencies within the personality (Chapter 3), but we must bear in mind Allport's doctrine of "congruence" whereby we search for key factors within the personality which may suggest greater consistency than is ostensibly present. Yet there are differences among results from tests especially of a more projective nature which at times can only be interpreted as manifesting central aspects of personality on the one hand and peripheral ones on the other.[3] Only one illustration of the apparent revelation of private and public domains by psychological instruments can be cited. Like other clinical cases offered in this text this one is not regarded as proof of a particular point. It is set against a background of similar cases and in some instances compared, as below, with normative populations.

An examinee showed relatively little anxiety, considerable ego strength, a balance of emotionality, and a lack of neurotic characteristics in general on several self-inventories. Even his sentence completion test, a semi-projective instrument, manifested relatively normal trends. Further, the Rorschach "psychogram" and formal scores with one single exception coincided with the objective tests; the exception was noted by the writer but was interpreted cautiously as a "possible psychotic indicator," inasmuch as the same sign had appeared in the

---

[1] The Rorschach Test (as suggested in Chapter 5) because of dozens if not hundreds of researches which have failed to find such correspondences has become open to suspicion; Raymond Cattell thinks that it was open to suspicion from its very inception. The Szondi Test has been suspect since its introduction by Susan Deri (1949) in this country without any validating data; later research has not found it to hold up well (*e.g.,* Fleishman, 1954; Gordon & Lambert, 1954). Gordon (1953) does find that Szondi factors have some relation to life factors, however.

[2] It seems that scientists have been busy trying to prove or disprove whether there are unconscious functions or not, almost disregarding the question of central and peripheral which are fully as important aspects of personality. Only tangentially does the research on "perceptual defense" (Chapter 11) bear on the problem at hand.

[3] Guilford (Thurstone, 1952) with much experience in subjecting projective and "superficial" approaches to statistical analysis remarks on disagreements between these approaches: "It may be well worth while to know about both the manifest and the latent traits of inconsistencies in overt behavior and of apparently sudden reversals of character. Clinical attention to individuals showing such disagreements might well prevent the scrupulously honest person suddenly becoming guilty of embezzlement and the sunny and cheerful person suddenly going on a homicidal binge."

records of several persons who were judged clinically normal (Dreger, 1952). To add to the normalcy picture, case data partially supported the inventories and general Rorschach interpretation. In particular those who worked closely with the testee in an academic capacity were convinced of his stability and normality. When, however, the Rorschach was reviewed for content rather than for formal scoring elements,[1] and when the Thematic Apperception Test was analyzed, anxiety and guilt trends showed up, although neither the examiner nor another clinician could find anything specific to indicate why anxiety and guilt should be present. On the basis of the tests, then, there *seemed* to be conscious feelings of security and poise and unconscious feelings of insecurity; the overt behavior *as far as ascertainable* was in keeping with both the objective test results and the projective data which suggested a normal personality.

Purely by chance, subsequently, the examiner stumbled onto the reasons for the "psychotic indicator" and the anxiety and guilt signs. When the young man was confronted with the interpretation of the tests, he readily —now—admitted that he had been engaging in sexual practices frowned upon by our society. Here was a case of a "private role," one that of necessity only a few perons could know was being played, but one so exceedingly important to the individual that it occasioned great anxiety and guilt. On account of the kind of training the young man had received whose rules he had transgressed, his superego was involved in accusations against his practices. Instead, however, of presenting a contrast between conscious and unconscious as the writer had first concluded, the examinee offered a contrast largely between central and peripheral, for the young man was aware of both the practice he had hidden and at least some of his anxiety and guilt.[2] The tests wholly or in part were sampling from different levels of personality; even the same test, which may be a composite of different tests, apparently succeeded in getting at the different levels, as in the case of the Rorschach and

TAT. Generally, however, the projective tests tapped "lower" levels or more private ones and the objective techniques public levels.

Interpretation of test results not only from the conscious-unconscious frame of reference, but from a central-peripheral frame as well, provides a means of assessing trends in a personality which appear contradictory or even sometimes falsely consistent with one another.

Predictability and Unpredictability of Functions. With some outstanding exceptions it must be acknowledged that prediction from tests to behavior and experience or vice versa is still a fairly hazardous pursuit (McClelland, Baldwin, Bronfenbrenner, & Strodtbeck, 1958), especially when we are dealing with normal individuals. Hartshorne and May (Chapter 3) discovered that moral knowledge as displayed on a test did not necessarily signify testable moral behavior. In other areas responses on either projective or objective tests may not signify similar behavior in "real life" situations. In making such pessimistic observations we are regarding only personological prediction, for group prediction has proved highly satisfactory at times (*e.g.*, Guilford & Lacey, 1947; Melton, 1947).

It might be expected (not ordinarily by a psychologist) that a person should know himself well enough to identify his own characteristics as abstracted from his test responses. After all, a person knows his private and public worlds to an extent, the former probably better than anyone else who has not made an intensive psychological study of it. Yet in one experiment (Forer, 1949) a teacher offered a general astrological description of personality to his students who had taken the Group Rorschach as if the description were a separate Rorschach picture of each one; every student accepted the astrological description as his own. It appears that knowledge of some portions of his private or public world does not prevent the individual from being deluded about himself.

Another experimenter (Sundberg, 1955) went further, however, in carrying out an

---

[1] The writer suspects that the value which most clinicians attach to the Rorschach rests on an analysis of content of responses rather than on the formal scoring, for the latter has failed in the majority of studies to manifest objective validity.

[2] Why this young man was forced to engage in the disapproved sexual practices is another story. The roots lay in his unconscious functions.

adaptation of the first experiment. He gave 44 students the Minnesota Multiphasic Personality Inventory. Two experienced psychologists using the students' MMPI records wrote individual interpretations of each record covering the areas of mood, physical and mental complaints, conflicts, and social attitudes and behavior. A sheet of paper was then presented to each subject containing his "bona fide" MMPI interpretation and another "fake" interpretation derived from the previous astrological description. The subject was first asked, "Which interpretation describes you better?" and then, "One of these interpretations is not yours; the other one is written from your tests especially. Which one is written for you?" By chance one would expect 22 correct choices for 44 individuals; actually only 18 correctly selected their own interpretation in answer to the first question and 20 in answer to the second question. These results cannot be considered any better than chance. Perhaps one's friends, though, do better in identifying "bona fide" test interpretations over "fake" ones. Close friends know something of the individual's private as well as much of his public world. The researcher continued his experiment by having each of 30 of the original 44 students give the two interpretations to several close friends with printed instructions to choose the one better suited to the subject. Here again identifications were not significantly different from what could be expected by chance. Assuming that the two psychologists were accurate in their précis of the MMPI record in each case, it seems that an individual knowing something of his own inner workings cannot predict his personality functioning as derived from a test; his friends likewise, knowing his overt behavior to some extent as well as some of his inner life, cannot predict what the person will do on a test. It is well to emphasize once more that these conclusions pertain to normal persons. Results of MMPI research on psychopathological groups yield better than chance matchings.

The MMPI is considered one of the best objective tests. What about projective tests in regard to prediction of central and peripheral regions? Although other tests and experiments could be cited, an experiment is instanced here with a test which was constructed on more adequate psychometric bases than are a good many projective tests. The test is the Rosenzweig "P-F Study." In the latter an individual is asked to fill in cartoon "balloons" as to what responses would be made by persons in the cartoons who are being subjected to obstructing, delaying, and generally frustrating circumstances (as interpreted by our culture). Although other experiments have been performed with the "P-F Study" on abnormal subjects, this one (Mehlman & Whiteman, 1955) is chosen in part because it employed normal subjects. The Rozenzweig was administered to 189 students who also were presented with one of three "real life" behavioral situations which corresponded to three of the artificial frustration situations on the test. Although there are reservations one wants to make about the treatment of the data, the conclusion derived from the study seems fairly well-substantiated that there was very little if any prediction from the test to the overt situation and from the latter to the test. As the authors state, one may argue that there should not be *direct* agreement between a projective test and overt behavior, but one may not reasonably argue that there should be *no* agreement. Although a couple of studies with psychopathological groups (Albee, 1950; Gatling, 1950) have demonstrated some predictability from maladjusted behavior to the "P-F Study," the results of the above experiment coincide with that of the writer (Dreger, 1952) who found that two normal subject groups could not be distinguished from each other by the Rosenzweig or other projective tests.

One other study follows on the heels of those just cited. When an intensive psychotherapeutic analysis has been conducted into an individual's central regions into which projective tests may be supposed to penetrate, there should be close agreement of the judgments of the therapist and of the patient with the results of a projective test. Accordingly, one psychologist (Ellis, 1953) administered the Blacky Test to a patient with whom he had engaged in over 200 hours of psychoanalytic therapy. The verbatim protocol of the patient's responses on the Blacky test was then submitted to 11 clinical psychologists and 11 psychological internes who had all been given a brief period of instruction specifically on the test in addition to their general psychological training. Even the originator of the test participated in the experiment. Each psychologist and interne filled out a rating-scale covering psychosexual and characterological aspects of the patient. Nineteen of the judges in addition wrote out summaries of the patient's behavioral characteristics as they inferred them from the protocol. Then, the therapist and the patient independently filled out the rating scale.

In about three-fourths of the ratings made by internes and psychologists, including the test originator, there was relative agreement, a rather high inter-rater reliability for the kind of task set the judges. When the others' ratings, however, were compared with the therapist's and the patient's, only about 60 per cent of these could be considered "successful" in the sense of agreeing with the ratings by the ones who presumably knew most about the patient, herself and her psychotherapist. The patient and therapist in contrast agreed with each other in all but three out of 38 questions on the rating scale. On the summaries of behavioral characteristics as derived from the Blacky Test the judges fared even less well than on the rating scales, for the patient and therapist could only agree with 90 out of 207 statements made in the summaries. The psychologist conducting the study concludes that the reliability of the Blacky Test is satisfactorily high in that raters agree among themselves on the basis of the test. But the *validity* of the instrument is low as a predictor of an actual person's functioning, central and peripheral, known from 200 hours of intensive psychotherapy.

If we take the results of the experiments cited immediately above as illustrative of how well tests perform in revealing central and peripheral portions of personality, we may be very much disappointed in the tests. To return to the thesis of this subsection, the statement can be easily upheld that it is a hazardous pursuit to predict from or to projective or other tests. If the results of the tests exemplified may be considered representative, we may conclude that objective and subjective tests are far from perfect in predicting the private or even the public functioning of an individual.

Score Patterns in Personality Functioning. Still another tentative conclusion related to the immediately preceding considerations is that sometimes when specific test indicators fail in assessing either inner or outer functioning adequately, a configuration or a pattern of scores from the tests may be more useful in predicting to some personality functions. Almost immediately when the personologist or psychological clinician has spoken of the value of a configuration, say on the Rorschach, after individual scores have proven to be inadequate predictors, "tough-minded" academic psychologists have retorted, "You are substituting for a definite, measurable set of observable and teachable indicators some vague, clinical intuition derived from a hazy impression of an individual's over-all test performance. You may be engaging in art with your 'total patterns,' but not in science." And far too often the academic psychologist has been right. "Tender-minded" clinicians or personologists have been content with a kind of mumbo-jumbo about configurations and patterns which seem to have little relation to specific scores on a test and little validation in observable behavior or even in an individual's introspective analysis of himself.

Nevertheless, psychological statisticians have become aware of the data issuing from clinics (Cronbach, 1949a, 1949b, 1950; Meehl, 1950). And there has been a movement in psychology to deal with whole test behavior rather than just specific scores isolated from one another. Despite the vagueness of many attempts at configurational thinking about personality, there is an attempt to do greater justice to the fact of personality, to an individual as a functioning whole (though not as a unit, as we have recognized previously), than does the atomistic test approach which considers only one score at a time. In recent years a number of mathematical methods of dealing with many scores from a test have been introduced. These methods range from simple ratios of individual scores on a test to complex multiple regression equations (Gaier & Lee, 1953). Analysis of the interrelations has been made not only of whole tests with one another but of single test items. Such paradoxical results are found to be possible as this: two items of a test, either one of which taken by itself has zero validity in distinguishing schizophrenics from normals, may distinguish these groups perfectly when scored as a pattern rather than only as individual items (Horst, 1954; Meehl, 1945, 1950).

How does this movement toward improved configurational analysis affect our understanding of the central and peripheral aspects of personality? At once we must recognize that these methods were not devised to give information directly relevant to public and private domains, even though there is a concerted attack, often unverbalized, on the problem of reaching the private world. Often the problem is confused with trying to unlock unconsciousness or even just "the unconscious." Ordinarily in interpreting research data which has not specifically endeavored to meet the problem at hand, we have to infer from research on related problems what the significance is for the immediate problem. Here we can at least tentatively suggest that related research gives ground for the belief that configurational scoring of tests allows better prediction to factors of overt behavior (whether one belongs in a certain group, conforms to certain roles, etc.) and to factors of private import (what one "really" believes, which attitudes one holds but conceals, etc.) than does the more particularistic approach of conventional test interpre-

tation. Two representative pieces of research may be adduced.

One of the experiments comes from a series of studies in personality, and especially its degree of integration (of being integrative). In the experiment (McQuitty, 1952) the primary aim was to discover items for an effective test rather than unearthing personality differences directly. The experimenter discovered facts about the latter from pattern-analyses of test items. A test consisting of 189 items distributed somewhat unevenly between "objective" and "subjective" questions was administered to male subjects, 130 mental hospital patients and 84 individuals from the community. Questions classed as "objective" were those which could be answered on the basis of objectively verifiable behavior, such questions as, "Do you laugh frequently?" "Subjective" questions were those answered on internal, less objective cues, such as "Do you have disturbing thoughts?" We may infer that those items which can be classed as subjective correspond to what we have identified as central or private here and those which are objective correspond to public or peripheral as we have defined them. Two methods of scoring the tests and analyzing items were employed, both involving pattern scoring.

The subjective items, reaching into the regions of the personality which the individual does not (will not or cannot) ordinarily divulge, when analyzed by the method of pattern analysis, differentiated individuals into normal and schizophrenic better than did objective items which reach the public portions of the personality. The objective items also differentiated with either method of pattern scoring. Thus in this experiment, either items concerning the private regions of an individual or those concerning his peripheral regions allowed some prediction of public behavior, that is, being within or outside a mental hospital, *when these items were treated configurationally*.

The second experiment bears tangentially on the central and peripheral. The researchers (Rogers & Hammond, 1953) presented to three psychologists with several years' Rorschach experience apiece Rorschach records of 59 patients classed as improved or slightly improved after psychotherapy, together with 50 records of unimproved patients. These psychologists judged improvement or unimprovement first on the basis of a two or three minute *snap* judgment, secondly on the basis of *studied* judgment allowing all the time necessary for examination of the record, and then on the basis of the Rorschach record plus the name of the therapist who worked with the patient. Results of these judgments were all negative; although each psychologist agreed strongly with himself, he did not agree well with the other two on any type of judgment, and none of the psychologists could distinguish improved from unimproved patients. Thus far one could say, "Score zero."

However, in another part of the experiment an examination of the records to determine single scores or combinations of scores which might distinguish the two groups revealed one particular score [1] plus several combinations of this score with other scores, and finally some combinations omitting the particular score, all of which showed promise of being a differential indicators. Following accepted scientific procedure, these experimenters did not allow their results obtained in this *a posteriori* fashion to stand without verification. Using the combinations of scores derived from the first groups as "empirical rules," they applied these rules to an entirely new group of 70 improved and 34 unimproved patients. The general conclusion to which the experimenters came was that in the new group the combinations of scores could predict improvement, though the same thing could not be said for predicting unimprovement. Cross-validation had then actually confirmed in part the empirical combinations of scores derived from individual Rorschach scores.

It may be concluded that at least em-

pirically-derived patterns of scores from a test which purports to reveal private, possibly unconscious portions of the personality, can predict with a fair measure of success to public behavior, that is, whether or not one is an improved patient. Crude as the over-all results may be, they are superior to the nonquantitative "total impression" of many clinical psychologists in making such predictions. There are still many problems to be solved in the use of patterns of scores from any one multi-score test or from many tests, but the efforts of recent years to use configurations of test scores to match the interrelated phenomena of personality will probably be continued and strengthened. More should be learned by means of improved configurational test scoring about the private and public domains of personality, which sometimes seem so hopelessly at odds.

Test Roles. One last brief but by no means minor conclusion relative to central and peripheral functions is that tests are sensitive to the roles played by the testee and by the administrator of the tests. This conclusion is of vast import, for it means that we have learned that personality testing is a social interactional process and not merely a transaction between a set of stimuli and a mechanical person.

Among representative experiments demonstrating the influence of the role of the examiner is one (Lord, 1950) in which Rorschach tests were administered by several examiners two times apiece to each of 36 male college sophomores. The administrators took on different affective roles, neutral, negative, or positive, toward the testee. Differences of performance on the same test between test and re-test showed up as functions not only of the repetition of the test, but also as functions of the administrator's attitude and the person of the administrator. The biggest differences could be traced to differences of examiners, an indication that the testing situation is an interpersonal one, involving more than testee and test. But a number of differences could be found emerging from the neutral, positive, or negative roles as-

---

[1] Human movement responses, *M*, of the so-called extensor variety.

sumed by the administrators. Those subjects who were warmly greeted understood instructions better than those greeted coldly, made no errors in following simple directions, and in general performed differently from those who received negative treatment. Although some of the differences of functioning were public, some differences in private functioning, if the Rorschach touches these as most clinicians suppose, also were effected by changes of role of administrators. That the role the testee plays in a testing situation may affect his responses has been suspected for some time by test administrators who are cross-culturally oriented. The story told by a missionary of Chinese children who would not answer test items in such a way as to "get ahead" of their comrades has the marks of credibility to anyone somewhat familiar with roles which Chinese are expected to fulfill.

A small but significant piece of research (Trent, 1954) tends to demonstrate the influence of the individual's role in a test. Two Negro and two white investigators were trained to administer a brief test consisting of pictures of three women judged "equally attractive" by 30 white and Negro judges, one picture of a decidedly light-skinned Negro, one of a white woman, and one of a decidedly dark-skinned Negro woman. The subjects were matched fairly evenly, 39 white and 42 Negro children, four- and five-year-old boys and girls in public schools in two New York cities. They were shown the pictures in random order, and asked simply; "See these three mothers? Which one is yours? Why?" The results confirmed within reasonable limits that some children respond to the test stimuli differently for administrators of different color. Of 20 white children ten selected the white "mother" for a white investigator, nine selected the light-skinned Negro "mother," none the dark-skinned, and one made no choice. Of the remaining 19 tested by a Negro investigator 12 chose the white "mother," none the light-skinned, but five chose the dark-skinned "mother," and two made no choice. Of 24 Negro children tested by a white investigator 12 selected the white "mother," five the light-skinned, only one the dark-skinned, and six made no choice. Of 18 Negro children tested by a Negro investigator eight chose the white mother, six the light-skinned, four the dark-skinned, and none made no choice.

It is fairly easy to pick methodological flaws in this particular experiment. But its results are in line with those expected by persons who are familiar with the role-playing activities of children even as young as four and five (Radke, Trager, & Davis, 1949; Radke & Trager, 1950). A conclusion that either white or Negro children's behavior manifests unconscious attitudes may not hold; at least private versus public behavior, however, seems to be represented, depending on what role the child plays in view of the color of the test administrator. As in other kinds of behavior, the role of the other and the role of the individual himself seem to affect what he can or will make known on a test.

SUMMARY

Besides the major cross-classifying of the topography of personality into id, ego, superego and role functions, and consciousness and unconsciousness, the Lewinian distinctions between central and peripheral can be observed. Literature has recognized that some portions of the personality, known in part to the individual, are withheld from others. Science, too, has taken account of this central portion of the personality. Stern set up an inward-outward dimension to account for surface and depth phenomena. Lewin also posited the central and peripheral defined by more or less permeable boundaries.

Both "objective" and "projective" tests have been devised by psychologists to penetrate the inner world "of the individual." "Personality inventories" of lesser or greater ingenuity can reveal far more of the personality than the taker may realize. Projective devices, although often thought to reveal unconscious processes, are useful in getting at both private and public domains.

Skilled interpretation of test data serves as a validation device for instruments in that persons may reveal and then admit to what to them is private but conscious. Of course, some functions are both private and unconscious as well as public and unconscious. Revelation of tests, coupled with other data, may help in determining consistency within the personality when otherwise only inconsistency could be postulated. However, prediction to "real life" from tests alone constitutes a hazardous pursuit at present. "Pattern analysis," employing a configuration of scores from tests rather than isolated indicators, or even "global judgment," has shown more promise. Some understanding of the dynamics of test administration, particularly in regard to the roles of examiner and examinee, is important in interpreting test results, and especially how much of the central portions of personality are revealed by tests.

QUESTIONS

1. How do conscious-unconscious and central-peripheral functions differ?

2. Give an example from literature, other than the examples cited in the text, of the central versus the peripheral.

3. Review briefly Lewin's distinctions between central and peripheral.

4. How do so-called "personality inventories" tap or fail to tap central portions of the personality?

5. In what ways do projective tests reveal conscious private areas of the personality and public unconscious ones?

6. Recalling the discussion on consistency in Chapter 3, how do you figure that tests may help in determining consistencies and inconsistencies?

7. Discuss "configurational analysis."

8. What effects do roles of examiner and examinee have upon test results?

PERSONALITY IN THE ADULT INDIVIDUAL: DYNAMIC STRUCTURE- FUNCTIONS: DIMENSIONAL: TRAITS

Before taking a further view of personality, a brief review of our approach to personality will provide orientation for the following chapters. In the first section of this text, frames of reference in general scientific and psychological concepts were provided for personology, the study of the person or the science of personality. Only after the general background had been delineated was an attempt made to define personality. For purposes of this text the simple definition was adopted: "Personality consists of the organized functions of the individual."

The succeeding sections including the present one constitute a detailed examination of these functions. The question first was raised as to the degree or degrees of consistency there is in personality in terms of the individual's history, *i.e.*, his "longitudinal continuity," and of his present functioning, his "cross-sectional consistency." Assuming some measure of consistency to personality, we made inquiry into the manner in which functions are related to one another in an over-all pattern. The discussion on personality structure presented the major ways (or theories) of the organization of personality in the adult individual primarily. In conceiving of personality structure as "a dynamic, multidimensional, topographical system," both a recognition of the legitimately different approaches to structure and a conscious attempt to emphasize the complexity of personality were incorporated in an eclectic but not atomistic concept of personality structure. Inasmuch as life in general and personality in particular do not lend themselves easily, if at all, to neat, mutually exclusive polychotomies, three broad cross-classifications of major functions were delineated, topographical, dimensional, and economic. These are called "dynamic structure-functions" in view of their relative permanency in the developed individual.

Within the topographical structure functions, further cross-classification revealed first those major functions roughly corresponding to the id, ego, and superego described by psychoanalysis plus roles as partially clarified by social psychology. In addition, consciousness and unconsciousness and the central and peripheral functions were considered in the topography of personality. In the final cross-categorizing group of dynamic structure-functions, the economic, the distribution and utilization of energy will be discussed in respect to changes within and movements of the personality.

Now, however, the second major set of dynamic structure-functions is presented. One of the oldest and in mathematical forms among the newest ways of describing functions of personality, traits are regarded here primarily as dimensional constructs.

There are scholars identified with trait theories of personality who will protest that no trait is essentially quantifiable. In this text, however, traits have been considered as "dimensions of personality." Each of these traits *may* be qualitatively distinct from others but most of them differ from individual to individual in such a way that persons may be ranked along a trait continuum. It is to factor analysis especially that we are indebted for material on dimensions of personality.[1] Much of the theory and many of the mathematical procedures have been developed by psychologists (Harmon, 1960; Holzinger & Harman, 1941; Thurstone, 1947).

[1] The Appendix presents a simplified description of factor analysis.

CHAPTER 13

THE NATURE OF TRAITS OF PERSONALITY

In the treatment of the over-all structure of personality it was necessary to speak of traits of personality. A review of the discussion there (Chapter 4) would be helpful as a background for the following, though some of the concepts and facts presented in the earlier discussion must be repeated.

FACULTIES AND FACTORS

The "faculties" of pre-scientific psychology have been fairly well discredited as traits of personality. They were impersonal entities scarcely needing a local habitation though having names like memory, will, judgment, imagination, and so forth.[1] To be sure, Franz Joseph Gall's faculty psychology, as explained in Chapter 4, does not fall under the same criticism, but is closer to modern trait psychologies than his contemporaries' faculty systems. "Faculties" shared at least one feature in common with traits as conceived by the modern discipline of factor analysis, that they could be possessed in greater or lesser quantity by an individual; if the individual can have more or less of a faculty, the latter can be represented dimensionally as can a trait.

[1] Allport, it will be recalled, gives a sympathetic critique of faculty psychology.

What difference is there, then, between faculties and factors? Are factors only mathematically-dignified restorations of Locke's faculties? There are similarities, it must be admitted. There is, however, what seems like one fundamental distinction between factor-traits dimensionally conceived and faculties so conceived. The difference may be symbolized by the two diagrams of Figure 17, p. 226. In Figure 17 (a) faculties are represented dimensionally, but the personality is conceived as a sum-total of the quantities of common faculties possessed by the person, as if an individual did not have organized functions but had instead a list of functions (actually, entities) which just happen to be together in the same individual.[2] On the other hand, Figure 17 (b) represents factors or traits also di-

[2] Long ago Herbart (1834) called attention to the need to distinguish the dynamic, "internal nature," which the faculties only manifested, from the faculties themselves. He wrote: "When in common life we hear it said that one man has more understanding, another more memory, a third more imagination, a fourth a sounder judgment, and yet upon the whole, no greater or less degree of mental health can be attributed to the one than to the other, then the conjecture arises that all this distinction of the so-called mental faculties has more to do with the products of mental activity than with the internal nature of the latter, whether this nature be sound or diseased. . . ."

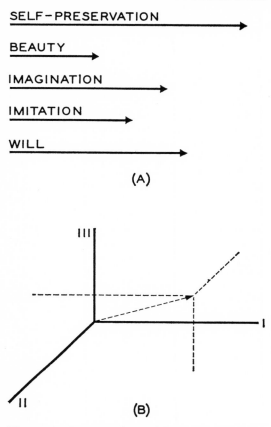

SELF-PRESERVATION

BEAUTY

IMAGINATION

IMITATION

WILL

(A)

III

I

II

(B)

Figure 17. A comparison of faculties and traits (factor-traits) as dimensions of personality.

mensionally, but the personality is conceived as a "vector resultant" of the differing amounts of different traits, a dynamic product of forces, a vector resultant rather than a static sum of qualities.[1] Only three traits or dimensions can be pictured here, yet the generalized notion of the personality as a *dynamic product* of many traits

possessed in varying degrees is not difficult to achieve.

Another fundamental distinction appears to hold in respect to faculties and factors. Faculties were regarded as virtually unchanged, except quantitatively, in their operation from individual to individual. Factors on the other hand are individualized in their operation according to factor theory. Any given piece of behavior is the resultant of a unique constellation of factors, each of which, sharing dynamically in the behavior, is modified in its operation *in the individual* by the other factors. A still further distinction may be found in the very important fact that faculties were logically derived and factors are derived empirically. As suggestions or hypotheses as to what basic functions exist in human beings, faculties have served a useful purpose. Actual research either of a factor-analytic variety or other controlled observation is necessary to determine more adequately which if any faculties stand up as basic functions.

TRAITS AS LOGICAL SUBSTRATA

If faculties were the forerunners of traits as conceived by modern personology, so too, logical definitions and analyses of traits, either prior to or contemporaneously with trait conceptions of factor analysis, have formed the necessary basis for factor-analytic investigations. In several systems of factor analysis, for example, a final procedure called "rotation of axes," is carried on until the factors (traits) which emerge are "psychologically meaningful,"[2] an expression which can in part be interpreted to signify "in accord with logical analyses of psychological traits." Further, when one of the most ambitious of factor-analytic studies was undertaken (Cattell, 1943a, 1946, 1957a), an investigation based on the list of several thousands of trait terms which Allport and Odbert (1936) had culled from an unabridged dic-

[1] If one takes a small object with smooth sides, like a small box, and pushes it first by a finger on one hand at one end and then by a finger on the other hand at the side, then pushes it with both fingers at the same time so that the object slides out from between his fingers, he will find the object moving, as one would suspect, in a diagonal direction in line with neither finger. The direction (and distance travelled) of the object can be represented by a directed line segment called the vector resultant. Factors are added, but added vectorially.

[2] Other criteria may also be used along with psychological meaning.

tionary, it was a logical not a statistical procedure at first. Therefore, nonfactor-oriented traits, as suggested by psychologists with wide experience in investigations of personality and with deep thought into the meaning of their findings, cannot be ignored. Among authorities who might be termed, "nonfactor-analytic"—though the term does not do justice to their positive contributions—four can be selected as fairly representative, G. W. Allport, J. R. Kantor, A. A. Roback, and William Stern. Each in turn can cast some light on the nature of traits.

Dynamic, Individualized Tendencies [1]

Allport (1931) whose personality structure concepts are given in Chapter 4, early in the modern era enunciated what he termed psychological criteria of traits. These are: (1) A trait has more than nominal existence, that is, it is something actually present in the individual, not a mere convenience for classifying behaviors which might seem similar. (2) A trait is more generalized than a habit; one may have a habit of going downtown every day at 4:00 which in turn manifests a trait of dependability. (3) A trait is dynamic or at least determinative; this concept is a key factor in Allport's system—the trait has "the capacity to. . . ." (4) The existence of a trait may be established empirically or statistically, may in other words be identified by inference from behavior or indirectly measured in terms of different quantities of similar behaviors. (5) Traits are only relatively independent of one another; being conservative politically may be related to being ethnocentric even though they are recognizably different traits. (6) A trait of personality is not the same as a moral quality; Allport excludes evaluative adjectives like "agreeable" or "asinine" from personality trait terms. (7) Acts or even habits which are inconsistent with a trait are not proof of the nonexistence of that trait; the possibility of "congruence" gives a foundation for this idea. (8) A trait may be viewed either in the light of the personality which contains it or in the light of its distribution in the population at large; although Allport insists on the individual nature of traits, the similarities of even individual traits can be assessed statistically.

With most of the eight criteria Allport suggests there seems little fault to be found. If traits are dimensional functions of personality, and quantifiable and measurable, all of the above characterizations can be considered applicable. Only two items seem somewhat unclear at this point. The third statement concerning the dynamic nature of traits is considered further under the discussion on Allport's concept of "functional autonomy" (Chapters 4 and 15). That the individual's behavior and his cognitive, conative, and emotional functions can become molded into more or less permanent forms is readily admissible; that there might be some special energy or capacity which makes the trait an "agent" to steer behavior is more difficult to believe. The other item, the sixth, has also received attention. Allport excludes moral qualities because they require another person's judgment. Today, however, it does not seem adequate to exclude interpersonal qualities from a concept of personality; "moral" qualities are as much functions of the individual as those which Allport rather artificially classes as "psychological."

In addition to characterizing traits in general, Allport makes several distinctions among traits. Along with Stern, Allport shows that traits can roughly be classified into *dynamic* and *stylistic*. The former are generally motivational: drive traits, interests, ambitions, tastes, values, and so forth. The latter are those which seem to direct but not drive behavior. Politeness, Allport indicates, is rarely a motivational trait—a polite person does not seek out others ordinarily in order to be polite to them as does a person with the trait of overt homo-

[1] Allport (1961) now terms these tendencies, which he formerly called traits, "personal dispositions." He distinguishes more sharply between the latter and common traits in his latest text than the discussion in our text, based on earlier writings, would imply.

sexuality who seeks out an object for his attentions. The difference between stylistic and dynamic traits is one of degree, however, for directive or stylistic traits may take on a drive character in certain instances.

Another distinction among traits is that between *genuine* and *pseudo-traits*. There is a difference between the Homeric "Greeks bearing gifts" who were bent on Troy's destruction and the giver of gifts who has the real interests of his donee at heart, although both actions could be superficially classed as springing from the trait of generosity. Still another distinction is between *individual* and *common* traits. In actuality every trait is individual in that no two persons have exactly the same trait even though the same word is used to describe what lies behind similar behaviors. Yet there are, because of common heredity, common physical conditions and common cultural pressures, similar modes of adjustment leading to traits which are approximately the same. On these common traits, Allport believes, there can be measurements and comparisons of individuals one with another. These various distinctions among traits which Allport suggests can be taken over into quantitative treatments of personality, though sometimes not very handily.

Sets of Reaction Systems

Kantor, the second of the "nonfactor analysts," writing prior to World War II seemed *in part* to hold to the "nominalist" viewpoint of traits against which Allport's first point above inveighed. "The exigencies of description, of course," Kantor (1938) writes, "impose upon us the necessity of using such words as cunning, honesty, politeness, helpfulness, etc. In each case, however, we regard them as naming *classes* of actions which find their place in the repertoire of character behavior." Such an insistence does not mean that Kantor does not believe in traits, for he adds, "X not only has just performed an honest action, but you can depend upon him to do so." What Kantor seems to mean is that

there are consistencies of behavior, classes of *actions* which go together—in the observation of these classes we know objectively that a person has a trait of some kind. But also there is some tendency which is resident in the individual that regulates his actions somewhat consistently. These tendencies are traits which he calls "continually existing sets of reaction systems" (a rather broad definition to be sure).

Traits arise, according to Kantor, from three different general sources. (1) Universal situations which all mankind must face. (2) Social circumstances which would be alike for many persons in the same culture. (3) Individual behavior experiences. Such an analysis seems reasonable and assists us in accounting for general traits found among all men as well as for less widely spread traits and those which seem unique. In addition it must not be overlooked that genetic factors make us both alike and different in respect to traits. Kantor's analysis assumes these genetic factors, for in one place the continuously existing set of reaction systems is spoken of as based on both biological individuality and behavioral experiences which are more or less homogeneous. The reaction systems or classes of actions arising from common and unique sources are in turn, Kantor points out, classifiable into groups of traits which have been recognized as having logical distinctions from one another.

Kantor's specimen classification serves to illustrate both the recognition in language of classes of traits and also some of the lines of demarcation psychology has employed in studying human functions. These classes of traits are: (1) abilities, (2) skills, (3) capacities, (4) habits, (5) dispositions, (6) ideals, (7) tastes, (8) talents, (9) ambitions, (10) knowledge, (11) manners, (12) accomplishments, (13) mannerisms, (14) intelligence, (15) desires, (16) fears and phobias, (17) prejudices, (18) beliefs. As Kantor well knew when organizing his classes, anyone who endeavors to make such a list invites criticism concerning too much or too little inclusiveness, or failure to consider overlappings of classes, or other inadequacies. But we are interested in learning from Kantor's efforts. His list gives us an idea of what traits are and how they can be divided into groups for purposes of scientific study.

Individual Modes of Behavior

From both Allport's and Kantor's logical analyses of traits a richer concept of the nature of traits can be gained. Further insight can be found in Roback's discussion of traits (1950). In considering his views, it is well to know that Roback scorns some statistical and factorial analyses of tests and ratings [1] which purport to uncover traits. He defines trait as "a distinctive mode of behavior, of a more or less permanent nature, arising from the individual's native endowments as modified by his experience" (Warren, 1934). It is Roback's tendency to emphasize "native endowments" strongly, even to what seems like an exaggerated degree, as in maintaining that there is, for example, an inborn trait of braggadocio. However, the definition given is satisfactory in that it coincides with the functions of personality we are considering. Roback further sets forth several points which are sometimes neglected in mathematical analyses of traits, namely, the gathering of traits into a pattern in the individual, the effect the individual has upon others—his interpersonal functions—as well as the multiplicity of traits, and the relation of traits to habits. We read in Roback's *Personality*:

We all have an assemblage of traits going to make up our personality. One pattern is different from every other. In other words, as the fashion advertisers say, 'only one of a kind is made.' Our traits are the same, but they appear not only in different proportions but in different groupings and settings. In the one case we have wisdom, perspicacity, intuition; in another the principal direction of intelligence lies in craftiness, cunning and scheming. One set of traits will affiliate with another which is kindred to it; and thus we may truly say that we are like loaded dice, not only loaded, but

magnetized so as to attract or repel (Roback, 1950).[2]

Each of us has thousands of traits, some relating to the physique or appearance (tall, short; stout, slim; fair, dark) others belonging to the intelligence department (bright, dull; acute, obtuse; cultured, philistine) while many traits deal with the emotional, social, and characterial phases of man. Every deliberate act points to a trait, and even habits can be subsumed under the same category. When it is said of someone that 'he makes a habit of not paying his debts,' it is not the habit which is significant, but the trait of irresponsibility. The incorporation of the word 'habit' is only for the sake of emphasis, to show that the trait has had several occasions for manifestation. A trait will, in general, show its true colors through the repeated behavior, but it may not have had the opportunity or else it might have been checked or disguised, so that it is not detectable to the 'naked' or inexperienced eye (Roback, 1950).[3]

One aspect, recognized in both Kantor's listing of classes of traits and in the above quotation, is that physiological functions such as mannerisms and those traits related to physique must be included in personality. While strictly speaking being tall, short, stout, or slim, fair, or dark is not a personality function, indicating instead possession of a physical trait, the physiological and psychological functions inextricably bound up with these physical traits differentiate individuals from one another. To take one example, a study of the effects in personality functioning of the nose (Holden, 1950) reveals what tremendous changes are made when plastic surgery alters the structure of an individual's nose. Either because the person feels that his nose is unsightly, even hideous, or because others actually look on it thus, he bears a seemingly inescapable burden. There is no reason to doubt the depth and breadth of the relief described in the study, or the consequent altering of the self and other concepts, when one no longer plays the role of "a

---

[1] ". . . very frequently one finds that this mountain of work has given birth to a puny mouse" (Roback, 1950).

[2] Roback, A. A. *Personality in theory and practice.* Cambridge: Sci-Art Publishers, 1950. Reprinted by permission.

[3] *Ibid.* Reprinted by permission.

person with a hideous nose." A depth analysis would probably uncover a body image which still persists in including the abhorred nose (Fisher, 1958; Schilder, 1950), but vast changes in the personality reaching deep and wide would not be unexpected.

Dispositions

The last of the logical trait analysts with whom we are concerned, William Stern, has been met several times throughout this book. His influence has been much more extensive than the actual references to his work. Again, only a small portion of this work is cited here partly because Stern's is not a trait psychology. He does, however, in his concept of "dispositions" bridge some of the gaps among the "mental faculties" of an older psychology, a doctrine which he declared had been "shipwrecked" in nineteenth-century psychology, and both the nonfactor-analytic trait psychologies and factor-analytic concepts of traits,[1]

Experience patterns are only activities of the moment. But a language usage, which Stern accepts, long ago recognized that *potential experience* must be reckoned with as well, tendencies or readiness or "dispositions" for the production of present experience. The doctrine of faculties which sought to account for those tendencies differs in several ways from the modern concept of dispositions, to which psychology has had to come after a period of trying to get along without them. (1) Unlike faculties, "dispositions are not rigid and compartmentalized mental powers" but are instead aspects of a person's total life. Although separable analytically for scientific purposes, various dispositions enter into an individual's present experiences in a relatively unified fashion. (2) A disposition does not perform one function only but may issue in a wide range of activities, partly if not largely as a resultant of the convergence of external world factors with

dispositions. (3) Rather than being fixed "powers of the mind," dispositions may have instrumental qualities; for instance, intelligence may be a disposition which is primarily ability to use what is at hand. Dispositions also may have directional qualities; *e.g.*, interests are primarily dispositions toward certain aims or objects.

Stern continues his comparison of faculties and dispositions with two other contrasts: (4) Dispositions are unlike faculties in being able to vary from time to time, some being fairly lasting throughout the life of the person but having different potency at some times than others. Some dispositions are rather short-lived even though possibly highly potent, such as dispositions during the pubertal or adolescent period. Perhaps only a vague potentiality at first, a disposition may crystallize into a definitive trait with very definite aims. But in the course of life a disposition may change its tendency or directional quality from one aim to others. (5) Dispositions are not only mental, for they apply to tendencies which utilize bodily actions as well. Manifestations of dispositions can be thus "psychophysically neutral" as in so-called "acts of will" where the disposition is manifested indistinguishably in bodily actions and conative experience, or in verbal memory where both readiness for speech movements and word images are found.

Aside from a possible misunderstanding arising from the third point above, that dispositions might be little generators or dynamos apart from the general energies available to the human being as a psychophysiological organism, Stern's presentation of the concept of "disposition" gears in well with the trait concepts of factor analysis. There is especially a parallel to numbers (1) and (2) above in the recognition by factor analysis that an action, for example performance on a test, has contributions from several factors.

One warning which Stern voices in connection with traits is definitely in order in a text on personality. Dozens of studies have issued recently from psychological laboratories containing enumerations of traits;

[1] As far as the writer can tell from Spoerl's translation (Stern, 1938), Stern used *Disposition*, rather than *Eigenschaft* or *Charakterzug*, but his discussion implies "trait."

often it is difficult to tell where all these traits fit into the individual. Stern's words are as apropos today as when written:

... the scientific urge to analyze and the logical urge to demarcate fixed traits lead to a *list* of the 'traits' being regarded as a 'character analysis.' In reality the proper task of the characterologist only begins at this point. The enumeration must be transformed into an actual joint survey, every item on the list becoming a personal component of this properly focussed total picture (Stern, 1938).

A clinical psychologist who sits with the results of a number of tests before him, some yielding a dozen or more standings of the person on different trait continua is sometimes put to it to make sense out of the varied scores as far as *this* individual is concerned. Yet for personality diagnosis and prediction, the most necessary task is not to get the listing of scores showing the presence or absence of certain traits or how much of each trait is possessed—vital as these facts are—but to get the "focussed total picture." One caution must be added, however, that without the factual data provided in the listing of traits and their relative weighting in the individual, obtaining the "focussed total picture" is more of an elaborate guessing procedure than it is science.

Although Allport, Kantor, Roback, and Stern have much more to offer to personology, their contributions given above are sufficient to further an understanding of traits. These authorities have not dwelt on the dimensional character of traits but instead upon qualitative distinctions among persons in respect to traits; nevertheless, their concepts do not exclude quantification and measurement. It is well to keep these qualitative aspects in our thinking, however, even as we deal with scores and "factor loadings" and correlation coefficients. Recognizing that the tyrant may possess a trait of sadism which on a mathematical scale is only different in degree from the similar trait of a gentle man, we cannot help judging at times that the difference in *degree* amounts to a difference in *kind* as well.

TRAITS AS FACTORIAL CONTINUA [1]

To make comparisons and contrasts such as we have made between faculties and factors and to dismiss logically-derived traits with little discussion does not necessarily commit us to the factor-analytic conception of the personality. The writer frankly accepts this conception as among the most fruitful for a scientific view of personality. Most of the succeeding two chapters are devoted to the results of research with factor-analytic procedures. Yet there must be just as frank an admission that in the present stage of factorial investigation a clinical psychologist gets from factor-analytically-derived tests less help in understanding his counselees than from logically-derived tests such as the Thematic Apperception Test. Except in the area of mental abilities, trait scores from the former type of tests are oftentimes not as enlightening as is a verbal description in terms of, say, Allport and Odbert's (1936) individualized traits which, though quantifiable, are taken mainly in a qualitative way.

In the long run, as measurements become more precise and traits are further clarified, factor-analytic methods—or their successors—should yield much more accurate information about the individual than clinical, logical, and "intuitive" methods can possibly yield. As this time approaches, there will still be room for clinical judgment and theories of personality interpretation. In medicine the basal metabolic rate may be measured with considerable exactness,[2] although the meaning of the rate for any one individual may not be clear; clinical judgment is necessary in interpreting his BMR. So, too, in personality interpretation scores will become more precise,

[1] Consult the Appendix for a rudimentary discussion of factor analysis.

[2] Of course, depending on the method used. The illustration is chosen deliberately because of the precisions and indecisions which surround the BMR. DuBois (1936) reviews theories of the BMR up to the mid-nineteen-twenties. Modern physiologists make use of the work of DuBois, but offer greater certainty in their discussions than he did.

but the personologist will probably never become a glorified bookkeeper.

Whatever logical and qualitative aspects there are to traits, we turn now to the more surely dimensional concepts of traits which have been accumulating in recent years. In a clear discussion of traits in his chapters on the organization of personality Stagner (1948) writes:

Traits cannot be conceived as existing on an all-or-none basis. In everyday speech we are prone to deal in absolutes: John is aggressive, Bill is submissive; Mary is cheerful, Susan is gloomy. Any intensive study of an individual, however reveals a tendency rather than absolute uniformity. John may be aggressive in 90 per cent of observed situations, submissive in 10 per cent of them. Bill may be aggressive in 25 per cent and submissive in 75 per cent. Comparison of a random group of people (on common traits) will reveal the presence of a continuum from one polar extreme to the other.[1]

Stagner speaks generally for many if not most trait theorists today. The production of questionnaires and rating scales and various other kinds of tests, a thriving occupation among psychologists, is based upon the premise that the addition of (usually weighted) units of a test indicates more of the trait purportedly being measured. The Rorschach test (cf. Chapter 5), though dealt with qualitatively by most clinicians, is scored by the addition of different responses to the ink-blots in order to determine the strength of certain traits like keenness of form perception, anxiety, originality, conformity, rigidity, or intellectual ability. A pencil-and-paper test like the "Guilford-Zimmerman Temperament Survey" adds positive and negative responses to individual statements in order to ascertain how much restraint, ascendance, objectivity, friendliness, or other trait the individual possesses. The whole factor-analytic movement initiated by Spearman has made the same assumption concerning the dimensionality of traits of person-

[1] Stagner, R. *Psychology of personality.* New York: McGraw-Hill Book Co., 1948. Reprinted by permission.

ality. Therefore, we keep the characteristics of traits in mind which are suggested in the preceding pages, the qualitative distinctions in particular. But we shall proceed on the assumption that traits are dimensional and draw most heavily from research employing quantitative methods. In describing traits from a dimensional standpoint, the terms "factor-trait" and "trait" are used here interchangeably. The former term means those traits which correspond to factors. The term trait may also refer to the hypothetical underlying quality which the individual possesses; actually we probably never can get to that quality but can only approximate it.

Traits regarded as factorial continua may be discussed in various ways. Here the method is chosen of presenting different views of factor-traits held by three outstanding authorities. An attempt is made to keep the unique individual in mind, as has been the aim throughout this text, by weaving together concepts from other sources. But factorists do disagree and perceive the same individual in different fashion. These facts are reflected in the following pages.

Operational Unities of Response

In the clarification of the meaning of traits, especially in their relation to the mathematical constructs known on factors, Raymond Cattell has done yeoman service. Cattell identifies a trait as ". . . a collection of reactions or responses bound by some kind of unity which permits the responses to be gathered under one term and treated in the same fashion for most purposes." (Cattell, 1946) With this semi-operational definition Eysenck, the outstanding personality factor analyst of Great Britain, and Guilford, who with Cattell ranks highest among American factorists in the realm of personality, agree substantially. The former, for example, defines a trait "as a co-variant set of behavioral acts." (Eysenck, 1953) And Guilford summarizes among other aspects of traits another's early advice to constructors of trait rating scales in these words: "Each trait should refer to a single type of activity or to the results of a single type of activity." (Guilford, 1954) As suggested, however, Cattell brings a major contribution [1] in amalgamating logical analysis of traits with the mathematical treatment of measurements which purportedly relate to these traits. What is stated of Cattell's concepts of traits (Cattell, 1946, 1950, 1957a) in the following paragraphs is over-simplified. Some of the cautions which Cattell observes in his extended explanations cannot be repeated here.

Common and Unique. Cattell first adopts the distinction among traits which Allport recognized, that between common and individual, or in Cattell's terms, common and unique traits. The latter are really rare traits, for as Allport insists, all traits are unique in one sense, and there is only a relative difference between common and unique or rare traits. For practical purposes we can say that the approximately similar response patterns which show up only once in a while are indicative of so-called unique traits. From a logical standpoint the same kinds of distinctions can be made between common and unique traits as Allport made. One may have a perceptual alertness (common) trait and also a (unique) trait of collecting Korean butterflies.

From a mathematical standpoint Cattell matches common traits, in part at any rate, with the factors derived by means of what he calls R-technique, a method of analyzing the ordinary correlation matrix. This method of factor analysis is that in which a series of tests is given to a *group* of persons and the tests correlated with one another. Unique traits on the other hand are matched, again in part, with the factors derived from an analysis of a matrix in which are found the correlations of a series of tests on the *same individual* over a number of days (or other units of time.) This method of factor analysis Cattell calls P-technique to refer to its emphasis on the *person*.

[1] William Stephenson does not think so. Cf. his article, "A note on Professor R. B. Cattell's methodological adumbrations" (1952).

Unique and common traits are given much fuller treatment in Chapter 14. The essential point to recognise now is that personalities may be studied and compared both quantitatively and qualitatively in terms not only of unique traits, but also in respect to common traits. An actual set of functions which may be designated as operational unities of responses can at one and the same time be *relatively* unique in any one individual and also be sufficiently like such operational unities in other individuals to be regarded as a common trait. Varying in degrees from individual to individual, these common traits in pattern with varying numbers of unique traits (which also can vary in degrees) help in our understanding both how we can be alike and how we can be different.

Modalities: Constitutional and Environmental. Besides distinguishing common and unique traits, Cattell draws into a general schema dynamic and stylistic traits differentiated by Allport, those hierarchies of temperaments, sentiments, attitudes, and traits suggested by several theorists, and heredity-environment influences which have to be incorporated if more than immediate behavior is considered important. Figure 18 presents Cattell's classification [2] of traits by "modalities" and constitution-environment categories.

"Modality" is merely a convenient term to be used here for dividing traits into those which are: (1) Dynamic or goal-directed: ergs,[3] drives, needs, interests, sentiments, attitudes, some of which are native (Constitutional Dynamic) and others of which

[2] Actual traits derived from factor analysis seem better classified as we have categorized them in the text. Cattell's scheme preserves the unity and congruence we hope for personality, but in actuality his own factor-analytic work does not utilize his six-fold scheme to any major extent. In fact, in his *Personality and motivation structure and measurement* (1957) he does not allude to it. When research is done on traits, they spill over from one "modality" to another and from constitutional to environmental mold so easily that the classification scheme soon has little use. For a logical classification to assist in categorizing behaviors it is still of some use.

[3] Cf. Chapter 4 for "erg."

	CONSTITUTIONAL UNITY	ENVIRONMENTAL MOLD UNITY	
Dynamic Modality	1. Ergs, Needs, Drives (Constitutional Dynamic)	4. Metanergs, Sentiments, Attitudes (Environmental Mold Dynamic)	
Temperament Modality	2. Constitutional Temperament	5. Modified Temperamental Tendencies	
Ability Modality	3. Constitutional Abilities and Capacities (Intelligence, Memory, Musical Ability)	6. Acquired Skills and Information	
		Conscious	Unconscious

Figure 18. Constitutional and environmental trait modalities. (From R. B. Cattell, *Description and Measurement of Personality*, p. 74)

are acquired (Environmental Mold Dynamic). Of course, these dynamic traits overlap one another in terms of subsidiation, and no one item of behavior can be strictly classed as constitutional or environmental mold. (2) Temperamental and temper traits: those basic patterns of reactivity such as high-strungness, general energy, irritability, fatigability, and tolerance of excitement and adventure, which supposedly also can be molded by the environment, though Cattell is somewhat vague at this point. And (3) Cognitive or Ability traits: some of these are native, potential capacities, and others are achievements or skills. These three modalities are further subdivided, but the major areas are sufficient for our purposes.

This logical classification may serve as a convenient framework for ordering the welter of factor-traits which confuse the student in their multiplicity and apparent disorganization. In actual practice factor analysts pay little attention to such a schema, preferring to derive classification systems from their data. Yet they do use some preliminary set of categories as a guide to research. And since there has as yet been no generally accepted factor-analytically-derived schema, Figure 18 can be utilized as one tentative classification scheme.

Surface and Source. One other distinction among traits, however, which is utilized in the succeeding pages despite some of its difficulties is Cattell's final classifying of traits into "surface" and "source" traits. The former refer to sets of empirically observable behaviors which go together, the "syndrome" of obsessional-compulsive neurosis in abnormal psychology, the patterns of behavior which go to make up a role such as being a banker or a bricklayer, or the exhibitions of courage in heroic activity. Source traits are the elemental functional unities which underlie different kinds of empirically co-varying behaviors. For example, recognizably courageous behavior may, as common sense has sometimes recognized, be compounded of fear (*Anxious Emotionality*, among Cattell's basic factors) and devil-may-careness (Guilford's *Rhathymia*) plus a need to be dominant (*Dominance* need or factor).

In conjunction with his treatment of traits in terms of the distinctions outlined above, Cattell very usefully identifies what he calls "trait elements." These are measurable constituent behaviors by which a trait may be expressed. The "literal trait element" is the whole behavior, some of which escapes the measurement process. A trait element like talkativeness or sourness or painstakingness may contribute variance to either surface or source traits and to several factor-traits rather than to just one. These trait elements have sometimes been classed as traits, but in factor-analytic research they constitute the behavior patterns whereby traits, co-varying patterns underlying the specific behaviors, are identified.

Personality Sphere. A further useful concept which Cattell introduced serves as a guiding model in the understanding of traits. This is what he names the "personality sphere."[1] In trying to get a com-

[1] Thurstone's (1947) spherical model of factors was a direct forerunner of Cattell's concept.

pleteness of coverage of the personality in terms of trait elements Cattell conceives of language as supplying not all aspects of personality but the most important ones. Therefore, he draws on Allport and Odbert's list of trait names to construct a personality sphere in *n*-dimensional space. We cannot visualize the sphere because it goes beyond the three dimensions in which an ordinary sphere is found. Cattell (1946) describes the sphere thus:

The personality sphere may be considered to present a complete surface, constituted by many small "trait areas," each trait area defined by a trait term and abutting on traits most closely resembling it, the whole constituting an endless but finite continuum of behavior meaning. If trait character is represented by direction as in factor-analytic representation, the sphere must be considered as one in *n*-dimensional space. There is no guarantee, in the axioms of this formal system, that the trait terms in language will be absolutely evenly distributed over the spherical surface. Intercorrelation must decide the actual closeness of different trait-term areas. However, it is part of our assumption from the study of language that no large area is completely neglected by vocabulary and that all dimensions of personality receive some representation.[1]

Cattell points out that if machines and animals could talk there would be additional terms describing traits observable to them and not to human beings, or not important to human beings. Beyond the language to which Cattell refers, however, there are terms which *are* observable to human beings describing traits or trait-elements relating man to animals or machines, as well as physiological and role terms which differentiate individuals characteristically from one another. Take the way in which some persons seem to get the "feel" of a horse or a machine almost immediately while others never seem to be able to "empathize" in this manner. John Wesley, the founder of Methodism, is said to have ridden 100,000 miles on horseback

in his lifetime, but despite his other sterling qualities he never made a good horseman. There are individuals with many years of experience driving an automobile for whom the automobile has never become an extension of themselves. Like Carlyle's workmen, about whom he complained that they violate the Ten Commandments with every blow of their hammers, these drivers frustrate those who do have the "feel" for machinery. Certainly horseback riding and other interactions with animals, automobiles, airplanes,[2] and other machinery have been and are both socially and materially important to humankind. Terms, or traits or trait-elements, representing such functions should be accordingly important for the personality sphere.

Before turning to others' contributions, it is well to pause and recall that the work of Cattell, though given in part above as if it were only a logical analysis of traits, is nevertheless posited on and permeated with the concept of the dimensionality and thus measurability of traits. No armchair analyses suffice, excellent as any thoughtful personologist gladly acknowledges many of them to be; traits must be determined, in Cattell's thought, by exact measurement and correlational procedures.

Connotative Concepts

Just as Cattell has had wide influence on American studies of personality—though his first work was done in Great Britain, and he is not uninfluential there—so Eysenck whose structure concepts of personality were presented earlier in this text (Chapter 4) has been taking a leading part in Great Britain, although here, too, his influence is strong. Eysenck's psychological position is more of a typology than a trait psychology, but this chapter would not be complete without referring to his contribution to our knowledge and understanding of traits. Eysenck is one who tries to clarify the relation between the actual trait as presumed to exist in persons and the measurements and factors which supposedly parallel the trait. He applies the

[1] Cattell, R. B. *Description and measurement of personality.* Yonkers-on-Hudson, N. Y.: World Book, 1946. Reprinted by permission.

[2] Some pilots "fly by the seat of their pants."

differentiation made by a modern philosopher, T. S. C. Northrop, between *denotative* and *connotative* concepts; the denotative is that which is directly observable or experienced, the connotative that which is derived from the assumptions and postulates of a theoretical system. These kinds of concepts are related to each other, as for instance observed (sensed or denoted) space and time are related to mathematical (derived or connotated) space and time. Eysenck writes:

> Now clearly, a statistical factor is a connotative concept, not a denotative one; yet much criticism of factorial work has been based on a misunderstanding of this position. The intelligence and suggestibility, the sense of humour and persistence which are observed and talked about by the man in the street are denotative concepts; stripped by experimental and factorial studies of popular misconceptions closely bound up with them, and of emotional elements inevitably mixed with them, they become *connotative* concepts. Certainly, Spearman's "g" bears some relation to the popular concept of "intelligence," just as Newton's or even Einstein's concept of space bears some relation to popular notions. . . .
>
> When, therefore, we find factors in our work which bear certain resemblances to such denotative concepts as "neuroticism" or "introversion," it should be borne in mind that these terms are not used in their ordinary, denotative meaning, but that they are connotative concepts, designated by the basic assumptions and postulates of factorial theory (Eysenck, 1947).[1]

Following logically on Eysenck's concept of factor-traits as derivative, connotative rather than denotative, is his stricture against accepting a distribution of scores on a test as necessarily paralleling the distribution of a trait in the real-life population. Tests are usually constructed to yield normal curves, though they could be made to yield almost any kind of a distribution, J-shaped, bimodal, rectangular, U-shaped, or other types. Accordingly, when scores from a test are employed as a basis for de-

riving factor-traits, they may misrepresent the actual distribution of the real-life behavior or experience and thus distort greatly the estimate of the trait. Ingenious means of overcoming measurement problems (Guilford, 1954) do not entirely exorcise the demon of lack of correspondence between measurement and reality in any science, in the behavioral sciences least of all.[2]

Factor and Trait

In discussing contributions of factor analysts to the dimensional concept of personality traits, we should be remiss in not speaking of Guilford specifically. His work has been primarily in the field of temperament and ability traits, among which he has uncovered a large number of factors. A rough comparison [3] of Cattell's, Eysenck's, and Guilford's concepts of traits as determined by factor analysis brings out one of the problems in the study of factors of personality. Eysenck's efforts seem to be directed to finding as few factors as possible by logically or factorially combining traits and factors from many research sources. Guilford's investigations have led to the finding of many factors. Somewhere in between, Cattell has endeavored to keep to as few factors as possible, but he has had to extend his factor lists to more than just a few. In practice each system has proved useful in selection procedures, indicating once again the general scientific principle that different theoretical models may be applicable to real life situations.

Guilford's work has probably had the widest application through the Air Force

---

[1] Eysenck, H. J. *Dimensions of personality.* London: Routledge & Kegan Paul, 1947. Reprinted by permission.

[2] Eysenck rightly points out that a trait theory of personality is usually related to a unimodal distribution and a type theory often related to a bimodal distribution. To accept a trait theory because it seems to be related to unimodality and accordingly to reject a type theory for its seeming bimodality is to place too much dependence on score distributions which may merely be artifacts of test construction.

[3] This comparison was suggested by Guilford to the writer in private conversation, but the responsibility for the text statement rests with the writer.

selection program during World War II (Guilford & Lacey, 1947) and numerous research projects under contract with the Office of Naval Research and the Air Research and Development Command, projects leading in part to post-World War II selection procedures. His projects illustrate among other things the practical value of factor analysis in measuring traits of personality.

In our consideration of the nature of traits we have taken account of the oft-repeated criticism of factor analysis: Does a mathematical factor derived from tests and therefore even further removed from the behavior of an individual than the tests themselves have any real relation to the trait the person is supposed to have? Are psychologists who manipulate calculators and employ computing equipment merely engaging in a kind of mathematical solitaire, autistically manufacturing factors out of, if not thin air, thin figures?

In actuality the large scale selection programs of the armed services constitute adequate proof that factors derived mathematically have a direct, though not perfect, relation to the way men, millions of men, behave. Test programs from World War I to the present have been useful in classifying men; but the factor analyses of tests between the World Wars enabled selection procedures to be administered far more economically in time and money. Ability traits especially were pinpointed so that tests could be discarded which did not clearly mark out the abilities required in certain jobs and other tests devised which did. The mass demonstration of the validity of factors in relation to traits made a profound impression not only upon psychologists.

Both prior to and subsequent to World War II, Guilford's analyses of temperament traits gave a sharper outlining to these basic functions which are often classed as "personality traits." Among other major research results in this field that Guilford and his associates [1] have effected is the breakdown of the gross traits of *Introversion* and

[1] Including his wife, Ruth B. Guilford, who has been a contributor in her own right.

Extroversion into constituent unitary traits. (Cf. Chapter 14).

Problems in Regard to Factor-Traits

As hinted in the preceding paragraphs, there are differences among the three men whose work has been briefly discussed, in regard to their methods of factor analysis and their conclusions concerning factor-traits of personality. And these men differ from others in the field. Since we are discussing the nature of traits, some statements are required concerning these differences which plague even experts in personology.[2]

Factor-Trait Names. First there are naming problems. Eysenck, in keeping to a few well-recognized factors, employs the British terms like "g" and "c" and "e" and "w." Cattell employs several systems, identifying factors sometimes by letters, sometimes by their test origin, as behavior ratings (BR, I, for example), questionnaires (QP, V, for example), or objective tests (Factor T. XII, for example), plus names added to the symbol designations, and in the last few years he has followed a system of Universal Index Numbers in addition to verbal labels. Guilford has employed letters, like S, T, D, C, R, plus verbal labels for naming the factors he has brought to light. Other factor analysts designate their factors by name and/or number.[3]

[2] For the student in personality this confusion of factorial tongues ought not be a problem, for the textbook should present an ordered overview of the complex field of factors. Students in various sciences who go beyond the first courses often complain that their introductions to the science did not prepare them for the uncertainties and complexities they find in their later work. The writer is of the opinion that the student beyond the first course or so should be given an inkling of the unsettled nature of certain areas of science to present an honest picture of the present state of that science. Each personologist appears to be pursuing a kind of solipsistic program of his own instead of engaging in a cooperative enterprise. Several attempts have been made to bring order out of chaos, but thus far there has not been even a satisfactory attempt to establish a universally accepted taxonomy and nomenclature.

[3] One first major consideration has to be stated at this point: Factor authorities are agreed that

Multiplication of Factors. Besides naming problems, there are problems of multiplication of factors.[1] Most psychological journals and, increasingly, journals in other sciences contain research articles announcing the discovery of more and more factors. There are factors derived from the Rorschach test, from the Bernreuter Personality Inventory, from the Minnesota Multiphasic Personality Inventory, factors of physical prowess and intellectual abilities by the score, and temperament factors of many,

_____

their verbal labels are often if not usually misleading and that the important matter is that a factor-trait is defined not by a formal Aristotelian definition but by the operations by which it is revealed. Operations in this case refer to the observable test behaviors of an individual. Sometimes there is no adequate verbal label for the factor which underlies diverse kinds of behavior, so that each man does his best to label it. When different tests are employed, or different methods of factor analysis, or different populations, for revealing somewhat the same traits, the factors may appear somewhat different also; thus even fairly accurate verbal labels may differ.

A second major consideration is that despite the different designations and labels there is more agreement than appears among the heterogeneous labelings. One aspect of the labeling problem concerns more than mere labeling; it concerns description as a whole of which naming is only one portion. Partly because many of our trait designations have come from the clinic there is a tendency to name or describe traits in terms of neurosis or psychosis. Thus an individual is described as "healthy" by having low scores on *Nervousness, Depression, Demoralized Emotionality,* or *Withdrawn Schizothymia.* Cattell tries to overcome this tendency by use of "health" terms as well as "illth" terms for his factor-traits. Guilford, too, names some of his temperament traits in "normal" words. Often, however, the trait designations are such that describing a personality in terms of a temperament test has to conform to the crude definition of health as "The absence of disease symptoms."

[1] Some of the multiplication may be the rediscovery of already known factors, so that the problem is not so much one of addition as identification of old and new. But there can also be multiplying of factors to an absurd extent by splitting old factors. One analysis (Educational Testing Service, 1954–55) reveals one of two taste factors to be "liking berries for dessert vs. liking melons for dessert." Possibly, of course, for completeness of description such fine distinctions are necessary.

many kinds. Sometimes factors once considered unitary, that is indivisible, have been split into further subdivisions.

At times the multiplication is only seeming, for careful comparison often reveals that two independently discovered factors are really one. But where genuine multiplication occurs, we should not be surprised by the appearance of so many factors. Personality is a highly complex affair; even if we restrict ourselves, as in most factor analyses, to common traits, the possibility of discovering many "functional unities" should be expected.

In addition, we can expect a number of unique factors which come from analyses of one individual's behavior. After all, Allport and Odbert's list of traits derived from English language usage contains over 4,000 terms; logical and mathematical analyses may reduce these to far fewer than 4,000, but there is still room for many factor-traits. Cattell considered at first that 12 factors cover all the source traits. However, it is notable that the 12 which he felt exhaustively represented personality (temperament) traits became 16 for his "Sixteen Personality Factor Questionnaire." And more recently close to double that number have been recognized by Cattell.

Sooner or later, however, it is to be expected that there will be a slowing down of the discovery of new factors, for the personality, though complex, is limited. It may very well be, though, even after such a stabilization, that further division of "unitary" factors will occur as refinement of measurement and theory takes place; experience in the field of physics and chemistry in respect to the "indivisible" atom suggests that psychology should not be surprised by such a trend of events.

Second-Order Factors; Rotation. A third major problem in factor-trait work is that of what second-order factors[2] may be identified, if there are any. This problem is especially related to the methods of factor analysis employed by different investi-

_____

[2] Second-order or higher-order factors are first mentioned and given meaning in Chapter 4.

gators (Holzinger & Harman, 1941) and centers in large part in the "rotation of axes." (Cf. Appendix.) Rotation is a technical process directly related to transformation of axes by rotation in analytic geometry. The logic of rotating axes does not concern us at this point, but the results of rotating or not rotating, or whether the factorist has employed one or another kind of rotation, seriously concern us. If no rotation occurs, one interpretation is placed upon factors derived from a matrix of intercorrelations. If any rotating takes place at all, considerably different factors may emerge. And if one method of rotating is employed rather than another, still a different set of factors may emerge.[1]

When one form of rotation (oblique) is used to transform a matrix of factor loadings (the initial result of a factor analysis), the resulting factor loadings may themselves be correlated and factored. The second set of factors from such a procedure are known as second-order factors, which in themselves may represent "operational unities of responses." After many years of debate across the Atlantic Ocean with Spearman, Thurstone (1941) discovered that by factoring his Primary Mental Abilities factors, he came up with a general second-order factor very much like Spearman's "g" which had seemed to be just an artifact of Spearman's method of factoring. Not all issues arising from the use of different methods or use or disuse of certain procedures can be so easily resolved.

From the preceding discussion on the problems in factor-trait investigation, the conclusion may be drawn that there are methodological difficulties in finding and interpreting factors which represent traits of personality. But the real difficulties which face factor analysis are those faced by any trait investigation. As Eysenck suggested and as F. H. Allport (1937) warned long ago, traits of any kind, verbalized or factorized, are abstractions from the personality, not a description of the individual. Whether

a trait is defined verbally or mathematically, it is a distortion of personal reality. If we accept the principle of psychology that the measurement of behavior is a desirable goal, then we may believe too, that factor-traits will become closer approximations to personal reality than verbal, armchair traits can be.

SUMMARY

Much may be learned from viewing personality topographically. But dimensional analysis of personality yields further understanding. In line with recent thinking traits are regarded not as fixed faculties but as dimensions of personality, with the individual personality as a vector resultant of his various trait or dimensional scores. Before factor analysis undertakes mathematical definition of its factor-traits, logical analysis has been necessary to locate meaningful areas of research. Among the outstanding "nonfactor-analytic" trait concepts are Allport's dynamic, individualized tendencies which may be dynamic or motivational and stylistic or primarily descriptive, genuine or pseudo-traits, and individual or common. Also, in the group of trait concepts which view traits as logical substrata is Kantor's "continually existing sets of reaction systems." Thousands of traits are possessed by everyone, according to Roback, who regards traits as rather permanent "distinctive modes of behavior." The last of the logical trait concepts named, that of Stern, offers "dispositions" or tendencies which may contribute to a wide variety of activities. Stern warns that listing of traits for anyone is not the end but the beginning of personality study.

Turning from the more qualitative aspects of traits to the quantitative, factor-analysis undertakes to determine mathematically the "operational unities of responses." Cattell especially has given service in classifying and cross-classifying these operational unities or basic dimensions of personality. Common and unique traits are distinguished in part by the correlational method used to derive them. At times traits can be cate-

---

[1] Roff (1952), however, found approximately the same factors by orthogonal and oblique transformations. (Cf. Chapter 15.)

gorized according to constitutional and environmental determination and in turn cross-classified into dynamic (ergic), temperament, and ability traits. Empirically co-varying behaviors may be regarded as surface traits, and the underlying elemental functional unities as source traits. To obtain completeness in coverage of dimensions the "personality sphere" draws on all language descriptive of trait elements; even language is not exhaustive in this respect.

Eysenck supplies a useful distinction between denotative traits, which are the man on the street's notion of personality functions, and connotative traits which are the mathematician's "model" of the observable behavior. As demonstrated by Guilford, however, in large-scale factor analyses, the factor, connotative as it is, represents the "actual" personality trait closely enough to allow scientific prediction for groups of persons.

Factor analysis faces problems in its endeavor to determine the dimensions of personality: The very naming of factor-traits is difficult because a verbal label may be misleading. Further, multiplication of factors has continued at so rapid a pace it is hard to know what to make of the multiplicity of supposed traits. More technical difficulties such as whether to derive second-order factors and how to rotate axes are part of the problem of factor analyzing to determine traits.

QUESTIONS

1. Give two fundamental distinctions between faculties and factors.

2. Outline briefly the trait concepts of Allport, Kantor, Roback, and Stern.

3. State briefly Cattell's distinctions between common and unique traits, constitutional and environmental modalities, and surface and source traits. What does he mean by the "personality sphere"?

4. How does Eysenck employ the terms "connotative" and "denotative" in respect to traits?

5. To what practical use did Guilford put factor-analytic discoveries during World War II?

6. What are some of the problems in connection with factor analysis and personology?

7. Are factors more useful than logical traits?

CHAPTER **14**

OBSERVED
TRAITS OF
PERSONALITY

In this chapter representative traits of personality, especially those derived by factor analysis, illustrate the functions of personality conceived dimensionally. Just as with topographical analysis of personality, the dimensional cross-classification of functions may in turn be subdivided into minor classifications. And the complex divisions can themselves be combined and recombined as Eysenck has done with temperament traits (Eysenck, 1953) and Guilford with traits of intellect (Guilford, 1957). In a somewhat simplified fashion, however, traits of personality are discussed as "unique" and "common" with full recognition that other categorizations could serve just as well for some purposes.

UNIQUE TRAITS

From some standpoints all traits are unique. Even so-called common traits take on unique forms in each individual. Guilty as we may be of "raising a superlative to the nth degree," it is appropriate to emphasize that in personology there are degrees of uniqueness. Some traits of certain individuals are indeed "one only" (the original meaning of unique), but others are similar to traits found in other persons, even though these latter traits may distinctly classify as "unique." Those traits which we are considering here have been discovered in part by

P-technique factor analysis, but research of a nonfactor-analytic nature is given due recognition.

Factor-Traits of a Clinically Normal Person

In order to demonstrate in part how unique traits are determined and what they are like, a representative study (Henrietta Williams, 1954) employing P-technique factor analysis is sketched here. Because of the expense in time and money to complete a P-technique analysis, such studies are almost as rare as the factor-traits they uncover! Consequently, "representative" means a sample from a very small population.

The subject in the investigation was a clinically normal male graduate student.[1] For each of 110 days this 23-year-old subject was measured on 54 objective physiological and psychological variables. One other rated variable, degree of stuttering,[2] was included also in the P-technique analysis. Test sessions varied from 7 A.M. to 10 P.M. in order to establish a pattern of fatigue. When a factor analysis was made of the correlation matrix of variables measured across the 110 days, and further treatment

[1] Parallel to an emotionally disturbed individual likewise studied (Cattell & Luborsky, 1950).

[2] If marked, stuttering might vitiate the use of the term "normal" for this subject.

of the data effected, 13 factor-traits appeared. The most interesting, if not important, of these traits are:

2. A drive or self-imposed emergency state with emphasis on perseverance and self-sufficiency.

3. An emotional trend similar to a therapeutic trend factor found in an emotionally disturbed person but differing in ways expected for a person not undergoing therapy.

4. A lateness of hour factor not identifiable with any fatigue factors which are found in some other studies.

5. Seemingly a trend to suspicion, withdrawing, and frustration.

10. An emotional state of some kind, perhaps the positive end of a factor opposing neurasthenia to obsessional determination of character.

12. Low physical resistance.

13. A condition of being jaded and apprehensive.

Others of the traits discovered in this "normal" male can be matched with common factors revealed by analyses of groups of persons. It is evident that the list of traits above are "unique" in the individual investigated, even though they could be found in varying amounts in other persons.

Listing traits is only the beginning of a psychological analysis, as Stern declared (1938). In drawing a "clinical picture" of the young man whose factor-traits are enumerated above, a fairly consistent pattern emerges, with enough inconsistencies to show that we are dealing with life and not an idealized "total personality." The first portion of the picture which is not made clear from the above factors is a fairly large (overt) trend toward being a *cyclothymic* individual. There is a common trait disclosed by R-technique factor analysis called *Cyclothymia-Schizothymia*. In the common factor cyclothymia refers to genial adaptability, warm-hearted emotional expressiveness; general approach behavior, good-naturedness, and easy-goingness. Our young man leans toward this "pole" of the factor.

The measurements reveal the young man as a fairly cheerful and nondepressed person with a tendency toward a stable personality configuration. On the other hand, there are trends that seem less positive in a mental hygiene sense, a paranoid trait, some anxious emotionality, neurasthenia, and low physical resistance. In interpreting these negative traits two features should be remembered. We are, first, dealing with a nonclinical individual—he is functioning in society in a normal adjustive way. Secondly, the young man's "neurotic" factor scores do not signify that he is neurotic. Nevertheless, examining the list of traits and coupling negative traits with one another and with the stuttering indicate that this personality is not a placid, unconflicted one. Perhaps it is too philosophical to state that enough tension is present in this personality to show that it is alive. Biological considerations lead us to conclude also that without tension (tonus) the organism is dead.

The trait pattern found (too simply) in the young man only represents the same kind of synthesizing of factor-traits possible whenever there is a series of traits derived from an analysis of one personality. When the analysis is accomplished by means of advanced methods like factor analysis, there should be a more adequate basis for forming a trait pattern than unaided intuitive analysis. But the putting together of factor-traits into a comprehensive pattern requires the skill of an expert possessed of "intuitive" capacity. As science advances, less and less of "intuition" will be called for; probably there will never be, however, a completely automated interpretation.

Special Forms: Genius

There are some special forms of unique traits which have not been investigated by factor analysis, but in several cases have had quantitative methods applied to them. Although there are a number of areas where such special forms of unique traits exist, only one is taken up here. A discussion of genius, brief as it must be in a general personality text, can illustrate the possession of unique traits in their special forms. Ever since ancient times geniuses have been considered to have traits of personality different from those of ordinary men. In one of its original senses the term "genius" referred to an attendant deity, as now the plural "genii" still refers to superhuman beings like the Arabian jinni. The use of the word and the concept of "genius" has never quite escaped this supernatural connotation. There is a carryover into modern times of the ancient elements, including the notion that genius is heaven-inspired, and that heavenly inspiration is akin to madness. Thus that genius possesses the traits descriptive of madness is not a defunct idea.[1]

In more recent times the term "genius" has come to mean the individual possessed of very special abilities, extraordinary talents, and/or great originality and creativeness. Sometimes, of course, the meaning has simply boiled down to the special talent itself as in reference to a musician (McLeish, 1950; Seashore, 1919). More naturalistic meanings have sometimes centered in the trait of patience or perseverance. Buffon wrote in the eighteenth century, "*La génie n'est autre chose qu' une grande aptitude á la patience*," or "Genius is nothing but a great aptitude for patience." The modern statements, "Genius is an infinite capacity for taking pains," and "Genius is ninety-five per cent perspiration and five per cent inspiration," possibly take their cue from Carlyle's statement that genius ". . . is the transcendent capacity for taking trouble first of all." Thus instead of inspiration-madness the qualities of the genius have come in some places to be considered unique only in the sense of being "more than" the similar qualities or traits of the ordinary man.

This dimensional concept of genius has been carried out in very recent times in respect to intellectual traits in the work of Leta S. Hollingworth (1942) and Terman (1925, 1926, 1930, 1947, 1959) who have tied the concept to persons with a Stanford-Binet I.Q. in the superior ranges. The uniqueness of the traits of these individuals consists of a superior quantity (and somewhat different quality) of intellect as determined by the Stanford-Binet tests, a higher score presumably indicating more of the trait. Research on individuals with high I.Q.'s tends to indicate that not only are the "geniuses" possessed of unique traits of intellect, uniqueness defined as above, but also they are beyond the average in temperamental-social traits as well. In this way genius may be considered close to divinity, if divinity is characterized by the possession of the nth degree of traits described as "psychologically healthy" by a mental hygienist; but certainly by the same standards genius is far from madness.

Whether, however, this quantitative delineation of genius is satisfactory or not to fulfill the concept which has been employed throughout history to set apart certain persons who possessed "something higher *and* different" is another matter. Perhaps the possession of a high I.Q., or in trait language high scores in a number of intellectual traits, does not qualify one as a genius. In Catherine Cox's (1926) retrospective assignment of I.Q.'s to 300 geniuses of history some of the persons whose accomplishments undoubtedly make them *bona fide* geniuses proved to have not very remarkable I.Q.'s. Of course, Cox could very well have missed many signs which would have given them higher scores. Nevertheless, of the 1500 children selected for intensive study as "geniuses" by Terman from the top one per cent of Stanford-Binet I.Q.'s not a very large number could be classed as geniuses in the sense of Cox's 300, even though the very top I.Q.'s in the Terman's

[1] Plato in the *Phaedrus* has Socrates declare that madness is not simply an evil, but that "there is also a madness which is the special gift of heaven, and the source of the chiefest blessings among men." As in the biblical tradition, madness and prophecy, Socrates declares, are really the same words, μαυτίκή or "prophecy" and μάνίκή or "madness," only differing by the "tasteless insertion of τ." He says that madness of this sort is superior to sanity, for one is of divine origin, the other only human. Seneca in his *Moral Essays* stated, "There is no great genius without some touch of madness." Possibly the same notion was in Festus' mind when he said to the Apostle Paul, "Thou art beside thyself; much learning doth make thee mad" (Acts 26:24b).

group match those in Cox's group. *Some* of Terman's "geniuses" will probably be judged by history as being "geniuses" in the older sense, but not *all* or even very many most likely (Terman, 1954). There may be other traits which make for genius other than high intellectual traits, or even other than high temperamental traits; there may be some traits of genius which are unique in the literal sense of the word.

It is not necessary in attempting to distinguish unique traits which are genuinely different from those of ordinary persons, to go along with students of personality who have claimed even in the present day a close alliance of genius and madness. Cesare Lombroso's main thesis in *The Man of Genius*, published about the turn of the century, is that "genius is a degenerative psychosis of the epileptoid group" (1905). He even maintained that the coincidence of the characteristics of genius and mental aberration was intended by nature to make us respect the misfortunes of insanity and to keep us from being dazzled by the brilliance of "men of genius who might well be compared, not to the planets which keep their appointed orbits, but to falling stars, lost and dispersed over the crust of the earth" (Lombroso, 1905). We cannot, of course, dismiss this view lightly, that the traits of genius are similar to the traits of insanity. Respected authorities like Wilhelm Lange-Eichbaum and in a modified form Ernst Kretschmer have held it. The former wrote:

But among geniuses (considered to the number of from three to four hundred individuals) we find that from 12 to 13 per cent have been psychotic at least once during their lifetime. Confining our examination to the 'very greatest' names, numbering seventy-eight in all, we find that more than 37 per cent have been psychotic once during their lifetime; that more than 83 per cent have been markedly psychopathic; that more than 10 per cent have been slightly psychopathic; and that about 6.5 per cent have been healthy. The proportion of diseased persons becomes a little greater still, if we select thirty-five persons who are regarded as 'the greatest geniuses of all;' the psychotic number 40 per cent; the psycho-

pathic more than 90 per cent; the healthy 8.5 per cent (Lange-Eichbaum, 1932).[1]

Lange-Eichbaum's contention is that genius is a social product—different from Lombroso's genetic concept; it is produced by a civilization which could not tolerate too many geniuses, and in fact may doom itself by producing them.

Rejecting Lombroso's concept that genius is madness and not regretting genius as does Lange-Eichbaum, Kretschmer considers the genius a bringer of values[2] derived from a fortunate combination of "opposed inheritances." To be sure, the genius is psycho-pathological, possessing the traits of "daemonic unrest," instability, hypersensitivity, and emotional exuberance.[3] But it is the very traits which in psychotic persons classify them as psychotic which make the genius a genius, when they are cou-

[1] Lange-Eichbaum, W. *The problem of genius.* (Trans. by Eden Paul & Cedar Paul.) New York: Macmillan, 1932. Reprinted by permission.

[2] ". . . we shall give the name of genius to those men who are able to arouse permanently, and in the highest degree, that positive, scientifically-grounded feeling of worth and value, in a wide group of human beings. But we shall do so only in those cases where the value arises with psychological necessity, out of the special mental structure of the bringer of value, not where a stroke of luck or some coincidence of factors has thrown it into his lap" [Kretschmer, 1929. Reprinted by permission from Kretschmer, E. *The psychology of men of genius.* (Trans. by R. B. Cattell.) London: Kegan Paul, Trench, Trubner, 1931.]

[3] "Any man with an apparently normal mental constitution, however, who continually fails to adjust himself is really no healthy-minded being at all. One can think of such careers as those of Michelangelo or Feuerbach—a constant, abrupt alteration of success and failure, a chain of exasperation, despair, and disappointment, of violent scenes and a staggering out of one conflict into another. Now this is the surest medical test for the irregularly-constructed personality, the psychopathic individual; that in normal, everyday life he is constantly kicking against the rules and running off the rails. And among men of genius we find a considerable number who are certainly unbalanced according to any reliable token. We find them inclined to delusions of persecution, possessed of tendencies to pathological affect reactions, with pronounced mental disease in the next of kin, and the like" (Kretschmer, 1929. Reprinted by permission.)

pled with the traits of close application, constancy, "spiritual activity," versatility, and whatever specific abilities he may possess.[1] The normal traits—common we might say—which the man of genius shares with his more normal brother keep him in contact with normal people and enable him to be a genius, not merely a brainy crank.[2]

Since Lange-Eichbaum's apparently exact percentages are not backed by adequate definitions of psychosis or psychopathic states, since his exactness is betrayed by his "three to four hundred," and furthermore since Cox's survey of 300 men of genius does not reach similar conclusions to Lange-Eichbaum, Kretschmer's analysis of genius seems to be more in keeping with the data. Whether genius arises principally from genetic factors or from social forces it is not at present possible to decide. The principle source of scientific information for historical characters we have, however, that of Cox, agrees to a greater degree with Kretschmer than with Lange-Eichbaum. Cox was trying to estimate I.Q.'s, but her detailing of childhood and adult lives yielded evidence of precocity and difference among

geniuses, but not much of madness, unless we define psychosis or psychopathologic states as mere deviance from a norm. But that the manifestations of the traits of genius are sometimes akin to those of emotional aberration seems fairly well established. And that *some* geniuses have had psychotic episodes and some have been neurotic can scarcely be doubted. Examples from Lange-Eichbaum and Kretschmer can be supplemented by such carefully documented studies as that of Sterba and Sterba (1954) on Beethoven in his relation to his nephew.

Research on gifted persons, especially children, has been accelerated under the influence of post-World War II concern over wastage of intellectual resources, and from a scientific urge to increase knowledge about important subjects. Two sets of investigations of adults (McClelland, *et. al.*, 1958; Roe, 1949, 1950, 1951, 1953) have concentrated on nonintellective aspects of personality in talented individuals. There are feelings of aloneness and apartness and a tendency toward over-intellectualization among topflight research scientists, who may be classified as geniuses in their respective fields. And talented persons may be different from their compeers in other ways. But neither of these studies suggests that high talent, even amounting to genius, in the present day allies itself closely with psychosis. Disturbance they may have, but not madness.

It seems, then, that the unique traits of genius can be considered as: (1) In some cases an uncommon, even unique *degree* of the traits possessed by ordinary individuals. (2) In other cases traits which resemble at times those of psychopathological states. Although much study is needed in the lives of those who can be classed as geniuses in the restricted sense, it seems also reasonable to add that there are probably many common traits possessed by the genius which are not in excess of those the ordinary person has, traits which are only unique as are all traits when found in their variations from individual to individual.

---

[1] "There arises a complicated individual psychology in which two abruptly opposed inheritances provide the main structural components and stand, throughout life, in constant mutual strain. This tension works in the first place as a dynamic affect factor. It also produces the unstable equilibrium, the emotional exuberance, and the restless inner drive which lifts genius high above the peaceful exercise of traditional occupations and forbids it satisfaction with the ordinary pleasures of life. In the realm of the intellect, it produces a great breadth of spiritual activity, a versatility and complex richness of talent and a certain formidableness of personality" (Kretschmer, 1929. Reprinted by permission.)

[2] ". . . it is that (the sound half) which enables him to round off and mature his creations, and which, above all, enables him to make wide and effective contact with the spiritual life of sound normal people" (Kretschmer, 1929). ". . . precisely this large ingredient of the normal citizen, with its contribution of close application, constancy, quiet reserve and fresh naturalness, lifts the true genius in all his effects, far above and beyond the noisy and transient attacks of those who are merely brilliant" (Kretschmer, 1929. Reprinted by permission.)

COMMON TRAITS

Of the hundreds of common traits which have been proposed by logical analysis or factor analysis it will only be possible in these pages to present the ones most widely accepted or those best attested by research. First, a few instances of surface and source traits (Cattell's distinctions to which we were introduced in the last chapter) are given. Then a rough division of traits is illustrated in terms of psychophysiological, psychophysical, intellectual, and temperamental-social traits. The last category is purposely broadened beyond the basic constitutional functions usually regarded as temperament. Further refinement may be called for later, but not at our present stage of understanding of personality.

Surface and Source Traits

Surface Traits. The gathering together of a number of easily identifiable trait elements into a "syndrome" or into a restricted "type" may give substance to the concept of surface trait. When Freud (S. Freud, 1925, 1950) in his classic paper on "the anxiety-neurosis" set forth in detail the characteristic symptoms of this hitherto undifferentiated syndrome, he was setting up a non-mathematical cluster of behavioral and ideational elements, like general irritability, anxious expectation, anxiety-attacks, and so on, a cluster of symptoms which could be considered today a surface trait. Examples of such traits developed by various methods are:

Psychoticism and *Neuroticism* are traits which Eysenck (1947, 1953) believes to be basic dimensions of personality but which also appear to be accumulations of elements going together empirically. Another trait regarded as basic or source in Eysenck's system (1947) comes under the appelation of surface trait in American analyses; this is the well-known *Extraversion-Introversion.* Some regard this latter trait to be the representation of types of persons (Jung, 1926; Mullahy, 1948; Munroe, 1955). Cattell (1943) at first considered it to be a cluster of a number of dimensions of per-

sonality such as personal attractiveness, sociability, pleasure seeking, and frivolity vs. earnestness, ascetism, and mirthlessness. Later he found the trait as a second-order factor (Cattell, 1957a).

Guilford (1945) has broken the over-all trait (*E-I*) into *Social Introversion-Extraversion* and *Thinking Introversion-Extraversion* (among other traits). These components of the surface trait serve to distinguish what even the nonscientific observer sometimes recognizes. A person may see himself as a socially approachable and overtly congenial, sociable individual, while at the same time he withdraws from people in his thought and feeling, or vice versa. *Extraversion and Introversion* may be a second-order factor which is just as much a source trait as those Cattell classifies as such; the preponderance of evidence does not, however, support it as one single dimension (Carrigan, 1960).

The most extensive attempt to identify surface traits is Cattell's (1943, 1946). Employing Allport and Odbert's list of trait names (Allport & Odbert, 1936) Cattell grouped 4,504 terms into 160 traits, then added 11 more from typology, mental ability research, interest measurement, and from special psychological concepts such as frustration tolerance, perseveration, level of aspiration, etc. These descriptive variables were considered to be a complete, though overlapping, coverage of the entire "personality sphere."

By comparing the results of a large number of correlation and cluster analyses,[1] Cattell found about 50 clusters which roughly grouped themselves together. These in turn seemed to form 20 major sectors of personality into which the various clusters grouped themselves, often overlapping one another. An example of such sectors is *Sector A. Character-Personality Integration or*

[1] Cluster analysis is a way of analyzing a correlation matrix by means of grouping together variables which "go together." Different systems of cluster analysis have been developed, but they all depend to some extent on putting tests together according to the degree of their correlations with one another (Fruchter, 1954; Holzinger & Harman, 1941).

Development vs. Moral Character Defect, Neurosis, Psychosis. These sectors are probably the ones employed by the average individual in his estimate of other persons and by employers or those who write letters of recommendation. We cannot pass off such sectors lightly, for our everyday judgments of others tend to be in these global terms. Yet even the novice in scientific study of personality should recognize that a host of dimensions is represented in such a conglomeration as *Sector A.* Two of the sectors in Cattell's 20 are broken down into sub-sectors, but even these are far from being single dimensions. These sectors represent patterns of variables which, though not single dimensions, do go together in some real fashion.

As the name implies, surface traits are often what are visible to the eye in the rough correlation of traits which a non-scientific, intelligent observer makes as he puts various pieces of behavior together with a fine astuteness, or in the clinical psychologists' rough nonmathematical factor analysis (Eysenck, 1953) of symptoms to form a syndrome. These cluster traits are dimensional in that they can be measured as "more" or "less"; they are, however, demonstrably multi-dimensional, so that they do not constitute the basic traits which factor-traits are claimed to be, for they are not as close to being "functional unities" as are the latter.

Source Traits. Long before scientific psychology came into existence and since then, men have tried to discern the irreducible elements of personality, the source traits in factor-analytic language. Aristotle and Plato spoke of "the parts of the soul." Faculty psychology sought universal elements supposed to be alike in all persons, Memory, Will, Courage, and so forth. McDougall (1923) sought the most important mammalian instincts, parental, combat, curiosity, escape, gregarious, and so on. In "character" McDougall's sentiments or complexes served as units, that is, hatred, love, self-regard, and many more. These sentiments are possibly source traits, but they are hardly the same as traits, for they

have not been shown to mark off a single individual from others, as Allport declared. When psychologists discovered the method of putting behavioral responses together mathematically rather than simply by clever but unaided analysis and synthesis, the search for source traits continued with increasing tempo. In 1942 one of the first attempts to summarize the results of factor-analytic research up to that time (Wolfle, 1942) revealed that only seven "personality factors" could be regarded as established. To these we could add the Primary Mental Abilities totaling seven also and about eight perceptual traits, both groups of factor-traits discovered by Thurstone (1938, 1944).

With the addition of from half a dozen to nine psychophysiological traits (Darrow, 1932) the list of all factor-traits up to the beginning of World War II included about 30 *in toto.* By 1951, following the intensive investigations of the AAF (Guilford & Lacey, 1947) and other research, a survey (French, 1951) disclosed 24 factor-traits in the aptitude and achievement areas alone. By 1959 Guilford (1957, 1959) reported 50 factors of intellect, out of a theoretically possible 120, in addition to more than a dozen temperament traits (Guilford & Zimmerman, 1949) and a number of interest traits (Guilford, Shneidman, & Zimmerman, 1949; Guilford, Christensen, Bond, & Sutton, 1954).

Obviously, in a survey of the kind we can make, not all the traits discovered in recent years can be detailed. Especially is it impossible to include many factors being revealed in many areas of personality each year. Appropriately, however, we can give the "16 personality factors" delineated by Cattell (Cattell, Saunders, & Stice, 1950)[1] who suggested the distinction between surface and source traits. It is necessary to remember, however, that this list includes primarily temperamental-social factor-traits and excludes most intellectual and all psychophysiological traits. It cuts across

[1] The more complicated listings in Cattell's (1957a) more recent work would serve only to confuse the student.

the outline of temperamental-social traits given in the following pages. Some of these factor-traits may be identical with those others, many are not. Until factorists get together on methods and nomenclature, confusion will exist. The later listing is made from a survey of many men's factor studies. This is provided as an example of a system of source traits one authority has set forth.

Source Traits

A. *Cyclothymia vs. Schizothymia*
B. *General Intelligence vs Mental Defect*
C. *Emotional Stability or Ego Strength vs. Dissatisfied Emotionality*
E. *Dominance or Ascendance vs. Submission*
F. *Surgency vs. Desurgency or Depressive Anxiety*
G. *Character or Super-Ego Strength vs. Lack of Internal Standards*
H. *Adventurous, Autonomic Resilience vs. Inherent, Withdrawn Schizothymia*
I. *Emotional Sensitivity vs. Tough Maturity*
L. *Paranoid Schizothymia vs. Trustful Altruism*
M. *Hysteric Unconcern (or "Bohemianism") vs. Practical Concernedness*
N. *Sophistication vs. Rough Simplicity*
O. *Anxious Insecurity vs. Placid Self-Confidence*
Q_1. *Radicalism vs. Conservatism*
Q_2. *Independent Self-Sufficiency vs. Lack of Resolution*
Q_3. *Will Control and Character Stability*
Q_4. *Nervous Tension*

A simple listing may give the wrong impression, for the name of a factor can be misleading in terms of behavioral referents. Nevertheless, gross approximations in verbal terms to underlying realities such as the above offer some notion as to what factorists mean by source traits, or at least what Cattell means.

In several instances these "source traits" tend in subsequent research to break down into smaller component traits. Such an apparent contradiction, the dissolution of what has seemed to be unitary into parts, is not unknown in the history of other sciences. The molecule and the atom must

have seemed like "unitary factors" before being broken into lesser components. In factor analysis some of the contradiction is resolved in an understanding of certain technical points which do not concern us here.[1]

Patterns of Covariation

It has been seen that common traits may be divided into surface and source traits. In the following discussion this distinction is not observed with any strictness. Instead, traits are divided by a logical division according to more classical reasoning than is involved in Cattell's framework of traits. Because there is overlapping of functions just as there has been in a topographical view of personality, a measure of repetition is found between the patterns of covariation represented below and the traits discussed thus far.

Psychophysiological Traits. Pioneer research in traits of this nature by Herrington (1942) combined physiological measures and social ratings. Small as the sample in this study, only fourteen, the intensive cross-sectional and longitudinal nature of the investigation lends support to Herrington's cautious conclusion that a major psychophysiological trait exists which he called *Pressure of Activity.* The research reveals among other things that there is a characteristic rate of basal energy expenditure for each person, a characteristic rate of respiration and pulse rate, and characteristic patterns of systolic blood pressure. (Cf. Chapter 3 for details.)

Another pioneer investigation (Darrow & Heath, 1932) which sought interrelations among physiological and psychological functions has been recognized as a classical study in the field. Both laboratory tests and

---

[1] Estimation of communalities is one such point. The further problem of representatives and adequate size of sample as well as other statistical considerations should not be forgotten when differences appear between factor-analytic studies. Besides, there may have been a failure in early investigations to include all the essential trait elements that go to make up some traits. Cf. discussions in Cattell (1946) and Eysenck (1953) on these points.

tests for psychological traits were administered to several groups of subjects. A rather crude factor analysis yielded several traits participating in both temperament and physiological behavior patterns.

As stated previously (Chapter 3), two factors resulted from research on the level of muscle tension and its concomitant autonomic nervous system activity (Wenger, 1943): (1) An autonomic factor, and (2) a muscular factor. The latter correlated with the ratings of judges as to the level of muscular tension. A multiple regression equation employing six of the autonomic measures was derived for predicting the individual's score on the second factor. When applied to the subjects of the original experiment (not a sound procedure), a relatively normal distribution resulted, somewhat skewed toward tenseness. Whatever methodological questions one may ask concerning the prediction equation's use, it is worthwhile to know that the existence of the second factor of muscle tension was confirmed independently by another investigator (Duffy, 1946) from sixteen different measures of muscle tension induced under pressure or stress conditions.

More recent research by Cattell (Cattell, 1955; Cattell & Cross, 1952) has resulted in refinements of psychophysiological traits; but these are too detailed and sophisticated to be presented in a brief illustrative overview.

Psychophysical Traits. Three major sub-areas of personality, dimensionally considered, are subsumed under the general heading of psychophysical traits. The first consists of the relations obtaining between physique and temperament. A second area concerns itself with psychomotor traits, enlarging to some extent upon the discussion in Chapter 3. And third, perceptual traits are discussed, whose dimensions admittedly reach from the strictly physiological to the clearly intellectual (Helson, 1951).

Somatotype and Temperament. Phrenologists, physiognomists, and characterologists of various sorts have endeavored to establish relations between the temperamental and physical factors of the individual. Physique itself may not be a subject for discussion in personology, although Guilford (1959) does devote a brief section of his text to morphological factors: general head size; trunk length, depth, and width; general body length; and muscular thickness. The physique itself may be more of an anatomical study; but functions directly determined by the physique are decidedly of interest to personality students. We cannot take space to review Franz Joseph Gall's phrenological attempts to correlate anatomical structure (of the head) and psychophysiological functions. Neither is there room for physionomical investigations reported in four extensive volumes by John Caspar Lavater (1797) in which he illustrates by carefully drawn portraits a "Horrible face," an "Undefinable passion," "Goodness and candor," the "Face of a knave," "The Miser," "The Brute," and other supposed traits and types. Only one of the major modern attempts to correlate bodily structure and traits of personality is given here, one which has been reported in a number of psychology texts, that of Sheldon and his associates (Hunt, 1944, Ch. 17; Sheldon, 1940, 1942, 1949) who have endeavored to relate body type and temperament.

By means of examination of more than 4,000 photographs, Sheldon first set up morphological types, which are really continuous variables rather than true types; these are called by the well-known names of endomorph, mesomorph, and ectomorph, the terms derived from the primary germ layers out of which the organs and structures of the body develop. Each of these types can be rated on a seven-point scale, so that the individual can be given an index number, like 7–3–2, to show the relative strength of each component or type. Temperament in turn was investigated by culling the literature on temperament, especially on the measurement of introversion and extraversion. An initial large list of traits was devised from this reading of the literature, then boiled down to fifty traits.

Thirty-three young men were then studied by Sheldon in intensive weekly interviews, and at the end of a year were rated on each of the fifty traits on the seven-point scale. Intercorrelations were entered in a matrix and clusters of traits determined. Three distinct trait clusters emerged, again well-known as visceratonia, somatotonia, and cerebrotonia. The first cluster groups together traits like relaxation, love of comfort, pleasure in eating, warmth toward people, and need for affection. The second includes, among other traits, those of being energetic, having assertiveness of posture and movement, a need for exercise, physical courage for combat, and indifference to pain. The last, cerebrotonia, combines restraint, inhibition, secretiveness of feeling, shyness, and need for solitude with overly fast reactions and hypersensitivity to pain, together with other inhibiting reactions. A final step was taken by Sheldon and his co-workers that brings his investigation into the realm of what we have called psychophysical; intercorrelations were computed on 200 additional subjects among the six patterns, three somatotypes and three temperament components. While most of the correlations run from $-.63$ to $-.23$, those between specific body types and temperaments are high positive: endomorphy and visceratonia, .79; mesomorphy and somatotonia, .82; and ectomorphy and cerebrotonia, .83.

We are indeed indebted to Sheldon for his massive work. The acceptance of Sheldon's work has been widespread and his terms have become part of the psychological patter of the day. A movement known as "constitutional psychology" [1] stemming in part from Sheldon's work has a number of adherents. Nevertheless, there are grave questions in connection with the results summarized above. One major methodological difficulty which has been pointed out is the lack of independence among the various ratings. When one man rates all the subjects in an experiment on all the patterns which are to be related, unless very special precautions are taken, there is almost always a tendency toward correlation among the ratings, whether actually present or not, either according to the "halo effect" or the prior belief of the rater that certain traits or items go together. Sheldon's work *seems* to suffer from this defect. More convincing criticism, however, is the accumulating evidence from research other than Sheldon's which does not support his original results (Adcock, 1948; Child, 1950; Fiske, 1944; Lubin, 1950; Smith, 1949). "Something peculiar about" Sheldon's intercorrelations found by one investigator (Adcock, 1948) led another (Lubin, 1950) [2] to discover they are virtually impossible, apparently the result of a computational error.

From the mounting research in somatotype and temperament it appears that some relation is allowable but not necessarily a determinantal relation (Child, 1950). For one thing, body type may *not* be hereditary, but could conceivably arise from environmental influences. Thus, both body type and temperament could develop in response to the same influences and show a resultant correlation. Even should it be shown conclusively that physique is primarily hereditarily determined, traits of temperament could arise as a result of the individual's reactions to his own body type as well as his reaction to others' reactions to his body type.

If we could prove a direct relation between physique and temperament, however, the task of the psychologist would be simplified immensely. If it can be shown, as Sheldon thought he had shown, that traits like "ruthlessness, freedom from squeam-

[1] The writer once attended a conference on "Constitutional Psychology" for a brief time. It seemed like a combination of scientific psychology, religious cult, and physical culture movement. Lectures on Sheldon's somatotyping and temperament testing and on some other rather unusual psychological concepts were interspersed with creative dance and group calisthenics. It was a memorable experience. An earnestness and devotion to a cause were manifest, together with an acceptance of a cult of psychology which was very different from the academic psychology with which the writer was familiar.

[2] The writer has not been able to examine Lubin's article, but takes this reference from Eysenck (1953).

ishness," "physical courage for combat," "Sociophilia," and "sociophobia" can be predicted with a fairly high degree of accuracy by measuring a person's nude photograph, one of the principles of psychology concerning prediction and control would be relatively easily fulfilled, the only limitation arising from considerations of modesty in our still somewhat puritanical society.[1] The clinician puts down Sheldon's works with a sigh, wishing all were as simple as that. The body type could be gotten readily and objectively according to Sheldon's directions; Rorschach, MAPS, TAT, Sentence Completions, questionnaires, and ratings of temperament would then be only adjunctive or confirmatory to the somatotyping. At present the evidence leads us to say, however, that the relation is possibly the other way around, that somatotyping is an adjunct to the direct tests of temperamental-social traits. There are most likely relations between body type and temperament which will yet prove useful to personality investigation (Cattell, 1950; Eysenck, 1953), for the views of many scholars past and present who believe that there are such relations cannot be taken lightly.[2] Thus far scientific investigation has not given adequate expression to these possible correlations.

Psychomotor Traits. The psychomotor traits constitute one special branch of those which can roughly be classified as psychophysical. These functions could be called perceptual-motor in part, but by custom they are labeled psychomotor. Air Force psychologists especially have been active

[1] Witness the furore raised by female students and their parents when the students were photographed ostensibly as part of their medical examination but really for purposes of somatotyping by Sheldon.

[2] Eysenck (1953) lists authorities from Hippocrates to Kretschmer and Burt who have set up physique classifications; some of these authorities have also divided psychological functions into corresponding types with characteristic traits. Eysenck believes that Kretschmer's work, though handicapped by inadequate statistical methods, has merit in associating schizothymes and cyclothymes with leptosome and pyknic body builds respectively.

in trying to find basic factor-traits in this area of the personality, beginning with the epoch-making aviation personnel testing program in World War II (Melton, 1947; Guilford & Lacey, 1947). Further research has added to the list of factors. A series of studies (Fleishman, 1953, 1954; Hempel & Fleishman, 1955), to part of which we have alluded in Chapter 4, contributed sufficient knowledge to enable us to say that there are probably at least 26 factors in the psychomotor abilities. Representative factors serve to illustrate the extent and complexity of this area of the personality which to the uninitiated appears fairly simple and uncomplicated.

Wrist-Finger Speed—requiring rapid wrist flexing and finger movements.

Psychomotor Coordination—either an integration of moderate muscle movements or coordination of eye and muscle movements. (This factor has been separated into a I and II, the first involving fine adjustments, the second suggesting gross, yet precise, adjustments.)

Manual Dexterity—arm-hand coordination and speed in action not emphasizing finger movements and not involving visual coordination.

Steadiness—the ability to make precise, steady arm-hand movements minimizing speed and strength.

Perceptual Speed—facility in making rapid comparisons of visual forms and noting similarities and differences in form and detail. (This factor suggests one reason for calling psychomotor traits perceptual-motor.)

Integration—ability to employ disparate cues and coordinate them with disparate activities quickly and accurately for an integrated response.

Rate Control—ability to make continual adjustments relative to comparatively unpredictable changes in speed and direction of a moving object.

Gross Body Coordination—simultaneous employment of trunk and limbs.

Leg Suppleness—flexibility and strain endurance of leg muscles.

Both the original AAF research and subsequent investigations (Ammons, 1954; Fleishman & Hempel, 1954) limit the generality of these psychomotor traits to a degree, in that the stage of practice must be taken into account when endeavoring to determine what factor-traits there are in this area. Most of the factors have shown up in sample after sample, so that we can be fairly certain that factors like those above represent basic dimensions. What we can say is that at different stages of individuals' practice different factors may contribute different proportions of variance to a test, while the factor-traits themselves remain relatively stable.

Perceptual Traits.[1] Several perceptual factors have been mentioned among psychomotor abilities even though they belong to a different realm of functions, for the former are associated with receptors and the latter with effectors. Yet in reality it is only possible in most instances to make an artificial distinction between perceptual and motor functions; it is difficult to think of motor behavior which does not involve preparatory perceptual functioning. All the tests employed to discover psychomotor traits involve perception of some sort. It is easier to think of perceptual tasks which do not involve immediate motor behavior as a direct result of the perceptual process; but here again motor behavior in the form of postural adjustments, proprioceptive activity, or other voluntary or involuntary muscle movement is part of the perceptual-motor process. Nevertheless, with general psychology we make the valid distinction between perceptual and motor responses and take up briefly the factor-traits revealed in studies of perception. Two major factorial experiments in the area of perception have been undertaken whose results can be summarized here.

In an investigation by Thurstone (1944) both perceptual tasks and mental ability as well as psychomotor tests were included to determine centrally determined perceptual

[1] Material incorporated in this section is taken from an article by the author (Dreger, 1961) and is used by permission of The Journal Press, copyright owners.

functions, as opposed to those peripherally determined (e.g., visual acuity). The factors which were disclosed by the experiment were not named by Thurstone because of their tentative nature; but a number of these with psychological significance have been verified separately.

A. *Speed and Strength of Closure*—forming and holding perceptual closure against distortion.

B. *Geometrical Design Illusions*—inhibitions of realistic perception by optical illusions.

C. *Reaction Time*—auditory and visual.

D. *Rate of Alternations*—reversals of ambiguous figures like the Necker Cube.

E. *Changing Gestalts*—flexibility in manipulating several irrelevant or conflicting configurations, a freedom from rigidity in changing one Gestalt for another.

F. *Speed of Perception*—facility in recognizing visual forms coupled with rapid adaptation.

G. *General Intellective Factor*—general intelligence as represented by Spearman's "g."

H. *Color-Form Dominance*—dominance of color or form in determining perception. (Very limited in Thurstone's results, but included here because European and Rorschach psychologists have stressed, probably inaccurately, its importance.)

J. *Speed of Judgment*—speed of making a judgment about an already clearly perceived situation.

One important fact to which Thurstone calls attention is that individuals may vary from one another in not just one gross perceptual speed function, but in five distinguishable functions, signified here by A, C, D, F, and J. Each of these seems to involve a differing amount of central participation, with simple reaction time, C, seeming to require the least, and E probably requiring most. When we consider the complexity of functioning in the limited segment of personality which may be called general speed of perception, it is easy to see how we may differ so vastly from one another in overall functioning. If an individual is high in the factor-trait, *Speed and Strength of Clo-*

sure, slow in general *Reaction Time*, fair in *Rate of Alternations*, high in *Speed of Perception*, and medium high in *Speed of Judgment*, his performance in a sudden emergency in automobile traffic may be vastly different from that of another whose scores on these traits differ by appreciable amounts at all, even if the emergency performance depended on perceptual factors only. Some of the peculiarities of conduct we observe in ourselves and others are probably the resultant of differing amounts of perceptual speed functions. Of course, our behavior is not so simply predicted as by scores on these restricted functions. Yet that they are important functions we cannot doubt; the Air Force has regarded these and other perceptual traits of sufficient import in aircraft operation and maintenance to devote much time to research in this area.

The other major perceptual trait research (Roff, 1952) utilized one of the largest peacetime samples in factorial investigations. From this study further factor-traits emerged which can be represented by the following more interesting ones:

M. *Sequential Perception*—ability to identify forms presented in moving trace or briefly flashed (presumably an important ability in plane-spotting).

N. *Movement Detection*—determination of direction of movement or whether movement is occurring.

P. *Perception Through Camouflage*—recognizing objects against a concealing background.

Perceptual traits take their place alongside those relating physique and temperament, together with physiological and psychomotor traits, as products in part of psychophysical research of traditional experimental psychology and in part of the more recent attacks on fundamental problems of relations among variables by factor analysis. The outlines of early German and American psychophysics laboratories show through the findings in perceptual functions particularly.

Personological Significance of Psychophysiological and Psychophysical Traits. If in the recital of separate factor-traits the individual seems to have been neglected, the neglect has been only temporary for scientific dissection purposes. That the individual is the locus of these as well as all human functions cannot be forgotten in a text on personality. Far from being irrelevant to the study of the individual, however, knowledge of the traits described thus far assists us in predicting individual behavior. If by testing a person for the possession of certain amounts of the traits represented here, we can gain a more accurate notion of what he will do under certain circumstances, we are certainly in a better position to understand his personality as a whole than if we make unguided (or misguided) judgments about him without knowledge of the intricate patterns of traits possible in his or any case.

Take the example of an apparently promising young man applying for a pilot's position in the Air Force. Suppose the selection officers are not aware of separate factor-traits, but go on their "global judgment" as to the capabilities of a man for piloting a plane. Our young man makes a good impression on those whom he meets; in common terms, he has a "pleasing personality." He possesses the air of a self-confident, intelligent man. Furthermore, the selection officers are not willing to trust their unaided judgment entirely—though after all, are they not good judges of human nature?—and so they make use of the information gathered independently, that the candidate has shown remarkable industry in playing quarterback on his high school football team, has made excellent grades in school, and has the recommendation from his high school principal as to his honesty and good judgment. "He'll make a good pilot" is the unanimous verdict of the selection board. And the young man proceeds to "wash out" miserably!

Why this failure in the face of so much apparent evidence to the contrary? Assuming that the young man's temperament traits are all the necessary ones for success in being a pilot, and that his higher intellectual traits are satisfactory, and further that his instructors are all fair-minded men and that there were no significant chance "flukes" in any of the training or extra-training situations—the writer recognizes the measure of unrealism in some of his assumptions—assuming "other things being equal" in other words, the reason for the failure can be most likely traced to the nearly complete lack of a trait called *Psychomotor Coordination I*, the ability to make fine, sensitive and highly controlled adjustments in movements that are restricted in scope, a trait which was found to correlate .64 with Navy midshipmen success in flight training when eliminations were due to flying deficiency. But the "global judgment" and high school teachers' grades and the football coach's perfectly justified praise could hardly have taken this lack into account. Some kind of test would have been necessary to discover the inadequacy; but unless factor analysis had broken down the gross "flying ability" into component factor-traits, the specific lack could not be ferreted out.

More is actually known about any one personality by having exact measurements for that one in the various factors described in the foregoing pages than by failing to take them into account. With all the limitations to which tests are subject and with due recognition of the need for a skillful clinician or personality expert to interpret individual scores in terms of a general pattern, in the long run a more scientific knowledge of the *individual* may be gained by knowing his relative strengths and weaknesses in as specific functions as factor analysis can delineate.

We scarcely need to state that these functions are not the only ones or yet the most important ones in personality. Indeed, some have not classed them as personality functions at all; on examination, however, we find that they are very significant portions of personality. On the other hand, those functions classified as intellectual and temperamental-social are probably more important in the over-all adjustments of human life.

Intellectual Traits. Studied more exten-

sively than traits already discussed, intellectual traits of personality reveal the same complexity found whenever we investigate any sub-area of personality. Except by gross over-simplification it is no longer possible for us to dismiss an individual with an offhand remark, "Oh, he's smart," or "He's stupid." Even when we employ Spearman's concept of a general intellective factor, it is necessary to keep in mind Spearman's notion that each task requires a special kind of intelligence as well as sharing in "*g*." An I.Q. no longer represents, if it ever did, a dead-level of intelligence applicable to any kind of task whatever. Instead, an I.Q. is now recognized as an average of many kinds of often widely diverging abilities tapped by the specific test. In the history of intelligence testing in general, divergencies and "scatter" of test performances were taken account of on a general intelligence test. Sometimes this "scatter" of performances has been interpreted as consisting of chance deviations. But a scientific view of intelligence appears to lie in the position to which factor-analytic research has arrived.

The history of factor analysis of intellectual functions can be summarized briefly: At first came Spearman's concept of general intelligence plus specific intelligences. Then came a break-down of general intelligence into the so-called primary mental abilities. Recently not only has there been a further breakdown and extension of the primary mental abilities, but a "breakthrough" has occurred into the previously untapped realms of creative-thinking aptitudes lying beyond the more reproductive types of abilities represented in earlier research. The following discussion of intellectual traits is outlined in terms of the natural historical divisions of factor-analytic history.

General Intelligence "*g*." When Spearman (1904) published his long article on "General intelligence objectively determined and measured," a new era was born in psychology. It was probably not coincidental that Spearman's initial contribution to the discovery of elementary traits of intellect came when it did. In America J. McKeen Cattell and others had been trying for a number of years to measure abilities by laboratory tests and other procedures. In Germany William Stern published a text in 1900 on individual differences. From France in 1905 came the greatest contribution to mental testing of the decade, Alfred Binet's scale of intelligence for school children. As Boring (1950) in his history of experimental psychology declares, the *Zeitgeist* of testing for individual differences was present in the psychological world. But with the establishment of "g" and the creation of a new method of measuring intellectual functioning the era of determining the functional unities of personality began. Even so, it was not for many years that the use of factor-analytic methods extended beyond the intellectual sphere.

McDougall (1934) tried to interpret and extend Spearman's general factor in terms of a general level of energy which manifests itself in cognitive, conative, and affective actions. According to McDougall, there is a reciprocal inhibition of different mental actions, demonstrating a common supply of available energy which in turn, may be concentrated in the dominating system, either cognitive or other. Thus "g" is not merely the quantity of energy available, but also represents a concentration of energy in specific functions. However, although clinicians of psychoanalytic persuasion are favorable to the concept of an available supply of energy which may be used in maintaining normal or abnormal adjustments, the research on "g" does not lend itself to McDougall's interpretation. The general intellective factor "g" is apparently not related to other functions in the way McDougall thought. It is not negatively correlated with conative and affective traits as would be expected if the "available energy" concept held, but instead has positive relations with them.

Primary Mental Abilities. Following Spearman's lead, others (Burt, 1941; Garnett, 1919; Holzinger & Harman, 1941; Thomson, 1939) have continued to expand

the general intelligence factor concept. But the apparently more fruitful approach is that of Thurstone (1934, 1935, 1936) which has led to greater understanding of both intellectual functions and other personality traits as well. Thurstone succeeded in establishing, at least for those not averse to his methods, the major outlines of primary mental abilities.[1]

In the initial experiment (Thurstone, 1938) to establish these abilities, 56 tests were given to 240 volunteer student subjects, 218 of whom completed the entire battery; the subjects were on the whole above the average in general school ability as measured by the A.C.E. test, but formed a distribution on the test similar in form to the distribution of students throughout the country. When the test results were factor-analyzed and the axes rotated orthogonally to obtain the best solution,[2] seven clear factors appeared plus two that seemed to be interpretable less readily, and four relatively uninterpretable or merely resulting from error. Several of these factors split into subfactors, according to research summarized later in this chapter. In this grouping of PMA, however, it is well to have Thurstone's original list of ability traits from which have developed the finer distinctions among intellectual traits in recent years.

S. *Spatial* or Space
P. *Perceptual* or Perceptual Speed
N. *Numerical* or Number
V. *Verbal* or Verbal Comprehension
M. *Memory* or Associative Memory
W. *Word Fluency*
I. *Induction*

---

[1] Thurstone was not the only one to make such a study. Truman L. Kelley (1928) distinguished among kindergarten, third grade, and seventh grade children the following "differentiable mental abilities": 1. General factor—heterogeneity, maturity, sex, and race. 2. Verbal. 3. Number. 4. Memory. 5. Spatial (in the third grade analysis divided into: a. sensing and retention of geometrical forms; b. manipulation of geometrical forms). 6. Speed. 7. Vivacity or ebullience (in one seventh grade only).

[2] The best here in terms of "simple structure" and "positive manifold."

Another similar experiment (Thurstone, 1941) confirmed the results of the first analysis. Thurstone did not believe, however, that the seven factors are irreducible atoms of intellect. His monograph contains these words:

It should not be assumed that the primary mental abilities are elemental and indivisible. For example, the primary ability that has been called "verbal comprehension" is almost certainly not an indivisible element of any kind. But in a wide variety of psychological examinations it behaves as *a functional unity that is strongly present in some tests and almost completely absent in many others.* This is the fundamental idea of a primary mental ability. (Thurstone, 1941).[1]

In this way he signified the meaning of a primary mental ability and at the same time left room for future possible divisions of those functional unities. Ironically, the one factor-trait which appears to be the most indivisible element, if any is, is *Verbal Comprehension.* Virtually all the others have been broken down into component traits.

Additional Factor-Traits of Intellect. Following the United States' entry into World War II, the Army Air Force set up a huge practical research program for the improvement of selection procedures for pilots, bombardiers, and navigators, plus some research in selection and training of flexible gunners, and in selection of radar operators (Guilford & Lacey, 1947; Melton, 1947). The emphasis here is on the term "practical," for the planning and execution of a research program of the magnitude of the Aviation Psychology Program in peacetime would have called for many more checks and careful testing of hypotheses than were possible in the exigencies of wartime. Nevertheless, the results both in betterment of selection and in delineation of personality traits in factors of a psychomotor and intellectual nature were of a high order. When by a combination of ap-

paratus and printed classification tests the prediction of pilot success rose to about 0.60 (validity coefficient, which means that about 36 per cent of the variance in pilot success can be accounted for by the tests) and that even greater predictability resulted for navigators, anyone who knows much about personnel selection is properly impressed. And the discovery of new factors, together with sharpening and confirming of ones already known, is heartening to personality trait psychologists. Some of the most important and interesting factor-traits added to the primary seven are:

V. *Judgment*—practical judgment and estimation, making wise choices from alternative solutions in terms of a judgmental and criticizing function.

M_2 (VM). *Visual Memory*—ability to keep a visual memory of pictorial stimuli following short intervals. Possibly the short time interval is unimportant. This is distinct from Thurstone's *Memory* factor which involves retention and recognition immediately of pairs of associated items.

ME. *Mechanical Experience*—a factor comprised at least of mechanical information, tool and driving skill.

V_2. *Visualization*—the ability to transform a stimulus presented pictorially or verbally to another visual arrangement.

In the period following World War II, Guilford [2] who took a major share of di-

---

[1] Thurstone, L. L., & Thurstone, Thelma G. Factorial studies of intelligence. *Psychom. Monogr.*, No. 2. Chicago: The Univer. of Chicago Press, 1941. Reprinted by permission.

[2] Reports have been issued regularly from the Psychological Laboratory of the University of Southern California giving information on one of the most complete and intensive investigations in any field of science. Those reports examined for the summary in the text are: Allen, Guilford, & Merrifield (1960); Green, Guilford, Christensen, & Comrey (1953); Guilford (1950, 1953, 1957, 1959); Guilford, Berger, & Christensen (1954, 1955); Guilford & Christensen (1956); Guilford, Christensen, Frick, & Merrifield (1957); Guilford, Christensen, Kettner, Green, & Hertzka (1954); Guilford, Comrey, Green, & Christensen (1950); Guilford, Fruchter, & Zimmerman (1952); Guilford, Green, & Christensen (1951); Guilford, Hertzka, Berger, & Christensen (1952); Guilford, Hertzka, & Christensen (1953); Guilford, Kettner & Christensen (1954, 1955a, 1955b, 1956); Guilford & Merrifield (1960); Guilford, Merrifield,

rection for the AAF Psychology Program has been the outstanding leader in the search for greater precision in our knowledge of the factors representing intellectual abilities. Since 1940 when he summarized the progress until that time on the "thinking abilities" (Guilford, 1940), his work has been recognized in the field of intellectual traits, concomitantly with his breaking down temperamental-social traits into primary factors (Guilford & Zimmerman, 1949).

Begun about 1950, a new venture into the realm of human creativity and its associated functions has advanced the frontier of knowledge of personality [1] in the intellectual area with a potential of profound consequence to society (Guilford, 1950). The primary problem of society is to discover creative youth and to develop creative personalities. But the first objective of the scientist is to discover empirically what creativity is. A very rough opera-

Christensen, & Frick (1960); Guilford, Wilson, & Christensen (1952); Guilford, Wilson, Christensen, & Lewis (1951); Hertzka, Guilford, Christensen, & Berger (1954); Merrifield, Guilford, Christensen, & Frick (1960); Wilson, Guilford, & Christensen (1953); Wilson, Guilford, Christensen, & Lewis (1954). Other research pertaining to breakdowns of primary abilities is found in the following references: Adkins & Lyerly (1952); Fiske (1949); Guilford & Lacey (1947); Michael, Zimmerman, & Guilford (1950, 1951).

[1] Other projects than Guilford's have advanced our knowledge of the traits of high-level intellectual individuals. Terman's *Genetic Studies of Genius* (1925, 1926, 1930, 1947, 1959) have added greatly to understanding as have Leta S. Hollingworth's studies of individuals above 180 I.Q. Research in the "Conservation of Human Resources" has been undertaken at Columbia University with a large aim of discovering and making intensive investigation of high-level performers in various fields of endeavor (Bray, 1954). Anne Roe's (1949, 1950, 1951a, 1951b, 1951c, 1953) research into characteristics of top producers in the field of science gives insight into traits found in some of the most brilliant men of today. One result Terman and others have brought forth is that high-level individuals are better "all-around" persons than the average, healthier both mentally and physically. Roe's top men, however, prove to have a number of reclusive characteristics which may differentiate them from others whom Kretschmer called the "merely brilliant."

tional definition states that creativity is what is most characteristic of creative people. The task then is to find what individuals of a high level of accomplishment or promise do in situations which call for responses beyond the range of stereotyped, unimaginative, and sterile reactions.

Judging that creativity may include traditionally measured intellectual functions, the primary mental abilities, Guilford maintained that it also extends beyond the domain of intelligence as conceived previously. As has been argued in these pages, genius, according to Guilford, is not synonymous with a high I.Q. Nor is it synonymous with even creativity amounting to less than genius, the creativity which may very well be a common possession of every man in greater or lesser degree. Creativity seems to be found among the various "thinking abilities," however, so any research which investigates creativity in the whole personality must at least relate creative abilities to the other intellectual functions. Thus the research which was actually planned was intended to cover the entire field of intellectual abilities. Initially, Guilford outlined the scientific method to be utilized, a research design which also serves as a model for other factorial investigations. Briefly the steps are: (1) The domain of investigation is chosen; (2) hypotheses are stated, including alternative hypotheses as to expected outcomes; (3) tests are selected for the postulated traits, with "reference tests" if possible which have been shown to measure known factors; (4) the battery of tests is administered to a representative sample of a population having certain specified characteristics (age, educational level, sex, etc.); (5) factors are extracted from the correlation matrix and axes rotated.[2] Of course, there follows what Thurstone called the most interesting part of the procedure, the interpretation of factors in terms of psychological theory and understanding.

It was postulated on the basis of previous

[2] Guilford rotates orthogonally, but takes account of psychological meaningfulness.

research and theory that there are four major domains in the area of thinking abilities: (1) reasoning abilities, which have been extensively explored, (2) creative abilities, (3) evaluative abilities, and (4) planning abilities. To determine the nature of these postulated domains or abilities, Guilford began a large-scale research into the "aptitudes of high-level personnel" under a contract with the Office of Naval Research which has been sponsoring such "basic research" in recent years. With the cooperation of the Human Resources Research Center of the Air Training Command at Lackland Air Force Base in Texas an intensive investigation of hundreds of Air Cadets and student officers at various air bases was undertaken.

The results of such an extensive research project have been eminently satisfying. Over-all, our knowledge about the structure of intellect has been radically altered. Long before Guilford's work, traditional distinctions between inductive and deductive thinking had been blurred almost beyond recognition. Now, however, even the divisions proposed as a framework for research, abilities categorized into thinking, creative, evaluative, and planning, have had to be realigned. Such realignment is on the basis of empirical findings now, not from armchair speculating. Besides the emergence of gross outlines of intellect, many new factors of intellectual abilities have been discovered.

According to Guilford's schema, the intellect can be cross-categorized in three ways: by its operations, by its contents, and by its products. Operations are the major kinds of intellectual activities, what the organism does with information; contents are the varieties of information; and products are the results of processing information.

Each cross-classification is divided into subcategories. Operations include factors in five areas: *Cognition* refers to the discovery or rediscovery of information; *memory* to the retention of information in any form; *divergent production* (or divergent thinking) to the generation of a variety of

information from one source, as in finding new ways of doing things or reaching alternate solutions; *convergent production* (or convergent thinking) to the generation of specific outcomes (the "right" answer, *e.g.*) from given information; and *evaluation* to making decisions concerning relative goodness (suitability, adequacy, etc.) of information in terms of specified criteria.

Contents may be *figural*, *i.e.*, having concrete form or images; *symbolic*, or having signs such as numbers, musical notations, mathematical symbols or others having no significance in themselves; *semantic*, referring to meanings, primarily those to which words may be attached; or *behavioral*, essentially nonverbal information relating to human interactions where awareness of one's own and others' responses is called for ("social intelligence").

Products of thinking are found in terms of *units*, items of information of a circumscribed nature; *classes*, groupings of items having common properties; *relations*, connections between or among units of information; *systems*, more highly organized aggregates of items of information; *transformations*, changes made in existing information; and *implications*, extrapolations in the form of predictions or expectancies from known information.

Guilford symbolizes the above categories and subcategories in the form of a master cube composed of minor cubes (Figure 19). Operations, contents, and products form the three dimensions of the cube. The columns and rows are the subclassifications. Each minor cube thus represents the confluence of an operation, a content, and a product. For example, one cube stands for memory-symbolic-systems, *i.e.*, "memory of certain symbols which form a system." Another cube is evaluation-behavioral-implications, or "judgment that this kind of behavior will lead to such-and-such consequences."

It is necessary to recall that even though this model of the intellect is a theoretical one, it has resulted from research on factors. It does not arise from armchair speculation but from many years of experiment-

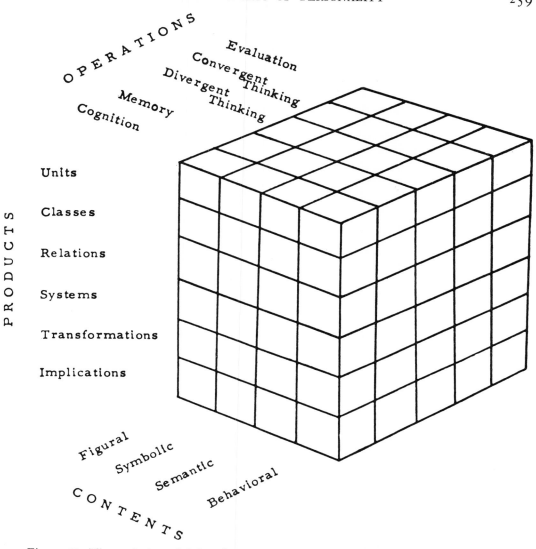

Figure 19. Theoretical model for the complete "Structure of Intellect." (From J. P. Guilford, *The Structure of Intellect Model*, p. 4)

ing and revising of the model in the light of empirical findings (Guilford, 1959a, 1959b; Guilford & Merrifield, 1960).

Only representative factors defining several "cubes" of intellectual functioning can be mentioned here. Indeed, not all of the 120 minor cubes (*i.e.*, 5 × 4 × 6) have been identified yet in terms of experimentally-derived factors; so in one sense even listing all of the factors thus far identified would yield only a representative set.

One factor, identifying the category cognition-figural-transformations (CFT), is *Visualization*, a well-known factor which we have defined before (p. 256); this factor loads on tests like the Guilford-Zimmerman Spatial Visualization Test in which the examinee indicates the position a clock would have after being rotated. In the memory-semantic-units (MSU) cube another familiar factor, *Memory Span*, is found, the ability to recall a series of items after one presentation. *Figural Spontaneous Flexibility*, which corresponds to the factor *Rate of Alternations* in the perceptual trait area (p. 252), a capacity to reverse ambiguous figures like the Necker Cube, identifies the divergent production-figural-classes (DFC) cube. Convergent production-symbolic-relations (NSR) is shown by the factor *Symbolic Correlates*, an ability to give an item when one knows another item and the relation holding between the two (Spearman's "eduction of correlates"). *Sensitivity to Problems* is the factor in the cube evaluation-memory-implications (EMI), a factor showing an ability to recognize a problem in connection with common practices and to suggest ways of improving the situation.

The neat schema symbolized by the master cube and its minor cubes is recognized by its creator as a tool for research, an heuristic model, and not a permanent picture of intellectual functions. (If we should take the model literally, it might signify that we are all blockheads!) Even in his most comprehensive discussions of his model, Guilford maintains that it needs changes, that interactions among categories alter the meanings of these categories individually considered, and that factors may be misplaced in their present categories. As an heuristic device, however, the model has served to foster discovery of hitherto unsuspected factors; and it brings some order out of the apparent chaos of the multiplied factors coming out of recent research.

New vistas have been opened up by Guilford's and others' work, going beyond the pedestrian abilities tapped by most conventional intelligence tests. A more accurate picture of the individual's personality in its intellectual functioning can be gained by determining his scores on a large number of factors than by merely obtaining a gross average of academic abilities, an intelligence quotient or mental age. Identification of those with special talents is more feasible with measures of specific factors. In a civilization that seeks desperately for higher level talents the identification of those who possess special abilities useful in complex tasks is coming to be—literally—a life saving occupation.

Temperamental-Social Traits. More important to the individual and to society from many standpoints than even the vastly important traits so far discussed are the temperamental-social functions. It is the temperamental-social traits which the man on the street considers most important when he says of another, "He has a sparkling personality." It is the temperamental-social traits to which some scientists have limited their study of personality; most "personality inventories" bear witness to this limitation. It has been, however, one contention of this text that psychophysiological, psychophysical, and intellectual functions, in whatever manner they are conceived, are as much portions of the personality as are temperamental-social functions or traits, for they, too, make an individual what he is and distinguish individuals from one another.

For some persons the intellectual, psychomotor, and psychophysiological traits may be more important, if they make the difference between having or not having capacity to hold out for the duration of a task, or to perform or to perceive in special ways, or where they make the difference between being able or not able to reason or to evaluate significant materials. But for the large majority of persons, doing the workaday jobs of the world, growing up in families, courting and/or marrying, begetting children and rearing families, growing old, getting or losing friends, dealing with joys and sorrows, meeting with victories and defeats, it is probably true that those traits which assist or hinder us directly in getting along with others and ourselves are more important. It is not too much to suggest that even for those whose patterns of intellectual, psychomotor, and psychophysiological traits far exceed the normal ranges there are more significant temperamental-social traits as well.[1]

[1] Actual correlations between temperament tests and job effectiveness or success in pilot-training run no higher than .40 in most cases (Thurstone, 1952). Only 16 per cent of the vari-

As in the other sections of this text, the social nature of personality is recognized in the very labeling of this group of traits. Very few if any of the traits described in the following pages can be regarded as "within the skin." On the whole they require a society in which to originate and operate. Like roles, which serve as interpersonal functions when we view personality topographically, temperamental-social traits, as personality is viewed dimensionally, cannot be intra-individual only.

Both so-called "personality" traits and interests and values are reported in this final section of the chapter. Popular usage in psychological literature has been acceded to in naming the first group of factor-traits even though they are more strictly dimensions of temperament.

"Personality" Traits. A great volume of literature on these traits exists, many factors have been discovered, and new factors and sub-factors are being announced each year. Sometimes these factors are dependent on the medium used to measure them, such as the Rorschach Test (Wittenborn, 1950), the Allport-Vernon "Study of Values" (Brogden, 1952), interest tests (Guilford *et. al.*, 1953), or objective, rating, or questionnaire tests (Cattell & Saunders, 1950; Cattell, 1955, 1957a). Sometimes the factors depend on the field being investigated, such as that of psychosexual development (Barnes, 1952) or social attitudes (Ferguson, 1939, 1940, 1941, 1944). Here more than in any other area there is a confusion of tongues. Not only is there somewhat of an autism in each authority's naming of the factors he has discovered, but sometimes one wonders whether the babel

of divergent languages even has reference to the same human personalities.[1]

Altogether there is need for a harmonization which at present does not exist. Rather than resigning ourselves to the seeming chaos, however, we shall find it more expedient to present as much order as there is. Complete harmonization of any field of science has never been achieved; but by seeing what order there is we may hope for greater order to be effected in the perspective thus obtained. The following traits are those which have received most prominence in the literature of "personality" study. No claim is made that all of these are source traits. All that is claimed is that in a number of studies they have been shown to be major dimensions in the

---

[1] The listing of traits in the text will not be satisfactory to any authority not only because each one names traits differently but because he has his own listing. For the record the traits set forth by the three outstanding authorities are presented here.

Eysenck (1947, 1952b, 1953c) appears to find only three major dimensions, *Introversion-Extraversion, Neuroticism,* and *Psychoticism.* However, he investigates *Radicalism-Conservatism, Cyclothymia-Schizothymia* and various forms of *Suggestibility* (Eysenck, 1950, 1952a, 1953c; Eysenck & Furneaux, 1945).

The student may wish to turn to Cattell's discussions (especially 1955b, 1956; Cattell & Cross, 1952; Cattell & Saunders, 1950; Cattell, Saunders, & Stice, 1950), but his original list (1946) is presented in the text. In his further detailing of traits not only is there autism about naming but there is a similar tendency toward factorial solipsism.

Guilford has several inventories which overlap to some degree. The latest names are given here except where older terms make for more clarity:

S—*Sociability* (Social Introversion-Extraversion)
T—*Thinking Introversion-Extraversion*
D—*Depression*
C—*Cycloid* tendencies
R—*Rhathymia* (happy-go-luckiness)
G—*General Activity*
A—*Ascendance-Submission*
M—*Masculinity-Femininity*
I—*Inferiority Feelings*
N—*Nervousness*
O—*Objectivity*
F—*Friendliness*
C—*Cooperativeness*
E—*Emotional Stability* (D and C combined.)

---

ance of the job criterion can thus be accounted for by the tests—at a maximum. Nevertheless, if the cost of administering such a test is small in terms of a battery of tests, even one or two per cent of predictable variance is welcome. And 16 per cent is really a respectable amount. The high importance of temperamental-social variables in business and industrial output has been recognized at least since the Hawthorne Study (Roethlisberger & Dickson, 1939).

temperament area—not always by the name assigned here. It is well for the student to recognize here that the name of a factor or trait is not important. What is important is that the behavioral indices or test items to which responses are made be specified. Numbers would be perfectly acceptable to identify the traits treated here in the way Cattell (1957a) has already done in his indexing of factors. The traits are numbered here, but only arbitrarily; the common designation by which a factor or trait has come to be known is employed.

1. *"w"* or *Will.* Discovered many years ago in the first factor analysis of nonintellectual functions (Webb, 1915), *"w"* should be recognizable by layman and scientist alike as equivalent to the persistence of motives. Scientist and layman part company in that the former does not regard *"w"* as will or will power in the layman's sense. Emphasis is rather on the will*ing*, a process fitting into a naturalistic conception of man's behavior, not upon will as an "uncaused causer" or source of energy. Probably related to several of the source traits Cattell describes,[1] the trait is regarded by Vernon (1953), the British psychologist as one of two main dimensions found by factor analysis. (The other is *Introversion-Extraversion.*)

One American psychologist (Moore, 1948)[2] defined the trait elements of this trait as: attention, truthfulness, self-control, will, reliability, stability, refinement, religion, response to reproof, attitude to work, and generosity. Both this authority and two English scientists (Burt, 1939; Eysenck, 1947, 1952, 1953) regard *"w"* to be the positive end of a pole with *Neuroticism* or *Emotionality* at the negative pole. This latter is sometimes called *"e"* or *Emotionality.* It refers, however, to an "emotional immaturity" or a general emotionality

in which persons may vary somewhat independently from *"w."* In one investigation (Burt, 1939) it was discovered that observers, even teachers, who are inexperienced in judging personality in terms of strictly observable data, rated a child high on joy and then automatically low on sorrow or vice versa. In actuality, when the same child's *behavior* was assessed directly he was seen to be excessively gay and merry on one occasion and excessively grieving on another. In this respect both children and adults may manifest this trait as a kind of general stability or general emotionality.

2. *"p"* or *Perseveration.* This trait has had a checkered career in the history of psychology, whatever it may be in the individual. It has been thought of as an intellectual rigidity, a tendency to perseverate in responses. Spearman thought that a general law of inertia holds in intellection, "Cognitive processes always both begin and cease more gradually than their apparent causes" (Spearman, 1927). Actually, subsequent research has made this apparently simple "law" appear like a very complex function of temperament. Each of us has probably known (or is) someone who seems generally rigid in his dealings with others. Arguing with him is like arguing with a mountain—but the fact that the mountain sometimes turns out to be a volcano suggests even to commonsense observation that this trait cannot be a completely unitary function.

In his excellent review of research on perseveration Eysenck (1953c) details evidence which shows how hard it is to hold to a concept of a unitary trait of perseveration or rigidity. For one thing there seem to be at least four basic kinds of perseverative behavior—whether there is correlation among them, of course, is the major question. (1) Ideational—for example, the obsessional tendency to repeat words or tunes. (2) Emotional—continuing of affective reactions following the initial stimulus. (3) Sensory—continuance of sensation, for example, the "persistence of vision" when a point of light is swung in a circle before

---

[1] C. *Emotional Stability or Ego Strength vs. Dissatisfied Emotionality.* G. *Character or Superego Strength vs. Lack of Internal Standards.* Q. *Will Control and Character Stability.*

[2] Correlation coefficients in this study by Moore (1948) are "out of this world."

one's eyes. (4) Motor—inability to shift rapidly from one psychomotor task to another or to its opposite. Some researchers have confused, Eysenck declares, persistence and perseveration, whereas these appear to be experimentally two different traits; persistence correlates positively, for instance, with "w," and perseveration negatively (to an extent) with "w." There is an apparent lack of relation among various kinds of perseveration, so that Eysenck insists there is no general factor of perseveration. Probably this one factor which seems so obviously unitary at first glance consists of several basic dimensions called variously *Rigidity* (Lewin, 1935), *Personality Rigidity* (Fisher, 1949), *Einstelling Rigidity* (Luchins, 1942, 1947) and *Disposition Rigidity* or *Structural Rigidity* (Cattell & Tiner, 1949) the relations among which are not at all understood.[1] A factor analysis of 21 tests of perseveration (Rim, 1955) tentatively revealed four factors, one of which may be a basic temperament dimension which excludes ability, motivational, and interest features; a second of which has "creative effort" aspects; the third is "cognitive or ideational"; and the fourth is probably related to an intellectual factor called here "alternation or speed."

3. *Persistence.* As suggested above, *Persistence* and *Perseveration* are sometimes mistaken for each other. This factor trait, also a multiple one, refers to the tendency not to abandon a task. In one early study (Fernald, 1912) 12 manual training school senior class members and 116 reformatory prisoners were given instructions to stand with their heels off the floor until they felt they must give up. It is recognized that motivations appealed to the subjects' su-

peregos, so that results may be attributed in part to differential responses to authority figures. Whatever the basis, however, the highly variable results are important from a personological standpoint. Reformatory prisoners ranged in time of standing from two and one-half minutes to almost 53 minutes. The class members ranged from 12 minutes to two and one-half hours. This "willingness to withstand discomfort to achieve a good" (Thornton & Guilford, 1938) may be placed alongside (Eysenck, 1947, 1953) "keeping on at a task (plodding)," ideational persistence, "group prestige persistence" and even a reputation for persistence. This multiple factor has been related to what is called "level of aspiration" (Lewin, Dembo, Festinger, & Sears, 1944). It has been found (Ausubel & Schiff, 1955) that individuals tend to be relatively consistent in the discrepancy between what they say they are going to achieve on a task, like shooting targets, and what they actually have achieved in the past. One major aspect of the experiments on "level of aspiration" is that persistence of this variety has both socio-cultural elements and deep-lying intrapsychic elements. An individual may persist in some activity either because of his need to maintain his standing in a group or because of inner compulsions not immediately related to his present social groups.

4. "f" or *Fluency.* Although this is another multiplex of subfactors in the intellectual realm (Guilford, 1947; Guilford & Christensen, 1956), it also seems to be a composite of several dimensions of temperament, elation-depression, confidence-diffidence, talkativeness-tendency to be silent, activity-inactivity, and excitability-inexcitability (Studman, 1935). Even in intellectual functions like *Ideational Fluency* and *Associational Fluency* emotional and motivational features may be recognized. Deeply buried and persistent fears, for example, may affect the actual abilities to be fluent in such a way that the cognitive and orectic aspects cannot be disentangled.

5. *Tender-Minded vs. Tough-Minded.* It was William James who described this

[1] The student should refer to the many studies (Applezweig, 1954; Cattell & Tiner, 1949; Cowen, 1952; Cowen & Thompson, 1951; Cowen, Wiener, & Hess, 1953; Forster, Vinacke, & Digman, 1955; Goodstein, 1953; Kounin, 1941a, 1941b; Levitt & Zelen, 1953; Luchins, 1942, 1947, 1949; Pitcher & Stacey, 1954; Rim, 1955; Rokeach, 1949; Schroder & Rotter, 1952; Weisgerber, 1955; Zelen, 1955) and the reviews (Cattell & Winder, 1952; Fisher, 1949) which leave the confusion confounded. Perseveration's name is Legion.

syndrome of general aggressiveness toward the world coupled with a somewhat hard attitude, as opposed to a submissive and tender attitude. Along with *Conservatism-Radicalism* this trait or group of traits ·is regarded by Eysenck (1953) as one of two attitude factors showing up repeatedly in Western countries. An English study (Burt, 1939) has, to be sure, revealed a factor, having both positive and negative loadings on trait elements, one pole of which represents joy, sex, sociability, self-assertion, anger, and curosity, and the other represents disgust, fear, sorrow, tenderness, and self-submission.

American research, on the other hand, tends to fractionate these elements and make a number of traits out of the one which seems to support James. However, the massive (but vulnerable) research on the "Authoritarian Personality" (Adorno, Frenkel-Brunswik, Levinson, & Sanford, 1950) regards one of the characteristics of an authoritarian personality to be:

Power and 'toughness': Preoccupation with the dominance-submission, strong-weak, leader-follower dimension; identification with power figures; overemphasis upon the conventionalized attributes of the ego; exaggerated assertion of strength and 'toughness.'

The researchers considered that the toughness really serves as a defense against various sorts of weakness. Whether they are right or not, their contention does reveal the possibility that there may very well be a distinction between possession of a trait and the dynamics underlying such trait possession. This distinction is very close to the one Cattell makes between surface and source traits, suggesting that *Tender-Minded vs. Tough-Minded* is a surface rather than a source trait.

6. *Ascendance-Submission.* One of the few traits proposed on logical grounds which also remains substantially unitary in factor-analytic research, this factor represents the manner in which a person responds to others as above or below (or equal). Somewhat ironically, Allport (1928) in presenting a rationale for the A-S Scale

thought of this as two traits which nevertheless can be measured on a linear continuum. Factor analysis has, however, come to regard it as a bipolar trait having positive loadings on ascendant items and negative ones on items of submission. In line with his strongly individual-centered personology, Allport emphasizes that a person is not always consistently dominant or submissive, but that each person may have both dominance and submission trends, usually in unequal measure.

7. *Conservatism vs. Radicalism.* A factor which shows up in research of both non-factor-analytic and factor-analytic varieties as a general temperamental-social trait, this is possibly best described in the terms of one substantial study (Kane, 1950) as "liking the world already planned" versus "liking the world being planned." General as this factor-trait may be, however, it does not reach into all areas of the personality, even in temperament, for a number of factors of conservatism-radicalism relating to religion, politics, and social action have been described (Ferguson, 1939, 1940, 1941, 1942, 1944).

8. *I-E or Introversion-Extraversion.* Along with "*w*," *I-E* has been thought to be one of two primary personality dimensions by some British authorities (Eysenck, 1953; Vernon, 1953). American factorists have not generally followed the British inclination to regard *I-E* as a typological continuum along which individuals may be ranged from true introverts to true extraverts. They have instead tended to look upon this trait as a composite of several virtually independent traits, so that an individual can be an introvert in respect to some behavior and experience and an extravert in other ways (Carrigan, 1960). In reality, Jung (1926) upon whose typology both views depend gives bases for both interpretations.

The student may think that the division of thought on this factor is between British and American temperaments, rather than upon varying research results and theoretical interpretations. Actually, Cattell, who has been among the foremost critics of a unitary trait, began his work in Great Britain. And two British scientists (Reyburn & Taylor, 1940) found three factors in the supposedly unitary *I-E*. Cattell (1947, 1957a) has come around to regarding *I-E* as a second-order factor on account of intercorrelations of primary factors, but with great reluctance he has striven to rescue the original concept from what he calls "scientific disrepute." On the other hand, an American student (Lovell, 1945) of Guilford's took the latter's extensive breakdown of *I-E* and intercorrelated the results which can easily be interpreted (Eysenck, 1953c) to mean that just two factors, "*w*" and *I-E* underlie all 13 temperament factors in some of Guilford's breakdown.

Introversion-Extraversion is certainly complex if not multiplex (Carrigan, 1960). Most persons have a confusion in thinking about this widely known but possibly little understood trait. Everyone, both scholar and lay person, seems to agree that sociability of some kind is found in extraversion. But the introverted end of the continuum is a compounding of lack of sociability and neuroticism. This confusion may be part of the explanation that a number of popular psychologies urge their adherents to become more extraverted, as if being introverted were something bad. Neuroticism is, of course, "bad." In a different sense lacking sociability is "bad" in the eyes of some as well. So on either or both views introversion should be avoided. The historic basis for the confusion is shown by Eysenck (1947) to stem from Freud's concept of neuroticism as the extreme of introversion and Jung's identification of introversion not with neuroticism but with withdrawing. Research in recent years tends with some exceptions to follow Jung's tendencies rather than Freud's. Both Guilford and his associates (Guilford, 1945, 1930, 1934, 1936) and Cattell (1946, 1950, 1957c) accept the Jungian position, but they do not follow Jung's typology to any extent.[1]

[1] Identification of *I-E* with psychasthenia and hysteria respectively by Jung (1926) appears to

9. *Suggestibility*. Following a suggestion (!) by McDougall (1908), we may roughly identify this trait as the readiness to accept a conviction or engage in behavior without logically adequate grounds or because of motivations of which the individual is unaware. It is assumed here, as with most of these gross traits that there are several different varieties of *Suggestibility*, some of which may not be correlated closely with one another. In a sample of institutional patients Eysenck (1943, 1947, 1945) recognized at least two kinds of *Suggestibility*:[2] (1) "Primary" which has to do with motor behavior involuntarily performed by one person at the suggestion of another. Eysenck relates this type to a fairly old concept, "ideo-motor response," which is supposed to relate to the actions of a "dowser" seeking water with a "divining rod," or other similar supposedly involuntary responses. (2) "Secondary" suggestibility consists of following indirect suggestions. False perceptions may be induced in which equal weights are perceived as unequal or false judgments may be suggested in which the person is made to describe "the color of the tie the man was wearing" when in actuality the man was wearing no tie.

A third type of *Suggestibility* is not really separate from the second, but as a variant is called "prestige suggestibility." A long line of experimenters, following Sherif (1935) have set up conditions in which a person makes a judgment as to the

be both refuted (Eysenck, 1947) and accepted (Eysenck, 1953c) by Eysenck. Eysenck employs the term "dysthymia" to refer to the psychasthenic end of continuum, *Hysteria-Dysthymia*. Heron (1954) supports Eysenck's notion of a continuum running from dysthymic through normal introvert through normal extrovert to hysteric. Cattell follows Kretschmer's (1951) division of persons into schizothymes and cyclothymes with schizophrenics and manic depressives at their respective extremes. His factors A and F serve to cross-classify schizothymes and cyclothymes with introverts and extraverts.

[2] In a normal group (Benton & Bandura, 1953) the traits of "primary" and "secondary" suggestibility could not be identified; methodological difficulties in the study, however, leave doubt as to the validity of the results.

distance a point of light "travels" in the so-called autokinetic phenomenon (Chapter 3), or as to the length of certain lines, or as to the value of certain political opinions, art objects, or personages. After the subject is exposed to "prestige suggestion" in the form of real or invented judgments of people who could be considered important in the eyes of the subject, a final test of his judgment measures his change following "prestige suggestion." Much advertising and propaganda of other kinds depend on a widespread possession of this latter type of suggestibility.

Accepting the strong probability that there are a number of kinds of the trait *Suggestibility*,[1] we may suppose with Allport (1954) that it (or they) may have various relations: to hypnotism in that hypnotism does seem to be a result of direct or indirect suggestion; to "ideomotor response" in that sometimes some of us, if not all of us, move involuntarily under suggestion;[2] to hysterical dissociation in its response to direct suggestions; to conditioning in which suggestions of a direct

or indirect nature may be conditioned ones; to propaganda and crowd behaviors with their various kinds of suggestions; and finally to individual differences in interpretation of a situation facing an individual who is "suggestible," in that he may react to a stimulus in different ways depending on his understanding of it.

10. *Cyclothymia-Schizothymia*. Kretschmer (1925) believes this to be a major dimension of temperament, perhaps the major dimension, running from manic-depressive through cycloid through schizoid to schizophrenic. Correlated with this temperament dimension, according to Kretschmer are body types.[3] The pyknic, associated with cycloid disposition, is short and tends toward stoutness. The leptosome or asthenic, corresponding to schizoid, is lean and taller. The athletic body type is supposed to be emotionally different in physiological and psychological ways from the others, according to Kretschmer. It is the psychological dimension in which we are primarily interested, however, and it is here that we find that Kretschmer's position is not supported.

Eysenck (1950) reviews the evidence for the existence of a *Cyclothyme-Schizothyme* dimension and comes to the conclusion that the proof is not adequate despite an impressive group of experiments yielding positive results by Kretschmer and his followers. Schizothymes are supposed to be dissociators in contrast to cyclothymes who are supposed to be integrators. The

---

[1] As with other traits, the arguments over the generality of *Suggestibility* sometimes bog down in disputes over the value of certain tests presumably measuring the trait. Steisel (1952) reports that there is no relation between Rorschach indices of *Suggestibility* and other indices, including the autokinetic phenomenon. Harriet B. Linton (1954a, 1954b), however, criticizes Steisel's method and emphasizes the subtleties of the Rorschach and of the autokinetic phenomenon as a reason for Steisel's negative results, whereas her experiment found positive results. Young and Gaier's work (1953) cited in the text (Chapter 3) is more relevant to the problem of the generality of *Suggestibility*. Young and Gaier are careful to point out that their consistent results in comparing other variables of personality with *Suggestibility* in the autokinetic situation do not necessarily mean a comparable trait in other situations.

[2] An example of the direct suggestion of this type and its ideomotor response was cited some years ago when the great Notre Dame football coach, Knute Rockne, was addressing a group of men who asked him how he inspired his football players to such heroic action. Rockne responded by addressing the men as if they were his team, starting in a soft voice, then increasing its tempo and volume, and ending after a brief but intense speech with "Are you with me, men?" They rose and shouted, "Yes!" then looked at one another sheepishly realizing what had happened.

[3] Kretschmer has another general division of "viscous" or consistent temperament—like the viscosity of motor oil—which lies between explosive and phlegmatic. In private conversation a psychologist who worked with Kretschmer in the post World War II period assured the writer that Kretschmer has abandoned his contentions that temperament and body build are correlated. No retraction of the position has appeared in the psychological literature with which the writer is familiar. Confirmation of the possible retraction by Kretschmer himself may be disconcerting to some who have built hopeful systems on the Kretschmerian model. Of course, either the report may be incorrect—though it had all the earmarks of veracity—or if correct, Kretschmer may be wrong now, not the first time a man has abandoned a "true" position he once held.

former are presumed to be possessed of greater sensitivity to form and the cyclothyme to color in color-form tests. A higher "personal tempo" as shown in their motor behavior supposedly characterizes schizothymes than cyclothymes. Greater motor coordination, greater perseveration, and a higher level of autonomic reactivity to stimuli were believed to be possessed by schizothymes. Sad to say, the elaborate temperamental superstructure which Kretschmer built on his body-type theory turns out to be somewhat chimaerical. Eysenck's elaborate investigation (1952a) of normal persons, schizophrenics, and manic-depressives, demonstrates in a fairly convincing manner, through the use of many tests which should have revealed the existence of a dimension of *Cyclothymia-Schizothymia*, its nonexistence as a unitary factor. Another study (Brengelmann, 1952) cited by Eysenck, employing tests which were designed directly from Kretschmer's suggestions, produced a correlation matrix in which only two out of 28 intercorrelations were significant statistically, not a matrix from which a factor like the supposed dimension could be extracted.[1]

Is there, then, no meaning to the *Cyclothyme-Schizothyme* concept? We may suppose that there is, but not as the unitary function to which Kretschmer has held. In Cattell's research (1946, 1957a) three traits have emerged each of which has some characteristics of *Cyclothymia-Schizothymia*. Factor A in Cattell's system is named for Kretschmer's and is very much like the latter's clinical syndrome: Easygoingness, genial adaptability, trustfulness, warmhearted, emotional expressiveness, and generosity are opposed to coldness, suspicion, secretiveness, inflexibility, timidity, cynical hostility, and pessimism in this trait. (Other characteristics are named by Cattell, but these are sufficient to give the general flavor of the trait.) A second factor, H. *Adventurous, Autonomic Resilience v. Inherent, Withdrawn Schizothymia* loads positively on items of adventurousness,

love of excitement, impulsiveness, and limelight tendencies, as well as frankness and kindness, and negatively on fearfulness, withdrawness, inhibition, and obstructiveness. Factor L. *Paranoid Schizothymia v. Trustful Altruism* represents the withdrawnness of a frustrated, suspicious, hostile individual as opposed to gregariousness of a liking, trustful, unmalicious person. Factors A and H complement each other with the latter regarded by Cattell as more of a genetically determined trait than A. Like so many other clinically derived traits, *Cyclothymia-Schizothymia* represents real aspects of personality but turns out to be multiple rather than a single dimension.

Other "personality" traits in addition to those detailed here are found in the research literature. Some of them could be included rather than these which are here. One gross dimension which resembles a trait only roughly should be mentioned, *i.e.*, *Authoritarianism*. This over-all construct purports to be characteristic of an "anthropological species" (Adorno, *et. al.*, 1950) with high ethnic prejudice, conventionalism, power and toughness orientation, and hostility patterns generally. The "trait" is so multiplex a dimension and has so many ramifications that a whole book would be required to do justice to the research concerning it.[2] Other traits like *Variability, Insight, Personal Tempo,* and *Carefulness* are described by Eysenck. Research (Barnes, 1952) on psychosexual development employing factor analysis brings out two traits beyond the ones mentioned elsewhere in the text, *Externalized Aggression,* characterized by overt aggression and sadism, and *Exhibitionism,* which links impatience and a belief in the importance of money in an exhibitionistic pattern.

Interests and Values. Traits in this area of temperament-social functions overlap to a large degree those of the immediately preceding section of this chapter. Nevertheless, there is sufficient distinction to warrant separate examination. The over-

---

[1] The writer has not examined this study, but takes it from Eysenck (1953).

[2] Research can be followed in part in the following references: Frenkel-Brunswik (1949); Hofstaetter (1952); Jones (1953); Rokeach (1948, 1955); Siegel (1954); Sullivan & Adelson (1954).

lap is seen in a series of studies (Ferguson, 1939, 1940, 1941, 1942, 1944) on "primary social attitudes." These attitudes are designated as *Religionism, Humanitarianism,* and *Nationalism.* They are presumably attitudes toward social institutions but in reality probably have "personality" sources of a structural nature (Dreger, 1952; Guilford, Christensen, Bond, & Sutton, 1953, 1954). In addition to other studies making use of Strong's Interest Inventory, the Kuder Preference Record, and the Allport-Vernon (-Lindzey) Study of Values, several factorial researches have brought out factor-traits in the realm of interests and values. One such study (Sternberg, 1955) among college men, employing the Kuder, Study of Values, and the Minnesota Multiphasic Personality Inventory uncovered six trait patterns of which the following are the most clearcut:

I. *Aesthetic Communication vs. Practical Science*—an interest in humanities at one pole compared to a scientific, practical, but not untheoretical orientation at the other.

IV. *The Driven Extravert vs. the Pure Scientist*—a hypomanic overexpansiveness compared to a controlled scientific outlook.

VI. *Quantitative Detail vs. Social Welfare*—an interest in numerical and computational work compared with involvement in others' problems.

Another study (Brogden, 1952) utilized the Study of Values to determine the factorial nature of the scale. The latter is based on Spranger's "types of men," the Theoretical, Economic, Aesthetic, Social, Political, and Religious. A majority of the types appeared in the investigation, but the value-traits cut across the logically-derived types. This result is exemplified by citing three factors of the eleven found:

I. *General Aesthetic Interest*—which appears to coincide with the Aesthetic type.

II. *Interest in the Fine Arts*—which is distinguished from Factor I by representing a less general and a more Bohemian set of value reactions.

VIII. *Tendency toward Liberalism*—with Social and Theoretical items identifying the positive pole and Economic items the negative.

One of the most extensive factor analyses ever attempted (Guilford, *et. al.,* 1954), performed under Guilford's direction, employed 1,000 test items with over 1,300 subjects. Two factor analyses, each with 95 variables, were run; each correlation matrix contained over 9,000 coefficients! Seventeen factors could be identified positively from one analysis to the other. Guilford distinguishes among interest or motivational variables and temperament factors, but the sample of factors below distinguishes only between vocational and general:

1. *Vocational*
   A. *Mechanical Interest*—appearing in many studies, this factor is bipolar, opposing interest in mechanical apparatus and manipulations to sedentariness and cleanliness.
   D. *Social Welfare*—which unites a strong interest in the welfare of others with a nearly equally strong interest in wanting to dominate them;[1] a well-developed social conscience and need for explaining things to others are represented.
   M. *Business Interest*—administration, selling, and commercial contacts, a not inconsequencial interest pattern in our society.

[1] Another confirmation of the belief that egoism and altruism are not contradictory but complementary needs. The need to serve coupled with the need to dominate is evident in a number of persons who have made significant contributions to the welfare of mankind. Probably no other man of the twentieth century has stirred both religious and nonreligious persons as much by self-sacrificing labors as has Albert Schweitzer, who is justly acclaimed a modern Francis of Assisi. In his autobiography (1949), however, it is evident that he is not averse to being in command of others. In addition, he defends colonialism with some of the same paternalistic arguments colonialists with consciences of a tender variety have always employed. This combination of social service and dominance motives has in Schweitzer's case resulted in the production of remarkable achievements.

2. *General*

C. *Adventure vs. Security*—a caring for adventure and risk-taking as opposed to a need for comfort, system, and security.

F. *Cultural Conformity*—the assurance that one is abiding by his conscience (culturally conditioned superego) and by prevailing custom, together with a belief in competition.

O. *Outdoor-work Interest*—both outdoor and manual activity interest, with farming, forestry, and construction items represented.

It seems evident that the interest and value factors cited above are to be regarded as personality functions as fully as those which are usually thought of as "personality" traits. Whether these traits have deeper roots in drives and control functions or are close to being "functionally autonomous," they differentiate individuals from one another and are often more important in the workaday world than others more usually regarded as "personality" variables. *Mechanical Interest* and *Scientific Interest* as reported by a number of studies may be composites of other source traits, but their lasting nature in many individuals and the pervasiveness of their influence qualify them fully as "organized functions of the individual."

Before concluding this section, it is well to remind ourselves that a list of traits only begins the study of personality. Suppose then, that we have a list of traits of some individual, with the relative strength of each trait indicated by a score on an appropriate test. From this point we have two major, not entirely independent, directions we may wish to go. We may be interested in going in both directions for some purposes, but for others we need only pursue one course.

The first is that which clinical psychology employs very often, which is the discovery of why the individual is possessed of just these traits, and which ones are capable of being changed for the better. This is the way of psychodynamic investigation. A good share of the discussion in Section V

of this text is concerned with the psychodynamics of behavior. Not all psychotherapists are in agreement that it is necessary to trace present traits to their roots in order to achieve success in therapy. Some do believe that the way to relieve present inadequate traits is to expose their sources. Beyond psychotherapy, however, there is an interest today in the psychodynamics of normality, in tracing the taproots of traits of personality in the "normal" person, whose problems have not brought him to a psychologist or psychiatrist. This type of investigation gears in with child psychology or developmental psychology in general in the broad field of "personality development."

The other direction which we may take is to ignore for practical purposes how our individual came by his traits, confining our interest to what he can do with the traits he now has. This task is by far the more extensive one today. Personnel psychologists working in business and industry, school psychologists in academic settings, vocational and guidance psychologists in both schools and private settings, military psychologists in selection programs in peace and wartime, all make use of traits of personality derived from testing the person where he is and predicting where it is probable that he may go.

Many traits both common and unique have been discussed in this chapter. A review of individual traits here would be superfluous. One final observation, however, can be made in the light of the revelation of the large number of factors reported in these pages. After the reader has grasped the extensiveness of a list of traits necessary to describe any one personality, that is, a recognition of the many dimensions along which a person's characteristics may vary, some of these dimensions virtually independent of one another, he can no longer think in absolutistic terms of anyone. Only very roughly can one describe a person as "dumb" or "bright" unqualifiedly, or "slow" or "fast," or "radical" or "conservative" without specifying the degree of the supposed quality and sometimes even the particular brand, for there may be several different, possibly independent kinds of traits which go broadly by a general name. It is constantly necessary to emphasize that science in opposition to common practice finds the personality a very complex affair.

SUMMARY

By means of a factor analysis of one person on a number of variables measured each day for many days, meaningful factors have been derived which are unique, yet possess common features with those derived from analyses of groups of persons. These unique traits can be put together to make a "clinical picture" that is also meaningful. Other unique traits, not usually factorially-derived, include musical genius and other forms of genius. High (test) intelligence may be reported for some purposes as a composite unique trait of genius. At times genius may be related to madness, but no general rule by any means holds establishing traits of genius as equivalent to traits of psychosis.

Common traits may be of the surface variety, like *Character Personality Integration or Development versus Moral Character Defect, Neurosis, Psychosis*, or of the source variety like Cattell's "16 personality factors."

Behaviors may covary in patterns of a mathematically determined nature. A psychophysiological trait like *Pressure of Activity* differentiates persons, as do a number of psychomotor traits uncovered by the AAF. Relations between temperament and somatotype purportedly found by Sheldon have not been supported to the degree one might hope. Deriving from Thurstone originally, research in perceptual traits has broken up what appeared to be unitary functions into more specific traits of psychological import. Knowledge of factor-traits in these realms yields increased understanding of an individual personality.

Intellectual traits, starting first with Spearman's "g," have been multiplied by Thurstone into the Primary Mental Abilities, and by the AAF (and Guilford especially) into a much larger number than ever anticipated prior to factor analysis. Creative abilities have been described which have opened a vista of research and use of talent.

Temperamental-social traits have been proliferated, but certain basic traits are discernible, even though these may be divided by research. Representative of these are *"w" or Will, "p" or Perseveration, Ascendance-Submission*, and *Conservation vs Radicalism*. Factor-traits denoting dimensions of interests and values, like *The Driven Extravert vs the Pure Scientist*, represent important personality functions.

All these traits may be utilized in a psychodynamic investigation of personality.

QUESTIONS

1. How can factor analysis be used to investigate the characteristics of a single individual?

2. Discuss the unique traits of genius.

3. Give some instances of common surface traits.

4. Name several of Cattell's source traits.

5. What relation seems to obtain between somatotype and temperament?

6. Describe some of the psychomotor traits.

7. Describe some of the perceptual traits.

8. In what way are psychophysical traits important to the entire personality?

9. Relate "g" to the Primary Mental Abilities.

10. What are the Primary Mental Abilities?

11. Discuss Guilford's schema of the intellect. Describe several of the factors in the different areas of abilities.

12. Briefly summarize information concerning the most important so-called "personality traits." Which of these traits are the most practically important?

13. Discuss interest and value traits. Of what value are the analyses of the several interest traits?

SECTION **V**

PERSONALITY IN THE ADULT INDIVIDUAL: ECONOMIC STRUCTURE-FUNCTIONS: DISTRIBUTION AND UTILIZATION OF ENERGY

In our overview of personality in Section II the general structure of personality was described as conceived in different systems. At the beginning of Section III the one common theme of practically all of the systematic attempts to order data of personality was expressed, namely, that the functions are organized into larger and larger units. The largest groupings appear to be topographical, dimensional, and economic which constitute major cross-classifications of personality functions. To the first of these major sub-functions, a large portion of this book has been devoted. Within the topographical classification of functions we have found minor personality functions cross-classified into id, ego, superego, and role functions, into conscious and unconscious, and into central and peripheral functions.

Section IV regarded personality from a dimensional standpoint. Recognizing traits to be the basic functions of the personality enables the personologist to utilize the results of trait psychology and factor analysis to gain a deeper understanding of his subject. Although it is more difficult to hold the over-all personality of any one person in mind when enumerating either logical or factor-traits, precision is increased in regard to specific functions by taking advantage of the refinements introduced especially by factor analysis into personality research.

In the section which follows, gross economic structure-functions are broken down. This time, however, topographical and dimensional schemas are set aside to a degree and the personality regarded as a system distributing and utilizing energy. "Economic" is thus employed to refer to the manner in which balance—and imbalance—of functions obtains among the parts of the personality, in much the same fashion as economics as a science refers in part to the distribution of goods in a society. In addition, the term has the meaning here of the ways the person proceeds toward certain goals, how in this case he utilizes his energies in a directional manner.

"Energy" is admittedly hypothetical when referred to personality. It signifies a presumed quantity of capacity-for-action, displaceable from one function to another. Objection may be raised to a "mechanical pump" concept of personality supposedly implied by the use of an idea like "mental energy." But as long as the concept is recognized as having no real explanatory value, serving only as an analogy, there is no reason to deny its usefulness on the grounds that it was first suggested by nineteenth century physics. Although there has been a serious attempt in the preceding chapters to convey the impression that personality is dynamic, both dimensional and topographical concepts tend to suggest a static condition. Use of the term energy, figurative or otherwise, forces attention to the dynamic nature of personality. In considering personality from this standpoint alone, on the other hand, the opposite notion might prevail, that personality is not merely dynamic, but fluid, having no form or pattern in its movements.

Psychoanalysis introduced the concept of mental economics to psychologists. The presumed quantity of energy mentioned above is assumed to vary from time to time within any one person and to vary decidedly from person to person. This concept is a fruitful one in dealing with both neurotic and psychotic individuals. If, the theory goes, the individual's available supply of energy is consumed in conflict, he has little left over for the ordinary pursuits of life; that is, the energy is withdrawn from ordinary functions to carry on the extraordinary one of inner conflict. And the symptomatology of psychopathological persons seems to bear out the theory. Neurasthenia is one of the most characteristic symptoms of many such persons. And when the manic-depressive loses his conflicts temporarily, a surge of energy enables him to operate at greatly increased tempo (Hartmann, 1948).

The concept of psychological economics is also applicable to normal persons in terms of the distribution of available energy throughout the personality. We can think beyond traditional psychoanalytic exchanges of energy within the skin to the entire personality as conceived by modern personology. For example, whether agreeing with its originator or not, we can discuss the concept of a "style of life," of the movement of the entire personality in certain psychological directions as a result of the various energy exchanges within the personality (which includes interpersonal functions as well as intrapersonal ones).

It may not be obvious that the subject of psychological or mental economics is directly related to that of motivation. It is very definitely, for how the individual utilizes his energies within and without constitutes the very stuff of why he does what he does. It is well to remember, though, that despite the legitimate place for a specific discussion of motivation, anywhere one touches on personality, whether in its overall structure, or in any major or minor functions, he is dealing with motivation.

Although many aspects of psycho-economics could be taken up, only the most general functions of over-all distribution of energy and the general psychological movement of the individual are presented. The first general functions are called "autonomy and homonomy"; any other designation could have been used which would convey the movements within personality toward self-governing and toward relatedness with others. The second, dealing with constancy principles, is motivation in a relatively narrow sense. The third general function is termed "style of life"; but again any term could have been employed which conveys the concept of general psychological directions of the personality discernible by the individual or others.

CHAPTER **15**

AUTONOMY-HOMONOMY AND CONSTANCY FUNCTIONS

AUTONOMY, HETERONOMY, AND HOMONOMY [1]

More than any other personality theorist, Angyal (1941) whose concept of personality structure has already been presented (Chapter 4), has given us a generalized view of the economics of the personality in respect to what might be called centripetal and centrifugal energy distribution. Angyal speaks of the "trend toward autonomy" and the "trend toward homonomy" within the personality.[2] He does not restrict the meaning of "within the personality" to intra-organismic functions; Angyal, it may be recalled, thinks of personality as "a superindividual whole."

Trend Toward Autonomy

The term "trend toward autonomy" means both the utilization of energy within the personality toward self-government

and the use of the (assimilated) environment for self-maintenance and adaptation. Speaking of biological processes Angyal (1941) declares,

One of the essential features of living organisms, whereby they differ from any other object in nature, is what we might call their *autonomy*. By this is meant that the organism does not represent merely an inactive point, in which various causal chains intersect—as mechanistic philosophy assumes—but is, to a large extent, a *self-governing* entity. The biological process is not a resultant of external forces, but is, in part, governed by specifically biological endogenous factors. The organism itself is, to a large extent, the cause of its functions, that is, it is endowed with spontaneity. We could also say that the organism possesses a certain degree of 'freedom,' if we use the term in the sense of Spinoza and call free that which acts according to its own inherent nature, according to its intrinsic law, and not under the compulsion of exogenous forces.[3]

And again:

Selection, choice, self-regulation, adaptation, regeneration are phenomena which logically

[1] More than half a generation ago Stern (1935) employed similar terms to convey somewhat similar ideas. He referred to the self-preservative, self-developing portions of the personality as "autotelic," and the portions related to the environment as "heterotelic." In the latter are included "hypertelos," the personal regions of membership, "syntelos," persons of significance to the self, and "ideotelos," ideas and ideals.

[2] The terms are derived from Greek: *autos,* self; *nomos,* law; and *homos,* the same or like.

[3] Angyal Andras. *Foundations for a science personality*. New York: The Commonwealth Fund, 1941. Reprinted by permission from Harvard University Press.

274

imply an autonomy of the organism. Selection, that is, the search for certain environmental conditions and the avoidance of other conditions, is only possible in a being capable of self-directed activity. The various functions usually comprised under the term 'self-regulation' are another group of phenomena which clearly demonstrate the autonomy of the organism (Angyal, 1941).[1]

The caution must be interpolated here that Angyal's words do not imply a retreat from the principle of psychology, "Psychological events are caused." As his text demonstrates, Angyal believes in this principle too. "The organism," Angyal writes, "is subjected to the laws of the physical world just as is any other object of nature, with the exception that it can oppose self-determination to external determination." Self-determination may be just as lawful and "deterministic" as is external regulation; indeed a good part of Angyal's book which outlines his position is devoted to establishing laws of the autonomous behavior of the individual. Self-determined behavior is not capricious behavior of a hypothetical "free will" variety. Angyal's concept of autonomy accords well with Lecky's doctrine of self-consistency. Lecky (1945) wrote, "There is a coherence in the behavior of any single organism which argues against an explanation in terms of chance combinations of determiners and points to an organized dynamic system which tends toward self-determination."

Both Lecky and Angyal have stressed the process of assimilation, beginning with food itself but going on to psychological objects to be absorbed by the personality. Assimilation is regarded as a function (or set of many functions) of the individual whereby the environment is not just passively absorbed, but actively transformed by the individual for his own self-regulatory purposes. In the assimilation of food there is a process of energy transformation and utilization for building up and maintaining of the organism. Beyond the intake and utilization of food, Angyal cites sensory adaptations as autonomous functions which are important in the individual's adjustments as self-regulatory functions.

Lecky, carrying the concept of assimilation beyond its physiological meanings, points out that in conflict situations the individual endeavors to "take in" the environment in doses sufficient to handle and thereby overcome the conflict, growing psychologically as it were, just as the infant takes in food of a more and more varied nature and grows physiologically. Work by Mary C. Jones (1924) is cited by Lecky to support his psychological assimilation idea. The Jones' experiment is almost as well-known as Watson's (Watson & Raynor, 1920) study of Albert on "Conditioned emotional reactions." Peter, the subject of Jones' conditioning experiment, was a three-year old who had gained a fear of furry, woolly, feathery creatures and objects. In true Watsonian fashion Jones placed a rabbit near, but not too near, to Peter as he ate; presumably eating was a pleasurable situation. Gradually the rabbit was brought closer to Peter until he lost his fear and handled the rabbit easily. Generalization occurred to other objects as well. Lecky gives other examples of the psychological assimilation process, in one of which a two year old girl had been frightened when a police dog knocked her down in the street. She would often say, "Doggie won't bite me, Doggie won't bite me." Her father encouraged her to speak to small dogs while in his arms, until she could pat a dog's head and lose her fear.

These psychological assimilative efforts are recognized by clinicians in repetition phenomena in which a person may repeatedly carry out an activity which he fears in order to prove to himself that he can master it. As Freud noted, children may engage in play whose subject is a frightening or painful experience.

To be sure, the psychodynamics of fear behavior are not anywhere nearly as simple as Jones' or Lecky's experiments would imply—too many phobias have been so "extinguished" only to reappear in disguised form some other way. But even this kind

---

[1] *Ibid.* Reprinted by permission.

of process illustrates the main point Lecky intended, that the individual is seeking to master (assimilate) the situation for self-regulatory purposes. And the transfer of phobic energy to some other symptom tends to demonstrate the distribution and exchange of energy as conceived by psychoanalysts.

Heteronomy

Interfering to a degree with the trend toward autonomy is that which Angyal calls the "heteronomous," which he defines as "governed from the outside." The self-regulation of the individual is limited by heteronomous or outside influences. As is evident, Angyal is thus taking account of environment in the determination of life processes, but his is a more dynamic concept than that of a simple additive relation of H(eredity) + E(nvironment) or even of a multiplicative relation, H × E. For Angyal, life is a process taking place between the individual and the environment, which are the two indispensable poles of the life process. Not only is the autonomous trend *limited* by that which is heteronomous, however, but it is also *furthered* by the latter. The illustrations used by Angyal to demonstrate the trend toward autonomy even in lower organisms serve likewise to show how heteronomy both restricts and promotes autonomy. In geotropism, for example, the turning or involuntary movement of an organism earthward, a plant in response to gravitation sends its roots downward, a *positive* geotropism, but also sends its stems upward, a *negative* geotropism.[1] On the animal level a cat falls as a mass rather than as an organism, but by means of the "righting reflexes" succeeds in landing upright. These organismic activities are not to be viewed as suspensions of the law of gravity, only as additional determinants of the individual's behavior. Gravity acts upon the organism in a manner that facilitates the organism's activities, as for example, in the cat's

falling (though what the cat might think about such "facilitation" is a different matter). Gravity acts as well in a way that restricts activities. Albert and Peter were hindered by the heteronomous influences which engendered fear in them, but likewise heteronomy in the form of Watson and Jones facilitated the removal (or as least conscious lessening) of their fears. The normal trend in the life process, Angyal argues convincingly, is toward an increase in the relative value of autonomy over heteronomy in the "Autonomy: Heteronomy ratio," a ratio which differs markedly from individual to individual and species to species.

Trend Toward Homonomy

Before pointing out other than obvious implications for personology of the trend toward autonomy, which is limited or facilitated by heteronomy, the seemingly opposite "trend toward homonomy" needs to be considered. At the same time as the individual possesses and develops self-regulatory capacities and behavior, he is likewise a social being and developing superindividual functions. Even on a biological level the individual is not truly individual. Uterine existence is a process of interchange and mutual influence of mother and child.[2] Lactation in the mother after biological separation has meaning only in terms of the child. Human beings and creatures close to men have long maturational periods in which, as Angyal phrases it, parental care is, figuratively speaking, "counted upon" by nature. Psychological development inevitably includes development of functions beyond the organism, that is, roles, group membership and status. On this point the whole discussion on *roles* should be recalled (Chapter 10) as well as Angyal's statement quoted among definitions of personality (Chapter 2) concerning the superindividual functions of the personality. But the individual is more than an integral participant in social groupings,

[1] Lapsed-time photography, one method of studying plant "behavior," demonstrates dramatically both positive and negative tropisms.

[2] Therese Benedek (1952) calls the symbiotic relation of mother-child the "primary unit."

he is also part of a universe. We quote again from Angyal (1941), "For this principle we propose the term 'trend toward homonomy,' that is, a trend to be in harmony with superindividual units, the social group, nature, God, ethical world order, or whatever the person's formulation of it may be."

Complementary Nature of Autonomy and Homonomy

Although autonomy and homonomy seem to be contradictory movements within the personality, actually they may be complementary. Self-regulatory activities become in general more autonomous, paradoxical as it seems, as they are utilized for homonomous ends. Childhood and adult identifications with others, and especially the higher form of love which psychoanalysts have designated as object-relationships, do not rob the personality but enlarge it, to an extent limiting but also making its area of autonomy greater than before. Fundamental biological functions like sexual behavior find their self-regulation primarily in a social setting. The one who, for example, like Don Juan moves from person to person seeking sexual satisfaction and caring not at all about his partners' welfare or their existence as personalities, as long as they provide bodies, is among the least free, the least autonomous in his sexual life. On the other hand, he who merges his personality with that of his loved one in sexual union gains autonomy Don Juan can only long for.

So it is with other functions; in general, depending upon certain conditions, the one who partakes of group and ultragroup solidarities gains autonomy by his homonomous movements. The conditions presupposed are, to be sure, exceedingly important in respect to certain functions. For the autonomous exercise of political, religious, and educational liberties a culture and a society which foster some measure of independence are required. If this over-all matrix is absent, partaking in homonomous movements may suppress rather than enhance autonomy in political, educational,

and religious roles. Nevertheless, even in totalitarian societies the general principle of complementariness of autonomy and homonomy would appear to hold for most biological and psychological functions. The child psychologist thinks of the immense freedom for individual fulfillment which comes from learning to talk, a result of social life. And skills all the way from hunting, trapping, and fishing to unravelling knotty philosophical and mathematical problems are at the same time products of social living and productive of individual fulfillment.

Here it is necessary to call attention to deeper psychological meanings in these trends of the personality toward autonomy and homonomy. The issues which are raised in personology in connection with these trends are too basic to have escaped the keen minds of philosophers and psychologists throughout the ages. Ethical philosophers particularly have faced problems of egoism versus altruism, self-centeredness versus other-centeredness, self-love and love for others. The answers of ethicists and religionists have been varied, but the preponderance of opinion has been about the same as that to which psychologists have arrived, that man fulfils or "realizes" himself (Urban, 1930) in his larger, superindividual attachments.

There is a fundamental difference between ethics (or religion) and psychology at this juncture, however. That difference, which holds between psychology and many other fields of endeavor, is well-demonstrated in regard to the major life trends of autonomy and homonomy. In the philosophic tradition descriptions of behavior may occur which would prompt the psychologist also to conclude that autonomy and homonomy are generally complementary processes. But the philosopher is approaching such behavior from the standpoint of its oughtness, while the psychologist sees it as data to be classified and related to other psychological functions in a scientific rather than an ethical system. As an acute observer of men, Aristotle described the "lover of self" and the "just man" fairly accurately. The former is one who works to get an unfair share of the gratifications of his appetites and emotions: "People ordinarily apply the term 'self-love' to those who snatch for themselves an unfair share of these things." Aristotle continues in the *Nicomachean Ethics*,

> But a man who sets his heart always on doing above all what is just or temperate or virtuous in any respect, and who always and in every way chooses for himself the noble part, is never accused of self-love or blamed for it. Yet such a man, more than the other, would seem a lover of himself. At all events, he takes for himself what is noblest and best, and gratifies the highest part of his nature and yields it unqualified obedience. . . . He is then in the truest sense a lover of himself, who loves and gratifies the higher part of his being. . . .

So far Aristotle's position coincides fairly well with that of Angyal or Freud or others in psychology. But his description is in answer to the question, "Whether a man should love himself or someone else most," and he concludes that "In this sense (that of acting 'justly') then a man should be a lover of self, but not in the sense in which ordinary people love themselves."

To psychology such descriptions as Aristotle gives are not bases of ethical judgment but serve as data in a scientific system or in the clinic to be used for diagnosis.[1] That Don Juan is failing to achieve autonomy in failing to achieve homonomy is a matter of record, not of reproach. That Aristotle's just man is a better lover of himself than the selfish individual is a fact coinciding with multiplied clinical investigations, not a fact for congratulating the just man for his greater homonomy and consequent (or antecedent or simultaneous) autonomy. To psychology Don Juan's crippled sexuality is no more basis for condemnation than Byron's crippled body. The just man's nobility is no more reason for congratulation than his possession of a beating heart. The fact that a psychologist may and does condemn or congratulate testifies to his membership in the human race and to his inability to escape his cultural traditions; as pointed out in the early part of this text, he cannot so escape, and there is good reason for believing it better that he cannot. Yet the behavior which he and his fellow human beings exhibit has been better understood in many ways when approached scientifically rather than judgmentally—although psychology grants the ethical approach as a legitimate one as well.[2]

Thus autonomy and homonomy are viewed here not as ethical ideals but as gross functions of the human personality, ways of distributing (directing) the available energy of the individual in more or less self-regulatory and supra-self-regulatory activity. Whether psychologists agree with the distribution of energy concept, they are agreed on the fundamental movements of the individual toward self-determinative and other-determinative behavior. This agreement is found in the use of variants of S-O-R (stimulus-organism-response) rather than merely S-R as in the heyday of a naïve behaviorism. It is found in the burgeoning of social psychology along with the traditional emphasis on "individual" psychology. The agreement is found likewise in the enlarging theories of personality of recent years (Lewin, Murphy, Angyal, *et al.*).

---

[1] One point of disagreement between ethicists and psychologists very closely related to this basic disagreement is in the degree of ability an individual has to alter his patterns of behavior as deeply-ingrained as the ones under discussion. The ethicist *seems* to think that an intellectual analysis of the man's condition should lead to the man's changing for the better; if he does not change, he has "willed" not to, and is "bad." The psychologist believes that an intellectual analysis is not enough, for it does not penetrate to what makes the man act as he does. The philosopher thinks the psychologist is dangerously muddleheaded, condoning evil and incapable of ethical judgment, while the psychologist thinks the other is dangerously ignorant, priding himself on and in turn projecting his thoughts onto others in terms of a freedom neither he nor they possess.

[2] Commandments such as the New Testament's "Judge not" indicate that religion too has held to a nonjudgmental attitude at times.

Homeostasis and Constancy Functions

It was suggested previously that in the study of economic structure-functions of the personality, we are dealing with motivation more or less distinctly, even though we recognize that wherever we touch on personality, motivation is involved. The whole concept of motivation is so complex and so fraught with difficulties that to say we uncover some bases of motivation here is possibly presumptive. However, ignoring the many complications, we may venture to state that a great many personality data fall into place if we conceive of them generally as fulfilling the individual's movement toward self-regulation and regulation within larger than individual wholes. If we look upon energy-exchanges from a motivational standpoint, then, the biological concept of *homeostasis* proposed by Claude Bernard and elaborated by Cannon (1932) is suggestive as an explanatory key in self-regulation. Attention has been called to the fact that psychologists are more enamored of the concept of homeostasis than are biologists. Nevertheless, if an idea serves as a fruitful lever in understanding personality functioning as a whole, its specific applicability to physiological functioning of the organism may not be necessary.

Biological Homeostasis

On the biological level there has to be some term to describe the equilibrium process occurring within and between cells whether it *explains* this process or not. In blood and cell chemistry, for example, both clotting and anti-clotting factors are produced in such a way that an excess of clotting substances tends to produce anti-coagulants and vice versa (Heilbrunn, 1952). There seems to be a dynamic balance which makes life possible, an interactional equilibrium of forces which constitutes a self-regulating activity; called whatever physiologists may choose, the facts seem well-attested. Beyond the intraorganismic are balances achieved by the

organism with its physical environment, a process to which Cannon explicitly referred as homeostasis. The most commonly cited example here is temperature regulation; no matter what the outside temperature, within certain limits, the body tends to retain a relatively stable temperature (with diurnal fluctuations). Angyal, as we noted previously, suggests that homeostatic functions[1] are good examples of self-regulating functions along with selection, choice, adaptation, and regeneration.

While accepting homeostasis as a general biological concept, Nissen (1951) who qualified as a biologist as well as a psychologist, presents arguments against relating homeostasis *directly* to some forms of sub-human behavior. The bee builds hives and stores honey, even though a state of hunger may not exist, or if there is a state of hunger, the activity does not satisfy present hunger. The elaborate ritual of carnivore in selecting a site for elimination and covering it over, seems to serve no direct homeostatic function. Nissen does add, however, that the nervous system seems to operate homeostatically, so that functional expressions of nervous structure—in such apparently nonhomeostatic behavior as building nests, brooding, and feeding

---

[1] Freud and Breuer (1895) in *Studies in Hysteria* spoke of a *constancy principle*. Later, in *Beyond the Pleasure Principle* (Freud, 1920) Freud's summary of the meaning of the *pleasure principle* is referred back to the *constancy principle*. The *pleasure principle* could be given as an explanation of behavior but seems rather limited. Even Freud (1920) himself had to say: ". . . it is incorrect to talk of the dominance of the pleasure principle over the course of mental processes. If such a dominance existed, the immense majority of our mental processes would have to be accompanied by pleasure or lead to pleasure, whereas universal experience completely contradicts any such conclusion. The most that can be said, therefore is that there exists in the mind a strong *tendency* toward the pleasure principle, but that tendency is opposed by certain other forces or circumstances, so that the final outcome cannot always be in harmony with the tendency towards pleasure." (Reprinted from Freud, S. *Beyond the Pleasure Principle*. London: Hogarth Press, 1920 & 1950, by permission of Liveright Publishing Corp.)

young—may be homeostatic activity for the nervous system. We may add that if the research of the Danish naturalist Tinbergen (1951, 1953) is to be substantiated on "trigger mechanisms," in which one activity releases the next one which releases the next one and so on in ever more complex behavior patterns, the relevance of homeostasis to the kinds of behavior which Nissen regards as possible exceptions to homeostasis may be greater than is at present observable.

Psychological and Psychosocial Equilibria

Constancies. A logical extension of homeostasis as a *unifying concept* (Stagner, 1951, 1952, 1954) seems justified, despite criticisms of the concept as an explanatory force. Besides the usual biological processes classed by Cannon under the rubric of homeostasis, we may instance the perceptual constancies, as examples of homeostatic equilibrating processes. Size, color, and shape of objects tend to remain constant to the perceiving individual under most normal circumstances, despite objectively measurable differences and the corresponding alterations of retinal images which occur. Even classes of objects appear to have constancy properties for the perceiver. The possession [1] of such constancies has survival value, making them another facet of homeostasis in a large sense of balance achieved between organism and world.

---

[1] Stagner (1951) maintains that these constancies are learned. As Maze (1953) points out, this contention is not necessary. The mere possession of them is all that is necessary to consider them of survival value, regardless of whether learned or native. Maze's argument against homeostasis at this point, therefore, is not more cogent than Stagner's insistence that the constancies are learned. Maze's objections to Stagner's formulations help to prevent making an all-explanatory principle out of homeostasis, but Stagner justly considers Maze's view too atomistic. Regardless of considerable lack of correlation from one function to another, there is some unity to the individual which cannot be dismissed in a specificity of reactions that virtually have no relation to one another, as Maze seems to contend. Cf. the discussion on specificity in Chapter 3.

It is at this point, however, that there is hesitancy on the part of some psychologists to make inferences from internal biological processes which serve to keep the organism in a dynamic equilibrium as the external environment alters, to physically and socially adaptive behavior *between* the organism and the environment.

Whether biological constancy can be equated with the balancing process which obtains between the organism and its physical and/or social environment, *some* type of constancy principle or principles does appear to be operating in the individual's adjustments to his physical and social milieu. There is no need to strait-jacket many different kinds of constancy into one term, homeostasis, especially if the latter has to be stretched even to be called a "principle" in biological functioning. Nevertheless, some dynamic equilibria are present beyond biological processes. Social perceptions and social behavior generally may, in analogy to psychophysical functions, achieve constancy properties (Stagner, 1951, 1954). Patterns of dominance and submissiveness, for example, develop in some if not most social groupings in a kind of homeostatic way. In one coop four chickens inadequately provided with food developed a "peck order" in so exact a hierarchy that each chicken lower in the order showed a greater proportion of featherless skin than the one higher in the scheme of things. The nethermost hen had to be removed or it would have perished. Killing the one of lowest order is one way of maintaining equilibrium in the coop; when the lowest was removed, the other three could keep the dynamic balance in the dominance-submission pattern without complete loss to the lower hens.

A number of objections (Maze, 1953) have been raised to applying a constancy concept to more general personality processes. Only one is considered here. The first objection is that some behavior seems to be indulged in for the sake of bringing about not equilibrium but disequilibrium (*e.g.* Kluckhohn, *et al.*, 1953). This statement may be fairly easily answered, as

Freud (1950) suggested briefly in *Beyond the Pleasure Principle*, by calling attention to long-term equilibria versus short term equilibria. Freud spoke of the "reality principle" as operating to complicate the simple operation of a constant level of excitation; reality considerations may demand a short-term disturbance of the individual's balance with his physical and social environment in order to achieve a long-term balance.

A closely related set of processes is represented in Selye's (1936, 1950) "general adaptation syndrome." This syndrome is represented in animals and human beings by loss of appetite, aches and pains, loss of weight, and (as reported by human beings) by a feeling of being ill; it has other features not specific to any one disease. All of these symptoms may be in response to "nonspecific stress" which differs from the "specific stress" of oxygen lack or loss of blood, for example, which initiates specific homeostatic reactions. Certain endocrine changes are characteristic of the syndrome, especially in the anterior portion of the pituitary gland, affecting its production of ACTH (adrenocorticotropic hormone) and in the adrenal cortex to which ACTH serves as stimulant. In addition, the other master integrating system, the nervous system, seems to be involved also. Under nonspecific stress the organism first has an "alarm reaction" before adaptation has occurred, then the organism builds up endocrinological (and other) defenses whereby the stress can be handled. However, there are further reactions which may occur if the stress, like continued exposure to cold, is carried beyond the ability of the organism to "adapt" and the adaptation is lost in a stage of exhaustion (Selye, 1955). It is as if the organism had overreached itself in trying to meet the stress conditions. That there is a failure of the equilibration process does not disprove the existence of the latter in most cases.

Likewise in the breakdown of psychological equilibria no basis is found for denying the existence of a normal constancy process. In experiments with altered rooms where men look larger or smaller than we know they are or in illusions the constancy functions serve only to play tricks on us. They "overreach" themselves and create imbalance rather than the balance they usually subserve. But aberrations of a process do not negate its normal functioning.

Auto-Correctivism. On the psychosocial plane the individual may engage in behavior presumed to reduce his tensions externally and internally, but as with biological and psychological balancing attempts, his very behavior "unintentionally" upsets his social relations even more. A fellow or girl who longs desperately for others' approval and affection may drive others away by loud, braggart behavior. Fisher's (1937) "auto-correctivism" seems applicable here in that Fisher has shown that neurotic and even psychotic behavior can be understood to a large extent as attempts to secure a balance of forces within oneself and between oneself and others, attempts which "overshoot the mark." However, even these "over-shootings" strangely may be themselves ways of balancing the individual, of seeking adjustment of a sort.

A significant study (Michaux, 1955) illustrates what the experimenter terms a breakdown in "psychological homeostasis" which may occur in psychotic individuals, but also demonstrates auto-corrective processes in both normal and psychotic behavior. Matched groups of 48 normal male hospitalized or hospital employee controls and 48 variously classified schizophrenic subjects were presented two word lists. Each word list consisted of 40 words lacking a first letter, 15 of which could be completed by making a food word or a nonfood word; for instance "–orn" could be completed as "corn" or it could be "horn" or another nonfood term. Twenty-five words were "dummy" items which could not be completed as food words, *e.g.*, "–old." One list was administered just after the subjects had finished eating and the other just before a meal, with an effort made to fit the testing unobtrusively into an individual's routine. The general hypothesis on which the experiment operated was that normal homeostatic functions do not remain intact in schizophrenia. Experiments (Blake & Ramsey, 1951) preceding this one had indicated that normal subjects give more food responses in perceptual tasks when hungry than when satiated. This increase may be viewed as a homeostatic function: as the need for food increases, the perceptual threshold for food items is lowered. On a common experience level, any automobile traveler may ignore the dozens of eating places he passes until he begins to be hungry, when he then takes notice of them. But normal homeostatic fluctuations in many functions, including perception and apperception are said to break down in schizophrenia (Hoskins, 1946). The expectation, then, was that schizophrenics would differ from normals in *not* increasing their food responses when hungry.

Table 1 summarizes the results of this experiment. Mean numbers of food responses (word-completions) of normals

TABLE 1. MEAN NUMBER OF FOOD RESPONSES OF NORMALS AND SCHIZOPHRENICS UNDER SATIATION AND HUNGER CONDITIONS [1]

Psychiatric Status	N	Food Need			
		Satiation		Hunger	
		Mean	SD	Mean	SD
Patient	48	4.46	2.23	4.06	2.34
Normal	48	4.75	2.16	5.71	2.35

[1] Adapted from Michaux (1955).

and patients under satiation conditions (just following a meal) are different, but not statistically different; when not hungry, in other words, the two groups react equivalently to the word-stimuli as far as food responses are concerned. However, under hunger conditions, the normal subjects reacted as expected from previous experiments, with a significant rise in the number of food responses, while at the same time patients actually decreased their mean number of food responses. The decrease from satiation to hunger conditions in the patients is not significant, so all that

can be said is that there was no *increase* for the schizophrenics as there was for the normals. The hypothesis of a breakdown of *normal* homeostatic processes among the patients seems fairly well sustained.

An additional analysis of the data throws light on both the general homeostatic principle and also on the specific personality dynamics of schizophrenia which broadly represents a breakdown in "social homeostasis." When neologisms, defined for the purposes of the experiment as word completions not in an unabridged dictionary and occurring where food response was possible, were totaled and compared, these results among others obtained: (1) Controls (normals) gave 30 neologisms, patients gave 178. (2) In the patient group in satiation tests there was no significant relation between the number of food responses and the number of neologisms. (3) In hunger tests, however, patients scoring *high* on neologisms scored *low* on food responses, and vice versa.

In terms of individual personality reactions, what do these results mean? First, according to expectation, schizophrenics seem to have more need to distort perceptively than do normals. Second, and more pertinent to our present line of investigation, schizophrenics seem to be operating defensively (homeostatically?) against their own hunger needs. There are probably some very intricate psychodynamics [1] involved; but from the less abstract dynamic interpretation which the experimenter gives to his results we can see how another kind of homeostasis may be operating, even though under hunger conditions "psychological homeostasis" may break down in psychotics. In addition to the familiar withdrawal of the schizophrenic into autistic (self-oriented) behavior regardless of hunger or satiation, in his hun-

[1] According to psychoanalytic theory psychosis is determined principally in the oral period of psychosexual development, so that fixations occurring in and regressions to the oral period might engender abnormal attitudes toward food. Whether the theory holds or not, eating disturbances are not at all uncommon in psychoses.

ger state there appears to be a suppression of the homeostatically increased responsiveness to food found in normals; it is as if the neologizing were held in readiness to operate as a suppressor. Another authority (Abt & Bellak, 1950) is given credit for the idea that there appears to be a new "lawful" response pattern which takes over when the normal, homeostatically operating response patterns break down. This process seems to illustrate Fisher's principle of auto-correctivism.

In the light of biological, psychological, and psychosocial evidence there is, then, reason to hold that some constancy principle is operating in the personality. At any rate there appear to be similar constancy principles beginning with biological, even cellular, balancing factors, which within limits act as automatic checks upon one another. These principles extend to the psychological and psychosocial functioning of the individual. It may not be necessary to think of these operations as one principle; indeed, the differences between blood chemistry and schizophrenic behavior are great enough to make us question the unity of operations. But there are enough parallels in the various constancies to justify their being classified under some general category of behavioral tendencies.[1]

Need-Tension-Reduction

Although we may well suppose that homeostatic operations are present in all personalities, it is possible to fill in the general concept of homeostasis with specific terms, which we may with Murray, (1938) call "needs";[2] though much alike from individual to individual, especially where so-called "basic needs" are concerned, they are as individually tailored as features and fingerprints. Generally, the need-tension-reduction theory holds that (1) a need of some sort exists, anything from a physiological need for water to a feeling of wanting to protect animals or becoming a missionary; (2) either periodically or apperiodically the need is unsatisfied so that some balance of the individual is disturbed; (3) a tension is felt by the individual; and (4) the individual behaves in such a way as to meet his need and restore the balance. The cycle is usually illustrated by thirst or hunger; in the former case (1) a general level of water content is necessary for cell functioning (balance), (2) periodically the cells are depleted and the balance of cell and blood chemistry is upset, (3) through the failure of the buccal glands, the buccal and pharyngeal regions of mouth and throat become dry so that tension is felt locally in these areas, and (4) the individual engages in behavior (of varied kinds) leading to drinking water and restoring the water balance in the body (Cannon, 1929).[3]

[1] To go beyond the personality to larger societal units as Cannon and Dempsey (1951) do is to undertake a task not subsumed under personology. Historians, sociologists, and economists may take up where we leave off, asking whether there are homeostatic mechanisms operating in large social groupings and across major temporal spans. Arnold Toynbee (1947) in *The Study of History* seems to hold to some kind of homeostatic philosophy of history. Physicists and chemists also extend the question in another direction in respect to self-balancing cycles of atomic, sub-atomic, and super-atomic processes. Very close to organismic concepts of homeostasis are electronic concepts of feedback mechanisms such as are elaborated by Norbert Wiener (1948) in *Cybernetics*.

[2] Cf. Chapter 5 for Murray's system of personality structure. Prior to Murray, Freud (1925, Vol. IV, ch. 3) suggested that instead of his term "instinct" which had been misunderstood in many places the term "need" would be better. Murray himself traces the concept in some measure to Ach's "determining tendency" and to James' notion of instinct, as well as in larger measure to McDougall whose "instincts" and "sentiments" have the dynamic character of needs. Although Murray's is the most complete treatment of the need concept, Maslow (1943a, 1943b, 1948a, 1948b, 1950, 1954) has extended the treatment even beyond Murray, especially to those he terms "self-actualizing people."

[3] Some associationist learning theories (Hull, 1951; Hull, Hovland, & Ross, 1940; Miller & Dollard, 1941; Thorndike, 1938) lean heavily on this paradigm for explanation of how learning occurs. Thorndike's "Law of Effect" as finally stated maintains that acts which are followed by states of affairs, called "satisfiers," which the individual does not avoid or may even try to preserve or

There are difficulties in the way of utilizing this general theory, possibly of terminological origin (Cf. Chapter 5). Confusion results from the use of the term "need" to apply both to the state of the organism and to the object which complements the state of the organism. Sometimes we say loosely that water is a need of the individual, at other times that the individual has a need for water, need in this case referring to his physiological state. And going on to psychosocial relations the same confusion exists in saying that the individual has dependency needs or that a certain amount of dependency is a need on everyone's part. To clear up the terminological difficulty is a responsibility of need theorists. For clarity in the following discussion, the term need refers to the state of the individual; it may not be possible to be entirely consistent in this usage, yet virtually always the meaning can be reduced to a person's (dynamic) state.

Needs: Constant and Temporary. Another major difficulty in the need concept is not so easily dismissed. We may speak of a need as a state of the individual, but when there has been satisfaction of a need, can it be said that there is still a need in the individual? Say that the individual has drunk his fill of water so that he has met the water depletion of his cells. Does he still have a need for water? A mother has carefully fulfilled all the tasks called for by her love need for her child. Does she still have a need for caring for her child? This difficulty may be a terminological one also, though it is more, too. As states of the organism, some needs are constants of the individual, being relatively satiated or unsatiated, but in either case needs that continue. We can see how this principle holds for water need. In the case of a single cell, when the cell's quota is completely filled, the state of the cell is such that it does not at the moment demand water. But there is probably no time when some cells of the multi-celled organism do not demand water. Again, because we fill our stomachs and thus roughly "meet our need" for food, the organism's metabolic processes are still in need of the food stored in stomach or intestine. In the case of "vital needs," a need may be constant even though fluctuating in its demands.

Other needs may be constant only for a certain period of the individual's life. A need such as the demand for increased insulin in diabetes may be considered a "constant" of this nature when for some reason the islets of Langerhans fail to function properly; such a need continues throughout the remainder of an individual's life. More temporary, yet "constant" during the period of its existence, may be the feeling of oughtness a person has in regard to usage of forks at a formal dinner; this particular constant is part of a more general need which manifests itself rather permanently, that of desiring to abide by the social amenities. Some of the acquired needs (as opposed to innate or vital needs) may not be constants of the same kind as the vital needs, but they may be stronger at

---

attain, are selected and fixated. Consequently, conditions of satisfaction of needs are important in learning. Going a step further, Hull felt that learning can occur only when reinforcement occurs, that is, when either drive-reduction or drive-stimulus reduction accompanies an activity. The former, drive-reduction, is the satisfaction of a need; the latter is the direct release of tension by the application of a rewarding stimulus or removal of a noxious one. (Dollard and Miller (1950) call the drive-stimulus simply a drive. What is usually called drive, the inner urges which we classify as id, the physiological need, they call primary or innate drive.) Hull's statement of the principle of primary reinforcement is his famous Postulate III, the last formulation of which is: "Whenever an effector activity (R) is closely associated with a stimulus afferent impulse or trace (s) and the conjunction is closely associated with the rapid diminution in the motivational stimulus (S_D or S_G), there will result an increment (Δ) to a tendency for that stimulus to evoke that response" (Hull, 1951). No matter which way one conceives of the learning process in this type of association theory, needs ranging from primary drives to the most remote learned or secondary drives are postulated. Accordingly, the discussion on need in the text can be regarded as congenial to reinforcement learning theory. However, the text does not intentionally ally itself with one or another learning theory. For various, sometimes quite conflicting learning theories, the student should consult Bugelski (1956), Hilgard (1956), or Stolurow (1953).

times. It is not uncommon for a man to give his life for (thwart his vital needs in favor of) his country, his family or friend. These loves and others are states of the individual, needs which even when satiated still exist.

There are, of course, some needs which cannot be classed as constants, either as vital needs or as long-term acquired needs. Although each of these may be subsumed under some constant need, as a temporary expression of the latter, specifically such a need may be regarded as a temporary rather than constant need. When some physiological process is somewhat out of balance and the individual craves a special kind of food, he may temporarily have a very strong special need. Or a person may have a passing desire for a "splurge" in bright, gaudy clothing; once having indulged the desire, he may never again care to do so. The multiplicity of needs of this sort is evident; they seem not to be constants of the need structure of the personality. Accordingly, we may recognize temporary as well as constant needs.

Needs and Energy-Exchanges. When a need is inordinately thwarted ("inordinately" being a relative matter to the individual and to his various states), there is too great tension which either makes for major readjustments among the balances of needs or leads to breakdown. Several principles concerning the operation of needs in producing tension or too-great a tension and their balance or overbalance with one another, were suggested some years ago in an important but little known article on "needs and need-energy" (Skard, 1937). The author pointed out that an unsatisfied need "stores its energy," in that the energy available for the satisfaction is not discharged. Also the stronger the need, the less particular is the individual about its "satisfiers." A starving man is not "choosy" about the food set before him; the king in straits is not particular about the horse, "My kingdom for a horse." Further, when strong needs are unsatisfied, other needs tend to be neglected, and the desire to satisfy one need may prevent the satisfaction of another. And finally, within limits different needs may replace one another. This last point is illustrated by the replaceability of one form of sexual urge by another urge seemingly far removed from the original direct libidinal need. A hand-washing compulsion, a foot fetishism, a nervous tic, indeed almost any symptom of neurosis or psychosis has been shown by psychoanalysis to be a possible substitute for direct sexual gratification (Fenichel, 1945).

Basic Needs: Personological Meanings. It is not necessary or desirable here to list various needs except representatively. We should first have to start out with "basic needs," according to Murray's (Chapter 5) or another authority's listing. One child psychologist, for example (Thorpe, 1946), gives three basic needs which the child and presumably the adult has: (1) The organic need, to safeguard physical well-being and satisfy physiological requirements. (2) The self or ego need, to be recognized as an individual of worth. (3) The social or mutuality need, to be meaningfully related to others. Rosenzweig (Hunt, 1944, Ch. 11) believes that needs lie along a continuum: (1) needs for protection against loss or impairment of structures and functions; (2) needs for maintaining the individual's growth level; (3) needs for reproduction of the organism and a certain degree of self-expansion; and (4) needs for expansion in creativity involving symbolical as well as biological behavior.

To these lists could be added other variants. However, it is enough for us first to recognize that in general all such lists take cognizance of what Murray terms "biogenic" and "psychogenic" needs; the latter might more accurately be called "psycho-sociogenic" needs, if a parallel to "biogenic" is needed. Second, we are principally concerned with the personological significance of these needs.

Individualized, Culturally-Conditioned Expressions. One of the features in recent years characterizing the study of needs is the recognition that needs are not fixed entities unvarying from person to person but that these "basic needs" are all individually expressive of a person. Employing the more general term "motives," but referring to classes of needs among other factors, one writer states,

Any catalogue of human motives must involve an oversimplification of the unique processes of living organisms. Motives to which names have been applied are, in actual operation, unique processes, exhibiting manifold individual differences, as well as differences from time to time in the same individual (Sappenfield, 1954).

Another feature recognized today is suggested by, but not limited to, the use of "psychosociogenic" above. Even so-called "biogenic" needs are understood now to be "culturally conditioned." While it remains true that "Culture cannot create needs and drives out of nothing" (Brand, 1954), the anthropological and clinical facts which have been accumulating in respect to the psychosocial expressions of "basic needs," even the most "biogenic" ones, reveal many individual patterns from one culture to another as well as from one individual to another. Still another feature of basic needs, stressed by Murphy, (1947) in particular, is the interactional nature of the organism's need systems one with another and with the environment. We are carried back here to the extended discussion on consistency and integration of functions in the early portion of this text and to later discussion of roles (Chapters 3 and 11).

Cognitive-Conative Needs; Functional Autonomy. One exceedingly important consideration concerning needs is implied in much of the previous discussion. There are needs which are above the biological, most of which are more important to *human* life than the essential biogenic ones. These are the so-called "cognitive needs" (Maslow, 1948; Scheerer, 1954) which are better termed "cognitive-conative." For example, a thirst for knowledge may be psychodynamically related to organic oral, anal, or genital functioning; and yet, the intellectual pursuit of truth may have a tension in its own right that is fully as real as

is the libidinal tension in respect to sexual gratification.

Both opponents and proponents of need-tension theories have misunderstood these "higher needs" and their relation to "lower needs" at times. Opponents have claimed, because we cannot perceive the connections between cognitive and biogenic strivings that cognitive needs are virtually unrelated to the biogenic ones, or more specifically that tension-reduction does not apply to cognition. But clinical observation as represented by Freudian psychoanalysis and other kinds of analysis (Fenichel, 1945) can find devious but genuine ties between, say, a strong ambition to make a literary name for oneself and one's shame reactions to urinary practices. And learning theory analysis (Dollard & Miller, 1950) reveals the possibility that a professional man who supposed that his colleague envied and feared him for his superior intelligence developed dislike for his colleague basically as a homosexual reaction to the colleague. However, proponents of tension-reduction theories have sometimes erred when, having discerned in biogenic needs the roots of even highly complex intellectual functioning, they suppose that the higher are "explained" by the lower. To carry out the implied analogy of the previous sentence, it must be stated that the roots are not the tree.

That complex intellectual and social behavior has organic, biogenic components seems to be a fact, if we can generalize from hundreds of analyses of creative artists, topflight physical and biological scientists (Roe, 1953), and others whose labors are essentially cognitive. That thereby the cognitive endeavors are "explained" is to violate what explanation means in science, specifically, that "explanation . . . consists of describing *as fully as possible* the relations among variables." For an example, seeking a stamp collection may have anal-retentive needs in its composition,[1] but it also has a genuine curiosity about the geo-

[1] The psychoanalytic concept is that sexual pleasure derived from retention of feces is generalized to other activities of a retaining nature.

graphic originations of the stamps, an eagerness to find something new, a hope for satisfaction of esthetic needs, a desire to show philatelic friends one's new acquisitions, a longing for completion of a stamp set, a need to own something for "pride of possession," and so on. Each of these individual cognitive-conative elements probably has biological origins, but the very fact that the intellectual components are so prominent and the biological so hidden to most philatelists bespeaks manifold layers covering the latter, making the need a different one from a two-year old's simple anal-retentiveness, or a five-year old's genital exhibitionism.

If there is value to Allport's "functional autonomy" concept (Chapter 4), it should be found at this point.[1] Some activities, it will be recalled, are considered by Allport as being so distantly related to their original biological sources that they are to all intents and purposes autonomous. Allport agrees that theoretically all adult purposes can be traced to infant needs. But it does appear to be a process of unnecessary reductionism to insist that the highest cognitive needs are explainable only in terms of biological needs. William James, writing about the so-called "genetic fallacy," said, "By their fruits ye shall know them, not by their roots" (1902). Civilized man's activities are often far removed from their biogenic bases and even from their basic approach-withdrawal needs. A passion for studying and teaching history may, for instance, have originated in a reaction formation against the hostility generated by a history teacher who reminded the individual unconsciously of a hated aunt and may have been continued partly from sexual exhibitionistic needs fulfilled in the teaching profession. And yet, history and its teaching may have acquired positive interest values of their own, presently giving delight, yielding genuine social status, and providing bread and butter. The overlayings of learning and social interactional components of the activity are so prominent that the cognitive needs are relatively functionally autonomous, and the activity only very incidentally satisfies the original needs.

Stress should be placed on the relative nature of this autonomy, and recognition given to large components of the original needs in some activities which appear to satisfy "higher needs" only. Too much evidence is at hand today to deny that many interests and motives which seem to be autonomous are still in a very real sense functions of deep-lying fundamental needs. Allport's own illustration of workmanship in which the workman sets himself high standards even when it is to his economic disadvantage to do so can be shown in some instances to be very directly related to childhood needs. "I am a good boy, Papa. Look how hard I work." Or in another instance it may be, "I am not impotent. I am really fully capable, a real man. Just look at my work." Or even, "See how neatly I do things. I make nice little piles, real neat ones." These illustrations come from the clinic. The clinic can also provide a test as to the genuineness of the so-called "functional autonomy." If the individual has had some kind of analysis in which he has gained an insight of more than an intellectual nature into the biogenic bases of his behavior—he has seen the connections between his covert and overt functions according to what philosophers call "knowledge by acquaintance" as opposed to "knowledge by description"—what happens subsequently yields the test. If the person loses taste for the activity, as often

---

[1] Murphy's (1947) concept of "canalization" has similarities to Allport's "functional autonomy." Pierre Janet first spoke of "canalization," but Murphy's exposition is more widely known to American psychologists. It is a process of developing specific satisfiers for general motives, as in the familiar change from satisfaction of hunger by a general class of stimuli to satisfaction by specific foods. Murphy distinguishes canalization from conditioning by the criterion of degree of continuing satisfaction an object may provide. The hungry dog may become conditioned to a tuning fork, but he cannot eat it, so his response extinguishes; he may, however, develop canalization in respect to a special kind of dog biscuit. Interests which have become "functionally autonomous" may be said to be canalized.

happens after such an analysis, presumably the activity is not "functionally autonomous." If, however, as happens just as often, he carries on the activity, sometimes with even greater satisfaction than before, it has the relative functional autonomy recognized here.

Personalized Needs. Beyond so-called "basic needs," including both "biogenic" and "psychogenic" needs which in their various alterations can still be considered common to all persons, personology is interested in those which are unique to individuals, the ones which may be termed the "personalized needs." Physiological functions, including self-regulative and reproductive functions, express themselves in the psychoeconomics of the individual in *relatively* the same manner as in other individuals, despite the "cultural conditioning" mentioned above. It is in the "personalized" needs that we often find the more important movements of personality.

While we could break down an individual's life into specific activities and class every one of these activities as a response to a specific need, such as "the need to walk to the corner to pick up a newspaper," "the need to dig a spade into the ground to unearth some fishing worms," "the need to run a bit faster to catch the 8:05," and so forth, no science of personality could survive the overwhelming multiplicity of such categories. Instead in the life of the individual we concentrate on his major, long-term needs, like that of the man vitally interested in politics; for him tension mounts until he satisfies his curiosity and reads the speech by a prominent politician which was only barely mentioned by a radio commentator but which he knows is printed in full in the *New York Times*. Such long-term needs may be represented in the person who has to seek the retreats of Izaak Walton; he feels a mounting tension until, after engaging in myriad preliminary activities he can sit beside a stream with a pole in his hand or stand on slippery rocks in hip boots casting a fly downstream. Or—in a neurotic condition—the "personalized need" is seen in the individual who has to linger over his morning coffee longer than is necessary so that habitually he must run in order to catch a train which he knows comes at a certain time every morning and when he knows the distance between his home and the station and how long it takes to get there.

It is these longer-term "personalized" needs which are more important for an understanding of the person than either the normally operating basic needs (including general cognitive ones) or the specific tensions which may loosely be said to be his needs. As Allport states in connection with functional autonomy, ". . . the differentiating course of learning (reflecting ever more diversified environmental influence), acting upon divergent temperaments and abilities, creates individualized motives" (Brand, 1954). It is not only the *existence* of such "personalized" needs or individualized motives which is of importance. It is also the *individual patterns* of these needs which give us understanding of the person. On the whole the clinician working with projective techniques has found them of most assistance in working with an individual in revealing to some extent the dynamic balancing of his needs. In the normal person some needs, which in some other person might signify gross imbalance, are counter-balanced by other needs so that the first person remains "normal." But in the patients usually studied by clinicians certain needs, perhaps normal in themselves, are out of all proportion to the remainder of the need pattern. (It is well to recall here that we are speaking of *dynamic* patterns, distribution of energy.) And some peculiar personalized need may show up as a nearly integral function of a healthy personality or it may represent a whole area of maladaptive functions in an unhealthy individual.

A case picked by random numbers from the writer's file of "normal subjects" illustrates patterns of needs as well as some specific needs which stand out as "personalized." The individual, a married man 23 years of age, a college Junior, volunteered to serve in an experiment the writer was conducting. Just to volunteer might be considered serving an unusual need, although a college Junior today has been exposed under ordinary circumstances to sufficient social research in texts and other information media that it is safe to assume it is fairly normal for a person of this educational level to volunteer. However, the first characteristic which strikes the examiner going over this young man's file is the number of times he postponed or "forgot" or was late for his appointments. The first appointment was met satisfactorily, but from then on the record reads, "Second appointment—cancelled"; "Third appointment—late; called by telephone, he responded, 'I'm just getting ready to come'"; "Fourth appointment—failed to show up—though appointment made less than twenty-four hours previously; though stated he had called to get E(examiner)"; "Fifth appointment—made other commitments and did not show up." The requisite tasks were completed, but only by dint of repeated reminders from the examiner. And yet, the young man expressed strong interest in the research project. At a behavioral level we might in terms of need-tension say he was manifesting a need to be late. There are deeper level meanings most likely to such behaviors; perhaps a further examination of the record will help to reveal those meanings.[1]

The second characteristic of our young man's record to which our attention is called is a notation, "Keeps mentioning how tired the examiner must get writing. 'Do you use shorthand?' Seems to be dictating for literary purposes." And the style of the stories which were told in response to the TAT cards indicates partially the meaning of the notation. He said in part to one picture, "It wasn't long after their vacation started when word arrived from him, by telegram indirectly—better rewrite that—word arrived from his buddy, etc." Another place he said, "This is supposed to be written for kids. I'm not used to writing stuff like this, throwing big words around." Another note in between TAT stories states, "Subject made practice of taking picture, glancing at it, and putting it down on table. Examiner reminded him, picture was to be held in hand. Subject would pick up pic-

ture and look away while telling story." (For experimental purposes a strictly standard procedure had to be followed with all subjects.)

Already before analyzing the tests themselves, it seems that we can say several things about our young man's needs. He appears to have had tensions of an anxious nature which were aroused by the testing situation in which he found himself. Lateness and forgetting of appointments in clinical work usually manifests a hostility to the therapist or an excess of anxiety in respect to the counseling period. From the procrastination itself we could not infer that the same reactions held here. But we add the "distance" mechanism of making a literary game out of the TAT task, a not unheard-of procedure among neurotic subjects but very uncommon among normal subjects. And it seems important that our subject shoved aside the stimulus materials even when reminded repeatedly that he was to hold them in his hand. It is not unreasonable to hypothesize that the research project in which the subject was engaging was anxiety- or hostility-provoking. We are still only vague about what needs were served by his behavior, but we might venture the further hypothesis that he felt basically more insecure than do many individuals who are functioning normally. We can put our hypotheses to one test by examining the subject's projective protocols.

An important factor immediately confronts us in the number of words used to present the subject's Thematic Apperception Test stories in contrast to the variety in his stories. While he was fourth out of 30 subjects in word productivity, he was nineteenth in terms of the number of categories of response he employed. In other words, for all his need to be a producer of stories of high excellence, his record shows a relative paucity of content, too many words to say too few things. This poverty could be a mark of anxiety, especially in view of the young man's intelligence rating in the upper tenth of persons of his educational background.

Another important factor stands out boldly in the TAT record. The majority of the responses were concentrated in the following areas:[2] asserting adequacy and certainty; asserting the lack of anxiety, confusion, conflict, and distress; referring to dependency feelings and to the needs for affection, for help, for empathy; an excessive use of defense mecha-

---

[1] Of course, this analysis was made prior to the writing of these paragraphs. It is necessary to reiterate that the case was picked *randomly* for the purpose of illustration. But the analysis originally employed followed approximately the order as given in the text.

[2] Responses in the scoring system employed are comparable to Rorschach responses (Dreger, 1952).

nisms; and finally feelings of being persecuted and dominated. These concentrations were high relative to his own remaining response areas, but showed up as excessive also in contrast to other subjects, for out of 30 persons he ranked first in two of the areas listed and not lower than eleventh in the others. When we put the Rorschach results with those of the TAT, there is a balancing of the need picture to a considerable extent. Agreeing with the intelligence test, the Rorschach estimates the level of intelligence of our young man as high, and his *capacity* for productivity is higher than the rather thin output on the TAT would imply. There appear to be, as we guessed from his procrastinative performance in respect to the testing situation, hostile tensions of a strong nature within him. His capacities to handle his hostilities, however, are adequate, so that one would not expect him to "lose his grip." Anxiety is not absent from his Rorschach, but is not beyond normal bounds.

In any of the data gathered from and about the subject are there hints as to why there might be insecurity, hostility, and as much anxiety as there is? There are a few such hints. In the first place, he comes from and participates actively in a religious group which denies that a religious person has feelings of hostility. When a person is "born again," he loses the old, sinful feelings of hate and is always loving toward everybody. As a very intelligent and earnest believer this young man may well be trying to live up to these principles more consistently than others with less intelligence or less ability to see their implications, or than others with less earnestness. This last observation, of course, is inference rather than data of observation. It is borne out partly, however, by the behavior of the young man toward the examiner; even though the procrastination and postponements almost forced a conviction on the examiner's part that the tasks set were distasteful, the subject remained very polite in his demeanor.

There are many other facets to the test and interview results obtained from our subject, but enough have been presented to illustrate several principles set forth in the need-tension-reduction schema of energy exchange. First there are "personalized" needs, like his "literary drive" and the special forms of procrastinative hostility he appears to have. Second, there seem to be insecurities and anxieties which interfere with the utilization of his best potentialities, as manifested in the failure to produce a richly varied TAT record in spite of his intellectual capacity and his wordiness. Yet there is likewise a balancing of needs against one another, a dynamic pattern well off-center as far as the majority of normal subjects are concerned but one which prevents his functioning as an "abnormal personality." On the basis of his various test and interview profiles, it seems that as long as only normal stress conditions obtain—not too-great thwarting of his needs—the subject's need pattern is adequate for him; whether it is optimum or not is another question.

The need-tension-reduction concept provides us thus with an individualizing of homeostasis. Needs may be present as constants of individuals, all possessing biogenic needs, yet each having his own quantity and pattern of biogenic and psychosociogenic needs. As the individual interacts with other people and things, he develops his own "personalized" needs, many of which become for most purposes relatively functionally autonomous. Needs of all kinds unite in various patterns within the personality, including needs to play certain roles, which make the person an individual. For one person the appearance of a certain set of needs would portend abnormality; for another the same set is sufficiently well-balanced by other needs that it is balanced *for him*. Emphasis must again be laid on the fact that these needs and need patterns are dynamic; needs as "constants" are ever-changing interacting constants.

SUMMARY

The distribution and use of psychic energy is the concern of an economic viewpoint of personality. Following Angyal, we can consider the personality as utilizing its energy for autonomy or self-governing, assimilating the environment for self-regulatory purposes. Opposing autonomy trends is that which is heteronomous, governed from the outside. Homonomy tendencies are also found in the personality, those functions which fulfill the individual's superindividual needs. Autonomy and homonomy are complementary in that the individual realizes himself most in his super-individual attachments. Psychology views these trends not as ethical ideals but as gross personality functions to be described.

Understanding the exchanges of energy in biological homeostasis also aids in understanding motivation of behavior. Likewise, psychological and psychosocial exchanges which maintain a dynamic balance among forces appear to operate, giving us a greater understanding, even when "overshooting" occurs. In pathological states, normal constancy principles seem to break down. Individualization of constancy concepts can be obtained by viewing the need-tension reduction process in terms of both the constant and temporary needs of each individual, and the manner in which his needs are satisfied. Individualization of these processes can be realized also in recognizing what each culture pattern needs, as does each individual. "Higher needs" which are relatively "functionally autonomous" also allow for individualization of need patterns arising out of common "lower needs." With a recognition of these "personalized needs," of which there may be a great number, the personologist individualizes motivation studies; and a recognition of a dynamic pattern of needs yields a rich understanding of a personality.

QUESTIONS

1. Distinguish in some detail among autonomy, heteronomy, and homonomy.

2. In what ways do autonomy and homonomy serve as complementary functions?

3. How can homeostatic concepts be extended into psychological and psychosocial realms of personality? What is the evidence for some type of constancy principle?

4. In what way do need concepts provide understanding of the manner in which personality operates? How do the "higher needs" enter into this operation?

5. What is meant by "personalized needs"?

6. Compare concepts of need and trait.

CHAPTER 16

STYLE OF LIFE— CHARACTERISTIC MANNERS OF BEHAVING

Distribution and utilization of energy available to the personality has been regarded in terms of the functions of autonomy and homonomy—sometimes opposed, but usually complementary. Self-balancing and need-tension-reduction mechanisms have been discussed, which like autonomy and homonomy serve to move the person in internally-oriented and/or externally-oriented psychological directions. After a fashion, study of these functions assists the student of personality in answering the question of motivation, "Why do we do what we do?" And yet, these functions alone are not sufficient to explain the utilization of an individual's resources. Operating autonomously-homonomously or in a need-tension-reduction cycle, the personality could be but an ebb-and-flow process. While it may be true that a number of persons appear to be "going around in circles," for most normal individuals deeper and larger directional trends seem to be visible to the understanding eye. These trends are actually implied in the autonomy-homonomy concept and to a lesser degree in cycles of tension-reduction. But a more explicit inquiry is called for to determine the reality, if any, of such trends and their nature if they are more substance than superficial appearance. This investigation, then, concerns an alleged "style of life" or possibly "styles of life."

"What manner of man is he?" constitutes a fundamental question in personology as it does in ethics, literature, and religion. In the study of personality we are primarily concerned, however, with the dynamic aspects of a person's ongoing "style of life," his general, over-all directional functioning, if there is an "over-all functioning" characteristic of the individual. If there is not such an over-all functioning, then we should like to know the general resultant (in the mathematical sense) of his several major trends or, if they in turn cannot be identified, of his many minor trends. In using the term "style of life" there is a presumption that a style of life exists which the investigator may discern by more or less careful observation, or that he could discern if his instruments of observation were sensitive enough. It may be, however, that in the lives of many if not most people there is a lack of a single style and that "styles of life" would be a better designation.

DIRECTIONAL TRENDS IN GENERAL

There may be a "closure" capacity of a highly complex nature whereby students of human personality *must* find a unified striving in the personalities they study. It may also be that there *is* some such major directional trend in each individual personality. Or, as seems more in keeping with actual facts, some major directional trends have been discovered in many persons who have been investigated closely, and thus personologists have assumed similar trends in all persons. At any rate, a number of authorities have expressed the idea of a style of life in the individual in similar language.

Unitary Process or Characteristic Modus Operandi

Alfred Adler, whose expression "style of life" has come to be employed generally to designate "the individual's central, unitary, indivisible, striving process," as Murphy (1947) describes it, did not consider the existence of this process to be an assumption made about a person, but a fact demonstrated by investigation:

Individual Psychology, therefore, creates for itself a heuristic [1] system and method: to regard human behavior and understand it as though a final constellation of relationships were produced under the influence of the striving for a definite goal upon the basic inherited potentialities of the organism. Our experience, however, has shown us that the assumption of a striving for a goal is more than simply a convenient fiction. It has shown itself to be largely coincident with the actual facts in its fundamentals, whether those facts are to be found in the conscious or unconscious life. The striving for a goal, the purposiveness of the psychic life is not only a philosophic assumption, but actually a fundamental fact (Adler, 1927).[2]

This fundamental striving, for Adler, is the dynamic core of the person's individual style of life. Formed by the age of four or five (Adler, 1927), this style carries through all of life as a master purpose. At least this master purpose is pursued under

---

[1] Heuristic devices may serve to guide to further discovery.

[2] Adler, Alfred. *Understanding Human Nature.* (Trans. by W. B. Wolfe.) New York; Greenberg, 1927. Reprinted by permission of Chilton Co., Book Div.

ordinary rather than extraordinary stress conditions. By many devious ways, the individual strives toward his goal, to compensate for his original feelings of inferiority. But devious as the ways may be, a discerning investigator, Adler contends, finds that all of them in some way portend the goal. It is true that, given certain conditions in which the old established personal ways no longer subserve their purpose, conditions of extreme stress, for example, the old style of life may be changed and a new one substituted. But the essential fact in this view of Adler's is that there is *a* style of life, a life direction or dominant behavior pattern.

Others have expressed similar convictions about personality. Roback (1950) speaks of the "personal idiom," a characteristic *modus operandi.* Despite seeming contradictions of behavior and lack of integration of personality, the "personal idiom" reveals itself in nervous habits, in idiosyncratically stereotyped behavior, in greetings, salutations, handshakes, gait, posture, and in tone, modulation and articulation of voice and language. Angyal, too, in speaking of "the course of life as a Gestalt" implies that, though there are many digressions and imperfections in the process, the self-realization of a person as he strives toward becoming a meaningful whole is his recognized or unrecognized purpose; "To make of one's life course a meaningful coherent whole, a work of art which one creates by living, seems to be the greatest concern of the person, although he may be only vaguely aware of such purpose" (Angyal, 1941). In William Stern's (1935, 1938) discussion of "telic types," general purposive patterns or telic character types are considered which may not issue as a "pure" type in any one individual, but may constitute the general direction of the person's life.

Wolff (1933, 1935, 1946, 1948) likewise seems to imply that there is a major directional trend in a personality as seen in a person's gait and other expressive movements such as handwriting. Wolff's claims in respect to what might be termed a life style in the individual seem less extensive than those of the others mentioned above. Murray's contribution to the concept typified by "style of life" is the "unity-thema." In "The Case of Earnst" Murray writes:

Experience was to teach us that, though the reasons for many of the subject's responses were mysterious and much of his past entirely out of reach, it was possible to find in most individuals an underlying reaction system, termed by us *unity-thema*, which was the key to his unique nature. I say 'key' because if one assumed the activity of this unity-thema many superficially unintelligible actions and expressions became, as it were, psychologically inevitable. A *unity-thema* is a compound of interrelated—collaborating or conflicting—dominant needs that are linked to press to which the individual was exposed on one or more particular occasions, gratifying or traumatic, in early childhood. The thema may stand for a primary infantile experience or a subsequent reaction formation to that experience. But, whatever its nature and genesis, it repeats itself in many forms during later life (Murray, 1938).[1]

It is only fair to say that psychologists were not the first proponents of some major directional trend in the personality. There is literary precedent for psychologists' insistence on a life style, just as for most of the unifying concepts which personology employs. Novelists and dramatists have found dominant purposes overshadowing all minor trends of their characters' lives. In *The Brothers Karamazov* Mitya (Dmitri) manifests a driving purpose in first fighting his father and then carrying out self-punishment (by others' hands in part) because of guilt over his rebellion. With greater insight than that of lesser novelists Dostoevsky gives Mitya the Karamazov two-fold character, possessing love as well as hate. In the defense of Mitya against the charge of killing his father, the distinguished Fetyukovitch declares:

[1] Murray, H. A. *Explorations in personality, a clinical and experimental study of fifty men of college age by the workers at the Harvard Psychological Clinic.* New York: Oxford Univer. Press, 1938. Reprinted by permission.

Gentlemen of the jury, people like my client, who are fierce, unruly, and uncontrolled on the surface, are sometimes, most frequently indeed, exceedingly tender-hearted, only they don't express it. Don't laugh, don't laugh at my idea! The talented prosecutor laughed mercilessly just now at my client loving Schiller—loving the sublime and beautiful! I should not have laughed at that in his place. Yes, such natures—oh, let me speak in defense of such natures, so often and so cruelly misunderstood—these natures often thirst for tenderness, goodness, and justice, as it were, in contrast to themselves, their unruliness, their ferocity—they thirst for it unconsciously. Passionate and fierce on the surface, they are painfully capable of loving woman, for instance, and with a spiritual and elevated love. Again do not laugh at me, this is very often the case in such natures. But they cannot hide their passions—sometimes very coarse—and that is conspicuous and is noticed, but the inner man is unseen. Their passions are quickly exhausted; but, by the side of a noble and lofty creature that seemingly coarse and rough man seeks a new life, seeks to correct himself, to be better, to become noble and honorable, 'sublime and beautiful,' however much the expression has been ridiculed (Dostoevsky, 1879–1880).

Thus beneath the external, observable trends and even the less obvious guilt reactions, Mitya's style of life is one of seeking love and affection denied him by his dissolute father. Subtly and with great psychological understanding Dostoevsky moves Mitya through vast episodes but keeps the "unity-thema" as an often hidden but ever present *leitmotif* characteristic of the young Karamazov. Other instances from literature could be cited, but this one suffices to represent the littérateur's need to delineate a character's style of life which shows through his vagaries and seeming inconsistencies. Indeed, without such a binding thread a literary production seems like a collection of news items.

Styles of Life

Is the scientific evidence sufficient to justify the literary writer's more or less disguised assumption that there is a characteristic style of life or to justify the psychologist's construct of a unity-thema in each person? The answer has to be in the negative. A review of the pros and cons of the continuity and consistency of personality functions (Chapter 3) as well as other considerations, does not warrant our supposing a high enough degree of unity to the personality to be able to subsume all minor trends under one grand theme, call it what we may. Terming Adler's concept of the style of life the greatest effort at unity thus far encountered in defining the personality, Murphy points out difficulties with the idea. The major objection Murphy offers concerning the generality of the style of life is summarized drily by the statement, "The generality is less than one hundred per cent in reality . . ." (Murphy, 1947).

Perhaps Adler's experience reveals that the striving for *a* goal in a purposive way is a fundamental fact and not a philosophic or poetic assumption. Other clinicians with perhaps less brilliant intuition than Adler's are hard put to it to discover in every one of their clients a dominant trend subordinating all other trends to itself. Even with modern techniques of analysis which multiply one's diagnostic powers the clinician sometimes finds himself with personalities that appear not to be moving in one direction but in many directions, sometimes opposed and sometimes parallel, but scarcely reducible to one. Using the language of trait psychology Allport (1937) contends that solely in the unusual personality is one and only one "cardinal trait" or "radix" or "master-sentiment" found. Most persons instead, he declares, have several "central traits," together with other secondary ones. Allport's statements are tantamount to saying that there is not one style of life, but rather there are a number of styles of life in the individual.

Though some clinical and experimental evidence favors the unity-theme as a basic purpose of the personality by which most if not all functions of the personality may be interpreted, in part the assertion of such a life-purpose for every individual falls in the category of faith analogous to that of the last century preacher who maintained

that "Every man's life is a plan of God." It is difficult to see how the proposition, "Every man has a master purpose in life," could be proved or disproved. If we say that in many cases we have not been able to find a single style of life, the answer could be that we have not tried hard or skillfully enough. If all we can find is a set of master-sentiments in a dynamic lattice as Cattell might say, or a number of major factors from a factor analysis, or a handful of central traits, or only a group of dominant needs, reply may be made that our mistake is that we have not *yet* discovered the ruling passion, the style of life. But an hypothesis which has not *yet* been supported by the best scientific endeavor must be regarded for the time being as scientifically unproved, not disproved, but unproved. On the other hand, the opposite view, that there is *no* such style of life, is unprovable; as statisticians say, "The null hypothesis cannot be proved." Far from denying the possibility, the scientist instead hopes Adler and others are right in their contention, for if one master urge is present in everyone, the task of the scientist for prediction, understanding, and control is immensely simplified. Until however, a reasonable amount of evidence —it is hard to determine how much—enables us to make the inductive leap, Adler's position appears to be more faith than science.

A view more in line with evidence now at hand is that most individuals possess several main trends of personality. And we are forced to conclude that some persons are just drifters, moved this way and that, first in an autonomous path then a homonomous one, or in various vector resultant directions depending on the dominance of one need at one time and another at another time. Although general autonomy-homonomy trends may be discernible, many persons may never develop what might truly be called a style of life.

Furthermore, as Murphy declares in connection with Adler's concept of a style of life, if any generality of purpose or general movement of a whole personality does arise in anyone, it does not come into existence all at once but slowly—it seems to be a dynamic pattern developed over a period of years, an achievement of adulthood, not as Adler felt, something clearly apprehensible (to qualified observers) in childhood. The facts gathered from most fields of investigation do not appear to bear out the contention that every man can say consciously or unconsciously, "This *one* thing I do——." As an heuristic device in the hands of a clinician the concept of a style of life may serve to bring together seemingly disparate portions of the personality in a meaningful whole; as an actuality in *every* case it is questionable. Perhaps billions of persons of past and present have never been dominated by any single style of life even though they may have had several major sentiments or central traits. For the remainder of this chapter we should translate style of life into "styles of life" if the latter term is not used explicitly, inasmuch as the presence of several trends or movements is here assumed.

Style of Life and Type

The concept of type has been scorned in modern American psychology, while at the same time in Great Britain Eysenck has sought to undergird a typology of a sort by factor analysis and inferences from factor-analytic studies. In this text it is assumed that there are no true types, for there seem to be too many opposing movements in the personality to classify any person as one type or another. However, gross tendencies of an individual may give some justification for characterizing him more by certain relatively consistent patterns than by others. In this sense only does an individual classify as a "type." On the "Guilford-Zimmerman Temperament Survey" he may have enough extraverted characteristics in both thought and behavior (as he perceives them) to show that he is moving generally in an extravert direction, so that for convenience we may call him an extravert type. It is somewhat disconcerting, to be sure, to recall that Jung's theory of types, on which the GZTS is

based, forces us to consider whether our man is basically extravert or whether his responses on the test are only overt manifestations constituting one end of the axis whose other end is a basic introversion.

Another man may score high on the Allports' "Ascendance-Submission Scale" as an ascendant individual. For convenience we may classify him as an ascendant type—though again we bear in mind that the Allports do not deal in types, but in traits, so that an "ascendant type" is contrary to the theory of the very test whose results we take to classify the individual. If in our analysis of any one personality there seems to be enough evidence to classify a man loosely as a type, two cautions must be kept in mind: We mean that his general directions of life (styles of life) seem to point in one direction more than in others, but that there are many other directions in which his energies are diverted which are not the main one. And second, as some (Cole & Bruce, 1950) point out, if we utilize the type concept, a type is not a pigeon hole but a point of vantage from which to make further investigation of the individual. With these strictures in mind, then, certain more or less commonly directed styles of life may in some instances be so pronounced that a man may be regarded as a type.

GOALS AND SUBGOALS

No value seems to be found in asserting a single, all-encompassing purpose, yet personology does not deny the existence of goals and sub-goals in the personality. Homeostatic and need-tension-reduction biological exchanges of energy can be described in terms of goals and sub-goals. General autonomous and homonomous movements may be subsumed under goal-seeking behavior. The principle accepted in scientific investigation that psychological events are caused is not a denial of the existence of consciously or unconsciously selected goals. Nor is that principle in contradiction to the existence of strivings of the individual (conative tendencies) in one direction or another. When an individual says, "I am going downtown now," or "I have made up my mind to marry Jim" or "It will take us twenty years to pay it out, but it's worth the effort," the least that can be said is that there exist certain goals or sub-goals for the individual whose decisions have been made at these junctures, certain directions of movement toward destinations either consciously or unconsciously selected. A half century of clinical research and another (concurrent) half century of animal and human experimentation on the astoundingly complex bases of goal-directed behavior, whether the turning of a rat at the choice-point in a maze or a man's vocational decision to be an engineer, have taught us that extra energies or supposed powers like "will-power" have little to do with the realities of conation. But the movement of the individual in the direction of either certain perceived or unknown goals (in psychoeconomic terms the flow of his available energies in definable channels) can scarcely be doubted.

Teleonomic Trends

One of the most fruitful concepts for expressing what personology means by goal-seeking is Floyd Allport's (1937) "teleonomic trends." Somewhat in contradiction to his brother, Gordon, he contends that "traits" are only abstractions from personality, not descriptive of anything within the individual; designating a trait merely gives an individual's position along a social continuum. Therefore, a scientific study of the individual can only be made by positing a "telic continuum" of behavior trends which describe a person not just in terms of traits, i.e., his various positions along social continua, but in terms of the purpose or purposes his behavior fulfills for him. These teleonomic trends are conceived by Allport neither as teleological or purposive in any supernatural or nondeterministic sense nor as consciously purposeful, but instead as descriptive of *what the behavior accomplishes for the individual*. The test of whether a teleonomic

trend covering wide or limited areas of the personality actually is present is to set up the apparent trend as an hypothesis and test the hypothesis.

Teleonomic Trends in "Senseless Behavior." This concept of teleonomic trends is especially helpful in dealing with behavior that seems to serve no logical purpose. People's tics and phobias and compulsions and amnesias *appear* to be senseless. Many of the "slips of speech"; the unreasonable forgettings ("I know it as well as I know my own name") of normal persons; and catatonic, homicidal, or suicidal behavior; hallucinations; delusions; and "crazy ideas" of those not so normal *appear* to be senseless.

When one asks what purpose the behavior serves, what the behavior accomplishes for the individual, then he is in a position to discover some sense in the "senseless behavior." Freud found in the "psychopathology of everyday life" and in other behavior which appears meaningless, meanings which make sense of such behavior. But even behavior which on the surface makes some sense but not enough becomes more meaningful if we consider the direction in which the behavior is tending.

In a counseling session one counselee failed to produce anything of significance for a long time. The counselor, then, asked him to free associate. At first he stayed silent for a period. Then he began to pour out words, expressing a number of ideas to which he had not given voice previously, but meticulously including in his stream of thought everything of such a minute nature that the production came out in a torrent of trivia which concealed more than it revealed. As the counselor picked out the few salient objects to comment upon or question, the counselee responded as if to a third party. "Why does he say that?" or "Why does he ask that?" and continued pouring forth a host of words. The schizoid pattern of employing the third person was duly noted by the counselor with the mental note, "What is the meaning of this—do we actually have incipient schizophrenia here?" As for the free— too free—association itself, the only interpretation the counselor could place on the entire performance was that it hinted at a strong trend of resistance in the dynamic processes of the personality. It was a clear demonstration of resistance in the psychoanalytic sense; an individual may overtalk in free association and then inquire with injured innocence when apprised of the fact, "But you told me to say everything, didn't you?" The counselee's use of the third person and his over-production appeared to mean, "All right, I have to free associate, do I? I'll do it—with a vengeance. *He* is not making me—I prove it by not even addressing *him*—I am doing this for myself."

Without further supporting evidence an interpretation of a "teleonomic trend" could not be sustained. Other evidence was available, fortunately, including a previous counselor's description of the hours the two sat and sat, while the counselee said absolutely nothing, and a pattern of refusal to conform to many male requirements in our society, together with other negativistic factors, made the interpretation plausible. Behavior in the one session taken by itself might have been chalked up as peculiar or unusual, but with other data in the background it seemed to reveal a teleonomic trend: the behavior appeared to serve a purpose, even though the counselee seemed unaware of its deeper nature. The obvious purpose was to comply with instructions; a relatively widespread inner purpose was probably to refuse to comply with these and many other extra-counseling instructions.

Having reasonable evidence of a broad trend of resistance running through a good portion of the personality, one turns to the next question logically following, "As many pieces of behavior fit into the pattern which this young man seems to have, what further purpose does this trend serve? Is it but a subgoal which points in the direction of even a more general goal? Are there other trends which taken with this one will serve to illuminate the more obscure but more important purposes these behaviors and trends subserve?" Unfortunately, in this particular case not much more opportunity was given to gather data. The young man withdrew from counseling which was getting too close to his sensitive spots. When he requested counseling again, the counselor had moved from the city. Enough progress had been made, however, in uncovering other "teleonomic trends" lying behind his academic and religious behavior to convince the counselor of the strong possibility of a major trend, that many of the disparate behaviors, traits, and trends served the purpose of striving to break the psychological symbiotic relation established in infancy between the boy's mother and himself and apparently never broken. This notion had to remain in the hypothesis stage because of the circumstances.

Many more similar examples are necessary, gathered with the express intent of testing hypotheses of hidden trends where the more obvious trends do not adequately explain some form of behavior, in order to sustain the concept of underlying teleonomic trends. But there is too great an accumulation of clinical data, to say nothing of literary instances, yielding "motives behind motives" to dismiss the concept summarily. Behavior which seems to serve no logical purpose may become amenable to explanation if one seeks for trends which are not readily observable.

Teleonomic Trends and Character. Another aspect of goal-seeking behavior and teleonomic trends should be brought out here. This is the relation of these trends to *character*. From the economic viewpoint character may be conceived of as the persistence of trends, the continued expenditure of energy in constant directions. Indeed Stern (1935) included his "telic types" under the section on character in his famous text. Kipling's expression of the requirements of being a Man, although definitely not phrased to the liking of psychologists, includes the maintenance of effort in the direction of a goal. "You'll be a Man, my son!" Kipling avers, in part:

If you can force your heart and nerve and sinew
  To serve your turn long after they are gone,
And so hold on when there is nothing in you
  Except the Will which says to them: 'Hold on!' [1]

Character has been discussed more fully in Chapters 8 and 9, so there is no need to elaborate here beyond pointing out that

[1] From: Rudyard Kipling's Verse Inclusive Edition. Copyright 1910 by Rudyard Kipling. Reprinted by permission of Mrs. George Bambridge and Doubleday & Co., Inc.

character regarded as a group of persisting teleonomic trends is not essentially different from character regarded topographically or dimensionally (*Persistence, Character* or *Superego Strength, et. al.*)—the viewpoint is different and probably the preciseness of a factor approach pinpoints more accurately the characteristics of these long-term trends.

Persistence of Goals

In the context of styles of life as expressed in teleonomic trends, an old, familiar question arises which was discussed in Chapter 3 at length. The question asked before was essentially how consistent is an individual from one time to the next and from one place to the next. From a goal-seeking standpoint the problem presents itself in the form: How persistent are specific goals? To illustrate the opposed answers two almost contradictory interpretations of the same data to which reference has been made before, may be cited. (Cf. Chapter 10.) Gordon Allport and his colleagues (Allport, *et. al.*, 1941) made a study of refugees who had fled Nazi persecution. To these investigators the outstanding characteristic of the refugees was their resistance to social catastrophe. Though they had been subject to intense suffering and hardship and to being uprooted from their homeland, there really had been few basic changes in their personality structures, or so concluded the original investigators. Where changes did take place in what we might call the trends of behavior, these changes invariably seemed to accentuate trends in the personality already present. On the other hand, the critical review (Newcomb, 1950) of the refugee study, making use of the very data provided in the report of the investigation, concluded that most likely much more basic changes took place than Allport *et al.* believed. The reviewer for the sake of argument granted that there were no catastrophic changes in those who managed to escape, for they fled rather than change. But who knows what changes took place in those who remained? Bettelheim's

(1943) study of concentration camp prisoners and Curle's (1947) analysis of British returnees from enemy prison camps are cited to support the possibility of fundamental changes which can occur.

Although these matters with which we are dealing are partly speculative, if we combine need concepts with goal-seeking behavior concepts like that of teleonomic trends, we find some tentative answers, perhaps only as good guesses to be tested by further investigation. The combination of need and goal concepts suggests: (1) That as long as a need persists the individual moves in the direction of the satisfying goal; in case frustrating or blocking obstacles become too great, more potent needs are generated so that the individual moves in other psychological directions. The combination also suggests: (2) That if the need persists, even though other stronger needs supervene the general direction prompted by that need may be maintained. Finally, there is a suggestion: (3) That when the need no longer exists for the individual, or the goal is no longer achieved by his action, the individual *may* not continue to move in the direction of the goal which serves as a satisfier of the need.

The possibility that persistence of certain behaviors may be present without the existence of need or purpose is suggested by Maier's experiments (1949, 1954). These studies represent a host of learning experiments on the persistence of behavior under normal and abnormal conditions. Maier trained rats in discrimination problems, requiring them, or forcing them with an air-blast, to jump from a Lashley jumping stand to a goal consisting of two cards, one in an upright position. Roughly, with various adaptations, rats learned to choose a card in either of two positions or with either of two designs, regardless of position, by being rewarded for success and punished for failure. When the rats had learned the discrimination thoroughly, the experimenter then altered the reward-success sequence so that for the previously rewarded behavior the rat was sometimes punished and sometimes rewarded. In this conflict situation many rats developed "neurotic" behavior, peculiar patterns very similar to that of human psychotics. When conditions were stabilized, following the inconsistent or frustration type of reward and punishment situation, it was found that a number of rats had become "fixated" on their neurotic behavior. A rat, for example, may have produced in the frustration period what has been called "neurotic-anxiety-to-fail" behavior; this type consisted of jumping with his body turned so that he could not possibly get through the opening where the card was placed. Such a rat may have continued to exhibit this paradoxical behavior, each time falling down into a net, even when the frustration conditions were no longer present. Maier terms the "fixated" kind of activity "behavior without a goal."

Maier's explanation, that the compulsive neurotic behavior produced in his rats is a different kind of behavior from that with goals involved, may be valid. In such a case there must be recognized a class of behaviors, probably including the vast majority of neurotic and psychotic processes, which are goalless in the sense that they serve no recognizable purpose of the individual. On the other hand, another explanation [1] of compulsive neurotic behavior is that it tends to reduce tension, and is thus rewarded behavior, or in other words it does serve a purpose, it does have a goal. In the rat on the jumping stand, there is observable tension built up when the conflict occurs. Doing something, anything, jumping to a card or to a design or compromising by jumping abortively, is successful in relieving tension; the animal is at least out of the conflict situation and thus is rewarded, despite the punishment he may suffer in striking the wall, the unyielding card, or the net below. A new situation is created, with the goal *now* a partly punished escape from the conflict situation. As long as the tension created by the

conflict is greater than the punishment accruing from the escape activities, the rat will continue to try to escape, because his greater tension is relieved. He has "learned" in a twisted way that his escape attempts are rewarded. His neurotic persistence of goals is satisfying his need to be free from excessive tension. That this latter explanation is preferred to Maier's in this text does not detract from the immense value of Maier's work, especially in defining "fixated" behavior of the kind which he found in his rats and in experimentally producing the kind of behavior that parallels so much of that found in human beings.

Although Maier's experiments have been presented in general psychological and not directly personological terms, there are individual patterns of rat behavior which fit into further analysis from a personological viewpoint. In the Maier experiments differences from rat to rat may first be found in the form of stereotyped "neurotic" behavior developed in the no-solution problem situation: Most rats develop a position habit, invariably jumping to the right or left position no matter what the correct card may be, but the rest ordinarily develop a habit of jumping to one of the symbols regardless of position. Again, in one of the experiments rats learned two tasks of discrimination, the first different from the second, then they were subjected to a frustration situation of random reward and punishment. Out of 60 rats 54 persisted in their second response for 160 trials (though seven varied once out of the 160 trials), but six of the animals abandoned their second response and developed other responses. One animal showed variability of response for 30 of the experimental trials, and one showed variability for all 160 trials. Other kinds of differences among rats subjected to the same stimuli show up in the other experiments.

In some ways the rat's behavior throws light on human behavior. One of the favorite questions students ask is, "If such-and-such happens, an individual's loved one dies, he 'goes crazy,' he is put in a con-

[1] There may be other different interpretations of Maier's work.

centration camp, etc., what will he do?" Although caution must be exercised in extrapolating from rat to human behavior, an *a fortiori* argument may be used in the answer to this question. If there are many individual exceptions to a general rule of response among rats to stimuli which are as nearly alike as experimentally possible, then how much greater should be the individualized reactions of human beings, who have so many more complex drives, needs, and purposes than have rats, to situations which are not as similar to one another as the standardized conditions of the rat laboratory. An adequate answer to the question includes a statement that a person's response depends in part upon what he brings to the situation. In terms of the economics of personality, responses depend in part upon what teleonomic trends are found in the individual, what his long and short term needs and goals are. It is fortunate, of course, for a science of personality that these trends and goals and needs are somewhat similar from person to person, much more so in respect to basic id factors, yet also to a degree in the realm of higher mental processes and roles.

Looking back over the preceding discussion, we can conclude that possibly only a few, if any, individuals possess a master motive or single style of life. Nevertheless, that behavior is motivated by long-term and short-term goals, teleonomic trends or whatever they are called, is not denied by personologists. A possible exception may be observed in neurotic behavior of a "fixated" variety, yet even such behavior may yield to analysis in terms of goal-seeking.

REPRESENTATIVE STYLES OF LIFE

Even though the evidence does not allow us to accept for most persons a style of life which can be said to be *the* trend of his life, to which all else is subordinated, there are certain representative styles which tend to characterize many individuals. If we recognize that opposing or at least somewhat inconsistent trends may also be found, it may be hazarded that some individuals are characterized at any one time as possessing a major trend or style of life. In considering such representative styles, we shall first discuss generic patterns, then special patterns within the generic and finally, illustratively, certain individual patterns.

Generic Trend Patterns

William Stern's "telic types" were mentioned briefly above. The first "type" which Stern depicts is that of the *autistic* individual whose movements seem predominantly to be in the direction of himself as the goal of his own acts. He is an individualist, a subjectivist, an egoist (not necessarily egotist), whose emphases are on what events and individuals mean to him personally and whose environment is utilized to gratify his own aims. The second telic type is the *heteristic* individual whose orientation is toward other people and toward abstract ideals. He is characterized by movements away from self to the extent sometimes of "selfless" behavior; he conforms to group expectations in a manner similar to Riesman's (1950) "other-directed type" who operates by the process of paying close attention to "signals from others." Stern emphasizes that autistic and heteristic telic types are limiting cases, that in any one case the type may be only the predominating tendency. Intermediate between these extremes is a kind of ideal telic type, the *introceptive* who combines both autistic and heteristic tendencies operating together to bring about self-realization in the process of serving others. The introceptive person does have ideals—ideatelic trends in Stern's terms, keeping the original concept that these are not types in any static sense, but *movements* of the individual—ideals of an abstract nature, principles and norms of behavior like "a sense of justice," but the introceptive person is not a slave to them. He organizes them and subordinates them in accord with his own self organization and the concrete demands of the situation.

Others besides Stern have offered designations of generic trend patterns in the light of clinical or experimental observation. One fairly well-known classification of behavior trends in children (McKinnon, 1942) is based on observation over a period of five years of 16 children from a beginning age of three to age eight. In this small group four general patterns were found: (1) *Conforming*, behavior which is molded by others, though including much constructive activity. (2) *Caution*, manifesting a lack of confidence, and signifying dependence. (3) *Invasiveness*, aggressive and self-assertive behavior. (4) *Withdrawal*, or unresponsiveness. Ten of the children continued in the same pattern of behavior from three to eight. Where there was change from one pattern to another, it tended to be toward conforming. The least likely to change was the withdrawal pattern. Although the N was small, the conclusions have been regarded with respect because of the extensive longitudinal nature of the observations and because others' observations seem to fit in with these conclusions. The classification needs cross-validation on another sample of children, for it is a notorious fact that patterns of behavior which correlate well in one sample tend to prove less well correlated in a second sample.

Another widely cited classification of major dynamic trends is Horney's (1945). Horney claimed that an individual may be generally: (1) moving *toward* other people, (2) Moving *away from* other people, or (3) Moving *against* other people. These movements may be roughly equated with the above-mentioned trends. It is not necessary to say that they all fit precisely into a similar classificatory schema; according to the understanding of scientific models set forth in the early pages of this text (Chapter 1), different classification schemes, not precisely identified with one another, can be expected to be applied to generic behavior trends. Yet it is significant that, among many others, three authorities with heterogeneous approaches should derive general trend patterns of a somewhat allied nature. Stern's telic types appear to be the most general set of such trends.

All of these general personality trends or movements are extremes or ideals of directional trends, scarcely if ever represented in any one individual. Both common and scientific (especially clinical) observation of human nature unite sometimes in purportedly discovering generic trend patterns in many persons, autistic or heteristic or introceptive or whatever terms may designate similar patterns. In respect to any one personality, we may well ask, "Are there enough evidences of individual trends to consider that this individual has a major direction in life which could be characterized by one of Stern's or others' dynamic trend patterns?" If we do not expect every minor trend to subserve a master trend, if we can recognize that in most persons several major trends may be descernible, and if we are not surprised to find some individuals with contradictory trends, a cautious affirmative answer may be given in a number of cases. We do not have to surrender the hard won specificity of science from Hartshorne and May to factor analysis to answer in the affirmative for some one person. Intensive analysis has usually thus far revealed contradictory patterns of thought, feeling, and behavior which run counter to the observable generic trend in an individual. Enough is known now of personality to know that extraverted role behaviors may very well, as Jung maintained, serve almost antipodally to an introverted feeling structure within the same personality, that central and peripheral may be looking different ways, that various levels of the personality, conceived dynamically, pull in different directions.

The very existence of conflict within the personality shows that there are opposing trends. If, however, we borrow the figure of speech from matrix algebra of a vector resultant, we may obtain a picture of some generic trend in the personality. Vectors (lines with both measured length and direction) issue from a common point of origin. They may point in any direction, positive or negative, but they may be added (vectorially) in such a manner that a single line may represent all the different lengths and directions. So in personality a "vector resultant," as Lewin believed, may represent all the contradictory trends issuing as a generally autistic or heteristic or introceptive style of life or any similar general trend pattern. It is a different thing to say that a life style is such a vector resultant of many often opposing trends than to say that all the subordinate movements of the personality join in a single grand movement. The latter, as conceived by Adler, signifies a purposiveness to personality neither proved nor proveable. The former is a manner of assessment of personality trends which has no more teleological significance than the physicist's vector diagram of positive and negative physical forces.

Special Trend Patterns

To have greater understanding of an individual not only must we know the over-all direction of his movements, if any are present and discernible, but we must also know something of special major trends within his over-all directional tendencies. There are so many of these particular trends which research has revealed that only two representative patterns are given.

Leadership and Followership. Vital to any society is the problem of leadership and followership and the question as to what makes a good leader or a good follower. Leadership has been investigated intensively by social scientists, followership not nearly as intensively or extensively, a contrast suggested by the two references to followers in the index of Lindzey's *Handbook of Social Psychology* (1954) compared to 18 on leadership. Too many thorny problems are present in research on leadership and followership to detail them now.[1] It is enough to say that leadership

seems to be a role function of the personality which depends on both ego, id, and superego factors as well as on situational determinants. Although definitions are exceedingly difficult in this area, roughly we may say that a leader is one who is voluntarily accepted in a group as an initiator and sustainer of group endeavor. Such a definition may subsume headship. Technically, a head is one whose exercise of leadership is the result of his official position guaranteed by a group's structure; however, the head may not be a leader even though he initiates and sustains group endeavor, for the group may not willingly accept him.

A follower may roughly be identified as one who accepts voluntarily another's leadership in group endeavor. A slave would not necessarily be a follower in this sense, although since the time of the ancient Hebrews, who longed to return to the fleshpots of Egypt, it has been recognized that a slave's dependency needs may be satisfied by following his master.

Leaders' and followers' roles may be interchanged from time to time as the situation calls for one kind of leader and then another. "The Admirable Crichton" can be a butler (and, according to his own expressions of belief, is a follower in the sense of the definition above). He may then assume the role of leader on the castaways' island, only to return again to his followership status after the return to England. Sir James Barrie's dramatic genius recognized the interaction of role and situation before modern research undergirded the principle that different occasions call for different kinds of leaders.

The fact, however, that certain individuals tend to become leaders under a variety of circumstances, and most individuals generally play the role of follower, no matter what the circumstances, gives us the right to consider that leadership and followership may be personality trend patterns of a more specific nature within the generic trend patterns. Most communities in the Western world if not everywhere contain persons who are "naturally" looked

[1] Freud's (1922) early discussion on *Group Psychology and the Analysis of the Ego* gives fruitful psychoanalytic suggestions. The best review with which the writer is acquainted of both empirical studies and theory of leadership-followership is found in Gibb's article in Lindzey's (1954, ch. 24) *Handbook of Social Psychology*. Stogdill (1948) gives a review of personal factors in leadership.

to for decisions in important community affairs. "Before we do anything about this matter I think we ought to hear what Ned Smith has to say about it." And these individuals may be the ones who are counted on to carry out the leadership functions of the community. "We have come to you, Mr. Jones, because we know you can secure the cooperation of the town better than anyone else." These leaders may be ones who have moved from one community to another and have gained a similar kind of leadership in their new locations to that which they had in the old. College and university campuses also know those who were leaders in high school and who have become the same in college.

Yet in village or campus affairs the nature of leadership activities must be specified or else the leader is not a leader. A local "town leader" who is elected to offices in civic clubs and benevolent enterprises, is (probably) not the leader in the local saloon where a group gathers every afternoon for a poker game and defers to the opinions of *their* acknowledged leader who never attends a Rotary Club luncheon. Although a campus leader may be president of his fraternity, elected to the student body government, even be sought out for study help by his fellow students, in most cases he has little aptitude for gross motor coordination in sports, seeks no berth on the football team, and has no leadership role at all on the football field, a very important adjunct to most campuses. In reality, an over-all view of leadership and followership, especially in the light of research data, leads us to believe that in most activities most of us, including those who may seem to be generally classed as leaders, are followers, though in specified areas some of us adopt leadership roles more often and for a longer time than the majority.[1]

[1] As stated in the text there are few researches on followership other than clinical reports. There is, however, a unique military report of leadership research which also includes investigation of the function of followership. In a study of leadership, followership, and friendship (Hollander & Webb,

Cognitive Styles. Another instance of special trend patterns has been called "cognitive style." Reseach in this area (Holzman, 1959; Klein, 1953, *e.g.*) reveals some persons as *levelers* or *sharpeners* in their perceptual-cognitive behavior. *Levelers* tend to "play down" new features of their environment, feeling a need to assimilate new things as just examples of older experiences. In clinical investigation these persons are found to depend on external supports and authority and tend to be repressers (Holzman, 1959). In the laboratory in discrimination of tunes they hear the "figure" tone so much like the

1954) two investigators administered a sociometric test to 187 Naval Aviation Cadets in eight sections during the last week of a 15-week pre-flight training course. Three questions constituted the test. Assuming that he was assigned to a special military unit having an undisclosed mission, each cadet was asked to nominate from his section, with which he had had intensive group interaction, three cadets whom he considered best qualified to lead the unit, and three least qualified. Second, the cadet was to assume that he himself was the assigned leader of the special unit and to nominate three whom he would want as part of his unit and three he would not want. A third nomination form asked for the names of three cadets from his section he considered his best friends. Scores were assigned to each man on the three variables on the basis of the nominations, and these scores were intercorrelated. The results are shown below.

The most obvious relation observed in the table

INTERCORRELATIONS AMONG LEADERSHIP, FOLLOWERSHIP, AND FRIENDSHIP

Variables	r[1]
Leadership and Followership	.92
Followership and Friendship	.55
Leadership and Friendship	.47

[1] All coefficients are significant beyond the 0.1 per cent level. Differences between coefficients are significant beyond the one per cent level. Table adapted by permission from Hollander and Webb (1954).

is that leadership and followership are so highly related. Eighty-five per cent of the variance of the leadership nominations is associated with the variance of the followership nominations. For the followership and leadership questions high reliabilities "ground" tone they tend not to be able to discriminate. *Sharpeners* have contrasting tendencies. Other "styles" of this nature are found in those who tend to be relatively undisturbed by distracting stimuli, *focusers*, and those who are distracted easily by internal or external stimuli. Still others have other "styles" of a perceptual-cognitive nature, such as being users of broad or narrow categories in estimating as diverse ranges of phenomena as the number of minutes the average person spends in eating per day and the number of ships entering or leaving New York harbor per day (Pettigrew, 1958).

Further special trend patterns could be cited besides leadership and followership and "cognitive styles." These could be as particular as the consistency of reproduction of filled and unfilled time intervals (Young & Sumner, 1954) or the judgment of the upright by visual or postural cues (Witkin, *et al.*, 1954) or as general as orientation toward originality (Wilson, Guilford, & Christensen, 1953). All of these may still be viewed as special trends in the ongoing life of an individual, possibly correlated with other factors to make up a general "life style," though on the whole, modern research tends to regard them as limited in scope. However, these trends *may* be consistent for an individual across several related tasks and from time to time.

(for this kind of test) strengthen any conclusion which might be drawn from this very strong relation. What broad conclusions can be drawn from this experiment? The sociometric technique is only one method for assessing leadership and followership, yet, insofar as it represents the major aspect of leadership and followership, voluntary acceptance, we are justified in affirming the well-known dictum, that good followers make good leaders. There must be an emphasis on a person's being a *good* follower, for others who would not be chosen either as good followers or as good leaders may still be followers of a sort, and those chosen as "bad followers" may also be followers. In other words merely being a follower does not make one a good leader. Additionally, we may say with the investigators that leadership as measured by sociometry cannot be equated with popularity; others (Stogdill, 1948) had found before that leadership selections are not "mere popularity contests."

Trend Patterns of Individuals

It would be a bit ironical if there were not included in the discussion of life styles, in addition to generic and special trends, some instances of individuals in whom such life styles can be observed. In our consideration of "personality" we cannot allow ourselves to lose sight of "personalities." The larger patterns of trends or the less general ones are not disembodied dynamic patterns but are found in persons if at all; they are not patterns of feeling, thought, and behavior divorced from flesh and blood.

Patterns Discerned by Psycho-Literary Methods. As indicated previously, characters in literature may be permitted greater over-all unities of purpose and general styles of life than science is at present prepared to find. Van Dyke's "Other Wise Man" though passing through all the vicissitudes of three-and-thirty years of travel and toil can be seen from time to time taking out his remaining precious jewel; we know the jewel is for the King and that the divagations of life have not obscured his consuming purpose, to find the King. The "Other Wise Man" is devoted to a purpose to which his major energies are directed no matter what his temporary aims may be. In an opposite vein Sammy in *What Makes Sammy Run?* pursues his relentless way, however generous his actions at any one time may seem to be. He schemes without principle, is ruthless, and carries out his only real aim in life—to aggrandize Sammy at whatever cost.

There have been a number of psycho-literary studies, especially by psychoanalysts who have followed Freud [1] in trying to find the deep meanings of the life of a literary or historical character and to discover his "main springs of action." One of

---

[1] A contrast between Freud's convincing arguments and lesser attempts can be seen in comparing Freud's analysis of Dostoevsky (Freud, 1952, Vo. V, ch. 21) and Fingert's (1954) study of Jonah. The latter is one of a number of psychoanalytic attempts combining brilliant insight with questionable allegorical interpretation.

Freud's (1925, 1950) major efforts in such studies is contained in a book preface written in 1928 on "Dostoevsky and parricide." Freud discusses some of the same factors in relation to *The Brothers Karamazov* that are mentioned earlier in this chapter. In addition, however, he cites the parallels between Sophocles' *Oedipus Rex*, Shakespeare's *Hamlet*, and Dostoevsky's work. In each the (mostly unconscious) aim of destroying the father and possessing the mother, or mother-substitute, is found. As a consequence, guilt over potential or actual incest manifests itself. Only literary characters are represented in Freud's analysis at first, each character being conceived as having a directional pattern of hating-father-and-feeling-guilty that dominates his entire personality. Freud then goes beyond the fictitious characters to the historical character, Dostoevsky himself, and gives fair evidence of the same life thema in the novelist which is found in the novel. If the "projective hypothesis" holds, that each of a man's creative works is a revelation of himself, there is good reason from Dostoevsky's works to accept Freud's contention that the novelist's trend was a lifelong attempt to escape the guilt of the oedipal situation; Freud adds substantiating data from Dostoevsky's life, especially in the brilliant Russian's gambling mania which calls for other than a "reasonable" explanation.

Another psychoanalytical attempt to show a directional trend of over-arching importance, in a great littérateur's life is found in the book, *Mr. Carlyle My Patient* (Halliday, 1950). Here the thema of a lifelong obedience to the domination of his mother is traced through Thomas Carlyle's life. The interpretation is extensively documented from Carlyle's own work and biographies of his life. Many of the apparently contradictory facets in the life of the irascible genius become contributing factors to a major life style when viewed in the light of psychoanalytic insights.

From a more academic psychological position an attempt (Squires, 1938b) has been made to analyze the "creative psychology"

of the musician, Cesar Franck.[1] Minor characteristics, such as a marked tone and luminosity synesthesia and a strongly developed kinesthetic factor in his musical memory—not at all minor characteristics viewed from some angles—were subordinated to a perfectionist trend in Franck's personality which issued in regularity and conscientiousness and a compulsive drive in his work. These behavior and attitudinal characteristics could be considered as delineating the life style of the famed composer.

Also in the academic psychological tradition, but employing psychoanalytic concepts, another writer (Moore, 1937) extracts what might be called the psychological essence of Algernon Charles Swinburne. According to this study, Swinburne was a sado-masochist who in his Eton days enjoyed being whipped by the school master. The relation of constitutional factors to the patterns of his personality extending beyond physiological functions can be found in the correlation between his exceedingly sensitive skin and the pleasure he derived from pain; swimming in the surf, Swinburne responded pleasurably to "the scourging of the sea." Intellectually he took delight in shocking the world with his "vice-virtue" philosophy. But his exceeding sensitivity was revealed one time when a mild criticism from his tutor regarding a manuscript occasioned the writer's tearing up the entire manuscript —and then sitting up all night writing it from memory! As anyone who has dealt with sado-masochistic individuals might suspect, Swinburne had a strong sexual component in his painful pleasure; indeed, he was strongly influenced by the writings of the Marquis de Sade. The hymn to "Notre Dame de Sept Douleurs" is addressed to a personification of the harlot of pain. Even the paradoxical drive to murder one's love object found in the sexual sadistic-masochistic character is found expressed in "I would my love could kill thee" from

---

[1] The same service was performed in relation to Carl Maria von Weber (Squires, 1938a).

Delores. Finally, perhaps the most puzzling of psychological reactions, necrophilia, a sometimes fulfilled desire to have sexual union with corpses, was part of Swinburne's make-up. Sado-masochistic life style is thus described in Swinburne; of course, it is a different one from what would be evident in England of the late nineteenth century which so avidly—for a time—drank in the strange poet's words.

It is not necessary to accept the interpretations of the authors of the preceding studies who claim discovery of a major life trend in the personality of each individual under discussion. Some of these representative life styles are presented convincingly, others not so convincingly. Together with other studies they give us a basis for surmising that there are many individuals whose major life trend patterns may be discerned. Further, it seems that many apparently disparate functions of the personalities described may have contributed to a basic pattern. It is well to bear in mind, however, that these are *ex post facto* observations: it may be that the materials remaining for examination from the almost limitless number of incidents occurring in any person's life are one-sided in emphasis or that the biographer or psycho-literary student consciously or unconsciously selects his data to suit a purpose held, again consciously or unconsciously. Perhaps instead of one major life style, each person discussed had two or three or more styles unrecorded or unrecognized.

There would be greater scientific validity, even to the positing of one among several life styles, should the analyst of a real or fictitious character predict the pattern of a man's life elsewhere from certain independent knowledge at hand. Prediction need not be to individual events, for these depend too greatly upon fortuitous external circumstances. It would be enough to predict some gross behavior patterns. An example of such prediction from one pattern to another comes from the writer's files; it can illustrate the possibilities of such an approach to the life styles or major dynamic trends of individuals.

An article in the *Reader's Digest* (Sondern, 1949) reprinted from *Argosy* and entitled "The Doctor Who Hated Murder," gave a number of details about the life of Sir Bernard Spilsbury, the renowned pathologist for the British Home Office and "father of modern legal medicine." The unusual statement which Sir Bernard is quoted as saying, "I hate murder," coupled with several incidents reported by the writer of the article without seeming recognition of their deeper significance attracted attention. A tentative hypothesis was set up to the effect that one underlying life style of Sir Bernard was directed towards mastering strong hostility feelings. One of the incidents recorded in the *Digest* concerned a far-famed court case which became known as the "Brides in the Bath" murder case and in which the pathologist testified brilliantly. In the course of his testimony, during which the ingenious and convincing deductions for which he was noted were explained, Sir Bernard re-enacted in the courtroom the method of the "bath murder" by bringing a bathtub full of water before the court and employing the assistance of one of his nurses. While he held the nurse by her ankles with her head under water, he calmly lectured the jury how in the murderer's tub death would occur in a few minutes. Then, in the words of the original *Argosy* article, "Suddenly someone in the stunned courtroom yelled, 'Good, God! *She's* drowning, too!' The unfortunate nurse was hastily dragged from the tub and had to be revived by artificial respiration" (Sondern, 1949).

To test the hypothesis arising from the *Digest* article, the original *Argosy* article was secured and read carefully. At the close of the *Argosy* article came a report of the end of Sir Bernard's life. He tipped a Bunsen burner toward himself in his laboratory and turned the petcock, ending his own life within a few minutes. This action seemed to be partial corroboration of the hypothesis set up, inasmuch as there seems to be in suicide a turning of hostile feelings inward upon oneself; to accomplish the suicidal act these hostile feelings must be very strong in the first place. One can only take this as possible corroboration in view of the fact that the theory of suicide as a resultant of inward-directed hostility is not acceptable to all psychopathologists.[1]

[1] Cf., *e.g.*, Freud in "Mourning and melancholia" (S. Freud, 1925, Vol. IV, ch. 8) with Cameron (1947), Maslow & Mittelmann (1951), and White

It was supposed on the basis of the evidence presented in the *Digest* article that the man who said, " 'I hate murder, . . . and I have devoted my life to making that most unforgivable of all crimes unprofitable' " (Sondern, 1949), did have a life style which moved overtly in the direction of crime-detection and prevention, while at the same time this basic direction of his life was aimed at the mastering of his hostile, sadistic impulses. The overt behavior was taken to be a life-long endeavor to overcome the pathologist's exceedingly strong hostile trends. Such a supposition was not, and was not intended to be, a disparagement of the work or character of the justly famous Sir Bernard; after all, if he had such inner trends, he was one who turned his feelings into activities of social usefulness, as contrasted with others whose similar feelings are turned to society's hurt. But the supposition would only stand unsupported without further evidence and would be no more scientifically convincing than most psycholiterary studies. Their conclusions may very well rest on good evidence, but they fail to meet one of the requirements of science in general and of psychology in particular, the requirement of predictability. Accordingly, the writer held that further evidence, independent of that offered in the *Digest* article was demanded. Such evidence would have to consist of further fresh events not recorded in the *Digest* article, events which would manifest the same impulses which in others would lead toward crime but which in Sir Bernard's case were sublimated into crime detection. An effort was made not to overlook negative instances which would controvert the hypothesis: no such negative evidence seemed present. The events which were sought were not found either; but in the heart of the article lay the following words:

"In later years, a colleague asked why he had ever taken up his macabre specialty, which never paid him more than a small income, when he could have had an extremely lucrative practice in Harley Street. 'It came from reading too much about Sherlock Holmes as a boy,' the doctor said, 'I also seem to have a sort of criminal mentality myself that makes it possible for me to imagine so clearly what a vil-

lain has done and why. I have an insatiable curiosity about villainy' " (Sondern, 1949).[1] Thus, although the actual events were not recorded, there appeared to be confirmation of the hypothesis concerning Sir Bernard's strivings. The eminent doctor affirmed in his own words the thesis that he possessed impulses—or a mentality—which in others leads to villainy.

The illustration here is not an adequately controlled experiment; it does, however, indicate the possibilities in discovering basic directional tendencies in studies of literary and historical characters. The possibility of finding such tendencies does not exclude, of course, other tendencies which may be parallel to or even contradictory to such trend patterns.

Patterns Derived from Direct Investigation. If we now turn from literary and historical attempts at discovering dominant life styles to investigations of persons directly, patterns can be traced in individuals which seem to disclose fairly basic individualized directional tendencies. It seems well to start with several twin studies, for if there should be patterns which are alike, those of twins, especially identical twins, should be most similar. As will be seen, however, even between twins there are marked basic directional trends which differentiate these individuals from each other. In addition to the twin studies there could be any number of case studies cited which have uncovered at least what seem to the observer to be dominant directional patterns. Instead, however, the final example of direct investigation is a report on an individual which places him against a background of group-derived patterns and suggests the complexity of trends derived by objective measurement. Out of this complexity perhaps one or a few dominant trends could be chosen as a life style or life styles. The reported study concludes with the short-term temporal fluctuations of these trends.

(1948). Hereditary factors may enter into determination of depressive tendencies, though to argue as White does that familial patterns of depression suggest a somatogenesis of depression is inadequate, for *familial* does not necessarily mean *hereditary*.

[1] Only the sentences about Holmes and about Spilsbury's "insatiable curiosity" were included in the *Digest* article. The most significant sentence on the "criminal mentality" was omitted.

First, we turn to the twin studies. In the familiar study of Johnny and Jimmy by Myrtle McGraw (1935), the investigator makes the point that even monozygotic twins are not the same at birth; only at conception are they the same, for intra-uterine life is experience of an environment. McGraw doubted after some time that Johnny and Jimmy were monozygotic, even though they were assumed to be because of the single placenta present at birth. Whether one-egg twins or not, however, they can be for our purpose treated as very closely alike in many ways; and indeed they were handled by their parents as though they were identical not fraternal twins. Within 15 minutes following birth there was a noticeable difference between Johnny and Jimmy, not so much in pattern or form of behavior but in degree of the same kind of behavior. Johnny was very flaccid, while Jimmy was possessed of much greater muscle tone; he was better developed than Johnny, though not necessarily with superior endowment. In a period of 780 days there were 25 occasions in which Jimmy cried enough to preclude his being tested by the examiner; Johnny had only seven similar occasions in the same period. One of the tests was a slight pin-pricking; during one series of tests there were 73 times when the pricking did not stimulate Johnny to cry while there were only 23 times for Jimmy. Indeed, in the last six months of testing Johnny took the pin from the experimenter and gently pricked himself, laughing the meanwhile; such behavior was not observed in Jimmy or any of the other babies under observation at the time.

When so-called "ontogenetic behavior" was compared for the twins, differences of a characteristic nature manifested themselves. Walking up an incline found Jimmy somewhat uncooperative. One kind of behavior which appeared to show both the principle of "readiness" and differences in the psychomotor patterns underlying the life trends of the twins was roller skating. Johnny started skating at 350 days, but Jimmy was held back from starting until 687 days of age; the former was slower in developing the skill, but achieved a higher degree of skill finally than did his brother. On the whole, with a number of exceptions faithfully reported by McGraw, there emerge pictures of two individuals, not merely distinguished by so-called "individual differences," but by behavior patterned in two fairly recognizable directional trends even at this very early age, with Johnny moving in directions characterized by his being easy-going, cooperative, and less sensitive, and with Jimmy's being more high-spirited, even "touchy" in respect to external stimuli of human or inanimate nature.

Another investigator (Schwesinger, 1952) followed the life careers of identical twin girls who were reared partly in the same environment and partly separated. Elvira and Esther were born to an unmarried American-born Mexican girl, 18 years of age. The father was deported and was never contacted afterward. The mother married another Mexican after nine months in a maternity home where she worked following the birth of the twins. According to the mother's report, both girls were breast-fed until two months, talked at 11 months, walked at 16 months, were toilet trained at one year "without tension," and engaged in various forms of sympathetic behavior such as vomiting together in the early months, sharing children's diseases, ear aches, and headaches—the last carrying into maturity. When the mother married, she placed both girls with relatives, though not for adoption, then in a few months took Elvira back with her, leaving Esther in the home of her husband's step-mother who lived in a neighboring house a few hundred feet from the original mother's home in a small desert town. The girls were aware that they were twins and that they were treated somewhat alike in the way of clothes and amusements. The twins' mother asserted that at the time she took Elvira back into her own home Esther objected to leaving her foster home. Further, she stated that Esther early liked her foster mother despite the latter's outbreaks of temper and the fact that she probably struck the child a great deal. The mother did not interfere with the foster mother's harsh treatment of Esther since she felt that the foster mother had the rights that go with responsibility. Both Esther and her mother declared that the girl had very heavy household chores which ran until relatively late at night, after which she had to do her homework. Elvira on the other hand had a comparatively easy life in her own mother's home. At school Esther showed more aptitude than did Elvira; her intelligence rating obtained later bore out her greater intellectual capacities.

At the age of nine the girls were separated by the removal of the mother's family to a distant city. The girls were not re-united until they were 16. About the time of adolescence, partly as a resultant of friction with her step-father, Elvira left home and became delinquent. Esther, too, at 15 years of age left the foster home for her mother's and though welcomed by her mother also had difficulty with her step-father; leaving the home, she likewise became delinquent. After several separated correctional school experiences, the girls were united at the school where the investigator became acquainted with them. At the school they were devoted to each other, Elvira being the stronger character, Esther the brighter. Tests at school confirmed the identical twin presupposition, with finger, palm, and foot prints closely resembling each other, a number of dental similarities (though a number of dissimilarities also), and identical electroencephalograms. Reported observation by their teachers as to the greater stability of Elvira, her more expressive and aggressive (not necessarily hostile) nature, and the more tense, sensitive and easily upset nature of Esther were supported by psychological test data, although the girls revealed similar traits on the Rorschach. When the girls were paroled to their home, social workers commented on the close attachment of mother and girls to one another. Within a few months Esther was married. Elvira planned marriage, but according to

the record her plans came to naught through no fault of her own. Esther, although she had been devoted to her fiance before marrying, started to "go on the loose" again, and finally disappeared. Her husband sought her in vain. After some time, unspecified, she was found dead in a hotel hall, the inside of her arms punctured by morphine injections. The presumption was that she had died from self-inflicted morphine poisoning. Elvira, though suffering much from the loss of both her fiance and her beloved sister, continued to show good adjustment. How long such ability to absorb shocks would continue is, of course, not indicated, for as has been said before there are breaking points for all of us.

Here, then were identical twins, carrying the physiological and psychological similarities which stem from developing out of the same egg. They were alike in many ways also because they had similar treatment in part but unlike in many ways because of dissimilar treatment. Their general life trend patterns, insofar as one can discern an over-all trend in each of them, ran parallel to each other even to the necessity of resisting society's regulations to the extent of requiring correctional efforts. Yet each had differences distinct enough to be observed by both untrained and trained observers and deep enough to be revealed on psychological tests which probe below the surface of behavior. In the framework of our discussion we may say that their directional trends were very much alike and yet measurably different.

A final illustration of scientific studies of life styles is found in one of the experiments from the University of Illinois' Laboratory of Personality Assessment and Group Behavior. We can see here some of the principles which have been expressed in the preceding pages. Not only are different directional trends noticeable in the same individual in this experiment, but also, something important to which we have not devoted much attention thus far: temporal fluctuations in strength of these trends is made evident. In a study similar to

Williams' (1954), Cattell and Cross (1952) made use of the correlation technique (P-technique) which discerns factors or traits *in an individual* when occasions in the ongoing life of the individual are correlated, rather than employing the usual type of correlation between tests on a group of persons. (Cf. Chapter 13.)

A male, unmarried graduate student, 24 years of age, was given a series of tests twice a day for 40 days for a total of 80 sessions. During the six-weeks period he kept a diary as well. Two outstanding external events occurred in this period: approximately in the middle of the forty-day period, the subject performed in a play for several nights, and shortly afterward his father suffered a fractured pelvis. In the testing series the young man gave his reactions to a group of statements of important life attitudes which were presented under differing experimental conditions. Most of the statements were derived from factor-analytic studies of groups of persons. Presentation of these statements guaranteed more objective measurement than the usual method of having an individual endorse or reject a statement or indicate approval in varying degrees. For example, the experimental conditions allowed the subject to view six three-digit numbers for one second apiece; then he was given 15 seconds to write them down. For 30 seconds he then wrote all the satisfactions of which he could think which stem from the activity suggested by a given attitude statement. Following this period he again wrote as many of the three-digit numbers as he could recall. His score was the difference between his recall before and after his writing of satisfactions, the theory being that greater retroactive inhibition would occur in the case of those attitudes in which the subject had a keener interest. Other similar objective measures were employed.

One of the strengths of the Cattell and Cross study is that most of the factors discovered by analyzing the intercorrelations of measures on the individual subject compare meaningfully with factors resulting from correlations among groups.[1] When the intercorrelations of the succeeding sessions were subjected to factor analysis, eight fairly clear factors—or in our present terms, dynamic trend patterns—appeared. These are:

    I. Mating or sex.
    II. Parental-protective.
    III. Self (regarding)-sentiment.
    IV. Narcism.
    V. Appeal-dependence.
    VI. Fear-anxiety.
    VII. Self-assertion.
    VIII. Fatigue.

What can be said about a life style or life styles of this person? We may speculate that generally he seems to be moving centrifugally, that is, towards others (Factors I, II, and V). But he also seems to be moving centripetally (Factors III, IV, and VII). The fear factor (VI) may represent a directional trend of withdrawal, although in this case the items which point up the factor suggest withdrawal from terrifying events, not from people. Factor VIII may be named misleadingly, for the items having the heaviest factor loadings betoken a need for rest *and* relaxing recreation. Thus the eighth factor could be a measure of a movement toward indulgence in passive as well as restful pursuits in the spirit of the laconic statement, "I was born lazy, and I've worked hard at it ever since." Possibly if a factor analysis of the factors were performed, functional unities (second-order factors) would be discovered among the eight trends above which might enable us to do more than speculate about the *major* directional trends of the young man. As it is, on relatively objective measurements covering important attitudes there are a number of distinct trends, if not opposed at least aiming in different directions. Perhaps more refined measurement techniques, more complete measurement, and more comprehensive statistical tools would reveal *a* life style which would correspond to a genuine Adlerian life style. The actual data at

[1] According to Cattell, P-technique factors range about R-technique factors as means.

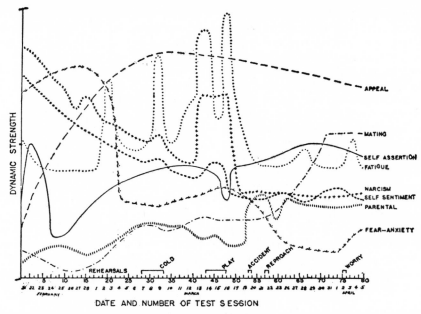

Figure 20. Temporal variations in individual factors. (From R. B. Cattell and K. P. Cross, "Comparison of the ergic and self-sentiment structures found in dynamic traits by R and P techniques," *J. Pers.*, 1952, 21, 268)

hand, however, give little reason to contradict the suggestions made previously concerning the presence of *styles* of life rather than *a* style; even more adequate data might not support the latter. A clinician who claims that he has found *the* life style of an individual may only be finding such a singular style by ignoring many directional trends of the personality he is studying.

By the nature of the experiment not only the presence of certain factors or trends could be ascertained but also fluctuations in these trends from day to day for the entire six weeks. A scoring system was devised to compare the varying strengths of the trend from beginning to end of the experiment. Results of the analysis are shown in Figure 20. Days are shown on the abscissa, but no numerical values are given on the ordinate, for the scores from variable to variable are not comparable. A given curve should not be compared with other curves but only with itself. Cattell and Cross point out that the trends in the diagram agree well with incidents known from

the subject's diary and otherwise. The fluctuations in the Fatique factor coincide in time with both strenuous play rehearsals, the play itself, and the diary complaint of tiredness. The relative strength of this trend shows clearly from period to period. Events preceding the six weeks started the Fear-anxiety trend high; no specific reason is given for its sudden drop about March 1, but worry over falling behind in school work on account of the play is reflected in the slighter rise starting March 8. Toward the end of the six weeks the diary records a worry over the way the subject's faculty advisor was behaving, as if hostile to the subject for some reason. Parental-protective trends were suddenly increased at the time of the accident to the subject's father, then decreased temporarily on receipt of a letter from the young man's aunt reproaching him for not giving up his personal interests for the sake of his family. The Mating or sex urge rises after the play, coincident with increased "dating"; an interpretation might be made that the sublimatory or substitutionary qualities of the excessive work surrounding the play can be observed here, but neither the actual upward trend during the play situation nor any other presented data could support such an interpretation.

How trends may vary together at some times and not at others is seen in the manner in which the Narcissistic trend and the Self (regarding)-sentiment fall jointly until the play and then rise together along with the Fatigue factor at the time of the play. Mating or sex and Parental-protective urges have a general common trend. Other joint action of trends could probably be abstracted from the diagram. Indeed, if objective measurements such as were employed in the study of this one subject could be continued over a much longer period of time and with more measurements, there might be discerned long-term patterns which could be woven together to make *a* style of life; on such a basis rather than on the unaided clinical observations usually employed to determine a life style we could be more certain of our generalizations about the individual. There exists a strong suspicion however, that even though more general trend patterns would most likely emerge from a longer period of observation, together with more measurements, there would still be some trends as anomalous as the Appeal-dependence trend in Figure 20. It is only fair to state in this connection that the latter trend is considered as a very basic urge which would probably not be much affected by passing events of every-day living.

SUMMARY

Economic factors are not only present in energy-exchanges within the personality, but likewise in movements of the entire personality in any (psychological) direction. Adler and Murray, especially, have hypothesized a single "style of life" or "unity-thema" for each person; but research only allows us at present to refer to "styles of life," and the concept as a single style can be employed merely as an heuristic device. A general trend or type may be granted as long as it is recognized that many opposing and inconsistent trends may be found in a personality.

To deny *a* style does not mean that goals are not present toward which an individual moves. Teleonomic trends, seen in the purposes behavior accomplishes for an individual, help explain neurotic and psychotic behavior patterns which appear to be utterly illogical, and give a dynamic outlook on character.

Persistence of goals may be understood in part as a persistence of needs; as long as needs persist, the individual moves in the direction of satisfying goals. A possible exception is found in "fixated" behavior, in which the person or animal engages in repetition of behavior which no longer reaches satisfying goals. A need-tension explanation of such persistence is possible, however. Goal-persistence is individualized to the extent that differences among responses of individuals to relatively the same stimuli may be explained in terms of the teleonomic trends of each individual.

Basic patterns of life styles may be recognized, but as vector resultants of different minor trends, rather than as grand patterns subordinating all minor trends. Many special trend patterns can be discerned, of which leadership and followership may be instanced as characterizing persons under certain conditions.

Psycho-literary methods have been used to ferret out individual trend patterns. Only if prediction from some evidence concerning a person's life can be made to other portions of that life can such investigations meet the standards of science. Some studies of twins have yielded individual trend patterns differentiating even identical twins. Factor analysis of an individual's behavior patterns has also thrown light on several dominant styles of life in an individual.

QUESTIONS

1. Describe the "style of life" as expressed by different authorities.

2. Why cannot the term "style of life" mean a unified goal-striving?

3. Relate style of life and type.

4. Discuss "teleonomic trends." How can "senseless behavior" and character be understood in view of these trends?

5. How persistent are specific goals?

6. Discuss several representative generic trend patterns and their application to individuals.

7. How much truth is there to the contention that "Good followers make good leaders"?

8. Instance styles of life in psycho-literary studies. Describe the prediction and fulfillment in the case of "The Doctor Who Hated Murder."

9. In what way may twin studies and factor analysis serve to illuminate styles of life?

CONCLUDING REMARKS

The fundamentals of personality have been examined in the pages of this text. There is much more to be said beyond the fundamentals which cannot be included in a text like this. But if the student has mastered the basic principles enunciated here, he has the foundation for a scientific understanding of the human personality. Only a few words need to be added. One of the principles of psychology, it may be recalled, is that "The aim of psychological investigation is to predict and control behavior." Although many advances have been made in this direction—far more probably than the man on the street knows—personology cannot yet predict, still less control the man in his emotional responses with the accuracy which the older sciences can boast. In the deep emotional experiences of mankind, there are overtones of personality functioning which have not been captured by our finest measuring instruments and perhaps never will be. Explain the heights and depths of emotion as one will, they are part of us, too real to be denied, despite their eluding our measurement so far.

We may hope that more of these subtle portions of the personality will be measured. And yet most likely some aspects will never yield to prediction and control. If we can rely on the experience of other sciences, as more areas of personality are discovered, new insights will be made. Already the complexities of personality have made themselves apparent as science has advanced in its investigations. What further complexities there are, what superfunctions beyond those manifest thus far, what dimensions unrealized as yet, in the nature of the case we cannot know. If there are extra-sensory functions as some psychologists maintain, or if there are "spiritual dimensions" as religious people believe, or if certain functions of the personality have survival value beyond this life, the scientist cannot say and still remain scientific, "These things are impossible." One would hesitate to think of philosophical and religious concepts as being mainly "untestable hypotheses," as some have claimed they are. The personologist who is aware of recent research knows that it has not yet gone out of fashion for some psychologists to say, "The propositions of psychoanalysis are untestable hypotheses." But other psychologists without this preconception have gone ahead to test psychoanalytic concepts, in a manner not unlike that of the bumblebee who was unaware that at one time the understanding of the "laws of aerodynamics" predicted the impossibility of his flying.

315

DIMENSIONS
AND FACTOR
ANALYSIS

Factor-analytic concepts of personality traits depend on mathematical notions possibly unfamiliar to the student. In psychological factor-analytic theory, geometrical dimensions are regarded as mathematical representations of traits. Thus, some measure of comprehension of geometrical dimensions is necessary to understand the text discussion on traits. Also, a brief introduction to factor analysis itself is in order.[1]

A dimension refers to measurement in a single line or direction so that larger quantities are represented as farther along the line than are smaller quantities. Usually, the convention has been adopted of depicting a dimension by a directed line segment like that in Figure 21(a). In most graphs the arrowheads are omitted. The graphs in Figure 21 retain the arrowheads to remind us that we are dealing with directed line segments.

One dimension is represented by Figure 21(a), and two dimensions by Figure 21(b). The line segments of the latter mark off a plane which coincides with the paper on which the lines are printed. Figure 21(c) shows three line segments or dimensions which mark off three planes, the plane indicated by the lines X and Z, that indicated by lines X and Y, and that indicated by lines Y and Z. The observer is, as it were, looking into the corner of a room formed by the three planes or walls which are at right angles to one another. X and Y lines in Figure 21(b) and X, Y, and Z in Figure 21(c) are said to be orthogonal to one another.

Orthogonality has two related meanings in mathematics: It is the generalization of

---

[1] With the advent of electronic computers the more mathematically satisfactory methods of factor analysis which were previously impractical have become usable for psychological investigation. These methods attempt to solve the rotational problem (Chapter 14) by analytical rather than graphical methods. Two especially have appealed to factor analysts, the quartimax (Neuhaus & Wrigley, 1954) and the varimax (Kaiser, 1958) methods. The first has a tendency to yield one general factor, although the writer obtained two general factors from a series of items designed to reveal only one general attitude. The varimax method seems to result in rotated factors somewhat similar to those derived from graphical rotation, but still different enough to suggest that the latter is not an exact approximation of the analytic pattern. Most of the factorial results in personology have come about from graphical rotations of axes. Consequently, the text materials depend on the methods of what might be called classical factor analysis, principally Thurstone's with some reference to the pioneer work of Spearman. In future editions of this textbook the contents of the Appendix will be changed to accommodate the more elegant mathematical methods of rotation. It is not expected that many basic changes in the conclusions of factorial investigations will take place as a result of the more refined machine methods (Cf. Harmon, 1960).

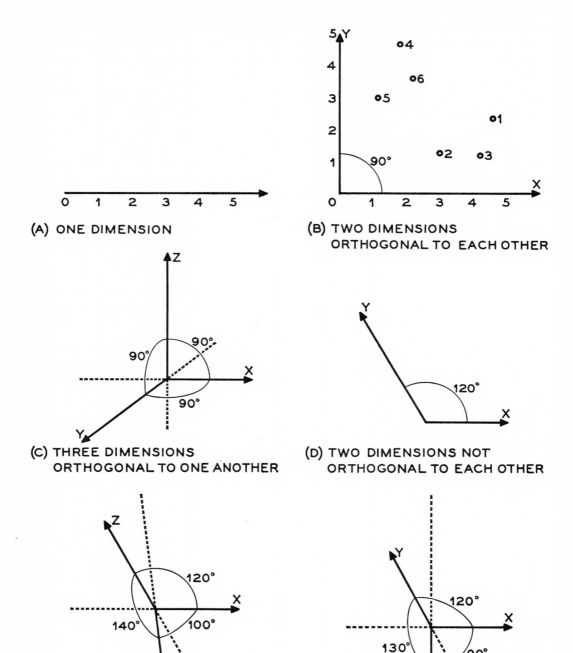

Figure 21. Dimensions represented geometrically.

the notion of *perpendicularity*, and it is the mark of *independence*. As long as we are thinking of two or three dimensions, the physical idea of perpendicularity suffices; but in personality study, as in higher mathematics, we have to think of many more than three dimensions. How can four or more dimensions be literally perpendicular to one another? We cannot conceive of perpendicularity in this case; but we can conceive of four or more dimensions being independent, just as the three dimensions in Figure 21(c) are independent. We can see in Figure 21(b) that the circlet numbered "2" has a score of about 3.0 on the X-axis or dimension. If circlet "2" is moved up and down an imaginary line perpendicular to X, *i.e.*, parallel to Y, its Y-score of about 1.3 could change to any value whatsover from minus infinity (below the X-axis) to plus infinity (above the X-axis), *but its X-score would still be 3.0.* Similarly, if the circlet, "2," moves along a line perpendicular to the Y-axis, staying the same distance from X, the Y-score would always remain about 1.3, no matter what its X-score would become. The X and Y dimensions are therefore considered independent, because scores on each are independent from one another. Dimensions X and Y are thus orthogonal, independent of each other, as are X, Y, and Z in Figure 21(c). In the same way, more than three dimensions can be considered orthogonal to one another.

In trigonometric terms, the cosines of the angles between orthogonal axes are zero, for cos 90° = .00. Under appropriate conditions, the cosine of the angle between two lines is the correlation between two sets of measurements represented by the two lines. It is this fact which is brought into factor analysis for representing factors. Orthogonal axes represent uncorrelated (orthogonal) factors. Axes which are at more or less of an angle than 90° are correlated and represent correlated factors (oblique factors).

If, as some believe, traits of personality can be represented by orthogonal dimensions, we need only Figure 21(a), (b), and (c) and their nongraphical extensions into multidimensional space. But if traits are not completely independent of one another, as some personality authorities are convinced, diagrams in Figure 21(d), (e), and (f) are necessary to represent the possibilities in two or three dimensions. In Figure 21(d), X and Y are not orthogonal to each other. Their lack of independence is expressed by saying that these two dimensions (in personological terms, traits) are correlated with each other. Likewise, X, Y, and Z are nonorthogonal or correlated with one another in Figure 21(e). And in Figure 21(f), X and Z are orthogonal to each other, but Y is correlated with each of them. Extending these principles to more than three dimensions, we can understand how hypergeometry (geometry of more than three dimensions) gives us a means of representing traits of personality which may or may not be independent of one another.

The logic of factor analysis may not be completely tied up with hypergeometric concepts. But if some measure of understanding has been gained from a reading of the foregoing paragraphs, the following may be more comprehensible. For more complete treatments of the subject of factor analysis, various references may be consulted (Burt, 1941; Cattell, 1952a; Fruchter, 1954; Harmon, 1960; Holzinger & Harman, 1941; Thurstone, 1935, 1947).

In the most common type of factor analysis, a number of tests are administered to a fairly large sample of persons, and the resulting scores intercorrelated. That is, the scores on each test are correlated with the scores on each of the other tests. In general, there are $\frac{1}{2}n(n-1)$ correlation coefficients for n tests. By certain arithmetical operations, the correlation coefficients, placed in a square matrix like the following,

	.16	.41	.38	.09
.16		.23	.24	.15
.41	.23		.31	.55
.38	.24	.31		.20
.09	.15	.55	.20	

are made to yield factor loadings, which represent the correlations of the tests with the underlying factors (or in geometrical terms, dimensions). The square of the factor loading is the proportion of test-score variance associated with that particular factor; in the statistical sense, the square of the factor loading is the proportion of the test score determined by the underlying factor.

TABLE A1. FACTOR LOADINGS OF THREE ABILITY FACTORS ON EIGHT TESTS

Test	Factor Loadings		
	R	N	V
1	.462	.389	.101
2	−.052	.801	.474
3	.282	.285	.521
4	.298	.064	.715
5	.096	.003	.683
6	.406	.528	.192
7	.803	−.054	.416
8	.044	.027	.648

Reprinted by permission from Guilford, J. P. *Psychometric Methods*. (2nd ed.) New York: McGraw-Hill Book Co., 1954.

Table A1 illustrates three factors derived from eight subtests of the Army Alpha Examination. Factor R stands for ability in seeing simple relations. Factor N is the well-known number ability factor, and V the even more widely known verbal comprehension ability factor. It can be seen that Factor N correlates with Test 2 .80 and Factor V correlates .47 with Test 2. These facts suggest that number ability plays a more important part in performance on Test 2 than does verbal comprehension ability. Actually, Test 2 is an arithmetic test, so we should expect numerical facility to be important. But it is not unexpected for verbal ability to be represented, for arithmetic directions require an ability to understand words. However, the near-zero correlation (or loading) of Factor R with Test 2 suggests that the ability which R symbolizes must be related to seeing relatively simple relations, as indicated above, because arithmetic does involve seeing relations, evidently of a more complex variety.

The factor loadings such as those in Ta-

ble A1 are usually not the original correlations between dimensions and tests. They are instead what are termed the rotated factor loadings, derived directly from the original ones. In getting the latter, an arbitrary set of axes is used. Then, to get the rotated factor loadings the axes are swung about the zero point until they are in a pre-determined "correct" position. (The criteria of correctness, as suggested in Chapter 14, is one of the major points of debate in factor-analytic theory.) The rationale for the rotation or swinging around of axes is fairly easily seen if one looks at Figure 21(b). Consider each circlet to be a star in the sky in a constellation and the axes (extending Y below zero and X to the left of zero) as the crosshairs of a telescope. No matter which way one rotates the crosshairs, the relative positions of the stars do not change. So, too, the relative positions of the circlets are determined by the basic correlations of one test with another; where the axes are makes no difference as long as they rotate about the zero point. The original position of the axes is arbitrary; and so are the factor loadings which are determined by dropping perpendiculars from the circlets to the axes. With a little imagination, it can be seen that as the axes are rotated, the factor loadings will vary inversely on axes X and Y. (This latter applies for orthogonal rotation; the situation is a bit more complicated for oblique rotation, rotation of one axis at a time.) When the appropriate rotations of axes are effected, the final rotated factor loadings are read off the axes, which now are regarded as geometrical representations of the dimensions or factors.

If it is assumed that the underlying factors are not correlated one with another, the rotation of axes is done by pairs, like the fixed crosshairs of a telescope. But if they are assumed to be correlated, only one axis is rotated at a time. Factor loadings may be somewhat different for orthogonal (90° axes) rotations from those derived by oblique rotations, though the differences may be slight (Roff, 1952).

Oblique rotation allows for obtaining

second-order factors. If the axes come out at odd angles to one another (more or less than 90°), each two columns of factor loadings can be correlated and the correlation coefficients placed in a correlation matrix which itself can be factored. It was by doing a second-order factor analysis that Thurstone achieved, to his own satisfaction at any rate, a resolution of the conflict between the Spearman "*g*" advocates and his own "primary mental abilities" concepts. By finding a second-order factor which accounted for all the variance of first-order obliquely-determined factors, Thurstone believed he had found Spearman's "general intellective factor."

Thurstone, the originator of the method of factor analysis which informs most of the above discussion, thought that factor analysis has its principal usefulness as an exploratory technique. He expected more rigorous experimenting to follow the tentative results of factor analysis "which enables us to make only the crudest first map of a new domain." But in the intervening years factor analysis has come to serve as a powerful experimental tool in its own right. In some instances it seems that it has been glorified beyond its actual value. And yet, when dealing with complex, multi-faceted behavior, the only tool possible is one which can reduce a multitude of interacting variables to manageable proportions. Factor analysis is one such tool.

BIBLIOGRAPHY

Several titles not directly consulted are included for the sake of completeness.

Abernathy, Ethel M., & White, J. C., Jr. Correlation of a self-inventory of personality traits with laboratory measures of vigor and motility. *J. soc. Psychol.*, 1954, *40*, 185–188.

Abraham, K. Selected papers of Karl Abraham, M.D. Trans. by Douglas Bryan & Alix Strachey. New York: Basic Books, 1954. (First publ., 1927)

Abramson, H. A. (Ed.) *Problems of consciousness. Transactions of the first conference, March 20–21, 1950.* New York: Josiah Macy, Jr., Foundation, 1951. (a)

Abramson, H. A. (Ed.) *Problems of consciousness. Transactions of the second conference. March 19–20, 1951.* New York: Josiah Macy, Jr., Foundation, 1951. (b)

Abramson, H. A. (Ed.) *Problems of consciousness. Transactions of the third conference, March 10 and 11, 1952.* New York: Josiah Macy, Jr., Foundation, 1952.

Abramson, H. A. (Ed.) *Problems of consciousness. Transactions of the fourth conference, March 29, 30, & 31, 1953.* New York: Josiah Macy, Jr., Foundation, 1954.

Abramson, H. A. (Ed.) *Problems of consciousness. Transactions of the fifth conference, March 22, 23, & 24, 1954.* New York: Josiah Macy, Jr., Foundation, 1955. (a)

Abramson, H. A. Lysergic acid diethylamide (LSD-25): III. As an adjunct to psychotherapy with elimination of fear of homosexuality. *J. Psychol.*, 1955, *39*, 127–155. (b)

Abt, L. E., & Bellak, L. (Eds.) *Projective psychology, clinical approaches to the total personality.* New York: Knopf, 1950.

Adams, D. K. Conflict and integration. *J. Pers.*, 1954, *22*, 548–556.

Adams, J. K. Laboratory studies of behavior without awareness. *Psychol. Bull.*, 1957, *54*, 383–406.

Adcock, C. J. A factorial examination of Sheldon's types. *J. Pers.*, 1948, *16*, 312–319.

Adkins, Dorothy C., & Lyerly, S. B. *Factor analysis of reasoning tests.* Chapel Hill, N. C.: The Univer. of No. Carolina Press, 1952.

Adler, Alfred. *The neurotic constitution, outline of a comparative individualistic psychology and psychotherapy.* (Trans. by Bernard Glueck & J. E. Lind.) New York: Dodd, Mead, 1926 (Orig., 1912).

Adler, Alfred. *The practice and theory of individual psychology.* (Trans. by P. Radin.) London: Routledge & Kegan Paul, 1925. (1st ed., 1920)

Adler, Alfred. *Understanding human nature.* (Trans. by W. B. Wolfe.) New York: Greenberg, 1927.

Adler, Alfred. *The science of living.* New York: Greenberg, 1929.

Adorno, T. W., Frenkel-Brunswik, Else, Levinson, D. J., & Sanford, R. N., in collaboration with Aron, Betty, Levinson, Maria H., & Morrow, W. *The authoritarian personality*. New York: Harper, 1950.

Aginsky, B. W. Psychopathic trends in culture. *Char. & Pers.*, 1939, 7, 331–343.

Aiken, L. R., Jr. *The identification of number anxiety in a college population*. Unpublished master's thesis, Florida State Univer., 1956.

Akhilananda, S. *Hindu psychology, its meaning for the west*. New York: Harper, 1946.

Albee, G. W. Patterns of aggression in psychopathology. *J. consult. Psychol.*, 1950, 14, 465–468.

Aldrich, C. A., Sung, C., & Knop, C. The crying of newly born babies. II. The individual phase. *J. Pediat.*, 1945, 27, 89–96.

Alexander, F. Fundamental concepts of psychosomatic research. In Franz Alexander & Thomas M. French (Eds.), *Studies in psychosomatic medicine, an approach to the cause and treatment of vegetative disturbances*. New York: Ronald, 1948.

Alexander, G. H. An unexplained death coexistent with death wishes. *Psychosom. Med.*, 1943, 5, 188–194.

Allen, M. S., Guilford, J. P., & Merrifield, P. R. The evaluation of selected intellectual factors by creative research scientists. *Rep. from the Psychol. Lab.*, No. 25. Los Angeles: Univer. of Southern Calif., 1960.

Allen, R. M. *Introduction to the Rorschach technique, a manual of administration and scoring*. New York: International Universities Press, 1953.

Allen, R. M. *Personality assessment procedures: psychometric, projective, and other approaches*. New York: Harper, 1958.

Allport, F. H. *Social psychology*. Cambridge, Mass.: Houghton Mifflin, 1924.

Allport, F. H. The J-curve hypothesis of conforming behavior. *J. soc. Psychol.*, 1934, 5, 141–183.

Allport, F. H. Teleonomic description in the study of personality. *Char. & Pers.*, 1937, 5, 202–214.

Allport, F. H., & Allport, G. W. Personality traits: their classification and measurement. *J. abnorm. soc. Psychol.*, 1921, 16, 6–40.

Allport, G. W. A test for ascendance-submission. *J. abnorm. soc. Psychol.*, 1928, 23, 118–136.

Allport, G. W. What is a trait of personality?

J. abnorm. soc. Psychol., 1931, 25, 367–372.

Allport, G. W. *Personality: a psychological interpretation*. New York: Holt, 1937. (a)

Allport, G. W. The personalistic psychology of William Stern. *Char. & Pers.*, 1937, 5, 231–246. (b)

Allport, G. W. The ego in contemporary psychology. *Psychol. Rev.*, 1943, 50, 451–478.

Allport, G. W. *The nature of personality: selected papers*. Cambridge, Mass.: Addison-Wesley, 1950.

Allport, G. W. The historical background of modern social psychology. In G. Lindzey (Ed.), *Handbook of social psychology*. Vol. I. *Theory and method*. Cambridge, Mass.: Addison-Wesley, 1954.

Allport, G. W., *Pattern and growth in personality*. New York: Holt, Rinehart & Winston, 1961.

Allport, G. W., & Allport, F. H. *A-S reaction study: a scale for measuring ascendance-submission in personality*. New York: Houghton Mifflin, 1928.

Allport, G. W., Bruner, J. S., & Jandorf, E. M. Personality under social catastrophe: ninety life-histories of the Nazi revolution. *Char. & Pers.*, 1941, 10, 1–22.

Allport, G. W., & Odbert, H. S. Trait-names, a psycho-lexical study. *Psychol. Monogr.*, 1936, 47, No. 1 (Whole No. 211).

Allport, G. W., & Schanck, R. L. Are attitudes biological or cultural in origin? *Char. & Pers.*, 1936, 4, 195–205.

Allport, G. W., & Vernon, P. E. *Studies in expressive movement*. New York: Macmillan, 1933.

Allport, G. W., Vernon, P. E., & Lindzey, G. *Study of values*. (Rev. ed.) Boston: Houghton Mifflin, 1951.

Alschuler, Rose H., & Hattwick, La Barta W. *Painting and personality, a study of young children*. Vol. I. Chicago: Univer. of Chi. Press, 1947.

Altschul, E., & Biser, E. The validity of unique mathematical models in science. *Phil. Sci.*, 1948, 15, 11–24.

American Psychiatric Association. *Proceedings, first colloquium on personality investigation held under the auspices of the American Psychiatric Association and the Committee on Relations with the Social Sciences. December 1, 2, 1928*. Baltimore: Lord Baltimore Press, 1929.

American Psychiatric Association. Committee on Relations with the Social Sciences. *Proceedings, second colloquium on personality investigation held under the joint auspices of the American Psychiatric Association, Committee on Relations of Psychiatry and the Social Sciences and of the Social Science Research Council, November 29–30, 1929, New York City.* Baltimore: Johns Hopkins Press, 1930.

American Psychological Association. *Ethical standards of psychology, a summary of ethical principles.* Washington, D. C.: American Psychological Association, 1953.

American Psychological Association. *Psychology and its relations with other professions.* Washington: American Psychological Association, 1954.

American Psychological Association, Committee on Ethics and Standards. Standards of ethical behavior for psychologists. *Amer. Psychologist*, 1958, *13*, 268–271.

Ames, Louise B., Learned, Janet, Metraux, Ruth W., & Walker, R. N. *Child Rorschach responses: developmental trends from two to ten years.* New York: Hoeber, 1952.

Ammons, R. B., Ammons, Carol H., & Morgan, R. L. Movement analysis of the performance of a simple perceptual-motor task under various conditions. *WADC Tech. Rep. 54–36.* Wright-Patterson Air Force Base, Ohio: Wright Air Develpm. Center, Air Res. and Develpm. Command, USAF, 1954.

Anastasi, Anne, & Foley, P., Jr. *Differential psychology; individual and group differences in behavior.* New York: Macmillan, 1949.

Anderson, H. H., & Anderson, Gladys L. (Eds.) *An introduction to projective techniques, and other devices for understanding the dynamics of human behavior.* New York: Prentice-Hall, 1951.

Angyal, Andras. Review of Dunne, J. W., *An experiment with time. Char. & Pers.*, 1940, *8*, 264–265.

Angyal, Andras. *Foundations for a science of personality.* New York: The Commonwealth Fund, 1941.

Ansbacher, H. L., & Ansbacher, Rowena R. *The individual psychology of Alfred Adler: a systematic presentation in selections from his writings.* New York: Basic Books, 1956.

Anonymous. *Hypnosis symposium manual.* Los Angeles: Hypnosis Symposium, c. 1957. (a)

Anonymous. *A seminar on hypnosis.* N. Y. Seminars on Medical and Dental Hypnosis, c. 1957. (b)

Applezweig, Dee G. Some determinants of behavioral rigidity. *J. abnorm. soc. Psychol.*, 1954, *49*, 224–228.

Argelander, A. The personal factor in judging human character. *Char. & Pers.*, 1937, *5*, 285–295.

Aristotle. *Nicomachean ethics.*

Arlow, J. A. The consecration of the prophet. *Psychoanal. Quart.*, 1951, *20*, 374–397.

Aron, Betty. *A manual for the analysis of the Thematic Apperception Test, a method and technique for personality research.* Berkeley, Calif.: Willis E. Berg, 1949.

Arthur, Grace. *A point scale of performance tests. Vol. I. Clinical Manual. Vol. II. The process of standardization.* New York: The Commonwealth Fund, 1930, 1933.

Arthur, R. P., & Shelley, W. B. Experimental evidence for an enzymatic basis for itching in man. *Nature*, 1955, *175*, 901–902.

Asch, S. E. Forming impressions of personality. *J. abnorm. soc. Psychol.*, 1946, *41*, 258–290.

Ausubel, D. P., & Schiff, H. M. A level of aspiration approach to the measurement of goal tenacity. *J. gen. Psychol.*, 1955, *52*, 97–110.

Axline, Virginia M. *Play therapy, the inner dynamics of childhood.* Boston: Houghton-Mifflin, 1947.

Bach, G. R. Some diadic functions of childhood memories. *J. Psychol.*, 1952, *33*, 87–98.

Bain, A. *On the study of character, including an estimate of phrenology.* London: Parker, Son, & Bourn, 1861.

Bain, A. *Mental science, a compendium of psychology and the history of philosophy, designed as a text-book for high-schools and colleges.* New York: Appleton, 1888.

Baker, L. M., & Taylor, W. M. The relationship under stress between skin temperature, electrical skin resistance, and pulse rate. *J. exp. Psychol.*, 1954, *48*, 361–366.

Bakwin, Ruth M. The comics. *J. Pediat.*, 1953, *42*, 633–635.

Baldwin, A. L. The study of individual personality by means of the intra-individual correlations. *J. Pers.*, 1946, *14*, 151–168.

Baldwin, J. M. *Handbook of psychology,*

senses, and intellect. (2nd ed., Rev.) New York: Holt, 1890.

Baldwin, J. M. *Mental development in the child and race.* New York: Macmillan, 1895 (Rev. Ed., 1906).

Baldwin, J. M. *The individual and society, or psychology and sociology.* London: Rebman, 1911.

Bales, R. F. *Interaction process analysis: A method for the study of small groups.* Cambridge, Mass.: Addison-Wesley Press, 1950.

Baltzell, E. D. "Who's Who in America" and "The Social Register": elite and upper class indexes in metropolitan America. In R. Bendix & S. M. Lipset (Eds.), *Class, status, and power, a reader in social stratification.* Glencoe, Ill.: Free Press, 1953.

Barker, R., Dembo, Tamara, & Lewin K. Studies in topological and vector psychology: II. Frustration and regression. *Univer. Iowa Stud. Ch. Welf., 18,* No. 1, 1941.

Barker, R. G., & Wright, H. F. *One boy's day, a specimen record of behavior.* New York: Harper, 1951.

Barnes, C. A. A statistical study of the Freudian theory of levels of psychosexual development. *Genet. Psychol. Monogr.,* 1952, *45,* 105–175.

Barnes, E. Books and pamphlets intended to give sex-information. *Studies in Education.* Vol. I. Stanford Univer., 1896–1897.

Barnett, J. H. Personality in primitive society. *Char. & Pers.,* 1933, *2,* 152–167.

Barron, F. Some test correlates of response to psychotherapy. *J. consult. Psychol.,* 1953, *17,* 235–241. (a)

Barron, F. An ego-strength scale which predicts response to psychotherapy. *J. consult. Psychol.,* 1953, *17,* 326–333. (b)

Barron, F., & Leary, T. F. Changes in psychoneurotic patients with and without psychotherapy. *J. consult. Psychol.,* 1955, *19,* 239–245.

Bartlett, F. C. *Remembering, a study in experimental and social psychology.* Cambridge, Eng.: At the Univer. Press, 1932.

Bartlett, F. C. *Thinking, an experimental and social study.* London: Allen & Unwin, 1958.

Bash, K. W. *Consciousness and the unconscious in depth and Gestalt psychology.* Amsterdam: Acta Psychologica, North Holland Pub. Co., 1949.

Bates, F. S. Position, role, and status: A reformulation of concepts. *Soc. Forces,* 1956, *34,* 313–321.

Baumgarten, F. Character traits derived from biographies. *Char. & Pers.,* 1937, *6,* 147–149.

Bayley, Nancy. *Studies in the development of young children.* Berkeley, Calif.: Univer. of Calif. Press, 1940.

Beach, F. A., & Jaynes, Julian. Effects of early experience upon the behavior of animals. *Psychol. Bull.,* 1954, *51,* 239–263.

Beaver, W. C. *The science of biology.* (4th Ed.) St. Louis: Mosby, 1952.

Bechterev, V. M. *General principles of human reflexology, an introduction to the objective study of personality.* (4th Ed.) (Trans. by Emma Murphy & William Murphy.) New York: International Publishers, 1932 (Orig. 4th Ed., 1928).

Beck, L. F. Unconscious motivation. New York: Association Films, 1949. (Film)

Beck, S. J. *Rorschach's test.* Vol. I. *Basic processes.* Vol. II. *A variety of personality pictures.* Vol. III. *Advances in interpretation.* New York: Grune & Stratton, 1944, 1949, 1952.

Bell, J. E. *Projective techniques, a dynamic approach to the study of the personality.* New York: Longmans, Green, 1948.

Bender, I. E., Iruns, H. A., Rothney, J. W. M., Kemple, Camilla, & England, Mary R. *Motivation and visual factors, individual studies of college students.* Hanover, N. H.: Dartmouth College Publ., 1942.

Bendix, R., & Lipset, S. M. *Class, status and power, a reader in social stratification.* Glencoe, Ill.: The Free Press, 1953.

Benedek, Therese. *Studies in psychosomatic medicine. Psychosexual functions in women.* New York: Ronald, 1952.

Benedict, Ruth. *Patterns of culture.* Boston: Houghton Mifflin, 1934.

Benedict, Ruth. A reply to Dr. Aginsky. *Char. & Pers.,* 1939, 7, 344–345.

Benne, K. D., & Sheets, P. Functional roles of group members. *J. soc. Issues,* 1948, *4,* 41–50.

Benton, A. L., & Bandura, A. "Primary" and "secondary" suggestibility. *J. abnorm. soc. Psychol.,* 1953, *48,* 336–340.

Berenda, Ruth W. *The influence of the group on the judgments of children, an experimental investigation.* New York: King's Crown Press, 1950.

Berg, I. A. Observations concerning obsessive tunes in normal persons under stress. *J. clin. Psychol.*, 1953, *9*, 300–302.

Berg, I. A. The unimportance of test item content. In Bernard M. Bass & Irwin A. Berg (Eds.), *Objective approaches to personality assessment.* Princeton, N. J.: Van Nostrand, 1959.

Bergler, E. *The battle of the conscience, a psychiatric study of the inner working of the conscience.* Washington: Washington Institute of Medicine, 1948.

Bergler, E. *The basic neurosis, oral regression and psychic masochism.* New York: Grune & Stratton, 1949.

Berlyne, D. E. Conflict and information-theory variables as determinants of human perceptual curiosity. *J. exp. Psychol.*, 1957, *53*, 399–404.

Bernard, L. L. *Instinct, a study in social psychology.* New York: Holt, 1924.

Bernreuter, R. G. The theory and construction of the personality inventory. *J. soc. Psychol.*, 1933, *4*, 387–405.

Best, H. L., & Michaels, R. M. Living out "future" experience under hypnosis. *Science*, 1954, *120*, 1077.

Bettelheim, B. Individual and mass behavior in extreme situations. *J. abnorm. soc. Psychol.*, 1943, *38*, 417–452.

Bettelheim, B. *Symbolic wounds, puberty rites and the envious male.* Glencoe, Ill.: The Free Press, 1954.

Betts, G. H. *Foundations of character and personality, an introduction to the psychology of social adjustment.* Indianapolis: Bobbs-Merrill, 1937.

Bidwell, C. E. Some effects of administrative behavior: A study in role theory. *Admin. sci. Quart.*, 1957, *2*, 163–181.

Bindra, D., & Cameron, Lois. Changes in experimentally produced anxiety with the passage of time: incubation effect. *J. exp. Psychol.*, 1953, *45*, 197–203.

Binet, A. *Alterations of personality.* (Trans. by Helen G. Baldwin.) London: Chapman & Hall, 1896 (Orig., 1891).

Binet, A., & Simon, T. *A method of measuring the development of the intelligence of young children.* (3rd Ed.) (Trans. by Clara H. Town.) Chicago: Chicago Medical Book Co., 1915.

Bird, C. Suggestions and suggestibility, a bibliography. *Psychol. Bull.*, 1939, *36*, 264–283.

Bitterman, M. E., & Kniffin, C. W. Manifest anxiety and "perceptual defense." *J. abnorm. soc. Psychol.*, 1953, *48*, 248–252.

Blackwood, Beatrice. A study of mental testing in relation to anthropology. *Ment. Measmt. Monogr.*, Serial No. 4, Dec., 1927.

Blake, R. R., & Ramsey, G. V. *Perception, an approach to personality.* New York: Ronald, 1951.

Blatz, W. E., Chant, N., Charles, M. W., & others. *Collected studies on the Dionne quintuplets.* Toronto: St. George's School for Child Study, Univer. of Toronto Press, 1937.

Bleuler, M., & Bleuler, R. Rorschach's ink-blot test and racial psychology: Mental peculiarities of Moroccans. *Char. & Pers.*, 1935, *4*, 97–114.

Block, Jack. An experimental investigation of the construct of ego control. Stanford Univer. dissertation abstracts, 1950.

Block, Jack, & Block, Jeanne L. H. An investigation of the relationship between intolerance of ambiguity and ethnocentrism. *J. Pers.*, 1951, *19*, 303–311.

Block, Jack, & Thomas, H. Is satisfaction with self a measure of adjustment? *J. abnorm. soc. Psychol.*, 1955, *51*, 254–259.

Block, Jeanne L. H. An experimental study of a topological representation of ego-structure. Stanford Univer. dissertation abstracts, 1950.

Block, Jeanne L. H., & Block, Jack. An interpersonal experiment on reactions to authority. *Hum. Relat.*, 1952, *5*, 91–98.

Block, Jeanne L. H., & Morton, B. Predicting the behavior of children under frustration. *J. abnorm. soc. Psychol.*, 1955, *51*, 281–285.

Blum, G. S. A study of the psychoanalytic theory of psychosexual development. *Genet. Psychol. Monogr.*, 1949, *39*, 3–99.

Blum, G. S. Perceptual defense revisited. *J. abnorm. soc. Psychol.*, 1955, *51*, 24–29.

Blum, G. S., & Hunt, H. F. The validity of the Blacky pictures. *Psychol. Bull.*, 1952, *49*, 238–250.

Boas, F. The social organization and the secret societies of the Kwakiutl Indians. *U. S. National Museum, Annual Report*, 1894–1895, Washington, 1897. (Cited in part in Margaret Mead & N. Calas, *Primitive Heritage.* New York: Random House, 1953.)

Boas, F. *The mind of primitive man.* (Rev. Ed.) New York: Macmillan, 1938.

Boothby, W. M., Berkson, J., & Dunn, H. L. Studies of the energy of metabolism of normal individuals: a standard for basal metabolism with a nomogram for clinical applications. *Amer. J. Physiol.*, 1936, *116*, 468–484.

Boring, E. G. *A history of experimental psychology.* (2nd Ed.) New York: Appleton-Century-Crofts, 1950.

Boring, E. G. A history of introspection. *Psychol. Bull.*, 1953, *50*, 169–189.

Bosanquet, B. *Psychology of the moral self.* London: Macmillan, 1897.

Bossard, J. H. S., & Boll, Eleanor S. *Family situations, an introduction to the study of child behavior.* Philadelphia: Univer. of Pennsylvania Press, 1943.

Bowley, Agatha. *Modern child psychology.* London: Hutchinson's University Library, 1948.

Bowne, B. P. *Philosophy of theism.* New York: Harper, 1887.

Bowne, B. P. *Personalism.* Boston: Houghton Mifflin, 1908.

Brachfield, O. *Inferiority feelings in the individual and the group.* New York: Grune & Stratton, 1951.

Brackett, Catherine W. Laughing and crying of preschool children, a study of the social and emotional behavior of young children as indicated by laughing and crying. *Ch. Develpm. Monogr.* No 14. New York: Bureau of Publications, Teachers College, Columbia University, 1934.

Braden, S. R. *The psychology of character, some psychological aspects of moral training.* Columbia, Mo.: Univer. of Missouri, 1924.

Brand, H. (Ed.) *The study of personality, a book of readings.* New York: Wiley, 1954.

Bray, D. W. *Issues in the study of talent.* New York: King's Crown Press, 1954.

Breese, B. B. *Psychology.* New York: Scribners, 1917.

Brengelmann, J. C. Kretschmer's zyklothymer und schizothymer Typus im Bereich der normalen Persönlichkeit. *Psychol. Rund.*, 1952, *3*, 31–38.

Breuer, J., & Freud, S. *Studies in hysteria.* New York: Nervous & Medical Diseases Publ. Co., 1936. (1st ed., 1895)

Bridges, Katherina M. B. *Social and emotional development of the preschool child.* London: Kegan Paul, 1931.

Bridgman, P. W. *The logic of modern physics.* New York: Macmillan, 1927.

Brillouin, L. *Science and information theory.* New York: Academic Press, 1956.

Brodbeck, A. J. Learning theory and identification: IV. Oedipal motivation as a determinant of conscience development. *J. genet. Psychol.*, 1954, *84*, 219–227.

Brodbeck, A. J., & Perlmutter, Howard V. Self-dislike as a determinant of marked ingroup-outgroup preferences. *J. Psychol.*, 1954, *38*, 271–280.

Brogden, H. E. A factor analysis of forty character tests. *Psychol. Monogr.*, 1940, *52*, No. 3 (Whole No. 234).

Brogden, H. E. The primary personal values measured by the Allport-Vernon test, "A Study of Values." *Psychol. Monogr.*, 1952, *66*, No. 16 (Whole No. 348).

Brown, F. J. *The sociology of childhood.* New York: Prentice-Hall, 1939.

Brown, R. Explanation by laws in social science. *Phil. Sci.*, 1954, *21*, 25–32.

Brown, R. W. A determinant of the relationship between rigidity and authoritarianism. *J. abnorm. soc. Psychol.*, 1953, *48*, 469–476.

Brown, R. W. Mass phenomena. In G. Lindzey (Ed.), *Handbook of social psychology.* Vol. II. Cambridge, Mass.: Addison-Wesley, 1954.

Brown, W. *Science and personality.* (The Terry Lectures) New Haven: Yale Univer. Press, 1929.

Brown, W., & Gilhousen, H. C. *College psychology.* New York: Prentice-Hall, 1950.

Brown, W., & Thomson, G. H. *The essentials of mental measurement.* (4th Ed.) Cambridge: At the Univer. Press, 1940.

Brownfain, J. J. Stability of the self-concept as a dimension of personality. *J. abnorm. soc. Psychol.*, 1952, *47*, 597–606.

Bruner, J. S., & Goodman, C. D. Value and need as organizing factors in perception. *J. abnorm. soc. Psychol.*, 1947, *42*, 33–44.

Bruner, J. S., & Krech, D. *Perception and personality, a symposium.* Parts I. & II. Durham, N. C.: Duke Univer. Press, 1949, 1950.

Bryn, D. The problem of human types: comments and an experiment. *Char. & Pers.*, 1936, *5*, 48–60.

Bugelski, B. R. *The psychology of learning.* New York: Holt, 1956.

Bugelski, B. R. *An introduction to the principles of psychology.* New York: Rinehart, 1960.

Buhler, Charlotte. *The first year of life.*

(Trans. by Pearl Greenberg & Rowena Ripin.) New York: John Day, 1930.

Buhler, Charlotte. The ball and field test as a help in the diagnosis of emotional difficulties. *Char. & Pers.*, 1938, *6*, 257–273.

Buhler, Charlotte. *The child and his family.* New York: Harper, 1939.

Buhler, Charlotte, LeFever, D. W., Kallstadt, Frances E., & Peak, H. M. *Rorschach standardization study. Development of the Basic Rorschach Score, supplementary monograph.* Los Angeles: Privately mimeographed, 1952.

Buhler, K. The skywise and neighborwise navigation of ants and bees. *Acta Psychol.*, 1951, *8*, 225–263.

Burlingham, Dorothy. *Twins, a study of three pairs of identical twins.* New York: International Universities Press, 1952.

Burnham, W. H. *The wholesome personality, a contribution to mental hygiene.* New York: Appleton-Century, 1932.

Buros, O. K. (Ed.) *The fourth mental measurements yearbook.* Highland Park, N. J.: Gryphon, 1953.

Burroughs, E. R. *The mucker.* New York: McClurg, 1921.

Burrow, T. *The social basis of consciousness.* New York: Harcourt, Brace, 1927.

Burrow, T. The autonomy of the "I" from the standpoint of group analysis. *Psyche*, 1928, *8*, 35–50.

Burrow, T. *The neurosis of man, an introduction to a science of human behavior.* New York: Harcourt, Brace, 1949.

Burt, C. *The young delinquent.* London: Univer. of London Press, 1925.

Burt, C. The factorial analysis of emotional traits. *Char. & Pers.*, 1939, 7, 238–254. (a)

Burt, C. The factorial analysis of emotional traits. Part II. *Char. & Pers.*, 1939, *1*, 285–299. (b)

Burt, C. *The factors of the mind: an introduction to factor-analysis in psychology.* New York: Macmillan, 1941.

Burton, R. *The anatomy of melancholy.* London: George Bell, 1903 (Orig., 1651–1652).

Caille, Ruth K. *Resistant behavior of preschool children.* New York: Bureau of Publications, Teachers College, Columbia University, 1933.

Calkins, Mary W. *The persistent problems of philosophy, an introduction to metaphysics through the study of modern systems.* New York: Macmillan, 1907.

Calkins, Mary W. The self in scientific psychology. *Amer. J. Psychol.*, 1915, *26*, 495–524.

Cameron, N. Deterioration and regression in schizophrenic thinking. *J. abnorm. soc. Psychol.*, 1939, *34*, 265–270.

Cameron, N. *The psychology of behavior disorders, a biosocial interpretation.* Boston: Houghton-Mifflin, 1947.

Campbell, C. M., Langfeld, H. S., McDougall, W., Roback, A. A. & Taylor, E. W. (Eds.) *Problems of personality, studies presented to Dr. Morton Prince, pioneer in American psychopathology.* New York: Harcourt, Brace, 1925.

Cannicott, R. G., & Umberger, J. P. An investigation of the psychoanalytic "mechanism" of repression: the retention of verbal material associated with noxious stimulation. *Proc. Okla. Acad. Sci.*, 1950, *31*, 176–178.

Cannon, W. B. *Bodily changes in pain, hunger, fear, and rage.* New York: Appleton, 1929.

Cannon, W. B. *The wisdom of the body.* New York: Norton, 1932.

Cantril, H. *The "why" of man's experience.* New York: Macmillan, 1950.

Cantril, H., & Allport, G. W. *The psychology of radio.* (2nd Ed.) New York: Harper, 1935.

Cantril, H., & Rand, H. A. An additional study of the determination of personal interests by psychological and graphical methods. *Char. & Pers.*, 1934, *3*, 72–78.

Cantril, H., Rand, H. A., & Allport, G. W. The determination of personal interests by psychological and graphological methods. *Char. & Pers.*, 1933, *2*, 134–143.

Carlson, A. J., & Johnson, V. *The machinery of the body.* (3rd Ed.) Chicago: Univer. of Chicago Press, 1948.

Carmichael, L. (Ed.) *Manual of child psychology.* New York: Wiley, 1946.

Carmichael, L., Hogan, H. P., & Walter, A. A. An experimental study of the effect of language on the reproduction of visually perceived form. *J. exp. Psychol.*, 1932, *15*, 73–86.

Carnegie, D. *How to win friends and influence people.* New York: Simon & Schuster, 1936.

Carr, H. A. *Psychology, a study of mental activity.* New York: Longmans, Green, 1925.

Carr, R. M., & Williams, C. D. Exploratory behavior of three strains of rats. *J. comp. physiol. Psychol.*, 1957, *50*, 621–623.

Carrigan, Patricia M. Extraversion-introversion as a dimension of personality: A reappraisal. *Psychol., Bull.*, 1960, *57*, 329–360.

Cartwright, D. S. Note on "changes in psychoneurotic patients with and without psychotherapy." *J. consult. Psychol.*, 1956, *20*, 403–404.

Case, Virginia. *Your personality—introvert or extravert?* New York: Macmillan, 1944.

Cash, W. J. *The mind of the south.* New York: Knopf, 1941.

Cattell, Psyche. *The measurement of intelligence of infants and young children.* New York: The Psychological Corporation, 1940.

Cattell, R. B. Friends and enemies: a psychological study of character and temperament. *Char. & Pers.*, 1934, *3*, 54–63.

Cattell, R. B. The measurement of interest. *Char. & Pers.*, 1935, *4*, 147–169.

Cattell, R. B. Sentiment or attitude? The core of a terminology problem in personality research. *Char. & Pers.*, 1940, *9*, 6–17.

Cattell, R. B. The. description of personality: basic traits resolved into clusters. *J. abnorm. soc. Psychol.*, Clin. Suppl., 1943, *38*, 476–506. (a)

Cattell, R. B. The description of personality. I. The foundations of trait measurement. *Psychol. Rev.*, 1943, *50*, 559–594. (b)

Cattell, R. B. *Description and measurement of personality.* Yonkers-on-Hudson, N. Y.: World Book, 1946.

Cattell, R. B. Confirmation and clarification of primary personality factors. *Psychometrika*, 1947, *12*, 197–220.

Cattell, R. B. *Personality, a systematic theoretical and factual study.* New York: McGraw-Hill, 1950.

Cattell, R. B. *Factor analysis, an introduction and manual for the psychologist and social scientist.* New York: Harper, 1952. (a)

Cattell, R. B. P-technique factorization and the determination of individual dynamic structure. *J. clin. Psychol.*, 1952, *8*, 5–10. (b)

Cattell, R. B. The chief invariant psychological and psychophysical functional unities found by P-technique. *J. clin. Psychol.*, 1955, *11*, 319–343. (a)

Cattell, R. B. The principal replicated factors discovered in objective tests. *J. abnorm. soc. Psychol.*, 1955, *50*, 291–314. (b)

Cattell, R. B. Second-order personality factors in the questionnaire realm. *J. consult. Psychol.*, 1956, *20*, 411–418.

Cattell, R. B. *Personality and motivation structure and measurement.* Yonkers-on-Hudson, N. Y.: World Book, 1957. (a)

Cattell, R. B. The conceptual and test distinction of neuroticism and anxiety. *J. clin. Psychol.*, 1957, *13*, 221–233. (b)

Cattell, R. B., Beloff, J., Flint, D., & Gruen, W. *Handbook for the Junior Personality Quiz ("the J.P.Q.").* Champaign, Ill.: Institute for Personality and Ability Testing, 1953.

Cattell, R. B., Cattell, A. K. S., & Rhymer, R. M. P-technique demonstrated in determining psycho-physiological source traits in a normal individual. *Psychometrika*, 1947, *12*, 267–288.

Cattell, R. B., & Cross, K. P. Comparison of the ergic and self-sentiment structures found in dynamic traits by R- and P-techniques. *J. Pers.*, 1952, *21*, 250–271.

Cattell, R. B., & Gruen, W. Primary personality factors in the questionnaire medium for children eleven to fourteen years old. *Educ. psychol. Measmt.*, 1954, *14*, 50–76.

Cattell, R. B., & Luborsky, L. B. P-technique demonstrated as a new clinical method for determining personality symptom structure. *J. gen. Psychol.*, 1950, *42*, 3–24.

Cattell, R. B., & Saunders, D. R. Inter-relation and matching of personality factors from behavior rating, questionnaire, and objective test date. *J. soc. Psychol.*, 1950, *31*, 243–260.

Cattell, R. B., Saunders, D. R., & Stice, G. *Handbook for the Sixteen Personality Factor Questionnaire. "The 16 P.F. Test." Forms A & B.* Champaign, Ill.: Institute for Personality and Ability Testing, 1950.

Cattell, R. B., & Tiner, L. G. The varieties of structural rigidity. *J. Pers.*, 1949, *17*, 321–341.

Cattell, R. B., & Winder, A. E. Structural rigidity in relation to learning theory and clinical psychology. *Psychol. Rev.*, 1952, *59*, 23–39.

Chapanis, A. How we see: A summary of basic principles. In National Research Council, Human factors in undersea warfare, 1949.

Chapman, P. W. *Your personality and your job.* Chicago: Science Research Associates, 1944.

Charnwood, G. R. B. *Abraham Lincoln*. London: Constable, 1917 (New York: Garden City, 1938).

Charters, W. W. *Motion pictures and youth, a summary*. New York: Macmillan, 1933.

Chave, E. J. *Personality development in children*. Chicago: The Univer. of Chicago Press, 1937.

Chessman, C. *Cell 2455 Death Row*. New York: Prentice-Hall, 1954.

Chickering, A. W. Self concept, ideal self concept, and achievement. *Dissertation Abstr.*, 1958, *19*, 164.

Child, C. M. *Individuality in organisms*. Chicago: The Univer. of Chicago Press, 1915.

Child, C. M. *Patterns and problems of development*. Chicago: The Univer. of Chicago Press, 1941.

Child, I. L. The relation of somatotypes to self-ratings on Sheldon's temperament traits. *J. Pers.*, 1950, *18*, 440–453.

Child, I. L., & Sheldon, W. H. The correlation between components of physique and scores on certain psychological tests. *Char. & Pers.*, 1941, *10*, 23–34.

Chodorkoff, B. Adjustment and the discrepancy between the perceived and ideal self. *J. clin. Psychol.*, 1954, *10*, 266–268. (a)

Chodorkoff, B. Self-perception, perceptual defense, and adjustment. *J. abnorm. soc. Psychol.*, 1954, *49*, 508–512. (b)

Chodorkoff, B. A note on Bitterman and Kniffin's "Manifest anxiety and perceptual defense." *J. abnorm. soc. Psychol.*, 1955, *50*, 144.

Clarapède, E. *Experimental pedagogy and the psychology of the child*. (Trans. by Mary Louch and Henry Holman.) London: Edward Arnold, 1913.

Clark, R. A. The problem of closure in mental organization. Unpublished Honors thesis. Middletown, Conn.: Wesleyan Univer., 1947 (Cited by McClelland, D. *Personality*. New York: Wm. Sloane Associates, 1951).

Coffin, T. E. Some conditions of suggestion and suggestibility: a study of certain attitudinal and situational factors influencing the process of suggestion. *Psychol. Monogr.*, 1941, *53*, No. 4 (Whole No. 241).

Coggan, W. Choices of comics by delinquent and non-delinquent boys. Paper read at the Florida Psychol. Assoc., St. Petersburg, Fla., 1955.

Cohen, M. R., & Nagel, E. *An introduction to logic and scientific method*. New York: Harcourt, Brace, 1934.

Cohn, R. On certain aspects of the sensory organization of the human brain. *J. nerv. ment. Dis.*, 1951, *113*, 471–484.

Cole, L. E., & Bruce, W. F. *Educational psychology*. Yonkers-on-Hudson, N. Y.: World Book Co., 1950.

Coleman, J. C. *Abnormal psychology and modern life*. (2nd ed.) Chicago: Scott, Foresman, 1956.

Collier, R. M. Outline of a theory of consciousness as a regulatory field: Preliminary statement. *J. Psychol.*, 1955, *40*, 269–274.

Collier, R. M. Consciousness as a regulatory field: A theory of psychopathology. *Psychol. Rev.*, 1956, *63*, 360–369.

Combe, G. *The constitution of man considered in relation to external objects*. (3rd ed.) New York: Collins, Keese, 1835.

Combs, A. W., & Snygg, D. *Individual behavior; a perceptual approach to behavior*. (Rev. ed.) New York: Harper, 1959.

Connor, Ruth, Greene, Helen F., & Walters, J. Agreement of family member conceptions of "good" parent and child roles. *Soc. Forces*, 1958, *36*, 353–358.

Cooley, C. H. *Human nature and the social order*. New York: Scribner's, 1902.

Cooley, C. H., Angell, R. C., & Carr, L. J. *Introductory sociology*. New York: Scribner's, 1933.

Coover, J. E. *Experiments in psychical research at Leland Stanford Junior University*. Stanford University, Calif.: Stanford Univer. Press, 1917.

Corrie, C. C. Aspiration, self acceptance and acceptance of others in normal and neuropsychiatric groups. *Dissertation Abstr.*, 1958, *18*, 1855.

Couch, C. J. A study of the relationships between self-views and role-taking accuracy. *Dissertation Abstr.*, 1957, *17*, 687.

Courtis, S. A. The rate of growth makes a difference. *Phi Delta Kappan*, 1949, *30*, 316–323.

Cowen, E. L. The influence of varying degrees of psychological stress on problem-solving rigidity. *J. abnorm. soc. Psychol.*, 1952, *47*, 512–519.

Cowen, E. L. The "negative self concept" as a

personality measure. *J. consult. Psychol.*, 1954, *18*, 138–142.

Cowen, E. L., & Thompson, G. G. Problem solving rigidity and personality structure. *J. abnorm. soc. Psychol.*, 1951, *46*, 165–176.

Cowen, E. L., Wiener, M., & Hess, Judith. Generalization of problem-solving rigidity. *J. consult. Psychol.*, 1953, *17*, 100–103.

Cox, Catherine M. *The early mental traits of three hundred geniuses.* (Vol. 2, *Genetic studies of genius.*) Stanford, Calif.: Stanford Univer. Press, 1926.

Cronbach, L. J. Pattern tabulation: a statistical method for analysis of limited patterns of scores, with particular reference to the Rorschach test. *Educ. psychol. Measmt.*, 1949, *9*, 149–171. (a)

Cronbach, L. J. Statistical methods applied to Rorschach scores: a review. *Psychol. Bull.*, 1949, *46*, 393–429. (b)

Cronbach, L. J. Statistical methods for multi-score tests. *J. clin. Psychol.*, 1950, *6*, 21–26.

Cronbach, L. J. & Gleser, Goldine C. *Psychological tests and personnel decisions.* Urbana: Univer. of Illinois Press, 1957.

Cronbach, L. J., & Meehl, P. E. Construct validity in psychological tests. *Psychol. Bull.*, 1955, *52*, 281–302.

Cross, Hildreth. *An introduction to psychology, an evangelical approach.* Grand Rapids, Mich.: Zondervan, 1952.

Crumpton, Evelyn, Cantor, J. J. & Batiste, C. A factor analytic study of Barron's Ego Strength Scale. *J. clin. Psychol.*, 1960, *16*, 283–291.

Culbertson, J. T. *Consciousness and behavior, a neural analysis of behavior and of consciousness.* Dubuque, Ia.: Brown, 1950.

Cunningham, G. W. *Problems of philosophy.* New York: Holt, 1924.

Curle, A. Transitional communities and social reconnection: a follow-up study of the civil resettlement of British prisoners of war, Part I. *Hum. Relat.*, 1947, *1*, 42–68.

Curran, C. A. *Personality factors in counseling.* New York: Grune & Stratton, 1945.

Curtis, Q. F. Frustration as an experimental problem. IV. Some physiological consequences of frustration. *Char. & Pers.*, 1938, *7*, 140–144.

Dana. R. M. Personality orientation: an organizational focus for current research. *J. Psychol.*, 1954, *37*, 139–150.

Darrow, C. W., & Heath, L. L. Reaction tendencies relating to personality. In K. S. Lashley (Ed.), *Studies in the dynamics of behavior.* Chicago: Chicago Univer. Press, 1932.

Darwin, C. *The expression of the emotions in man and animals.* London: John Murray, 1872.

David, H. P., & von Bracken, H. (Eds.) *Perspectives in personality theory.* New York: Basic Books, 1957.

Davis, A., & Havighurst, R. J. *Father of the man. How your child gets his personality.* Boston: Houghton Mifflin, 1947.

Davis, A., & Havighurst, R. J. Social class and color differences in child-rearing. In C. Kluckhohn, H. A. Murray, & D. M. Schneider (Eds.) *Personality in nature, society, and culture.* (Rev. ed.) New York: Knopf, 1953.

Dearborn, W. F., & Rothney, J. W. M. *Predicting the child's development.* Cambridge, Mass.: Sci-Art, 1941.

Debs, E. V. *Writings and speeches of Eugene V. Debs.* New York: Hermitage, 1948.

Dember, W. N., & Earl, R. W. Analysis of exploratory, manipulatory, and curiosity behaviors. *Psychol., Rev.*, 1957, *64*, 91–96.

Dempsey, E. W. Homeostasis. In S. S. Stevens (Ed.), *Handbook of experimental psychology.* New York: Wiley, 1951. Pp. 209–235.

Dennis, Wayne (Ed.) *Current trends in psychological theory.* Pittsburgh: Univer. of Pittsburgh Press, 1951.

Deri, Susan. *Introduction to the Szondi test, theory and practice.* New York: Grune & Stratton, 1949.

De Sanctis, Sante. So-called "reactions" in characterology and psychology. *Char. & Pers.*, 1934, *3*, 40–53.

Dessoir, M. Character types. *Char. & Pers.*, 1935, *3*, 214–221.

Deutsch, F. *Applied psychoanalysis, selected objectives of psychotherapy.* New York: Grune & Stratton, 1949.

Deutsch, Helene. *The psychology of women, a psychoanalytic interpretation.* New York: Grune & Stratton, 1944. 2 vols.

Devereux, G. Cultural and characterological traits of the Mohave related to the anal stage of psychosexual development. *Psychoanal. Quart.*, 1951, *20*, 398–422.

Dewey, J. *Psychology.* (3rd rev. Ed.) New York: American Book Co., 1891.

Dexter, E. G. *Weather influences, an empirical study of the mental and physiological ef-*

fects of definite meterological conditions. New York: Macmillan, 1904.

Dexter, Emily S. Personality traits related to conservatism and radicalism. *Char. & Pers.,* 1939, 7, 230–273.

Diamond, S. *Personality and temperament.* New York: Harper, 1957.

Diggory, J. C. Responses to experimentally induced failure. *Amer. J. Psychol.,* 1949, *62,* 48–61.

Dingle, H. Science and modern cosmology. *Science,* 1954, *122,* 513–521.

Diven, K. Certain determinants in the conditioning of anxiety reactions. *J. Psychol.,* 1937, *3,* 291–308.

Dockeray, F. C., & Lane, G. G. *Psychology.* New York: Prentice-Hall, 1950.

Dollard, J. *Caste and class in a southern town.* New Haven: Yale Univer. Press, 1937.

Dollard, J., & Miller, N. *Personality and psychotherapy.* New York: McGraw-Hill, 1950.

Doris, J., & Sarason, S. Test anxiety and blame assignment in a failure situation. *J. abnorm. soc. Psychol.,* 1955, *50,* 335–338.

Dostoevsky, F. *The brothers Karamazov.* (Trans. by Constance Garnett.) New York: Modern Library, n.d. (Orig., 1879–1880).

Downey, June E. *The will-temperament and its testing.* Yonkers-on-Hudson, N. Y.: World Book Co., 1924.

Downey, June E. Familial trends in personality. *Char. & Pers.,* 1932, *1,* 35–47.

Dreger, R. M. Erythrophobia, stage fright, and examination anxiety. Unpublished manuscript, 1949.

Dreger, R. M. Some personality correlates of religious attitudes as determined by projective techniques. *Psychol. Monogr.,* 1952, *66,* No. 3 (Whole No. 335).

Dreger, R. M. Different I.Q.'s for the same individual associated with different intelligence tests. *Science,* 1953, *118,* 594–595.

Dreger, R. M. Spontaneous conversation and story-telling of children in a naturalistic setting. *J. Psychol.,* 1955, *40,* 163–180.

Dreger, R. M. The GE Scale: Measurement of custom and conscience functions of the superego. Unpublished res., Jacksonville Univer., 1960. (a)

Dreger, R. M. Perceptual closure in recognizably incomplete *Gestalten.* Unpublished res., Jacksonville Univer., 1960. (b)

Dreger, R. M. Perception in the context of social and personality theory. *J. gen. Psychol.,* 1961, *64,* 3–30.

Dreger, R. M., & Aiken, L. R. The identification of number anxiety in a college population. *J. educ. Psychol.,* 1957, *48,* 344–351.

Dreger, R. M., & Miller, K. S. Comparative psychological studies of Negroes and Whites in the United States. *Psychol. Bull.,* 1960, *57,* 361–402.

Dreger, R. M., Smith, W. D., & Wieland, R. Changes in dating attitudes and practices in the first semester of the college Freshman year. Unpublished manuscript, 1954.

Dreger, R. M., & Sweetland, A. Traits of fatherhood as revealed by the factor-analysis of a parent attitude scale. *J. genet. Psychol.,* 1960, *96,* 115–122.

Drevdahl, J. E. Factors of importance for creativity. *J. clin. Psychol.,* 1956, *12,* 21–26.

DuBois, E. F. *Basal metabolism in health and disease.* (2nd & 3rd Eds.) Philadelphia: Lea & Febiger, 1927, 1936.

Dudycha, G. J. An objective study of punctuality in relation to personality and achievement. *Arch. Psychol.,* 1936, *29,* No. 204.

Dudycha, G. J. A qualitative study of punctuality. *J. soc. Psychol.,* 1938, *9,* 207–217.

Dudycha, G. J. The dependability of college students. *J. soc. Psychol.,* 1939, *10,* 233–245.

Dudycha, G. J. Self-estimates and dependability. *J. soc. Psychol.,* 1940, *12,* 39–53.

Dudycha, G. J. A scale for measuring attitude toward dependability. *J. soc. Psychol.,* 1941, *13,* 59–69.

Duffy, E. Level of muscular tension as an aspect of personality. *J. gen. Psychol.,* 1946, *35,* 161–171.

Dugdale, R. L. *The Jukes, a study in crime, pauperism, disease, and heredity.* (4th Ed.) New York: Putnam's, 1910.

Dumas, G. *Traité de psychologie.* Paris: Librarie Félix Alcan, 1924.

Dunlap, K. *Personal adjustment.* New York: McGraw-Hill, 1946.

Dunlap, K. *Habits, their making and unmaking.* New York: Liveright, 1949.

Durdin, Peggy. "Face" is a basic issue in Asia. *The New York Times Magazine,* Jan. 23, 1955.

Ebbinghaus, H. *Memory, a contribution to experimental psychology.* (Trans. by Henry Ruger & Clara Busenius.) In *Educational Reprints.* No. 3. New York: Teachers College, Columbia Univer., 1913 (Orig., 1885).

Educational Testing Service. Annual report to the Board of Trustees, 1954–1955. Princeton, N. J.: Educational Testing Service, n.d.

Edwards, W. The theory of decision making. *Psychol. Bull.*, 1954, *51*, 380–417.

Eells, K., Davis, A., Havighurst, R. J., Herrick, V. E., & Tyler, R. W. *Intelligence and cultural differences*. Chicago: The Univer. of Chicago Press, 1951.

Einstein, A., & Infeld, L. *The evolution of physics*. New York: Simon & Schuster, 1938.

Eiselen, F. C., Lewis, E., & Downey, D. G. (Eds.) *The Abingdon Bible Commentary*. New York: Abingdon, 1929.

Eisenberg, P. Expressive movements related to feeling of dominance. *Arch. Psychol.*, 1937, No. 211. (a)

Eisenberg, P. A further study in expressive movement. *Char. & Pers.*, 1937, *5*, 296–301. (b)

Ellis, A. The validity of personality questionnaires. *Psychol. Bull.*, 1946, *43*, 385–440.

Ellis, A. An introduction to the principles of scientific psychoanalysis. *Genet. psychol. Monogr.*, 1950, *41*, 147–212.

Ellis, A. The Blacky Test used with a psychoanalytic patient. *J. clin. Psychol.*, 1953, *9*, 167–172.

Epstein, S. Unconscious self-evaluation in a normal and a schizophrenic group. *J. abnorm. soc. Psychol.*, 1955, *50*, 65–70.

Erickson, M. H. Experimental demonstrations of the psychopathology of everyday life. *Psychoan. Quart.*, 1938, *8*, 338–353.

Eriksen, C. W. Perceptual defense as a function of unacceptable needs. *J. abnorm. soc. Psychol.*, 1951, *46*, 557–564.

Eriksen, C. W. Discrimination and learning without awareness: A methodological survey and evaluation. *Psychol. Rev.*, 1960, *67*, 279–300.

Eriksen, C. W., & Kuethe, J. L. Avoidance conditioning of verbal behavior without awareness: A paradigm of repression. *J. abnorm. soc. Psychol.*, 1956, *53*, 203–209.

Eriksen, C. W., Lazarus, R. S., & Strange, J. R. Psychological stress and its personality correlates. Part II. The Rorschach test and other personality measures. *J. Pers.*, 1951, *20*, 278–286.

Evans, B. *The psychiatry of Robert Burton*. New York: Columbia Univer. Press, 1944.

Eysenck, H. J. Some factors in the apprecia-tion of poetry, and their relation to temperamental qualities. *Char. & Pers.*, 1941, *9*, 160–167.

Eysenck, H. J. Suggestibility and hysteria. *J. Neurol. Psychiat.*, 1943, *6*, 22–31. (Cited in Eysenck, H. J., & Furneaux, W. D. *J. exp. Psychol.*, 1945, *35*, 485–503)

Eysenck, H. J. *Dimensions of personality*. London: Routledge & Kegan Paul, 1947.

Eysenck, H. J. Cyclothymia and schizothymia as a dimension of personality: I. Historical review. *J. Pers.*, 1950, *19*, 123–152.

Eysenck, H. J. Schizothymia-cyclothymia as a dimension of personality: II. Experimental. *J. Pers.*, 1952, *20*, 345–384. (a)

Eysenck, H. J. *The scientific study of personality*. London: Routledge & Kegan Paul, 1952. (b)

Eysenck, H. J. Social attitude research. In C. A. Mace & P. E. Vernon, *Current trends in British psychology*. London: Methuen, 1953. (a)

Eysenck, H. J. The logical basis of factor analysis. *Amer. Psychologist*, 1953, *8*, 105–114. (b)

Eysenck, H. J. *The structure of human personality*. New York: Wiley, 1953. (c)

Eysenck, H. J. The science of personality: nomothetic! *Psychol. Rev.*, 1954, *61*, 339–342.

Eysenck, H. J., & Furneaux, W. D. Primary and secondary suggestibility: an experimental and statistical study. *J. exp. Psychol.*, 1945, *35*, 485–503.

Eysenck, H. J., & Prell, D. B. The inheritance of neuroticism: an experimental study. *J. ment. Sci.*, 1951, *97*, 441–465 (*Psychol. Abstr.*, 1952, *26*, No. 2347).

Eysenck, H. J., Granger, G. W., & Brengelmann, J. C. *Perceptual processes and mental illness*. Maudsley Monogr., No. 2. New York: Basic Books, 1957.

Farber, L. H., & Fisher, C. An experimental approach to dream psychology through the use of hypnosis. *Psychoan. Quart.*, 1943, *12*, 202–216.

Faris, R. E. L., & Dunham, H. W. *Mental disorders in urban areas*. Chicago: The Univer. of Chicago Press, 1939.

Fantham, H. B. Charles Dickens: a biological study of his personality. *Char. & Pers.*, 1933, *2*, 222–230.

Fay, P. J., & Middleton, W. C. Judgment of Spranger personality types from the voice as transmitted over a public address system. *Char. & Pers.*, 1939, *8*, 144–155.

Feibleman, J. K. The rational unconscious. *J. gen. Psychol.*, 1955, *52*, 157–162.

Feigl, H., & Brodbeck, May (Eds.). *Readings in the philosophy of science.* New York: Appleton-Century-Crofts, 1953.

Fenichel, O. *The psychoanalytic theory of neurosis.* New York: Norton, 1945.

Fenichel, O. *The collected papers of Otto Fenichel.* First Series. New York: Norton, 1953.

Ferenczi, S. *Further contributions to the theory and technique of psycho-analysis.* (Trans. by Jane Isabel Suttie.) London: Hogarth & Institute of Psycho-Analysis, 1950.

Ferguson, L. W. Primary social attitudes. *J. Psychol.*, 1939, *8*, 217–223.

Ferguson, L. W. The measurement of primary social attitudes. *J. Psychol.*, 1940, *10*, 199–205.

Ferguson, L. W. The stability of the primary social attitudes: I. Religionism and II. Humanitarianism. *J. Psychol.*, 1941, *12*, 283–288.

Ferguson, L. W. The isolation and measurement of nationalism. *J. soc. Psychol.*, 1942, *16*, 215–228.

Ferguson, L. W. A revision of the primary social attitude scales. *J. Psychol.*, 1944, *17*, 229–241. (a)

Ferguson, L. W. Socio-psychological correlates of the primary attitude scales: I. Religionism; II. Humanitarianism. *J. soc. Psychol.*, 1944, *19*, 81–98. (b)

Ferguson, L. W. *Personality Measurement.* New York: McGraw-Hill, 1952.

Fernald, G. G. An achievement capacity test. *J. educ. Psychol.*, 1912, *3*, 331–336.

Fernberger, S. W. The prestige and impact of various psychologists on psychology in America. *Amer. J. Psychol.*, 1954, *2*, 288–298.

Fey, W. F. Acceptance by others and its relation to acceptance of self and others: A revaluation. *J. abnorm. soc. Psychol.*, 1955, *50*, 274–276.

Fidelity of report. State College, Pa.: Pennsylvania State College Psychological Cinema Register, 1946. (Film)

Fields, P. E. Discrimination. In F. A. Moss (Ed.), *Comparative psychology.* (Rev. ed.) New York: Prentice-Hall, 1942.

Fingert, H. H. Psychoanalytic study of the minor prophet, Jonah. *Psychoanal. Rev.*, 1954, *41*, 55–65.

Fink, D. H. *Release from nervous tension.* New York: Simon & Schuster, 1943.

Fisher, C. Studies on the nature of suggestion. Part II. The transference meaning of giving suggestions. *J. Amer. psychoanal. Ass.*, 1953, *1*, 406–437.

Fisher, G. P. *The beginnings of Christianity.* New York: Scribner's, 1916.

Fisher, R. A. *The design of experiments.* (6th ed.) New York: Hafner, 1951.

Fisher, S. An overview of trends in research dealing with personality rigidity. *J. Pers.*, 1949, *17*, 342–351.

Fisher, S., & Cleveland, S. E. *Body image and personality.* Princeton, N. J.: D. Van Nostrand, 1958.

Fisher, V. E. *Auto-correctivism: the psychology of nervousness.* Caldwell, Idaho: Caxton Printers, 1937.

Fisher, V. E., & Marrow, A. J. Experimental study of moods. *Char. & Pers.*, 1933, *2*, 201–208.

Fiske, D. W. A study of relationships to somatotypes. *J. appl. Psychol.*, 1944, *28*, 504–519.

Fiske, D. W. Consistency of the factorial structures of personality ratings from different sources. *J. abnorm. soc. Psychol.*, 1949, *44*, 329–344.

Flanagan, J. C. *Factor analysis in the study of personality.* Stanford, Calif.: Stanford Univer. Press, 1935.

Fleege, U. H. *Self-revelation of the adolescent boy, a key to understanding the modern adolescent.* Milwaukee: Bruce, 1945.

Fleishman, E. A. A factor analysis of intra-task performance on two psychomotor tests. *Psychometrika*, 1953, *18*, 45–55. (a)

Fleishman, E. A. Testing for psychomotor abilities by means of apparatus tests. *Psychol. Bull.*, 1953, *50*, 241–262. (b)

Fleishman, E. A. A factorial study of psychomotor abilities. *Res. Bull.*, AFPTRC-TR-54-15.

Fleishman, E. A., & Hempel, W. E., Jr. A factor analysis of dexterity tests. *Personnel Psychol.*, 1954, *7*, 15–32. (a)

Fleishman, E. A., & Hempel, W. E., Jr. Changes in factor structure of a complex psychomotor test as a function of practice. *Psychometrika*, 1954, *19*, 239–252. (b)

Fleishman, E. A., & Hempel, W. E., Jr. Factorial analysis of complex psychomotor performance. *Res. Bull.*, AFPTRC-TR-54-12.

Fleishman, M. The discriminative power of

Szondi's syndromes. *J. consult. Psychol.*, 1954, *18*, 89–95.

Fliess, R. *The psychoanalytic reader.* Vol. 1. New York: International Universities Press, 1948.

Flowerman, S. H., Stewart, Naomi, & Strauss, Marion. Further investigation of the validity of "authoritarianism" as predictive of ethnic prejudices. *Amer. Psychologist*, 1950, *5*, 307–308. (Abstract)

Flugel, J. C. *Men and their motives, psychoanalytic studies.* New York: International Universities Press, 1947 (Orig., 1934).

Flynn, J. T. *God's gold, the story of Rockefeller and his times.* New York: Harcourt, 1932.

Forel, A. *Hypnotism or suggestion and psychotherapy.* (Trans. from 5th German ed. by H. W. Aronit.) New York: Rebman, 1907.

Forer, B. R. The fallacy of personal validation, a classroom demonstration of gullibility. *J. abnormal soc. Psychol.*, 1949, *44*, 118–123.

Forster, Nora C., Vinacke, E. W., & Digman, J. M. Flexibility and rigidity in a variety of problem situations. *J. abnorm. soc. Psychol.*, 1955, *50*, 211–216.

Frank, L. K. *Projective methods.* Springfield, Ill.: Charles C. Thomas, 1948.

Franz, S. I. Handbook of mental examination methods. *Nerv. & Ment. Monogr. Ser. No. 10.* New York: Journal of Nerv. & Ment. Dis. Publishing Co., 1912.

Franz, S. I., & Gordon, Kate. *Psychology.* New York: McGraw-Hill, 1933.

Fraser, R., & Sargant, W. The subjective experience of a schizophrenic illness: Personal records written at the end of the illness by some patients who were treated with insulin. *Char. & Pers.*, 1940, *9*, 139–151.

Frazer, J. G. *The golden bough, a study of magic and religion.* (Abridged ed.) New York: Macmillan, 1940 (Orig., 1922).

Freedman, M. B., Leary, T. F., Ossorio, A. G., & Coffey, H. S. The interpersonal dimension of personality. *J. Pers.*, 1951, *20*, 143–161.

Freeman, F. S. *Individual differences; the nature and causes of variations in intelligence and special abilities.* New York: Holt, 1934.

Freeman, F. S. *Mental tests, their history, principles, and applications.* Boston: Houghton Mifflin, 1936.

Freeman, J. T. Set or perceptual defense? *J. exp. Psychol.*, 1954, *48*, 283–288.

French, J. W. The description of aptitude and achievement tests by means of rotated factors. *Psychometr. Monogr.*, No. 5. Chicago: The Univer. of Chicago Press, 1951.

French, J. W. *The description of personality measurements in terms of rotated factors.* Princeton, N. J.: Educational Testing Service, 1953.

Frenkel-Brunswik, Else. Intolerance of ambiguity as an emotional and perceptual personality variable. *J. Pers.*, 1949, *18*, 108–143. (Reprinted in J. S. Bruner, & D. Krech, *Perception and Personality, a symposium.*)

Freud, Anna. *The ego and the mechanisms of defence.* New York: Stechert, 1937.

Freud, Anna. *The psycho-analytical treatment of children. Technical lectures and essays.* (Parts I & II trans. by Nancy Proctor-Gregg. London: Imago Publishing Co., 1946 (Lectures, 1926–1945).

Freud, Anna, & Burlingham, Dorothy. *Infants without families, the case for and against residential nurseries.* New York: International Universities Press, 1944.

Freud, S. *The Interpretation of dreams.* (Trans. by J. Strachey.) New York: Basic Books, 1955 (Orig., 1900).

Freud, S. *On the psychopathology of everyday life.* New York: Macmillan, 1914 (Orig., 1904).

Freud, S. *Wit and its relation to the unconscious.* In A. A. Brill (Ed.), *The basic writings of Sigmund Freud.* New York: Modern Library, 1938 (Orig., 1905).

Freud, S. *Totem and taboo.* (Trans. by J. Strachey.) New York: Norton, 1952 (Orig., 1913).

Freud, S. On narcissism: an introduction. *Collected papers.* Vol. IV. London: Hogarth Press & Institute of Psycho-Analysis, 1925 (Orig., 1914).

Freud, S. Mourning and melancholia. *Collected papers.* Vol. IV. London: Hogarth Press & Institute of Psycho-Analysis, 1925 (Orig., 1917).

Freud, S. *A general introduction to psychoanalysis.* (Trans. by Joan Riviere.) New York: Perma Giants, 1949 (Orig., 1917). (a)

Freud, S. *Beyond the pleasure principle.* London: Hogarth Press, 1950 (Orig., 1920).

Freud, S. *Group psychology and the analysis of the ego.* (Trans. by J. Strachey.) The

Psychoanalytical Library, No. 6. London: Hogarth Press & Institute of Psycho-Analysis, 1922 (Orig., 1921).

Freud, S. *The ego and the id.* (Trans. by Joan Riviere.) London: Hogarth Press & Institute of Psycho-Analysis, 1927 (orig., 1923).

Freud, S. *Collected papers.* (Vols. trans. under superv. of Joan Riviere: I, II, IV. Vol. III trans. by Alix & J. Strachey. Vol. V edited by J. Strachey.) London: Hogarth Press & Institute of Psycho-Analysis. Vols. I, II, 1924; Vols. III, IV, 1925; Vol. V, 1950.

Freud, S. *An outline of psychoanalysis.* (Trans. by J. Strachey.) New York: Norton, 1949 (1st German printing, 1940). (b)

Freud, S. *New introductory lectures on psychoanalysis.* (Trans. by W. J. H. Sprott.) London: Hogarth Press, 1949 (Orig., 1932).

Freud, S. *The origins of psychoanalysis; letters to Wilhelm Fliess, drafts and notes, 1887–1902.* New York: Basic Books, 1954.

Freyd, M. The graphic rating scale. *J. educ. Psychol.*, 1923, *14*, 83–102.

Friedenberg, E. Z., & Havighurst, R. J. An attempt to measure strength of conscience. *J. Pers.*, 1948, *17*, 232–243.

Friedgood, H. B. On the psychological aspects of authoritarianism and democratic political systems. *Amer. Scientist*, 1951, *39*, 432–440, 451.

Fromm, E. *Escape from freedom.* New York: Rinehart, 1941.

Fromm, E. *The forgotten language, an introduction to the understanding of dreams, fairy tales, and myths.* New York: Rinehart, 1951.

Frosch, J. (Ed.) *The annual survey of psychoanalysis, a comprehensive survey of current psychoanalytic theory and practice.* Vol. I, 1950. New York: International Universities Press, 1952.

Frosch, J., Ross, N., Tarachow, S., & Arlow, J. (Eds.) *The annual survey of psychoanalysis, a comprehensive survey of current psychoanalytic theory and practice.* Vol. II, 1951. New York: International Universities Press, 1954.

Fruchter, B. *Introduction to factor analysis.* New York: Van Nostrand, 1954.

Fulton, J. F. (Ed.) *A textbook on physiology.* (17th ed.) Philadelphia: Saunders, 1955.

Gaier, E. L., & Lee, Marilyn C. Pattern analysis; the configurational approach to predictive measurement. *Psychol. Bull.*, 1953, *50*, 140–148.

Galton, F. *Inquiries into human faculty and its development.* London: Macmillan, 1883.

Gandine-Stanton, Dorothy C. A study of failure. *Char. & Pers.*, 1938, *6*, 321–334.

Gannon, J. T. *A statistical study of certain diagnostic personality traits of college men.* Washington, D. C.: The Catholic Univer. of America Press, 1939.

Gantt, W. H. *Experimental basis for neurotic behavior, origin and development of artificially produced disturbances in dogs.* New York: Paul B. Hoeber, 1944.

Gardiner, Mary S. *The principles of general biology.* New York: Macmillan, 1952.

Garfinkle, M. The relationship between general self concept, role self concept and role behavior in high school. *Dissertation Abstr.*, 1958, *19*, 897–898.

Garnett, M. General ability, cleverness, and purpose. *Brit. J. Psychol.*, 1919, *9*, 345–366.

Gatling, F. P. Frustration reactions of delinquents using Rosenzweig's classification system. *J. abnorm. soc. Psychol.*, 1950, *45*, 749–752.

Geldard, F. A. Explanatory principles in psychology. *Psychol. Rev.*, 1939, *46*, 411–424.

Gesell, A. *The embryology of behavior, the beginning of the human mind.* New York: Harper, 1945.

Gesell, A., & Amatruda, Catherine S. *Developmental diagnosis, normal and abnormal child development, clinical methods and pediatric applications.* New York: Paul B. Hoeber, 1947.

Gesell, A., Amatruda, Catherine S., Castner, B. M., & Thompson, Helen. *Biographies of child development, the mental growth careers of eighty-four infants and children.* New York: Paul B. Hoeber, 1939.

Gesell, A., & Ilg, Frances L. *Infant and child in the culture of today.* New York: Harper, 1943.

Gesell, A., & Thompson, Helen. *The psychology of early growth, including norms of infant behavior and a method of genetic analysis.* New York: Macmillan, 1938.

Gill, M. Ego psychology and psychotherapy. *Psychoanal. Quart.*, 1951, *20*, 62–71.

Glaser, E. M., & Maller, J. B. The measurement of interest values. *Char. & Pers.*, 1940, *9*, 67–81.

Glover, E. War and pacifism: some individual

(unconscious) factors. *Char. & Pers.*, 1936, *4*, 305–318.

Goddard, H. H. *Feeblemindedness, its causes and consequences.* New York: Macmillan, 1914.

Goddard, H. H. *Two souls in one body, a case of dual personality.* New York: Dodd, Mead, 1927. (a)

Goddard, H. H. *The Kallikak family, a study in the heredity of feeblemindedness.* New York: Macmillan, 1927. (b)

Goldiamond, I. Indicators of perception: 1. Subliminal perception, subception, unconscious perception: An analysis in terms of psychophysical methodology. *Psychol. Bull.*, 1958, *55*, 373–411.

Goldman, A. E. Studies in vicariousness: degree of motor activity and the autokinetic phenomenon. *Amer. J. Psychol.*, 1953, *66*, 613–617.

Goldstein, K. *The organism, a holistic approach to biology derived from pathological data in man.* New York: American Book, 1939.

Goldstein, K., & Scheerer, M. Abstract and concrete behavior. *Psychol. Monogr.*, 1941, *53*, No. 2 (Whole No. 239).

Goldstein, S. B. A projective study of psychoanalytic mechanisms of defense. *Dissertation Abstr.*, 1952, *12*, 218. Ann Arbor, Mich.: Univer. Microfilms, Publ. No. 3501. (Abstract)

Goodenough, Florence L. Anger in young children. *Univer. Minn. Inst. Ch. Welf. Monogr.* Ser., No. 10. Minneapolis: The Univer. of Minnesota Press, 1931.

Goodenough, Florence L. *Developmental psychology, an introduction to the study of human behavior.* (2nd ed.) New York: Appleton-Century, 1945.

Goodstein, L. D. Intellectual rigidity and social attitudes. *J. abnorm. soc. Psychol.*, 1953, *48*, 345–353.

Gordon, L. V. A factor analysis of the 48 Szondi pictures. *J. Psychol.*, 1953, *36*, 387–392.

Gordon, L. V., & Lambert, E. J. The internal consistency of the Szondi factors. *J. soc. Psychol.*, 1954, *40*, 67–71.

Gordon, R. G. *Personality.* New York: Harcourt-Brace, 1926.

Gordy, J. P. *Lessons in psychology, designed especially as an introduction to the subject for private students, and as a text-book in normal and secondary schools.* Athens, Ohio: Ohio Publishing Co., 1890.

Gouldner, A. W. Cosmopolitans and locals: Toward an analysis of latent social roles. *Admin. sci. Quart.*, 1957, *2*, 281–306.

Graham, W. C., & May, H. G. *Culture and conscience: an archeological study of the new religious past in ancient Palestine.* Chicago: The Univer. of Chicago Press, 1936.

Gray, P. H. Theory and evidence of imprinting in human infants. *J. Psychol.*, 1958, *46*, 155–166.

Green, R. F., Guilford, J. P., Christensen, P. R., & Comrey, A. L. A factor-analytic study of reasoning ability. *Psychometrika*, 1953, *18*, 135–160.

Greenspoon, J. The reinforcing effect of two spoken sounds on the frequency of two responses. *Amer. J. Psychol.*, 1955, *68*, 409–416.

Gregg, J. E. Comparison of races. *Sci. Mon.*, 1925, *20*, 248–254.

Griggs, E. H. The development of personality in children. *Studies in Education*, Vol. I. Stanford Univer., 1896–1897.

Grinker, R. R., & Spiegel, J. P. *Men under stress.* Philadelphia: Blakiston, 1945.

Gross, K. *The play of man.* (Trans. by Elizabeth L. Baldwin.) New York: Appleton, 1901.

Grosz, H. J., & Levitt, E. E. The effects of hypnotically induced anxiety on the manifest anxiety scale and the Barron Ego-Strength Scale. *J. abnorm. soc. Psychol.*, 1959, *59*, 281–283.

Grummon, D. L., & Butler, J. M. Another failure to replicate Keet's study: "Two verbal techniques in a minature counseling situation.' *J. abnorm. soc. Psychol.*, 1953, *48*, 597.

Guerber, H. A. *Myths of Greece and Rome, narrated with special reference to literature and art.* New York: American Book, 1921.

Guilford, J. P. Human abilities. *Psychol. Rev.*, 1940, *47*, 367–394.

Guilford, J. P. *An inventory of factors STDCR.* Beverly Hills, Calif.: Sheridan Supply Co., 1945.

Guilford, J. P. Creativity. *Amer. Psychologist*, 1950, *5*, 444–454.

Guilford, J. P. *Fundamental statistics in psychology and education.* (2nd ed.) New York: McGraw-Hill, 1952. (a)

Guilford, J. P. Some recent findings on thinking abilities and their implications. *Informational Bull.*, Air Training Command,

Training Analysis and Development, 1952, *3*, No. 3, 48–61. (b)

Guilford, J. P. Validation of measures of interest and temperament. In L. L. Thurston (Ed.), *Applications of psychology.* New York: Harper, 1952. (c)

Guilford, J. P. Thinking abilities. *Res. Rev.*, Office of Naval Research, Department of the Navy, Nov., 1953, 6–10.

Guilford, J. P. *Psychometric methods.* (2nd ed.) New York: McGraw-Hill, 1954.

Guilford, J. P. A revised structure of intellect. *Rep. from the Psychol. Lab.*, No. 19. Los Angeles: Univer. of Southern Calif., 1957.

Guilford, J. P. *Personality.* New York: McGraw-Hill, 1959. (a)

Guilford, J. P. Three faces of intellect. *Amer. Psychologist*, 1959, *14*, 469–479. (b)

Guilford, J. P., Berger, R. M., & Christensen, P. R. A factor-analytic study of planning. I. Hypotheses and descriptions of tests. *Rep. from the Psychol. Lab.*, No. 10. Los Angeles: Univer. of Southern Calif., 1954.

Guilford, J. P., Berger, R. M., & Christensen, P. R. A factor-analytic study of planning. II. Administration of tests and analysis of results. *Rep. from the Psychol. Lab.*, No. 12. Los Angeles: Univer. of Southern Calif., 1955.

Guilford, J. P., & Braly, K. W. Extroversion and introversion. *Psychol. Bull.*, 1930, 27, 96–107.

Guilford, J. P., & Christensen, P. R. A factor-analytic study of verbal fluency. *Rep. from the Psychol. Lab.*, No. 17. Los Angeles: Univer. of Southern Calif., 1956.

Guilford, J. P., Christensen, P. R., Bond, N. A., Jr., & Sutton, M. A. A factor analysis of human interests. *Res. Bull.*, 53–11. San Antonio, Tex.: Human Resources Research Center, Air Research & Development Command, Lockheed Air Force Base, 1953.

Guilford, J. P., Christensen, P. R., Bond, N. A., Jr., & Sutton, M. A. A factor analysis study of human interests. *Psychol. Monogr.*, 1954, *68*, No. 4 (Whole No. 375).

Guilford, J. P., Christensen, P. R., Frick, J. W., & Merrifield, P. R. The relations of creative-thinking aptitudes to non-aptitude traits. *Rep. from the Psychol. Lab.*, No. 20. Los Angeles: Univer. of Southern Calif., 1957.

Guilford, J. P., Christensen, P. R., Kettner, N. W., Green, R. F., & Hertzka, A. F. A factor-analytic study of Navy reasoning tests with the Air Force Aircrew Classification Battery. *Educ. psychol. Measmt.*, 1954, *14*, 301–325.

Guilford, J. P., Comrey, A. L., Green, R. F., & Christensen, P. R. A factor-analytic study of reasoning abilities. I. Hypotheses and descriptions of tests. *Rep. from the Psychol. Lab.*, No. 1. Los Angeles: Univer. of Southern Calif., 1950.

Guilford, J. P., Fruchter, B., & Zimmerman, W. S. Factor analysis of the Army Air Forces Sheppard Field battery of experimental aptitude tests. *Psychometrika*, 1952, 17, 45–68.

Guilford, J. P., Green, R. F., & Christensen, P. R. A factor-analytic study of reasoning abilities. II. Administration of tests and analysis of results. *Rep. from the Psychol. Lab.*, No. 3. Los Angeles: Univer. of Southern Calif., 1951.

Guilford, J. P., Green, R. F., Christensen, P. R., Hertzka, A. F., & Kettner, N. W. A factor-analytic study of Navy reasoning tests with the Air Force Aircrew Classification Battery. *Rep. from the Psychol. Lab.*, No. 6. Los Angeles: Univer. of Southern Calif., 1952.

Guilford, J. P., & Guilford, R. B. An analysis of the factors in a typical test of introversion-extroversion. *J. abnorm. soc. Psychol.*, 1934, *28*, 377–399.

Guilford, J. P., & Guilford, R. B. Personality factors S, E, and M, and their measurement. *J. Psychol.*, 1936, *2*, 109–127.

Guilford, J. P., & Guilford, R. B. Personality factors, D, R, T, and A. *J. abnorm. soc. Psychol.*, 1939, *34*, 21–36. (a)

Guilford, J. P., & Guilford, R. B. Personality factors N and GD. *J. abnorm. soc. Psychol.*, 1939, *34*, 239–248. (b)

Guilford, J. P., Hertzka, A. F., Berger, R. M., & Christensen, P. R. A factor-analytic study of evaluative abilities. I. Hypotheses and description of tests. *Rep. from the Psychol. Lab.*, No. 7. Los Angeles: Univer. of Southern Calif., 1952.

Guilford, J. P., Hertzka, A. F., & Christensen, P. R. A factor-analytic study of evaluative abilities. II. Administration of tests and analysis of results. *Rep. from the Psychol. Lab.*, No. 9. Los Angeles: Univer. of Southern Calif., 1953.

Guilford, J. P., Kettner, N. W., & Christensen, P. R. A factor-analytic study across the domains of reasoning, creativity, and evaluation. I. Hypotheses and description of tests. *Rep. from the Psychol. Lab.*, No. 11. Los Angeles: Univer. of Southern Calif., 1954.

Guilford, J. P., Kettner, N. W., & Christensen, P. R. The relation of certain thinking factors to training criteria in the U. S. Coast Guard Academy. *Rep. from the Psychol. Lab.*, No. 13. Los Angeles: Univer. of Southern Calif., 1955. (a)

Guilford, J. P., Kettner, N. W., & Christensen, P. R. A factor-analytic investigation of the factor called General Reasoning. *Rep. from the Psychol. Lab.*, No. 14. Los Angeles: Univer. of Southern Calif., 1955. (b)

Guilford, J. P., Kettner, N. W., & Christensen, P. R. A factor-analytic study across the domains of reasoning, creativity, and evaluation. II. Administration of tests and analysis of results. *Rep. from the Psychol. Lab.*, No. 16. Los Angeles: Univer. of Southern Calif., 1956.

Guilford, J. P., & Lacey, J. I. (Eds.) *Printed classification tests.* Army Air Forces Aviation Psychology Program Research Reports, No. 5. Washington, D. C.: U. S Government Printing Office, 1947.

Guilford, J. P., & Martin, H. G. *The Guilford-Martin Personnel Inventory I.* Beverly Hills, Calif.: Sheridan Supply Co., 1943.

Guilford, J. P., & Martin, H. G. *The Guilford-Martin Inventory of Factors GAMIN.* (Abridged ed.) Beverly Hills, Calif.: Sheridan Supply Co., 1948.

Guilford, J. P., & Merrifield, P. R. The structure of intellect model: Its uses and implications. *Rep. from the Psychol. Lab.*, No. 24. Los Angeles: Univer. of Southern Calif., 1960.

Guilford, M. P., Merrifield, P. R., Christensen, P. R., & Frick, J. W. An investigation of symbolic factors of cognition and convergent production. *Rep. from the Psychol. Lab.*, No. 23. Los Angeles: Univer. of Southern Calif., 1960.

Guilford, J. P., Shneidman, E., & Zimmerman, W. S. *The Guilford-Shneidman-Zimmerman Interest Survey.* Beverly Hills, Calif.: Sheridan Supply Co., 1949.

Guilford, J. P., Wilson, R. C., & Christensen, P. R. A factor-analytic study of creative thinking. II. Administration of tests and analysis of results. *Rep. from the Psychol. Lab.*, No. 8. Los Angeles: Univer. of Southern Calif., 1952.

Guilford, J. P., Wilson, R. C., Christensen, P. R., & Lewis, D. J. A factor-analytic study of creative thinking. I. Hypotheses

and descriptions of tests. *Rep. from the Psychol. Lab.*, No. 4. Los Angeles: Univer. of Southern Calif., 1951.

Guilford, J. P., & Zimmerman, W. S. The Guilford-Zimmerman Aptitude Survey. *J. appl. Psychol.*, 1948, *32*, 24–34.

Guilford, J. P., & Zimmerman, W. S. *The Guilford-Zimmerman Temperament Survey.* Beverly Hills, Calif.: Sheridan Supply Co., 1949.

Gullahorn, J. T. Measuring role conflict. *Amer. J. Sociol.*, 1956, *61*, 299–303.

Haggard, E. A., Experimental studies in affective processes: I. Some effects of cognitive structure and active participation on certain autonomic reactions during and following experimentally induced stress. *J. exp. Psychol.*, 1943, *33*, 247–284.

Haggard, H. W., & Fry, C. C. *The anatomy of personality.* New York: Harper, 1936.

Hall, C. S. *The meaning of dreams.* New York: Harper, 1953.

Hall, C. S., & Lindzey, G. *Theories of personality.* New York: Wiley, 1957.

Hall, G. S. *Adolescence, its psychology and its relations to physiology, anthropology, sociology, sex, crime, religion, and education.* Vols. I, II. New York: Appleton, 1904.

Halliday, J. L. *Mr. Carlyle, my patient, a psychoanalytic biography.* New York: Grune & Stratton, 1950.

Hampton, Barbara J. An investigation of personality characteristics associated with self-adequacy. *Dissertation Abstr.*, 1955, *15*, 1203–1204.

Hardee, Melvene D. Moral guidance—our responsibility. *Personnel Guid. J.*, 1953, *31*, 220–223.

Hare, A. P., Borgatta, E. F., & Bales, Robert F. (Eds.) *Small groups, studies in social interaction.* New York: Knopf, 1955.

Harlow, H. F. Primate learning. In C. P. Stone (Ed.), *Comparative psychology.* (3rd ed.) New York: Prentice-Hall, 1951.

Harlow, H. F. Mice, monkeys, men, and motives. *Psychol. Rev.*, 1953, *60*, 23–32.

Harlow, H. F., Harlow, Margaret K., & Meyer, D. R. Learning motivated by a manipulation drive. *J. exp. Psychol.*, 1950, *40*, 228–234.

Harlow, R. G. The perception of persons: An exploratory study of some of the determinants of self perception and social perception. *Dissertation Abstr.*, 1956, *16*, 2220–2221.

Harmon, H. H. *Modern factor analysis.* Chicago: Univer. of Chicago Press, 1960.

Harmon, F. L. The reliability of metabolism measurements by the closed circuit method. *J. appl. Physiol.,* 1953, *5,* 773–778.

Harrison, R. Studies in the use and validity of the Thematic Apperception Test with mentally disordered patients. II. A quantitative validity study. *Char. & Pers.,* 1940, *9,* 122–133.

Harrower, Molly R., & Steiner, M. E. *Large scale Rorschach techniques, a manual for the Group Rorschach and multiple choice tests.* (2nd ed.) Springfield, Ill.: Charles C. Thomas, 1951.

Harsh, C. M., & Schrickel, H. G. *Personality development and assessment.* (2nd ed.) New York: Ronald, 1959.

Hartmann, G. W. *Gestalt psychology.* New York: Ronald, 1935.

Hartmann, H. On rational and irrational action. In Geza Roheim (Ed.), *Psychoanalysis and the social sciences, an annual.* Vol. I. New York: International Universities Press, 1947.

Hartmann, H. Comments on the psychoanalytic theory of instinctual drives. *Psychoanal. Quart.,* 1948, *17,* 368–388.

Hartmann, H. Technical implications of ego psychology. *Psychoanal. Quart.,* 1951, *20,* 31–43.

Hartshorne, H., & May, M. A. *Studies in deceit; studies in the nature of character by the Character Education Inquiry.* Vol. I. New York: Macmillan, 1928.

Hartshorne, H., May, M. A., & Maller, J. B. *Studies in service and self-control; studies in the nature of character by the Character Education Inquiry.* Vol. II. New York: Macmillan, 1929.

Hartshorne, H., May, M. A., & Shuttleworth, F. F. *Studies in the organization of character; studies in the nature of character by the Character Education Inquiry.* Vol. III. New York: Macmillan, 1930.

Harvey, O. L. The measurement of handwriting considered as a form of expressive movement. *Char. & Pers.,* 1934, *2,* 310–321.

Haslerud, G. M. Frustration as an experimental problem. III. Some interrelations of behavioral measures of frustration in chimpanzees. *Char. & Pers.,* 1938, *7,* 136–139.

Hathaway, S. R. Increasing clinical efficiency. In Bernard M. Bass & Irwin R. Berg (Eds.), *Objective approaches to personality assessment.* Princeton, N. J.: Van Nostrand, 1959.

Hathaway, S. R., & Meehl, P. E. *An atlas for the clinical use of the MMPI.* Minneapolis: Univer. of Minnesota Press, 1951.

Hathaway, S. R., & McKinley, J. C. *The Minnesota Multiphasic Personality Inventory Manual.* Rev. ed. New York: Psychological Corp., 1951.

Haverland, E. M. An experimental analysis of P-technique of some functional unitary variables of fatigue. Unpublished master's thesis, Univer. of Ill., 1954. (Cited in Cattell, R. B. The chief invariant psychological and psycho-physical functional unities found by P-technique. *J. clin. Psychol.,* 1955, *11,* 319–343.)

Havighurst, R. J., & Taba, Hilda. *Adolescent character and personality.* New York: Wiley, 1949.

Hayes, K. J., & Hayes, Catherine. *Vocalization and speech in chimpanzees.* State College, Pa.: Psychological Cinema Register, The Pennsylvania State College, 1950. (Film)

Hayes, K. J., & Hayes, Catherine. Imitation in a home-raised chimpanzee. *J. comp. physiol. Psychol.,* 1952, *45,* 450–459.

Hayes, K. J., Thompson, R., & Hayes, Catherine. Discrimination learning set in chimpanzees. *J. comp. physiol. Psychol.,* 1953, *46,* 99–104. (a)

Hayes, K. J., Thompson, R., & Hayes, Catherine. Concurrent discrimination learning in chimpanzees. *J. comp. physiol. Psychol.,* 1953, *46,* 105–107. (b)

Healy, W., & Bronner, Augusta F. *Delinquents and criminals, their making and unmaking.* New York: Macmillan, 1926.

Healy, W., & Bronner, Augusta F. *New light on delinquency and its treatment.* New Haven, Conn.: Yale Univer. Press, 1936.

Healy, W., Bronner, Augusta F., & Bowers, Anna Mae. *The structure and meaning of psychoanalysis, as related to personality and behavior.* New York: Knopf, 1930.

Heilbrunn, L. V. *An outline of general physiology.* (3rd ed.) Philadelphia: Saunders, 1952.

Helson, H. (Ed.) *Theoretical foundations of psychology.* New York: Van Nostrand, 1951.

Hempel, W. E., Jr., & Fleishman, E. A. A factor analysis of physical proficiency and manipulative skill. *J. appl. Psychol.,* 1955, *39,* 12–16.

Hendrick, I. Early development of the ego:

identification in infancy. *Psychoanal. Quart.*, 1951, *20*, 44–61.

Henry, J. The personality of the Kaingang Indians. *Char. & Pers.*, 1936, *5*, 113–123.

Hepner, H. W. *Psychology applied to life and work.* (2nd ed.) New York: Prentice-Hall, 1950.

Herbart, J. F. *A text-book in psychology, an attempt to found the science of psychology on experience, metaphysics, and mathematics.* (Trans. by Margaret K. Smith.) New York: Appleton, 1891 (Orig. rev. ed., 1834).

Heron, A. The objective assessment of personality among factory workers. *J. soc. Psychol.*, 1954, *39*, 161–185.

Herrington, L. P. The relation of physiological and social indices of activity level. In Q. McNemar & Maud A. Merrill (Eds.), *Studies in personality, contributed in honor of Lewis M. Terman.* New York: McGraw-Hill, 1942.

Hertz, Marguerite R. *Frequency tables for scoring responses to the Rorschach Inkblot Test.* Cleveland, O.: The Press of Western Reserve Univer., 1951.

Hertzka, A. F., Guilford, J. P., Christensen, P. R., & Berger, R. M. A factor-analytic study of evaluative abilities. *Educ. psychol. Measmt.*, 1954, *14*, 581–597.

Herzberg, A. Dreams and character. *Char. & Pers.*, 1940, *8*, 323–334.

Hildreth, Gertrude. *The child mind in evolution, a study of developmental sequences in drawing.* Morningside Heights, N. Y.: King's Crown Press, 1941.

Hilgard, E. R. *Theories of learning.* (1st & 2nd eds.) New York: Appleton-Century-Crofts, 1948, 1956.

Hilgard, E. R. Human motives and the concept of the self. *Amer. Psychologist*, 1949, *4*, 374–382.

Hilgard, E. R. *Introduction to psychology.* (2nd ed.) New York: Harcourt, Brace, 1957.

Hilgard, E. R., Kubie, L. S., & Pumpian-Mindlin, E. *Psychoanalysis as science. Hixon Lectures on the Scientific Status of Psychoanalysis.* Stanford, Calif.: Stanford Univer. Press, 1952.

Hillyer, Jane, *Reluctantly told.* New York: Macmillan, 1931.

Hoch, P. K., & Zubin, J. (Eds.) *Anxiety. The proceedings of the thirty-ninth annual meeting of the American Psychopathological Association, held in New York City, June, 1949.* New York: Grune & Stratton, 1950.

Hocking, W. E. *What man can make of man.* New York: Harper, 1942.

Höffding, H. *Outlines of psychology.* (Trans. by Mary E. Lowndes.) London: Macmillan, 1891.

Hofstaetter, P. R. A factorial study of prejudice. *J. Pers.*, 1952, *21*, 228–239.

Holden, H. M. *Noses.* Cleveland, O.: World Publishing, 1950.

Hollander, B. *The mental functions of the brain, an investigation into their localization and their manifestation in health and disease.* New York: Putnam's, 1901.

Hollander, E. P., & Webb, W. B. Leadership, followership, and friendship. *Res. Rep.*, No. NM 001 058.16.03, Contract No. NR 154–098. Pensacola, Fla.: U. S. Naval School of Aviation Medicine, 1954.

Hollingworth, H. L. *Psychology and ethics; a study of the sense of obligation.* New York: Ronald, 1949.

Hollingworth, L. S. *Children above 180 IQ, Stanford-Binet, origin and development.* Yonkers-on-Hudson, N. Y.: World Book Co., 1942.

Holt, E. B. *Animal drive and the learning process, an essay toward radical empiricism.* Vol. I. New York: Holt, 1931.

Holt, R. R. Clinical and statistical prediction: A reformulation and some new data. *J. abnorm. soc. Psychol.*, 1958, *56*, 1–12.

The Holy Bible, Revised Standard Version, containing the Old and New Testaments. New York: Thomas Nelson, 1953.

Holzinger, K. J. Recent research on unitary mental traits. *Char. & Pers.*, 1936, *4*, 335–343.

Holzinger, K. J., & Harman, H. H. *Factor analysis, a synthesis of factorial methods.* Chicago: Univer. of Chicago Press, 1941.

Holzman, P. S., & Gardner, R. W. Leveling and repression. *J. abnorm. soc. Psychol.*, 1959, *59*, 151–155.

Hoppe, F. *Erfolg und Misserfolg.* In K. Lewin (Ed.), *Untersuchungen zur Handlungs- und Affectpsychologie: IX. Psychol. Forsch.*, 1930, 14, 1–62. (Cited in Lewin, K., Dembo, Tamara, Festinger, L., & Sears, Pauline S. Level of aspiration. In Hunt, J. McV. *Personality and the behavior disorders.* New York: Ronald, 1944. 2 vols.)

Horney, Karen. *The neurotic personality of our time.* New York: Norton, 1937.

Horney, Karen. *Our inner conflicts, a con-*

structive theory of neurosis. New York: Norton, 1945.

Horst, P. Pattern analysis and configurational scoring. *J. clin. Psychol.,* 1954, *10,* 3–11.

Hoskins, R. G. *The biology of schizophrenia.* New York: Norton, 1946.

Howard, R. C., & Berkowitz, L. Reactions to the evaluators of one's performance. *J. Pers.,* 1958, *26,* 494–507.

Hovell, F. An exploratory study of behavioral correlates of personal constructs: IV. An analysis of differences in role-conceptualizations as a function of several personality variables. *Dissertation Abstr.,* 1955, *15,* 2576.

Howells, T. H. *Hunger for wholiness, man's universal motive.* Denver, Colo.: World Press, 1940.

Howes, D. H. A statistical theory of the phenomenon of subception. *Psychol. Rev.,* 1954, *61,* 98–110.

Howes, D. H., & Solomon, R. L. A note on McGinnies' "Emotionality and perceptual defense." *Psychol. Rev.,* 1950, *57,* 229–234.

Hull, C. L. *Hypnosis and suggestibility.* New York: Appleton-Century, 1933.

Hull, C. L. *Essentials of behavior.* New Haven, Conn.: Yale Univer. Press, 1951.

Hull, C. L., Hovland, D. I., Ross, R. T., & others. *Mathematico-deductive theory of rote learning; a study in scientific methodology.* New Haven, Conn.: Yale Univer. Press, 1940.

Hull, C. L., & Montgomery, R. B. An experimental investigation of certain alleged relations between character and handwriting. *Psychol. Rev.,* 1919, *26,* 63–74.

Hume, D. *A treatise of human nature.* Reprinted from the original edition in three volumes, and edited with an analytical index, by L. A. Selby-Bigge. Oxford: Clarendon Press, 1896 (Orig. *Treatise on human nature,* 1739–1740).

Humm, D. G. Personality and adjustment. *J. Psychol.,* 1942, *13,* 109–134.

Humm, D. G., & Wadsworth, G. W. The Humm-Wadsworth Temperament Scale. *Amer. J. Psychiat.,* 1935, *92,* 162–200.

Humphrey, Betty M. Introversion-extraversion ratings in relation to scores on ESP tests. *J. Parapsychol.,* 1951, *15,* 252–262.

Hunt, J. McV. (Ed.) *Personality and the behavior disorders.* New York: Ronald, 1944. 2 vols.

Hunt, W. A. An actuarial approach to clinical judgment. In Bernard M. Bass & Irwin A. Berg (Eds.), *Objective approaches to personality assessment.* Princeton, N. J.: Van Nostrand, 1959.

Hunter, W. S. The sensory control of the maze habit in the white rat. *J. genet. Psychol.,* 1929, *36,* 505–537.

Huxley, A. L. *Brave new world.* New York: Harper, 1946.

Icheiser, G. Real, pseudo, and sham qualities of personality: an attempt at a new classification. *Char. & Pers.,* 1941, *9,* 218–226.

Isaacs, Susan. *Intellectual growth of young children.* New York: Harcourt, Brace, 1930.

Isaacs, Susan. *Social development in young children, a study of beginnings.* New York: Harcourt, Brace, 1937.

Isaacs, Susan. *Childhood and after, some essays and clinical studies.* New York: International Universities Press, 1949.

Isham, A. C. The ego, consciousness, motor processes, and thought. *Psychoanal. Rev.,* 1955, *42,* 61–71.

Jacobson, A. C. *Genius, some evaluations.* New York: Greenberg Publishers, 1926.

Jacobson, E. *Progressive relaxation.* Chicago: The Univer. of Chicago Press, 1929.

Jacobson, E. Electrophysiology of mental activity. *Amer. J. Psychol.,* 1932, *44,* 677–694.

James, W. *Psychology, briefer course.* New York: Holt, 1920 (Orig., 1892).

James, W. *Talks to teachers on psychology: and to students on some of life's ideals.* New York: Holt, 1900.

James, W. *The varieties of religious experience. Gifford Lectures on Natural Religion.* New York: Longmans, Green, 1929 (Orig., 1901–1902).

Janet, P. *The mental state of hystericals: a study of mental stigmata and mental accidents.* New York: Putnam's, 1901.

Janet, P. *The major symptoms of hysteria.* New York: Macmillan, 1907.

Jaynes, J. Imprinting: The interaction of learned and innate behavior: I. Development and generalization. *J. comp. physiol. Psychol.,* 1956, *49,* 201–206.

Jaynes, J. Imprinting: The interaction of learned and innate behavior: II. The critical period. *J. comp. physiol. Psychol.,* 1957, *50,* 6–10.

Jennings, H. S. *Behavior of the lower organisms.* New York: Columbia Univer. Press, 1906.

Jersild, A. T., & Holmes, Frances B. Children's fears. *Child develpm. Monogr.* No. 20. New York: Bureau of Publications, Teachers College, Columbia Univer., 1935.

Johnson, H. M. Pseudo-mathematics in the mental and social sciences. *Amer. J. Psychol.*, 1936, 48, 342–351.

Johnson, Winifred B. Euphoric and depressed moods in normal subjects. *Char. & Pers.*, 1937, 6, 79–98.

Johnson, Winifred B. Euphoric and depressed moods in normal subjects. *Char. & Pers.*, 1938, 6, 188–202.

Jones, E. *The life and work of Sigmund Freud.* Vol. 1. *The formative years and the great discoveries, 1856–1900.* Vol. 2. *Years of maturity, 1901–1919.* Vol. 3. *The last phase, 1919–1939.* New York: Basic Books, 1953, 1955, 1957.

Jones, E. The genesis of the superego. In Clara Thompson, M. Mazer, & E. Witenberg (Eds.), *An outline of psychoanalysis.* (Rev. ed.) New York: Modern Library, 1955.

Jones, E. E., & deCharms, R. The organizing function of interaction roles in person perception. *J. abnorm. soc. Psychol.*, 1958, 57, 155–164.

Jones, H. E. *Motor performance and growth, a developmental study of static dynamometric strength.* Berkeley, Calif.: Univer. of Calif. Press, 1949.

Jones, L. M. *A factorial analysis of ability in fundamental motor skills.* Contrib. to Educ., No. 665. New York: Teachers College, Columbia Univer., 1935.

Jones, M. B. Aspects of the autonomous personality: I. Manifest Anxiety. *Res. Rep.*, U. S. Naval School of Aviation Medicine, Proj. No. NM 001058.25.03, 1953.

Jones, Mary C. A laboratory study of fear: the case of Peter. *J. genet. Psychol.*, 1924, 31, 308–315. (a)

Jones, Mary C. The elimination of children's fears. *J. exp. Psychol.*, 1924, 7, 382–390. (b)

Joseph, Alice, & Murray, Veronica F. *Chamorros and Carolinians of Saipan; personality studies.* Cambridge, Mass.: Harvard Univer. Press, 1951.

Jourard, S. M. Identification, parent-cathexis, and self-esteem. *J. consult. Psychol.*, 1957, 21, 375–380.

Jourard, S. M., & Remy, R. M. Perceived parental attitudes, the self, and security. *J. consult. Psychol.*, 1955, 19, 364–366.

Joyce, J. *Ulysses.* New York: Random House, 1934.

Judd, C. H. *Psychology, general introduction.* (2nd rev. ed.) Boston: Ginn, 1917.

Jung, C. G. *Psychological types, or the psychology of individuation.* (Trans. by H. G. Baynes.) New York: Harcourt, Brace, 1926.

Jung, C. G. *Contributions to analytical psychology.* (Trans. by H. G. Baynes & Cary F. Baynes.) New York: Harcourt, Brace, 1928.

Jung, C. G. *Two essays on analytical psychology.* (Trans. by R. F. C. Hull.) New York: Pantheon Books, 1953 (Orig. trans., 1928).

Jung, C. G. *The integration of personality.* New York: Farrar & Rinehart, 1939.

Jung, C. G. *The development of personality.* New York: Bollingen Foundation, 1954.

Kagan, J. Differential reward value of incomplete and complete sexual behavior. *J. comp. physiol. Psychol.*, 1955, 48, 59–64.

Kaiser, H. F. The varimax criterion for analytic rotation in factor analysis. *Psychometrika*, 1958, 23, 187–200.

Kallman, F. J. The genetic theory of schizophrenia. *Amer. J. Psychiat.*, 1956, 103, 309–322.

Kane, Janet P. *A bipolar general factor influencing specific attitudes and opinions.* New York: New York Univer., 1950.

Kantor, J. R. Character and personality: their nature and interrelations. *Char. & Pers.*, 1938, 6, 306–320.

Kardiner, A. *The individual and his society, the psychodynamics of primitive social organization.* New York: Columbia Univer. Press, 1939.

Kardiner, A. Hysterias and phobias. In S. Lorand, *Psychoanalysis today.* New York: International Universities Press, 1944.

Karon, B. P. *The Negro personality, a rigorous investigation of the effects of culture.* New York: Springer, 1958.

Karpf, Fay B. *Personality from the standpoint of Rankian "will" or "dynamic relationship" psychology.* Los Angeles: Social Work Technique, 1940.

Karvonen, J. J., & Kunnas, M. Factor analysis of haemotological changes in heavy manual work. *Acta physiol. Scandinavica*, 1953, 29, 220–231. (Cited in Cattell, R. B. The chief invariant psychological and psycho-physiological functional unities found by P-technique. *J. clin. Psychol.*, 1955, *11*, 319–343.)

Katona, G. *Psychological analysis of economic behavior.* New York: McGraw-Hill, 1951.

Katz, D. Some fundamental laws of the psychology of need: hunger. *Char. & Pers.*, 1935, *3*, 312–326.

Kawin, Ethel. *The wise choice of toys.* Chicago: The Univer. of Chicago Press, 1938.

Keet, C. D. Two verbal techniques in a miniature counseling situation. *Psychol. Monogr.*, 1948, *62*, No. 7 (Whole No. 294).

Kelley, D. M. Note on the symbol interpretation of the word crap in coprophilia. *Psychoanal. Rev.*, 1950, *37*, 71–72.

Kelley, T. L. *Crossroads in the mind of man, a study of differentiable mental abilities.* Stanford Univer., Calif.: Stanford Univer. Press, 1928.

Kellogg, W. N. Ultrasonic hearing in the porpoise, *Tursiops Truncatus. J. comp. physiol. Psychol.*, 1953, *46*, 446–450.

Kellogg, W. N. On the psychological study of small whales. *J. Psychol.*, 1958, *46*, 97–100.

Kellogg, W. N., & Kellogg, Luella A. *The ape and the child, a study of environmental influences upon early behavior.* New York: McGraw-Hill, 1933.

Kelly, E. L. Consistency of adult personality. *Amer. Psychologist*, 1955, *10*, 659–681.

Kelly, E. L., & Fiske, D. W. The prediction of success in the VA training program in clinical psychology. *Amer. Psychologist*, 1950, *5*, 395–406.

Kelly, E. L., Miles, Catherine C., & Terman, L. M. Ability to influence one's score on a typical pencil-and-paper test of personality. *Char. & Pers.*, 1936, *4*, 206–215.

Kelly, G. A. *The psychology of personal constructs.* Vol. I. *A theory of personality.* New York: Norton, 1955.

Kempf, E. J. *The autonomic functions and the personality.* Nerv. & Ment. Dis. Monogr. Ser., No. 28. New York: Nerv. & Ment. Dis. Publ. Co., 1921.

Kent, Grace H. Oral test for emergency use in clinics. *Ment. Measmt. Monogr.*, 1932, No. 9.

Kent, Grace H., & Rosanoff, A. J. A study of association in insanity. *Amer. J. Insanity*, 1910, *47*, Nos. 1 & 2. (Reprinted, Baltimore: The Lord Baltimore Press, 1910.)

Kerr, M. *Personality and conflict in Jamaica.* Liverpool: Univer. of Liverpool Press, 1952.

Keys, A., Brožek, J., Henschel, A., Mickelson, O., & Taylor, H. L. *The biology of human starvation.* Minneapolis: Univer. of Minnesota Press, 1950. 2 vols.

King, G. F. A theoretical and experimental consideration of the Rorschach human movement response. *Psychol. Monogr.*, 1958, *72*, No. 5 (Whole No. 458).

King, Marian. *The recovery of myself, a patient's experience in a hospital for mental illness.* New Haven, Conn.: Yale Univer. Press, 1931.

Kinget, G. Marian. *The Drawing-Completion Test, a projective technique for the investigation of personality based on the Wartegg Test Blank.* New York: Grune & Stratton, 1952.

Kinsey, A. C., Pomeroy, W. B., & Martin, C. E. *Sexual behavior in the human male.* Philadelphia: Saunders, 1948.

Kinsey, A. C., Pomeroy, W. B., Martin, C. E., & Gebhard, P. H. *Sexual behavior in the human female.* Philadelphia: Saunders, 1953.

Klein, A. F. *Role playing in leadership training and group problem solving.* New York: Association Press, 1956.

Klein, G. S. The Menninger Foundation research on perception and personality, 1947–1952; a review. *Bull. Menninger Clin.*, 1953, *17*, 93–99.

Klein, Melanie. The early development of conscience in the child. In S. Lorand (Ed.), *Psychoanalysis today.* New York: International Universities Press, 1944.

Kleitman, N. *Sleep and wakefulness as alternating phases in the cycle of existence.* Chicago: The Univer. of Chicago Press, 1939.

Kleitman, N. The sleep-wakefulness cycle. In H. A. Abramson (Ed.), *Problems of consciousness. Transaction of the first conference, Mar. 20–21, 1950.* New York: Josiah Macy, Jr., Foundation, 1951.

Kleitman, N. Sleep, wakefulness, and consciousness. *Psychol. Bull.*, 1957, *54*, 354–359.

Kleitman, N., Mullin, F. J., Cooperman, N. R., & Titelbaum, S. *Sleep characteristics, how they vary and react to changing conditions in the group and individual.* Chicago: The Univer. of Chicago Press, 1937.

Klineberg, O. *Negro intelligence and selective*

migration. Morningside Heights, N. Y.: Columbia Univer. Press, 1935.

Klopfer, B., Ainsworth, Mary, Klopfer, W. G., & Holt, R. R. *Developments in the Rorschach technique*. Vol. I. *Technique and theory*. Yonkers-on-Hudson, N. Y.: World Book, 1954.

Kluckhohn, C., Murray, H. A., & Schneider, D. M. (Eds.) *Personality in nature, society, and culture*. (2nd ed.) New York: Knopf, 1953.

Klüver, H. The study of personality and the method of equivalent and non-equivalent stimuli. *Char. & Pers.*, 1936, *5*, 91–112.

Koch, S. Review of H. Helson (Ed.), *Theoretical foundations of psychology*. New York: Van Nostrand, 1951. *Psychol. Bull.*, 1952, *49*, 349–355.

Koffka, K. On the structure of the unconscious. In *The unconscious, a symposium*. New York: Knopf, 1927.

Kohs, S. C. *Intelligence measurement, a psychological and statistical study based on the block-design tests*. New York: Macmillan, 1923.

Korner, Anneliese F. *Some aspects of hostility in young children*. New York: Grune & Stratton, 1949.

Kounin, J. S. Experimental studies of rigidity. I. The measurement of rigidity in normal and feebleminded persons. *Char. & Pers.*, 1941, *9*, 251–272. (a)

Kounin, J. S. Experimental studies of rigidity. II. The explanatory power of the concept of rigidity as applied to feeblemindedness. *Char. & Pers.*, 1941, *9*, 273–282. (b)

Kraepelin, E. *Manic-depressive insanity and paranoia*. (Trans. by R. Mary Barclay.) Edinburgh: Livingstone, 1921.

Krech, D., & Klein, G. S. *Theoretical models and personality theory*. Durham, N. C.: Duke Univer. Press, 1952.

Kretschmer, E. *Physique and character, an investigation of the nature of constitution and of the theory of temperament*. (Trans. by W. H. Sprott.) New York: Harcourt, Brace, 1925. (Latest ed., *Körperbau und Charakter*. Berlin: Springer-Verlac, 1951.)

Kretschmer, E. *The psychology of men of genius*. (Trans. by R. B. Cattell.) London: Kegan Paul, Trench, Trubner, 1931 (Orig., 1929).

Krikorian, Y. H. An empirical definition of consciousness. *J. Phil.*, 1938, *35*, 156–161.

Kris, E. On preconscious mental processes. *Psychoanal. Quart.*, 1950, *19*, 540–560.

Kroeber, A. L. Psychosis or social sanction. *Char. & Pers.*, 1940, *8*, 204–215.

Krugman, M. Out of the inkwell: the Rorschach method. *Char. & Pers.*, 1940, *9*, 91–110.

Krus, D. M., Werner, H., & Wapner, S. Studies in vicariousness: motor activity and perceived movement. *Amer. J. Psychol.*, 1953, *66*, 603–608.

Kurth, Gertrude M. The Jew and Adolph Hitler. *Psychoanal. Quart.*, 1947, *16*, 11–32.

Kutash, S. B. Performance of psychopathic defective criminals on the Thematic Apperception Test. *J. crim. Psychopathol.*, 1943, *5*, 319–340. (Cited in S. S. Tomkins. *The Thematic Apperception Test, the theory and technique of interpretation.* New York: Grune & Stratton, 1947)

Lacey, J. I. Individual differences in somatic response patterns. *J. comp. physiol. Psychol.*, 1950, *43*, 338–350.

Lacey, J. I., Bateman, D. E., & Van Lehn, R. Autonomic response specificity. An experimental study. *Psychosom. Med.*, 1953, *15*, 8–21.

Lacey, J. I., & Smith, R. L. Conditioning and generalization of unconscious anxiety. *Science*, 1954, *120*, 1045–1052.

Lacey, J. I., & Van Lehn, R. Differential emphasis in somatic response to stress. *Psychosom. Med.*, 1952, *14*, 71–81.

Ladd, G. T. *Psychology, descriptive and explanatory, a treatise of the phenomena, laws, and development of human mental life*. (4th ed.) New York: Scribner's, 1894.

Laird, D. A., & Laird, Eleanor C. *The technique of building personal leadership, proved ways of increasing the powers of leadership*. New York: McGraw-Hill, 1944.

Lambert, W. W. Stimulus-response contiguity and reinforcement theory in social psychology. In Gardner Lindzey (Ed.), *Handbook of social psychology*. Vol. I. *Theory and method*. Cambridge, Mass.: Addison-Wesley, 1954.

Landes, Ruth. The personality of the Ojibwa. *Char. & Pers.*, 1937, *6*, 51–60.

Landis, C., & Hunt, W. A. *The startle pattern*. New York: Farrar & Rinehart, 1939.

Landis, C., Landis, A. T., & Bolles, M. Marjorie. *Sex in development, a study of the growth and development of the emotional and sexual aspects of personality together with physiological, anatomical, and medical information on a group of 153 normal women and 142 female psychiatric patients.* New York: Paul B. Hoeber, 1940.

Lange-Eichbaum, W. *Genie-Irrsinn und Ruhm.* Munich: Verlag von Ernst Reinhardt, 1927.

Lange-Eichbaum, W. *The problem of genius.* (Trans. by Eden Paul & Cedar Paul.) New York: Macmillan, 1932 (Orig., 1930–1931).

Langer, W. C. *Psychology and human living.* New York: Appleton-Century, 1943.

Langworthy, O. R., & Betz, Barbara J. Narcolepsy as a type of response to emotional conflicts. *Psychosom. Med.,* 1944, *6,* 211–236.

Lapin, Joseph H. Common errors in infant feeding. *J. Pediat.,* 1954, *45,* 583–589.

Larrabee, H. A. *Reliable knowledge.* Boston: Houghton Mifflin, 1945.

Larson, Leroy. Preschool experiences of physically handicapped children. *Except. Child.,* 1958, *24,* 310–312.

Laughlin, H. P. King David's anger. *Psychoanal. Quart.,* 1954, *23,* 87–95.

Lavater, J. C. *Essays on physiognomy calculated to extend the knowledge and the love of mankind.* (Trans. by C. Moore.) London: Symonds, 1797. 4 vols.

Lazarus, R. S., Eriksen, C. W., & Fonda, C. P. Personality dynamics and auditory perceptual recognition. *J. Pers.,* 1951, *19,* 471–482.

Lazarus, R. S., & McCleary, R. A. Autonomic discrimination without awareness: A study of subception. *Psychol. Rev.,* 1951, *58,* 113–122.

Leary, T., & Coffey, H. S. Interpersonal diagnosis: some problems of methodology and validation. *J. abnorm. soc. Psychol.,* 1955, *50,* 110–124.

Leavitt, H. C. Organized qualities of the id structure. *Psychoanal. Rev.,* 1953, *40,* 295–303.

Lecky, P. *Self-consistency, a theory of personality.* New York: Island Press, 1945.

Leeper, R. W. *Lewin's topological and vector psychology, a digest and critique.* Eugene, Ore.: Univer. of Oregon, 1943.

Leeper, R. W. Theories of personality. In Dennis, W. (Ed.), *Current trends in psychological theory.* Pittsburgh: Univer. of Pittsburgh Press, 1951.

Lehner, George F. J. Personal adjustment scores and assigned "average" scores. *J. Psychol.,* 1956, *42,* 227–236.

Leiter, R. G. *The Leiter International Performance Scale.* Vol. I. *Directions for the application and scoring of individual tests.* Santa Barbara, Calif.: Santa Barbara State College Press, 1940.

Lepine, L. T., & Chodorkoff, B. Goal setting behavior, expressed feelings of adequacy, and the correspondence between the perceived and ideal self. *J. clin. Psychol.,* 1955, *11,* 395–397.

Le Senne, R. *Traité de caractérologie.* Paris: Presses Universitaires de France, 1945.

Leventhal, A. M. The effects of diagnostic category and reinforcer on learning without awareness. *J. abnorm. soc. Psychol.,* 1959, *59,* 162–166.

Levine, A. S. Perseveration, rigidity, and persistence. *Psychol. Rep., Monogr. Suppl.,* 1955, No. 1. (a)

Levine, A. S. "Perseveration" or "the central factor." *Psychol. Rep., Monogr. Suppl.,* 1955, No. 5. (b)

Levitt, E. E., & Zelen, S. L. The validity of the *Einstellung* test as a measure of rigidity. *J. abnorm. soc. Psychol.,* 1953, *48,* 573–580.

Levy, L. H. Sexual symbolism: a validity study. *J. consult. Psychol.,* 1954, *18,* 43–46.

Lévy-Bruhl, L. *How natives think (Les fonctions mentales dans les sociétiés inférieures).* (Trans. by Lilian A. Clare.) New York: Knopf, 1925.

Lewin, B. D. Obsessional neuroses. In Sandor Lorand (Ed.), *Psychoanalysis today.* New York: International Universities Press, 1944.

Lewin, H. S. Facts and fears about comics. *Nation's Sch.,* 1953, *52,* 46–48.

Lewin, K. *A dynamic theory of personality.* New York: McGraw-Hill, 1935.

Lewin, K. *Principles of topological psychology.* (Trans. by F. Heider & Grace M. Heider.) New York: McGraw-Hill, 1936. (a)

Lewin, K. Some social-psychological differences between the United States and Germany. *Char. & Pers.,* 1936, *4,* 265–293. (b)

Lewin, K. Level of aspiration. In J. McV. Hunt, *Personality and the behavior disorders.* Vol. I. New York: Ronald, 1944.

Lewin, K. Behavior and development as a function of the total situation. In Leonard Carmichael (Ed.), *Manual of child psychology.* New York: Wiley, 1946.

Lewin, K. *Field theory in social sciences, selected theoretical papers*. Edited by Dorwin Cartwright. Published for the Research Center for Group Dynamics, University of Michigan. New York: Harper, 1951.

Lewin, K., Dembo, Tamara, Festinger, L., & Sears, Pauline S. Level of aspiration. In J. McV. Hunt (Ed.), *Personality and the behavior disorders, a handbook based on experimental and clinical research*. Vol. I. New York: Ronald, 1944.

Lewin, K., Lippitt, R., & White, R. K. Patterns of aggressive behavior in experimentally created "social climates." *J. soc. Psychol.*, 1939, *10*, 271–300.

Lewis, Claudia. *Children of the Cumberland*. New York: Columbia Univer. Press, 1946.

Lewis, H. K. *The child, its spiritual nature*. London: Macmillan, 1896.

Lewis, N. D. C., & Pacella, B. L. (Eds.) *Modern trends in child psychiatry*. New York: International Universities Press, 1945.

Lieberman, S. The effects of changes in roles on the attitudes of role occupants. *Hum. Relat.*, 1956, *9*, 385–402.

Liebman, J. L. *Peace of mind*. New York: Simon & Schuster, 1946.

Lief, A. *The commonsense psychiatry of Dr. Adolph Meyer*. New York: McGraw-Hill, 1948.

Ligon, E. M. *Dimensions of character*. New York: Macmillan, 1956.

Lindner, R. M. *Rebel without a cause; the hypnoanalysis of a criminal psychopath*. New York: Grune & Stratton, 1944.

Lindzey, Gardner (Ed.) *Handbook of social psychology*. Vols. I. & II. Cambridge, Mass.: Addison-Wesley, 1954.

Linton, Harriet B. Rorschach correlates of response to suggestion. *J. abnorm. soc. Psychol.*, 1954, *49*, 75–83. (a)

Linton, Harriet B. Autokinetic judgments as a measure of influence. *J. abnorm. soc. Psychol.*, 1954, *49*, 464–466. (b)

Linton, R. Status and role. In Edgar F. Borgatta & Henry J. Meyer (Eds.), *Sociological theory, present-day sociology from the past*. New York: Knopf, 1956.

Livingston, S. *Must men hate?* New York: Harper, 1944.

Lombroso, C. *The man of genius*. (2nd ed.) London: Walter Scott Publishing Co., 1905.

London, I. D. Psychologists' misuse of the auxiliary concepts of physics and mathematics. *Psychol. Rev.*, 1944, *51*, 266–291.

London, I. D. The role of the model in explanation. *J. genet. Psychol.*, 1949, *74*, 165–176.

Lorand, S. (Ed.) *Psychoanalysis today*. New York: International Universities Press, 1944.

Lord, Edith. Experimentally induced variations in Rorschach performance. *Psychol. Monogr.*, 1950, *64*, No. 10 (Whole No. 316).

Lovell, Constance. A study of the factor structure of thirteen personality variables. *Educ. psychol. Measmt.*, 1945, *5*, 335–350.

Lubin, A. A note on Sheldon's table of correlations between temperamental traits. *Brit. J. Psychol.*, *Stat. Sect.*, 1950, *3*, 186–189. (Cited in Eysenck, H. J. *The structure of human personality*. London: Methuen, 1953.)

Luchins, A. S. Mechanization in problem solving: the effect of *Einstellung*. *Psychol. Monogr.*, 1942, *54*, No. 6 (Whole No. 248).

Luchins, A. S. Proposed methods of studying degrees of rigidity. *J. Pers.*, 1947, *15*, 242–246.

Luchins, A. S. Rigidity and ethnocentrism: a critique. *J. Pers.*, 1949, *17*, 449–466.

Lufton, R. J. Thought reform of Chinese intellectuals: A psychiatric evaluation. *J. soc. Issues*, 1957 (3), *13*, 5–20.

Lundholm, H. Mark Antony's speech and the psychology of persuasion. *Char. & Pers.*, 1938, *6*, 293–305.

Luria, A. R. *The nature of human conflicts, or emotion, conflict and will, an objective study of disorganization and control of human behavior*. (Trans. by W. H. Gantt.) New York: Liveright, 1932.

Luria, A. R. The development of mental functions in twins. *Char. & Pers.*, 1936, *5*, 35–47.

Lurie, W. A. A study of Spranger's value types by the method of factor analysis. *J. soc. Psychol.*, 1937, *8*, 17–37.

McClelland, D. C. *Personality*. New York: Wm. Sloane Associates, 1951.

McClelland, D. C., Atkinson, J. W., Clark, R. A., & Lowell, E. L. *The achievement motive*. New York: Appleton-Century-Crofts, 1953.

McClelland, D. C., Baldwin, A. L., Bronfenbrenner, U., & Strodtbeck, F. L. *Talent and society, new perspectives in the iden-*

tification of talent. Princeton: Van Nostrand, 1958.

McDougall, W. B. *Introduction to social psychology*. London: Methuen, 1908.

McDougall, W. B. *Body and mind, a history and defense of animism*. New York: Macmillan, 1913.

McDougall, W. B. *Outline of psychology*. New York: Scribner's, 1923.

McDougall, W. B. *Outline of abnormal psychology*. New York: Scribner's, 1926. (a)

McDougall, W. B. The "Margery mediumship." *Psyche*, 1926, 7, 15–30. (b)

McDougall, W. B. Of the words character and personality. *Char. & Pers.*, 1932, *1*, 3–16. (a)

McDougall, W. B. *The energies of men, a study of the fundamentals of dynamic psychology*. New York: Scribner's, 1932. (b)

McDougall, W. B. On the nature of Spearman's general factor. *Char. & Pers.*, 1934, *3*, 127–143.

McElvaney, C. T. Recall of positively and negatively affective material related to self-esteem. *Dissertation Abstr.*, 1958, *18*, 1495–1496.

McFarland, Margaret B. Relationships between young sisters as revealed in their overt responses. *Child Develpmt. Monogr.*, No. 23. New York: Bureau of Publications, Teachers College, Columbia Univer., 1938.

McGehee, T. P. The stability of the self-concept and self-esteem. *Dissertation Abstr.*, 1957, *17*, 1403–1404.

McGinnies, E. Emotionality and perceptual defense. *Psychol. Rev.*, 1949, *56*, 244–251.

McGinnies, E., & Sherman, H. Generalization and perceptual defense. *J. abnorm. soc. Psychol.*, 1952, *47*, 81–85.

McGraw, Myrtle B. *Growth, a study of Johnny and Jimmy*. New York: Appleton-Century, 1935.

McIntyre, C. J. Acceptance by others and its relation to acceptance of self and others. *J. abnorm. soc. Psychol.*, 1952, *47*, 624–625.

McKellar, P. *Imagination and thinking, a psychological analysis*. New York: Basic Books, 1957.

Mackenzie, J. S. *Manual of ethics*. (4th ed.) New York: Noble & Noble, 1925.

MacKinnon, D. W. Tests for the measurement of personal effectiveness. In *Invitational Conference on Testing Problems, 1951*. Princeton, N. J.: Educational Testing Service, 1951.

MacKinnon, D. W. Fact and fancy in personality research. *Amer. Psychologist*, 1953, *8*, 138–145.

McKinnon, Katherine Mae. Consistency and change in behavior manifestations, as observed in a group of sixteen children during a five-year period. *Child Develpmt. Monogr.*, No. 30. New York: Bureau of Publications, Teachers College, Columbia Univer., 1942.

McLeish, J. The validation of Seashore's measures of musical talent by factorial methods. *Brit. J. Psychol., Stat. Sect.*, 1950, *3*, 129–140. (Cited in *Psychol. Abstr.*, 1951, *25*, No. 6043.)

McNemar, Q. *The revision of the Stanford-Binet Scale, an analysis of the standardization data*. Boston: Houghton-Mifflin, 1942.

McNemar, Q. Review of Stephenson's *The study of behavior*. *Psychol. Bull.*, 1954, *51*, 527–528.

McNemar, Q., & Merrill, Maud A. (Eds.) *Studies in personality. Contributed in honor of Lewis M. Terman*. New York: McGraw-Hill, 1942.

McQuitty, L. L. An approach to the measurement of individual differences in personality. *Char. & Pers.*, 1938, 7, 81–95.

McQuitty, L. L. Effective items in the measurement of personality integration—I. *Educ. psychol. Measmt.*, 1952, *12*, 117–125.

Mace, C. A., & Vernon, P. E. (Eds.) *Current trends in British psychology*. London: Methuen, 1953.

Maier, N. R. F. *Frustration, the study of behavior without a goal*. New York: McGraw-Hill, 1949.

Maier, N. R. F. The premature crystallization of learning theory. In *Learning theory, personality theory, and clinical research, the Kentucky Symposium*. New York: Wiley, 1954.

Malinowski, B. *Sex and repression in savage society*. New York: Harcourt, Brace, 1927.

Maller, J. B. General and specific factors in character. *J. soc. Psychol.*, 1934, *5*, 97–102.

Mann, J. H. Experimental evaluations of role playing. *Psychol. Bull.*, 1956, *53*, 227–234.

Manson, W. The Gospel of Luke. In James Moffatt (Ed.), *The Moffatt New Testa-*

ment commentary. New York: Harper, 1930.

Marcovitz, E. The meaning of déjà vu. *Psychoanal. Quart.,* 1952, *21,* 481–489.

Margolin, S. G. The behavior of the stomach during psychoanalysis. *Psychoanal. Quart.,* 1951, *20,* 349–373.

Marston, W. M., & King, C. D. The psychonic theory of consciousness—an experimental study. *Psyche,* 1929, *10,* 39–57.

Martin, B. A factor analytic study of anxiety. *J. clin. Psychol.,* 1958, *14,* 133–138.

Maslow, A. H. A theory of human motivation. *Psychol. Rev.,* 1943, *50,* 370–396. (a)

Maslow, A. H. Preface to motivation theory. *Psychosom. Med.,* 1943, *5,* 85–92. (b)

Maslow, A. H. "Higher" and "lower" needs. *J. Psychol.,* 1948, *25,* 433–436. (a)

Maslow, A. H. Some theoretical consequences of basic need-gratification. *J. Pers.,* 1948, *16,* 402–416. (b)

Maslow, A. H. Self-actualizing people: a study of psychological health. *Pers. Monogr., Symposium,* No. 1, 1950, 11–34.

Maslow, A. H. *Motivation and personality.* New York: Harper, 1954.

Maslow, A. H., & Mittelmann, B. *Principles of abnormal psychology, the dynamics of psychic illness.* (Rev. ed.) New York: Harper, 1951.

Mateer, Florence. *The unstable child, an interpretation of psychopathy as a source of unblanced behavior in abnormal and troublesome children.* New York: Appleton, 1924.

Matthews, S. *Jesus on social institutions.* New York: Macmillan, 1928.

May, R., Angel, E., & Ellenberger, H. F. (Eds.) *Existence: a new dimension in psychiatry and psychology.* New York: Basic Books, 1958.

Mayer, M. S. *They thought they were free: the Germans, 1933–1945.* Chicago: The Univer. of Chicago Press, 1955.

Maze, J. R. On some corruptions of the doctrine of homeostasis. *Psychol. Rev.,* 1953, *60,* 405–412.

Mead, G. H. *Mind, self, and society, from the standpoint of a social behaviorist.* (Edited by C. W. Morris.) Chicago: The Univer. of Chicago Press, 1934.

Mead, Margaret. *Male and female, a study of the sexes in a changing world.* New York: W. Morrow, 1949.

Mead, Margaret, & Calas, N. (Eds.) *Primitive heritage: an anthropological anthology.* New York: Random House, 1953.

Mead, Margaret, & Macgregor, Frances C. *Growth and culture, a photographic study of Balinese childhood.* New York: Putnam's, 1951.

Meehl, P. E. The dynamics of "structured" personality tests. *J. clin. Psychol.,* 1945, *1,* 296–303.

Meehl, P. E. Configural scoring. *J. consult. Psychol.,* 1950, *14,* 165–171.

Meehl, P. E. *Clinical versus statistical prediction.* Minneapolis, Minn.: Univer. of Minnesota Press, 1954.

Meehl, P. E., & Dahlstrom, W. G. Objective configural rules for discriminating psychotic from neurotic MMPI profiles. *J. consult. Psychol.,* 1960, *24,* 375–387.

Mehlman, B., & Whiteman, S. L. The relationship between certain pictures of the Rosenzweig Picture-Frustration Study and corresponding behavioral situations. *J. clin. Psychol.,* 1955, *11,* 15–19.

Meloun, J. Does drawing skill show in handwriting? *Char. & Pers.,* 1934, *3,* 194–213.

Melton, A. W. (Ed.) *Apparatus tests.* AAF Aviation Psychology Program Research Reports, No. 4. Washington, D. C.: U. S. Government Printing Office, 1947.

Menninger, K. A. *Man against himself.* New York: Harcourt, Brace, 1938.

Menninger, K. A. *Love against hate.* New York: Harcourt, Brace, 1942.

Mensh, I. N., & Wishner, J. Asch on "Forming impressions of personality": Further evidence. *J. Pers.,* 1947, *46,* 188–191.

Merrifield, P. R., Guilford, J. P., Christensen, P. R., & Frick, J. W. A factor-analytic study of problem-solving abilities. *Rep. from the Psychol. Lab.,* No. 22. Los Angeles: Univer. of Southern Calif., 1960.

Merrill, R. M. On Keet's study, "Two verbal techniques in a miniature counseling situation." *J. abnorm. soc. Psychol.,* 1952, *47,* 722.

Merton, R. K. *Social theory and social structure.* (Rev. ed.) Glencoe, Ill.: Free Press, 1957.

The Methodist hymnal. Nashville, Tenn.: Publishing House of the Methodist Episcopal Church, South, 1935.

Meyer, M. F. *Psychology of the Other-One, an introductory textbook of psychology.* Columbia, Mo.: The Missouri Book Co., 1921.

Michael, W. B., Zimmerman, W. S., & Guilford, J. P. An investigation of two hypotheses regarding the nature of spatial-relations and visualization factors. *Educ. psychol. Measmt.*, 1950, *10*, 187–213.

Michael, W. B., Zimmerman, W. S., & Guilford, J. P. An investigation of the nature of the spatial-relations and visualization factors in two high school samples. *Educ. psychol. Measmt.*, 1951, *11*, 561–577.

Michaux, W. Schizophrenic apperception as a function of hunger. *J. abnorm. soc. Psychol.*, 1955, *50*, 53–58.

Miller, J. G. *Unconsciousness.* New York: Wiley, 1942.

Miller, N. E., & Dollard, J. *Social learning and imitation.* New Haven, Conn.: Yale Univer. Press, 1941.

Minard, R. D. Race attitudes of Iowa children. *Univer. Ia. Stud., Studies in character,* 1931, *4*, No. 2, New Series No. 217.

Minehan, T. *Boy and girl tramps of America.* New York: Farrar & Rinehart, 1934.

Mode, E. B. *Elements of statistics.* New York: Prentice-Hall, 1951.

Monnier, M. Experimental work on sleep and other variations of consciousness. In H. A. Abramson (Ed.), *Problems of consciousness. Transactions of the third conference, March 10 and 11, 1952.* New York: Josiah Macy, Jr., Foundation, 1952.

Mons, W. *Principles and practice of the Rorschach personality test.* Philadelphia: Lippincott, nd. (Proba., 1949).

Montaigne. *The essays of Montaigne.* (Trans. from the French by E. J. Trechmann.) New York: Modern Library, 1946 (Orig., 1580).

Moore, H. T., & Gilliland, A. R. The measurement of aggressiveness. *J. appl. Psychol.*, 1921, *5*, 97–118.

Moore, T. V. A study in sadism: The life of Algernon Charles Swinburne. *Char. & Pers.*, 1937, *6*, 1–15.

Moore, T. V. The prepsychotic personality and the concept of mental disorder. *Char. & Pers.*, 1941, *9*, 169–187.

Moore, T. V. *The driving forces of human nature and their adjustment, an introduction to the psychology and psychopathology of emotional behavior and volitional control.* New York: Grune & Stratton, 1948.

Morgan, J. J. B. *Child psychology.* (3rd ed.) New York: Rinehart, 1942.

Mosier, C. I. A factor analysis of certain neurotic symptoms. *Psychometrika*, 1937, *2*, 263–286.

Moss, F. A. Study of animal drives. *J. exp. Psychol.*, 1924, *7*, 165–185.

Moss, F. A. (Ed.) *Comparative psychology.* New York: Prentice-Hall, 1942.

Mountford, E. G. An experimental study of some German type-theories. *Char. & Pers.*, 1940, *8*, 271–280.

Moustakas, C. E. (Ed.) *The self: explorations in personal growth.* New York: Harper, 1956.

Mowrer, O. H., & Kluckhohn, C. Dynamic theory of personality. In J. McV. Hunt (Ed.), *Personality and the behavior disorders, a handbook based on experimental and clinical research.* Vol. I. New York: Ronald, 1944.

Mullahy, P. *Oedipus, myth and complex, a review of psychoanalytic theory.* New York: Hermitage Press, 1948.

Munn, N. L. *Psychology, the fundamentals of human adjustment.* Boston: Houghton Mifflin, 1946, 1951, 1956.

Munroe, Ruth L. *Schools of psychoanalytic thought, an exposition, critique, and attempt at integration.* New York: Dryden, 1955.

Münsterberg, H. *Psychotherapy.* New York: Moffatt, Yard, 1909.

Münsterberg, H. *Psychology and social sanity.* Garden City, N. Y.: Doubleday & Page, 1914. (a)

Münsterberg, H. *Psychology, general and applied.* New York: Appleton, 1914. (b)

Münsterberg, H. *On the witness stand, essays on psychology and crime.* New York: Clark Boardman Co., 1930 (Orig., 1908).

Murchison, C. (Ed.) *The case for and against psychical belief.* Worcester, Mass.: Clark Univer. Press, 1927.

Murphy, G. *Personality; a biosocial approach to origins and structure.* New York: Harper, 1947.

Murphy, G., & Jensen, F. *Approaches to personality, some contemporary conceptions used in psychology and psychiatry.* New York: Coward-McCann, 1932.

Murray, H. A. *Explorations in personality, a clinical and experimental study of fifty men of college age by the workers at the Harvard Psychological Clinic.* New York: Oxford Univer. Press, 1938.

Musgrave, R. S., & Allport, F. H. Teleonomic description in the study of behavior. *Char. & Pers.*, 1941, *9*, 326–343.

Mussen, P. H., & Newman, D. K. Acceptance of handicap, motivation, and adjustment in physically disabled children. *Except. Child.*, 1958, *24*, 255–260, 277–279.

Myers, F. W. H. *Human personality and its survival of bodily death.* London: Longmans, Green, 1903.

Myerson, A. *The foundations of personality.* Boston: Little, Brown, 1922.

Myrdal, G. *An American dilemma; the Negro problem and modern democracy.* New York: Harper, 1944.

Nadel, S. F. The typological approach to culture. *Char. & Pers.*, 1937, *5*, 267–284.

Neiman, L. J., & Hughes, J. W. The problem of the concept of role—a re-survey of the literature. *Soc. Forces*, 1951, *30*, 141–149.

Nelson, Janet F. Personality and intelligence, a study of some responses other than intellectual noted in a simple mental test situation. *Child Develpm. Monogr.*, No. 4, New York: Bureau of Publications, Teachers College, Columbia Univer., 1931.

Neuhaus, J. O., and Wrigley, C. The quartimax method: an analytical approach to orthogonal simple structure. *Brit. J. statist. Psychol.*, 1954, *7*, 81–91.

Neumann, E. *The origins and history of consciousness.* (Trans. by R. F. C. Hull.) New York: Bollingen Series XLII [Pantheon Books, 1954] (Orig., 1949).

Newburg, E. Current interpretation and significance of Lloyd Morgan's Canon. *Psychol. Bull.*, 1954, *51*, 70–74.

Newcomb, T. Role behaviors in the study of individual personality and of groups. *J. Pers.*, 1950, *18*, 273–290. (Reprinted in Howard Brand (Ed.), *The study of personality, a book of readings.* New York: Wiley, 1954)

Newman, H. H. *Twins; a study of heredity and environment.* Chicago: The Univer. of Chicago Press, 1937.

Newton, N. R. The relationship between infant feeding experience and later behavior. *J. Pediat.*, 1951, *38*, 28–40.

Niemöller, M. *The Gestapo defied.* London: The Religious Book Club, 1942.

Nimkoff, M. F. *The child.* Chicago: Lippincott, 1934.

Nissen, H. W. Phylogenetic comparison. In S. S. Stevens (Ed.), *Handbook of experimental psychology.* New York: Wiley, 1951.

Nissen, H. W. The nature of the drive as innate determinant of behavioral organization. In M. R. Jones (Ed.), *Nebraska symposium on motivation, 1954.* Lincoln: Univer. of Nebraska Press, 1954.

Norton, Fay-Tyler M., & Kenshalo, D. R. Incidental learning under conditions of unrewarded irrelevant motivation. *J. comp. physiol. Psychol.*, 1954, *47*, 375–377.

Notcutt, B. *The psychology of personality.* New York: Philosophical Library, 1953.

Nowlis, V. The development and modification of motivational systems in personality. In *Current theory and research in motivation: a symposium.* Lincoln, Nebr.: Univer. of Nebraska Press, 1953.

Nuttin, J. *Psychoanalysis and personality, a dynamic theory of normal personality.* (Trans. by G. Lamb.) New York: Sheed & Ward, 1953.

Nuttin, J. Consciousness, behavior, and personality. *Psychol. Rev.*, 1955, *62*, 349–355.

O'Connor, J. P., Lorr, M., & Stafford, J. W. Some patterns of manifest anxiety. *J. clin. Psychol.*, 1956, *12*, 160–163.

Odbert, H. S. Trends in the study of personality (as revealed in the 1936 meeting of the American Psychological Association). *Char. & Pers.*, 1936, *5*, 149–154.

Oeser, O. Typological methods in experimental psychology. *Psyche*, 1930, *10*, 80–89.

Ogden, R. M. *An introduction to general psychology.* New York: Longmans, Green, 1914.

Olmsted, D. W. Inter-group similarities of role correlates. *Sociometry*, 1957, *20*, 8–20.

Olsen, M. W., & Marsden, S. J. Natural parthenogenesis in turkey eggs. *Science*, 1954, *120*, 545–546.

Omwake, Katherine T. The value of photographs and handwriting in estimating intelligence. *Publ. personnel Stud.*, Jan., 1925.

Omwake, Katherine T. The relation between acceptance of self and acceptance of others shown by three personality inventories. *J. consult. Psychol.*, 1954, *18*, 443–446.

Omwake, Katherine T., Dexter, Emily S., & Lewis, L. W. The interrelations of certain physiological measurements and aspects of personality. *Char. & Pers.*, 1934, *3*, 64–71.

O'Neil, W. M., & Levinson, D. J. A factorial exploration of authoritarianism and some of its ideological concomitants. *J. Pers.*, 1954, *22*, 449–463.

Orgel, A. R., & Smith, J. C. Test of the magnetic theory of homing. *Science*, 1954, *120*, 891–892. (Also, Orgel, A. R., & Smith, J. C. A test of the magnetic theory of homing in pigeons. *J. genet. Psychol.*, 1956, *88*, 203–210.)

O. S. S. Assessment Staff. *Assessment of men.* New York: Rinehart, 1948.

Otto, R. *The idea of the holy.* London: Oxford Univer. Press, 1924.

Over-dependency. New York: McGraw-Hill, 1948. (Film)

Overton, R. K. An effect of high- and low-calcium diets on the maze performance of rats. *J. comp. physiol. Psychol.*, 1958, *51*, 697–700.

Pace, D. M., & McCashland, B. W. *College physiology.* New York: Crowell, 1955.

Palmer, S. *Understanding other people, the motives behind their behavior.* New York: Crowell, 1955.

Panton, J. H. MMPI profile characteristics of physically disabled prison inmates. *Psychol. Rep.*, 1958, *4*, 529–530.

Pap, A. Does science have metaphysical presuppositions? In H. Feigl & May Brodbeck (Eds.), *Readings in the philosophy of science.* New York: Appleton-Century-Crofts, 1953.

Parker, J. W., Jr. Psychological and personal history data related to accident records of commercial truck drivers. *J. appl. Psychol.*, 1953, *37*, 317–320.

Parmelee, Maurine. *The science of human behavior, biological and social foundations.* New York: Macmillan, 1913.

Parsons, T. Consciousness and symbolic processes. In H. A. Abramson (Ed.) *Problems of consciousness, transactions of the fourth conference, March 29, 30, & 31, 1953.* New York: Josiah Macy, Jr., Foundation, 1954.

Pascal, G. R., & Suttell, Barbara. Testing the claims of a graphologist. *J. Pers.*, 1947, *16*, 192–197.

Pascal, G. R., & Suttell, Barbara J. *The Bender-Gestalt Test, quantification and validity for adults.* New York: Grune & Stratton, 1951.

Paterson, D. G. *Physique and intellect.* New York: Century, 1930.

Paterson, D. G., & Elliott, R. M. *Minnesota Mechanical Ability Tests.* Minneapolis: The Univer. of Minnesota Press, 1930.

Pavlov, I. P. *Conditioned reflexes; an investigation of the physiological activity of the cerebral cortex.* (Trans. and edited by G. V. Anrep.) London: Oxford Univer. Press, 1927.

Payne, D. E. Role constructs versus part constructs and interpersonal understanding *Dissertation Abstr.*, 1957, *17*, 1127–1128.

Pearl, D. Ethnocentrism and the self concept. *J. soc. Psychol.*, 1954, *40*, 137–147.

Pearson, K. Some recent misinterpretations of the problem of nature and nurture. *Eugenics Lab. Lecture Series*, III, Part 2. Cambridge, Eng., 1915.

Peck, R. F. Family patterns correlated with adolescent personality structure. *J. abnorm. soc. Psychol.*, 1958, 57, 347–350.

Pederson-Krag, Geraldine. Review of J. L. Moreno, *Psychodrama*, Vol. I. *Psychoanal. Quart.*, 1947, *16*, 265–267.

Penfield, W. Mechanisms of voluntary movement. *Brain*, 1954, 77, 1–17. (Montreal Neurological Inst., Reprint No. 457)

Penry, J. *How to read character from the face, a complete explanation of character as it is shown by the size, proportion, and texture of each feature.* New York: Fortuny's Publisher, n.d. (proba., 1940)

Perls, F. S., Hefferine, R. F., & Goodman, P. *Gestalt therapy, excitement and growth in human personality.* New York: Julian Press, 1951.

Perry, J. W. *The self in psychotic processes; its symbolization in schizophrenia.* Berkeley, Calif.: Univer. of California Press, 1953.

Peterson, C. H., & Spano, Frances L. Breast feeding, maternal rejection and child personality. *Char. & Pers.*, 1941, *10*, 62–66.

Peterson, J., & Lanier, L. H. Studies in the comparative abilities of whites and negroes. *Ment. Measmt. Monogr.*, 1929, No. 5.

Pettigrew, T. F. The measurement and correlates of category width as a cognitive variable. *J. Pers.*, 1958, *26*, 532–544.

Philblad, C. T. Possible applications of mental tests to social theory and practice. Unpublished doctor's dissertation, Univer. of Missouri, 1925.

Phillips, B. S. A role theory approach to adjustment in old age. *Amer. sociol. Rev.*, 1957, *22*, 212–217.

Phillips, E. L. *Psychotherapy, a modern theory and practice.* Englewood Cliffs, N. J.: Prentice-Hall, 1956.

Piaget, J. *The language and thought of the child.* (Trans. by Marjorie Warden.) New

York: Harcourt, Brace, 1926 (Orig., 1924).

Piaget, J. *The child's conception of the world.* New York: Harcourt, Brace, 1929.

Piaget, J. *The child's conception of physical causality.* New York: Harcourt, Brace, 1930.

Piaget, J. *The moral judgment of the child.* New York: Harcourt, Brace, 1932.

Piaget, J. *Play, dreams and imitation in childhood.* (Trans. by C. Gattegue & F. M. Hodgson.) New York: Norton, 1951.

Piaget, J. *The origins of intelligence in children.* (Trans. by Margaret Cook.) New York: International Universities Press, 1952.

Pickford, R. W. Imagination and the nonsense syllable, a clinical approach. *Char. & Pers.,* 1938, 7, 19–40.

Pickford, R. W. Three related experiences of *déjà vu. Char. & Pers.,* 1941, *9,* 152–159.

Pierce, F. *Dreams and personality, a study of our dual lives.* New York: Appleton, 1931.

Pillsbury, W. B. *The essentials of psychology.* New York: Macmillan, 1911.

Pillsbury, W. B., & Pennington, L. A. *Handbook of general psychology.* New York: Dryden, 1942.

Pintner, R., Eisenson, J., & Stanton, Mildred. *The psychology of the physically handicapped.* New York: F. S. Crofts, 1941.

Pintner, R., & Paterson, D. G. *A scale of performance tests.* New York: Appleton, 1923.

Pitcher, Barbara, & Stacey, C. L. Is *Einstellung* rigidity a general trait? *J. abnorm. soc. Psychol.,* 1954, *49,* 3–6.

Plant, J. S. *Personality and the culture pattern.* New York: Commonwealth Fund, 1937.

Plant, J. S. *The envelope, a study of the impact of the world upon the child.* New York Commonwealth Fund, 1950.

Polansky, N. A. How shall a life-history be written? *Char. & Pers.,* 1941, *9,* 188–207.

Porteus, S. D. *Primitive intelligence and environment.* New York: Macmillan, 1937.

Porteus, S. D. *Qualitative performance in the Maze Test.* Honolulu (?): S. D. Porteus, 1942.

Porteus, S. D., & Babcock, Marjorie E. *Temperament and race.* Boston: Richard G. Badger, 1926.

Postman, L. On the problem of perceptual defense. *Psychol. Rev.,* 1953, *60,* 298–306.

Postman, L. Review of Witkin, *et al., Personality through perception. Psychol. Bull.,* 1955, *52,* 79–83.

Postman, L., Bronson, Wanda C., & Gropper, G. L. Is there a mechanism of perceptual defense? *J. abnorm. soc. Psychol.,* 1953, *48,* 215–224.

Postman, L., & Egan, J. P. *Experimental psychology: an introduction.* New York: Harper, 1949.

Potter, E. G., & Fiedler, F. E. Physical disability and interpersonal perception. *Percept. mot. Skills,* 1958, *8,* 241–242.

Pratt, J. G., Rhine, J. B., Smith, B. M., Stuart, C. E., & Greenwood, J. A. *Extrasensory perception after sixty years; a critical appraisal of the research in extra-sensory perception.* New York: Holt, 1940.

Preston, G. H. *The substance of mental health.* New York: Farrar & Rinehart, 1943.

Preyer, W. *The mind of the child.* Part I. *The senses and the will; observations concerning the mental development of the human being in the first years of life.* Part II. *The development of the intellect.* (Trans. by H. W. Brown.) New York: Appleton, 1888, 1889.

Price, G. R. Science and the supernatural. *Science,* 1955, *122,* 359–367.

Prince, M. *The dissociation of a personality.* New York: Longmans, Green, 1913.

Prince, M. *The creed of Deutschtum, the other war essays, including the psychology of the Kaiser.* Boston: Richard G. Badger, 1918.

Prince, M. *Clinical and experimental studies in personality.* Cambridge, Mass.: Sci-Art, 1929.

Prothro, E. T., & Teska, P. T. *Psychology, a biosocial study of behavior.* Boston: Ginn, 1950.

Pullias, E. V. Masturbation as a mental hygiene problem—a study of the beliefs of seventy-five young men. *J. abnorm. soc. Psychol.,* 1937, *32,* 216–222.

Purcell, K. Some shortcomings in projective test validation. *J. abnorm. soc. Psychol.,* 1958, *57,* 115–118.

Purdy, D. M. The biological psychology of Kurt Goldstein. *Char. & Pers.,* 1937, *5,* 321–330.

Putnam, D. *A text-book of psychology for secondary schools.* New York: American Book., 1901.

Quay, H. The performance of hospitalized psychiatric patients on the ego-strength scale of the MMPI. *J. clin. Psychol.*, 1955, *11*, 403–405.

Rabban, M. Sex-role identification in young children in two diverse social groups. *Genet. psychol. Monogr.*, 1950, *42*, 81–158.

Radke, Marian, Trager, Helen G., & Davis, Hadassah. Social perceptions and attitudes of children. *Genet. psychol. Monogr.*, 1949, *40*, 327–447.

Radke, Marian, & Trager, Helen G. Children's perceptions of the social roles of Negroes and whites. *J. Psychol.*, 1950, *29*, 3–33.

Rall, H. F. *Christianity: an inquiry into its nature and truth.* New York: Scribner's, 1940.

Rank, O. *The trauma of birth.* New York: Harcourt, Brace, 1929.

Rapoport, Rhona, & Rosow, I. An approach to family relationships and role performance. *Hum. Relat.*, 1957, *10*, 209–221.

Razran, G. The conditioned evocation of attitudes (cognitive conditioning?) *J. exp. Psychol.*, 1954, *48*, 278–282.

Razran, G. Conditioning and perception. *Psychol. Rev.*, 1955, *62*, 83–95.

Redl, F., & Wineman, D. *Children who hate, the disorganization and breakdown of behavior controls.* Glencoe, Ill.: Free Press, 1951.

Redl, F., & Wineman, D. *Controls from within, techniques for the treatment of the aggressive child.* Glencoe, Ill.: Free Press, 1952.

Reich, W. *Character-analysis.* (Trans. by T. P. Wolfe.) (3rd enlarged ed.) New York: Orgone Inst. Press, 1949.

Reich, W. On the technique of character-analysis. In Clara Thompson, M. Mazer, & E. Witenberg, *An outline of psychoanalysis.* (Rev. ed.) New York: Random House, 1955.

Reider, N. The concept of normality. *Psychoanal. Quart.*, 1950, *19*, 43–51.

Rethlingshafer, Dorothy. The relation of tests of persistence to other measures of continuance of action. *J. abnorm. soc. Psychol.*, 1942, *37*, 71–82.

Rexroad, C. N. *Psychology and personality development.* Boston: Christopher Publishing House, 1940.

Reyburn, H. A., & Taylor, J. G. Some factors of personality: a further analysis of some of Webb's data. *Brit. J. Psychol.*, 1939, *30*, 1, 151–211.

Reyburn, H. A., & Taylor, J. G. Factors in introversion and extraversion. *Brit. J. Psychol.*, 1940, *31*, 335–340.

Reyburn, H. A., & Taylor, J. G. Some factors of temperament: a re-examination. *Psychometrika*, 1943, *8*, 91–104.

Reymert, M. O. (Ed.) *Feelings and emotions, the Wittenberg Symposium.* Worcester, Mass.: Clark Univer. Press, 1928.

Reymert, M. L., & Kohn, H. A. An objective investigation of suggestibility. *Char. & Pers.*, 1940, *9*, 44–48.

Reymert, M. L., & Speer, G. S. Does the Luria technique measure emotion or merely bodily tension? A re-evaluation of the method. *Char. & Pers.*, 1939, 7, 192–200.

Rhine, J. B. Telepathy and clairvoyance in the normal and trance states of a "medium." *Char. & Pers.*, 1934, *3*, 91–111.

Rhine, J. B. Comments on "Science and the supernatural." *Science*, 1956, *123*, 11–14.

Riesman, D. *The lonely crowd, a study of the changing American character.* New Haven, Conn.: Yale Univer. Press, 1950.

Riesman, D. *Faces in the crowd, individual studies in character and politics.* New Haven, Conn.: Yale Univer. Press, 1952.

Rim, Y. Perseveration and fluency as measures of introversion-extraversion in abnormal subjects. *J. Pers.*, 1955, *23*, 324–334.

Rioch, Janet M. The transference phenomenon in psychoanalytic therapy. In Clara Thompson, M. Mazer, & E. Witenberg (Eds.), *An outline of psychoanalysis.* (Rev. ed.) New York: Modern Library, 1955.

Roback, A. A. Character and adjustment. *Psyche*, 1925, *6*, 67–79.

Roback, A. A. *The psychology of character, with a survey of temperament.* New York: Harcourt, Brace, 1927.

Roback, A. A. Writing slips and personality. *Char. & Pers.*, 1932, *1*, 136–146. (a)

Roback, A. A. Personality tests—whither? *Char. & Pers.*, 1932, *1*, 214–224. (b)

Roback, A. A. Personalysis: a study in method. *Char. & Pers.*, 1934, *3*, 144–156.

Roback, A. A. Race and mode of expression: a preliminary investigation in collective personality. *Char. & Pers.*, 1935, *4*, 51–60.

Roback, A. A. Review of G. W. Allport, *Personality, a psychological interpretation. Char. & Pers.*, 1938, *6*, 243–249.

Roback, A. A. *Personality in theory and practice.* Cambridge, Mass.: Sci-Art, 1950.

Robinson, D. S. *The principles of reasoning, an introduction to logic and the scientific method.* (2nd. ed.) New York: Appleton, 1930.

Robinson, Mary Frances, & Freeman, W. *Psychosurgery and the self.* New York: Grune & Stratton, 1954.

Roe, Anne. Analysis of group Rorschachs of biologists. *J. proj. Tech.,* 1949, *13,* 25–43.

Roe, Anne. Analysis of group Rorschachs of physical scientists. *J. proj. Tech.,* 1950, *14,* 385–398.

Roe, Anne. A psychological study of eminent biologists. *Psychol. Monogr.,* 1951, *65,* No. 14 (Whole No. 331). (a)

Roe, Anne. A psychological study of physical scientists. *Genet. psychol. Monogr.,* 1951, *43,* 121–239. (b)

Roe, Anne. Psychological tests of research scientists. *J. consult. Psychol.,* 1951, *15,* 492–495. (c)

Roe, Anne. A psychological study of eminent psychologists and anthropologists, and a comparison with biological and physical scientists. *Psychol. Monogr.,* 1953, 67, No. 2 (Whole No. 352).

Roethlisberger, F. J., & Dickson, W. J. *Management and the worker.* Cambridge, Mass.: Harvard Univer. Press, 1939.

Roff, M. A factorial study of tests in the perceptual area. *Psychometr. Monogr.,* No. 8. Chicago: The Univer. of Chicago Press, 1952.

Rogers, C. R. Persons or science? A philosophical question. *Amer. Psychologist,* 1955, *10,* 267–278.

Rogers, L. S., & Hammond, K. R. Prediction of the results of therapy by means of the Rorschach test. *J. consult. Psychol.,* 1953, *17,* 8–15.

Róheim, G. (Ed.) *Psychoanalysis and the social sciences, an annual.* Vol. 1. New York: International Universities Press, 1947.

Róheim, G. *Psychoanalysis and anthropology; culture, personality, and the unconscious.* New York: International Universities Press, 1950.

Róheim, G. The anthropological evidence and the Oedipus complex. *Psychoanal. Quart.,* 1952, *21,* 537–542.

Rokeach, M. Generalized mental rigidity as a factor in ethnocentrism. *J. abnorm. soc. Psychol.,* 1948, *43,* 259–278.

Rokeach, M. Rigidity and ethnocentrism: a rejoinder. *J. Pers.,* 1949, *17,* 467–474.

Rokeach, M. Religious and political commitment in relation to dogmatism and the authoritarian personality. *Amer. Psychologist,* 1955, *10,* 340–341. (Abstract)

Romano, J. (Ed.) *Adaptation.* Ithaca, N. Y.: Cornell Univer. Press, 1949.

Rosenman, S. Toward a theory of the ego. *Psychoanal. Rev.,* 1955, *42,* 142–159.

Rosenzweig, S. Frustration as an experimental problem. VI. A general outline of frustration. *Char. & Pers.,* 1938, 7, 151–160.

Rosenzweig, S., & Sarason, S. An experimental study of the triadic hypothesis: reaction to frustration, ego-defense, and hypnotizability. I. Correlational approach. *Char. & Pers.,* 1942, *11,* 1–19.

Ross, V. R. *Relationships between intelligence, scholastic achievement, and musical talent.* Claremont, Calif.: California Bureau of Juvenile Research, 1937.

Rowland, L. W. Will hypnotized persons try to harm themselves and others? *J. abnorm. soc. Psychol.,* 1939, *34,* 114–117.

Ruch, F. L. *Psychology and life.* (4th ed.) Chicago: Scott, Foresman, 1953.

Rundquist, E. A., & Sletto, R. F. Personality in the depression, a study in the measurement of attitudes. *Univer. of Minn. Inst., Child Welf. Monogr. Ser.,* No. 12. Minneapolis: Univer. of Minnesota Press, 1936.

Sadger, J. Sleep walking and moon walking; a medico-literary study. (Trans. by Louise Brink.) *Nerv. & Ment. Dis. Monogr. Ser.,* No. 31. New York: Nerv. & Ment. Dis. Publishing Co., 1920.

Sainte-Beuve, C. A. *Derniers portraits littéraires.* Paris: Didier, 1858.

Salisbury, H. E. Enigma of the Russian character. *The New York Times Magazine,* Oct. 23, 1955, 11 ff.

Samuels, Myra R. Judgments of faces. *Char. & Pers.,* 1939, *8,* 18–27.

Sanborn, H. An examination of William Stern's philosophy. *Char. & Pers.,* 1939, 7, 318–330.

Sanford, N. The dynamics of identification. *Psychol. Rev.,* 1955, *62,* 106–118.

Sanford, N. Surface and depth in the individual personality. *Psychol. Rev.,* 1956, *63,* 349–359.

Sanford, R. N., Adkins, M. M., Miller, R. B., & Cobb, E. A. Physique, personality, and scholarship, a cooperative study of school children. *Monogr. Soc. Res. Child Develpm.* 1943, No. 34. (Cited in *Psychol. Abstr.,* 1943, *13,* No. 4319.)

Sappenfield, B. R. *Personality dynamics, an*

integrative psychology of adjustment. New York: Knopf, 1954.

Sarbin, T. R. Adjustment in psychology. *Char. & Pers.*, 1940, 8, 240–249.

Sarbin, T. R. Role theory. In Gardner Lindzey, *Handbook of social psychology.* Vol. I. *Theory and method.* Cambridge, Mass.: Addison-Wesley, 1954.

Sarbin, T. R., & Jones, D. S. An experimental analysis of role behavior. *J. abnorm. soc. Psychol.*, 1955, 51, 236–241.

Sargent, S. S., & Smith, Marian W. (Eds.) *Culture and personality. Proceedings of an interdisciplinary conference held under the auspices of the Viking Fund.* New York: Viking Fund, 1949.

Saudek, R. *Experiments with handwriting.* New York: William Morrow, 1929.

Saudek, R. Identical twins reared apart. *Char. & Pers.*, 1933, 2, 22–40.

Saudin, A. A. Social and emotional adjustments of regularly promoted and non-promoted pupils. *Child Develpm. Monogr.*, No. 32. New York: Bureau of Publications, Teachers College, Columbia Univer., 1944.

Savage, L. J. *The foundation of statistics.* New York: Wiley, 1954.

Saxer, Gertrud. Emotionelle Schwierig-keiten des körperbehinderten Kindes. *Heilpadag. Workbl.*, 1958, 27, 50–53. (*Psychol. Abstr.*, 1959, 33, 8931.)

Schafer, R. *The clinical application of psychological tests, diagnostic summaries and case studies.* New York: International Universities Press, 1948.

Schafer, R. *Psychoanalytic interpretation in Rorschach testing, theory and application.* New York: Grune & Stratton, 1954.

Schaffner, B. *Father land, a study of authoritarianism in the German family.* New York: Columbia Univer. Press, 1948.

Scheerer, M. Problems of performance analysis in the study of personality. *Annals of the New York Acad. of Sci.*, 1946, 46, 653–678.

Scheerer, M. Personality functioning and cognitive psychology. *J. Pers.*, 1953, 22, 1–16.

Scheerer, M. Cognitive theory. In Gardner Lindzey (Ed.), *Handbook of social psychology.* Vol. I. *Theory and method.* Cambridge, Mass.: Addison-Wesley, 1954.

Scheide, Elizabeth J. Anxiety: Its relationship to self-evaluation. *Dissertation Abstr.*, 1955, 15, 880.

Schein, E. H. Reaction patterns to severe, chronic stress in American Army prisoners of war of the Chinese. *J. soc. Issues*, 1957 (3), 13, 21–30.

Scher, S. C. Some group attitudes related to expressed acceptance of self and others. *Dissertation Abstr.*, 1955, 15, 2579.

Schilder, P. *Goals and desires of man, a psychological survey of life.* New York: Columbia Univer. Press, 1942. (a)

Schilder, P. *Mind: perception and thought in their constructive aspects.* New York: Columbia Univer. Press, 1942. (b)

Schilder, P. *The image and appearance of the human body.* New York: International Universities Press, 1950. (Previous publ., 1935)

Schmeidler, Gertrude R. Personality correlates of ESP as shown by Rorschach studies. *J. parapsychol.*, 1949, 13, 23–31.

Schmidt-Koenig, K. The sun-azimuth compass: One factor in the orientation of homing pigeons. *Sci.*, 1960, 131, 826–828.

Schnier, J. The cornerstone ceremony. *Psychoanal. Rev.*, 1947, 34, 357–369.

Schroder, H. M., & Rotter, J. B. Rigidity as learned behavior. *J. exp. Psychol.*, 1952, 44, 141–150.

Schulberg, B. W. *What makes Sammy run?* New York: Random House, 1941.

Schweitzer, A. *Out of my life and thought, an autobiography.* (Trans. by C. T. Campion.) Postscript 1932–1949 by Everett Skillings. New York: Holt, 1949.

Schwendener, Norma. *Game preferences of 10,000 fourth grade children.* New York: No publisher cited, 1932.

Schwesinger, Gladys C. The effect of differential parent-child relation on identical twin resemblances in personality. *Acta geneticae medicae et Gemellologiae*, 1952, 1, 40–47.

Sears, R. R. *A survey of objective studies of psychoanalytical concepts.* Soc. Sci. Res. Council, Bull. 51. New York: Social Science Research Council, 1943.

Sears, R. R. Experimental analysis of psychoanalytic phenomena. In J. McV. Hunt (Ed.), *Personality and the behavior disorders, a handbook based on experimental and clinical research.* Vol. I. New York: Ronald, 1944.

Sears, R. R. A theoretical framework for personality and social behavior. *Amer. Psychologist*, 1951, 6, 476–483.

Seashore, C. E. *Manual of instructions and interpretations for Measures of Musical Talent.* New York: Columbia Graphophone Co., 1919.

Seeman, E., & Saudek, R. The self-expression of identical twins in handwriting and drawing. *Char. & Pers.*, 1932, *1*, 91–128, 268–285.

Segal, J. Correlates of collaboration and resistance behavior among U. S. Army POW's in Korea. *J. soc. Issues*, 1957 (3), *13*, 31–40.

Selye, H. A syndrome produced by diverse nocuous agents. *Nature*, 1936, *138*, 32.

Selye, H. *The physiology and pathology of exposure to stress; a treatise based on the concepts of the general-adaptation syndrome and the diseases of adaptation.* Montreal: Acta, 1950.

Selye, H. Stress and disease. *Science*, 1955, *122*, 625–631.

Sen, A. A statistical study of the Rorschach test. *Brit. J. Psychol., Stat. Sect.*, 1950, *3*, 21–39. (Cited in *Psychol. Abstr.*, 1950, *24*, No. 5260)

Seward, Georgene H. *Sex and the social order.* New York: McGraw-Hill, 1946.

Seward, J. P. Psychoanalysis, deductive method, and the Blacky Test. *J. abnorm. soc. Psychol.*, 1950, *45*, 529–535.

Shakow, D., & Rosenzweig, S. The use of the tautophone ("verbal summator") as an auditory apperception test for the study of personality. *Char. & Pers.*, 1940, *8*, 216–226.

Shand, A. F. *The foundations of character, being a study of the tendencies of the emotions and sentiments.* (2nd ed.) London: Macmillan, 1920.

Sharma, A. K. Auto-suggestion and Hindu psychology. *Psyche*, 1924, *4*, 204–212.

Sharpe, Ella F. *Collected papers on psychoanalysis.* Edited by Marjorie Brierly. London: Hogarth Press & Institute of Psycho-Analysis, 1950.

Shayon, R. L. *Television and our children.* New York: Longmans, Green, 1951.

Sheldon, W. H. Constitutional factors in personality. In J. McV. Hunt (Ed.), *Personality and the behavior disorders, a handbook based on experimental and clinical research.* Vol. I. New York: Ronald, 1944.

Sheldon, W. H., with the collaboration of E. M. Harth, & E. McDermott. *Varieties of delinquent youth; an introduction to constitutional psychiatry.* New York: Harper, 1949.

Sheldon, W. H., & Stevens, S. S. *The varieties of temperament, a psychology of constitutional differences.* New York: Harper, 1942.

Sheldon, W. H., Stevens, S. S., & Tucker, W. B. *The varieties of human physique; an introduction to constitutional psychology.* New York: Harper, 1940.

Sherif, M. A study of some social factors in perception. *Arch. Psychol.*, 1935, No. 187.

Sherif, M., & Cantril, H. *The psychology of ego-involvements; social attitudes and identifications.* New York: Wiley, 1947.

Sherman, M. *The development of attitudes, a study of the attitudes of mountain children.* New York: Payne Fund, 1933.

Shinn, Milicent W. *The biography of a baby.* Boston: Houghton Mifflin, 1900.

Shneidman, E. S., with the collaboration of W. Joel & K. B. Little. *Thematic test analysis.* New York: Grune & Stratton, 1951.

Shorr, J. E. An analysis of the rationalization and explanations of test behavior. *J. clin. Psychol.*, 1954, *10*, 29–34.

Shuey, Audrey M. *The testing of Negro intelligence.* Lynchburg, Va.: J. P. Bell, 1958.

Sidgwick, H. *Outlines of the history of ethics for English readers.* With an additional chapter by A. G. Widgery. (6th enlarged ed.) London: Macmillan, 1931.

Sidis, B. *An experimental study of sleep.* Boston: Richard G. Badger, Gordon Press, 1908.

Sidis, B., & Goodhart, S. P. *Multiple personality.* New York: Appleton, 1909.

Siegel, S. Certain determinants and correlates of authoritarianism. *Genet. psychol. Monogr.*, 1954, *49*, 187–229.

Silverberg, W. H. Review of *Psychiatry: its evolution and present status* by Wm. C. Menninger. *Psychoanal. Quart.*, 1949, *18*, 370–372.

Simmel, Marianne L. The conditions of occurrence of phantom limbs. *Proc. Amer. Phil. Soc.*, 1958, *102*, 492–500.

Simpson, D. C. First and Second Kings. In F. C. Eiselen, E. Lewis, & D. G. Downey (Eds.), *The Abingdon Bible commentary.* New York: Abingdon, 1929.

Sisam, C. H. *Analytic geometry.* (Rev. ed.) New York: Holt, 1949.

Skard, Å. G. Needs and need-energy. *Char. & Pers.*, 1937, *8*, 28–41.

Skinner, B. F. *The behavior of organisms; an experimental analysis*. New York: Appleton, 1938.

Skinner, B. F. *Science and human behavior*. New York: Macmillan, 1953.

Slotkin, J. S. *Personality development*. New York: Harper, 1952.

Smith, E. E. The effects of clear and unclear role expectations on group productivity and defensiveness. *J. abnorm. soc. Psychol.*, 1957, *55*, 213–217.

Smith, G. M. A phobia originating before the age of three—cured with the aid of hypnotic recall. *Char. & Pers.*, 1937, *5*, 331–337.

Smith H. C. Psychometric checks on hypotheses derived from Sheldon's work on physique and temperament. *J. Pers.*, 1949, *17*, 310–320.

Smith, M. B., Bruner, J. S., & White, R. W. *Opinions and personality*. New York: Wiley, 1956.

Smithies, Elsie M. *Case studies of normal adolescent girls*. New York: Appleton, 1933.

Smuts, F. C. *Holism and evolution*. New York: Macmillan, 1926.

Snygg, D., & Combs, A. W. *Individual behavior, a new frame of reference for psychology*. New York: Harper, 1949.

Soal, S. G. On "Science and the supernatural." *Science*, 1956, *123*, 9–11.

Soal, S. G., & Bateman, F. *Modern experiments in telepathy*. New Haven, Conn.: Yale Univer. Press, 1954.

Solley, C. M., & Murphy, G. *Development of the perceptual world*. New York: Basic Books, 1960.

Solomon, J. C. *A synthesis of human behavior, an integration of thought processes and ego growth*. New York: Grune & Stratton, 1954.

Sondern, F., Jr. Twentieth Century Sherlock Holmes. *Argosy*, 1949, *328*, 36–37, 71–72.

Sondern, F., Jr. The doctor who hated murder. *Reader's Digest*, 1949, *55*, 65–68.

Sonnemann, U. *Existence and therapy, an introduction to phenomenological psychology and existential analysis*. New York: Grune & Stratton, 1954.

Soper, E. D. *The religions of mankind*. (Rev. ed.) Nashville, Tenn.: Abingdon-Cokesbury, 1938.

Sorokin, P. C. *Man and society in calamity: the effects of war, revolution, famine, pestilence upon human mind, behavior, social organization and cultural life*. New York: Dutton, 1942.

Soskin, W. F. Frames of reference in personality assessment. *J. clin. Psychol.*, 1954, *10*, 107–114.

Spearman, C. General intelligence, objectively determined and measured. *Amer. J. Psychol.*, 1904, *15*, 201–293.

Spearman, C. *The nature of 'intelligence' and the principles of cognition*. London: Macmillan, 1923.

Spearman, C. *The abilities of man*. New York: Macmillan, 1927.

Spearman, C. German science of character. Part I. Approach from experimental psychology. *Char. & Pers.*, 1937, *5*, 177–201. (a)

Spearman, C. German science of character. Part II. Approach from typology. *Char. & Pers.*, 1937, *6*, 36–50. (b)

Spelt, D. K. The conditioning of the human fetus "in utero." *J. exp. Psychol.*, 1948, *38*, 338–346.

Spence, K. W. Theoretical interpretations of learning. In Moss, F. A. (Ed.) *Comparative psychology*. (Rev. ed.) New York: Prentice-Hall, 1942.

Spencer, D. *Fulcra of conflict, a new approach to personality measurement*. Yonkers-on-Hudson, N. Y.: World Book, 1938.

Spencer, H. *The principles of psychology*. (3rd ed.) Vol. I. New York: Appleton, 1895.

Spiegelman, M., Terwilliger, C., & Fearing, F. The content of comics: goals and means to goals of comic strip characters. *J. soc. Psychol.*, 1953, *37*, 189–203.

Spitz, R. A. Authority and masturbation, some remarks on bibliographical investigation. *Psychoanal. Quart.*, 1952, *21*, 490–527.

Spock, B. McL. *The common sense book of baby and child care*. New York: Duell, 1946.

Spoerl, Dorothy T. Personality and drawings in retarded children. *Char. & Pers.*, 1940, *8*, 227–239.

Spoerl, H. D. Faculties versus traits: Gall's solution. *Char. & Pers.*, 1936, *4*, 216–231.

Sprague, E. M. An appraisal of Freud's concept of the superego and an analysis of its relationship to ethical value-systems. *Dissertation Abstr.*, 1958, *18*, 1504–1505.

Squires, P. C. The creative psychology of Carl Maria von Weber. *Char. & Pers.*, 1938, *6*, 203–217. (a)

Squires, P. C. The creative psychology of Cesar Franck. *Char. & Pers.*, 1938, 7, 41–49. (b)

Stacey, C. L., & Goldberg, H. D. A personality study of professional and student actors. *J. appl. Psychol.*, 1953, 37, 24–25.

Stadler, L. J. The gene. *Science*, 1954, *120*, 811–819.

Stagner, R. *Psychology of personality*. New York: McGraw-Hill, 1948.

Stagner, R. Homeostasis as a unifying concept in personality theory. *Psychol. Rev.*, 1951, *58*, 5–17.

Stagner, R. Homeostasis: corruptions or misconceptions?—a reply. *Psychol. Rev.*, 1954, *61*, 205–208.

Stagner, R., & Karwoski, T. F. *Psychology*. New York: McGraw-Hill, 1952.

Stanton, M. O. *The encyclopedia of face and form reading, a complete summary of character analysis, the only modern and comprehensive textbook showing "the logical method" of character analysis, with answers to every question on the subject carefully grouped and arranged for quick reference, physical and mental traits revealed.* (5th Rev. ed.) Philadelphia: Davis Co., Publishers, 1919.

Stein, A. Guilt as a composite emotion: The relationship of child-rearing variables to superego response. *Dissertation Abstr.*, 1958, *19*, 863–874.

Stein, M. H. Premonition as a defense. *Psychoanal. Quart.*, 1953, 22, 69–74. (Cited in *Psychol. Abstr.*, 1954, *28*, No. 1251)

Stein, M. I. *The Thematic Apperception Test, an introductory manual for its clinical use with adult males.* Cambridge, Mass.: Addison-Wesley, 1948.

Steiner, I. D. Interpersonal behavior as influenced by accuracy of social perception. *Psychol. Rev.*, 1955, *62*, 268–274.

Stein-Levinson, Thea. An introduction to the graphology of Ludwig Klages. *Char. & Pers.*, 1938, *6*, 163–176.

Steisel, I. M. The Rorschach test and suggestibility. *J. abnorm. soc. Psychol.*, 1952, *47*, 607–614.

Stephenson, W. Correlating persons instead of tests. *Char. & Pers.*, 1935, *4*, 17–24. (a)

Stephenson, W. Perseveration and character. *Char. & Pers.*, 1935, *4*, 44–52. (b)

Stephenson, W. Some recent contributions to the theory of psychometry. *Char. & Pers.*, 1936, *4*, 294–304.

Stephenson, W. A note on Professor R. B. Cattell's methodological adumbrations. *J. clin. Psychol.*, 1952, *8*, 206–207.

Stephenson, W. *The study of behavior; Q-technique and its methodology.* Chicago: The Univer. of Chicago Press, 1953.

Sterba, Edith, & Sterba, R. *Beethoven and his nephew; a psychoanalytic study of their relationship.* (Trans. by W. R. Trask.) New York: Pantheon, 1954.

Sterba, R. A case of brief psychotherapy by Sigmund Freud. *Psychoanal. Rev.*, 1951, *38*, 75–80.

Stern, G. S., Stein, M. I., & Bloom, B. S. *Methods in personality assessment; human behavior in complex situations.* Glencoe, Ill.: Free Press, 1956.

Stern, W. *Der Intelligenzquotient als Mass der kindlichen Intelligenz, inbesondere der Unternormalen. Z. angewand. Psychol.*, 1916, *11*, 1–18.

Stern, W. *Psychology of early childhood, up to the sixth year of age, supplemented by extracts from the unpublished diaries of Clara Stern.* (Trans. from the third edition, revised and enlarged, by Anna Barwell.) New York: Holt, 1924.

Stern, W. On the nature and structure of character. *Char. & Pers.*, 1935, *3*, 270–289.

Stern, W. Cloud pictures: a new method for testing imagination. *Char. & Pers.*, 1937, *6*, 132–146.

Stern, W. *General psychology from the personalistic standpoint.* (Trans. by H. D. Spoerl.) New York: Macmillan, 1938.

Sternberg, C. Personality trait patterns of college students majoring in different fields. *Psychol. Monogr.*, 1955, *69*, No. 18 (Whole No. 403).

Stevens, S. S. (ed.) *Handbook of experimental psychology.* New York: Wiley, 1951.

Stockard, C. R. *The physical basis of personality.* New York: Norton, 1931.

Stogdill, R. M. Personal factors associated with leadership: a survey of the literature. *J. Psychol.*, 1948, *25*, 35–71.

Stolurow, L. M. *Readings in learning.* New York: Prentice-Hall, 1953.

Stott, L. H. General home setting as a factor in the study of the only versus the non-only child. *Char. & Pers.*, 1939, *8*, 156–162.

Stouffer, S. A. An analysis of conflicting social norms. *Amer. sociol. Rev.*, 1949, *14*, 707–717.

Stout, G. F. *A manual of psychology.* New York: Hinds, Noble, & Eldredge, 1899.

Stout, G. F. *Analytic psychology*. New York: Macmillan, 1918. 2 vols.

Strauss, A. The learning of roles and of concepts as twin processes. *J. genet. Psychol.*, 1956, *88*, 211–217.

Strong, E. K. *Vocational interests of men and women*. Stanford, Calif.: Stanford Univer. Press, 1943.

Strongin, E. I., Strongin, J., & Bull, Nina. Visual changes and affective states. *J. nerv. ment. Dis.*, 1954, *119*, 344–348.

Studman, L. G. The factor theory in the field of personality. *Char. & Pers.*, 1935, *4*, 34–43.

Stutsman, Rachel. *Mental measurement of preschool children, with a guide for the administration of the Merrill-Palmer Scale of Mental Tests*. Yonkers-on-Hudson, N. Y.: World Book, 1931.

Sullivan, H. S. Multidisciplined coordination of interpersonal data. In S. S. Sargent, & Marian Smith (Eds.), *Culture and personality*. New York: Viking Fund, 1949.

Sullivan, H. S. *The interpersonal theory of psychiatry*. (Ed. by Helen S. Perry, & Mary L. Gamel.) New York: Norton, 1953.

Sullivan, P. L., & Adelson, J. Ethnocentrism and misanthropy. *J. abnorm. soc. Psychol.*, 1954, *49*, 246–250.

Sumner, W. G. *Folkways; a study of the sociological importance of usages, manners, customs, mores, and morals*. Boston: Ginn, 1906.

Sumner, W. G., & Keller, A. G. *The science of society*. New Haven, Conn.: Yale Univer. Press, 1927.

Sundberg, N. D. The acceptability of "fake" versus "bona fide" personality test interpretations. *J. abnorm. soc. Psychol.*, 1955, *50*, 145–147.

Sutcliffe, J. P., & Haberman, M. Factors influencing choice in role conflict situations. *Amer. sociol. Rev.*, 1956, *21*, 695–703.

Symonds, P. M. *Diagnosing personality and conduct*. New York: Century, 1931.

Symonds, P. M. *Psychological diagnosis in social adjustment, including an annotated list of tests, questionnaires, and rating scales for the study of personality and conduct*. New York: American Book, 1934.

Symonds, P. M. *The dynamics of human adjustment*. New York: Appleton-Century-Crofts, 1946.

Symonds, P. M. *The ego and the self*. New York: Appleton-Century-Crofts, 1951.

Symonds, P. M. *Dynamic psychology*. New York: Appleton-Century-Crofts, 1959.

Szasz, T. S. On the psychoanalytic theory of instincts. *Psychoanal. Quart.*, 1952, *21*, 25–48.

The Tallahassee Democrat, July 13, 1955, 41, No. 187, 2.

Taft, R. The ability to judge people. *Psychol. Bull.*, 1955, *52*, 1–23.

Taft, R. Some characteristics of good judges of others. *Brit. J. Psychol.*, 1956, *47*, 19–29.

Taft, R. The validity of the Barron Ego-Strength Scale and the Welsh Anxiety Index. *J. consult. Psychol.*, 1957, *21*, 247–249.

Taft, R. Multiple methods of personality assessment. *Psychol. Bull.*, 1959, *56*, 333–352.

Taft, R. & Coventry, J. Neuroticism, extraversion, and the perception of the vertical. *J. abnorm. soc. Psychol.*, 1958, *56*, 139–141.

Tamkin, A. S. An evaluation of the construct validity of Barron's Ego-Strength Scale. *J. clin. Psychol.*, 1957, *13*, 156–158.

Tamkin, A. S., & Klett, C. James. Barron's Ego-Strength Sale: A replication of an evaluation of its construct validity. *J. consult. Psychol.*, 1957, *21*, 412.

Tarachow, S. Circuses and clowns. In Géza Róheim (Ed.), *Psychoanalysis and the social sciences*. New York: International Universities Press, 1951.

Taylor, Janet A. A personality scale of manifest anxiety. *J. abnorm. soc. Psychol.*, 1953, *48*, 285–290.

Taylor, W. S. Changing attitudes in a conflict of cultures. *Char. & Pers.*, 1941, *10*, 87–108.

Technical recommendations for psychological tests and diagnostic techniques. Psychol. Bull., 1954, *51* (2), 1–38.

Terman, L. M. *The measurement of intelligence, an explanation of and a complete guide for the use of the Stanford Revision and Extension of the Binet-Simon Intelligence Scale*. New York: Houghton Mifflin, 1916.

Terman, L. M. (Ed.) *Genetic studies of genius*. Vol. I. *Mental and physical traits of a thousand gifted children*. Vol. II. Cox, Catherine M., *The early mental traits of three hundred geniuses*. Vol. III. *The promise of youth*. Vol. IV. *The gifted child grows up, twenty-five years' follow-up of a superior group*. Vol. V.

Gifted group at mid-life: thirty-five years' follow-up of the superior child. Stanford, Calif.: Stanford Univer. Press, 1925, 1926, 1930, 1947, 1959.

Terman, L. M. Scientists and nonscientists in a group of 800 gifted men. *Psychol. Monogr.*, 1954, *68*, No. 7 (Whole No. 378).

Terman, L. M., & Merrill, Maud A. *Measuring intelligence: a guide to the administration of the new Revised Stanford-Binet tests of intelligence.* Boston: Houghton Mifflin, 1937.

Terman, L. M., & Miles, C. C. *Sex and personality: studies in masculinity and femininity.* New York: McGraw-Hill, 1936.

Thompson, Clara. *Psychoanalysis: evolution and development.* New York: Hermitage House, 1950.

Thompson, Clara, Mazer, M., & Witenberg, E. *An outline of psychoanalysis.* (Rev. ed.) New York: Modern Library, 1955.

Thompson (Woolley), Helen B. *The mental traits of sex.* Chicago: The Univer. of Chicago Press, 1903.

Thomson, G. H. *The factorial analysis of human ability.* New York: Houghton Mifflin, 1939.

Thorndike, E. L. *The psychology of arithmetic.* New York: Macmillan, 1922.

Thorndike, E. L. A theory of the action of the after-effects of a connection upon it. *Psychol. Rev.*, 1933, *40*, 434–490.

Thorndike, E. L., Bregman, E. O., Cobb, M. O., & Woodyard, Ella. *The measurement of intelligence.* New York: Bureau of Publications, Teachers College, Columbia Univer., 1927.

Thorndike, R. L. *Personnel selection: test and measurement techniques.* New York: Wiley, 1949.

Thorndike, R. L. The psychological value systems of psychologists. *Amer. Psychologist*, 1954, *9*, 787–789.

Thornton, G. R. A factor analysis of tests designed to measure persistence. *Psychol. Monogr.*, 1939, *51*, No. 3 (Whole No. 229).

Thornton, G. R., & Guilford, J. P. A factor analysis of some tests purporting to measure persistence. *Psychol. Bull.*, 1938, *35*, 708–709.

Thorpe, L. P. *Personality and life, a practical guide to personality improvement.* New York: Longmans, Green, 1941.

Thorpe, L. P. *Child psychology and development.* New York: Ronald, 1946.

Thorpe, L. P., & Katz, B. *The psychology of abnormal behavior, a dynamic approach.* New York: Ronald, 1948.

Thorpe, L. P., & Schmuller, A. M. *Personality: an interdisciplinary approach.* Princeton, N. J.: Van Nostrand, 1958.

Thrasher, F. M. *The gang, a study of 1,313 gangs in Chicago.* Chicago: The Univer. of Chicago Press, 1927.

Thurstone, L. L. A law of comparative judgment. *Psychol. Rev.* 1927, *34*, 273–286.

Thurstone, L. L. Attitudes can be measured. *Amer. J. Sociol.*, 1928, *33*, 529–554.

Thurstone, L. L. Theory of attitude measurement. *Psychol. Rev.*, 1929, *36*, 222–241.

Thurstone, L. L. *The reliability and validity of tests.* Ann Arbor, Mich.: Edwards Bros., 1931.

Thurstone, L. L. The vectors of the mind. *Psychol. Rev.*, 1934, *41*, 1–32.

Thurstone, L. L. *The vectors of the mind; multiple-factor analysis for the isolation of primary traits.* Chicago: The Univer. of Chicago Press, 1935.

Thurstone, L. L. The factorial isolation of primary abilities. *Psychometrika*, 1936, *1*, 175–182.

Thurstone, L. L. Primary mental abilities. *Psychom. Monogr.*, No. 1. Chicago: The Univer. of Chicago Press, 1938.

Thurstone, L. L. A factorial study of perception. *Psychom. Monogr.*, No. 4. Chicago: The Univer. of Chicago Press, 1944.

Thurstone, L. L. *Multiple-factor analysis.* Chicago: The Univer. of Chicago Press, 1947.

Thurstone, L. L. (Ed.) *Applications of psychology; essays to honor Walter V. Bingham.* New York: Harper, 1952.

Thurstone, L. L., & Chave, E. J. *The measurement of attitude, a psychological method and some experiments with a scale for measuring attitude toward the church.* Chicago: The Univer. of Chicago Press, 1929.

Thurstone, L. L., & Thurstone, Thelma G. Factorial studies of intelligence. *Psychom. Monogr.*, No. 2. Chicago: The Univer. of Chicago Press, 1941.

Tinbergen, N. *The study of instinct.* Oxford: At the University Press, 1951.

Tinbergen, N. *The herring gull's world; a study of the social behavior of birds.* London: Collins, 1953.

Titchener, E. B. *An outline of psychology.* New York: Macmillan, 1899.

Tolman, E. C. *Collected papers in psychology.* Berkeley, Calif.: Univer. of California Press, 1951. (a)

Tolman, E. C. *Purposive behavior in animals and men.* Berkeley, Calif.: Univer. of California Press, 1951. (b)

Tolman, E. C., & Honzik, C. H. Introduction and removal of reward, and maze performance in rats. *Univer. Calif. Publ. Psychol.,* 1930, *4,* 257–275.

Tomkins, S. S. (Ed.) *Contemporary psychopathology.* Cambridge, Mass.: Harvard Univer. Press, 1947. (a)

Tomkins, S. S. *The Thematic Apperception Test, the theory and technique of interpretation.* New York: Grune & Stratton, 1947. (b)

Toynbee, A. *The study of history.* Abridgment of Vols. I–VI by D. C. Somervell. New York: Oxford Univer. Press, 1947.

Travis, L. E., & Baruch, Dorothy W. *Personal problems of everyday life, practical aspects of mental hygiene.* New York: Appleton-Century-Crofts, 1941.

Trent, R. D. The color of the investigator as a variable in experimental research with Negro subjects. *J. soc. Psychol.,* 1954, *40,* 281–287.

Trueblood, C. K. Sainte-Beuve and the psychology of personality. *Char. & Pers.,* 1939, *8,* 120–143.

Tsai, C. The relative strength of sex and hunger motives in the albino rat. *J. comp. Psychol.,* 1925, *5,* 407–415.

Tuddenham, R. D. The influence of a distorted group norm upon individual judgment. *J. Psychol.,* 1958, *46,* 227–241. (a)

Tuddenham, R. D. The influence of an avowedly distorted norm upon individual judgment. *J. Psychol.,* 1958, *46,* 329–338. (b)

Tuddenham, R. D. The constancy of personality ratings over two decades. *Genet. psychol. Monogr.,* 1959, *60,* 3–29.

Tuddenham, R. D., MacBride, Philip, & Zehn, Victor. The influence of the sex composition of a group upon yielding to a distorted norm. *J. Psychol.,* 1958, *46,* 243–251.

Tulane factors of liberalism-conservatism. Chicago: Psychometric Affiliates, n.d.

Turney, A. H. *Factors other than intelligence that affect success in high school.* Minneapolis: Univer. of Minnesota Press, 1930.

Tuttle, H. S. *How emotions are educated.* New York: Edwards Bros., 1941.

Tyler, L. E. *The psychology of human difference.* New York: Appleton-Century-Crofts, 1947. (2nd ed., 1956)

Urban, W. M. *Fundamentals of ethics, an introduction to moral philosophy.* New York: Holt, 1930.

Vaihinger, H. *The philosophy of "as if," a system of theoretical, practical and religious fictions of mankind.* (Trans. by C. K. Ogden.) London: Routledge, 1949 (Orig., 1911).

Van Ophuijsen, J. H. W. The technique of psychosomatic therapy. In S. Lorand (Ed.), *Psychoanalysis today.* New York: International Universities Press, 1944.

Van Zelst, R. H., & Kerr, W. A. Personality self-assessment of scientific and technical personnel. *J. appl. Psychol.,* 1954, *38,* 145–147.

Veblen, T. *The theory of the leisure class, an an economic study of institutions.* New York: Modern Library, 1934 (Orig., 1899).

Vernon, M. D. *A further study of visual perception.* Cambridge, Eng.: Cambridge Univer. Press, 1952.

Vernon, M. D. Cognitive inference in perceptual activity. *Brit. J. Psychol.,* 1957, *48,* 35–47.

Vernon, P. E. Can the "total personality" be studied objectively? *Char. & Pers.,* 1935, *4,* 1–10.

Vernon, P. E. An analysis of the conception of morale. *Char. & Pers.,* 1941, *9,* 283–294.

Vernon, P. E. *Personality tests and measurements.* New York: Holt, 1953.

Vinacke, W. E. *The psychology of thinking.* New York: McGraw-Hill, 1952.

Von Bertalanffy, L. *Problems of life: an evaluation of modern biological thought.* London: Watts, 1952.

Wade, T. L., & Goodner, D. B. *Advanced calculus.* Unpublished prospectus, Florida State Univer., 1953.

Waelder, R. Authoritarianism and totalitarianism: psychological comments on a problem of power. In G. B. Wilbur, & W. Muensterberger (Eds.), *Psychoanalysis and culture; essays in honor of Géza Róheim.* New York: International Universities Press, 1951.

Warden, C. J., Jenkins, T. N., & Warner, Lucien H. *Comparative psychology, a com-*

prehensive treatment: Vertebrates. New York: Ronald, 1936.

Warner, W. L., & Lunt, P. S. *Yankee City series:* I. *The Social life of a modern community;* II. *The status system of a modern community.* New Haven, Conn.: Yale Univer. Press, 1941, 1942.

Warren, H. C. *Dictionary of psychology.* Boston: Houghton Mifflin, 1934.

Warren, H. C., & Carmichael, L. *Elements of human psychology.* (Rev. ed.) Boston: Houghton Mifflin, 1930.

Watson, G. B. *Experimentation and measurement in religious education.* New York: Association Press, 1927.

Watson, J. B. *Behavior, an introduction to comparative psychology.* New York: Holt, 1914.

Watson, J. B. *Psychology from the standpoint of a behaviorist.* Philadelphia: Lippincott, 1929 (Orig., 1919).

Watson, J. B. *Behaviorism.* (Rev. ed.) New York: Norton, 1930 (Orig., 1924).

Watson, J. B., & Raynor, R. Conditioned emotional reactions. *J. exp. Psychol.,* 1920, *3,* 1–4.

Webb, E. Character and intelligence, an attempt at an exact study of character. *Brit. J. Psychol., Monogr. Suppl.,* 1915, *1,* No. III.

Weber, A. *History of philosophy.* (Trans. by F. Thilly, with philosophy since 1860 by R. B. Perry.) New York: Scribner's, 1925.

Wechsler, D. *The range of human capacities.* Baltimore: Williams & Wilkins, 1935.

Weinfield, G. F. Self-demand feeding. *Med. Clin. N. Amer.,* 1950, *34,* 33–40.

Weisgerber, C. A. Factor analysis of a questionnaire test of perseveration. *J. gen. Psychol.,* 1955, *53,* 341–345.

Weiss, E. *Principles of psychodynamics.* New York: Grune & Stratton, 1950.

Weitzenhoffer, A. M. *Hypnotism, an objective study of suggestibility.* New York: Wiley, 1953.

Wells, W. R. Experiments in the hypnotic production of crime. *J. Psychol.,* 1941, *4,* 63–102.

Wenger, M. A. An attempt to appraise individual differences in level of muscular tension. *J. exp. Psychol.,* 1943, *32,* 213–225.

Wenger, M. A., & Irwin, O. C. Fluctuations in skin resistance of infants and adults and their relation to muscular processes. *Univer. Iowa Stud.,* 1936, *12,* 145–178.

Werner, H. William Stern's personalistics and

psychology of personality. *Char. & Pers.,* 1938, 7, 109–125.

Wertheimer, M. *Productive thinking* (Enlarged ed., edited by Michael Wertheimer). New York: Harper, 1959.

Westcott, B. F., & Hort, F. J. A. *The New Testament in the original Greek.* New York: Macmillan, 1921.

Wheeler, R. H. *The laws of human nature, a general view of Gestalt psychology.* New York: Appleton, 1932.

Whisler, L. D. A multiple-factor analysis of generalized attitudes. *J. soc. Psychol.,* 1934, *5,* 283–297.

White, R. W. *The abnormal personality.* New York: Ronald, 1948.

White, R. W. *Lives in progress, a study of the natural growth of personality.* New York: Dryden, 1952.

White, R. W. Motivation reconsidered: The concept of competence. *Psychol. Rev.,* 1959, *66,* 297–333.

White House Conference on Child Health and Protection. The adolescent in the family, a study of personality development in the home environment. Report of the Subcommittee on the function of home activities in the education of the child. New York: Appleton-Century, 1934.

Wickes, Frances G. *The inner world of childhood, a study in analytical psychology.* New York: Appleton, 1929.

Wiener, N. *Cybernetics; or control and communication in the animal and the machine.* Cambridge, Mass.: Technology Press, 1948.

Wilbur, G. B., & Muensterberger, W. (Eds.) *Psychoanalysis and culture; essays in honor of Géza Róheim.* New York: International Universities Press, 1951.

Williams, H. L., & Lawrence, J. F. Further investigation of Rorschach determinants subjected to factor analysis. *J. consult. Psychol.,* 1953, *17,* 261–264.

Williams, H. L., & Lawrence, J. F. Comparison of the Rorschach and MMPI by means of factor analysis. *J. consult. Psychol.,* 1954, *18,* 193–197.

Williams, Henrietta V. A determination of psychosomatic functional unities in personality by means of P-technique. *J. soc. Psychol.,* 1954, *39,* 25–45.

Williams, R. J. *Free and unequal, the biological basis of individual liberty.* Austin, Tex.: Univer. of Texas Press, 1953.

Williams, R. J. Biochemical individuality—its

human implications. *Wiley Bull.*, 1959, *44*, 1, 7.

Willis, A. E. *Encyclopedia of human nature and physiognomy, treating of every character- istic, both good and bad, of the various types of man and woman as they exist, and as manifested in every day life, giving "The truth, the whole truth, and nothing but the truth."* Chicago: Loomis & Co., Publishers, 1889.

Wilson, R. C., Guilford, J. P., & Christensen, P. R. The measurement of individual dif- ferences in originality. *Psychol. Bull.*, 1953, *50*, 362–370.

Wilson, R. C., Guilford, J. P., Christensen, P. R., & Lewis, D. J. A factor-analytic study of creative thinking abilities. *Psy- chometrika*, 1954, *19*, 297–311.

Winship, A. E. *Jukes-Edwards, a study in edu- cation and heredity.* Harrisburg, Pa.: R. L. Myers & Co., 1900.

Wirt, R. D. Further validation of the ego- strength scale. *J. consult. Psychol.*, 1955, *19*, 444.

Wishner, J. Reanalysis of "Impressions of per- sonality." *Psychol. Rev.*, 1960, 67, 96–112.

Witkin, H. A., Lewis, H. B., Hertzman, M., Machover, K., Meissner, P. B., & Wap- ner, S. *Personality through perception, an experimental and clinical study.* New York: Harper, 1954.

Wittenborn, J. R. A factor analysis of Ror- schach scoring categories. *J. consult. Psychol.*, 1950, *14*, 261–267.

Witty, P. A. The only child of age five. *Psychol. Clin.*, 1933, 22, 73–87.

Wolberg, L. R. Hypnotic phenomena. In H. A. Abramson (Ed.), *Problems of conscious- ness, transactions of the third conference, March 10 and 11, 1952.* New York: Josiah Macy, Jr., Foundation, 1952.

Wolfe, B., & Rosenthal, R. *Hypnotism comes of age, its progress from Mesmer to psy- choanalysis.* Indianapolis: Bobbs-Merrill, 1948.

Wolfenstein, Martha. Trends in infant care. *Amer. J. Orthopsychiat.*, 1953, *23*, 120– 130.

Wolff, W. The experimental study of forms of expression. *Char. & Pers.*, 1933, 2, 168– 176.

Wolff, W. Involuntary self-expression in gait and other movements: an experimental study. *Char. & Pers.*, 1935, *3*, 327–344.

Wolff, W. Projective methods for personality analysis of expressive behavior in pre-

school children. *Char. & Pers.*, 1942, *10*, 309–330.

Wolff, W. *The personality of the preschool child, the child's search for his self.* New York: Grune & Stratton, 1946.

Wolff, W. *Diagrams of the unconscious, hand- writing and personality in measurement, experiment and analysis.* New York: Grune & Stratton, 1948.

Wolff, W. *Values and personality, an existen- tial psychology of crisis.* New York: Grune & Stratton, 1950.

Wolff, W. *The dream—mirror of conscience; a history of dream interpretation from 2000 B.C. and a new theory of dream syn- thesis.* New York: Grune & Stratton, 1952.

Wolff, W., & Precker, J. Success in psycho- therapy. *Pers. Monogr.*, Vol. 3. New York: Grune & Stratton, 1952.

Wolff, W. M. Certainty: generality and rela- tion to manifest anxiety. *J. abnorm. soc. Psychol.*, 1955, *50*, 59–64.

Wolfle, D. Factor analysis to 1940. *Psychom. Monogr.*, No. 3. Chicago: The Univer. of Chicago Press, 1940.

Wolfle, D. Factor analysis in the study of per- sonality. *J. abnorm. soc. Psychol.*, 1942, *37*, 393–397.

Woodworth, R. S. *Experimental psychology.* New York: Holt, 1938.

Woodworth, R. S. Reinforcement of percep- tion. *Amer. J. Psychol.*, 1947, *60*, 119–124.

Yerkes, R. M., Bridges, J. W., & Hardwick, Rose S. *A point scale for measuring ability.* Baltimore: Warwick & York, 1915.

Yoakum, C. S., & Yerkes, R. M. *Army mental tests.* New York: Holt, 1920.

Young, K. *Personality and the problems of ad- justment.* (Rev. ed.) New York: Ap- pleton-Century-Crofts, 1952.

Young, N., & Gaier, E. L. A preliminary in- vestigation into the prediction of suggesti- bility from selected personality variables. *J. soc. Psychol.*, 1953, *37*, 53–60.

Young, P. T. *Motivation of behavior, the fundamental determinants of human and animal activity.* New York: Wiley, 1936.

Young, Shirley A., & Sumner, F. C. Personal equation, frame of reference, and other observations in remote reproductions of filled and unfilled time-intervals. *J. gen. Psychol.*, 1954, *51*, 333–337.

Yule, G. U., & Kendall, M. G. *An introduction to the theory of statistics.* (13th ed., Rev.) London: Charles Griffin, 1949.

Zachry, Caroline B. *Emotion and conduct in*

adolescence; for the Commission on secondary school curriculum. New York: Appleton-Century, 1940.

Zeigarnik, Bluma. Ueber das Behalten von erledigten und unerledigten Handlungen. *Psychol. Forsch.*, 1927, *9*, 1–85. (Cited in K. Lewin, *Principles of topological psychology*. New York: McGraw-Hill, 1936.)

Zelen, S. L. Goal-setting rigidity in an ambiguous situation. *J. consult. Psychol.*, 1955, *19*, 395–399.

Zilboorg, G. *Sigmund Freud, his exploration of the mind of man*. New York: Scribner's, 1951.

Zimmer, H. Self-acceptance and its relation to conflict. *J. consult. Psychol.*, 1954, *18*, 447–449.

Zirkle, C. Citation of fraudulent data. *Science*, 1954, *120*, 189–190.

Zuckerman, M., Baer, M., & Monashkin, I. Acceptance of self, parents and people in patients and normals. *J. clin. Psychol.*, 1956, *12*, 328–332.